RENEWALS: 691-4574

ECONOMIC GROWTH AND
STRUCTURAL CHANGE IN TAIWAN

ECONOMIC GROWTH AND STRUCTURAL CHANGE IN TAIWAN

The Postwar Experience of
the Republic of China

edited by **WALTER GALENSON**

CORNELL UNIVERSITY PRESS
ITHACA AND LONDON

Dedicated to the memory of
our friend and colleague

TA-CHUNG LIU

Contents

Preface

The essays in this volume deal with various aspects of economic development in the Republic of China. The authors read and criticized one another's essays in preliminary draft and modified their own contributions in the light of the findings of their colleagues. An attempt was made to reconcile conflicts in the data, but differences in sources and interpretation at times prevented reconciliation. Each author has full and final responsibility for the contents of his chapter and no attempt has been made to reach a group consensus on the evaluation of Taiwan's policies and experience. Each one speaks for himself alone.

In planning the volume, we attempted to cover all major sectors and activities of the economy. But we did not intend, nor have we achieved, a complete history of Taiwan's economic development. Each author was encouraged to select, within the broad topics assigned, those elements in the growth process that impressed him as most interesting and as having the greatest potential value to students of economic development generally.

Many of the sources cited in English are printed in the Chinese language, and the authors did their best to obtain consistent translations. Some of the statistical material was provided by scholars in Taipei after discussion with the authors; these are mainly estimates not shown in regular statistical sources. For these reasons, and also because many of the publications are not available in the United States, it has not always been possible to achieve complete uniformity in citations.

This book could not have been written without the assistance and cooperation of scholars in the Republic of China. They interpreted the statistics in official yearbooks, provided bibliographical material, and arranged interviews and institutional visits during field trips to Taiwan. Their comments on preliminary drafts were very helpful. Among those most directly involved were Tzong-shian Yu, director of the Institute of Economics, Academia Sinica, who acted as coordinator in Taipei; Shirley W. Y. Kuo, Kuo-shu Liang, and

Chen Sun, National Taiwan University; Paul K. C. Liu, Institute of Economics, Academia Sinica; Yu-chu Hsu, National Cheng-chi University; and Yu-kang Mao, Division of Agricultural Economics, Joint Commission on Rural Reconstruction. None of the foregoing, however, is in any way responsible for the interpretations that appear in the text. The authors are also indebted to the Economic Development Council, which provided us with office space and other assistance during our visits to Taiwan.

This project was sponsored by the Joint Council on Sino-American Cooperation in the Humanities and Social Sciences. This organization is composed of the China Council on Sino-American Cooperation in the Humanities and Social Sciences in the Republic of China and the Joint Committee on Sino-American Cooperation in the Humanities and Social Sciences of the American Council of Learned Societies and the Social Science Research Council in the United States.

We have dedicated this book to our friend and colleague, the late Professor Ta-chung Liu of Cornell University. He helped plan the volume and facilitate its execution. Even more significantly, he played a major role in the actual course of Taiwan's economic development.

WALTER GALENSON

Ithaca, New York

Contributors

Walter Galenson. Jacob Gould Schurman Professor of Economics, Cornell University. Author of *Rival Unionism in the United States* (1940); *Labor in Norway* (1949); *The Danish System of Labor Relations* (1952); *Labor Productivity in Soviet and American Industry* (1955); *The CIO Challenge to the AFL* (1960); *Trade Union Democracy in Western Europe* (1961); *The Quality of Labor and Its Impact on Economic Development* (with F. G. Pyatt) (1964); *A Primer on Employment and Wages* (1966); *The Chinese Economy under Communism* (with N. R. Chen) (1971).

Simon Kuznets. Recipient of the Nobel Prize in Economics, 1971. George F. Baker Professor of Economics Emeritus, Harvard University. Author of *Cyclical Fluctuations* (1926); *Secular Movements in Production and Prices* (1930); *Seasonal Variations in Industry and Trade* (1933); *National Income and Capital Formation* (1937); *Commodity Flow and Capital Formation* (1938); *National Income and Its Composition* (1941); *National Product in Wartime* (1945); *National Income: A Summary of Findings* (1946); *National Product since 1869* (1946); *Economic Change* (1953); *Shares of Upper Income Groups in Income and Savings* (1953); *Six Lectures on Economic Growth* (1959); *Capital in the American Economy* (1961); *Postwar Economic Growth* (1964); *Economic Growth and Structure* (1965); *Modern Economic Growth* (1966); *Economic Growth of Nations* (1971); *Population, Capital, and Growth* (1973).

Ian M. D. Little. Special Adviser, World Bank. Formerly Professor of Economics of Underdeveloped Countries, University of Oxford, and Vice-President of the OECD Development Centre. Author of *A Critique of Welfare Economics* (1950); *The Price of Fuel* (1953); *Concentration in British Industry* (with Richard Evely) (1960); *International Aid* (with J. M. Clifford) (1965); *Manual of Industrial Project Analysis in Developing Countries* (with

J. A. Mirrlees) (1969); *Industry and Trade in Some Developing Countries* (with Maurice Scott and Tibor Scitovsky) (1970); *Project Appraisal and Planning for Developing Countries* (with J. A. Mirrlees) (1974).

Erik Lundberg. President, Royal Swedish Academy of Science. Formerly President of the International Economic Association; Professor at the University of Stockholm and at the Stockholm School of Economics. Author of *Wages in Sweden* (1933); *Studies in the Theory of Economic Expansion* (1937); *The Business Cycle Sensitivity of the Swedish Economy* (1945); *Business Cycles and Economic Policy* (1953); *Productivity and Profitability* (1961); *Instability and Economic Growth* (1968); *Swedish Fiscal Policy in Theory and Practice* (1971); *Inflation and Unemployment* (with L. Calmfors) (1974).

Gustav Ranis. Professor of Economics, Yale University. Formerly Director of the Economic Growth Center, Yale University; Assistant Administrator for Program, Agency for International Development. Author of *Development of the Labor Surplus Economy* (with J. C. H. Fei) (1964); "Equity with Growth: The Taiwan Case" (with J. C. H. Fei and S. M. Y. Kuo) (for the World Bank). Editor of *Government and Economic Development* (1971); *The Gap between Rich and Poor Nations* (1972); *Sharing in Development: A Programme of Employment, Equity and Growth for the Philippines* (1974).

Maurice FitzGerald Scott. Fellow in Economics, Nuffield College, University of Oxford. Author of *A Study of U.K. Imports* (1963); *Industry and Trade in Some Developing Countries* (with I. M. D. Little and Tibor Scitovsky) (1970); *Project Appraisal in Practice* (with J. D. MacArthur and D. M. G. Newbery) (1976). Coeditor of *Induction, Growth and Trade: Essays in Honor of Sir Roy Harrod* (1970); *Using Shadow Prices* (1976).

Erik Thorbecke. H. Edward Babcock Professor of Economics and Food Economics, Cornell University. Author of *The Tendency towards Regionalization in International Trade* (1960); *Employment and Output: A Methodology Applied to Peru and Guatemala* (with A. Stoutjesdijk) (1971); *The Theory of Quantitative Economic Policy with Applications to Economic Growth, Stabilization, and Planning* (with K. A. Fox and J. K. Sengupta) (1973); *Planning Techniques for a Better Future* (with F. G. Pyatt) (1976). Editor of *The Theory and Design of Economic Development* (with I. Adelman) (1966); *The Role of Agriculture in Economic Development* (1969).

**ECONOMIC GROWTH AND
STRUCTURAL CHANGE IN TAIWAN**

1 | Growth and Structural Shifts

SIMON KUZNETS

In this chapter I tried to organize the basic data on population, total product, and components, so as to present a consistent quantitative outline of the economic growth and structural shifts in Taiwan. Special emphasis is placed on the quarter of a century from the early 1950s to the middle 1970s.

The first two brief sections deal with the colonial period, 1895 to 1940, and the period of transition, 1945 to the early 1950s. The treatment is highly selective, noting a few major features required for better understanding of the remarkable growth accomplishment in the two and half decades that followed.

The next four sections deal, in some detail, with the quantitative framework of growth and structural change between 1951–53 and 1971–73. The account proceeds from the records of the aggregates, population, product, and product per capita, to changes in production structure, to movements in the structure of product by use, and to distributive aspects. A final section deals with changes since the peak of 1973—changes still unfolding, but deserving note because of the marked break in pace since that time.

My task—made possible by the abundance of basic data for Taiwan—encountered some difficulties. The very wealth and variety of the basic statistics, combined with the inappropriateness of some aspects of conventional national accounting to the realities of Taiwan's economy, resulted in several unresolved contradictions and questions. I hope that the somewhat arbitrary expedients that had to be employed do not limit unduly the validity and value of the discussion.

I have provided various analytical comments, suggested by the cast of the quantities and relating particularly to some implications of structural shifts associated with rapid growth. These comments present reflections rather than formal hypotheses and are offered only as possibly illuminating suggestions.

The Colonial Period, 1895–1940

In 1895, when the Japanese annexation began, Taiwan's population was probably well over 2.5 million.[1] This total included a small proportion of aborigines; at least 95 percent must have been accounted for by Chinese in-migrants and their descendants, of whom over eight-tenths were from Fukien and most of the remaining from Kwantung Province.[2] Migration from the Chinese mainland began in the early seventeenth century and accelerated after the Manchu dynasty extended its power to the island in 1683. Kowie Chang notes: "It is recorded in history that at the time the Manchu ruler first seized Taiwan, the total of population in Taiwan amounted only to 200,000 [presumably the aborigines are not included]; but in 1843, the sum total of Chinese, with the aborigines not excepted, rose to 2,500,000."[3]

These few figures indicate that by the start of the colonial period Taiwan had a sizable population of migrants (and their descendants) from the southern provinces of the Chinese mainland—migrants who, originally attracted by the richer supply of land, brought farming practices and skills with them and were settled in Taiwan for well over a century. Their agricultural and economic performance at that time was comparable with that of several countries in South Asia around 1960.[4]

Assumption of power by the Japanese, exercised over the next five decades, brought political and institutional changes that had a major economic impact. At the start of the annexation, the Japanese government was confronted by a rebellious population. It had to pacify the country and secure the cooperation of its Chinese inhabitants (if not of the aborigines, who were isolated in the mountains) in attaining its basic economic aims. This pacification task was not completed until the end of the second decade after occupation.[5] If only for

In addition to the helpful comments by the authors of the other chapters in this volume, I profited also from comments by a number of scholars in Taiwan. Particularly valuable comments were received from Minister T. H. Lee (formerly with the Joint Commission on Rural Reconstruction [JCRR]): Shirley W. Y. Kuo of the Economic Planning Council; and M. H. Hsing, formerly of the Institute of Economics of Academia Sinica and currently at the Chinese University of Hong Kong. My access to, and understanding of, the basic data and past analysis were greatly facilitated by the unfailing assistance of T. S. Yu, director of the Institute of Economics, Academia Sinica, and his associate, Paul K. C. Liu of that Institute. Mrs. Jacob Weksler, who had helped me in many past years, edited the text patiently and painstakingly.

1. According to the Japanese census as of October 1 of the year Taiwanese population (excluding Japanese and Koreans) rose from 2.97 million in 1905 to 3.33 in 1915. See George W. Barclay, *Colonial Development and Population in Taiwan* (Princeton, 1954), Table 2, p. 13. Extrapolating this rate of growth back to 1895, which may exaggerate the actual growth and underestimate the derived total for 1895, yields a population of 2.64 million.

2. According to the most complete enumeration of aborigines, that for 1935, they accounted for slightly over 4 percent of all Taiwanese (Barclay, Table 3, p. 16).

3. Kowie Chang, ed., *Economic Development of Taiwan* (Taipei, 1968), p. 7.

4. See the brief discussion in Teng-hui Lee, *Intersectoral Capital Flows in the Economic Development of Taiwan 1895-1960* (Ithaca, N.Y., and London, 1971), pp. 32–39.

5. See brief discussion of this task in the paper by Samuel Ho, cited in the note to Table 1.1.

security reasons, the first steps involved cutting the ties between the island and the Chinese mainland, a policy decision that did not change significantly through the five decades. The implied legal separation and identification of Taiwanese (those resident on the island at the time of occupation) and the clear line of distinction between them and the mainlanders (of whom there was subsequently only a handful, judging by the relatively accurate Japanese censuses) was initiated and maintained. The limited out-migration of Taiwanese from the island and the limited in-migration of Japanese and others (largely Korean, and in 1935 about 5 percent of total population) seems to have made the majority population an effectively closed group, isolated from direct flows of people in and out, and exposed to only limited contact with the small Japanese population concentrated in the cities. One may argue that the Taiwanese Chinese community was formed in these five decades of relative isolation. And yet the long-standing inherited Chinese institutions and social patterns remained because of the indirect nature of Japanese control, despite its effectiveness in shaping the economic growth of the island.

Given the economic aims of the annexation, the Japanese government faced the task of raising the productivity of Taiwan's dominant productive sector—its agriculture—to permit securing a steady and growing surplus at the disposal of the metropolitan country. This called for policies that would create sufficient control over the countryside and its institutions to facilitate increased use of more advanced agricultural technology, but would not disrupt the established institutions and provoke resistance. It also called for a mechanism by which the resulting increased volume of savings would be captured for the benefit of the metropolitan country and not diverted into higher levels of per capita consumption by the Taiwanese or into capital formation for the development of industries in Taiwan that might compete with those in Japan.

This policy (modified only belatedly and partially during the late 1930s in an attempt to extend the industrial base in Taiwan proper) had several important consequences. First, the Japanese government had to make a vigorous attempt to build up the transport and communication infrastructure to permit easier access to and open wider markets for the Taiwanese countryside. It had to make similar investments in raising health and sanitation standards indispensable for higher productivity, as well as for easier Japanese control. It had to make some initial capital investments in agriculture for needed technological innovations. Valuable material capital was accumulated and mortality reduced; both were positive aspects of the colonial period. Second, the productivity of agriculture rose considerably; and yet the patterns of institutions and community life apparently were not disrupted; the customary institutions and relations of power among the various groups were not significantly modified. Third, until quite late in the period, movement of capital into building up the industrialization base of Taiwan was restricted, whether it be material capital that tended to be concentrated in the hands of Japanese corporations, private or government (or exported, in effect, to Japan); or human capital that would serve to develop among the native groups leaders in modern technology and enterprise. Excluding the small Japanese nucleus of administrators, technicians, and entrepreneurs, even toward the end of the period Taiwan remained a largely agricultural country, with relatively high agricultural productivity, but with industrialization and modernization impulses and agents lying as it were, outside its mainstream.

A few major quantitative results for the five decades under Japanese occupation provide continuity with my discussion of recent economic growth and structural change. Table 1.1 indicates the change in the patterns of population growth in the transition from traditional to modern economic life. In interpreting Table 1.1, it should be noted that the small "other" group, not shown separately (the difference between column 1 and the sum of columns 2 and 3), consisted largely of mainland Chinese admitted by the Japanese authorities for special reasons; the Taiwanese in column 2 include the aborigines, although they never accounted for more than 5 percent of the total.

Several findings should be mentioned explicitly. First, the growth rate of the Taiwanese population, in column 4, and the rate of natural increase of the same stock, in column 8, show impressive agreement, confirming the hypothesis that the Chinese population on Taiwan formed a closed body scarcely affected by migration. The one discrepancy is in line 7, for which

Table 1.1. Population Growth, Taiwan, 1905–1944

		Population (thousands)			Annual growth per 1,000 col. 2	Dates for cols. 6–8	Birth rate	Death rate	Rate of natural increase
							(Crude rates, per 1,000 Taiwanese population)		
		Total (1)	Taiwanese (2)	Japanese (3)	(4)	(5)	(6)	(7)	(8)
1.	1905	3,040	2,973	57					
2.	1915	3,480	3,326	135	11.5	1906–15	42.3	31.0	11.3
3.	1925	3,993	3,775	184	12.7	1916–25	41.6	28.0	13.6
4a.	1930		4,219		22.5	1926–30	45.0	22.1	22.9
4b.	1930	4,593	4,314	228					
5.	1935	5,212	4,883	271	25.1	1931–35	46.0	21.2	24.8
6.	1940	5,872	5,510	312	24.5	1936–40	45.4	20.6	24.8
7.	1944	6,270	5,900	320	18.2	1941–43	42.1	18.5	23.6

For lines 1–6, population totals refer to October 1 of each year. For 1944 the total refers to July 15 and is based on a sample survey rather than a census. The totals through line 4a largely omit the aborigines, who are included in the totals in lines 4b through 7.

The entries in column 4 are calculated as geometric rates for the interval between the successive population totals in column 2. The entries in columns 6–8 are arithmetic means of annual crude rates for the years within the spans shown in column 5. Entries in columns 1–3 are from Samuel P. S. Ho, "The Development Policy of the Japanese Colonial Government in Taiwan, 1895–1945," Table 9.8, p. 307, in Gustav Ranis, ed., *Government and Economic Development* (New Haven and London, 1971). Entries in columns 5–8 are from George W. Barclay, *Colonial Development and Population in Taiwan* (Princeton, 1954), Table 74, p. 241.

there may be a question of comparability between the sample-derived total in 1944 and the census-derived total in 1940.

Second, the crude death rate (column 7) declined from above 30 per thousand in 1906–15 (and presumably at least as high if not higher for the first decade of occupation) to 22 by 1926–30, with a slow downdrift thereafter to 18.5 in 1941–43. This decline brought the death rates of the Taiwanese population close to those of Japan: for 1906–25, the rate for the Taiwanese averaged 29.5 per thousand, while that for the population of Japan was 22.0, or almost a third lower. For 1926–40 the two rates were 21.3 and 18.3 respectively, a minor difference.[6]

Third, if the decline in the death rates was the first step toward modernization, to be followed by the second after World War II, there was no such movement in the birth rate. The crude birth rate, at a high level above 40 per thousand, showed a rise. The average birth rate for the Taiwanese population, 42.0 for 1906–25, and 45.5 for 1926–40, can be compared with the rates of 34.7 and 32.0 for Japan for the two periods. The rise for the Taiwanese population is slight and may be partly due to improvements in registration. Clearly, modernization elements that usually result in a lower birth rate had little effect, despite some industrialization and urbanization.

Fourth, the combination of a high or slightly rising birth rate with a substantially declining death rate meant a sharp acceleration of the rate of natural increase, and thus of the rate of growth of the Taiwanese population. The rate of natural increase rose from an average of 12.5 per thousand for 1906–25 (and presumably somewhat lower for the first three decades 1896–1925) to 24.2 for 1926–40. This change is similar to that observed in many developing countries after World War II. As a result, Taiwanese population by the end of the occupation period was close to 6 million and somewhat more with the inclusion of residents classified as mainland Chinese and included among "others."

In turning now to the sectoral-occupational distribution of the occupied population of Taiwan (Table 1.2), we note first the declining ratio of all occupied (all ethnic groups, men and women) to total population. Relating the entries in lines 1–3, column 1, to total population, we find that the proportion of occupied to total population declined from 46 percent in 1905 to 39 percent in 1930 and 38 percent in 1940. This decline is due largely to the effects of a rising rate of natural increase and a declining death rate on the age composition of the population. The proportion of population below the working age of

6. The birth and death rates for Japan were calculated by relating the average annual number of births and deaths for the five periods shown in the table cited here, column 1 from 1906 to 1940, to the midperiod population, and then averaging again for the two long periods. The data for Japan are from Bank of Japan, *Hundred-Year Statistics for the Japanese Economy* (Tokyo, 1966), Table 1, pp. 12–13.

Table 1.2. Sectoral-Occupational Distribution of Occupied Population, Taiwan, 1905–1940*

	Total (in thousands) (1)	Percentage shares				
		A sector (2)	Industry sector (3)	Commerce (4)	Govt. and professions (5)	Other (6)
All occupied						
1. 1905	1,392	73.4	8.8	6.7	2.3	8.8
2. 1930	1,781	70.0	12.9	12.0	4.9	0.2
3. 1940	2,208	70.0	12.2	10.0	5.1	2.7
		Males Only				
Taiwanese						
4. 1905	1,046	72.7	8.3	7.4	1.8	9.8
5. 1915	1,088	73.4	10.1	7.3	1.8	7.4
6. 1920	1,100	71.1	12.5	7.6	2.2	6.6
7. 1930	1,265	70.1	12.8	10.2	2.7	4.2
Japanese						
8. 1905	27.8	1.6	39.5	16.5	41.3	1.1
9. 1915	53.4	7.6	44.7	17.8	28.7	1.2
10. 1920	63.9	6.4	41.0	15.0	37.2	0.4
11. 1930	75.8	6.7	29.7	14.6	45.6	3.4
Other						
12. 1905	8.2	1.5	64.8	26.5	1.8	5.4
13. 1920	16.6	3.6	62.3	27.3	2.7	4.1
14. 1930	28.9	3.4	61.2	29.2	3.0	3.2

*Domestic servants are excluded throughout. A sector includes agriculture, forestry, and fishing. Industry sector includes mining, manufacturing, and transportation.
Source: Barclay (see note to Table 1.1), Table 11, p. 58, and Table 16, pp. 71–72.

fifteen increased from about 37 percent in 1905 to 43 percent in 1940; that of population sixty-five and over rose from about 2 to 3 percent. The proportions in the age brackets fifteen to sixty-four, the working ages, must have declined from 61 to 53 percent, or 8 percentage points.[7] This drop in the proportion of occupied persons was not due to the prolongation of the educational and training period of the young or to the reduction of propensity to work at the older ages—both trends that emerge with transition to the modern pattern of organization of society and of the labor force.

In view of the uncertain classification of women in the occupational and labor force, the remainder of the table is limited to males, who accounted for 1.08 of the 1.39 million for 1905 and for 1.37 of the 1.78 million for 1930. The sectoral and occupational distribution even for males is crude, and "other" occupations, the share of which behaves erratically, may contain, in addition to an "occupation unknown" group, some specific occupations that could not be allocated to any other category. It seems most plausible to view this group as part of service, not easily assigned to either commerce or government and professions, although this is only a conjecture.

7. Barclay, Chart 16, p. 100.

Even with the limitations of the data, two major findings loom significantly. The first is the distinctive sectoral-occupational structure of the dominant Taiwanese population with seven-tenths or more in the A sector (agriculture and related industries) and particularly limited shares in government and professions. By contrast, the Japanese group, with a proportion to the Taiwanese total growing from less than 3 percent in 1905 to about 6 percent in 1930, is largely concentrated in industry and the government-professional sectors— together about seven to eight-tenths of the total. The structure of the much smaller other group, largely mainland Chinese, is concentrated largely in industry and commerce, these two accounting for nine-tenths of the total.

Second is the stability over time in the sectoral-occupational structure of each of the three groups. For the dominant Taiwanese male labor force, the A sector share declined by just a few percentage points and that of the non-A sector rose largely in industry (mining, manufacturing, and transportation)— but the movements were limited and hardly significant; and lines 2 and 3, indicate little such movement between 1930 and 1940. In short, any trend toward industrialization—a shift away from agriculture—was extremely limited for the Taiwanese population over the long period from the late nineteenth century to 1940.

Finally, the Taiwanese were dominant not only among male workers, accounting for 97 percent in 1905 and 92 percent in 1930,[8] but also within each broad sectoral-occupational group. Even in 1930, Taiwanese accounted for one-half of the relatively small group of government and professional male workers. Of all the A sector male workers, Taiwanese accounted for between 99 and 100 percent in both the early and late years; of all the non-A male workers, Taiwanese accounted for 89 percent in 1905 and 79 percent in 1930.

Trends in total output cannot easily be established because of the divergence among the available estimates and the difficulty of evaluating their data bases. Table 1.3 summarizes the estimates of gross national expenditures (GNE) (or product) by Toshiyoki Mizoguchi and of net domestic product (NDP) by T. H. Lee, both given in constant prices of the mid- or later 1930s. Despite the wide gap[9] in the absolute levels between the two series, it is possible to discern a common set of findings relating to the average growth rates over the period and to an intriguing pattern of these growth rates over time, particularly in the per capita or per worker series.

The growth rates in per capita product in Table 1.3 average between 1.9

8. These and other ratios in this paragraph are computed from Barclay, Table 16, pp. 71–72.

9. The price levels for 1934–36 averaged 85.2, the 1937 prices taken as 100 (from the annual "deflator" series for T. H. Lee's estimates, cited in the Ho manuscript table mentioned in the notes to column 2, Table 1.3). For totals in comparable prices, the NDP estimates in column 2 are short of the GNE estimates in column 1 by percentages ranging from 40 to 50. The difference in concept (indirect taxes minus subsidies and the allowance for capital consumption) should have yielded a differential of about 20 percent at most.

Table 1.3. Growth of Product, Total, Per Capita, and Per Employed Worker, 1903-1938 (gross national expenditure [GNE] in 1934-36 market prices; net domestic product [NDP] in 1937 factor costs)

	Total product		Population (mill.)	Employed workers (mill.)	Per capita		Per worker	
	mill. O.T.$				O.T.$		O.T.$	
	GNE	NDP			GNE	NDP	GNE	NDP
	(1)	(2)	(3)	(4)	(5)	(6)	(7)	(8)
	Absolute volume, average per year							
1. 1903-10	382	n.a.	3.16	1.40	121	n.a.	272	n.a.
2. 1911-20	514	316	3.56	1.61	144	88.5	320	196
3. 1921-30	848	480	4.16	1.69	204	115	502	284
4. 1931-38	1,041	743	5.20	2.13	201	143	489	349
	Growth rates, per year							
4. Lines 1-2 (9 years)	3.35	n.a.	1.33	1.53	1.99	n.a.	1.79	n.a.
5. Lines 2-3 (10 years)	5.13	4.27	1.57	0.51	3.50	2.66	4.60	3.74
6. Lines 3-4 (9 years)	2.30	4.97	2.51	2.59	−0.20	2.40	−0.28	2.32
7. Lines 2-4 (19 years)	3.78	4.60	2.02	1.49	1.73	2.54	2.26	3.06
8. Lines 1-4 (28 years)	3.65	n.a.	1.68	1.50	1.94	(2.21)	2.12	(2.55)

Column 1: The estimates of GNE, in 1934-36 prices, are from Toshiyoki Mizoguchi, *The Economic Growth of Taiwan and Korea* (Tokyo, 1975), p. 150, quoted from Table A-2 of Samuel P. S. Ho, *Economic Development of Taiwan, 1860-1970* (New Haven, 1978).

Column 2: From annual estimates by Teng-hui Lee, "Intersectional Capital Flows in the Economic Development of Taiwan, 1895-1960" (Ph.D. dissertation, Cornell University, 1968), cited in Table A-1 of Ho's manuscript.

Column 3: The estimates are from the annual, end-of-year series published by the Statistical Office of Taiwan Province, in *Statistical Summary of the Past 51 Years* (Taipei), pp. 76-77, quoted in Table A-11 of Ho's manuscript. The entries here relate to the middle of the period (calendar years) the dates of which are set in the vertical stub of lines 1-4.

Column 4: For 1911-20 and 1921-30, taken directly from S. C. Hsieh and T. H. Lee, *Agricultural Development and Its Contribution to Economic Growth in Taiwan*, JCRR Economic Digest Series, no. 17 (Taipei, April 1966), Appendix Table 2, p. 108. The same table was used to estimate the average for 1931-38 by simple interpolation using the quinquennia 1931-35 and 1936-40. For extrapolating the estimates to 1903-10 the rate of change for 1905-30 in total occupied persons in Table 1.2 above was applied (with due allowance for the period) to the entry for 1921-30 (thus extrapolating it back over nineteen years).

Lines 4-8: All growth rates are calculated from the midpoint of one period to that of the next (or further removed), on the basis of a straight log line connecting the values for the two time points. The averages in parentheses in line 8, columns 6 and 8, were calculated by assuming that the entries in line 4, columns 6 and 8, would be in the same ratio to corresponding entries in line 5 as was the case for the GNE per capita or per worker (in columns 5 and 7, respectively). This provided the missing entries in line 4, columns 6 and 8, and was used with the two other entries, weighted by differing durations, to derive the weighted averages in line 8, columns 6 and 8.

and 2.2 percent per year for the three decades between the middle of the 1903-10 to the middle of the 1931-38 periods (see line 8, columns 5 and 6). By the standards of the time, this was a respectable rate of growth, but it excludes the long decade from 1895 to the midpoint of the 1903-10 span. Given the low rate of increase in product prior to 1911-15 (see Table 1.4), it is difficult to assume significant growth in per capita product over that early period. If we cumulate the 2 percent per year for the twenty-eight years and then spread it over a forty-year period (roughly between 1895 and the mid-1930s), the average drops to 1.4 percent per year, implying a rise of some 70 percent over the four decades. There would be a similar proportional reduction in the average rate of growth of product per worker, ranging for the twenty-eight year span between 2.1 and 2.5 percent per year (line 8, columns 7 and 8): it would drop from 2.3 to 1.6 percent per year.

Of somewhat more interest is movement of the growth rates over time. The pattern is one of from zero or slight growth in the first decade to decade and a half after annexation, to increasingly higher rates until the 1930s, and then a slowdown in that decade. This inverted U pattern is particularly discernible in the per capita and per worker product series, in which the acceleration in the growth rates of population clearly contributed to the slowdown of growth rates in per capita product in the 1930s. Further scrutiny and greater familiarity with the underlying data would be required to establish this pattern of movement as a firm finding. But it is an intriguing possibility because it suggests that the growth engendered and promoted by the colonizing government's economic policy might have been running out of steam—reflecting a combination of too long a concentration on the agricultural and raw materials sector with the effects of a rapid climb in the rate of natural increase resulting from a high birth rate and declining death rate. And it raises the question as to what might have happened if war preparations and the incipient world war had not intervened.

Table 1.3 and the related comments apply to the output produced in Taiwan, not that retained for use by the population of Taiwan. The relevant data on use are assembled in Table 1.4, taken largely from the Mizoguchi monograph but also including some more specific data on the supply and consumption of food.

Panel A demonstrates that, with the rapid rise of the proportions of foreign trade to gross national expenditures (lines 4 and 5), there was a marked shift in the balance of exports over imports—from negative and then minor positive fractions of GNE to substantial and positive fractions beginning with the 1911–15 quinquennium (line 6). These meant that an average of more than one-tenth of the total product of Taiwan was exported to other countries without a corresponding quid pro quo in imports. The shift toward adverse price terms began in 1911–15 with the much greater rise of import than of export prices; the results of this shift in price terms explain the lower positive balances in line 7 than in line 6, beginning in 1911–15. But in terms of real resources, the outflow was substantial.

This meant that the domestic uses, consumption, and domestic capital formation, which were close to total output before 1911–15, dropped, on the average, to 10 percent below gross product. And with the rise in the proportions of government consumption and of fixed gross domestic capital forma-

Table 1.4. Foreign Trade Balances, Domestic Uses, Private Consumption, and Consumption of Food, Various Periods, 1903–1940

A. Composition of GNE, 1934–36 prices, 1903–1938

	1903–05 (1)	1906–10 (2)	1911–15 (3)	1916–20 (4)	1921–25 (5)	1926–30 (6)	1931–35 (7)	1936–38 (8)
1. GNE per year, mill. O.T.$	356	386	449	579	770	927	1,040	1,044
2. GNE, per capita, O.T.$	116	124	129	158	195	211	208	189
3. Line 2, index, 1911–15 = 100	90	96	100	122	151	164	161	147
		Foreign trade as percentage of GNE						
4. Exports	11.1	14.9	22.0	28.2	23.5	28.4	32.2	36.1
5. Imports	12.6	15.5	20.6	15.7	13.9	18.6	20.7	26.1
6. Exports minus imports	−1.5	−0.6	1.4	12.5	9.6	9.8	11.5	10.0
7. Line 6, including changes in terms of trade	−0.3	1.1	2.1	6.3	7.6	7.9	8.1	8.3
	Domestic uses and private consumption as percentage of GNE							
8. Domestic uses	101.4	100.5	98.7	87.6	90.5	90.2	88.6	90.0
9. Private consumption	96.1	92.2	86.0	77.4	79.7	78.1	74.1	71.1
		Private consumption per capita						
10. O.T.$	111	115	111	122	156	165	154	134
11. Line 10, index, 1911–15 = 100	100	104	100	110	141	149	140	121

B. Supply and consumption of food, indexes 1911–15 = 100

	1911–15 (1)	1916–20 (2)	1921–25 (3)	1929–30 (4)	1931–35 (5)	1936–40 (6)
12. Supply, mill. O.T.$, 1935–37 prices	100.0 (158.2)	115.6	117.0	171.1	210.7	286.4
13. Net exports, percent of line 12	15.8	20.1	23.8	25.6	37.6	41.5
14. Consumption, line 12 reduced by 13	100.0 (133.3)	109.7	125.5	146.2	156.1	164.2
15. Food consumption per capita	100.0	104.0	109.9	114.6	107.3	99.5
16. Daily food availability, calories per capita*	100.0 (1,881)	101	107	110	103	99

*Relates to quinquennia beginning in 1910–14 and ending in 1935–39.
Panel A: All data relating to gross national expenditures and the components are from the Mizoguchi monograph cited in Table 1.3. The totals, in current and in 1934-36 prices, are given in Mizoguchi's Tables 5.1 (pp. 146–47) and 5.4 (pp. 150ff.) and so are the components (government consumption, fixed gross domestic capital formation (GDCF), private consumption, exports, and imports). The changes in terms of trade were calculated from the price indexes implicit in exports and imports, but the GNE totals were not adjusted to reflect these changes.
For the population series used to shift to a per capita basis in lines 2 and 11 see the source cited in Table 1.3.
Panel B: Entries in parentheses in column 1, lines 12, 14–16, are the average values, in relevant units, in the base quinquennium.
Lines 12–15: From the Hsieh and Lee monograph cited in Table 1.3, Table 32, p. 90; and the population data in Appendix Table 2, p. 108.
Line 16: From Samuel P. S. Ho, "Agricultural Transformation under Colonialism: The Case of Taiwan," *Journal of Economic History* 28, (September 1968), Table 5, p. 336. For the first five quinquennia I used the arithmetic mean of two variants, differing in the ratio of calories from rice and from sweet potatoes—the two basic calorie foods.

tion (the sum of which, as proportion of GNE, is the difference between lines 8 and 9), which together rose from about 5 percent of GNE in 1903–5 to about 19 in 1936–38, the share of household consumption in GNE declined drastically, particularly after 1906–10 (line 9).

The result was a far lower rate of growth in per capita consumption than in per capita product. A comparison of lines 3 and 11 shows that unlike product, per capita consumption failed to rise before 1916–20; that whereas product per capita rose from 90 in 1903–5 to over 160 in 1931–35, or over 80 percent, per capita consumption rose over the same span from 100 to about 140, or at about half the rate. But the estimate of household or private consumption is one of the weaker estimates in the Mizoguchi series; more data would be needed to be sure of the true magnitude of the trend, although the pattern is found also in the movements of food consumption in Panel B.

This panel summarizes indexes more directly related to consumption levels and more dominated by the weight of the majority Taiwanese population than might be true of other components of household consumption, namely, food consumption per capita (lines 12–15). The supply of food, overwhelmingly of domestic origin, shows substantial rise on a per capita basis. If the index of total supply, in line 12, column 6, is related to an index of population (also 1911–15 = 100), the result would be an index of per capita supply of 143. But an increasing proportion of that supply was exports (line 13), with the result that food available for consumption, on a per capita basis, shows a moderate rise of less than 15 percent over the first three quinquennia and then drops to slightly below the 1911–15 level by 1936–40.

This pattern of movement, a slight rise to the late 1920s and then a decline back to the initial level, or slightly lower, is shown also by the measure in line 16 of the calorie contents of daily food availability per capita. One should also note that the per capita daily calorie availability was not high: the peak 1925–29 level was reached in Taiwan as early as 1951 (2,070 calories), while the process of recovery and reconstruction was beginning, and then was followed by a rise to 2,754 by 1973.[10]

Given these low basic levels of food availability (as measured in calories) and the much greater levels of rise in per capita household consumption in the Mizoguchi index in line 11, the extremely moderate rise in food consumption is somewhat of a puzzle. Whether this was a reflection of the colonizing government's policy of forcing food exports or a result of the defects of the household consumption series is a matter for further exploration.

The preliminary conclusion that deserves at least provisional acceptance is that the impressive growth of product from 1910 onward was accompanied by

---

10. Directorate-General of Budget, Accounting, and Statistics (DGBAS), *Statistical Yearbook of the Republic of China, 1975* (Taipei, 1976), Consumption, Supp. Table 1, p. 169.

a much more limited rise in consumption per capita, particularly of foods, and, in general, more limited for the Taiwanese than for total population. This is also one aspect of the limited modernization that raised productivity but preserved many traditional demographic and social patterns and institutions within the colonial framework.

The Transition Period, 1945 to the early 1950s

This period began in September 1945, with the formal surrender of Japan to the victorious allies in World War II, the resulting retrocession of Taiwan to Nationalist China, and other consequences. It terminated in the early 1950s, when rehabilitation from the major ravages of the war was largely completed; and, more important, when it became clear to the Nationalist government, by then moved to Taiwan from the Communist-occupied mainland, that the separation from the mainland would be prolonged and that major growth-conditioning decisions bearing on the Taiwan economy and society would have to be made in a longer time perspective. Within this brief transition period, three major shifts occurred: (1) the shift in the locus of power responsible for making effective decisions; (2) inflow of a substantial and distinctive group from the mainland to Taiwan, largely in connection with the move of the Nationalist central government, thus providing additional means for implementing the shift under (1); (3) changes in aggregate output and structure of the economy needed to restore and rehabilitate the country and thus provide an adequate base for whatever subsequent long-term growth could be hoped for.

(1) In the first few years after 1945, Taiwan functioned as a liberated region of the country, and the mainland authorities operated through a military governor. But China as a whole was afflicted by disorganization produced by the civil war; and although substantial rehabilitation was attained almost immediately, the major change occurred in 1949 when the central government and its military forces relocated on the island, accompanied by substantial groups of mainlanders unwilling to remain under communist rule. Thereafter Taiwan was still viewed as a province of China; but it was also the seat of a Nationalist central government claiming sovereignty over the rest of the country and considering itself in a state of war with mainland authorities. This legal position, supported by Taiwan's allies in World War II (particularly the United States), along with the influx of experienced and educated personnel, allowed the central government, from 1950 onward, to be the major source of policy decisions, including those that helped to set the conditions for the economic growth that followed.

Economic growth is channeled through the political and institutional conditions of the country. Its sovereign government shapes these conditions, selecting from alternative modifications those that may be needed—because sources of, and obstacles to desirable economic growth changed with changes in technological innovations, shifts in relations of population to natural resources, and changes in the international constellation within which the country operates. The sovereign government is responsible for maintenance of, and change in, the political and social conditions within which economic growth takes place, conditions that affect the magnitude and structure of that growth. This key role of government was all the more important in Taiwan shortly after the war, when the departure of the Japanese personally and cancellation of their role legally left a vacuum, only poorly filled before 1949, while the immediate problems of production shortages, inflation, distorted agricultural structure, and the burdens of a substantially increased population were acute. The importance of government's role is indicated by the major decisions made during the 1950s—on land reform, on the public and private choices in industrial development, on curbing inflation through the control of money supply and government budgets, on regulating foreign exchange and controlling foreign trade, and, most recently, on major public projects that seemed advisable to cushion the shock of the recent world recession.

As will be seen under (2) below, the shift of population brought over a million and a half net migrants from the mainland (a conservative estimate, including the armed forces). At that time, after the departure of the Japanese, the Taiwanese population was somewhat over six million. The addition of this large group with similar cultural and historical background, but with different social and economic experience, was a major factor in the subsequent development of the economy and the community; and one wishes that data and analysis of the social and economic characteristics of both the majority islanders and minority mainlanders were available. But we are more interested in the small subgroup among the mainlanders who were in government and in the technically advanced positions and who became responsible for the growth decisions that followed. Our knowledge of their background and experience is even more limited.

Yet several preliminary impressions may be suggested. First, the policy interests of the decision-making group lay in attaining rapid economic progress in Taiwan, both to fulfill the party goal of people's livelihood that had been frustrated on the mainland and to provide a firm base for growing social consensus and cohesion in Taiwan as a source of economic and social power vis-à-vis the communist-dominated mainland. Second, this group had had a long and sobering experience with the economic and social problems generated by the traditional Chinese economy; and, despite the contributions and controls of the Japanese during the colonial period, Taiwan contained many elements of typical Chinese agriculture and its nonagricultural complements. Third, the governing group were largely newcomers to the island and had no substantial interest roots, no clear affiliation with any of the various Taiwanese interest groups, large and often absentee landlords, poor tenant farmers, rich merchants, or unskilled workers. They could, therefore, act as independent arbitrators attempting to achieve a long-term consensus and calling for sacrifices by some groups for the benefit of others for the long-term benefit of all. If we assume that there was substantial agreement among the decision-making groups and the larger groups that were being served, both islanders and mainlanders; that the historical and cultural community among all groups was an adequate basis for consensus; and that the decision-making group had enough experience and human capital for generating the required decisions promptly and efficiently, we can argue that this combination of the islanders and the mainlanders was favorable for a poor, developing country like Taiwan—and certainly not too common among the many developing countries that attained political independence after World War II.

These are all impressions, partly colored by the relative success of economic growth attained later, and they disregard the extra burdens of the shift of sovereign power to Taiwan. The purely economic burden of maintaining a large military establishment, although it eventually was decreased, can be measured. The more intangible burdens of maintaining a state of war, with the necessary restrictions of freedoms; of a central government that could not easily be renewed by direct contact with its wider constituency; and of the almost unavoidable concentration, in the earlier years, of government and private commanding jobs among the more educated and experienced mainlanders, are not easily weighed in any scale. It is beyond the competence of an economic analyst to attempt such a wider calculus and comparison. These comments are made to draw attention to the strategic role of the shift in the locus of power that occurred after 1949, which is indispensable for understanding how and why the growth-fashioning decisions (many of them discussed in the other chapters of this volume) have been made in Taiwan in the course of the last two and a half decades. A fuller analysis would have to include a view of the guiding social and party philosophy, the experience and training of the decision makers and workers involved, the mechanism by which the interests of various groups were satisfied and their responsiveness maintained, and, not the least, the characteristics of the native islander population that favored the positive response and outcome.

(2) Table 1.5 helps to explain the shifts in population during the transition period and reveals the complexities and difficulties in securing fully reliable population totals and trends.

The population total for the end of 1946 (column 1, line 1) may be compared with the total for Taiwan for mid-July 1944, excluding the Japanese, who would all have been gone and therefore could not have been included in the register total at the end of 1946. This 1944 comparable total is 5.95

Table 1.5. Population and Its Movements, 1946–1954

A. Population and the crude vital rates

	Population* end of year (thousands) (1)	Growth rate, percent per year (2)	Vital rates (crude, per 1,000)			
			Calendar years (3)	Birth (4)	Death (5)	Natural increase (6)
1. 1946	6,091		n.a.	n.a.	n.a.	n.a.
2. 1947	6,498	6.68	1947	38.3	18.1	20.2
3. 1948	6,808	4.77	1948	39.7	14.3	25.3
4. 1949	7,397	8.65	1949	42.4	13.1	29.2
5. 1950	7,554	2.12	1950	43.4	11.5	31.8
6. 1951–52	7,999	3.89	1951–52	48.3	10.8	37.5
7. 1953–54	8,594	3.65	1953–54	44.9	8.8	36.1

B. Estimates of net in-migration of mainlanders (thousands)

	1947 (1)	1948 (2)	1949 (3)	1950 (4)	1951–52 (5)	1953–54 (6)	1955–56 (7)	1947–56 (8)	1945–54 (9)
8. Derived from Panel A	280	142	382	−81	−16	48	−20	735	n.a.
9. Reported directly	34	99	304	81	24	34	30	606	640
10. Males, in line 9	26	62	199	59	15	25	17	400	425

C. Distribution of islanders and mainlanders among areas with differing economic structure

	Islanders			Mainlanders		
	1950 (1)	1955 (2)	1965 (3)	1950 (4)	1955 (5)	1965 (6)
11. Population* end of year (thousands)	7,028	8,225	10,908	525	853	1,721
Percent in areas:						
12. Metropolitan and industrial	22.2	23.3	26.6	66.1	66.8	62.6
13. Rural mixed	25.9	25.5	24.6	18.3	17.0	18.3
14. Agricultural, predominantly agricultural, and frontier	51.9	51.2	48.8	15.6	16.2	19.1

*Excludes military forces on bases and some institutional population.

Lines 1–7: From Directorate-General of Budget, Accounting, and Statistics (DGBAS), *Statistical Yearbook of the Republic of China, 1975* (Taipei, 1976), Table 18, pp. 2–3. The vital rates are computed to the midyear total of population as base.

Line 8: Calculated by applying the rates of natural increase shown in column 6 of Panel A to the midyear population and subtracting the addition thus estimated from the observed increment in the corresponding end-of-year population. The computations were done for each single year and then added or averaged for the two-year periods, 1951–52 and 1953–54, and 1955–56.

Lines 9–10: From Kowie Chang, ed., *Economic Development in Taiwan* (Taipei, 1968), Table 9-3, p. 532. The source cited is the 1956 census, and the data are presumably based on answers to questions concerning mainland origin and date of migration. This implies that the data are for net migration survivors, net of outflow and of deaths that may have occurred between the time of in-migration and the time of the census.

Lines 11–14: Taken or calculated from Paul K. C. Liu, "Population Redistribution and Economic Development in Taiwan, 1951–1965," particularly Table 4, p. 205, in John S. Y. Chiu, ed., *Proceedings of Conference on Economic Development of Taiwan* (Taipei, 1967). The grouping is for 361 area units, classified largely by the percent of males gainfully occupied in agriculture in 1965. Table 7, p. 221, of the source shows that of total population in 1965, population in areas with less than 20 percent of males in agriculture accounted for 27 percent of total, areas with 20 to 49 percent of working males in agriculture for 18 percent, and areas with 50 percent or more in agriculture for the remaining 55 percent. There is rough consilience between these three groups of areas and the three groups distinguished in Panel C (when observed for total population, that is, the sum of islanders and mainlanders).

million (see Table 1.1), suggesting a growth rate for the 2.46 years of 9.5 per thousand per year—far lower than the rate of natural increase shown for 1947 of 20.2 (see line 2, column 6) or than the growth rates shown in Table 1.1. There may have been a low rate of natural increase during these years; however, minor errors in the population totals for mid-1944 and end of 1946 could easily produce substantial errors in the growth rate derived for so short and turbulent a period.

A more important question raised by Panel A concerns the omission of military personnel and some institutional population. In later years the retirement from this substantial but omitted group meant an inflow into the civilian and hence recorded population, in addition to the natural increase, and in the early years, the magnitude of the group omitted suggested the additional burden imposed on the economy. Because there are no official and continuous estimates of the omitted group, several variants must be considered in attempting to derive a consistent series that would help to approximate the true movement of total population before 1969, the year when the group was first included in the official estimates.

The details and rationale of the adjustment for the omission are presented in section (3) dealing with growth of total product and population for the long period after the transition. Here it suffices to indicate that the adjustment raises the average total for 1950 from 7.475 to 8.134 million, or by almost 9 percent; and that the similarly adjusted figures for 1951–53 (calendar years) would raise the average from about 8.0 to about 8.65 million. Thus, the addition to the population of Taiwan (excluding the Japanese) from mid-1944 to 1951–53 was from below 6 million to 8.7, or somewhat short of 50 percent; and for the shorter period to 1950 it rose to 8.0 million, or well over a third. Because much of that influx came in about two years, the sudden addition to Taiwan's population created acute short-term pressures.

The crude death rates shown in Panel A hovered in the last few years of the colonial period around 18.5 per thousand (see Table 1.1). The entries in column 5, lines 2–7, show an immediate and sharp drop from 18 to less than half that level by 1953–54, a period of about seven years. If these data are acceptable, and there is no basis for suspecting a bias in the trend, they provide impressive evidence of the revolution in the technology of death prevention that occurred during and immediately after World War II and resulted in a strikingly prompt reduction of death rates in the economically less developed parts of the world.

The data in Panels B and C, bearing largely on the inflow and characteristics of the in-migrant population from the mainland, suggest several findings. First, the estimates of in-migration derived by subtracting additions through natural increase from the total additions to the registered population (line 8) and those reported in the census of 1966 (line 9) show a rough agreement in magnitude, allowing for some attrition by death in the census figures. They also agree roughly in showing a concentration of the flow in the early three to four years. Second, the census data (lines 9 and 10) show the dominance of male in-migrants, accounting for about seven-tenths of the total. Third, the number of mainlanders in Panel C is somewhat lower in 1950 than we would expect but shows a rapid rise, suggesting a substantial natural increase, but, more important, extensive marriage, with the wife, often an islander, acquiring the mainland status of the husband. There were also substantial additions by the retirement of many men from the military and their consequent shift to civilian status. Fourth, and of most interest, the mainlanders and the islanders were located in areas with distinctly different economic structures. The mainlanders were far more concentrated in the metropolitan and industrial areas and far less in the agricultural areas than were the islanders. There had been some convergence between 1950 and 1965, but the differences largely remained by that later date. This distribution of the mainlanders was similar to that of the small group of islanders, who could be identified as having migrated during the period under observation (see discussion in source cited in note to lines 11–14), indicating that mainlanders, the incoming mobile element, were moving into the same areas that were the destination of the migrant islanders.

(3) The movements of national or domestic product and of its important components over the transition years from 1946 to 1951–53 or 1951–55 are summarized in Table 1.6. The major underlying source of Panel A is apparently a June 1955 publication by the Directorate-General of Budget, Accounting, and Statistics (DGBAS) on *National Production and National Income in Taiwan* (in Chinese); but the data are available to me only in the Economic Commission for Asia and the Far East (ECAFE) and United Nations publications cited in the notes to Table 1.6.

Several findings in Panel A merit noting. First, total product was at an extremely low level in 1946 and 1947, at somewhat over half of the 1937 total; this is particularly striking for the industry component (mining, manufacturing, and construction). Obviously, the damage of the war and the dislocation of the economy and society in the rapid shifts immediately after the war adversely affected all production—but most disastrously the industry sector (I). Second, from the low levels of 1946 and 1947 there were extremely rapid relative rises, so that increases in output of 20 percent or more in a year were not uncommon (for example, the rise from 1948 to 1949 in the output of the A sector [about 20 percent] and of the I sector [over 30 percent]). This recovery tended to be relatively greater the lower the initial level and thus the greater the earlier decline. By 1954, the index for the industry sector, 132, was not much lower than that for the A sector, 137, although the 1946 index for the industry sector was only 25 and that for the agriculture sector was 64.

Table 1.6. Movements of Product and Components, 1946–1953 (constant prices)

A. Net domestic product and components, 1937 prices

Indexes, 1937 = 100

	1937 (1)	1946 (2)	1947 (3)	1948 (4)	1949 (5)	1950 (6)	1951-53 (7)
1. NDP Absolute value in mill. N.T.$	100.0 (842)	55	62	76	91	105	119
2. Agriculture, forestry, fishing	36.1	64	75	88	104	110	117
3. Mining, manufacturing, construction	27.1	25	29	46	61	70	92
4. All services	36.8	66	73	84	99	127	140
5. Transport, public utilities	7.5	62	73	90	103	111	132
6. Trade	17.2	48	56	71	86	94	108
7. Public administration, defense	5.1	84	84	77	107	240	240
8. Other services	7.0	102	107	115	120	142	150

B. Net national output: Gross value added in agriculture, food supply, and consumption, 1935-1937 prices

Indexes, line 9 = 100

	NNO (1)	Primary (2)	Secondary (3)	Tertiary (4)	Gross value added, agriculture (5)	Food supply (6)	Food consumption (7)
9. Absolute values 1936–40, per year, mill. N.T.$	797	280	270	247	303	374	219
10. 1946-50	50.6	57.8	38.8	66.1	70.0	77.7	122.9
11. 1951-55	91.5	91.2	63.1	122.8	120.5	114.9	184.9

Panel A: Taken or calculated from Economic Commission for Asia and the Far East (ECAFE), *Economic Survey of Asia and the Far East, 1955* (Bangkok, 1956), Table K, p. 208, Table L, p. 208, and Table O, pp. 211–12. Many of these indexes were reprinted in United Nations, *Statistics of National Income and Expenditure, Statistical Papers*, H-8 (New York, 1955), and H-9 (New York, 1956), Tables 1, 2, and 3. Entry in parentheses in column 1, line 1, is the volume of NDP in million of N.T.$. Entries in column 1, lines 2–8, are percentage shares of sectors and subsectors in NDP.

Panel B: Except for column 5, all entries are taken or calculated from the JCRR 1966 monograph by Hsieh and Lee, Appendix Table 1, p. 107, and Table 32, p. 90. Column 5 is taken or calculated from T. H. Lee and Y. E. Chen, *Growth Rates of Taiwan Agriculture, 1911–1972*, JCRR Economic Digest Series, no. 21 (Taipei, January 1975), Table 3, pp. 62ff.

Finally, one should note the distinctive behavior of two components of the services—public administration and defense, and other services. The public administration subdivision shows a large jump from 1949 to 1950, presumably reflecting the movement of the national government from the mainland in 1949 (line 7, columns 5 and 6). The other services subdivision, a mixed and residual category (line 8, columns 2-7), shows no decline from 1937 to 1946 and a moderate rise thereafter, suggesting that absence of better employment opportunities tended to swell the output of this component in poor times and that improvement in such opportunities tended to restrict its growth in better times. Thus, while the trade component tended to move roughly like the average of the A and I sectors, the remining service components, even transport and public utilities, tended to move differently.

The low initial levels after the war and the extremely high rates of increase thereafter for the important sectors of the economy, particularly the A and I sectors, illustrated in Panel A, lend meaning to the concept of recovery or rehabilitation, as distinct from that of normal growth. Recovery follows upon a violent dislocation, either in actual damage to material and to some human capital or in disturbance of the existing political and institutional patterns. Once the causes of such dislocation disappear, recovery can be rapid because human capital is largely preserved; because some parts of material capital are preserved and make material reconstruction much easier than building from scratch; and because experience has been accumulated in the past so that the human capital is of high level relative to the very low production levels attained in the first year after the war or dislocation is over. And, indeed, records such as those summarized in Table 1.6 for Taiwan can be observed for a number of other countries that suffered similar damage during World War II and then began the recovery period in the second half of the 1940s (for example, Germany and Japan). But once this process of rapid rehabilitation exhausts the easy reservoirs of immediate recovery, the extraordinary rates of relative increase end, until a further base for accelerated growth is achieved later. One should note that as compared with growth rates per year in total product ranging (in line 1) from 30 down to over 15 (from 1949 to 1950) and to less than 7 (over the two years from 1950 to 1951-53), the record for the decade that begins with 1951-53 shows annual growth rates of between over 6 to over 8.5 (see Table 1.8, Panel B). This would seem to justify terminating the recovery period in 1951-53, even though the income produced per capita of the much larger population then still fell substantially short of the product per capita of the much smaller population in 1937.

Most of Panel B is based on the 1966 JCRR estimates. Those for net national output, a concept assumed to be comparable with net domestic product, suggest greater declines and slower recovery from the prewar levels than is indicated in Panel A. Thus the index of total product for 1946-50 is about

51 (line 10, column 1), whereas in Panel A it would be about 78; and the index for 1951–55 of 91 (line 11, column 1) is appreciably lower than the average for 1951–54 from the source of Panel A (which would be well over 120). These differences would be only slightly affected by the use of 1938 (1936–40) prices in Panel B and of 1937 prices in Panel A. It is also puzzling that the JCRR estimate of gross value added in agriculture (which is properly a component of GDP) in column 5 shows much less decline and much greater recovery than GDP originating in the primary sector (agriculture, fishing, forestry) in column 2. However, with respect to the sharper decline in the secondary sector (industry) and the much greater recovery of the tertiary sector (services), the JCRR estimates reveal a pattern similar to that in Panel A.

The contrast between the movements of food supply and food consumption in columns 6 and 7 is similar to the difference between total product and its availability for domestic use, and the implicit contrast between the large excess of exports over imports in Taiwan as a colony in 1937 (or 1935–37) and the moderate excess of imports over exports in Taiwan in 1951–53 or 1951–55. On the basis of data to be discussed in the next section, the population of Taiwan may be assumed to have risen by 60 percent (including military and institutional personnel in the later date) between 1937 and 1952 (or between 1938 and 1953). If we take this population increase into account, NDP, or the output of agriculture per capita, would still fall short in 1951–53 relative to either 1937 or 1936–40, but food consumption per capita in 1951–55 would be more than 15 percent above that in 1936–40.

Two Decades of Growth: Population and Total Product

This section begins discussion of the central topic—growth and structural change in the economy of Taiwan over the two decades from 1951–53 to 1971–73. In this period the high rate of overall growth and the rapid rate of structural transformation were attained. The broader quantitative framework must be established as a background against which the analysis of the various aspects of Taiwan's economic growth may be more easily followed and evaluated.

The necessary consistent and comprehensive estimates of total population and product in constant prices are not directly available. The official estimates of population, summarized in Table 1.7, omit armed forces on military bases and the inmates of institutions (the latter not specified in the *Statistical Yearbook*) before the entry for the end of 1969. This omission is of some importance because large numbers were involved in the early years, and they contributed to the civilian labor force with the reduction in or their retirement from the armed forces. Although the adjustment needed to secure consistency over the period is necessarily approximately, it seems preferable to make it rather than try to derive trends from the unadjusted series.[11]

The subperiods within the span, three or four years each, were introduced to avoid the cumbersome detail involved in handling annual data and yet to provide enough detail to reveal the time pattern of the growth rates. The result, which might be called a growth calendar, was used in all subsequent tables. It omits the three years that follow 1973, which, covering the world recession phase, are discussed toward the end of this chapter.

The adjusted population record since the early 1950s, in Panel A, shows consistency between the totals for the successive subperiods, the growth rates over the intervals, and the rates of natural increase when related to the adjusted population bases (compare columns 4 and 6, lines 2–7). Such consistency indicates a largely closed population, in which changes are dominated by the differences between the birth and death rates.

Both the initially high population growth rate and its marked decline, caused largely by the decline of the birth rate, are clearly shown in Panel A. Two aspects of this record deserve particular notice. First, the steady and substantial reduction in the growth rate, or rate of natural increase, occurred despite marked reductions in the death rate. In relative terms, the decline in the latter from 7.5 in the first interval to 4.8 in the last, amounting to well over a third, is not much short of the relative decline in the crude birth rate from 42.1 to 26.0, or somewhat less than four-tenths. But it is the initially low level of the death rates that helped to translate declines in the birth rate into marked declines in the rate of natural increase. If the initial death rate had been in the upper 20s or close to 30 per thousand, it might have dropped more precipitously than the birth rate. In other words, success in reducing the death rate to lower absolute levels before 1950 made possible the marked slowdown of population growth over the two-decade period.

Second, the decline in the crude birth rate began after the first interval and before the effects of economic growth or of the population-planning programs could have been realized. To be sure, these are crude rates, and more detailed analysis of the sex and age composition of the population and the locus of

11. The results in column 3, lines 2-7, can be compared with the population totals implicit in the relation of total to per capita income (both in current factor costs) series published in DGBAS, *National Income of the Republic of China, December 1976* (Taipei, December 1976), Tables 7 and 10, pp. 21 and 25. Dividing the income total by per capita income for every calendar year, and averaging the resulting population totals for the periods shown in Panel A of Table 1.6, we obtain the following averages (in millions): 8.54; 9.64; 10.81; 11.89; 13.10; 14.28; and 15.22. These differ from the averages shown in column 3, lines 2-7, by an average of less than .1 million. The DGBAS series would presumably have been obtained by a procedure similar to that followed here, but the publication does not indicate the source of the underlying population figures.

Table 1.7. Population and Vital Rates, Unadjusted and Adjusted,* 1951-1973

A. Population (midyear) and vital rates

	Population					Vital rates (per 1,000)		
	Unadjusted (mill.) (1)	(percentage of column 1) (2)	Adjusted (mill.) (3)	Growth rate (per 1,000 per year) (4)	Percentage adjustment in base (5)	Natural increase (6)	Birth rate (7)	Death rate (8)
1. 1951-53	8.00	8.14	8.65	33.4	7.56	34.6	42.1	7.5
2. 1954-57	9.07	6.99	9.70	30.2	6.09	32.4	39.9	7.5
3. 1958-60	10.24	5.19	10.77	30.3	4.56	30.8	37.3	6.5
4. 1961-63	11.33	3.93	11.78	28.9	3.76	28.1	33.8	5.7
5. 1964-67	12.62	2.78	12.97	25.5	2.66	23.7	29.0	5.3
6. 1968-70	13.81	2.53	14.16	22.4	1.26	21.2	26.0	4.8
7. 1971-73	n.a.		15.13					
	Growth rates per year and average vital rates							
8. Lines 1-4				31.4		32.7	39.9	7.2
9. Lines 4-7				25.4		24.5	29.8	5.3
10. Lines 1-7				28.4		29.1	35.3	6.2

B. Distribution of population (adjusted) by age and sex

	Age 0-14		Age 15+	Males 15+		Females 15+		Males 15+
	Mill. (1)	Percent of total (2)	Mill. (3)	Mill. (4)	Percentage of total (5)	Mill. (6)	Percentage of total (7)	Unadjusted mill. (8)
11. 1951-53	3.37	39.0	5.28	3.01	34.8	2.27	26.2	2.36
12. 1954-57	3.94	40.6	5.76	3.25	33.5	2.51	25.9	2.61
13. 1958-60	4.58	42.6	6.19	3.41	31.6	2.78	25.8	2.88
14. 1961-63	5.19	44.1	6.59	3.59	30.5	3.00	25.4	3.15
15. 1964-67	5.64	43.5	7.33	3.94	30.4	3.39	26.1	3.59
16. 1968-70	5.80	40.9	8.37	4.48	31.7	3.89	27.4	4.13
17. 1971-73	5.80	38.3	9.34	4.98	32.9	4.36	28.8	4.98
	Growth rates, percent per year							
18. Lines 11-14	4.41		2.24	1.78		2.83		2.92
19. Lines 14-17	1.11		3.55	3.32		3.82		4.70
20. Lines 11-17	2.74		2.90	2.55		3.33		3.80

*Unadjusted figures exclude armed forces on military bases and inmates of institutions not reported prior to 1969 (end of year). Adjusted figures include these groups.

Panel A: Lines 1–6, column 1: The unadjusted population totals and vital rates are from DGBAS, *Statistical Yearbook, 1975*, Table 18, pp. 2–3. Population is given at end of year; midyear values were obtained by averaging. To end of 1968 the totals are unadjusted; military and some institutional population are included first at end of 1969. The unadjusted population total for end of 1969 and end of 1970 was approximated (to derive the average in line 6, column 1), by estimating the growth rate from end of 1968 to end of 1969 on the basis of the growth rates of comparable totals in the preceding and following two-year spans.

Lines 1–6, column 2: Three basic items of evidence underlie these estimates. One is the comparison for the end of 1966 of the census totals (including military) and the registered population totals (the continuous series), which shows a differential of about 350,000. The other is the comparison at end of 1969 between the new adjusted totals and the extrapolated unadjusted estimate (see note to lines 1–6, column 1) which yielded a difference of about 360,000. The third was the estimate by Paul K. C. Liu by the reverse survival method "applied to the 1970 registered population to estimate the number of those not retired from military forces for 1965, 1960, 1955, and 1950" (see his "The Population of Taiwan, 1945–1990," *Proceedings of Sino-American Conference on Manpower in Taiwan* [Taipei, 1972], p. 71). Liu's estimate, in Table 1, p. 85, shows an addition of 570,000 in 1950, 548,000 in 1955, 389,000 in 1960, and 235,000 in 1965. These estimates are clearly too low, considering the differentials of 350 to 360,000 noted above for end of 1966 and 1969, respectively; this may be due to inclusion of institutional population, which I estimated for 1969 at about 1.1 percent of the unadjusted population total. This percentage was applied to the unadjusted totals in column 1 and the result added to Liu's estimates of the discrepancy for the four base years (1950, 1955, 1960, and 1965). This revised proportion (relative) of additions to the unadjusted population was then extrapolated, linearly, to estimate the percentages in column 2, which refer to the midyear of each three- or four-year period.

Lines 2–10, column 4: Calculated from column 3, for the three- or four-year intervals in lines 2–7, the ten-year intervals in lines 8–9, and the twenty-year interval in line 10.

Lines 2–10, columns 5–8: The unadjusted vital rates, that is, to the base of unadjusted population as given in column 1, lines 1–6, are from the same source and table as the entries for unadjusted population. In all the averaging of vital rates, the additions of rates for single years are to make up the intervals as they extend from the midpoint of one three-year or four-year calculated (the midyear population) could be derived by simple averaging of the adjustment percentages in column 2 of Panel A. average to the midpoint of the next. This meant also that the adjustment in the base to which the unadjusted vital rates were In defining the averages for the longer periods (lines 8, 9, 10), the arithmetic means of rates shown in lines 2–7, columns 4–6, were weighted by the number of years in each interval (which varied from 3.5 to 3.0).

Panel B: The basic data here are partly those for unadjusted population by age and sex shown in DGBAS, *Statistical Yearbook, 1975*, Population Supplement Table 1, pp. 4–9; partly the estimate of the adjustment in Panel A. The governing assumption for use of the adjustment is that it applies to males aged fifteen and over, but does not affect either the population aged up to fifteen or females aged fifteen and over.

The unadjusted totals for males aged fifteen and over were derived by using the entries as shown through 1968 in the *Statistical Yearbook, 1975*, and then extrapolated by the rate of increase in that population on the basis of growth rates in it (unadjusted) in the two years preceding 1968 and in the two years (adjusted) following 1969.

The calculation of growth rates in lines 18–20 follows the procedure employed in the calculation of the growth rates in column 4, lines 8–10, except that they are stated in percent per year, rather than as per thousand per year.

birth-rate declines is required. But Panel B shows that the proportion in the total population of women age fifteen and over has declined but little within the period from 1951–53 to 1961–63 (lines 11–14, column 7), although it rose from 1961–63 to 1971–73 sufficiently to accentuate the decline in the birth rate, as we shift from ratios to total population to ratios to the population of females over fifteen. One should finally note that the initial level of the crude birth rate in Table 1.7, 42 per thousand, was already somewhat below that prevailing in Taiwan in the decades just before World War II.

A decline in the birth rate, when voluntary and occurring under conditions of an economy and society with consumer sovereignty, is a trend of major significance in modern growth, and not only because of its effects on capital formation and the allocation of material product. It is even more significant as an indication of changes in attitude of the population to future prospects as they bear upon the economic and social fortunes of both the parental generation and that of their children. For it is only the belief in a better social and economic status for both parents and children, with greater investment in fewer children (as well as a low death rate), that would result in a massive enough reduction of the birth rate to have a major effect on the aggregate vital rate.

Panel B illustrates the effects of the migration from the mainland (including the adjustment for armed forces) and of the changing birth rate on the sex and age structure of the population over the two-decade period. The inflow, preponderantly of men, produced, in the initial subperiod, 1951–53, a large excess of men over women in the age group fifteen and over. The differential, which amounts to 8.6 percentage points (in percent of total population) in 1951–53, declined steadily, but was still 4.1 points in 1971–73 (compare columns 5 and 7, lines 11 and 17). Since the participation rate in the labor force is so much higher for men than for women, these differentials made for a high ratio of labor force to population fifteen and over in the beginning, which declined over the period.

The effect of the changing birth rate was different. The high birth rate of the earlier years tended to raise the proportion of population aged under fifteen which increased from 39 percent in 1951–53 to 44 percent in 1961–63 (lines 11–14, column 2); and the decline in the birth rate caused, with some delay, this share to drop from 44 percent in 1961–63 to 38 percent in 1971–73 (lines 14 and 17, column 2). The share of the population aged fifteen and over, predominantly of working ages (the share of people aged sixty-five and over remained low) decreased from 1951–53 to 1961–63 and then rose to 1971–73.

These data explain the different time patterns shown by the growth rates in lines 18 and 19, relating to the first and second decades, respectively. The growth rate of population under fifteen years of age shows a sharp drop from 4.4 percent per year in the first decade to 1.1 percent in the second (lines 18 and 19, column 1). The growth rate of population aged fifteen and over rose from 2.2 percent in the first decade to 3.6 in the second (lines 18–19, column 3). The rates for men and women within the population fifteen and over differ because of the differential effect of the inflow of mainlanders; they also differ depending on adjustment for inclusion of the armed forces and institutional population. It is worthy of note that the growth rate for the unadjusted series of males fifteen and over (column 8) is much higher than that for the adjusted series (column 4), reflecting the effect of the flow from the omitted component into the civilian population.

In determining growth rates for total product, several problems arise in securing an acceptable series of estimates in constant prices. Given the complex problems of inclusion, netness, and valuation in national product aggregates, some of the resulting questions are not easily answered. They should be considered, however, if only to convey an adequate notion of the measures finally employed.

The official estimates available are of gross domestic product at market prices, "deflated" or adjusted to constant prices with 1971 as the base year. The deflation is carried through separately for the components and subcomponents of GDP: government consumption, with a distinction between employee compensation and goods purchased from other sectors; private consumer expenditures, subdivided into such categories as food, clothing, housing, etc.; gross domestic capital formation, subdivided into increase in stock (with six subgroups) and gross fixed capital formation, with building, transport equipment, and other machinery and equipment distinguished.[12] These three major components constitute the total that may be designated "domestic uses." To it are added exports, adjusted by price indexes for goods and services; and from it are subtracted imports, similarly adjusted. The resulting total, gross domestic product, is *gross* only in the sense that no deduction was made for the current consumption of durable, fixed capital, but it is net in all other respects; and it is *domestic* only in the sense that it disregards the net flow of factor income across boundaries, which is a relatively minor negative item in the Taiwan national accounts (although this is partly because some of the financial transfers to the country in the 1950s were in the form of grants).

In short, gross domestic product is a familiar concept in accepted national economic accounting and provides a good approximation to the relevant product of the Taiwan economy. It is subject to the usual limitations in that it excludes a variety of productive activities within the household and fails to recognize (and deduct) implicit costs associated with industrialization and the shift from the rural village to urban industrial conditions of life and work. But

12. For details on the procedure used in deriving product and income in constant prices, see DGBAS, *Statistical Yearbook, 1975*, pp. 383–85.

we have to use this concept and are concerned here only with the shift of the totals from current to constant prices. Three questions arise: (1) why was 1971 selected as the base year for converting the recent totals and those back to the early 1950s, although the older sources provide estimates in prices based on earlier years; (2) what was the method of adjusting the balance of exports and imports in current prices, included in the total (with a minus or plus sign), for price changes; (3) and what are the implications of the adjustment (in the official series) of the government consumption component for price changes.

(1) The use of 1971 prices implies that approximations to quantity indexes of output of the various goods are weighted by their 1971 prices. A current value series of a specific commodity or service deflated by a price index to the base of 1971 yields, for every year, the quantity of the good weighted by its 1971 price. It is generally true that if the volumes of some goods grow more rapidly than those of other goods, their prices rise less rapidly (or decline more) than those of other goods. This negative association over time between relative changes in quantities and prices is caused by the differential impact of technical change on costs, hence on prices, and hence on the differences in growth rates in the demand for various goods.

Because of this negative association, the growth rate of an aggregate in constant prices depends on the position of the base year within the growth period (and, of course, on the extent of structural change). The use of initial year prices yields higher growth rates over the period than the use of terminal year prices. The difference can be substantial, and is meaningful. It means that the rate of advance in total product is estimated more highly when viewed in terms of initial year prices, that is, evaluated by the community of that earlier year looking forward, than when viewed in terms of terminal year prices, that is, by the current generation looking backward. Given this difference in meaning and the analytical significance of each, no single way of choosing the base year for conversion of product to constant prices is "correct." One may, for the present, accept the more general practice of using a late or terminal base year—in this case 1971—thus appraising the rate of economic advance in the more conservative evaluation of contemporaries looking backward and dealing with the past advance, rather than the more exuberant evaluation that would be ascribed to the earlier generation if it could have foreseen the advance actually made.

(2) The conventional adjustment of the export-import balance involves converting both exports and imports to constant prices and taking the difference. But one may argue that for a country viewed as a national unit vis-à-vis others it is the difference between exports and imports (both including factor flows) in current prices that measures the change in obligations incurred or claims augmented, and that it is this difference in current prices that has to be deflated by an appropriate price index. The two approaches

would yield identical results only if the prices of inflows and outflows move at the same rate. Otherwise, the difference would reflect gains or losses from changes in relative prices.

In fact, the price movements for exports and imports were fairly similar over the long period covered, at least for the three- or four-year periods involved in this analysis (see columns 7 and 8, Panel A, of Table 1.8). And the adjustment for gains and losses caused by changes in terms of trade, actually calculated in the Taiwan economic accounts, when added to the official totals, would modify the growth rates only slightly: the average growth rate for the first period would remain at 7.0 percent per year (see line 18, column 4 of Table 1.8) and that for the second period would drop from 10.0 to 9.8.[13] The modifications did not seem sufficiently large to warrant complicating the presentation; therefore the item was omitted from further analysis.

(3) The deflation of the government consumption component raises questions of substantial effect on the movements of the product total in constant prices and the growth rates yielded by them. An examination of the implicit prices in Panel A of Table 1.8 indicates that those for government consumption, in particular those for the employee compensation part, show trends quite different from those for other domestic components (see lines 8, 9, and 10, columns 2 and 3 compared with columns 4–8).

The source of these data reveals that the price index used to deflate employee compensation in the government sector was that of compensation of government employees; that for government consumption of other goods was the price index of office supplies in Taipei. The former procedure assumes no increase in the productivity of labor employed by the government, which is difficult to accept considering the rise in productivity in the nongovernment parts of the economy. It is also surprising that the index of compensation of government employees rose by elevenfold from 1951–53 to 1971–73. Monthly earnings in manufacturing, a series that should fully reflect the rapidly rising productivity in that sector, rose from N.T.$ 335 in 1951–53 to N.T.$ 2,340 in 1971–73, only sevenfold.[14] And the deflation of the purchases component of government consumption by prices of office supplies may be questioned on the ground that such purchases are much more varied.

A questionable result of the deflation procedure is that whereas the share of government consumption in total gross domestic product ranges between 17

13. For the adjustment see DGBAS, *National Income of the Republic of China* (Taipei, December 1975), Tables 7 and 8, pp. 21–22.

14. See DGBAS, *Statistical Yearbook, 1975*, p. 384; Table 171, pp. 176–77. If the high rate of increase in the index of compensation of government employees is due to a rising quality mix, a corresponding rise in productivity would be implied, and the index should be adjusted accordingly.

Table 1.8. Gross Domestic Product in 1971 Prices, Alternative Totals, 1951–1973

A. Implicit price indexes, 1971 = 100

	Total (1)	Government consumption		Private consumption (4)	GDCF (5)	Cols. 4 and 5 (6)	Exports (7)	Imports (8)	GDP (9)
		Employee compensation (2)	Other (3)						
1. 1951–53	15.5	10.4	38.5	36.7	38.1	36.8	29.8	28.5	30.4
2. 1954–57	25.5	16.9	52.9	49.7	60.3	51.3	48.1	45.8	44.3
3. 1958–60	36.4	25.3	64.8	64.9	82.6	68.1	69.2	74.1	57.3
4. 1961–63	47.1	36.8	71.7	76.5	83.5	78.0	86.0	83.7	69.3
5. 1964–67	59.3	50.8	77.2	80.8	90.6	83.3	89.2	88.1	77.9
6. 1968–70	82.3	76.2	92.8	93.7	97.3	94.8	95.2	93.8	92.6
7. 1971–73	108.8	110.2	106.6	108.4	113.4	110.0	113.7	117.8	108.6
			Rates of increase, percent per year						
8. 1951–53 to 1961–63	11.8	13.4	6.4	7.6	8.2	7.8	11.2	11.4	8.6
9. 1961–63 to 1971–73	8.7	11.6	4.0	3.6	3.1	3.5	2.8	3.5	4.6
10. 1951–53 to 1971–73	10.2	12.5	5.2	5.6	5.6	5.6	6.9	7.4	6.6

B. Gross domestic product, 1971 prices, three variants (absolute totals in billions of N.T.$)

	Absolute totals			Growth rates, percent per year		
	As given (1)	Different price index for govt. cons. (2)	Omit govt. cons. (3)	Col. 1 (4)	Col. 2 (5)	Col. 3 (6)
11. 1951–53	57.52	46.66	38.78	7.49	8.79	7.68
12. 1954–57	75.26	62.66	50.24	6.24	6.98	7.00
13. 1958–60	93.02	79.34	63.66	6.83	8.27	8.54
14. 1961–63	113.4	100.7	81.41	9.76	11.35	12.01
15. 1964–67	157.1	146.7	121.1	9.20	10.49	10.14
16. 1968–70	213.8	208.0	169.8	11.20	12.15	13.15
17. 1971–73	294.0	293.4	246.0			
Growth rates, percent per year, longer intervals						
Total product						
18. 1951–53 to 1961–63				7.02	8.00	7.70
19. 1961–63 to 1971–73				10.00	11.29	11.69
20. 1951–53 to 1971–73				8.50	9.63	9.68
20a. Multiples, 1971–73/1951–53				5.1	6.3	6.3
Product per capita						
21. 1951–53 to 1961–63				3.76	4.71	4.42
22. 1961–63 to 1971–73				7.28	8.53	8.92
23. 1951–53 to 1971–73				5.50	6.60	6.65
23a. Multiples, 1971–73/1951–53				2.9	3.6	3.6

Panel A: The implicit price indexes were derived by dividing the current price totals for the periods indicated in the stub of lines 1–7 by the corresponding totals in 1971 prices. The underlying data for columns 1 and 4–9 are from DGBAS, *Statistical Yearbook, 1975*, National Accounts, Suppl. Tables 1–3, pp. 194ff. For columns 2–3 see DGBAS, *National Income of the Republic of China, December 1972* (Taipei, 1972) and *December 1975* (Taipei, 1975), Table XI, 1972, pp. 156ff., for current price totals through 1957; Table XI, 1975, pp. 120ff., for current price totals beginning in 1958; Table XIII, 1975, pp. 124ff., for 1971 price totals.

Panel B: From DGBAS, *Statistical Yearbook, 1975*, the tables indicated in notes to Panel A. The growth rates in per capita product (lines 21–23) use the growth rates of population, as adjusted, shown in Table 1.7 above.

and 20 percent in volumes in current prices, with no apparent trend, that in 1971 prices declines from 33 percent in 1954–57 (and 31 in 1951–53) to about half, 16.3, in 1971–73. The result is to reduce the overall rate of growth of GDP in constant prices. The effects would not have been so marked if the share of the government sector in current prices were smaller or the rise in productivity in the nongovernment sector so pronounced.

An intensive exploration of this problem is not feasible here and is beyond the competence of any individual scholar without access to the repositories of the detailed, underlying data. Under the circumstances, it seems worthwhile to suggest crude alternatives. One is to apply to the current price total of government consumption the general index of prices derived for the sum of private consumption and gross domestic capital formation (see Panel A, column 6, lines 1–7). The other is to omit government consumption entirely and deal with the remaining private components of the economy (including government enterprises not covered under government consumption). The former alternative seems more acceptable and less likely to disturb comparability with other countries.[15]

The implication of this alternative is suggested by comparing the price index for column 6 in Panel A, the new index used, with that in columns 1–3, used in the official estimates. The productivity rise in the government consumption component meant about doubling of ''real'' output per employee (derived from comparing the 5.6 percent rate of rise per year in the price index in column 6, line 10, with the 10.2 percent rate in line 10, column 1, and the 12.5 percent rate in column 2). Such a substantial rise is to be expected because of the change in the mix, with decline in proportion of the armed services and rise in the proportion of civilian government employees; because of the usual rise in the quality mix of civilian government employment; and because of the provision of more capital equipment in some branches of government activity. For the economy as a whole, largely dominated by the nongovernment sector, the rise in real product per employed was, over the period, substantially greater; but this might have been affected more by intersectoral shifts than would have been the case in government. This crude adjustment yields a more realistic trend in structure and results in aggregate

15. The choice was made despite a judgment that there are strong analytical reasons for viewing government activity, except that directly providing benefits to final consumers (education, health, recreation, and the like), as producing intermediate rather than final products, serving to maintain and lubricate the social and economic mechanisms which turn out the final goods. On this view, the only part of government consumption that should be included in total product (viewed as an aggregate of final goods) is the input of personnel and goods into the kind of services listed above. This alternative was not followed, for it would have impaired comparability with the conventionally derived totals for other countries.

growth rates quite close to those for the variant that completely omits the government-consumption component.[16]

Before passing on these results, we should note that the implicit price indexes for all components show a decline in the rate of increase in the second decade as compared with the first (lines 8 and 9, columns 1–8). These declines are quite marked (but most moderate in the index for employee compensation in government in column 2), to less than half the rate in the first decade. Of course, these indexes have been derived by dividing current price totals by 1971 price totals, and they reflect not only changes in prices of individual goods but also shifts of weights within the groups. But the trends are so conspicuous that they would persist in price indexes with internal weights constant. Thus, the general wholesale price index (1971 = 100) rises from an average of 40.6 in 1951–53 to 88.5 in 1961–63 and 110.9 in 1971–73, yielding rates of rise of 8.1 percent in the first period and of 2.3 percent in the second.[17] Panel B of Table 1.8 shows that the rate of growth of real output accelerated from the first to the second decades for total product and even more for per capita product. This negative association over time between the rate of growth of real product and the rate of price inflation is, of course, no accident. A greater growth in the supply of goods per capita will tend to constrain the rate of rise of prices, directly and indirectly (in suggesting conditions under which pressure for excess money and higher velocity would slacken).

Panel B reveals high growth rates, in total and per capita product, for all three variants—but they are distinctly higher when a more general price index for the government consumption component is assumed or that component is omitted entirely. For total product and the full period, the difference is between a growth rate of 8.5 percent per year for the official series, compared with more than 9.6 percent for the two alternative variants (line 20); on a per capita basis, the official series (using adjusted population totals) yields a growth rate of 5.5 percent per year, compared with more than 6.5 percent, a shortfall of almost a fifth.

The acceleration in the growth rate of total product from the first to the second decades is quite marked, especially in the rates for per capita product. The entries for six intervals in columns 4–6 of Panel B indicate that through

16. In his review of the original version of this chapter, Mo-huan Hsing, formerly of the Institute of Economics of Academia Sinica and currently at the Chinese University of Hong Kong, made several intriguing suggestions for alternative bases of deriving deflation indexes for government outlays on employee compensation and on purchases of goods. But their application would require access to the underlying data and greater familiarity with the value and reliability of these data than I was in a position to command. Like several other deviations from the official and other estimates in this chapter, the procedure followed here is an easy but crude expedient—preferred for analytical reasons, but not offered as a final substitute.

17. See *Statistical Yearbook, 1975,* Table 172-B, pp. 178–79.

the first decade none of the three intervals showed growth rates as high as they did in the second decade—demonstrating that the much higher growth rate in the second decade was not due to a limited, sharp, single aberration. A similar comparison would be even more impressive for the rates over the shorter intervals in per capita product. Finally, one should note that, although decadal rates were computed from the three-year terminal averages (1951–53, 1961–63, and 1971–73), the use of longer spans would not affect the result markedly.[18]

Rates of rise in per capita product of from 5.5 to 6.5 percent per year (implying a doubling every 13 or 11.5 years), over a period as long as two decades, are uncommon in the growth experience of either developed or less developed countries—even in the decades since World War II. These rates are at least three times as high as those that could be estimated for Taiwan during its colonial era; and as the comparisons in Table 1.9 show, they loom large among the high-level rates in the post–World War II experience.

In Table 1.9 the growth rates in the two variants for Taiwan of gross domestic product, total and per capita of population and of population aged fifteen and over, are compared with those for several neighboring countries in East Asia and with those for major less developed (LDC) regions and the group of developed market economies as a whole. Growth in total product was related not only to that in total population, but also to that in population of working ages (fifteen and over). To be sure, trends in employed labor force might differ from those in population fifteen and over because of possible movements in the age structure above fifteen, and particularly because of changing labor force participation rates, separately for men and women. Yet for Taiwan, as will be shown, there was a similar acceleration in growth rates of the labor force from the first to the second decades (from 1.6 to 2.8 percent per year), although the general level of these growth rates was somewhat below those for population fifteen and over.

The findings in Table 1.9 may be briefly indicated. First, for the period as a whole, the rate of growth in Taiwan's total product, from 8.5 to 9.5 percent per year, approached the high level for Japan of 9.7 percent per year and was

18. For the variant in column 2 of Panel B, calculation of a growth rate for the first decade between the geometric mean of 1951–53 and 1954–57 (with allowance for different durations) and 1958–60 and 1961–63 yielded a growth rate per year of 7.7 percent (compared with 8.0 in column 5, line 18); a similar calculation for the second decade yielded a growth rate per year of 11.3 percent (compared with 11.3 in line 19, column 5). For the total period, I then calculated the growth rate between the geometric mean for 1951–53 to 1968–70, and 1964–67 to 1971–73, segments of ten years each, obtaining a growth rate per year of 9.5 percent (compared with 9.6 percent in line 20, column 5).

Similar computations, or lines fitted by least squares, could have been attempted for other variants, or the diverse estimates presented later in the chapter. But it seemed best to keep the presentation simple and not to place much weight on small differences.

well above the rates for other countries in East Asia, in the LDC regions (in which East–Southeast Asia is dominated by India), or among the developed market economies. Second, the rate of growth of product per capita (either of total population or of population of working ages) remained high in Taiwan, in comparison with the rest of the world (although lower than in Japan). Third, the acceleration in the rate of growth in both total and per capita product from the first to the second decade also occurred in other countries in East Asia, except the Philippines, which also had a relatively low average growth rate (compared with other countries in Table 1.9).

Widening the comparison in Table 1.9 to include other countries would probably reveal cases of high growth rates similar to Taiwan's and might increase the number of exceptions to the finding of acceleration of growth rates from the first to the second decades, but would not likely change the broad conclusions suggested by Table 1.9. These conclusions are that the growth rates in Taiwan were high, but in other countries, particularly Japan, they were as high or higher and that the acceleration in the rate of growth from the first to the second decades, in total and per capita product, was, on the whole, fairly general, although the increase in the rate between the two decades was particularly large for Taiwan. In addition, the difference in movements between total population and population aged fifteen and over observed for Taiwan also occurred in other countries where birth rates had already begun to decline (for example, South Korea and the Latin American group among the less developed countries); but not where that decline was still to come (the Philippines, and the East–Southeast Asia LDCs) or has been in progress for a long time (Japan) (compare lines 10 and 11 with lines 12 and 13).

The attainment of high and accelerating growth rates in Taiwan, concurrently with those among some major neighbors, as well as in many other parts of the world, has a twofold analytical bearing in any attempt to explain these features of growth in Taiwan proper. First, given the expected economic flows among market economies, particularly those in geographical and historical proximity to each other, the fact that some of them experience a rapid rate of growth in total and per capita product makes it easier to explain a similar experience in other countries of the group. Thus Japan's spectacular economic growth from the early 1950s to the early 1970s is a significant factor in the high growth rates of Japan's trading neighbors, including Taiwan; reciprocally, the high growth rate in Japan's trading neighbors contributes to Japan's growth. In that sense, the growth experience of any single country is a function of the growth of others, especially if, because of its limited size, the country in question must rely heavily on the international division of labor through higher proportions of foreign trade to domestic product.

Second, the concurrent presence of other countries with high growth rates

Table 1.9. Growth Rates in Total and Per Capita Product, Taiwan and Other Countries Compared, The Two-Decade Span (1951-1953 to 1971-1973) and Subperiods

	Taiwan		Japan (3)	S. Korea (4)	Philippines (5)	Thailand (6)	ESE Asia (7)	Latin America (8)	Developed countries (9)
	Official estimate (1)	Revised estimate (2)							
	Full period, S—standard dates—1951-1953 to 1971-1973								
1. Dates	S	S	1952-54 1971-73	1953-55 1971-73	S	S	S	S	S
			Growth rates, percent per year						
2. Total product	8.50	9.63	9.74	7.49	5.70	6.71	4.38	5.73	4.35
3. Population total	2.84	2.84	1.08	2.37	3.11	3.03	2.39	2.77	1.09
4. Population fifteen and over	2.90	2.90	1.81	2.63	2.88	2.73	2.12	2.80	1.21
5. Product per cap.	5.50	6.60	8.57	5.01	2.51	3.57	1.94	2.88	3.22
6. Product per cap. fifteen and over	5.44	6.54	7.79	4.74	2.74	3.87	2.39	2.85	3.10
		Subperiods I and II, standard middle date 1961-1963							
7. Middle date	S	S	S	1962-63	S	S	S	S	S
			Growth rates, percent per year						
Total product									
8. Subper. I	7.02	8.00	9.27	4.94	5.96	5.51	4.06	5.46	3.85
9. Subper. II	10.00	11.29	10.17	10.10	5.45	7.93	4.71	6.01	4.85
Total population									
10. Subper. I	3.14	3.14	1.08	2.78	2.96	2.91	2.25	2.79	1.22
11. Subper. II	2.54	2.54	1.08	2.07	3.24	3.15	2.54	2.75	0.96
Population, fifteen and over									
12. Subper. I	2.24	2.24	2.03	2.33	2.69	2.40	1.91	2.94	1.21
13. Subper. II	3.55	3.55	1.60	2.85	3.08	3.06	2.34	2.65	1.21

Product per capita, total population

14. Subper. I	3.76	4.71	8.10	2.10	2.91	2.53	1.77	2.60	2.60
15. Subper. II	7.28	8.53	8.99	7.87	2.14	4.63	2.12	3.17	3.85

Product per capita, population fifteen and over

16. Subper. I	4.68	5.63	7.10	2.55	3.18	3.04	2.11	2.45	2.61
17. Subper. II	6.23	7.47	8.44	7.05	2.30	4.73	2.32	3.27	3.60

The entries for Taiwan in columns 1 and 2, the official estimate of gross domestic product at 1971 market prices, the revised estimate using a different deflation procedure for government consumption, and the population estimates, all of which were used to calculate the growth rates, are from Tables 1.7 and 1.8.

The underlying gross product estimates for other countries and regions are largely from United Nations, *Yearbook of National Accounts Statistics, 1969*, vol. II, *International Tables* (New York, 1970); and United Nations, *Yearbook of National Accounts Statistics, 1975*, vol. III, *International Tables* (New York, 1976). Table 6B, which gives indexes of gross domestic product at constant market prices for broad regions, such as East and Southeast Asia, Latin America, or all developed market economies (columns 7–9 here); and Table 7, which gives indexes, for selected individual countries, of gross domestic product at factor cost (for Japan, GNP at market prices; for the Philippines, NDP at factor costs; for Thailand, GDP at market prices). The 1969 *Yearbook of National Accounts Statistics* volume was used to calculate the growth rate for subperiod I. For Thailand the series was carried back to 1951 by the data in OECD Development Center, *National Accounts of Less Developed Countries, 1950–1966* (Paris, 1968), Table C, p. 21.

The underlying estimates of population, total and aged fifteen and over, for countries and regions other than Taiwan, were taken from United Nations, Population Division, "Selected World Demographic Indicators by Countries, 1950–2000," Working Paper ESA/P/WP.55 (mimeo, May 1975), which shows population for 1950, 1955, 1960, 1965, 1970, and medium projection to 1975, for a number of countries and regions, and the proportion of population fifteen and over for each of these years. The growth rates for subperiod I were calculated using the geometric mean for 1950 and 1955 as the initial date and 1960–65 mean as the terminal date; the geometric means for 1960–65 and 1970–75 were used as the data for subperiod II.

The totals for Japan, South Korea, the Philippines, and Thailand, and Latin America were available directly. For East and South East Asia two subregions were added—East South Asia and Middle South Asia. To derive the totals for the developed market economies I took the overall total for the more developed regions shown in the source, and subtracted those for USSR and eastern Europe. The residual is still somewhat wider than the coverage of the product total, since the former still includes temperate South America (Argentina, Uruguay, and Chile); but the discrepancy is minor.

The growth rates in per capita (total population) or in per capita of population aged fifteen and over were derived by division of the growth rates in product by the growth rates in population (each added to 100).

increases the number of cases in which the determining factors that explain the high growth results can be observed. Thus, any hypothesis formulated to account for Taiwan can be examined in the light of similar experience elsewhere. And, of course, as the averages for the Philippines suggest, and as many other cases would illustrate, some countries, not unlike Taiwan in relative economic standing, experienced different growth patterns. Here again any hypothesis formulated to account for Taiwan's growth performance can be examined to see whether it includes factors present, but inoperative, in countries with distinctly lower growth rates.

The implication is that an explanation of the high growth rates in the economy of Taiwan during the last two decades cannot be adequately tested without also examining similar and divergent experiences in other market economies. Given a strict definition of ''adequately tested,'' the implication is valid. Nevertheless, available knowledge of these experiences may be used to advance tentative hypotheses to provide a preliminary indication of the directions in which a fuller and more adequately tested theory should be sought.

Thus, in considering the factors that might have raised the growth rate to high levels during the last two to two and a half decades and observing first the developed market economies (disregarding the communist countries with their entirely different institutional and social organization), one may note that very high growth rates are found in countries like Japan and Germany (and also Italy and France). For a long period before World War II, these countries lost ground because of distortions in their institutional structure and war preparations; they were then subjected to wide destruction and collapse of their political structures during the war. This long withdrawal from participation in peacetime progress, which lasted from the early 1930s to the late 1940s in Japan and Germany, even longer in Italy, and also affected France, did not occur in developed market economies in North America or Oceania. Nor were the latter affected by the destructive impact of World War II or by any collapse of antecedent political and institutional structures. The two factors to be stressed are the increased backlog of new production opportunities that accumulated because of the long withdrawal from effective participation in peacetime progress before and during the war, and the drastic change in institutional structure after the war that was conducive to a better exploitation of the augmented growth opportunities. The increased backlog may be suggested by assuming that by the time prewar per capita levels were restored after the immediate postwar reconstruction, two decades had elapsed during which the country's peacetime production per capita was very low, thus failing to utilize the growth potential that in more normal times might have meant a rise in per capita product to about 2 percent per year. If new institutions enable a country to resume the old pace and also to catch up with the accumulated backlog in, say, about twenty years, a growth rate of 4.04 percent per year would be required.[19]

The additions to the backlog of unexploited production opportunities are provided by the forward movement of technology and economic efficiency in other countries not affected by the conditions that retarded progress elsewhere. This growth-stimulating effect of a widened backlog of unexploited production opportunities may be a factor even in LDCs. Though a backlog is presumably continuously present in them, even in some less developed countries per capita product may have grown in the past (as in Taiwan under Japanese occupation), a process that may have been interrupted by war preparations and war (again as in Taiwan since the early or middle 1930s). If, as noted above, Taiwan managed, even with Japanese dominance and constraints on domestic industrialization, to attain a growth rate of between 1 and 2 percent per capita per year before war preparations began, the interruption added to the effective backlog of production opportunities. Once the institutional and political conditions had changed, a much higher growth rate could be attained. The weight of this factor of additional backlog in other less developed countries after World War II clearly depended upon the specific growth history of the country; but it presumably had much less weight than in developed countries like Japan and Germany and perhaps also than in Taiwan.

The change in institutional structure was an important factor in developed countries that had lost the war and needed to replace outworn and unsuitable prewar institutions, but was even more important in the less developed countries. The latter needed to catch up not merely for the one and a half to two decades of lost time, but for a much longer period of falling behind and for a much wider spread between their economic performance and that of the developed economies. The importance of that far-reaching change in the political structure of Taiwan and the emergence of a group capable of guiding and manning the transformation of economic and social institutions have been noted in the discussion of the transition period.

In short, one could attempt to explain the high rate of aggregate growth in the last two to two and a half decades in Taiwan by examining the contributions of the stimulating effects of a wide backlog of unexploited new production opportunities, of the major structural changes in economic and social institutions, and of the effect of high growth rates generated for similar rea-

19. Assuming that a country's per capita product was 100 in 1933 and that it was still 100 in 1953 (a loss of growth over a two-decade period), the catching up (assuming a normal growth rate of 2 percent per capita per year) would require a level of 220.8 by 1973. To reach the latter level over the two decades from 1953 to 1973 would require a rate of growth averaging 4.04 percent per year. (Variations within this twenty-year period are, of course, compatible with such an average that would reach its aim by 1973.)

sons in important neighboring countries and in much of the world at large. Also the acceleration from the first to the second decade could be associated with the slowness with which the new reforms and institutional devices were introduced and accepted. It may also have awaited the flows of material and human capital that were rapidly built up during the first decade.

All of these are, of course, preliminary and general conjectures, useful in pointing direction but not in yielding firm analytical arguments. In particular, the conjectures neglect the possibility that even with these advantages, policy mistakes can be made and bottlenecks may develop that result in appreciably lower growth rates than might otherwise have been expected. In many both less and more developed countries in which the three sets of conditions existed, the growth record, while not negligible, was much below the high levels attained elsewhere. Clearly, the explanatory framework is incomplete; and the three sets of conditions are necessary, but not sufficient.[20]

One source of difficulty lies in the rapid changes in various structural aspects of the economy that are needed as a high rate of growth of per capita product is generated. These structural changes imply shifts in position of various groups in the population and may be resisted by those whose interests are relatively neglected or may cause bottlenecks by impeding the movement of resources from one part of the economy to others that require them for their greater contribution to growth. For these and other reasons, a summary discussion of the changes in production structure and in the use and distributive aspects of growth follows to supplement the bare picture of aggregate growth limited so far to total product and population, total or of working ages.

Changes in Production Structure

Increases in product per capita (and per worker) of the magnitude that occurred in Taiwan over the two recent decades were necessarily associated with rapid shifts in production structure. By the latter I mean the variety of industries comprising the nation's economy, namely, agriculture, manufacturing, transportation, trade, services, and their components. In gauging structure, we are concerned with the relative contribution of these industrial branches to total product and its growth and in their share in labor, capital, and enterprise. Production structure is important because industries differ in the kind of final product to which they contribute, in the technological process involved, in their contribution to growth at different stages of a country's

20. A different way of putting it is to say that none of the three complexes of variables—wider backlog, changes in institutions, and contribution of the rest of the world—were stated with sufficient precision. Hence we cannot tell whether the conditions have been met and thus whether the failure results from the absence of an additional factor that, when added, would have converted a necessary into a sufficient combination.

economic development, in relative proportions of labor and capital required, in the quality of labor needed, and in the conditions of work they entail.

Table 1.10 summarizes the distribution of gross domestic product at market prices and that of net domestic product at factor costs for the seven subperiods from 1951 to 1973. The shares of the various production sectors and components are in totals in current prices because the official series fails to provide estimates of shares in constant prices. But, as argued below, the differences in price trends, at least for the major sectors, are moderate compared with the differences in growth rates of the approximate quantity volumes; hence the changes in shares in Table 1.10 are suggestive of trends in the shares in constant price volumes.

The contribution of an industry to gross domestic product is the difference between the gross value of its output and the costs of goods and services purchased from other industries—in other words, value added gross of consumption of fixed capital, derived as the difference between total output and costs of purchases, both in market prices. The contribution of an industry to net domestic product at factor costs is the total compensation of the factors of production (labor, capital, and enterprise) engaged in that industry. It differs from the contribution to GDP in that indirect taxes minus subsidies and the allowance for consumption of fixed capital are excluded. Comparison of Panels A and B of Table 1.10 shows that gross domestic product at market prices exceeds net domestic product at factor costs by a relatively constant fraction, about a fifth of the smaller total or about a sixth of the larger. Also, because indirect taxes plus capital consumption are a larger component of market prices for the products of the I sector and are particularly low for the A sector, the shares of the A sector are higher in NDP than in GDP, and those of the I sector are lower. The differences, however, are not large (compare lines 2, 8, and 13, with lines 15–17); and the trends over time are roughly the same.

These trends in the shares of the various sectors and subsectors, if applied to constant price totals, would indicate major differences in growth rates. First, as would be expected, the share of the A sector declined substantially from a third or more to less than a seventh (lines 2 and 15). This is a marked decline by international standards over a period as short as two decades.

Second, within the I sector the subdivisions that show marked rises in shares (in GDP) are manufacturing, more than doubling; electric and related utilities, also more than doubling; and transport and communication, rising by a factor of 1.5 (see lines 4, 5, and 7). The shares of mining and construction do not show distinct trends (lines 3 and 6). But the share of the I sector, dominated by manufacturing, doubles (from 26 to 51 percent in line 8 and from 22 to 45 percent in line 16).

Third, within manufacturing, the distribution among industries showed significant and interesting changes over time (Panel C). The share of food and

Table 1.10. Changes in Production Structure, Gross Domestic Product at Market Prices and Net Domestic Product at Factor Costs, Current Prices, 1951–1973

	1951–53 (1)	1954–57 (2)	1958–60 (3)	1961–63 (4)	1964–67 (5)	1968–70 (6)	1971–73 (7)
A. Distribution of GDP by industrial origin							
1. GDP, average per year, bill. N.T.$	17.5	32.6	53.3	78.6	122.3	198.0	319.2
			Percentage shares in GDP				
2. Agriculture and related industries	33.2	27.8	27.2	24.9	22.4	16.5	13.1
Subgroups of I							
3. Mining and quarrying	1.8	2.1	2.5	2.2	1.8	1.4	1.1
4. Manufacturing	15.5	19.6	21.4	23.0	26.7	32.3	37.9
5. Electricity, gas, and water	1.0	1.1	1.5	1.9	2.0	2.3	2.2
6. Construction	3.8	4.6	3.8	3.9	4.0	4.1	4.1
7. Transport, storage, communication	4.1	4.4	4.6	5.1	5.4	5.9	6.0
8. Total I (lines 3–7)	26.2	31.8	33.8	36.1	39.9	46.0	51.3
Subgroups of S							
9. Commerce	17.8	17.4	16.2	15.4	14.3	13.1	11.1
10. Finance, insurance, real estate (net of bank service charges)	8.5	8.3	8.0	8.1	8.0	8.6	8.9
11. Community, social, and business service (incl. hotels and restaurants)	5.2	4.8	4.7	4.9	5.2	5.1	5.5
12. Government services	9.1	9.9	10.1	10.6	10.2	10.7	10.1
13. Total S (lines 9–12)	40.6	40.4	39.0	39.0	37.7	37.5	35.6

B. Distribution of NDP by major sectors of origin

14. NDP, average per year bill. N.T.$	14.9	26.7	43.0	63.7	99.8	156.1	250.6
			Percentage shares in NDP				
15. A sector	36.7	31.6	31.2	28.6	25.6	19.2	15.1
16. I sector	21.9	26.3	28.6	30.6	33.7	38.9	44.8
17. S sector	41.4	42.1	40.2	40.8	40.7	41.9	40.1
18. Commerce component in S	17.5	16.5	14.7	14.3	14.6	13.6	11.8

C. Distribution of GDP in manufacturing by origin in major branches

			Percentage shares in manufacturing GDP				
19. Food, beverages, and tobacco	47.1	48.3	46.3	43.0	34.8	26.3	18.6
20. Textiles and clothing	17.9	19.0	15.0	13.8	14.3	14.2	18.1
21. Wood and paper products	10.1	9.3	10.1	10.1	8.7	8.4	8.2
22. Chemical, incl. coal, petroleum, plastics	13.3	9.9	10.0	14.7	18.4	21.5	21.5
23. Metals (basic and others), incl. misc.	11.6	13.5	18.6	18.4	23.8	29.6	33.6

Taken or calculated from DGBAS, *Statistical Yearbook, 1975*, National Accounts Section, Supp. Tables 5-7, pp. 198-207. All percentage shares were calculated as ratios of the average volume of product per year in a given production branch to the average volume per year for the same period for the appropriate total. The difference between GDP at market prices and NDP at factor costs is the sum of allowance for capital consumption and of indirect taxes minus subsidies, included in GDP and excluded from NDP.

related industries declined sharply, particularly after 1961–63; that of more complex consumer goods industries (textiles and clothing and food and paper) remained relatively stable, at somewhat over a quarter of total manufacturing; and those of industries closer to producer and durable goods—chemicals, metals, and machinery—rose sharply from about a quarter to well over a half.

Fourth, within the S sector, a combination of diverse subcomponents, the share of commerce (wholesale and retail trade) declined perceptibly, both in the GDP and the NDP totals (lines 9 and 18). The remaining components do not show distinct trends when related to the GDP total, but may rise somewhat when related to the NDP total. The share for the sector as a whole declines slightly when observed for GDP in market prices and remains stable when observed for NDP (lines 13 and 18).

Finally, a most interesting feature of the movements in the shares of the sectors and subsectors is the widening of changes from the first to the second decades, paralleling the acceleration in the rate of growth of per capita product between these two decades (noted in Table 1.8). This finding can be summarized by adding the changes in shares, signs disregarded, these changes observed for the first decade (from 1951–53 to 1961–63), and then for the second decade (from 1961–63 to 1971–73) for the different percentage distributions in Table 1.10.

	Measures of total change in percentage shares			
	Shares in GDP Panel A		Shares in NDP Panel B	Shares in manufacturing Panel C
	Ten components (1)	Three components (2)	Three components (3)	Five components (4)
1. 1951–53 to 1961–63	22.8	19.8	17.4	16.4
2. 1961–63 to 1971–73	35.4	30.4	28.4	52.6
3. 1951–53 to 1971–73	55.0	50.2	45.8	60.8

For all of the groupings distinguished by the number of components and using total product as base, the shift in percentage shares accelerates appreciably from the first to the second decades. By and large, the subcomponents of the major sectors, when distinguished, do not move too differently, so that the measure declines only slightly with the shift from ten components in column 1 to three in column 2. Also, direction of change between the first and second decades tends to persist so that the totals in line 3 are the same or only slightly below the sum of the entries for the first and second decades. The association between growth rates in per capita product and the magnitude of structural shifts in the economy, observed here for the shares of production sectors and reflecting shifts in the production structure, will be noted repeatedly through-out this chapter.

In considering shares in constant price totals, we face a problem the diffi-culty of which should be noted to be appreciated. Gross value added in an industry in current prices is the difference between value of total output and value of purchases from other industries, with both the diminuend and sub-trahend in current prices. The defensible method of adjustment is to deflate both for price changes, which requires price data on an industry's product, on goods purchased from other industries, and on the weights of the two totals—a requirement that is unlikely to be met even in developed economies with rich statistical data. Net value added at factor costs would have to be deflated by indexes of changes of factor costs, with such indexes available separately for the various factors and reflecting prices per unit of service of factor (thus allowing for possible changes in quality over time) and weights available for the shares of these several factors. This requirement, too, is unlikely to be met. Therefore the adjustment for price changes of value added by the wide variety of production sectors among both the goods-producing and the service industries can, at best, be only a rough approximation.

Our choice of the price index of major domestic uses (private consumption and gross domestic capital formation) to deflate government consumption (see Table 1.8 and discussion above) eliminated a major differential in price trends in the official price adjustment of gross domestic product. With other relevant evidence to be noted presently, our rough approximation assumes that the price trends for the major production sectors (A, I, and S) were not so differ-ent as to bar the use of shares in current price totals as proxies for shares in constant, 1971 price totals.

Evidence to support this assumption is provided in Panel A of Table 1.8 and in Panel A of Table 1.11. In the former two important implicit price in-dexes—those for private consumption and for gross domestic captial forma-tion—show fairly similar rates of increase for each of the two decades (7.6 and 8.2 percent per year in the first decade and 3.6 and 3.1 percent per year in the second decade), while the rates for the full twenty-year period were identical at 5.6 percent per year (see Table 1.8, lines 8-10, columns 4 and 5). With the assumption concerning price adjustment for government consump-tion, this means that the implicit price indexes for all three groups of domestic uses of product are close to each other. In addition, lines 1 and 2 of Table 1.11 indicate that prices received by farmers and those paid by them (for means of subsistence and for producer goods) moved quite closely to each other.

A partial test of the assumption involves comparison of constant price value added, derived by applying the share of the sector in current price totals to GDP in constant 1971 prices, with the index of production of the sector derived from quantity indexes appropriately weighted. This comparison is

Table 1.11. Distribution of GDP in Constant (1971) Market Prices Among Major Production Sector of Origin (an approximation), 1951–1973

A. Test comparisons

	1951–53 (1)	1954–57 (2)	1958–60 (3)	1961–63 (4)	1964-67 (5)	1968–70 (6)	1971–73 (7)
	Indexes of prices received and paid by farmers, 1971 = 100						
1. Received	41.6	44.3	62.1	80.5	88.4	95.5	110.5
2. Paid	42.5	44.9	60.8	83.9	89.6	97.6	110.2
	Comparison for A sector						
3. Index of production, 1971 = 100	42.5	50.3	59.5	66.9	81.9	95.5	103.3
4. Estimate of GDP in 1971 prices, bill. N.T.$	15.49	17.42	21.58	25.07	32.86	34.32	38.44
5. Line 4 converted to base of line 3 for 1968–73	42.3	48.6	58.7	68.5	89.8	93.8	105.0
	Comparison for I sector (excl. transport subsector)						
6. Index of production, 1971 = 100	7.4	11.2	15.7	22.2	37.0	67.8	121.8
7. Estimate of GDP in 1971 prices, bill. N.T.$	10.31	17.17	23.17	31.22	50.61	83.41	132.9
8. Line 7 converted to base of line 6 for 1968–73	8.03	15.08	20.30	27.35	44.36	73.21	116.5

B. Sectoral GDP in constant prices and growth rates

	A sector		I sector		S sector	
	Absolute volume (1)	Growth percent per year (2)	Absolute volume (3)	Growth percent per year (4)	Absolute volume (5)	Growth percent per year (6)
9. 1951–53	15.49	3.4	12.22	15.0	18.95	8.6
10. 1954–57	17.42	6.3	19.93	8.9	25.31	5.9
11. 1958–60	21.58	5.1	26.82	10.7	30.94	8.3
12. 1961–63	25.07	8.0	36.36	14.6	39.27	10.3
13. 1964–67	32.86	1.3	58.53	15.1	55.31	10.3
14. 1968–70	34.32	3.8	95.68	16.3	78.00	10.2
15. 1971–73	38.44		150.51		104.45	
	Growth rates over longer periods					
Total product						
16. 1951–53 to 1961–63		4.93		11.52		7.56
17. 1961–63 to 1971–73		4.37		15.26		10.28
18. 1951–53 to 1971–73		4.66		13.38		8.91
Per capita						
19. 1951–53 to 1961–63		1.74		8.12		4.29
20. 1961–63 to 1971–73		1.79		12.41		7.55
21. 1951–53 to 1971–73		1.77		10.25		5.90

Lines 1, 2, 3, and 6: Calculated from the series shown in DGBAS, *Statistical Yearbook, 1975,* Wages and Prices Section, Supp. Table 6, p. 186; Agricultural Section, Supp. Table 1, p. 84; and Industry and Commerce Section, Supp. Table 1, pp. 118ff. Lines 4 and 7: Derived by applying the percentage share of the sectors in GDP in current prices (in Table 1.11) to the total GDP in constant prices (with the variant adjustment for prices of government consumption) in Table 1.8.

Lines 5 and 8: To facilitate comparison, the entries in lines 4 and 7 were converted to the base of the average of the last two entries in lines 3 and 6 (99.4 for the A sector and 94.8 for the I sector).

Panel B: The sectoral GDP totals were derived by applying the percentage shares in Table 1.11 to the 1971 prices total of GDP. The growth rates for per capita product were obtained by dividing the rate for total product by that for population (for latter see Table 1.7).

possible for the A sector, given a physical index of production available for it; and for a narrower version of the I sector, that excluding the transport and communication component (lines 3–5 and 6–8 of Table 1.11).

The comparison for the A sector reveals discrepancies over short intervals, but close agreement over the decades. Thus the assumption yields an estimate of growth for the A sector (line 5) of roughly 60 percent in the first decade, somewhat above 50 percent in the second decade, and a total increase by a factor of 2.5 in the two decades. Similar rates for the index of production (line 3) are 60 percent, somewhat over 50 percent, and a total increase again by a factor of 2.5.

The comparison for the I sector yields similar growth rates for the first decade, a tripling in the index of production and slightly more than tripling (3.4) in the measure derived by assumption (lines 6 and 8, columns 1 and 4). But there is a perceptible difference in the second decade, the index of production showing a rise by a factor of more than 5 (from 22.2 to 121.8, or 5.5, see line 6), whereas the measure derived by assumption rises by a factor of slightly more than 4 (from 27.35 to 116.5, see line 8). The reason, however, may lie in the weighting system used for the I production index from 1961: for the first decade the individual component series of physical production were weighted by 1957 value added; for the second decade the weights were the values added for 1971, a terminal year. Use of 1971 weights, with the high growth rates in the components, exaggerated the index (it is to be stressed that the weights were not prices but value added, thus partly reflecting quantity shares).[21]

If the assumption is accepted, and it seems valid at least for the three broad sectors, A, I, and S, with perhaps a slight bias toward underestimating the rise in the share of the I sector, we can observe the growth rates over the period in the GDP originating in each sector, total or per capita of aggregate population. Three conclusions may be noted.

First, the growth rate in GDP originating in the A sector, over 4.5 percent per year, is substantial, but only about a third of the rate of growth of the I sector.

Second, while the growth rates for the I and S sectors rise substantially

---

21. For discussion of the weighting systems for the production indexes for both the A sector, which used price weights, and the I sector, which used value-added weights, see *Statistical Yearbook 1975,* sources cited in the notes to Table 1.11.

An experimental calculation for the manufacturing subtotal of I, using the nine manufacturing branches distinguished, yielded, with 1971 value-added weights, a rise from 1961–63 to 1971–73 with a factor of close to 5.8; whereas with the use of 1966 value-added weights (given in the source), the rise was reduced to a factor of 4.6. The difference is of the order shown in the comparison for the I sector in Table 1.11 for the second decade. Unless errors crept into my interpretation of the procedures, this calculation supports the comments in the text and warrants a conclusion of substantial agreement between the I index properly weighted and the measure derived by assumption from GDP totals in current prices.

from the first to the second decades, that for the A sector does not. Total contribution to product of the A sector grew at a somewhat lesser rate in the second than in the first decade; and even on a per capita basis, the growth rate of product originating in the A sector was about constant in the two decades, at between 1.7 to 1.8 percent per year. The A sector did not contribute to the acceleration of the growth rate of total or per capita product observed in Table 1.10.

Third, even if the rates of increase in each of the three sectors had been at the same level in the two decades, the growth rate of aggregate product would still have accelerated—as long as the rate of growth was higher for one sector than for the others. With sectoral differences in growth rates of product, a constant or declining rate of aggregate product is possible only if the growth rate in some sectors actually declines. No such diminution in the growth rate was observed for Taiwan for the broad classification in Table 1.11.

Before considering the implied significance of marked differences among sectors in growth rates of their output and thus of marked shifts in the shares in aggregate product, we should note that by historical standards, shifts in sectoral shares of the magnitude revealed in Tables 1.10 and 1.11, with the share of the A sector declining by more than 20 percentage points in two decades, are major and rapid. A compilation of long-term trends in major sector shares in gross or net domestic product shows that even in Japan, declines of more than 20 percentage points over two decades were not reached in the past, whereas in most currently developed countries, these shifts away from the A sector and toward the I sector were long drawn out.[22] The United Nations *Yearbook of National Accounts* for the years since the late 1960s indicates that only the less developed countries that matched the high growth rates of per capita product of Taiwan (for example, South Korea) had as wide and rapid a shift in sectoral shares in total product.

Major differences in growth rates of quantity output among different production sectors and the resulting changes over time in the shares of these sectors in aggregate product mean that the proportions contributed by the sectors to additions to aggregate product differ substantially from their shares in aggregate product. Thus the finding in Tables 1.10 and 1.11 that GDP in the A sector in the first decade grew by only 4.93 percent a year, whereas GDP in the other sectors grew at much higher rates, and that the share of the A sector declined from 33.2 percent in 1951–53 to 24.9 in 1961–63, means that the proportional contribution of the A sector to the additions to total GDP over the decade were distinctly below 33.2 percent. A simple calculation shows that the share of the A sector in additions to GDP in the first decade was 17.7

22. See my *Economic Growth of Nations: Total Output and Production Structure* (Cambridge, Mass., 1971), Table 21, pp. 144–51.

percent (9.58 billion N.T.$ derived from lines 9 and 12, column 1, of Table 1.11, related to total additions of 54.04 billion N.T.$ derived from lines 11–14, column 2, of Table 1.8). Conversely, the contribution of the I sector to additions to total GDP over the first decade accounted for 44.7 percent, whereas the shares of the I sector in total GDP were only 26.2 percent in 1951–53 and 36.1 percent in 1961–63.

Gross value added in a sector is the outcome of activities of the productive factors engaged in it—labor, capital, and enterprise. The sector's contribution to additions to aggregate product is the result of additions to gross value added produced by factors attached to the sector. These additions may result from increased productivity of a constant volume of productive factors or from additions to the stock of factors by way of added labor and capital or usually from both. On the assumption, to simplify the argument, that factor productivity remains constant (or accounts for a limited fraction of the additional contributions of the various sectors), shifts in shares of sectors reflecting differences in growth rates of their contribution would represent additional productive factors assigned to the several sectors. Thus, assuming constant factor productivity and equal productivities among sectors, the share in additional factors (labor and capital) needed by the A sector in the first decade was only 17.7 percent, even though the implicit share of the A sector in total factor supply was a high as 33.2 percent at the beginning of the decade. In short, shifts in sectoral shares in GDP mean disparities between the initial (and even terminal) sectoral shares in total factor supplies and their shares in the required additions to these factors. In other words, sectors that lose shares in output need much smaller shares in *additional* factor supply than they currently use in *total* factor supply.

This truism, however, produces many transfer and friction problems because the sectors may themselves generate the additional factor supplies, and they may produce them in proportion to their current weight in the economy. Thus, if the A sector accounts for a third of GDP and, by our assumption, for a third of labor and capital engaged, it may also tend to produce a third of additions to labor and capital. But only a fifth of the total additions to labor and capital are needed in the A sector, whose share in the aggregate product is to decline. Hence, a significant portion of the additional labor and capital generated in the A sector will have to be transferred to other sectors, whose shares in aggregate output are to rise and whose contributions to additions to aggregate product cannot be attained by the additions to productive factor generated within the sectors. The crux of the problem raised by rapid shifts in shares of productive sectors in aggregate output lies in the double role of the sectors as producers of value added and as generators, through the population and capital attached to them, of additions to labor and capital supply.

The second role of the production sector as generator of additions to labor supply (including entrepreneurial) and to capital implies a wide meaning of the term "generator." Thus, the population attached to the A sector, in that the head of the family is predominantly engaged in agriculture, generates the additional labor supply by giving birth to the next generation and bringing it to working capacity at certain ages. Whether, in fact, the offspring are added to the labor force clearly depends on a variety of complementary factors, which may also determine quality of the eventual additions to the labor force. Yet a large A sector population would tend to generate large additional numbers of new potential entrants. Likewise, the economy of the population attached to the A sector, and deriving income from the latter, generates capital formation, if only in the sense of yielding savings or paying taxes that can finance capital investment, rather than actually producing new and additional capital goods. Of course, the propensity to generate additions to labor and capital need not be conceived as a simple proportion of the sector's share either in labor force or in gross value added; nor would such proportions be the same for population and value added in the several sectors. Thus, because of the greater rate of natural increase of the agricultural than of the urban population, the proportions of potential additions to the labor force generated in the A sector may be greater in relation to the labor force now engaged than would be true in the other sectors; and if the saving or tax propensity is higher (relative to, say, gross value added), the funds generated for capital formation would be a higher proportion of gross value added in the A sector. If so, the internal migration problems of labor and capital, with whatever mechanisms are devised to facilitate their solution, would be all the greater, given the shifts of the production structure away from the A sector.

The point stressed—the discrepancy between the two roles of sectors in their generation of and demand for additional supplies of factors—touches upon a major topic in the analysis of economic growth, namely, the implications of the major structural shifts for the movement of labor and capital among the sectors. It thus touches upon the voluminous literature on surplus labor and its movement from the A and related traditional sectors to more modern sectors and on the mobilization of capital for industrialization, drawing upon savings, through various mechanisms, in the A and other traditional sectors.[23] Of course, given the conditions under which structural shifts must occur, shifts of resources out of the more slowly to the more rapidly growing sectors are an economic necessity. But the mechanisms by which such shifts are accomplished are important, and the differences in these mechanisms may have a major effect on the costs and consequences of the shifts. Our interest here, however, is only to note the inevitability of the disparity between the

23. In connection with the latter, in the particular case of Taiwan, one should note the studies by T. H. Lee (1971) and by Rong-I Wu, *The Strategy of Economic Development: A Case Study of Taiwan* (Louvain, 1971).

two roles of the sectors in their supply of additional factors and in their demand for them. The analytical framework is complicated by the variable of factor productivity, which may differ among sectors and change differentially over time. But the double role of the sectors is only qualified, not denied, by the missing variable. We must bear this double role in mind as we turn now to the sectoral distribution not of product, but of labor force and of capital formation.

Table 1.12 summarizes data on the sectoral distribution of the total labor force, including the underemployed and unemployed. The overtly unemployed were estimated at about 6 percent of the labor force in the decade of the 1950s and about 3 percent in the 1960s (see Table 6.13 in Chapter 6 by Walter Galenson). The estimation of underemployment is closely connected with the wider problem of the proper definition of labor force in a less developed economy. In such an economy, much production and employment takes place within a family enterprise, with frequent use of unpaid family members and no clear line of distinction between the fully engaged, occupationally oriented worker in the prime working ages and the part-time participant in family production or the casual employee in another family's business. Even in a developed country marginal groups (such as teenagers and part-time workers) move in and out of the labor market, and their inclusion or exclusion from the total is largely a matter of society's view of the validity of the socially acceptable claim of right to work in application of the marginal group. For a rapidly changing LDC like Taiwan, the estimates of labor force, and hence also of its allocation among sectors, can be only approximate (further detail is provided by Walter Galenson in Chapter 6). The task is further complicated by the need to include servicemen, without adequate data for recent years and substantial relative magnitudes in the early years of the two-decade span.

Total labor force in line 3 rose by only 17 percent in the first decade; growth accelerated in the second decade to over 30 percent. The civilian labor force alone rose only 20 percent in the first decade and about 40 percent in the second. In either definition, the proportion of labor force to population fifteen years of age and over declined. Further analysis of this relation cannot be pursued here, but the omission of two groups from the labor force—family workers and servicemen—would raise the growth rate of the labor force significantly. Thus, if, using Panel B, we assume that for the labor force as a whole the share of family workers declined from at least 27 percent in the early 1950s to 25 percent in the early 1960s, and then down to 16 percent by 1971–73, while the share of servicemen declined from 15 to 12 to 6 percent, the civilian labor force, excluding family workers, would have changed from (3.57×0.58) to (4.17×0.63) and to (5.49×0.78). This would mean a rise of 27 percent over the first decade and of 63 percent over the second, while the ratios to population fifteen years of age and over (including servicemen)

Table 1.12. Changes in Sectoral and Status Structure of the Labor Force and Growth Rates in Total and Sectoral GDP per Worker, 1951–1973

A. Total labor force and structure by major sectors

	1951–53 (1)	1954–57 (2)	1958–60 (3)	1961–63 (4)	1964–67 (5)	1968–70 (6)	1971–73 (7)
1. Labor force, excl. servicemen, mill.	3.03	3.13	3.38	3.67	3.96	4.55	5.14
2. Servicemen, mill.	0.54	0.54	0.54	0.50	0.35	0.35	0.35
3. Total LF, lines 1 and 2	3.57	3.67	3.92	4.17	4.31	4.90	5.49
	Percentage shares of major sectors in line 3						
4. A	48.9	45.8	44.2	42.3	40.5	35.7	30.8
5. I	15.0	17.0	19.9	22.8	25.9	29.4	35.1
6. S total	36.1	37.2	35.9	34.9	33.6	34.9	34.1
6a. S excl. servicemen	21.0	22.5	22.1	22.9	25.5	27.8	27.7
6b. Servicemen	15.1	14.7	13.8	12.0	8.1	7.1	6.4

B. Structure by labor force status (incl. servicemen)

	Men only			Total labor force		
	1956 (1)	1966 (2)	1970 (3)	1964–67 (4)	1968–70 (5)	1971–73 (6)
7. Absolute totals, mill.	2.73	3.34	3.65	4.28	4.73	5.29
	Percentage shares in total in line 7						
8. Employers and own-account workers	35	32	33	29	27	26
9. Employees, private	17	28	29	27	34	40
10. Government employees	33	27	28	21	19	18
10a. Line 10, excl. servicemen	13	16	18	13	12	11
10b. Servicemen	20	11	10	8	7	7
11. Family workers	15	13	10	23	20	16

continued

Table 1.12. continued

C. Absolute volume of labor force (mill.), major sectors, and implicit displacement, by decades

	Absolute volumes, actual or assumed			Growth rates, percent per year, and total displacement		
	1951–53 (1)	1961–63 (2)	1971–73 (3)	Cols. 1-2 (4)	Cols. 2-3 (5)	Cols. 1-3 (6)
12. Total LF, actual and growth rates	3.57	4.17	5.49	1.57	2.79	2.18
A sector						
13. Actual and growth rates	1.75	1.76	1.69	0.06	−0.41	−0.35
14. Assumed and displacement	1.75	2.04	2.69	−0.28	−0.72	−1.00
I sector						
15. Actual and growth rates	0.54	0.95	1.93	5.81	7.35	6.58
16. Assumed and displacement	0.54	0.83	0.82	0.32	0.79	1.11
S sector total						
17. Actual and growth rates	1.28	1.46	1.87	1.32	2.51	1.91
18. Assumed and displacement	1.28	1.50	1.98	−0.04	−0.07	−0.11
S sector excl. servicemen						
19. Actual and growth rates	0.75	0.95	1.52	2.39	4.81	3.60
20. Assumed and displacement	0.75	0.88	1.15	0.07	0.30	0.37
21. Servicemen displacement (line 20, cols. 4-6 minus line 18, cols. 4-6)				−0.11	−0.37	−0.48

D. Gross domestic product (1971 prices) per worker

	Absolute volumes (000, N.T.$)			Growth rates, percent per year		
	1951–53 (1)	1961–63 (2)	1971–73 (3)	Cols. 1-2 (4)	Cols. 2-3 (5)	Cols. 1-3 (6)
22. Total	13.07	24.15	53.44	6.33	8.27	7.30
23. A sector	8.85	14.24	22.75	4.87	4.80	4.83
24. I sector	22.63	38.27	77.98	5.39	7.38	6.38
25. S sector	14.80	26.90	55.86	6.16	7.58	6.87

Line 1: Derived largely from an estimate by the Economic Planning Council for 1953 onward shown in Chen Sun, "The Trend of Economic Development and Productivity in Taiwan," in Institute of Economics, Academia Sinica, *Conference on Population and Economic Development in Taiwan* (Taipei, 1976), pp. 114–15. The annual series was extrapolated back to 1951 by comparison with the movement of gainfully occupied (derived from registration statistics) in DGBAS, *Statistical Yearbook, 1975*, Population Supplement, Table 8, pp. 20–21.

Line 2: Estimated from comparison of the series for population aged fifteen and over, including servicemen, in the Chen Sun paper cited for line 1 with that on population fifteen and over, excluding servicemen (to end of 1969) in the *Statistical Yearbook, 1975* used for Table 1.7. The comparison cannot be continued beyond the calendar year 1968, and a constant number at 0.35 million was assumed.

Lines 4–6b: Estimated from two distributions of labor force (both excluding military servicemen) by production sector. The first, by the Council of International Economic Cooperation and Development (CIECD), is found in Tzong-shian Yu, "Taiwan Employment and Productivity Trends since 1953," in *Proceedings of the Sino-American Conference on Manpower in Taiwan* (Taipei 1973). Appendix B, Table 1, p. 123. The series begins in 1952, and that year was used to represent the average for 1951–53. The second series, based on annual labor force surveys available beginning in 1966, is shown in DGBAS, *Statistical Yearbook of the Republic of China, 1976* (Taipei, 1976), Manpower, Suppl., Table 1, pp. 46–47.

Both series refer to civilian labor force and exclude servicemen. Shares in the annual total for each year were computed for the three major sectors; those for the recent series beginning in 1966 were taken as basic and then extrapolated back to 1952 on the basis of the average difference in shares between the two series in the five-year overlap, 1966–70.

The resulting percentages were applied, after averaging, to the civilian labor force total in line 1; the estimated number of servicemen in line 2 was added, for each subperiod, to the total and S sector of the civilian labor force; and the percentage shares were recalculated.

Panel B: The first part, for 1956, 1966, and 1970, is based on census data as summarized in DGBAS, *Statistical Yearbook, 1975*, Population, Table 9, p. 24, and the military servicemen in 1956 were added (the totals include them in 1966 and 1970). Because of the marked shortage in number of females reported as being in the labor force in 1956, only the data for males could be used (the shortage of males was much smaller). The second part, for 1964–67 to 1971–73, is from the data provided by labor force surveys (to which servicemen were added) reported by status in DGBAS, *Statistical Yearbook, 1975*, Manpower, Suppl., Table 3, p. 48.

Panel C: The actual absolute volumes in lines 12, 13, 15, 17, and 19, columns 1–3, were derived by applying to the totals in line 12 (taken from line 3) the percentage shares in the relevant columns in lines 4–6a. The growth rates per year relating to the absolute volumes, in lines 12, 13, 15, 17, columns 4–6, were derived from these volumes in the same lines.

The assumed volumes, in lines 14, 16, 18, and 20, columns 1–3, were calculated by applying the share in total labor force in the initial period, 1951–53, to the totals in 1961–63 and 1971–73—revealing what the sectoral labor force totals would have been with a constant sectoral allocation at the initial level. The displacement was measured by subtracting the actual values in 1961–1963 and 1971–73 from the assumed values, yielding the entries in columns 4 and 6; that for column 5, representing displacement over the second decade (including the "making up" for that in the first decade), was obtained as the difference between columns 4 and 6 (subtracting the former from the latter).

Panel D: The sectoral GDP totals needed for deriving sectoral GDP per worker were taken from Tables 1.8 and 1.11 using variant with different deflator for the government consumption component.

would be 40 percent in 1951–53 and 1961–63 and 46 percent in 1971–73.[24] The point of these rough calculations is that the moderate growth rate of the labor force and the decline in the ratio to population fifteen and over is largely associated with the weight of two groups, family workers and servicemen, who for different reasons are not full-fledged workers engaged in market-valued pursuits.

But our main interest here is in the changing allocation of the labor force among the major production sectors, and this is shown in Panel A, lines 4–6b, for the total, including servicemen and family workers. The exclusion of these two groups will only tend to widen the magnitude of changes in shares, when observed for the three major sectors.[25] But even as given in Panel A, the shares, particularly if we distinguish the servicemen component of the S sector, shift widely: the total of changes in percentage shares is 18 points for the first decade, 40 points for the second decade, and 58 points for the total span—magnitudes close to those shown for shifts in shares in gross or net domestic product in Table 1.11. And the changes are in the expected direction—declines in shares of the A sector and major rises in those of the I sector and of the civilian component of the S sector. Finally, as expected, the magnitude of the shifts is wider in the second decade as compared with those in the first.

Panel C illustrates the comment made above concerning the double role of sectors as contributors to aggregate product and the additions to it and, given a changing structure, as generators of additional labor and capital. The actual changes in sector labor force (lines 13, 15, 17, and 19) show that although the

24. The underlying totals for population aged fifteen and over, including servicemen, are 5.17 million in 1951–53, 6.64 million in 1961–63, and 9.34 million in 1971–73. They were derived from the Chen Sun series used for lines 1–3 (see reference in the notes to Table 1.12) and extrapolated to years before 1953 by using data for registered population (including addition of servicemen, all placed in the above fifteen age group).

25. This is shown by recalculating the shares for the A, I, and S sectors, first omitting servicemen and limiting the total to civilian labor force, then assuming a plausible allocation of family workers among the three sectors. (I assigned 17 percentage points of total labor force as family workers to the A sector in 1951–53 and 3 and 7 percentage points, respectively, to the I and S sectors. The allocation for 1961–63 was 16, 3, and 6 percentage points; for 1971–73, 9, 3, and 4 percentage points.) The assignment was based on data indicating that the largest group of family workers, almost two-thirds of all family workers, was in agriculture, and the next largest in services (commerce and personal).

The shifts among the three major sectors were then measured by the following totals of changes in percentages (all based on A-I-S):

	As in Panel A (1)	Excluding servicemen (2)	Also excluding family workers (3)
1. First decade	16	20	26
2. Second decade	24	30	28
3. Total span	40	50	54

A sector accounted for as much as 49 percent of the total in 1951–53 and more than 40 percent even in 1961–63, its contribution to additions to labor force was slightly negative; and the opposite contrast prevailed between the initial shares of the I sector of 15 percent in 1951–53 and 23 percent in 1961–63 and the shares in additions of almost 70 percent over the first decade and more than 70 percent in the second. The assumed changes in sectoral labor force (lines 14, 16, 18, 20, and 21) were calculated on a premise that the proportional increment in a sector's labor force generated was the same for all sectors and equal to the countrywide average proportion—a premise that underestimates the propensity of the A sector population and labor force to increase. The difference between the actual and assumed changes is the disparity between the sectoral shares in addition to labor force associated with changing demand in economic growth and the generation capacity of the sector to produce additions to the labor force. This disparity, referred to as displacement in Panel C, cumulated to a draft of 1 million of the agricultural labor force over the two decades from 1951–53 to 1971–73—a wide movement, considering the level of less than 2 million in the initial period (see line 14, columns 1 and 6). There were compensating displacements in the disparity between demand and generation for the I sector; these were somewhat less for the S sector.

The displacement totals shown in columns 4–6 of Panel C would be approximations to net internal migration of labor only if the sector's population could be assumed to generate additional labor force in identical proportions and if the effects of differentially changing labor productivities in the several sectors were not a major element. But there is little question that the magnitudes indicated strongly suggest wide disparities between the sectoral supply and demand for additional labor and the inevitability of major shifts (and associated migration) of labor generated in the slowly growing sectors to attachment to the more rapidly growing sectors.

With labor force allocated among the same sectors as GDP, we can relate gross product to numbers of workers; derive sectoral product per worker; and observe the growth rates in GDP per worker, total and by sectors (Panel D). An approximation to sectoral differences in product per worker (lines 23–25, columns 1–3) indicates that the product per worker in the A sector tends to be about a third that in the I sector and about half that in the S sector—an expected result. It would be reduced, but not fully offset, by allowance for sectoral differences in intensity of engagement and quality of labor.

Of more interest is the finding that the rates of growth in product per worker are all quite high, ranging among the sectors from 5 to over 6.5 percent per year for the total span (column 6, lines 23–25). Differences among sectors are not as wide as might be expected, and the growth rate in the S sector is higher than that in the I sector. The reason for the latter may lie in the greatly changing mix between the servicemen and the civilian components within the S sector, a mix that would tend to magnify the growth rate in product per worker in the sector as a whole. The narrow intersectoral differences in growth rates of product per worker, compared with the wide spread of these intersectoral differences in growth rate of total sectoral product, is, obviously, a reflection of the adjustment in the allocation of labor force to the changing sectoral composition of aggregate product.

Finally, there is an acceleration, from the first to the second decades, in the growth rate of product per worker in two of the three sectors and in the total (compare columns 4 and 5, lines 22-25). The stability of the growth rates per worker, at a fairly high level, in the A sector is not surprising; nor is the greater acceleration over the period in the growth rates in product per worker for the I sector. The high and accelerating growth rate in product per worker in the S sector is a finding that would require further exploration to render it more meaningful.

Because of differences in product per worker by sector and the greater growth of sectors with high product per worker, the combined measure, product per worker for the economy as a whole, can grow at a higher rate than any of its parts. Thus, in line 22, the growth rate for total GDP per worker, at 7.30 percent per year in column 6, is higher than the rate for any of the three sectors. This is a result of the changes in allocation of workers among sectors in favor of the sector with the higher product per worker—in this case largely the I sector. Total growth in product per worker is thus the sum of intersectoral shifts in the distribution of the labor force and the intrasectoral rates of growth of sectoral product per worker, with both sets of rates appropriately weighted. A simple calculation shows that in Panel D between a fifth and a seventh of total rise in product per worker is due to intersectoral shifts and the large remainder to a weighted rise in intrasectoral product per worker.

But this result, conveying the impression that the shifts among sectors in the distribution of the labor force (and of other production factors) contribute only a small fraction of the increase in aggregate product per worker, is misleading in that it is dependent upon a broad definition of sectors. A much needed disaggregation, distinguishing a variety of essentially different subsectors and subcomponents, would change the result. Because the total rise to be accounted for would remain unaffected by such further disaggregation, the weight of the intershift variable would necessarily rise and that of the intrasector trend variable would decline.

This caution against underestimating the contribution of intersectoral shifts to total growth, because of the wide character of the sectors that we can distinguish with the available data, is of substantial analytical import. For it is also a caution against overlooking the contribution, and hence the importance, of shifts of labor (and of other productive factors) from one subcomponent to another within the broad sectors. It is clear that the intrasectoral rises in product per worker now shown in the three major sectors in Panel D contain large contributions of intershifts of labor within each of the three major sectors, or even within subcomponents within each (such as manufacturing), and that without such shifts among narrower subdivisions within each sector, the sectoral product per worker would not have shown as high a rate of rise. The point is that a much greater rate of shift, of mobility of labor, and of other productive factors is required to obtain the aggregate rate of growth now suggested in the three-sector classification and that the shifts from old to new subbranches within these sectors are particularly neglected. And yet these shifts involve mobility of factors and availability of entrepreneurial resources that we tend to neglect in the temptation to think of the A or the I sector as a kind of homogeneous whole, in which the same kind of labor and capital with the same kind of process not involving changing differentiation somehow manages to raise factor productivity at the rates indicated. The underlying processes of change, differentiation, and mobility are far more pervasive and far more productive of strains and problems, the resolution of which may call for continuous adjustments in policy to relieve the strain, to minimize block- ages and resistance, and to encourage entrepreneurial venturesomeness.

In turning now to the sectoral structure of the other measurable production factor, reproducible capital, one would wish for data both on capital stock and on additions to it, capital formation. But there are puzzling aspects about the sectoral composition of the capital stock estimates that are available; and since they could not be resolved here, Table 1.13 summarizes the sectoral structure of capital formation, that is, of additions to capital stock, not of the stock itself.[26]

The periods used in Table 1.13 are intervals between the successive seven subperiods followed elsewhere, in order to compare more easily the additions to capital stock with additions to product, total and by sectors. We begin with the sectoral distribution of gross fixed capital formation in current prices,

26. In the most recently published series on capital stock, attributed to the Council of Interna- tional Economic Cooperation and Development (CIECD), in 1966 prices, the subsector of trans- port and communication accounts for as much as 42 percent of total fixed capital in 1952. (See the paper by Tzong-shian Yu, "Taiwan Employment and Productivity Trends since 1953," in the *Proceedings of the Sino-American Conference on Manpower in Taiwan* [Taipei, 1973], Table 2, p. 124.) The share then declines to 37 percent in 1958–60 and to 25 percent in 1968–70. The share of this subsector in GDP, also in 1966 prices, is somewhat over 4 percent in 1952, close to 5 percent in 1958–60, and close to 6 percent in 1968–70 (ibid., Appendix B, Table 3, p. 125). As Table 1.13 shows, the share of this subsector in current gross fixed domestic capital formation rose from less than 10 percent in the first interval to 18.5 percent in the last (see line 7). The use of these capital stock estimates would imply that the capital-output ratio in the subsector was more than 30 to 1 in 1952 and that the aggregate capital-output ratio declined from 3.45 in 1952 to 1.76 in 1968–70. These striking results would call for a close check on the capital stock estimates before they can be used here; their omission from the *Statistical Yearbook, 1975,* also suggests caution.

Table 1.13. Changes in Distribution of Gross Domestic Capital Formation among Sectors of Destination, 1951–1973

A. Distribution of fixed capital formation and of increase in stocks

	1951–53 to 1954–57 (1)	1954–57 to 1958–60 (2)	1958–60 to 1961–63 (3)	1961–63 to 1964–67 (4)	1964–67 to 1968–70 (5)	1968–70 to 1971–73 (6)
1. Duration of intervals, years	3.5	3.5	3.0	3.5	3.5	3.0
Fixed gross capital formation, current prices						
2. Cumulated total over interval, bill. N.T.$	10.39	20.94	31.82	53.11	103.84	168.67
Percentage shares in total in line 2, by sector of destination						
3. A sector	24.1	19.8	19.1	17.4	12.4	8.7
Subdivisions of I						
4. Manufacturing	22.2	24.1	22.4	27.4	32.3	33.2
5. Mining and construction	1.3	2.2	2.5	1.6	1.9	2.9
6. Electricity, gas, water	11.9	15.1	13.2	10.2	11.2	11.9
7. Transport, storage, communication	9.4	12.9	16.5	16.4	17.1	18.5
8. Total I (lines 4–7)	44.8	54.3	54.6	55.6	62.5	66.5
Subdivisions of S						
9. Commerce	10.1	4.7	3.9	5.5	5.4	3.8
10. Finance and housing	12.7	11.7	12.7	12.0	11.7	10.9
11. Government	6.2	8.0	7.3	6.0	5.0	5.9
12. Other	2.0	1.5	2.4	3.6	3.0	4.2
13. Total S (lines 9–12)	31.1	25.9	26.3	27.0	25.1	24.8
Increase in stocks, current prices						
14. Cumulative total, bill. N.T.$	2.20	3.72	6.82	15.27	22.41	18.84
Percentage shares in total in line 14						
15. A sector	6.5	11.7	−1.7	0.7	2.1	3.9
16. I sector	41.9	53.5	56.7	49.2	62.4	68.5
17. S sector	51.6	34.8	45.0	50.1	35.5	27.6

B. Approximation to distribution of gross domestic capital formation in 1971 prices among three major sectors of destination, cumulative totals, constant prices, bill. N.T.$

	Gross fixed capital formation				Gross total capital formation			
	All (1)	A (2)	I (3)	S (4)	All (5)	A (6)	I (7)	S (8)
18. First decade, 1951–53 to 1961–63	88.4	18.2	45.9	24.2	105.8	19.0	55.0	31.8

| | 19. Second decade, 1961–63 to 1971–73 | 351.9 | 40.5 | 222.4 | 89.0 | 409.9 | 41.8 | 257.6 | 110.5 |
| | 20. Both decades, 1951–53 to 1971–73 | 440.2 | 58.7 | 268.3 | 113.2 | 515.6 | 60.8 | 312.6 | 142.3 |

C. Shares of sectors in cumulative totals and ratios of GDCF to dGDP
Shares in cumulative totals

	GDP		dGDP		GDCF		Ratios, GDCF/dGDP	
	1st dec. (1)	2d dec. (2)	1st dec. (3)	2d dec. (4)	1st dec. (5)	2d dec. (6)	1st dec. (7)	2d dec. (8)
21. Total (mill. N.T.$, 1971 pr.) and ratios	71.0	180.2	54.0	192.7	105.8	409.9	1.96	2.13
			Percentage shares and ratios					
22. A sector	27.5	18.3	17.7	6.9	18.0	10.2	1.98	3.13
23. I sector	32.8	44.5	44.7	59.3	52.0	62.8	2.28	2.26
24. S sector	39.7	37.2	37.6	33.8	30.0	27.0	1.56	1.69

Panel A: Calculated from the annual series in DGBAS, *National Income of the Republic of China* (Taipei, 1972), Table VII, pp. 148–49 (for years 1951 through 1958) and ibid. (Taipei, 1975), Table VII, pp. 110–13 (for years beginning with 1958). The intervals are defined as extending from the midpoint of 1951–53 to the midpoint of 1954–57, and so on. This meant, for the first interval, adding one-half of capital formation for 1952 to the years 1953, 1954, and 1955. The purpose was to be able to compare cumulative capital formation over the interval, with net additions to GDP over the same interval (in Panel C).

Panel B: The approximation in lines 18–20 involves applying the percentage shares of the major sectors in GDCF in current prices to the totals in constant, 1971 prices separately to the total of fixed capital formation and that of increase in stocks, shown separately in the official estimates in constant, 1971 prices. For the constant price totals see DGBAS, *Statistical Yearbook, 1975*, National Accounts, Suppl. Table 2, pp. 194–95. The percent shares of Panel A were applied to the constant price totals for each of the six intervals; the results were then added to form two intervals of a decade each and the sum for the full twenty years.

Panel C: The decades refer to the spans from mid-1951–53 to mid-1961–63 (first decade) and from mid-1961–63 to mid-1971–73 (second decade), as in lines 18 and 19 of Panel B. The GDP, overall and sectoral totals (in columns 1–2), are derived from Table 1.11 (Panel B), with the terminal periods (1951–53, 1961–63, and 1971–73) assigned half of their year's weight (1.5 years each) and the other period averages weighted by the years covered (4 or 3). The cumulative total is the weighted sum of the averages for the subperiods, weighted by their duration as indicated. The additions to GDP (designated dGDP) are by direct subtraction of the values in 1971 prices given in Table 1.11 (value for 1961–63 minus that for 1951–53, for the first decade; and value for 1971–73 minus that for 1961–63 for the second decade). The totals and percentages in columns 5 and 6 are from Panel B, columns 5–8. The ratios in columns 7 and 8 are of cumulative GDCF to total addition to annual GDP, using the absolute figures in line 21 and the underlying absolute figures in lines 22–24.

given in fairly wide sectoral detail; consider the more approximate distribution of the lesser capital component, increase in stocks; and then apply the sectoral distribution of each to fixed capital formation and increase in stocks, given separately in constant 1971 prices, to derive an approximation to the sectoral distribution of gross capital formation in constant prices.

The detailed distribution of fixed capital formation in lines 3–13 and the less detailed allocation of increase in stocks are of interest here only as indicating which of the sectors and subdivisions secured the larger proportions of the total additions to capital stock. For fixed capital formation, the share of the A sector is moderate and rapidly declining, and this is even more true of commerce. These two subdivisions also showed marked declines in their shares of gross domestic product. The other components that account for substantial shares of fixed capital formation are the three subdivisions of the I sector—manufacturing; electricity, gas, and water; and transport and communication—and finance and housing, mostly the latter. The addition of the increase in stocks modifies the distribution somewhat, largely by further reducing the share of the A sector and raising that of the I sector. The final shares, derived for the distribution of total gross capital formation in constant prices (lines 22–24, columns 5–6) show a relatively low and declining share for the A sector, at less than a fifth in the first decade and only a tenth in the second; a substantial and slightly declining share for the S sector, at 30 percent in the first decade and 27 percent in the second; and a huge and rising share for the I sector, from over half in the first decade to close to two-thirds in the second.

Given these distributions of the total gross domestic capital formation among the three major sectors, two analytical comparisons become possible. First, the distribution of these additions to capital stock among the sectors can be compared with the distribution of gross domestic product, the shares in the latter suggesting the capacity to generate funds for new capital (lines 22–24, columns 1 and 2). This comparison shows, as would be expected, that the share of the slower growing A sector in gross capital formation is markedly below its share in total GDP and implicitly below the capacity to generate funds for capital investment, the shares in the first decade were 18 percent in GDCF compared with 28 percent in GDP and in the second decade 10 percent compared with 18 percent (see columns 1 and 2 compared with columns 5 and 6, line 22). It is of interest and significance that the sectoral distribution of GDCF is far closer to that of additions to GDP (in lines 22–24, columns 3–4) than it is to that of GDP. The sum of total differences in percentage shares in GDCF and in dGDP is 15.2 in the first decade and 13.6 in the second, compared with the measure comparing GDCF and GDP of 38.4 in the first decade and 36.6 in the second. The obvious implication is of considerable intersectoral displacement of additional capital flows, reflecting the disparity in the capacity to generate capital funds and the demand for them as they are compared for the major sectors (and as would become even more significant with greater disaggregation).

The second comparison is of the sectoral totals of gross domestic capital formation in constant prices with the additions to gross domestic product, also in constant prices, over comparable intervals of time. These comparisons, for decadal intervals to minimize erratic aspects of estimates over shorter intervals, yield the incremental capital-output ratios, both for the economy as a whole and for the three major sectors (lines 21–24, columns 7–8).

Although these results are necessarily crude (and no experimentation with leads and lags or greater disaggregation is feasible here), several conclusions may be reasonably suggested. First, a gross capital-output incremental ratio of about two appears generally low and would be even lower with a shift to a net capital-output basis. The official figures (in *National Income of the Republic of China,* 1972 and 1975, Table VI) show that capital consumption allowances averaged 33.7 percent of GDCF in the first decade and 27.8 percent in the second decade (both in current prices). Using the proportion of GDCF to GDP (in constant prices) shown in Table 1.15 below, we can estimate the proportion of capital consumption allowances to GDP at about 4.9 percent in the first decade and 6.1 percent in the second. Applying these two sets of percentages to ratios of GDCF to dGDP in line 21 (1.96 and 2.13), we derive net incremental capital-output ratios (ICORS) of 1.37 and 1.65 respectively. Yet an ICOR on a net basis of about 3 to 1 was frequently found and considered normal over long stretches of the past.[27] The suggestion is one of high efficiency in utilization of additional (and already existing) capital to induce growth—a finding that would have to be checked further for significant components of the sectors.

Second, there was a slight rise in the gross capital-output ratio, from 1.96 to 2.13, and a somewhat greater proportional rise in the net capital-output ratio. Such rises could be expected even with substantial growth rates of product; but their significance could be tested only with a more disaggregated analysis.

Third, as the capital-output ratios are distinguished for the three major sectors, differences emerge in the level and the movements of the ratios over time. These differences in levels would be far more striking if the comparison were disaggregated and extended to significant subdivisions of the major sectors. Thus, allowance for the apparently high capital-output ratios for the transport and the electric and other utilities subdivisions of the I sector would reveal that the ratios for manufacturing are quite low; and there may be effects also on movements of the ratios over time. As the crude comparisons now

27. See a summary of wealth estimates and ratios to product in Raymond Goldsmith and Christopher Saunders, eds., "The Measurement of National Wealth," *Income and Wealth Series VII* (London, 1959), pp. 1–34.

stand, there is generally a lower level of the ratios in the S sector than in the others; and associated with the low magnitude of additions to the A sector output in the second decade, there is a marked rise in the incremental capital-output ratio for that sector, from less than 2 in the first decade to over 3 in the second.

Much more detail would obviously be required for a more revealing analysis of the changes in sectoral structure of production, labor, capital, and other factors in the two decades of growth covered. But only the broad outlines are possible here; more intensive analysis is pursued in several of the chapters that follow.

In concluding this section on sectoral structure, we may note the levels and trends in the distribution of product and of capital formation by type of organization or enterprise—an aspect of changing organizational structure of production (Table 1.14).

The groups that require a more specific definition are public corporations, government enterprises, and general government. The others—private enterprises (business firms, whether or not incorporated), households, and private nonprofit institutions (usually included with households)—are self-explanatory. Household appears as a subgroup in connection with minor household production activities (outside the A sector), and it and the nonprofit institutions could be best viewed as parts of the private enterprise division.

"The public corporation is operated under registration according to the Law of Incorporation with more than 51 percent of its stock or capital owned by the government (if less than 51 percent, it will be classed as a private enterprise). The government enterprise is financed and run by the government," states the 1972 *National Income* volume. These enterprises are apparently largely public utilities and transport networks (waterworks, railways, electric power stations, and the like). "General government consist of public administration, national defense units, public non-profit institutions (school, hospital, etc.) and government small-scale establishments (printing shop, research institute, etc. whose budgets are included in the general government budget)."[28]

The line of division between government and private control is not sharply drawn, since government may have shares in private firms but less than 51 percent of holdings; and conversely, public corporations may (and perhaps should) allow for some influence of private enterprise on their management and policies. But the distributions in Table 1.14 can be viewed as at least roughly those between government and private sectors.

The interesting feature of the table is the relative long-term constancy of the shares, in rather sharp contrast with the rapid structural shifts among the A,

28. DGBAS, *National Income of the Republic of China, December 1972* (Taipei, 1972), pp. 90–91.

Table 1.14. Distribution of Net Domestic Product at Current Factor Costs by Type of Organization and of Gross Domestic Capital Formation at Current Prices by Type of Purchaser, 1951–1973

	1951–53 (1)	1954–57 (2)	1958–60 (3)	1961–63 (4)	1964–67 (5)	1968–70 (6)	1971–73 (7)
Distribution of net domestic product							
1. Absolute total, bill. N.T.$, per year	14.9	26.7	43.0	63.7	99.8	156.1	250.6
Percentage shares originating in							
2. Private enterprise	74.5	73.1	71.7	70.4	71.8	69.2	70.2
3. Households and private nonprofit institutions	3.9	3.7	3.6	3.6	3.5	3.9	4.0
4. Public corporations and government enterprises	10.9	11.1	12.3	13.0	12.2	13.4	12.9
5. General government	10.7	12.1	12.4	13.0	12.5	13.5	12.9
Distribution of gross domestic capital formation							
6. Absolute total, bill. N.T.$, per year	2.55	4.98	10.1	14.6	28.0	51.2	82.3
Percentage share purchased by							
7. Private enterprise	43.2	44.4	39.6	50.2	59.5	53.2	48.5
8. Households and nonprofit institutions	6.4	8.0	9.0	8.8	7.5	8.4	11.0
9. Public corporations and government enterprises	38.6	34.8	38.9	29.5	23.4	28.0	30.3
10. General government	11.8	12.8	12.5	11.5	9.6	10.4	10.2

Calculated from DGBAS, *National Income of the Republic of China, 1972 and 1975*, Table IV (for national income excluding net factor income from abroad, equal net domestic product) and Table VII (composition of gross domestic capital formation). The numbering of the tables is the same in both years. Percentage shares are derived from the absolute totals for the periods.

I, and S sectors or their subdivisions. The share in net domestic product of private enterprises and the small household–nonprofit institutions groups together was over 75 percent in 1951–53 and dropped to 74 percent in 1971–73 (lines 2 and 3). The government sector, taken widely, was somewhat over a fifth in 1951–53 and rose to about a quarter in 1971–73. These slight movements presumably reflect the more rapid rise of transport and public utility enterprises in the public corporations and enterprises subdivision and a somewhat variable trend with an approach to constancy in the share of general government (line 5).

The public sector accounts for a larger share in the distribution of gross domestic capital formation by destination, presumably reflecting the greater capital-intensity and demand of the transport and utility enterprises under public auspices. In general, the public sector absorbed between 40 and 50 percent of domestic capital formation (and contributed only half of that to net domestic product), whereas the share of the private sector in capital formation was distinctly below its share in product. There is here a trend in shares in GDCF, although of limited magnitude. The share of the private sector in capital formation rose from about 50 percent in 1951–53 to almost 60 percent in 1971–73, whereas that of the public sector declined over the total span from 50 to 40 percent. In general, one might argue that the public sector is more responsible for the capital infrastructure than is the private sector; that the share of the former had to be higher in the first decade when the infrastructure was being built up as a condition for the accelerated growth that would follow; and that this acceleration, once it occurred, shifted the demand for capital to the private sector, particularly the manufacturing industries, and to some extent to residential and related construction for the increasingly urban population.

Structure of Product by Use

The accepted broad categories of final use in an aggregate like gross domestic product are government consumption, consumption expenditures of households and nonprofit associations, gross domestic capital formation—the three constituting domestic uses; the balance of exports over imports indicating whether domestic uses were greater or smaller than total product, that is, were supported by excess imports or were moderate enough to permit net exports. These four categories are defined as final uses in that the three domestic uses are not for immediate further production (otherwise they would constitute intermediate inputs), whereas the export-import balance is a final use from the standpoint of the country's economy. Whether this view of the four categories, particularly the three domestic uses, is justified can be questioned, and some comments are presented below. But we are accepting the conventional view to preserve comparability.

Panel A of Table 1.15 summarizes the levels and movements of the shares of final use components in two totals: one is the familiar GDP; the other, more relevant for observing the weight of exports and imports, is that of uses-resources, which, being a sum of gross domestic product and of imports, gauges the total from which domestic uses and exports can be drawn. Both distributions are given in Panel B for totals in constant prices to facilitate comparisons of growth rates. But with our adjustment of the government consumption component for price changes, the shares in totals in current and constant prices differ only slightly, and there is little need to extend the table. The findings can be summarized seriatim.

First, for the GDP total, the share of government consumption—that is, purchases of services of government employees and of commodities and services from other sectors—is between a sixth and a fifth; that of households' and nonprofit associations' consumption expenditures is between one-half and three-quarters; and that of gross domestic capital formation is between a seventh and a quarter. The balancing item, exports minus imports, shows excess imports, ranging over 7 percent of GDP in early years, declining to a low percentage, and turning to excess exports in the early 1970s. The shares of exports and imports taken separately are best related to the wider aggregate of total uses-resources, and these shares of exports range from below 10 percent to over 30, while those of imports are between a seventh and a quarter.

Second, the share of government consumption, in either total, fails to show sustained movements, but those of other components show marked trends over the twenty-year span. The share of private consumption expenditures declines strikingly, in GDP from over three-quarters in 1951–53 to slightly over a half in 1971–73 (line 12); in total uses from about two-thirds to less than two-fifths (line 3). The shares of the other components, GDCF, imports, and exports, all rise substantially. It is particularly intriguing that the share of the large, private consumption expenditure component, perhaps the closest to a final use category, representing material returns to the population as the basic goal of economic activity, declines, reflecting a much lower rate of growth than the other, subsidiary components such as capital formation or imports and exports.

Third, like the shifts in production structure (discussed in the previous section), the shifts in the use structure are far greater in the second than in the first decade, in association with the higher growth rate of product per capita. Thus, the measure of total differences in percentage shares, for the four categories in total uses-resources (the three domestic uses and exports),

Table 1.15. Shares and Growth Rates of Components of Total Product by Use, 1971 Prices, 1951–1973

A. Shares of use components

	1951–53 (1)	1954–57 (2)	1958–60 (3)	1961–63 (4)	1964–67 (5)	1968–70 (6)	1971–73 (7)
1. Absolute totals, all uses, bill. N.T.$	55.34	72.94	93.40	118.5	176.4	266.7	396.9
Percentage shares			*Shares in total uses*				
2. Government consumption	14.2	17.0	16.8	16.3	14.5	14.3	12.0
3. Private consumption	64.3	63.9	60.5	57.6	52.5	45.2	39.2
4. GDCF	12.1	11.3	13.1	14.8	17.5	19.7	18.3
5. Domestic uses (lines 2–4)	90.6	92.2	90.4	88.7	84.5	79.2	69.5
6. Exports	9.4	7.8	9.6	11.3	15.5	20.8	30.5
7. GDP	84.3	85.9	85.0	85.0	83.1	78.0	73.9
8. Imports	15.7	14.1	15.0	15.0	16.9	22.0	26.1
9. Exports minus imports or GDP minus domestic uses	−6.3	−6.3	−5.4	−3.7	−1.4	−1.2	4.4
			Shares in GDP				
10. Absolute total bill. N.T.$	46.66	62.66	79.74	100.7	146.7	208.0	293.4
Percentage shares							
11. Government consumption	16.9	19.8	19.8	19.2	17.4	18.3	16.2
12. Private consumption	76.3	74.3	71.2	67.8	63.2	57.9	53.0
13. GDCF	14.3	13.2	15.4	17.4	21.1	25.3	24.8
14. Exports	11.1	9.1	11.3	13.3	18.6	26.7	41.3
15. Imports	18.6	16.4	17.7	17.7	20.3	28.2	35.3
16. Exports minus imports	−7.5	−7.3	−6.4	−4.4	−1.7	−1.5	6.0

B. Absolute volumes and growth rates of various totals and components, 1951–1953, 1961–1963, and 1971–1973

	Total uses (1)	GDP (2)	Government consumption (3)	Private consumption (4)	GDCF (5)	Domestic uses (6)	Exports (7)	Imports (8)
Absolute volumes, bill. N.T.$, 1971 prices								
17. 1951–1953	55.34	46.66	7.88	35.61	6.68	50.17	5.17	8.68
18. 1961–1963	118.5	100.7	19.32	68.36	17.51	105.2	13.37	17.83
19. 1971–1973	396.9	293.4	47.46	155.6	72.60	275.7	121.3	103.5
Growth rates, percent per year								
20. First decade	7.91	8.00	9.38	6.74	10.12	7.68	9.87	7.46
21. Second decade	12.85	11.29	9.40	8.57	15.26	10.11	24.66	19.23
22. Both decades	10.35	9.63	9.39	7.65	12.67	8.89	17.14	13.19
23. Multiple, line 19 to line 17	7.2	6.3	6.0	4.4	10.9	5.5	23.5	11.9

The underlying data are all from DGBAS, *Statistical Yearbook, 1975*, cited for Table 1.8. The same table indicates the adjustment for price changes adopted here for the deflation of the government consumption component. As usual, all percentage shares are calculated from the absolute totals for the given subperiod.

changes from 13.4 points for the first decade to 45.4 points for the second (based on lines 2–4 and 6). A similar measure for the shares of four components in GDP (three domestic uses and the export-import balance) changes from 17.0 percentage points for the first decade to 35.6 points for the second (based on lines 11–13 and 16). This association between rate of growth of product per capita and structural shifts will be observed again, particularly in the structure of the large component of private consumption expenditures.

Panel B reveals the implications of the trends in the several shares for the rates of growth of the volumes of the totals and use-components. The growth rate in private consumption, 7.7 percent per year, is the lowest of the high growth rates observed. Nevertheless, with population growing over the period at 2.8 percent per year, the growth rate in per capita household consumption would be 4.7 percent per year, implying that it would more than double over the twenty-year period from 1951–53 to 1971–73. The rates of growth of the other use components are substantially higher, particularly exports and imports. And all the rates, except that of government consumption, accelerate markedly from the first to the second decades (compare lines 20 and 21). With the decline in the growth rate of population, this would mean an even greater acceleration in the growth rate of aggregates or components per capita.

Before shifting to a comparison of the shares of the use components in Taiwan with those in relevant countries, we return to the question of the meaningfulness of the conventional categories as final use components. Some outlay, even among private consumption expenditures, may have been undertaken to facilitate work or to accommodate to the demands of work, rather than to satisfy consumer wants that would have existed without work requirements. Such items should be properly viewed as intermediate rather than as final products. Even more serious questions relate to government consumption in view of the later finding that most of it is either for administration and defense or economic purposes, rather than in services to ultimate consumers. As indicated above, much of government consumption may be viewed as intermediate input—sustaining and lubricating the economic and social machine. In the case of capital formation, there is merit in Irving Fisher's argument that capital exists to facilitate production of final consumer goods, that the latter are the proper measure of accomplishment of the economy in terms of its final goals, and that, in the long run, additions to capital should be translated into higher levels of final consumption. And clearly, imports and exports, taken by themselves, are tools in the facilitation of supply of final products—not unduplicated, final output of the economy.

There are counterarguments that justify the inclusion of government consumption, capital formation, and the export-import balance into a net aggregate such as NDP or GDP (gross only of capital consumption). Yet there is ground, from the long-run standpoint, for arguing that the final goal of economic development is to provide a greater volume and variety of material goods to the ultimate consumers under social conditions acceptable to them and that attainment of that goal is best measured by final consumption that takes account of all the externalities and the limiting conditions under which such consumption was provided for. From that standpoint, much of government consumption represents intermediate uses; capital formation is a measure of added capacity that is of interest only for shorter-term, not long-term measurement; and international flows, whether gross or in net balances, are, like capital formation, also a means rather than an end.

If so, the disparate behavior of final consumption, represented by private consumption expenditures (or some variant thereof) and the other use components, represents a natural shift in structure during periods of rapid growth. This rapid growth of final consumption is achieved by an even faster growth of the necessary tools. Clearly, the comparatively rapid growth of private consumption expenditures could not have been attained without the even more rapid growth of capital formation and a greater growth of imports and exports involving a greater involvement of Taiwan in the network of international division of labor. As a result, the growth rate of the grossest total, total uses, is distinctly higher than that of the netter aggregate, gross domestic product, and that of the latter is higher than the growth rate of the nettest aggregate, private consumption expenditures (compare columns 1, 2, and 4, lines 20–23).[29]

In comparing the levels and changes in the use structure of Taiwan with those in other countries, we are limited by the number of countries or regions with which comparison is relevant (Table 1.16). But some broad similarities and significant differences stand out.

First, with respect to the general structure, Taiwan is characterized by a

---

29. This comparison can be extended to even grosser totals, including the intermediate products purchased by the production sectors distinguished in the industrial classification. Thus, DGBAS, *National Income, 1975,* indicates that between 1968 (the first year shown) and 1974, the proportion of intermediate products in the total gross value of output (current prices) rose from 48.4 to 55.2 percent, whereas the share of the GDP part of gross output declined from 51.6 to 44.8 percent (Table XVII, pp. 140ff.). Assuming similar price trends for input and output, one would infer that the total gross output rose over these six years by a percentage substantially higher than that of the netter total, GDP, and that the intermediate components rose at an appreciably higher rate than the final components. A glance at Table XVIII, pp. 142 ff., in the same source, which shows the cost structure by industry sectors for 1974, reveals that the intermediate products–gross output ratio is lowest for the S sector (about a quarter), somewhat higher for the A sector (about four-tenths), and at its highest in the I sector (about two-thirds). Other conditions being equal, this cost structure would mean that the rise in the share of the I sector and the decline in the share of the A sector (and somewhat smaller decline in the share of the S sector) would lead to a long-term rise in the intermediate products proportionate to the country's net output.

This general impression of the elaboration of the underlying substructure that is implicit in high rates of growth of the final net product of the economy could be confirmed further in the input-output analysis of economies at different stages of development.

Table 1.16. Percentage Shares of Use Components in GDP, Taiwan and Selected Countries Compared (GDP in current prices, unless otherwise indicated)

	Government consumption (1)	Private consumption (2)	GDCF (3)	Domestic uses (4)	Exports (5)	Imports (6)	Balance, exports-imports (7)
Taiwan (constant prices)							
1. 1951–53	17	76	14	107	11	18	–7
2. 1961–63	19	68	17	104	13	17	–4
3. 1971–73	16	53	25	94	41	35	6
South Korea							
4. 1953–55	9	85	13	107	2	9	–7
5. 1962–64	11	84	16	111	5	16	–11
6. 1971–73	11	72	24	107	13	20	–7
Japan							
7. 1952–54	11	65	25	101	11	12	–1
8. 1961–63	9	55	37	101	9	10	–1
9. 1971–73	9	52	37	98	11	9	2
Phillippines (approximate)							
10. 1951–53	8	86	13	107	19	21	–2
11. 1961–63	9	79	19	107	14	14	–2
12. 1971–73	9	71	20	100	19	18	1

Thailand							
13. 1952–54	11	77	14	102	19	21	–2
14. 1961–63	10	73	19	102	17	19	–2
15. 1971–73	11	66	25	102	19	21	–2
East and Southeast Asia, except Japan (1970 prices)							
16. 1961–63	9.5	79.1	14.1	102.7	11.1	13.8	–2.7
17. 1971–73	10.6	76.7	14.6	101.9	14.5	16.4	–1.9
Caribbean and Latin America (1970 prices)							
18. 1961–63	11.1	71.1	17.8	100.0	13.5	13.5	0
19. 1971–73	10.4	70.3	21.5	102.2	12.2	14.4	–2.2
Developed market economies (1970 prices)							
20. 1961–63	19.0	60.1	20.6	99.7	10.0	9.7	0.3
21. 1971–73	16.4	60.1	23.3	99.8	14.5	14.3	0.2

Lines 1–3: Taken from Table 1.15. The shares in GDP in current prices would differ from the ones given by one or two percentage points; the structures in constant and in current prices, in the variant used, are close to each other.

Lines 4–15: Calculated from Table 2 of United Nations, *Yearbook of National Accounts Statistics, 1969*, Vol. II, ibid., *1975*, Vol. III (see references in the notes to Table 1.9). As in Table 1.9, 1969 *Yearbook* was used for the years to 1960 or 1961; and the 1975 *Yearbook* for the later years. In general, with the single exception of the Philippines, the difference between domestic uses and GDP checks with the difference between imports and exports (compare column 4 with column 7). For the Philippines there is a discrepancy because some components are derived as residuals, but the general order of magnitudes of the shares should not be greatly affected.

Lines 16–20: Calculated from Table 5, of United Nations, *Yearbook of National Accounts Statistics, 1975*, Vol. III, using the indexes (1970 = 100) for the several use components, calculating the average indexes for 1961–63 and 1971–73, applying them to the weights of the components, and deriving the time-specific shares for the two sub-periods. Only market economies are included.

high proportion of government consumption—almost twice as high as that in the other countries in its region and in East and Southeast Asia or the Latin American regions.[30] Otherwise, the use structure in Taiwan is similar to that of the other rapidly growing countries in the region. It differs most clearly from the much more slowly growing East Southeast Asia region, for which only the second decade can be covered (lines 16–17).

The more interesting comparison is of the changes in structure that occurred over the two-decade period. These, particularly in the shares of private consumption and the net export-import balance, appear to be far greater in Taiwan than in the four other countries of the region. Thus the share of private consumption in Taiwan dropped from 1951–53 to 1971–73 by about three-tenths, in South Korea by less than a fifth, in Japan by about a fifth, and in the Philippines and Thailand by lower proportions. Likewise, the export-import balance turned from a negative fraction of 7 percent in 1951–53 to a surplus in 1971–73—a reversal of a magnitude not observed elsewhere.

Despite the sharper drop in the share of private consumption in GDP than in the other countries, the growth rate in private consumption per capita in Taiwan probably remained higher, with the single exception of Japan. This impression can be checked by converting the changes in the shares in column 2 to rates of relative decline per year over the period covered and applying these rates of decline to the aggregate growth of gross domestic product per capita shown in Table 1.9. The calculation indicates that the rate of growth of GDP per capita in Taiwan, 6.51 percent in Table 1.9, is reduced to 4.61 percent (if we apply the percentage shares in lines 1 and 3, column 2). The converted growth rates for the other countries, in consumption per capita, are: Japan, 7.30; South Korea, 4.18; Philippines, 1.53; and Thailand, 2.73. This calculation, applied to shares in totals in current prices, assumes only minor differentials in price trends among the use components; and it is to be doubted that the price differentials would affect the substantial disparities in growth rates between Taiwan and the other countries.

Finally, the export-import ratios in Taiwan are very high, compared with the other countries, particularly in the second decade. This may be partly a matter of the country's size, the usual experience being that, all other conditions equal, the smaller country tends to have larger foreign trade proportions to total product; and Taiwan, in terms of population and partly of total product, is smaller than any of the other four countries in the region distinguished

---

30. The United Nations source used (see notes to Table 1.16) provides a breakdown for the second decade also for Africa, except South Africa. But the region is a combination of oil-rich and oil-poor states toward the end of the decade; and the data for it are not too trustworthy. The share of government consumption for that region moved from 13.8 percent in 1961–63 to 17.4 percent in 1971–73; the share of the export-import balance changed from −3.4 percent to +0.5 percent.

in Table 1.16. But the analysis of foreign trade is the subject of Chapter 5 in this volume, and the relative magnitude of foreign trade as well as the structure of exports and imports are among several topics covered here.

The remainder of this section is devoted to brief accounts of the structure of the three domestic use components: (1) private consumption expenditures; (2) government consumption; and (3) gross domestic capital formation.

(1) In beginning with the structure of private consumption expenditures, it would be useful to keep in mind three aspects of that use component. First, as shown in Table 1.15, this category accounts for from two-thirds to over half of total product (in 1971 prices), and thus its structure is of major importance in determining the composition of final demand in its effect on the production structure of the economy. Second, total population exercises this demand, not the much narrower groups involved directly in the demand for government consumption or for domestic capital formation. This total population of consumers is also the population of producers, and shifts in the composition of that population, in the conditions of work, the rise in per capita income available for consumer expenditures, and the differential price changes among various groups of consumer goods—all affect the structure of private consumption expenditures. Third, consumption outlays, in current prices, are based on prices paid by the final consumers. This means that, for example, outlay for food includes the price not only of food as originated on the farms, but of its transport to the urban consumers, of whatever fabrication may be involved, and of the trade distribution charges, including whatever sales or other indirect taxes may be imposed. By definition, the entry for outlays on food (and other items among the commodities and services included) would reflect, in current prices, the changing mix in the flow to rural and urban consumers with the changing weights of different prices for the same article of food.

The last comment suggests several problems in adjusting the current price totals of private consumption expenditures for price changes and the reasonable expectation that these adjustments are approximate. Nevertheless, the shifts are marked and rather similar for the structure in current and in 1971 prices (see Table 1.17).

In both current and constant price totals, the shares of two categories show sufficiently sustained marked declines to warrant note. These are the large food category and the much smaller one of fuel and power (lines 2 and 5 for current price totals and 15 and 17 for constant price totals). The decline in the share of food should have been expected, given the large rise in per capita income and in per capita consumer expenditures (for the latter see line 12, which shows a rise by a factor of almost 2.5 from 1951–53 to 1971–73). Greater detail would reveal that the shares of some food components declined sharply and those of other food components rose. The drop in the share of fuel

Table 1.17. Composition of Private Consumption Expenditures, Current and 1971 Prices, 1951–1973

A. Composition of expenditures

	1951–53 (1)	1954–57 (2)	1958–60 (3)	1961–63 (4)	1964–67 (5)	1968–70 (6)	1971–73 (7)
			Current prices				
1. Absolute volume, per year, bill. of N.T.$, total	13.07	23.20	36.70	52.32	74.99	112.7	168.7
Percentage shares							
2. Food	55.2	52.8	51.5	49.4	47.0	42.5	40.2
3. Beverages and tobacco	6.0	6.8	7.7	7.7	7.7	8.2	7.6
4. Clothing and footwear	5.7	6.1	5.6	5.2	5.5	5.3	5.5
5. Fuel and power	4.4	4.5	4.7	4.6	4.1	3.9	3.9
6. Household, total	12.1	13.0	13.2	13.3	14.4	16.4	17.5
6a. Rent and water	n.a	n.a	n.a	10.7	11.0	11.7	12.7
6b. Furniture, furnishings, equipment	n.a	n.a	n.a	0.9	1.4	2.7	2.8
6c. Household operation	n.a	n.a	n.a	1.7	2.0	2.0	2.0
7. Medical care and health	4.1	4.3	4.5	6.6	6.3	5.9	5.7
8. Recreation and amusement	2.8	2.6	2.3	2.3	2.8	3.5	5.0
9. Transport and communication	1.5	1.3	1.5	1.4	2.2	2.7	2.9
10. Miscellaneous, including education and services	8.2	8.6	9.0	9.5	10.0	11.6	11.7
			1971 prices				
11. Absolute volume, per year, billions of N.T.$	35.61	46.52	56.53	68.30	92.62	120.3	155.6
12. Cons. expenditures, per capita, thousands of N.T.$	4.12	4.80	5.24	5.80	7.14	8.50	10.28
13. Percent proportion of population in localities of 20,000 or more	19.9	27.6	32.8	34.3	36.5	42.7	46.7
Percentage shares, volumes in 1971 prices							
14. Food	59.5	57.9	55.3	51.4	48.1	42.8	39.3
15. Beverages and tobacco	7.2	7.3	7.2	6.3	6.3	7.8	8.1
16. Clothing and footwear	3.8	4.0	4.2	4.2	4.6	5.0	5.3

17. Fuel and power	4.7	4.6	4.4	4.5	3.9	3.8	4.1	
18. Household, total	11.1	11.4	12.0	13.5	14.6	16.3	17.6	
18a. Rent and water	n.a.	n.a.	n.a.	10.8	11.0	11.4	12.9	
18b. Furniture, furnishings, equipment	n.a.	n.a.	n.a.	0.8	1.2	2.6	2.7	
18c. Household operation	n.a.	n.a.	n.a.	1.9	2.4	2.3	2.0	
19. Medical care and health	4.4	4.2	4.6	6.9	6.9	6.2	5.6	
20. Recreation and amusement	2.4	2.6	3.0	2.9	3.3	3.7	5.0	
21. Transport and communication	1.1	1.3	1.4	1.2	2.0	2.6	3.0	
22. Miscellaneous, including education and cultural services	5.8	6.7	7.9	9.1	10.3	11.8	12.0	

B. Implicit prices, broader components, 1971 = 100

	Food (1)	Beverages, tobacco (2)	Clothing (3)	Fuel, power (4)	Household total (5)	Personal health (6)	All other (7)	Total (8)
23. 1951-53	34.0	30.6	55.7	33.9	40.1	34.7	49.5	36.7
24. 1961-63	73.6	92.8	93.4	78.8	76.2	72.5	76.7	76.5
25. 1971-73	110.7	101.1	112.2	103.7	107.9	110.3	106.7	108.4

Lines 1-11, 14-25: Calculated from DGBAS, *National Income of the Republic of China* for 1972 and 1975, Tables IX and XIII. The earlier volume was used for data in current prices through 1957. The 1971 price series is completely from the 1975 issue, Table XIII. To permit coverage of the more detailed classification for 1961-63, the missing breakdown for 1961 was estimated on the basis of the 1962 breakdown available in the source. Percentage shares were derived by relating the totals of each component within the period to aggregate of consumer expenditures for that period. Derived price indexes were calculated by dividing the current price totals by the 1971 price totals, for the given component and period. For more detail on composition of the categories see notes in the basic source and also reports on family income and expenditures, for Taiwan as a whole, and then separately for Taiwan Province and Taipei City, the former beginning in 1964 and the more recent series beginning in 1970.

Line 12: Calculated by dividing the totals in line 11 by the population averages for the same subperiods shown in Table 1.7.

Line 13: End-of-year population living in localities of 20,000 and over is given from end of 1955 onward in DGBAS, *Statistical Yearbook, 1975*, Population, Supp. Table 3, p. 12. The same table shows population living in localities of 100,000 and over back to the 1940s. The series were shifted to a midyear basis, and the ratios over the 20,000 and over to the 100,000 and over groups calculated for the years since 1955; the ratios gradually declined from 1.26 down to about 1.20. A ratio was assumed of 1.275 for 1951-53 and 1.265 for 1954-57, and thus population was derived in localities of 20,000 and over for the missing period. The ratios are to the population series in Table 1.7.

and power is less conspicuous and is perhaps due to the necessity character of this consumption item and its lesser response to the shift from country to city living—both features not characteristic of most other nonfood components distinguished in Table 1.17.

Of these other nonfood components, all, except beverages and tobacco, and clothing and footwear, show marked rises in shares in the totals in both current and 1971 prices. Some of these components are greatly affected by the urbanization of the consumer population, which progressed rapidly over the period, as indicated by the rise of the proportions living in localities with a population of twenty-thousand or over from about 20 percent in 1951–53 to about 47 percent in 1971–73 (line 13). Others are more accessible in the cities than in the countryside and have an income or expenditure elasticity of demand appreciably above 1. One example of the former is the large category of housing-related outlays, the share of which in current prices rose from 12 to 17.5 percent (line 6) and in 1971 prices from 11 to almost 18 percent (line 18); another is transport and communication, with a share rising from about 1 to about 3 percent (lines 9 and 21). Examples of the second type are the health and medical care items, recreation, amusement, and cultural outlays—all with income-elastic demand much more easily satisfied in the cities: the total share of these rose from about 15 to over 22 percent in aggregates in current prices (lines 7, 8, and 10) and from about 12.5 to 22.5 percent in the aggregates in constant prices (lines 19, 20, and 22).

Of the two components the shares of which show either uncertain trends or different trends in current and in 1971 prices, clothing and footwear are of most interest. Their share in the total in current prices is relatively constant at about 5.5 percent (line 4); but in 1971 prices it climbs fairly steadily from less than 4 to over 5 percent (line 16). The direct source of this disparity is in the implicit price index, which rises over the period less than those for other components: in lines 23–25, the index for clothing doubles between 1951–53 and 1971–73, whereas those for most other components triple, except for the housing outlays and recreation, transport, and miscellaneous. Testing the validity of these price differentials is not feasible here, except to note that the source places heavy reliance on consumer price indexes in Taipei City. This may well mean an understatement of the rise in the price of clothing and related items, when one considers their weighted price for the total population, rural and urban.

As in the case of shifts in other structures, those in the structure of private consumption expenditures widen from the first to the second decades. Using the categories in lines 2–10 and 14–22, we find that the changes in the shares in current prices add up to 13.8 points in the first decade and 21.8 points in the second; a similar measure for the shares in constant prices is 18.4 points in the first decade and 27.6 points in the second.

The fact that the structural shifts in the total of private consumption in 1971 prices were distinctly wider than those in the total in current prices suggests a negative correlation between the relative rise in the implicit price indexes and the relative change in the share of the component in totals in constant prices. And indeed, lines 23–25 reveal that for food and fuel and power, rates of price rise over the two decades were appreciably higher than for clothing or the housing outlays or all others—yet the shares of food and fuel and power in the constant price totals dropped and the shares of these other components rose. A simple rank correlation (C. Spearman's *rho*) for the nine components of private consumption expenditures between the percentage rises in the implicit price indexes and the relative changes in the shares in constant price totals, both measured for the two decades from 1951–53 to 1971–73, yield a coefficient of −0.7—suggesting a significant negative association.

This inverse relation between the degree of price rise and the relative change in percentage shares in the total in constant prices also means a negative association between differential price rises and the growth rates in the volume of the consumption components, total and per capita (since the percentage shares relate to the same constant price volumes, total or per capita). This negative association between price trends and growth rates of consumption components is similar to that usually observed between price trends and production components in the long run of economic growth. The connection between these two associations obviously lies in the effect of domestic consumption on domestic production.

(2) The distribution of government consumption by classes of purpose or function is shown in Table 1.18. By definition, the total comprises only outlays on government employment and on purchases of commodities or services from other sectors and excludes money transfers from the government to households or to individuals. The totals thus reflect absorption of goods and services by government, expressed in current prices. It would have been more informative to have the structure observed in constant prices, but, as already indicated, no adequate deflation is possible. A further complication is the anonymous category of "other purposes," the share of which gyrates from high in column 1 to a low in column 3 (most of the first decade) and then rises appreciably in the second decade.[31]

Given the limitations of the data, only a few conclusions can be safely

---

31. The description of this component in United Nations, *A System of National Accounts,* Revision 3 (New York, 1968), cited and followed in the Taiwan national accounts, is of little help. Category 9, "other purposes," is said to include, in addition to transfers on public debt and other categories not relevant here, "outlays in connection with disasters and other calamities" and "outlays not specified elsewhere" (p. 89). The Taiwan residual category may include some items from other classes, for which no entries in the source are shown: housing and community amenities and other community and social services. These two cover sanitary services and recreational and cultural activities, which could be allocated to direct services to households and other final consumers. If so, this might explain the rise of the "other services" proportion in line 7 in the second decade, but not its decline from its high level in 1951–53.

Table 1.18. Composition of Government Consumption by Class of Purpose, Shares in Totals in Current Prices, 1951–1973

	1951–53 (1)	1954–57 (2)	1958–60 (3)	1961–63 (4)	1964–67 (5)	1968–70 (6)	1971–73 (7)
1. Total per year, bill. N.T.$	2.90	6.37	10.68	15.07	21.30	36.17	52.23
Percentage shares							
2. General public services and defense	71.9	72.6	72.4	73.6	68.8	59.8	56.1
3. Education	6.4	11.1	12.3	11.8	13.8	15.5	16.4
4. Health, social security, and welfare	2.0	3.5	4.5	3.8	3.4	3.6	4.1
5. Services to consumers (lines 3 and 4)	8.4	14.6	16.8	15.6	17.2	19.1	20.5
6. Economic services	5.0	5.7	6.0	5.1	5.2	6.1	5.6
7. Other purposes	14.7	7.1	4.8	5.7	8.8	15.0	17.8
Services to consumers as percentage of private consumption expenditures							
8. Private consumption expenditure bill. N.T.$	13.1	23.2	36.7	52.3	75.0	112.7	168.7
9. Government direct services to consumers, bill. N.T.$	0.25	0.93	1.79	2.35	3.65	6.89	10.65
10. Line 9 as percentage of line 8	1.9	4.0	4.9	4.5	4.9	6.1	6.3

Lines 1–7 and 9: Calculated from DGBAS, *Statistical Yearbook, 1975*, National Accounts, Supp. Table 8, pp. 206–7.
Line 8: See Table 1.17, which relates to consumption expenditures by households and nonprofit institutions.

suggested. First is the large proportion of general public services and defense (including judiciary and police), as well as the marked decline in this share in the second decade, perhaps reflecting the reduction in the proportion of defense outlays. Second, the share of government outlays on direct services to consumers—education, health, welfare (in kind), and the like—shows a fairly steady upward trend, even disregarding the puzzling jump from 1951–53 to 1954–57 (lines 3–5). And it is not unlikely, as suggested in footnote 31, that additional items of direct services to consumers are included under the "other purposes" category in line 7. If so, the additions to private consumption expenditures that ought to be made to account for total consumption by individuals and households would be somewhat greater than the 4 to 6 percent shown in line 10. Finally, if one disregards the structure for 1951–53 in column 1, as perhaps for statistical reasons not comparable with those in the following subperiods, the shifts in the ratios from 1954–57 to 1964–67, and then to 1971–73, again show a widening in the magnitude, from a total of changes in percentages of 8.8 points in the initial decade to 25.4 points in the following span of some 6.5 years (based on lines 2, 3, 4, 6, and 7).

(3) The structure of gross domestic capital formation, total or fixed, by industrial classification and by type of organization of purchasers was shown in Tables 1.13 and 1.14. Here we are concerned with the structure by type of capital good, which suggests the function that the use is to satisfy (Table 1.19). The distribution is for totals in 1971 prices, but would not differ substantially from that for totals in current prices.

The allocation between fixed capital goods and increase in stocks indicates that over eight-tenths is accounted for by fixed capital (lines 1–4). Generally, in the long-run course of development the share of increase in stocks is fairly substantial in the beginning and declines as better transport and communication facilities and shifts in industrial structure toward sectors in which the demand for inventories is not large reduce the relative role of commodity stocks. The period covered here is far too short to allow observation of such a trend, even assuming adequate coverage of the increase in stock component, which is not easily attainable because of the dispersion of stocks among many small farms, craft shops, and retail stores and stalls, in addition to those in the hands of large firms or units.

More interest attaches to the structure of fixed capital formation divided among residential, nonresidential, and other construction, and total equipment, transport, or other equipment. Construction of residential and some other buildings can be linked directly to the demand of the population for housing, stores, and the like, affected as it may also be by urbanization and population mobility. Other parts of construction and much of the equipment results from demand by the producing enterprises and the social collectives and thus is only indirectly related to demand by ultimate consumers.

Table 1.19. Composition of Gross Domestic Capital Formation by Type of Capital Good, Volumes in 1971 Prices, 1951–1973

	1951–53 (1)	1954–57 (2)	1958–60 (3)	1961–63 (4)	1964–67 (5)	1968–70 (6)	1971–73 (7)	First decade (8)	Second decade (9)
1. Volume, GDCF bill. N.T.$	6.68	8.22	12.21	17.51	30.88	52.56	72.60		
2. Percent fixed CF	80.5	84.5	84.2	83.7	80.1	85.7	95.6	83.7	84.6
3. Percent increase in stocks	19.5	15.5	15.8	16.3	19.9	14.3	4.4	16.3	15.4
4. Volume, fixed CF, bill. N.T.$	5.38	6.95	10.28	14.65	24.73	45.02	69.44		
Percentage shares in line 4, by type of capital good									
5. Residential buildings	11.5	15.1	14.2	14.5	11.5	10.8	11.0	14.2	11.7
6. Nonresidential buildings	28.8	26.6	23.6	24.6	23.0	18.9	12.7	25.7	20.4
7. Other construction	26.2	23.5	23.3	23.5	19.0	15.0	13.1	23.8	17.6
8. Total construction (lines 5–7)	66.5	65.2	61.1	62.6	53.5	44.7	36.8	63.7	49.7
9. Transport equipment	7.8	5.2	7.8	8.5	10.1	11.9	14.2	6.9	11.0
10. Other equipment	25.7	29.6	31.1	28.9	36.4	43.4	49.0	29.4	39.3
11. Total equipment	33.5	34.8	38.9	37.4	46.5	55.3	63.2	36.3	50.3
Share of equipment in GDCF and in GDP									
12. In GDCF	27.0	29.4	32.8	31.3	37.2	47.4	60.4	29.3	42.9
13. Percent GDCF to GDP	14.3	13.2	15.4	17.4	21.1	25.3	24.8	14.7	22.4
14. Percent equipment to GDP	3.9	3.9	5.1	5.5	7.8	11.9	15.0	4.3	9.8

All except line 13 calculated from DGBAS, *Statistical Yearbook, 1975*, National Accounts, Supp. Table 10, pp. 212–13. Line 13 is from Table 1.15 above.

Line 12 was obtained by multiplying line 11 by line 2. Line 14 was derived by multiplying line 12 by line 13.

The entries in columns 8–9, shown only for the lines in which percentage shares (not absolute values) are entered, are averages of these percentages in the same line. In column 8 the averages are for the decade extending from the middle of 1951–53 to the middle of 1961–63, with the entries in the successive columns weighted 1.5, 4, 3, and 1.5 representing the years covered. In column 9 the averages are for the decade extending from the middle of 1961–63 to the middle of 1971–73, with the averages in columns 4–7 again weighted by 1.5, 4, 3, and 1.5.

The entries in columns 8 and 9 are calculated from the line entries, not, when it is possible, by dividing the averages in one line by those in another.

The shares of residential buildings, between a tenth and a seventh of the fixed capital formation total; of other building construction, between a third and a seventh; and of other construction, between a quarter and a seventh, all declined from the first to the second decades, particularly, after 1961-63 (lines 5-8). As a result, total construction, which accounted for over six-tenths of fixed capital formation in the first decade, dropped rapidly thereafter and declined to less than four-tenths by 1971-73 (line 8). In contrast, the share of equipment, about a third of the fixed capital total in 1951-53, rose slowly during the first decade and then rapidly in the second decade, with the share reaching almost two-thirds by 1971-73 (line 11). Here again, the shifts are far greater in the second decade: the sum of changes in percentage shares of the five subdivisions of fixed capital (lines 5-7 and 9-10) is 11.8 points in the first decade and 51.6 points in the second.

Two findings of interest are suggested by the distribution of fixed capital in Table 1.19. The first, already noted, is the shift away from construction and toward equipment. This trend parallels that found in the long-term course of economic growth in many countries and reflects the natural sequence of priorities in fixed capital investment in the growth process. The construction of the economic infrastructure—buildings, roadways, and public utilities all of which are capital-intensive—emerges fairly early, for they are the precondition for economic integration within a country by establishing adequate connections among the various parts of the economy. As this first priority is met, a substantial rate of economic growth is attained and greater resources become available for capital formation; there is a shift toward a larger share of equipment to increase the efficiency of the goods-producing industries and of various services—equipment that assists in raising the technical levels of already established branches of production and permits the creation of new, equipment-intensive branches. The one distinctive aspect about this shift in Taiwan is its high rate, the great speed at which it occurred over the relatively short period of two decades.

The second finding centers on the share of equipment in total product (lines 12-14). This component of capital formation presumably represents the part of capital that is likely to embody new technology, as distinct from construction of buildings, which, despite qualitative differences in the result, scarcely reflects major technological innovations in performance (of the buildings, not in the construction process in which equipment is involved); and as distinct from many other types of construction, although some of it is complementary to new types of equipment. If most equipment embodies new technology, whereas most construction does not, the equipment component is of particularly strategic value in the process of economic growth. Equipment also is more importable than construction, most of which must use local labor and capital (though not materials and parts). The observation stressed here is that the weight of equipment, as part of total product, is quite small, averaging less than 5 percent of GDP in the first decade (see line 14, column 8) on a gross (of capital consumption) basis. One could argue that it does not take very high proportions of savings or of total product to provide modern equipment, as long as the basic infrastructure is in place and as long as the complementary factors, labor and enterprise, are of a quality that permits effective utilization of equipment-embodied, more advanced, technology.

Distributive Aspects

The distributive aspects of aggregate growth concern the relative shifts in the shares of various groups of households—the recipients of the claims to the final product. I also discuss briefly some demographic changes, particularly fertility, perceived as a response by households to changes in their economic position and prospects as they view them. Granted the remarkable record of growth in total and per capita product over the scant quarter of a century under review, its distribution among various groups within the country's population is important, though it is difficult to establish these shares in a meaningful fashion.

Structure of Household Income by Type

The structure of income received by households (and nonprofit associations serving households, a minor component not separated in the available data), by type of income received, and by categories of disposition is shown in Table 1.20. The broader findings are fairly clear. First, of total factor incomes, which account for practically all income receipts (transfers averaging well below 1 percent), a growing proportion is accounted for by compensation of employees, its share rising from 43 percent at the beginning of the period to about 60 percent at the end (line 2). Second, this rise is offset by a decline of the same magnitude in the share of the mixed income of unincorporated entrepreneurs and own-account workers, from 32.5 to 13 percent (line 3). The share of property incomes, as defined here, remains fairly constant, fluctuating around 25 percent (line 4). Third, the structure by disposition shows that direct taxes formed a minor, if rising, fraction (line 8); that the share of consumer expenditures declined from 91 percent in the first decade to about 73 percent at the end—with a compensating rise in the share of savings from about 6 percent during the first decade to over 20 percent by the end of the period (lines 11 and 12). All these shifts have implications for income distribution, if we assume that property incomes tend to be distributed more unequally than earned incomes, especially than compensation of employees, and that direct taxes have a progressive impact, reducing inequality. Finally, as observed for other structural shifts, the changes in the structure of income of

Table 1.20. Structure of Income of Households (including nonprofit associations), by Type of Income and of Disposition, Current Prices, 1951–73

	1951–53 (1)	1954–57 (2)	1958–60 (3)	1961–62 (4)	1964–67 (5)	1968–70 (6)	1971–73 (7)
1. Total income, bill. N.T.$ per year	14.30	25.20	40.62	60.22	92.81	142.0	230.0
Percentage shares by type of income							
2. Compensation of employees	42.9	48.4	48.5	49.6	52.0	56.9	59.8
2a. Agriculture	2.2	3.5	3.8	3.2	3.2	3.3	3.3
3. Compound or entrepreneurial income	32.5	27.8	27.2	25.1	22.9	16.7	12.9
3a. Farm	31.0	26.3	25.6	23.7	21.2	15.0	10.8
3b. Other	1.5	1.5	1.6	1.4	1.7	1.7	2.1
4. Property incomes total	24.0	23.2	22.9	23.8	23.8	25.6	26.6
4a. Interest	2.7	2.6	4.1	4.9	5.2	5.9	5.0
4b. Rent	11.5	11.1	10.6	9.6	8.6	8.6	8.5
4c. Dividends, inc. savings of private enterprises	9.8	9.5	8.2	9.3	10.0	11.1	13.1
5. Total factor incomes (lines 2–4)	99.4	99.4	98.6	98.5	98.7	99.2	99.3
6. Social security and social assistance, receipts	0.3	0.5	0.5	0.5	0.4	0.4	0.4
7. Transfers from abroad	0.3	0.1	0.9	1.0	0.9	0.4	0.3
Percentage shares by type of disposition							
8. Direct taxes	1.3	1.5	1.4	1.4	1.3	1.9	2.5
9. Fees, social security contributions	1.7	1.6	1.8	1.2	2.0	2.4	2.1
10. Transfers to abroad	0.1	0.1	0.1	0.1	0.1	0.1	0.1
11. Consumer expenditures	91.0	91.9	90.3	86.9	80.7	79.4	73.4
12. Savings	5.9	4.9	6.4	10.4	15.9	16.2	21.9

The absolute totals underlying the percentage shares are either from DGBAS, *Statistical Yearbook, 1975,* National Accounts, Suppl. Table 14, pp. 222–23, or from DGBAS, *National Income of the Republic of China, 1972,* and *1975,* Table V, pp. 142–43 of the earlier source (used for years to 1958), and pp. 106–7 of the later source (used for 1958 onward). The dividends item is presumably inclusive of savings or private corporations only, since by definition the compound or mixed income of proprietors of unincorporated firms (or of own-account workers) includes whatever savings have materialized.

The percentage shares are, as usual, calculated by relating the average for the period of the particular component to the average of the total (the latter given in line 1).

households were far wider in the second decade of accelerated growth than in the first.

Although there is little unexpected about the findings, the estimates give rise to several questions, which indicate the need for further exploration. The first question relates to the extremely modest share in the total of mixed income other than farm—mixed income in the professions and in small firms engaged in nonagricultural sectors. The latter are of considerable importance in retail trade and repair and personal services. Lines 3a and 3b show that as compared with entrepreneurial incomes on farms including forestry and fishing, that in other sectors is below a fiftieth of total household income and between a twentieth and a fifth of farm entrepreneurial income. Yet the census of population data show that in 1956, of the total of employers and own-account workers of 1.04 million, 0.745 million were in agriculture and the remaining 0.295 million in other production sectors; a similar comparison for 1966 shows a total of employers and own-account workers of 1.18 million, of whom 0.73 million were in agriculture and 0.45 million in other sectors.[32] With a ratio of entrepreneurs outside of agriculture to those in the latter of between 0.4 to 0.6, at least as high a ratio of mixed income would have been expected in nonagriculture to that in agriculture. Unless the incomes of own-account workers outside of agriculture were classified under compensation of employees (and thus different from the classification in agriculture), the finding remains a puzzle.

The second question, closely linked with the first, bears on the meaning of the property income component entitled dividends, including savings of private enterprises (line 4). This designation, given in the official sources, must mean that only savings of private corporations are included, since, by definition, savings of unincorporated firms are already included in the mixed incomes of the individual entrepreneurs, and dividends, by definition, assume corporations in which separation between widespread ownership and nonowning management is clear. The question is: does the component so defined refer to payments by private corporations with the clear separation between management and ownership; or is the underlying economic universe largely comprised of essentially privately owned and managed enterprises, similar to unincorporated firms even if legally incorporated? This question was directly confronted in the presentation of the results of the first government countrywide sample of family income and expenditures for 1964. In one table mixed income from nonagricultural firms was given as N.T.$ 10.7 billion (compared with N.T.$ 17.7 billion for mixed income from agriculture), and among property income, the third component (besides interest and rent),

32. The figures are quoted from Kwok-Kwan Fung, "The Growth and Utilization of the Labor Force in Taiwan, 1956–1966" (Ph.D. dissertation, Harvard University, 1970), Appendix Tables 4-1A and 4-1B, pp. 87 and 88.

"investment income," was set at N.T.$ 0.35 billion. In another table mixed income from firms outside of agriculture was set at only N.T.$ 2.1 billion, and under property incoe, in addition to interest and rent, one item is entitled operation surplus (N.T.$ 8.9 billion), and the other, transfer from corporations, presumably dividends (N.T.$ 0.1 billion).[33] In the volume dealing with the next round, that for 1966, the analogous tables show an identical distribution by type of income; and it is the one in which the investment income among property incomes is quite small and mixed income of non-agricultural firms adequately large.[34]

A large proportion of the component in line 4c seems to be mixed income of entrepreneurs and therefore should be shifted from the pure property income category to that of mixed incomes; but how large the shift should be or how the correct proportion would vary over time is unknown. The only warranted judgment is that the pure property component under line 4c should be materially reduced, thus reducing significantly the share of property incomes in the total (and raising that of entrepreneurial mixed incomes). This is relevant because, with the structure as now given in Table 1.20, Taiwan shows an unusually high ratio of pure property incomes in the total of factor incomes.[35]

The final question concerns the size of the rent component of property income. The definition in the source refers to the rent component of property income as "*net* of costs of operation such as insurance, repairs, taxes, water charges, commissions, mortgage interest, and depreciation";[36] and this also applies presumably to imputed rental value of owner-occupied dwellings included in this item. But if this net item of rent, received by, or imputed to, households, is compared with the gross item of outlays by household on rent and water charges (the latter given beginning with 1961-63 in Table 1.17), we find that over the years 1961-63 to 1971-73, the net item in Table 1.20 and the gross item in Table 1.17 both account, on the average, for 11.5 percent of consumer expenditures—in other words, they are of roughly the same magnitude. This finding may be due to the receipt by households of rent on properties other than residential housing, but only to the extent that receipt of rent is not part of the mixed income of individual entrepreneurs. The question

---

33. DGBAS, *Report on the Survey of Family Income and Expenditures, 1964* (Taipei, December 1966), Table 6, pp. 218-ff., Table 21, pp. 288ff. The problem is discussed in the text of the report on pp. 126-27.

34. DGBAS, *Report on the Survey of Family Income and Expenditure in Taiwan, 1966* (Taipei, 1968), Table 7, pp. 164ff., and Table 21, pp. 352ff.

35. A comparison can be made for the early 1950s, utilizing the data and analysis in my "Quantitative Aspects of the Economic Growth of Nations, IV. Distribution of National Income by Factor Shares," *Economic Development and Cultural Change* 7, no. 3, part II (April 1959), 1-100. In Table 1, pp. 10-11, the share of property income in the total factor income of households varies from somewhat over 11 percent in the upper per capita income developed countries to about 10 percent in the lower per capita income countries.

36. DGBAS, *Statistical Yearbook, 1975*, p. 373.

calls for a scrutiny of the bases on which net rent has been estimated, a task not feasible here.

The conclusion suggested is that the distribution in Table 1.20 significantly overestimates the share of pure property incomes and underestimates that of the mixed incomes of entrepreneurs. Further analysis and allocation, like that presented in the study cited in footnote 35, may reveal whether the mixed income contains substantial components of property income over and above the labor compensation of the active entrepreneur or own-account worker. The reduction in the share of pure property incomes, even including the property income component of entrepreneurial incomes, may easily be to less than half of the share now shown in Table 1.20. If so, the resulting type of income structure would not differ substantially from those shown for other countries with similarly large shares of mixed entrepreneurial incomes. Presumably, the share of the adjusted pure property income might show a rise over time, but this is no more than a plausible conjecture; and given the much lower level of the share, such a trend is unlikely to have a significant impact on the income distribution by size among meaningful groups in the population.

Income Distribution among Households

The structure of household income by type provides only indirect suggestions of possible inequalities in the distribution of income among households. More direct evidence is needed, and such evidence must shed light on the long-term income levels of various groups in the population, taking into account the relevant household unit, its size, its age and stage in the life cycle, and several other variables that would make meaningful analysis possible. But there are major obstacles to obtaining such evidence, even in the developed countries with a rich body of statistical data; and efforts much beyond the feasibility of this study would be needed to assemble and distill such data for Taiwan. This subsection, therefore, deals with the available data on the conventional type of distribution, among households by size of current income per household. We consider, first, its purely statistical limitations, that is, deficiencies, even if we were to accept the conventional formulation and classification of the data; and then deal with the analytical deficiencies that force us to turn, in the next subsection, to income differentials among the major household groups by occupation of the household head.

Table 1.21 compares the population and income totals in the major source of data on size distribution of income among households, the surveys of family income and expenditures (FS), with the comparable totals in the national accounts (ND), for population and for income. The comparison is for selected years and is necessarily qualified by the limitations of my knowledge of, and access to, much of the underlying data and details—limitations that are unavoidable for an individual scholar dealing with the rich variety of basic data usually available for a country. But the comparison illustrates the difficulties in securing adequate coverage of the topic for international comparison and explains my reluctance to use the conventional size distribution of income among households for Taiwan.[37]

The findings in Table 1.21 are as follows. First, the total population yielded by the family surveys is significantly larger than the comparable national total, which should exclude the servicemen and other institutional population (hence the comparison of line 3 with line 4a rather than line 4b). This excess is particularly large for 1964, for which the number of persons was derived from that shown for various size-of-household or occupation-of-head groups; and there is a question whether this disparity affected the income totals. The reasons for such an excess of population yielded by the family surveys may lie either in inclusion of a good proportion of servicemen and members of institutional population (that is, inclusion of members of households living separately and contributing to, or dependent upon, income of the household) or in the overrepresentation of larger households in the sample. In the former case, the apparent exclusion from the family surveys of a part of the income-earning population should not be adjusted for in the comparison of family survey income totals with those in national accounts; in the latter case, the family surveys underestimate income if household income is related to number of persons because usually the larger households are characterized by lower per person income than are smaller households.

Second, for the strictly comparable groups of factor incomes—wages and salaries, net income from agriculture, and combined interest and rent—the evidence in lines 6–11 indicates a marked and fairly continuous shortage of the family survey income totals relative to those of national accounts. If 1964 is excluded, the shortages, in percentages of the larger national accounts totals, range from 22 to 33 percent for wages and salaries, 20 to 35 percent for net income from agriculture (mixed income), and from 31 to 51 percent for the total of interest and rent.

Third, the residual group of factor incomes (lines 12–14) combines, for the national accounts, mixed income from nonfarm entrepreneurial activities with dividends, the latter including savings of private corporations; for the family

37. The table omits reference to two earlier sample surveys, for 1953 and 1961. They are described and summarized in the paper by Shirley W. Y. Kuo, cited in the notes to line 1 of Table 1.21. These surveys cover only a few hundred families; show even larger deviations from the national totals than the larger samples that represent official surveys beginning in 1964; and suggest movements of inequality measures that are not easily defensible in the light of much narrower movements for the years beginning in 1964. Unless and until intensive analysis of these earlier samples indicates their reliability, an analysis not feasible here, their use is subject to too much question to be warranted.

Table 1.21. Comparison of Population and Income, Family Surveys of Income (FS) and National Accounts (ND), Selected Years, 1964–1975

A. Population (end of year)

		1964 (1)	1966 (2)	1968 (3)	1972 (4)	1974 (5)	1975 (6)
1.	Size of sample, number of households, thousands	3.00	3.00	3.00	5.76	5.87	9.46
2.	Total households as given in surveys, thousands	2,152	2,281	2,373	2,772	2,916	3,039
3.	Population, as given in surveys, mill.	13.75	13.36	13.84	15.47	15.55	16.03
4a.	Population, excl. military and some institutions, mill.	12.26	12.99	13.65	14.93	15.47	15.74
4b.	Total population, national accounts, mill.	12.75	13.45	14.10	15.37	15.92	16.20
5.	Percentage difference, lines 3 to 4a	+12.2	+2.8	+1.4	+3.6	+0.1	+1.8

B. Factor incomes (current prices, N.T.$ bill.)

		1964 (1)	1966 (2)	1968 (3)	1972 (4)	1974 (5)	1975 (6)
Wages and salaries							
6.	National accounts (ND)	39.49	50.27	69.70	132.15	234.33	253.41
7.	Family surveys (FS)	27.26	35.90	46.94	97.56	177.63	198.97
8.	Percentage difference, lines 7–6	−31.0	−28.6	−32.7	−26.2	−24.2	−21.5
Net income from agriculture							
10.	ND	18.55	20.37	21.23	23.69	46.32	49.40
11.	FS	17.72	16.20	14.68	17.24	29.97	35.82
12.	Percentage difference, lines 11–10	−4.4	−20.5	−30.9	−27.2	−35.3	−27.5
Interest and rent							
12.	ND	11.27	12.87	18.31	30.83	48.84	50.59
13.	FS	4.95	6.29	10.12	16.76	28.99	34.97
14.	Percentage difference, lines 13–12	−56.1	−51.2	−44.7	−43.6	−40.6	−30.9

*All other**						
15. ND	.58	11.41	14.66	30.76	40.40	35.38
16. FS	11.07	13.79	18.51	27.75	45.99	52.06
17. Percentage difference, lines 16–15	+29.0	+20.7	+26.3	–9.8	+13.8	+47.1
Total factor incomes (sum of above)						
18. ND	77.89	94.92	123.90	217.43	369.89	388.78
19. FS	61.00	72.18	90.25	159.31	282.58	321.82
20. Percentage difference, lines 19–18	–21.7	–24.0	–27.2	–26.7	–23.6	–17.2

*For ND: mixed income from professions and other nonfarm self-employment, plus dividends including savings of private corporations; for FS: mixed income from professions and nonagricultural employment, plus investment income.

Line 1: For years through 1972 from Shirley W. Y. Kuo, "Income Distribution by Size in Taiwan Area—Changes and Causes," in *Seminar on Income Distribution Employment and Economic Development in Southeast and East Asia: Papers and Proceedings of the Seminar Sponsored Jointly by the Japan Economic Research Center and the Council for Asian Manpower Studies, December 16–20, 1974* (Tokyo, July 1975), I, 83–84. For 1974 and 1975 from Taipei City govt., *Report on the Survey of Family Income and Expenditure and Personal Income Distribution in Taipei City, 1974* (Taipei, June 1975), and Taiwan Provincial govt., *Report on the Survey of Family Income and Expenditure, Taiwan Province, 1974* (Taipei, June 1975), and reports by the same titles for 1975.

Lines 2–3: From the single or double reports for each year as given for line 1. The number of persons reported appears to be for the end of the year, whereas income is for the year; but no adjustment was made for this slight discrepancy. For 1964, line 3, the total distributed among the various size or occupation-of-head household groups was appreciably greater than that obtained by multiplying total number of households by the average number of persons per household shown in the report (that is, 2.152 million households by 5.61 persons per household, or 12.07 million). The total used in line 3 was obtained by multiplying the average number of persons for the various occupation-of-head groups (shown in DGBAS, *Report on the Survey of Family Income and Expenditures, 1964*, [Taipei, 1966], Table 9, p. 140) by the number of households in these groups (shown in Table 4, p. 208). Approximations to the average number of persons per household had to be made for two small occupational groups, and these were based on analogous data for 1966.

Line 4a: For 1964, 1966, and 1968, these are the end-of-year series in DGBAS, *Statistical Yearbook, 1975*, Table 18, p. 2. For 1971 (not included here) the estimate was derived by applying to the 1968 total the ratio of change from 1968 to 1971 in female population, which was assumed to have been unaffected by the inclusion of military and some institutional population at the end of 1969. For 1972, 1974, and 1975, the 1971 total was extrapolated by the movement in the series for total population from line 4b.

Line 4b: Derived from DGBAS, *National Income of the Republic of China, December 1976* (Taipei, December 1976, dividing total national income (in current prices) in Table 7, p. 21, by per capita income (also in current prices) in Table 10, p. 25. The calendar-year results were then averaged to secure end-of-year totals.

Lines 6–20: All totals from national accounts (ND) are from DGBAS, *National Income of the Republic of China, December 1976*, Table V, pp. 116–17. All (FS) totals are from the successive volumes of reports for the years indicated. For 1972, 1974, and 1975, the results were derived by simple addition of the aggregates shown separately for Taipei City and Taiwan Province.

surveys, the combination is of mixed income from nonfarm entrepreneurial activities with an item defined as "investment income." The reason for using such combinations was indicated in the preceding subsection.

Here, unlike the result for the other three groups of factor incomes, the family survey totals tend to exceed those in the national accounts in most of the years, although greater detail for other years shows that in 1971 and 1973 the entry in line 14 was, like that in 1972, negative (it was −23 percent in both years). Whatever the reasons for the sign and movement of this discrepancy, it may represent a combination of excess in the family survey data of the mixed income component, with a shortage in the dividends—investment income components. But an answer could be secured only by a far more intensive analysis of the comparison than is feasible here.

Finally, for all factor incomes, the shortage in the totals in the family surveys relative to those in national accounts range from 17 to about 27 percent of the larger totals. If this comparison is to be accepted, it implies that from 20 to more than 30 percent of the smaller family survey totals would have to be added to attain relatively complete income coverage. The answer to how such an addition would affect the income distribution must remain speculative. The general indication is that the adjustment upward is likely to be greater at the higher than at the lower income levels.

Such shortages of family or household income survey totals relative to comparable totals in the national accounts are not uncommon.[38] Further analysis that might take into account some aspects neglected here (for example, that the national accounts totals of factor incomes relate to private households and nonprofit assiciations, while the latter are excluded from family surveys, an aspect of unknown magnitude) could narrow the disparity somewhat. But, for the present, we have to accept the major conclusions of the comparison, which suggest significant shortages in the family survey income totals; the possibility of wider inequalities in the conventional size distribution of income among households than are now indicated by the family survey reports; and some question about the possibility of deriving significant trends in income inequality from the conventional size distributions based on the survey reports from 1964 or 1966 to 1975.

These statistical difficulties should be viewed in the light of analytical criteria that data on income distribution should satisfy. By these criteria, the

---

38. Thus, in the United States, where both national accounts and family sample surveys (of sizable coverage) have been available for a number of years, a check of the comparable totals (limited to money incomes) showed that the family survey "during the past few years . . . obtained about 89 percent of the comparable total money income aggregates and about 97 percent of the comparable money wage or salary aggregates" in the personal income series of the national accounts (U.S. Bureau of the Census, *Income in 1969 of Families and Persons in the United States,* Current Population Reports, Series P-60, No. 75 [Washington, D.C., 1970], p. 12).

conventional distributions of income among households by income per household for a given year are inadequate in many respects.[39]

Because the family household is the major deciding unit on income acquisition and use, it is the proper recipient unit in a meaningful size distribution of income, but households differ widely in size, and there is usually a positive association between number of persons and total income per household. Yet income must be related to numbers of consumers dependent upon it (or, for some purposes, to numbers of income earners); the conventional size distribution by income per household must, therefore, be adjusted for differing size of households. When the proper adjustment is made, the smaller households usually are found to have higher per person income than the larger.

But even when household income is reduced to a per person or per consumer basis, the household's position in its life cycle, as reflected in the age of head, affects the income levels. Such income differentials are compatible with equality of lifetime income. All other conditions being equal, households with younger and older heads, at the beginning and end of their life cycles, will tend to show lower per unit income than those with middle-aged heads, who are at the peak of income-earning ability, and yet the number of children may have been reduced because they have reached the age of leaving and starting out for themselves (at least in developed countries). Any interpretation of household income distribution, even shifted to a per person or per consumer basis, must take cognizance of, and secure data on, the position of the household within the life cycle; and the latter may be quite different for less developed and for developed countries.

To determine the relation between economic growth and income inequality, we need income levels that are not affected by transitory disturbances. Yet the available data presumably reflect one year's income, with whatever nonsecular elements are embodied in it, and they affect the classification by income size. Whether consumption rather than income totals can be used to secure a better approximation to longer-term income levels is a question that is difficult to answer without further experimentation with the data.

The three aspects of the conventional distribution touched upon—differing size of family households, the effect of the position of the household in life cycle, and the distinction between longer-term income levels associated with growth and the more transient components—are all affected by economic

39. The present comments are a capsule summary, extended in application to the case of a rapidly growing country like Taiwan, of arguments and statistical illustrations presented by me in detail in two long papers. The first, entitled "Demographic Components in Size Distribution of Income," is in Vol. 2, pp. 389–472, of the monograph from which Kuo's paper was cited (see notes to Table 1.21). This paper, completed in late 1974, was substantially revised and modified for publication as "Demographic Aspects of the Size Distribution of Income: An Exploratory Essay," *Economic Development and Cultural Change* 25, no. 1 (October 1976), 1–94.

growth processes. The latter, through their effects on the demographic variables and family formation, modify the differentials among family households with respect to size; shape in different ways the life cycles of family households; and, through changes in technology and control over temporary disturbances, modify the incidence of transitory income changes. This means that any comparison between developed and less developed countries, or within the same country among different long periods, must shift from the conventional distribution by current income per household to account for these various effects of household size, phase of life cycle, and so forth.

In the case of Taiwan, the task is complicated by the rapidity with which its growth and structural shifts occurred over the last quarter of a century. The demographic components in the conventional size distribution also changed rapidly because of urbanization, decline in the birth rates, and their effects on family formation and the life cycle. Furthermore, in the light of the findings given below of the combination within the family households of income from different production sectors and of close relations between parental families and the next generation, one may ask what inequality would mean if it were observed between a parental household and the household of a son. Assume, for illustration, that the parental generation is in farming and the son is in industry with appreciably higher per unit income at a given time. Would such inequality, if wide or sidening, have a welfare meaning, or should we think of related clusters of households formed by blood ties?

In the papers referred to in footnote 39, the concluding comments suggested that in view of the difficulties of dealing directly with these problems by modifying conventional size distributions of income (a task that will take much time and effort), the analysis should emphasize data on interoccupational differences in income per household, adjusted for differences in household size among occupations. These data, usually provided in family income and expenditure surveys, do not answer all the questions and contain other difficulties. But we may follow this direction briefly for Taiwan.

Interoccupational Differences in Household Income

Table 1.22 summarizes selected data on farm households or families yielded by periodic farm income surveys by the JCRR. The possible value of these data is particularly high because they reach back to 1952 and extend, at five-year intervals, to 1972, thus spanning the period of coverage here. The sample is substantial, ranging from 4,000 families in 1952 to close to 2,000 in 1962 and 1,400 in 1957. Only households are included that cultivate land, and the farm families are grouped into classes by size of their land holdings (in four classes) and into thirteen agricultural regions. The difficulty is that the basis of selection appears to have varied among the years; and adequate tests of the representativeness of these sample data relative to the full universe of

Table 1.22. Trends in Per Person Income of Farmer Households Compared with Those for All Households, Current Prices, Selected Years, 1952–1972

	JCRR survey data					All households survey	
	1952 (1)	1957 (2)	1962 (3)	1967 (4)	1972 (5)	1966–68 average (6)	1972 (7)
1. Cropland per farm, chias	1.30	1.19	1.15	1.11	0.87	n.a.	n.a.
2. Cultivated land per farm, chias	1.27	1.11	1.05	1.01	0.99	n.a.	n.a.
3. Total income per farm household, N.T.$, thousands	7.36	14.15	24.11	40.39	49.06	32.17	49.10
4. Percent of total income from nonfarm sources	22.1	36.7	40.9	41.6	60.2	38.9	55.6
5. Persons per farmer household	8.14	8.39	8.58	8.34	7.50	6.94	6.51
6. Total income per person, N.T.$, thousands	0.90	1.69	2.81	4.84	6.54	4.64	7.54
7. Line 6, index, 1967 = 100	19	35	58	100	135	100	162.5
8. Total income of households (including nonprofit associations), N.T.$, bill.	14.03	30.54	59.27	100.35	219.13	100.35	219.13
9. Total population, mill.	8.54	10.13	11.86	13.62	15.26	13.62	15.26
10. Income per person, N.T.$, thousands	1.64	3.01	5.00	8.10	14.36	8.10	14.36
11. Line 10, index, 1967 = 100	20	37	62	100	177	100	177

Columns 6 and 7, lines 1–7, were derived from the *Report on the Survey of Family Income and Expenditures* for these years, the findings of which are covered in greater detail in Table 1.23 (see sources in the notes to that table).

Columns 1–5, lines 1, 3–6: Taken or calculated from three sources published by the Rural Economics Division of the JCRR, *A Summary Report on Farm Income of Taiwan in 1957 in Comparison with 1952*, JCRR Economic Digest Series, no. 13 (Taipei, December 1959); *Taiwan Income Survey of 1967*, JCRR Economic Digest Series, no. 20 (Taipei, January 1970); and a mimeographed release, "A Brief Report on Farm Income in Taiwan in 1972" (Taipei, 1976). A chia equals 0.97 of a hectare and 2.4 acres.

Line 2: Calculated from the series on cultivated land and number of farm households (averaged to yield the midyear entries) in DGBAS, *Statistical Yearbook, 1975*, Agriculture, Supp. Table 4, p. 91, and Supp. Table 5, p. 92.

Lines 8–10: total income of households derived from DGBAS, *National Income of the Republic of China, 1972*, and Table VIII; ibid, *1975* (Taipei, 1976), Table VIII for both years; total population derived from comparisons of total income and per capita income for the five selected years from the relevant tables in the same sources.

farm or agricultural families are not available. But the data can be linked with those on farmer households in the overall surveys of family income and expenditures and may be of interest as yielding preliminary approximations.

Before summarizing the findings, we note that the comparison in lines 1–2 for cultivated land per farm shows a fair agreement in the movement from 1952 to 1967; but in the sample in line 1, land per farm declines more sharply from 1967 to 1972 than in the estimates based on registered population in line 2. Likewise, the rise in total income per person from 1967 to 1972 in the JCRR sample (lines 6 and 7, columns 4 and 5) is not as large as that shown by the overall family surveys (lines 6 and 7, columns 6 and 7). finally, the JCRR sample shows a much larger number of persons per farm than either the overall households sample of farmer households or the registered agricultural or farm population totals in the *Statistical Yearbook*. For our purposes it is advisable to rely for the movements of per capita farm income from 1967 to 1972 on the overall family surveys and not to utilize the persons per farm data of the JCRR for deriving total disparity measures between farm and nonfarm populations in their income per capita.

Two findings deserve explicit note. The first relates to the comparative movements of income per person of the population comprised by farmer households and of income per person of the total population in all households (lines 6 and 11)—the former derived for 1952–67 from the JCRR sample and for 1967–72 from the overall households survey and the latter derived from the national accounts totals of income received by households (including nonprofit associations) and aggregate population. The income totals are not fully comparable, but they do indicate the broader trends. The significant finding is that the movements in per person current income (in current prices) of the farm households and of the total population were roughly the same, the former rising from an index of 19 in 1952 to one of 162.5 in 1972, the latter moving from an index of 20 to one of 177. Since the average income per person of the total population was a weighted mean of the lower per person income of farm population with the higher per person income of the nonfarm population, with the share of the farm population in the total declining, the finding implies that the ratio of per person income of the farm population to that of the nonfarm was rising (except perhaps from 1967 to 1972).[40]

40. Table 1.23 shows, for an average of 1966 and 1968, a share of 37 percent of farm households in total persons and a share of 27.3 percent in total income, yielding a ratio of per person income in farm households to that in all households of 0.74. If, for illustrative purposes, we assume a share of farm households in total persons in 1952 of 50 percent, and the 1966–68 income relative for per person income in farm households, the share of the latter in total income would be 37 percent, and the ratio of per person income of nonfarm households to that in farm households would be 1.70 in 1952, compared with 1.56 for 1967 (average of 1966 and 1968). The figures used are illustrative; but they are realistic and reveal the implications of the similarity in movement over time in per person income in the farm and total population, under the conditions

The second major finding is that this similarity in movement is associated with the marked rise of nonagricultural sources in the total income of farm households. The reduction of land per farm and other changes in income-earning opportunities were accompanied by a marked shift in the distribution of total income per farm between net receipts from farming and nonfarm income, the latter in the JCRR sample rising from about 20 percent of the total in 1952 to 40 percent in 1967 and about 60 percent in 1972 (see line 4, columns 1–5). This finding is confirmed by the overall household surveys of family income and expenditure. For farmer households defined by the occupation of the head of family, the proportion of income other than net income from agriculture rose from an average of 39 percent in 1966 and 1968 to 56 percent in 1972. Were such nonfarm sources of income absent, one or both of possible consequences might have followed: there might have been more out-migration from the farm household in search of other income sources, thus further reducing the size of farm households and adding a larger migrant group to nonfarm population; or there might have been a shrinkage of per person income, with migration from the farm household not matching the restriction of farm income opportunities. In either case, the results would have been different from those suggested in Table 1.22. Thus, the relative stability in the income distribution among households, if found, was probably associated with the increasing diversification of income sources that proved feasible within the households, farm or nonfarm.

In short, the evidence provides no basis for inferring adverse marked shifts in the farm–nonfarm relative differentials in per capita income over the long period from the early 1950s to the early 1970s. Unless further research modifies this finding substantially, the conclusion is of large potential importance, for it is the widening contrast between the agricultural sector, with its lagging productivity and increasing weight of surplus labor, and the more buoyant nonagricultural sectors that may contribute to widening the inequality in income levels between the two major components of a developing country's population. That this widening did not occur in Taiwan, despite rapid growth of productivity and hence widening productivity levels between the two sectors, may have resulted partly from the movement of the farm population out of agriculture and partly from a rapid decline in the rate of natural increase, but mostly from the capacity to secure income from sources other than farming while retaining, perhaps for more than accounting purposes, membership in the farm household.

The family income and expenditure surveys that were the source of the information (in Table 1.23) on total and per person income for households

---

stated—the lower level of per person income in farm households and a decline in the proportion of farm to total population.

grouped by occupation of the family head were also used to estimate shortfalls of total income compared with national accounts totals in Table 1.21. Hence the occupational group income totals and averages are, on the whole, short by the same relative proportions; but we do not know how the shortages should be apportioned among the occupations. Any inferences as to presence or absence of trends must be subject to the qualification that they could be modified in a further, and desirable, scrutiny of the specific loci of the shortfalls.

Panel A provides data on the two occupational classifications that were found in the tabulated data. There is an element of discontinuity that could not be eliminated short of a retabulation of data for one set of years by the occupational classification of the other. But there is some similarity between the two; and one may reasonably assume that for an aggregate measure of disparity, the noncomparability elements in the two classifications would not introduce major errors in comparison between 1966 and the later years. In Panel B, data for 1964 were omitted because of the difficulty of correcting for the overstatement on number of persons per household in the several occupation-of-head groups.

Our findings are summarized here in total disparity measures (TDM)—sums of differences, signs disregarded, between percentage shares of the relevant groups in the two related totals (e.g., totals of household and income, or of persons and income). TDM is a useful simple measure of inequality among groups with respect to the total distributed; and was extensively discussed, and compared with Gini coefficients, in the two papers cited in note 39.

Several probably valid findings can be suggested. First, per capita household income and the average size of the household in the occupational group are inversely correlated. This is largely because among professional, technical, and white-collar employees, with their relatively high per family incomes, the size of families tends to be smaller than among the farmers or manual laborers, with their lower per family incomes. As a result of this inverse correlation, total disparity measures for distributions among occupations by per person income are consistently wider than those for distributions among occupations by per household income (compare lines 14 and 15).

Second, the most relevant disparity measures, in line 15, fluctuate from year to year, but show no perceptible trend for the whole stretch, either to 1973 or to 1975. A slight rise occurs from the mid-1960s to 1973 (and a decline thereafter); but the movements are so slight that, given the limitations of the data, we can only assume long-term constancy in the inequality in interoccupational differentials.

Third, the farm–nonfarm differential in per capita income is a major factor in the total disparity measures. But this does not mean that interoccupational differences in per capita income among nonfarm occupations are negligible. Line 22 provides measures of total disparity in per capita income of households among nonfarm occupations. Because of the nonadditive nature of the TDM (true also of the Gini coefficients), the sum of the measures for the disparity between farm and nonfarm households, and that among nonfarm households (lines 18 and 22), exceed by a substantial margin the measures for the occupational distribution of the total universe of households (line 15). But, in itself, the TDM for the occupational differentials among the nonfarm households also shows no clear trend over time; the values range about 20, with the single exception of the low value for 1968. And the sum of lines 18 and 22, like the entries in line 15, show no marked trends over the period, adding to between 36 to 44 points, with no sustained movements in the changes in the single years.

To sum up, present indications are that no acceptable evidence exists for inferring significant trends in the inequality over the two to two and a half decades, either between farm and nonfarm households or among occupational groups, in distributions by household per capita income. There is also some indication that the magnitude of income disparities is not wide in Taiwan, but better data and analysis on the relative numbers involved and on the allocation of the shortfalls among the incomes of various population groups are required; and it might not be justified to advance this hypothesis until further work on the data has been done.

The Diffusion of Lower Fertility Patterns

A major demographic trend, the decline in fertility, is related to the broader topic of distributive aspects of economic growth in that a basic hypothesis links the two. This hypothesis can be briefly stated. Marked declines in fertility imply a wide diffusion of its reduction among the country's population. In societies that allow adequate freedom to consumers and families, such widespread reductions in fertility represent significant economically rational responses of the population to changes in economic and social conditions that favor fewer children and greater investment in their education and training. Hence, such wide diffusion of fertility reduction is a significant index of the extent to which the revised view on children and their future prospects has spread, and thus an index of the spread of the positive contributions of economic growth in their distribution among the population. Finally, wide diffusion of fertility reduction among all strata of the population prevents or minimizes the inequality effects of uneven diffusion, which in the past of many currently developed countries meant a gradual and slow spread of the pattern from the higher income brackets to the lower. This is a working hypothesis, and it places the potential effects of deliberate population control policies in free societies in the second rank, compared with the effects of changes in economic and social conditions. It does not deny, of course, the contribution of deliberate population policies, particularly to those limited

Table 1.23. Disparities in Income (current receipts), Per Household and Per Person, Households Grouped by Occupation of Head, Selected Years, 1966-1975

A. Percentage shares of occupational groups in total of households, persons, and income, illustrative years

Occupational groups, 1966 (1)	Percentage shares in			Occupational groups, 1968 (5)	Percentage shares in		
	Number of households (2)	Number of persons (3)	Total income (4)		Number of households (6)	Number of persons (7)	Total income (8)
1. Managers and professional	1.6	1.4	3.2	1. Professionals and technical	5.3	4.8	8.4
2. Government employees, including teachers, servicemen	11.6	10.1	12.7	2. Administrators and managers	2.5	2.7	4.7
				3. Clerical workers	8.9	8.1	10.9
				4. Sales workers	14.2	14.0	17.2
3. Employees, private, public, nonprofit	7.8	7.2	11.4	5. Farmers and related occupations	31.6	36.3	24.8
4. Owners of small firms	11.9	12.5	14.5	6. Craftsmen, workers, miners	18.5	18.1	16.7
5. Farmers and related occupations	30.9	37.8	29.8	7. Transport workers	6.4	6.7	7.5
6. Industrial laborers	15.2	13.7	11.7	8. Service, sports, recreation workers	6.0	5.0	5.1
7. General laborers	11.6	9.7	9.7	9. Unclassified industries, military, not working	6.6	4.3	4.7
8. Personal service and repair workers	6.9	6.4	5.2				
9. Unclassified, industries, unemployed, retired	2.5	1.2	1.8				

B. Data relating to overall totals and measures of disparity

	1966 (1)	1968 (2)	1971 (3)	1972 (4)	1973 (5)	1974 (6)	1975 (7)
10. Number of households, mill.	2.28	2.37	2.69	2.77	2.86	2.92	3.04
11. Number of persons, mill.	13.36	13.84	15.20	15.47	15.64	15.55	16.03
12. Persons per household	5.86	5.83	5.66	5.58	5.47	5.31	5.28
13. Household income (current receipts), N.T.$ bill.	76.5	96.4	141.6	167.7	213.1	294.5	337.7
Total disparity measures							
14. All households, income per household	17.8	22.8	23.2	21.2	23.8	21.0	22.5
15. All households, income per person	22.4	25.8	25.4	23.8	28.2	24.2	25.6
Farmer and nonfarmer households							
16. Farm households, percent of persons in total of persons	37.8	36.3	27.6	30.1	29.6	27.1	29.9
17. Farm households, percent in total income (current receipts)	29.8	24.8	18.5	21.0	18.6	18.9	20.3
18. Total disparity measures (TDM) (lines 16–17)	16.0	23.0	18.2	18.2	22.0	16.4	19.2
19. Income relative per person, farm households (F)	0.79	0.68	0.67	0.70	0.63	0.70	0.68
20. Income relative per person, nonfarm household (NF)	1.13	1.18	1.13	1.13	1.16	1.11	1.14
21. Ratio, income per person, NF/F (line 20 to line 19)	1.43	1.74	1.69	1.61	1.84	1.59	1.68
Total disparity, nonfarm occupations							
22. Total disparity measures (TDM), income per person	19.6	16.8	20.6	19.2	21.0	20.4	21.4

Based on data in the DGBAS and related statistical agencies' reports on family income and expenditures for 1966, 1968 (covering all Taiwan in one volume for each year), and annually for 1971–75, with separate volumes covering Taiwan Province and Taipei City. Panel A shows the two occupational classifications, one given for 1964 and 1966 and the other for 1968 and 1971–75.

Lines 14 and 15 are based on shares in the annual totals of income, households, and persons of the nine occupational groups distinguished in Panel A.

Lines 19 and 20 are calculated from lines 16 and 17, the former by dividing the shares in line 17 by those in line 16; the latter by dividing (100 minus the shares in line 17) by (100 minus the shares in line 16).

In line 22, the TDM is computed from the shares in the totals of persons and income, excluding the group of farmer households, with the shares recalculated as percentages of a new set of totals. The groups are those distinguished in Panel A.

groups within any society that are impeded from reducing fertility by lack of adequate knowledge of means and by social pressure (both relievable by population policy). At any rate, it is the hypothesis as to the major influence of aggregate and distributive economic and social changes on fertility that explains my use of these demographic data here.[41]

The evidence summarized in Table 1.24 relates to age-specific birth rates for all women and all men (including unmarried) and presents a fertility measure that more closely than the others, reflects decisions by the members of society involved as to intra- or extramarital births, qualified only by fecundity factors that vary with age (particularly of women). In the case of the crude birth rates used earlier, the effects of differences in age and sex structure of the population are involved, factors that are beyond control of decisions by individuals and families. If, then, we find, as we do, that the age-specific fertility rates and their unweighted sum (total fertility) decline sharply over the two-decade span, the implication is that either marriage rates or intramarital fertility— probably much more the latter than the former—have declined because of decisions within the marital life of the population. The rationale for those decisions, suggested by the hypothesis, makes these findings meaningful.

Total fertility rate (TFR) indicates the number of children that a cohort of one-thousand women would give birth to through the full span of their reproductive life, assuming complete survival and age-specific birth rates of the year to which the TFR relates. Thus, Table 1.24 shows that the average number of births per woman in this assumed cohort was as high as 6.7 in 1951–53 and about half that, 3.4, in 1971–73. This decline is over a span that differentiates in recent years the TFRs for more developed and less developed countries and is almost as wide as the decline that occurred in the currently developed countries in the long course of their economic growth.[42] Yet it occurred in Taiwan over the short span of about two decades.

Declines of such magnitude in countrywide measures indicate a widespread phenomenon that could not be limited to small fractions of the population, and

41. A vast literature exists on this topic. In the present connection see particularly the discussion in the Institute of Economics, Academia Sinica, *Conference on Population and Economic Development of Taiwan* (Taipei, 1976), of the paper by T. H. Sun, "The Prospects for Population Growth: Socio-economic Implications for Taiwan," pp. 37–99, by R. A. Easterlin, on pp. 157–58.

42. See my paper, "Fertility Differentials between Less Developed and Developed Regions: Components and Implications," *Proceedings of the American Philosophical Society* 110, no. 5 (October 1975), 363–96. Table 1, p. 364, shows an average total fertility rate (TFR) for less developed countries of 5,935 and for developed countries of 2,880 (market economies, early or middle 1960s). A recent working paper by the Population Division of the United Nations (*ESA/P/WP. 55,* May 1975, mimeographed) shows, for 1970, a TFR for all less developed regions of 5,267 and for the developed regions of 2,337 (both, medium variant, pp. 2–3). It took over a century for the fertility rates in the currently developed countries to decline as much relatively as they did in Taiwan since the early 1950s, although lack of age-specific rates in the earlier decades for the developed countries limits the comparison to crude birth rates.

Table 1.24. Age-specific and Total Fertility Rates, 1951–1973 (all rates per 1,000 of midyear population)

	15–19 (1)	20–24 (2)	25–29 (3)	30–34 (4)	35–39 (5)	40–44 (6)	45–49* (7)	Total fertility (8)
				All women				
1. 1951–53	56	275	346	299	221	118	30	6,708
2. 1954–57	48.5	262	335	290	214	101	23	6,365
3. 1958–60	46	253	334	269	186	85	14	5,932
4. 1961–63	44	252	339	237	147	65	10	5,470
5. 1964–67	38	260	321	189	95	40	6	4,740
6. 1968–70	40	246	300	153	63	26	4	4,145
7. 1971–73	35	212	261	119	43	14	2	3,427
Percentage decline from earlier level (rises marked +)								
8. Full period, lines 1–7	37.5	22.9	24.6	60.2	80.5	88.1	93.3	48.9
9. First decade, lines 1–4	21.4	8.4	2.0	20.7	33.5	44.9	66.7	18.5
10. Second decade, lines 4–7	20.5	15.9	23.0	49.6	70.7	78.5	80.0	37.4
Percentage contribution of age-class fertility to total fertility (cols. 1–7) and age at which 75 percent of total is reached (col. 8)								
11. 1951–53	4.2	20.5	25.7	22.2	16.4	8.8	2.2	35.1
12. 1961–63	4.0	23.0	31.0	21.7	13.4	6.0	0.9	33.9
13. 1971–73	5.1	30.9	38.0	17.4	6.3	2.0	0.3	30.3
				All men				
14. 1951–53	15	163	297	310	255	187	128	6,777
15. 1961–63	8	90	298	275	187	121	74	5,289
16. 1971–73	4	65	272	218	90	54	35	3,690
Percentage decline from earlier level (rises marked +)								
17. Full period	73.3	60.1	8.4	29.7	68.6	71.1	72.7	45.5
18. First decade	46.7	44.8	+0.3	11.3	26.7	35.3	42.2	22.3
19. Second decade	50.0	26.8	8.7	20.7	51.9	55.4	52.7	29.9
Percentage contribution of age-class fertility to total (col. 7) and age at which first 75 percent of total is reached (col. 8)								
20. 1951–53	1.1	12.1	21.9	22.9	18.8	13.8	9.4	39.5
21. 1961–63	0.8	8.5	28.3	26.1	17.8	11.5	7.0	38.2
22. 1971–73	0.5	8.8	36.9	29.5	12.2	7.3	4.8	34.9

*May be interpreted as including births occurring at ages over 49.

The underlying data are from DGBAS, *Statistical Yearbook, 1975,* Population, Supp. Table 11, p. 27, and Supp. Table 15, p. 31. Total fertility in column 8, lines 1–7 and 11–13, should add up to the sum of the entries for the age classes over the same period, multiplied by 5 (for the number of years in each age interval). A slight discrepancy is partly caused by errors of averaging.

The declines over the two- and one-decade intervals are in percentages to the level at the earlier of the two terminal periods.

The ages at which three-quarters of total fertility have been reached are obtained from the age limits of the age classes and by simple linear interpolation.

The source indicates that births in the age of mother (or father) unknown category were apportioned in proportion to the age distribution for the known categories (see DGBAS, *Statistical Yearbook, 1975,* p. 286).

indeed we shall find direct evidence on this in Table 1.25. Here we are more concerned with the large cumulative magnitude of the decline and its impact on the different age classes of women and men.

The rates of decline, in lines 8–10 and 17–19, are appreciably higher for almost all age classes and for the totals over the second decade than over the first. but the decline even in the first decade was already substantial before

Table 1.25. Age-specific and Total Fertility Rates, All Women, by Cities, Urban Townships, and Rural Townships, 1963-64 and 1973-1974 (rates per 1,000 of midyear population)

	Age classes							Total fertility
	15-19 (1)	20-24 (2)	25-29 (3)	30-34 (4)	35-39 (5)	40-44 (6)	45-49 (7)	(8)
1963-64								
1. Cities	41	237	304.5	190	98.5	39.5	9	4,598
2. Urban townships	34	249.5	341	222.5	128.5	55	8.5	5,195
3. Rural townships	40.5	267	357	247.5	154	69.5	9	5,722
4. Countrywide	39	253	336	222.5	129.5	56	9	5,225
1973-74								
5. Cities	28.5	179	222	92.5	31	9	2	2,820
6. Urban townships	32	197	251.5	103	35.5	9.5	1	3,148
7. Rural townships	39.5	226.5	265.5	110	42.5	14	2	3,500
8. Countrywide	32.5	198	239	98	34.5	10.5	1.5	3,070
Percentage decline over the decade								
9. Cities	nc*	24.5	27.1	51.3	68.5	77.2	nc	38.7
10. Urban townships	nc	21.0	26.2	53.3	72.4	82.7	nc	39.4
11. Rural townships	nc	15.2	25.7	55.6	72.4	79.9	nc	38.8
12. Countrywide	nc	21.7	28.9	56.0	74.9	81.2	nc	41.2
Percentage contribution of age class to total fertility (cols. 1-7) and age by which 75 percent of the total were reached (col. 8)								
1963-64								
13. Cities	4.5	25.7	33.1	20.7	10.7	4.3	1.0	32.8
14. Urban townships	3.3	24.0	32.8	21.4	12.4	5.3	0.8	33.5
15. Rural townships	3.5	23.3	31.2	21.6	13.5	6.1	0.8	33.9
16. Countrywide	3.7	24.2	32.1	21.3	12.4	5.4	0.9	33.5
1973-74								
17. Cities	5.0	31.7	39.4	16.4	5.5	1.6	0.4	29.9
18. Urban townships	5.1	31.3	39.9	16.4	5.6	1.5	0.2	29.8
19. Rural townships	5.6	32.4	37.9	15.7	6.1	2.0	0.3	29.9
20. Countrywide	5.3	32.2	38.9	16.0	5.6	1.7	0.3	29.8

*nc: not calculated.

Lines 1-3 and 5-7: Calculated from DGBAS, *Statistical Yearbook, 1975*, Population, Supp. Table 12, p. 28. "Cities covered include Taipei City, four provincial cities and the small cities under the jurisdiction of county governments. Urban and rural townships are the basic administrative units classified according to level of urbanization by the government" (ibid., p. 285).

Lines 4 and 8: Calculated from the source used for data on women in Table 1.24. For the calculation of other values, see notes to Table 1.24.

the population planning program and the educational attempts at spreading knowledge and acceptance of birth control devices. A drop of almost a fifth in total fertility in a decade is a major change; and its significance even in the first decade is augmented by its concentration in the upper age groups of women and in the younger and older age groups of men.

This concentration of the decline in fertility rate in specific age classes of women and somewhat older classes of men supports the argument that the trend was a rational response by the population to changed economic and social conditions and prospects. The age-specific fertility pattern in Taiwan, like that in some but not most LDCs, shows by 1951-53 low rates in the very young ages, below twenty for women (for evidence on other LDCs, with a different pattern, see Table 1 in the paper cited in footnote 42). If a marked reduction in total fertility were to occur, it would have to be for women above twenty. Theoretically it could be concentrated in the younger age classes, between twenty and thirty, or perhaps be in proportion to the initial age-specific rates. But this did not occur. Table 1.24 shows that in the first decade, the proportional declines in the two age classes in the twenties, for women, were quite moderate; the same was true of the corresponding age classes, five years older, for men (see line 9, columns 2 and 3; and line 18, columns 3 and 4). In the second decade, the declines were still greatest in the age classes above thirty for women and above thirty-five for men (see line 10, columns 2 and 3, and line 19, columns 3 and 4); but they were also substantial in the two younger age classes for women (line 10, columns 2 and 3) and the younger age class for men (line 19, column 4). It is only rational for the voluntary reduction in fertility to begin with older parents in families in which presumably a number of children have survived, and then to spread to the younger ages, as conditions led to further reducing the number of desired children.

One important consequence of such a reduction was to shorten appreciably the time span over which the childbearing processes extended, thus leaving room for a longer rearing and educational process and for a period when the older parental generation was still at high income-earning capacity but with consumption needs reduced by departure of children to form their own families. The percentage distributions in lines 11–13 (for mothers) and in lines 20–22 (for fathers) reflect this process of concentrating births into a narrowing range of years. Thus, births to mothers aged twenty to thirty accounted for less than half of all births in 1951–53 (line 11); by 1971–73, the births in that ten-year period were close to 70 percent of all births (line 13). The rough estimates suggest that the age by which three-quarters of total births had been attained had dropped for women from about thirty-five to thirty and for men from about forty to about thirty-five (lines 11–13 and 20–22, column 8). The lower incidence of births past these ages and of children to be reared by older parents is an important aspect of the trend in fertility reduction. In effect, it relieves the burdens on the parental generation at a younger age—and eventually at an age well before the pressure for retirement or before the incidence of a marked lowering in the parental generations' income-earning ability.

The evidence in Table 1.25 is limited to the last decade, when reduction in fertility was particularly marked. The most relevant findings are that the proportional decline in fertility was as large in the rural townships as in the urban townships and cities, thus confirming the widespread character of the process; and that the age-specific pattern of the decline was also similar, showing a somewhat greater movement toward concentration of births in the younger ages of the childbearing span in the rural townships than in the urban townships or cities.

The first finding is of obvious importance. It demonstrates that the experience of Taiwan was unlike that of many currently developed countries in their long-term movement toward lower fertility and perhaps unlike the recent experience of some other less developed countries. No perceptible element of inequality in incidence of childbearing and in the implications for income inequalities was introduced in Taiwan in the process of rapid reduction of fertility. There was no significant distinction of this respect between the rural and urban populations, and the initial relative discrepancies in fertility, narrow proportionally to begin with, remained unchanged, while the absolute differences shrank sharply.

Because of this wide diffusion, the shift of the population toward the cities had only a moderate effect on the countrywide reduction. To be sure, the overall rate of decline (line 12, column 8) for the country, 41.2 percent, is higher than the rate for any of the three components, which range from 38.7 to 39.4; and similar effects can be observed for several of the age classes (compare line 12 with lines 9-11 in columns 3, 4, and 5). But these excesses of the countrywide percentage declines, caused by shifting weights within the universe of women of childbearing ages, are narrow—even though in the nine years 1965 to 1974 the proportions of women in these ages in the cities (to all women in childbearing ages) rose from 30 to 41 percent, while those in the rural townships declined from 40 to 35 percent, and those in the urban townships from 30 to 24 percent.[43] If the current city-urban differentials in fertility had been wider, the effects of such shifts on the overall rate of decline would have been much greater.

The second finding shows that although the proportional differentials in fertility between rural and urban populations remained the same and overall fertility was reduced markedly, there was some convergence in the age-specific patterns between the countryside and the cities. This may be seen most clearly in the median ages at which three-quarters of total fertility are reached (lines 13-15 and 17-19, column 8). In 1963-64, these ages differed perceptibly, if only by a year, between the early age for cities, at 32.8 years, and the late age for rural townships, at 33.9 years, but by 1973-74 they were almost identical: 29.8 or 29.9 years. Another measure is provided by the sum of the differences in percentage contributions to total fertility of the different age classes within the women's childbearing ages. For 1963-64 these differences were 6.8 points between cities and urban townships; 11.0 points between cities and rural townships; and 4.6 points between urban and rural townships. By 1973-74 they were 1.4, 4.6, and 5.4 percent, respectively.

43. These percentages were calculated from the number of births and the general fertility rates given for 1965 and 1974 for the three groups of localities in Ministry of the Interior, *1974 Taiwan-Fukien Demographic Fact Book* (Taipei, December 1975), Tables 71 and 72, pp. 1004–7.

Except for the relation between urban and rural townships, the disparities between cities and either urban or rural townships were reduced markedly over the decade. Such convergence is another indication of the widespread character of the fertility decline; and of a growing similarity between the urban and rural populations in their changing views of the prospects of the younger generations under the changing economic and social conditions, as reflected in their familial decisions on childbearing and implicitly on child rearing.

Changes since 1973—A Postscript

The quantitative record discussed so far stops, with one or two exceptions, in 1971–73—the terminal period of a remarkable spurt in growth and structural change that extended for more than two decades. The worldwide depression that began by late 1973 brought that period to a halt. By mid-1977, current comprehensive data are not fully available, the adjustment process is still continuing, and more years will have to pass before we gain a proper historical perspective. Yet changes in pace since 1973 merit brief discussion of the data for Taiwan that are now available for 1974–76, in comparison with those for 1971–73 or 1973.

Table 1.26 summarizes the movements in population, aggregate product, and prices. Population, increasing at a rate below 2 percent per year, reveals continuation of the downward trend in the rate of growth (which was over 2.2 percent in the three-year span from 1968–70 to 1971–73, see Table 1.7). The changes in product and prices were most distinctive and deserve note.

Four comments should be made, though some are obvious. First, the years since 1971–73 or 1973 were marked by a perceptible drop in the growth rates of either total or per capita product and a conspicuous increase in the rate of rise of prices—both of them in comparison with the growth rates for product and rates of increase in price levels in the two decades preceding 1971–73 (see Table 1.8). For this longer period, growth rate per year for total product averaged over 9.6 percent per year and that for per capita product about 6.6 percent; whereas for the three-year span 1971–73 to 1974–76, the rates were between 3 and 4 percent for per capita product (column 7, lines 9 and 10). In contrast, the rate of rise in the price levels for the two-decade span averaged about 10 percent per year, whereas from 1971–73 to 1974–76 it was between 15 and 16 percent per year (column 7, lines 6 and 7). The two sets of changes were clearly associated, for it was the inflation initiated by the sudden rise in the price of oil in late 1973 that, in turn, contributed to disruption of internal flows, domestic inflation, and marked retardation in growth of product.

Second, the disparity in movements of export and import prices that resulted in a large negative adjustment for changes in terms of trade had to be

Table 1.26. Movement of Population, Product, and Prices, 1973–1976

| | Average, 1971–73 (1) | 1973 (2) | 1974 (3) | 1975 (4) | 1976 (5) | Average, 1974–76 (6) | Percentage change per year | |
							Columns 1–6 (7)	Columns 2–5 (8)
1. Population, midyear, mill.	15.22	15.51	15.79	16.06	16.34	16.10	1.9	1.8
2. GDP, current prices, N.T.$, bill.	319.2	388.7	524.7	560.0	655.9	—	—	—
3. GDP, 1971 prices, N.T.$, bill.	293.4	327.2	327.6	341.1	386.4	351.7	6.2	5.7
4. Adjustment for changes in terms of trade, N.T.$, bill	−3.8	−8.7	−13.8	−13.1	−16.2	−14.4	—	—
5. GDP, 1971 prices, adjusted, N.T.$, bill.	289.6	318.5	313.8	328.0	370.2	337.3	5.2	5.1
6. Implicit price index, GDP, lines 2 and 3	108.8	118.8	160.2	164.2	169.7	164.7	14.8	12.6
7. Implicit price index, GDP, lines 2 and 5	110.2	122.0	167.2	170.7	177.2	171.7	15.9	13.2
8. Consumer expenditures, 1971 prices, N.T.$, bill.	155.6	170.9	175.5	185.2	196.6	185.8	6.3	4.8
Per capita GDP and consumer expenditures, 1971 prices, indexes, average 1971–1973 = 100								
9. GDP, lines 3 and 1	100.0	109.4	107.6	110.2	122.7	113.5	4.3	3.9
10. GDP, lines 5 and 1	100.0	108.0	104.5	107.4	119.1	110.3	3.3	3.2
11. Consumer expenditures, lines 8 and 1	100.0	107.8	109.1	112.8	117.7	113.2	4.2	3.0

Line 1: By division of total income by per capita income, from DGBAS, *National Income of the Republic of China* (Taipei, December 1974), Tables 7 and 10, pp. 21 and 25.

Line 2: From ibid., Table I, pp. 106–7 (through 1974) and Table 1, pp. 98–99 (for 1975 and 1976).

Line 3: The GDP total at market prices follows the concept used in the preceding tables and excludes the adjustment for changes in terms of trade. The adjustment for price changes uses the implicit price index for the combined total of consumer expenditures and gross domestic capital formation to deflate the current price totals for government consumption. The totals in 1971 prices for the several components of expenditures on national income and the corresponding totals in current prices are given in ibid.; for the 1971 price totals, see Table XIII, pp. 134–37.

Line 4: Taken from ibid., Table XV, pp. 142–45.

Line 8: See the sources for line 3.

In deriving ratios, either of the current price totals to the 1971 price totals (to derive the implicit price indexes in lines 6 and 7), or of total GDP or consumer expenditures in constant prices to population to derive per capitas (in lines 9–11), annual ratios were calculated and the latter averaged. This departure from the procedure used in the earlier tables, in which ratios of averages of absolute totals were used, was because of the rapid changes in the underlying absolute totals within the short period covered here.

emphasized in Table 1.26 for recent years. The effect of the adjustment was to reduce the growth rate in total and per capita product by a full percentage point, by about a sixth for total product and by almost a quarter for per capita product. The adjustment remains proportionately large even in 1976, despite the marked recovery of the growth rate of product in that year.

Third, attention to single years reveals a decline in per capita product from 1973 to 1974 and no perceptible rise over the 1973 level until 1976 (lines 9-10, columns 3-5). Such a decline and failure to rise over a two-year period are not found in per capita product in constant prices over the record back to 1951. The relevant Tables 11 and 12 in *National Income, 1976* (pp. 26-27), on per capita income in 1971 prices, with and without adjustment for changing terms of trade, show not a single year in which per capita income did not rise by over 1 percent and no pair of years in which the combined rise was not over 4 percent. Thus the halt in 1974 and in part of 1975 was a sudden and unusual shock.

Still, observing the recent period as a whole, either from 1971-73 to 1974-76, or from 1973 to 1976, we find that, largely due to the marked recovery in 1976, the record is one of significant growth in total and per capita product. The recent growth appears limited only in comparison with the unusually high, and probably not sustainable in the longer run, growth rates of the span from 1951-53 to 1971-73, particularly over the decade preceding 1971-73. In terms of the long historical record of modern growth, rises in per capita product from 3 to 4 percent per year are impressive. And, one should note, consumer expenditures per capita, in constant prices, have continued to grow even after 1973 between 3 and 4 percent per year (see line 11). Significantly, the growth rate from 1971-73 to 1974-76 (line 11, column 7) of 4.2 percent per year is not much below that for consumer expenditures per capita from 1951-53 to 1971-73, which was 4.7 percent per year (see Tables 1.7 and 1.15). The economy apparently was capable of maintaining growth even in the disturbed conditions after late 1973.

Table 1.27 presents a condensed summary of changes since 1971-73 or 1973 in the structure of gross domestic product and of total uses. Two major conclusions can be tentatively suggested.

First, for the totals in 1971 prices, the recent changes appear to have continued the preceding long-term trends, even though the brief period was characterized by the slowdown and even temporary decline indicated in Table 1.26. Thus, the changes in the shares of the three major production sectors shown in lines 4-6 can be compared with the movements of the shares in Table 1.10 over the two-decade span from 1951-53 to 1971-73 (relating to shares in GDP in current prices and, by assumption, to those in constant prices). The long-term trends, as expected, were a continuous decline in the share of the A sector from over 33 percent in 1951-53 to about 13 percent in

Table 1.27. Changes in Structure of GDP and of Total Uses, 1973–1976

A. Shares of GDP originating in three major sectors, 1971 prices

	Average, 1971–73 (1)	1973 (2)	1974 (3)	1975 (4)	1976 (5)	Average, 1974–76 (6)
	Indexes, 1971–73 = 100					
1. GDP, 1971 prices	100.0	110.8	111.7	116.2	131.7	119.9
2. Index of agricultural, fishery, and forestry production	100.0	104.3	104.8	102.7	108.1	105.2
3. Index of industrial production I (−)*	100.0	118.5	116.8	123.6	154.4	131.6
	Approximation to percentage shares in GDP, 1971 prices					
4. A sector	13.1	12.3	12.3	11.6	10.8	11.6
5. I (−)* sector	45.3	48.5	47.4	48.2	53.1	49.5
6. S (+)* sector	41.6	39.2	40.3	40.2	36.1	38.9

B. Structure of total uses, 1971 prices

7. Total uses, per year, N.T.$, bill.	396.9	451.6	473.4	479.2	564.4	505.7
Percentage shares						
8. Government consumption	12.0	10.8	10.0	11.8	11.2	11.0
9. Private consumption	39.2	37.8	37.1	38.7	34.8	36.9
10. GDCF	18.3	18.1	23.6	19.9	18.2	20.6
11. Domestic uses (lines 12–14)	69.5	66.7	70.7	70.4	64.2	68.4
12. Exports	30.5	33.3	29.3	29.6	35.8	31.6
13. GDP	73.9	72.5	69.2	71.2	68.5	69.6
14. Imports	26.1	27.5	30.8	28.8	31.5	30.4
Exports minus imports as percentage of						
15. Total uses	4.4	5.8	−1.5	0.8	4.3	1.2
16. GDP	6.0	8.0	−2.2	1.1	6.3	1.7

C. Structure of total uses, current prices

17. Average per year, N.T.$, bill., total uses	441.1	557.7	805.4	806.9	981.9	864.7
Percentage shares						
18. Domestic uses	68.7	65.8	70.4	71.6	65.4	69.1
19. Exports	31.3	34.2	29.6	28.4	34.6	30.9
20. GDP	72.4	69.7	65.1	69.4	66.8	67.4
21. Imports	27.6	30.3	34.9	30.6	33.2	32.9
Exports minus imports as percentage of						
22. Total uses	3.7	3.9	−5.3	−2.2	1.4	−2.0
23. GDP	5.1	5.6	−8.1	−3.2	2.1	−3.0

*I (−) sector is the same as I, but excludes the transport and communication subdivision. S (+) sector is the same as S, but includes the transport and communication subdivision.

Line 1: From line 3 in Table 1.26, converted into an index, 1971–73 = 100.

Line 2: The index for 1971–75 is taken from DGBAS, *Statistical Yearbook, 1976,* Agriculture, Supp. Table 1, pp. 88–89. It is then extrapolated from 1975 to 1976 by movement of GDP in 1971 prices originating in the sector, shown in DGBAS, *National Income, 1976,* p. 101.

Line 3: For 1971–75 the underlying index is from DGBAS, *Statistical Yearbook, 1976,* Industry and Commerce, Supp. Table 1, pp. 120–21. For 1976 the index is from DGBAS, *Statistical Bulletin* 3, no. 1 (February 1977), 5. This index, like that in line 2, was to the base of 1971 as 100. The 1971–73 average was calculated and the annual indexes, 1973–76, converted to the base of that average.

Lines 4–6: The percentages in column 1 are from Panel A, column 7, of Table 1.10. Entries in columns 2–5, are the indexes in lines 2–3 multiplied by the shares in lines 4 and 5, column 1; the results in lines 4 and 5 are related to total GDP (indexes in line 1). This yielded the approximate shares of the A and I (−) sectors in total GDP in 1971 prices. The share of the S (+) sector was obtained by subtraction. The averages in column 6 were obtained by averaging the entries in columns 3–5.

Panel B: Column 1 is taken directly from Table 1.15. Columns 2–6, from DGBAS, *National Income, December 1976,* Table XIII, pp. 136–37 (through 1974) and Table 1, pp. 98–99, for 1975 and 1976.

Panel C: Calculated from the source given for Panel B, Table I, pp. 106–7, and Table 1, pp. 98–99. The averages in column 6, for both panels, were calculated directly from the percentages in the corresponding lines, columns 3–5.

1971-73; a more than compensating rise in the share of the I (−) sector from 22 to over 45 percent; and a relatively minor decline in the share of the S (+) sector from about 45 to somewhat less than 42 percent. Lines 4-6 show a decline in the share of the A sector by 1.5 percentage points, either from 1971-73 to 1974-76 or from 1973 to 1976; a rise in the share of the I (−) sector by over 4 percentage points over the same interval; and a decline in the share of the S (+) sector by between 2.5 and 3 percentage points. Likewise, the changes in the structure of total uses, in 1971 prices (Panel B), can be compared with movements in that structure over the two-decade span shown in Table 1.15. The major trends observed there were a marked decline in the share of private consumer expenditures, a marked rise in the share of GDCF, and marked upward trends in the shares of both exports and imports, with the balance of the former over the latter shifting toward the end of the period to the positive side. The shares in Panel B appear to repeat, or, in a way, continue these long-term trends, with the important exception of the share of the export-import balance.

The second major conclusion, partly suggested in discussion of Table 1.26, relates to the rise in the rate of increase of price levels, the implicitly wider magnitude of disparities of price trends among various groups of commodities and services (of particular bearing on prices of exports and imports), and the possibility that the structure of product or uses in current prices might, over this recent period, differ more significantly, or change in a somewhat different fashion, from that of product or uses in constant prices. Panel C illustrates this possibility when compared with Panel B. Whereas domestic uses accounted for a declining share of total uses in Panel B in constant prices (see line 11), the share in current prices shows a slight rise from 1971-73 to 1974-76 (line 18); correspondingly, the share of exports in total uses rises, when observed in the total in 1971 prices (line 12), but declines somewhat in the total in current prices (line 19). And, of course, there are more marked changes in the balance of exports and imports, as we shift from the calculation of both outflows and inflows in constant prices (lines 15-16) to that in current prices (lines 22-23).

The combination of these two sets of findings must be explored further before its implications can be fully established. On the one hand, the continuation of past trends, which changed the production and use structure of the economy drastically while total and per capita product were growing at relatively high rates, through a period in which growth slowed down perceptively is somewhat of a puzzle—for one would have expected the slowdown in growth to retard the pace of change in production and use structure. On the other hand, the effects of high and disparate rates of price rise over the few years on the structure in terms of current prices must be examined in much greater detail than is feasible here and perhaps over a longer period than is now available for study.

In conclusion, the disturbed years since 1973 were characterized, particularly including the strong recovery in 1976, by continuation of aggregate growth at rates more moderate than in the preceding two-decade span, but still significant; consumer expenditures per capita continued to grow at impressive rates; the long-term trends in the production and use structure continued; and, as noted in the discussion of interoccupational income disparities in 1974 and 1975, there were no marked changes in these disparities in the two recession years. Subject to qualifications imposed by the limitations on data supply, and even more those that the future may bring, the country's economy showed enough resilience since 1973 in its capacity not only to retain the growth and structural gains of the two decades back to the early 1950s, but to add to them.

Concluding Comments

Following two brief sections dealing with the colonial experience from 1895 to 1940 and the transition period from 1945 to the early 1950s, we concentrated in this chapter on the growth of, and structural changes in, Taiwan's economy from the early 1950s to the early 1970s. The detailed quantitative account is supplemented by a brief postscript, dealing with changes since 1973.

The major findings, by now familiar, can be briefly stated.

First, the growth rates from 1951–53 to 1971–73 in Taiwan's total product (GDP), at close to 10 percent per year, and of per capita product, at close to 7 percent per year, were among the highest observed since World War II. This period, in turn, was characterized by growth rates in most countries significantly above those found in the longer-run past among the developed as well as the less developed regions. The temporary halt in 1974 and 1975, followed by a sharp recovery in 1976, tempered the record only slightly.

Second, with the high rate of growth in product per capita (and per worker), shifts in the production structure—in the shares of major production sectors in output and in productive resources used—were necessarily rapid. Thus, over the two-decade span, the share of the A sector (agriculture and related industries) in GDP declined from over 33 to 13 percent; that of the I sector (all industry, including transport and communication) rose from 26 to 51 percent. Likewise, the share of the total labor force engaged in the A sector declined from 49 to 31 percent, and that engaged in the I sector rose from 15 to 35 percent. These shifts meant extensive movement of labor, capital, and enterprise from the more slowly growing sectors, the shares of which declined, to the more rapidly growing sectors, the shares of which rose.

Third, there were rapid shifts also in the structure of product by use. The share of private consumption in GDP declined from 76 percent in 1951–53 to 53 percent in 1971–73; the share of gross domestic capital formation rose from 14 to 25 percent; and, although the share of government consumption varied, with no clear trend, between 16 and 20 percent, its nondefense component must have accounted for a rising share of GDP. Furthermore, the share of exports rose over the two decades from 11 to 41 percent; that of imports from around 18 to 35 percent; and the balance of exports over imports, substantially negative at 7 percent of GDP in the first decade, was greatly reduced and turned into a surplus at the end of the second decade. In general, components like capital formation and the foreign trade flows, which can be viewed in the long run as tools for, or means of, attaining the end goal of economic activity—providing for satisfaction of consumer needs of the population—grew at higher rates than private consumption, the truly final product. This association between the greater relative supply of tools and higher per capita product and consumption was again to be expected.

Fourth, despite the rapid shifts in the production and use structure, there is no evidence of widening inequality in the sharing of gains from growth among various groups of households in the population. Such a widening was a likely possibility, with rapid changes in relative position of various production sectors (which are also complexes of workers and entrepreneurs and of population groups dependent upon the economic performance of the sector). Because of serious deficiencies in the data on this aspect of the country's growth— deficiencies widely prevalent among other countries, even developed ones— the conclusion just suggested is subject to particularly limiting qualifications. If confirmed in further and more intensive analysis, it may be credited, at least in part, to the widening diversification of industrial and type-of-income sources in the total income of the relatively large, average Taiwan household.

Fifth, an important corollary of, as well as major factor in, the high growth rate sustained over the long span and the marked structural shifts that were accomplished, possibly without widening income inequality, was the forward movement in Taiwan's demographic transition to modern population patterns. The death rates, already low in the early 1950s, declined further. More important, the initially high birth rate of 42 per thousand declined substantially in the 1950s and dropped to about 25 per thousand by the end of the period studied. This reduction in fertility was widespread among all the economic and social groups in the population and has a significant bearing upon problems of inequality. Such widespread trends, reflecting increasing confidence of the population in the advantages of a smaller but better brought-up and educated next generation, suggest that the effects of, and gains from, a technologically advancing economy have also been widespread.

Finally, significant variations over time occurred in the growth rates and in the rates of structural change. Thus, per capita GDP grew in the first decade at 4.7 percent per year, but in the second at over 8.5 percent per year—a marked acceleration. By contrast, the rise in the overall price level was at about 12 percent per year in the first decade, but down to less than 9 percent per year in the second decade—an expected negative association between time differentials in growth rates in output and in prices (which was particularly conspicuous in the recession after 1973). Acceleration in the growth of per capita product in the second decade was accompanied by a widely observed rise in the rate of structural shifts, in both the production structure and structure by use. Such acceleration of growth rates of product per capita between the first and second decades and of the associated shifts in structure are an important facet of the findings, in indicating changes of pace, possibly associated, at least in part, with changes in the country's economic and social policies.

This capsule summary omits a variety of details that may be of interest. Nor is it possible to note here the several analytical comments or hypotheses advanced at various points in the detailed presentation of the quantitative evidence in the chapter. It may be useful, however, to conclude with broad reflections on (1) the general context within which high and sustained rates of growth of the type that occurred in Taiwan over the last two to two and a half decades may be expected; and (2) the connection between such high growth rates and rapid shifts in the structure of product, resources, and population.

(1) If we observe rates of growth of total, particularly of per capita product, that are within a high range and are sustained over sufficiently long periods not to be viewed as a transitory aberration, the presumption is that the country had an unusually high growth opportunity. This follows by definition, since a high growth attained over the given period means, ipso facto, that an exceptionally high growth opportunity was exploited. Of course, such high growth opportunities may exist, as they do for all less developed countries; but they are not often converted into attained high growth.

The high growth opportunity may emerge because of some unforeseen discovery of hitherto unknown resources or some unexpected (but rarely found) transformation of the production drives of the population. But usually, particularly in less developed, lagging countries, this opportunity exists in the form of a large backlog of productively useful knowledge that has not been exploited and that, if exploited, could raise markedly and consistently the productivity of the country's resources, particularly human resources. An important corollary is that sustainable growth at high rates is contingent upon the existence and accessibility to the country in question of a stock of hitherto unused, or little used, relevant and tested knowledge. This knowledge has been developed, tested, and applied in the currently developed countries (which is why they are developed); and the coexistence of less developed, lagging countries with the developed countries provides the permissive condition of a large backlog and hence of a high growth opportunity.

But this is only a permissive condition, in the sense that in the absence of such a backlog of unexploited useful knowledge, high growth rates in the less developed countries would be technologically improbable, until they have slowly reached an effective, new-knowledge-producing phase of economic development. The useful knowledge must be accessible—through trade, capital flows, direct investments, and the like—transmission processes usually available within the framework of normal international relations among market economies. Even more important, given the accessibility of such new knowledge, the aspects of the economic and social structure of the less developed countries, which have evolved in adjustment to the earlier and less effective technology, must be modified so that historically inherited productive resources, convertible to more advanced and productive uses, can be applied to exploit the hitherto unused knowledge. For example, there would be little sense in trying to exploit the more modern agricultural technology in conditions of land tenure that fail to provide the tenants with economic incentives and resources to adopt the new technology.

This argument assumes two implications: that the less developed country in question possesses historically inherited resources, whether labor, land, reproducible capital, or entrepreneurship, that are potentially applicable to exploitation of new knowledge; and that the economic and social system within which they have been operating poses obstacles to such more productive use, obstacles that must be removed, however useful the institutions that contain them may have been in the past.

Thus the context within which high growth rates become feasible includes a backlog of applicable useful knowledge, usually greater (proportionally) for the countries that lag than for the developed countries; a lagging country, with historically inherited productive resources, convertible to new and much more productive uses; and elements in the inherited economic and social institutions that must be modified to allow the shift in uses of the resources to more advanced opportunities at an adequately high rate. The schema suggested is, obviously, quite general; and the more specific contents that would have to be fed into it would vary from one less developed country to another and from one historical period to the next. In the case of Taiwan, we noted some of the key productive resources historically conditioned from the colonial experience, from the experience of the incoming mainlanders, and from the common heritage further back; and mentioned the variety of institutional changes that were made within the first decade of the post-transition period. But, clearly, the combination of adequate, historically inherited resources, with the capacity to modify the institutional framework without endangering the social consensus and without destroying the conditions under which labor and enterprise can operate freely to exploit the new and changing opportunities, is not too common among the less developed countries, as it was not common among the currently developed countries in their early and yet protracted economic transition to modern high levels of economic performance.

(2)The bearing of the last comment becomes particularly relevant if we note that growth at high rates through the application of hitherto unexploited knowledge is a disruptive process because of the unequal impact on various sectors, that is, on various groups within the population. The connection between a high rate of growth in product per capita or per worker and the high rate of shift in production structure, in structure of use, and in other structural aspects of the economy, a connection repeatedly noted in the detailed quantitative account, is a necessary connection. Given the differing income elasticities of domestic demand for consumer goods, the changing relations between tools and final consumption at rising levels of economic productivity, and the changes in comparative advantages in foreign flows of a country growing more rapidly than its trading partners, it is impossible to attain high rates of growth of per capita or per worker product without commensurate substantial shifts in the shares of the various sectors. And if there are major obstacles to such shifts, to the movements of labor and other resources from one sector to another, from one type of use to another, the resulting bottlenecks would reduce the growth rate of overall and per capita product below the distinctively high levels assumed.

But if structural shifts are necessary corollaries of the high growth rate of per capita or per worker product, they are also disruptive, in that groups in the population attached to the more slowly growing sectors lose out relatively to those attached to the more rapidly growing sectors; in that the new sectors may, for technological reasons, impose work requirements that demand adjustment of the labor force to new conditions of work and life; and in that some new industries make individual firm entrepreneurship impossible and tilt the balance of the labor force away from small personal firms and toward employment by large, impersonal corporations. In short, the structural shifts impose a variety of new differentials and conditions to which the working and dependent population is pressed to adapt itself. And the difficulties and costs of the movements and adjustments required may, at times, be sufficiently great to create difficulties (such as a long-lasting surplus of labor in the lagging sectors, not necessarily compensated by the greater economic gains of the limited numbers who find employment in the new industries). If the costs of, and resistance to, the structural shifts implicit in, and required for, a high rate of growth of per capita or per worker product are to be minimized, policy action and institutional changes are required, as they were also involved in the context under which a shift toward high growth rates through the exploitation of hitherto unused knowledge could be assumed.

Thus a high rate of economic growth is a continuously disruptive process—disruptive of the older institutional patterns, of the older relations among economic groups, of the older conditions of work, and hence of life. The particular focus of the disruption always shifts as economic growth proceeds with the flow and absorption of new technological opportunities hitherto unexploited and as the level at which structural shifts occur changes.

How this disruption is channeled without affecting adversely the social consensus, without endangering the viability of the country as a coherent unit, and without damping the free economic and social drives that are needed to power growth is a broad question that cannot be answered here. Clearly, the complex of policies and policy actions—by the government, by other decision-making institutions, and by voluntary social and economic groups—is involved.

The quantitative account in this chapter deals amost wholly with the *results* of economic growth—total and for various significant components of the production and use structure; it reflects only obliquely the underlying causal factors. The speculative comments at some points in the detailed presentation, and even the broader reflections here, bear upon the general context within which rapid economic growth is feasible. But at best these comments deal only with the necessary, not the sufficient conditions. The immediately important part of what is missing would be the specific sequence of policy measures and alternatives, governmental and nongovernmental, that, when scrutinized, suggest more fully the conditions under which growth was accelerated or retarded. Many, although not all, of these policies are treated in the chapters that follow.

2 | Agricultural Development

ERIK THORBECKE

This chapter is subdivided into four major parts. The first part describes the aggregate performance of agriculture from 1895 to 1975, with a brief historical perspective of the colonial period and a broad outline of the structural transformation of agriculture since World War II, particularly the rapid shift in the center of gravity of the economy away from agriculture.

The second part is a detailed review and quantitative analysis of the changes within agriculture during the postwar period with respect to output, inputs, and regional and commodity composition. This part of the chapter contains the bulk of the statistical information required to understand the major shifts that occurred within agriculture. Three distinctive phases of agricultural development are identified in Taiwan between 1946 and the present.

The third part is an analysis of these three phases: the recovery period, 1946 to 1953; the growth period, 1954 to 1967; and the slowdown or stagnation phase, 1968 to 1975. This part attempts to identify the factors and policy measures that had the greatest influence on agricultural development during each of these phases. The final section argues that Taiwan's agriculture is presently at a crossroad and that difficult decisions must be made regarding its future direction.

The last part of the chapter tries to evaluate Taiwan's agricultural development strategy and to situate it within the context of a typology of alternative strategies. Because it is a prototype example of a unimodal strategy that appears to have been successful in achieving multiple policy objectives and, in particular, growth and an improved income distribution, major lessons can

I am deeply indebted to four individuals who taught me more about Taiwan's agricultural development than I ever hoped or expected. They represent different generations of leadership in the Joint Council on Rural Reconstruction (JCRR) from T. H. Shen, the dean of Taiwan agriculture, to T. H. Lee, the present spokesman for the interests of the farmers in the cabinet, to You-Tsai Wang and Yu-Kang Mao, present secretary general and chief of the Rural Economics Division of the JCRR, respectively. I would also like to thank Jackson Karunasekera for his dedication as a research assistant.

be drawn from its agricultural development process of possible use to other developing countries. In this connection, a number of potentially transferable and nontransferable elements of the Taiwanese experience are suggested.

The Aggregate Performance of Agriculture within the Context of the Economy, 1895–1975

A Brief Historical Perspective of Agricultural Development in the Colonial Period, 1895–1945

A strong case has been made by serious students of Taiwan's agricultural history, Teng-hui Lee and Samuel P. S. Ho, that the recent performance of agriculture in the post–World War II period can be understood only in the context and as a continuation of changes that occurred in the era of Japanese colonization.

During the colonial period, Taiwan became an important part of the agricultural sector of the Japanese economy. The major task of the colonial government was to transform Taiwan's subsistence agriculture into a more productive sector so that substantial food surpluses could be produced and transferred to Japan to support the latter's industrialization effort. The proximity and large size of the Japanese market meant that there was practically no constraint on the demand side. The fact that output growth was not limited by domestic demand is an important element in understanding the agricultural development process in this period.

Table 2.1 reveals the overwhelming importance of agriculture in Taiwan's economy during the colonial era. Almost three-fourths of the total labor force was employed in agriculture at the beginning of this period and two-thirds at the end of the 1930s; the share of agriculture in total net domestic product (NDP) went from about 42 percent to 35 percent over the same time span. Aggregate economic growth during this period was substantial as judged by the growth rates of NDP and agricultural NDP, which amounted to, respectively, 4.5 and 3.5 percent between 1911 and 1940 (see lines 4 and 5 in Table 2.1).

Three phases of agricultural development can be distinguished between 1913 and 1946: agricultural development under Japanese colonial rule, 1913–23; agricultural transformation under Japanese colonial rule, 1923–37; and depression under the impact of World War II, 1937–46.[1] Table 2.2 shows the significant differences in agricultural output performance that occurred in these three phases. Throughout this whole period the value of rice, sweet potatoes, and sugarcane consistently amounted to about 85 percent of total

1. See T. H. Lee and Y. E. Chen, *Growth Rates of Taiwan Agriculture, 1911–1972,* JCRR Economic Digest Series, no. 21 (Taipei, January 1975).

Table 2.1. Agriculture's Share in Net Domestic Product (NDP), in Labor Force, and in Total Exports and Growth Rates of NDP and Agricultural NDP, 1911-1973

	1911–20 (1)	1921–30 (2)	1931–40 (3)	1947 (4)	1951–53 (5)	1964–67 (6)	1971–73 (7)
1. Share of agricultural NDP in total NDP	41.8	39.4	35.2	43.9	36.7	25.6	15.1
2. Share of agricultural labor force in total	72.9	70.2	66.3	—	50.0	42.0	30.0
3. Share of agricultural exports in total exports	—	—	—	—	90.9	45.8	17.1

	1911–20 to 1921–30 (8)	1921–30 to 1931–40 (9)	1937 to 1946–48 (10)	1946–48 to 1951–53 (11)	1951–53 to 1964–67 (12)	1964–67 to 1971–73 (13)
4. Growth rate of NDP	4.3	4.6	–3.1	13.2	7.7*	10.1*
5. Growth rate of NDP in agriculture	3.7	3.4	–2.2	9.1	5.7*	2.4*

	1913–23 (14)	1923–37 (15)	1937–46 (16)	1946–48 to 1951–53 (17)	1951–53 to 1964–67 (18)	1964–67 to 1970–72 (19)
6. Growth rate of gross value added in agriculture	1.9	3.8	–3.9	10.1	4.0	2.1

*Growth rates of gross domestic product (GDP) rather than NDP.

Sources: Columns 1 to 3 and 8 and 9 calculated from Kuznets' Table 1.4, which in turn is based on S. C. Hsieh and T. H. Lee, Agricultural Development and Its Contributions to Economic Growth in Taiwan, JCRR Economic Digest Series, no. 17 (Taipei, 1966), Appendix Tables 1–3, pp. 107–9. Line 1, columns 5–7 calculated from Directorate-General of Budget, Accounting, and Statistics (DGBAS), Statistical Yearbook of the Republic of China, 1975 (Taipei, 1976), National Accounts, Supp. Tables 5–7, p. 207. Columns 10 and 11 and line 1, column 4, calculated from Kuznets' Table 1.7.

Line 5, columns 12 and 13 computed from Kuznets' Table 1.12. Growth rates refer to agricultural GDP rather than NDP.

Line 4, columns 12 and 13 computed from DGBAS, Statistical Yearbook, 1975, Supp. Table 2, pp. 194–95. Growth rates refer to GDP.

Line 2, columns 5–7 are the corrected estimates from Kuznets' Table 1.13 after allowance is made for servicemen.

Line 6, T. H. Lee and Yueh-eh Chen, Growth Rates of Taiwan Agriculture, 1911–1972, JCRR Economic Digest Series, no. 21 (Taipei, January 1975), p. 3.

Table 2.2. Growth Rates of Total Production, Total Output, and Gross Value Added in Agriculture (percent)*

Phase of development	Period	Total production	Total output	Gross value added
Initial phase of agricultural development under Japanese colonial rule	1913-23	2.7	2.8	1.9
Agricultural transformation under Japanese colonial rule	1923-37	4.0	4.1	3.8
Agricultural development under the impact of World War II	1937-46	-4.9	-4.9	-3.9
Recovery and rehabilitation after World War II	1946-51	10.3	10.2	9.2
Further development after rehabilitation	1951-60	4.6	4.7	4.1
Sustained development at the economic turning point	1960-70	4.1	4.2	3.3
Average of prewar period	1913-37	3.5	3.6	3.0
Average of postwar period	1946-70	5.5	5.6	4.8
	1951-70	4.3	4.4	3.7
Average of whole period	1913-70	3.0	3.0	2.6

*Growth rates are annual compound rates of increase between five-year averages of the data centered at the years shown.
Source: Lee and Chen, p. 3.

agricultural production expressed at constant prices. These crops occupied over 80 percent of the total crop area. The major shift in the commodity composition of agricultural output between 1910 and 1940 was the increase in the share of sugarcane in total crop production from about 11 percent to 22 percent.[2]

An attempt is made in the following part of this section to identify the major characteristics of these phases and the major factors that contributed to output growth.[3] Extension of the area of cultivated land appears to have been the main input contributing to the increase in agricultural output during the first phase above, in contrast with rice and sugarcane yields, which did not rise significantly. Labor inputs measured in terms of total working days increased moderately at an annual rate of 1.4 percent, caused exclusively by a rise in the number of average working days per worker per year (the number of agricultural workers actually fell slightly in this period). Production techniques in agriculture were traditional, relying on highly labor-intensive methods and farm-produced fertilizers.

The dramatic jump in the growth rate of agricultural output in the second phase indicates a turning point in the development of colonial agriculture. The

2. See Samuel P. S. Ho, "Economic Development of Taiwan, 1860-1970" (manuscript) chap. 4, pp. 74-75.
3. Three very good accounts of agricultural development during the colonial period, are: Lee and Chen; Ho, *Economic Development*; and Samuel P. S. Ho, "Agricultural Transformation under Colonialism: The Case of Taiwan," *Journal of Economic History* 28 (September 1968). My brief review relies extensively on these sources.

doubling of the growth rate of gross value added from 1.9 to 3.8 percent from the first phase to the second was the combined result of a rise in crop yields and an increase in multiple cropping (a more intensive use of the limited land base). The second phase was clearly characterized by a shift to a new technology based on modern, nontraditional inputs, which provided an important source of growth. Hence, on the basis of a Cobb-Douglas production function, only 80 percent of the increase in output over the second phase was calculated as caused by increases in inputs—the remaining 20 percent being the result of technological change.[4]

The new technology consisted of three crucial components: a new rice variety, the widespread use of chemical fertilizer, and irrigation. The major breakthrough in rice production came in the middle 1920s with the successful introduction of the higher-yielding Japonica varieties, commonly called Ponlai rice. Also, during this period, new high-yielding varieties of sugarcane were introduced and widely adopted. Rice yield per hectare, which had remained practically stagnant from 1913 to 1923, increased by about 50 percent in the second phase. The rate of adoption was reasonably fast—the proportion of total cultivated rice area using Ponlai rice increased from less than 5 percent in 1924 to about 21 percent in 1930 and 51 percent in 1940.

The consumption of fertilizer approximately tripled in the second phase, mainly because of the increased use of commercial fertilizer and purchased vegetable (mainly soybean) oil cakes. The third element in this early technological revolution was the significant increase in the amount of land under irrigation from 311,000 hectares in 1921 to 532,000 hectares in 1938 (the irrigated portion of the cultivated land area went up from 41 to 62 percent during the same period). It is remarkable, in retrospect, that these three inputs were effectively used in a complementary fashion long before the Green Revolution.

Taiwan's success in formulating and implementing a new agricultural technology depended on the existence of a set of appropriate rural institutions, particularly in the domains of agricultural research, farmers' associations, and rural credit and extension. Taiwan's Agricultural Research Institute was founded in 1903, and a number of experimental stations were established in strategic farming districts in subsequent years. With the help of skilled technicians and agronomists—many of whom came from Japan—and a network of experimental stations, improved seeds and modern intermediate inputs were developed as part of a labor-intensive package after controlled experimentation. This package became available to the farmers in the middle 1920s and

4. Ho, *Economic Development*, chapt. 4, p. 89. In contrast, in the previous phase (between 1910 and 1920) the totality of the growth in output is explained by increases in inputs, indicating that technological change was insignificant in this early period.

explains the sharp increase in labor productivity, growth, and employment up to the beginning of World War II.[5]

An important step toward the dissemination of agricultural technology was the establishment of the farmers' associations on an islandwide basis around the turn of the century. Within a few years, farmers' associations existed in every prefecture under the control of the colonial government. These associations eventually performed such important functions as the improvement of seeds and farming techniques, extension of knowledge to farmers, training of agricultural technicians, and purchase of fertilizers and farm equipment.

At about the same time, agricultural cooperatives, which provided credit and helped with the distribution of fertilizer, were set up as complementary and supporting institutions to the farmers' associations. The availability of credit was an essential factor in transforming Taiwan's agriculture because the new technology depended on a rising share of purchased (intermediate) inputs.

The importance the colonial government attached to rural organizations can be judged by the fact that in the early 1930s farmers' associations and agricultural cooperatives employed close to forty-thousand persons, of which thirteen-thousand were extension workers, according to Ho,[6] (or about one extension worker per thirty-two farm households, a level almost unequaled by international standards).

Two final characteristics of Taiwan's agriculture in the pre–World War II period should be highlighted. First, land was unequally distributed, and the majority of the farmers were tenants rather than owner-cultivators. According to the 1920 land registration survey, 42.7 percent of the owners held 5.7 percent of the land, and 11.5 percent of the owners possessed 62.1 percent of the land. Throughout that period, the share of tenants and part owners, part tenants, hovered around two-thirds of the agricultural population, only one-third were owner-cultivators.[7] Second, during most of the colonial period, Taiwan's agriculture performed a very important function of transferring resources to the rest of the economy. T. H. Lee has calculated that throughout this period, approximately one-fifth of total agricultural production was "squeezed out" as a net capital outflow through a variety of mechanisms such as agricultural taxes, the savings of individual and corporate landlords, and

5. S. P. S. Ho feels that, in retrospect, "the introduction of Ponlai rice may have been the single, most important agricultural innovation made during the Colonial period" (ibid., chap. 4, p. 95).

6. Ho, "Agricultural Transformation." The Rural Economics Division of the JCRR questions these figures since they imply that there were substantially more extension workers in the 1930s than in the 1960s.

7. See Ho, *Economic Development,* chap. 4, pp. 66–67.

the strong monopsonistic power of buyers of agricultural goods.[8] Lee's study reveals that a large part of the outflow out of agriculture consisted of exports. In fact, whereas in the period after World War II, agriculture generated a surplus for its own industrialization, in the prewar period the surplus favored the economic development of Japan.

During World War II (from 1937 to 1946), production decreased by 36 percent as a consequence of a major drop in yields per hectare and a slight reduction in both crop and cultivated land areas. Gross value added declined at a rate of almost 4 percent during this period (see Table 2.2). From a developmental standpoint, the second phase, from 1923 to 1937, was the crucial one because it entailed the transformation of an essentially traditional sector into one starting to use modern inputs.

In summary, by the end of the colonial period, a number of essential features were present that were conducive to a potential takeoff in the postwar era. These major elements were an appropriate labor-intensive technology relying on modern inputs, a physical infrastructure, particularly in terms of irrigation and drainage, which increased greatly the productivity of this technology, and, finally, a set of rural institutions that helped to disseminate knowledge, provide extension and credit services, and market both inputs and outputs.

Aggregate Agricultural and National Economic Performance in the Post–World War II Period

Immediately following World War II, Taiwan was still a predominantly agricultural economy with well over half of its labor force employed in agriculture and about 44 percent of NDP generated in that sector. The transformation of agriculture that had started in the colonial period had not altered significantly the agricultural shares in, respectively, NDP and the labor force, as can be judged from the first two lines of Table 2.1.

In contrast, the decline in these two shares after the end of the war was dramatic. Over the course of a quarter of a century (from 1947 to 1971–73) the contribution of agriculture to NDP dropped from 43.9 percent to 15.1 percent, and agriculture's share in the labor force fell from over half to 30 percent.[9] Taiwan moved from an agriculture-based economy to a semi-industrialized one in two decades.

8. See Teng-hui Lee, *Intersectoral Capital Flows in the Economic Development of Taiwan, 1895–1960* (Ithaca, N.Y., 1971). This key role of Taiwan's agriculture in providing capital resources for industrialization in the post–World War II period will be discussed later in the chapter.

9. Agriculture is defined here as including forestry and fishing in addition to crop and livestock production. For the post–World War II period, military personnel (servicemen) are included in the total labor force, which tends to reduce the share of agriculture in the labor force. Thus, if the labor force were defined exclusive of servicemen, the corresponding agricultural share would be 59 percent in 1951–53, 46 percent in 1964–67, and 32 percent in 1971–73.

Another indicator of the structural shift away from agriculture is the major drop in the share of agricultural exports in total exports from approximately 91 percent in 1951–53 to 17 percent in 1971–73. Even as late as the middle 1960s that share amounted to almost 46 percent. The significance of these data is that until the mid-1960s, agricultural exports played a major role in financing the required imports. In a sense, the agricultural sector was continuing until that time to perform its traditional role of transferring resources through exports, albeit in a more limited way than during the colonial period. In this connection, a comparison of total agricultural exports (including processed agricultural products) and total agricultural imports (including production inputs such as fertilizer) shows an increasing agricultural export surplus that rose from approximately U.S. $12 million in 1952 to $120 million in 1965, to be subsequently transformed into an import surplus in the neighborhood of $200 million in 1973–75.[10] Hence, from the late 1960s on, agriculture as a sector was a net drain on the economy from the standpoint of foreign resources.

The overall agricultural transformation is indicated by a comparison of the aggregate economic growth to that of agricultural output. Thus, if the post-World War II period is divided into three subperiods, 1946–48 to 1951–53, 1951–53 to 1964–67, and 1964–67 to 1971–73, the corresponding annual growth rates of NDP were, respectively, 13.2, 7.7, and 10.1 percent (see line 4, Table 2.1). The corresponding growth rates of agricultural NDP over the same three periods were, respectively, 9.1, 5.7 and 2.4 percent (line 5, Table 2.1).

These data suggest that in the recovery period, which lasted until the early 1950s, overall economic growth was largely fueled through agricultural growth. The former was clearly dependent on the restoration of a level of capacity utilization in agriculture at least equivalent to the one that had prevailed before the war. In the second phase, agriculture continued to play an important role in helping the economy achieve an impressive overall growth.

Finally, in the third subperiod, from the mid-1960s to the early 1970s, the growth rate of agricultural NDP dropped drastically to 2.4 percent annually, while that of aggregate NDP increased to a remarkable 10.1 percent—indicating that agriculture had reached an important turning point and was entering a slowdown, if not a stagnation phase. An alternative measure of the aggregate performance of agriculture is the growth rate of gross value added

10. These figures are based on T. H. Shen, ed., *Agriculture's Place in the Strategy of Development: The Taiwan Experience* (Taipei, July 1974), Tables 13 and 14, pp. 427–28, for the period 1962–72; and Maurice Scott, Chapter 5 of this volume, Table 5.13, for 1973–75. Scott shows an agricultural import surplus of $151 million in 1973–75, exclusive of imports of agricultural inputs. If the latter are included, the corresponding import surplus would be around $200 million.

Table 2.3. International Comparison of Growth of Agricultural Production in Selected Countries and Regions, 1952–1954 to 1966–1968 and 1967–1969 to 1972–1974 (annual percentage rates)

Period	Taiwan	Japan	South Korea	Philip-pines	Thailand	India	Pakistan	Far* East	Near† East	Africa	Latin America	Developed market economies
1. 1952–54 to 1966–68	4.4	3.5	4.5	3.3	5.5	2.1	2.9	2.8	3.2	3.0	3.0	.5
2. 1967–69 to 1972–74	2.6	–.3	2.7	4.0	3.3	2.1	4.1	2.6	3.1	2.2	2.2	.3

*Far East excludes mainland China and Japan and includes South Asia.
†Near East includes Israel.
Source: United Nations, Food and Agriculture Organization, *The State of Food and Agriculture* (Rome, 1968, 1970, and 1975).

(see line 6, Table 2.1), which reveals, even more strongly the sharp deceleration in the output performance of that sector.

The spectacular aggregate growth performance of Taiwan in the last three decades—as compared to other developing and developed countries—is well documented in other parts of this volume.[11] Table 2.3 provides an international comparison of agricultural output for two periods 1952-54 to 1966-68 and 1967-69 to 1972-74. These two periods were chosen to correspond to the previously identified second and third phases of Taiwan's postwar agricultural development process (the growth and slowdown phases, respectively.) Taiwan's agricultural performance was outstanding (with output increasing at 4.4 percent per annum) in the first subperiod, surpassed only by that of Thailand (5.5 percent) and South Korea (4.5 percent), but significantly better than that of Japan and the other developing countries in the sample.

In contrast, Taiwan's growth rate of agricultural output in the second phase (2.6 percent between 1967-69 and 1972-74) appears about average for the developing world but distinctly lower than that of Pakistan (4.1 percent) the Philippines (4.0 percent), Thailand (3.3 percent), and the Near East (3.1 percent).

Changes within Agriculture during the Development Process, 1946–1975

In this section I analyze first the output performance within the agricultural sector, as well as changes in the commodity composition of agricultural output. Three major phases of agricultural development are identified in the period following World War II. Second, I focus on the major shifts in the use of inputs during this same time span in an attempt to provide a better understanding of the production process in terms of changes in resource use and technology. Finally, I undertake an interregional, intercommodity analysis of agricultural production. By adding the spatial (geographical) dimension, some better insights into the location of production and the regional distribution of resources and cropping patterns are obtained.

Agricultural Output Growth: Changes in the Composition of Output and Phases of Agricultural Development

Table 2.4 summarizes the output performance of the agricultural sector, overall and in terms of its major components, between 1946 and 1975 in terms of volume indices of agricultural production.[12] It is based on three different

11. See, in particular, for international comparisons of output growth, Chapter 1 by Simon Kuznets in this volume, Table 1.10.

12. Throughout this analysis, agricultural production is defined as including crop and livestock but excluding forestry and fishing.

Table 2.4. Volume Indices of Agricultural Production, 1946–1975 (base 1971 = 100)

Year	Index of agric. production (1)	Index of agric. crop output (2)	Index of agric. production (3)	Index of agric. crop production (4)	Index of prod. of common crops of agriculture (5)	Index of rice production (6)	Index of prod. of other common crops (7)	Index of prod. of special crops (8)	Index of fruit production (9)	Index of vegetable production (10)	Index of mushroom production (11)	Index of livestock production (12)
1946	22.8	—	23.2	26.8	37.5	38.6	33.9	17.2	7.3	14.4	—	10.3
1947	27.7	—	28.7	33.5	44.0	43.2	46.6	24.2	15.5	21.4	—	12.1
1948	31.9	—	33.0	38.2	48.1	46.2	54.2	41.0	14.8	20.4	—	14.7
1949	37.1	—	38.0	44.6	53.5	52.5	56.5	62.7	13.3	22.1	—	15.0
1950	41.6	—	42.4	48.7	60.7	61.4	58.4	60.0	14.2	24.4	—	20.0
1951	42.7	—	43.7	48.7	61.9	64.2	54.7	54.9	13.8	25.5	—	26.2
1952	46.0	51.0	46.8	52.3	65.6	67.9	58.5	64.1	13.8	25.8	—	27.3
1953	51.2	55.5	51.6	56.7	68.8	70.9	61.9	81.3	13.4	25.8	—	33.8
1954	51.6	55.9	52.1	57.1	72.3	73.3	69.2	70.8	13.0	26.5	—	34.4
1955	51.0	54.4	51.7	56.3	69.6	69.8	69.1	73.1	15.0	27.3	—	35.7
1956	55.6	59.2	56.1	61.1	76.4	77.4	73.3	78.9	14.1	28.9	—	38.1
1957	59.1	62.4	59.7	64.6	78.9	79.5	77.1	88.3	17.3	30.5	—	42.6
1958	63.0	65.8	63.7	68.2	82.8	81.9	85.7	93.4	20.6	32.0	—	47.8
1959	63.0	65.7	63.5	68.0	81.4	80.2	85.2	97.2	20.9	32.3	—	47.4

Year	col 1	col 2	col 3	col 4	col 5	col 6	col 7	col 8	col 9	col 10	col 11	col 12
1960	63.4	66.8	64.0	69.1	83.9	82.6	88.1	90.5	23.7	34.9	—	45.8
1961	68.3	71.3	69.0	74.2	89.1	87.1	95.4	101.5	25.8	35.5	4.8	50.7
1962	69.2	71.7	70.7	75.2	91.6	91.3	92.4	91.3	28.9	37.2	22.4	55.0
1963	69.4	72.1	70.3	74.2	85.6	91.2	68.2	96.0	29.0	40.7	67.3	56.4
1964	76.6	81.6	78.3	83.5	97.3	97.1	98.1	101.8	43.1	47.6	39.6	59.9
1965	83.0	88.0	83.9	90.2	100.4	101.5	97.0	119.3	57.4	48.9	56.5	61.6
1966	85.8	90.6	86.4	91.6	102.8	102.9	102.8	110.0	65.4	50.5	67.0	68.3
1967	89.6	94.1	91.5	95.4	106.1	104.3	111.6	105.2	80.0	53.7	87.4	78.0
1968	94.6	98.2	95.8	99.3	107.7	108.8	104.1	109.8	88.2	63.2	91.3	83.5
1969	93.2	93.7	94.0	95.3	102.0	100.3	107.0	102.3	82.9	78.1	57.1	89.5
1970	98.3	98.9	99.5	99.9	105.4	106.4	102.1	100.3	86.9	93.8	68.0	98.3
1971	100.0	100.0	100.0	100.0	100.0	100.0	100.0	100.0	100.0	100.0	100.0	100.0
1972	103.5	100.8	102.6	101.1	102.3	105.5	92.3	95.1	98.8	95.1	149.0	107.9
1973	—	101.6	107.6	102.1	98.3	97.5	100.9	99.2	115.2	108.6	112.0	127.2
1974	—	107.1	109.8	107.6	103.0	106.0	93.4	106.6	129.2	110.6	107.0	117.5
1975	—	103.3	105.8	104.7	102.4	107.8	85.5	96.6	113.0	120.7	85.0	109.8

Source: Column 1: Lee and Chen (based on 1935–37 constant prices), Table 3, column 6, pp. 63–64.

Column 2: My computation (based on constant average prices for 1952–75).

Columns 3–12: DGBAS, *Statistical Yearbook, 1975,* Executive Yuan, The Republic of China (based on weights representing gross value added per unit of product in 1971). The indices in column 3 for 1972–75 were recomputed according to the most recent revisions in Department of Agriculture and Forestry, Provincial Government of Taiwan, *Taiwan Agricultural Yearbook, 1976* (Taipei, 1977).

output series using different weighting systems: (1) the output series compiled by T. H. Lee and Y. E. Chen, which was compiled for the period 1911–72 using as weights constant prices for 1935–37;[13] (2) a series computed by the Directorate-General of Budget, Accounting, and Statistics (DGBAS)—appearing in the *Statistical Yearbook* and the *Taiwan Agricultural Yearbook*—which uses as weights gross value added per unit of product in 1971 and is available from 1946 on; and (3) a series I computed for crop output (thus excluding livestock production) over the period 1952–75, which used average prices over this period as weights.

These different series provide remarkably similar trends, as shown by comparing, for instance, columns 1 and 3 in Table 2.4, which give volume indices of total agricultural production (crops and livestock) using two different weighting systems, (1) and (2) above, or, alternatively, columns 2 and 4, which yield volume indices of crop production, based on systems (2) and (3) above. Evidently, the use of substantially different weighting systems does not affect the yearly changes more than marginally and certainly does not affect the trends.

A careful examination of Table 2.4 indicates, first, that some discrete changes occurred in the growth rate of overall agricultural output during 1946 and 1975 which suggest that the overall output performance could best be analyzed in terms of a number of subperiods. Second, some marked differences are noticeable in the growth performance of different components (commodity groups) of agricultural output.

These two facts are clearly highlighted in Table 2.5, which gives the growth rate of output for different commodity groups in three subperiods based on the information in Table 2.4. Three distinctive phases of agricultural development are identified in Table 2.5: (1) a recovery period between 1947 and 1953 during which the growth rate of agricultural output amounted to a staggering 10.3 percent annually; (2) a phase of sustained growth between 1954 and 1967 during which output grew at 4.4 percent per year; and (3) a slowdown or stagnation phase after 1968 when output grew at only 2.3 percent annually. It will be seen subsequently that these phases correspond to, and are correlated with, important structural, institutional, and technological changes in the agricultural development process of Taiwan after World War II.

Table 2.5 also concisely brings to light the differential growth performance among groups of products. Thus, the annual growth rate of production of fruits, vegetables, and livestock over the period 1947–74—amounting, respectively, to 8.7, 6.9, and 8.7 percent—were considerably higher than the average rate of growth of agricultural output of 5.1 percent during the same

13. Lee and Chen.

Table 2.5. Growth Rates of Agricultural Output in Different Phases of Agricultural Development, 1946-1974 (annual percentage rates)

Phases*	Agri-cultural production (crop and live-stock)	Common crops		Special crops	Fruits	Vege-tables	Live-stock
		Total	Rice only				
I 1947-53 Recovery	10.3	8.1	8.8	17.4	1.2	5.7	17.0
II 1954-67 Growth	4.4	3.2	3.0	2.9	14.2	5.9	6.3
III 1968-74 Slowdown	2.3	-0.6	-0.1	-0.8	6.1	9.7	5.9
IV 1947-74 Average	5.1	3.2	3.3	4.9	8.7	6.9	8.7

*The annual growth rates prevailing in each phase have been computed on the basis of three-year averages centered on the first and last year of each period, that is, 1947 = average 1946-48, 1953 = average 1952-54, and so forth.
Source: The growth rates are computed on the basis of the index of agricultural production given in column 3 of Table 2.4.

period. In contrast, special crops[14] and, in an even more pronounced way, common crops[15] (in particular, rice) performed worse than the average (the corresponding growth rate of output of these three groups were, respectively, 4.9, 3.2, and 3.3 percent). Table 2.5 also shows that significant changes occurred in the growth of these various commodity groups during the three phases. These changes are discussed in detail in the section on phases of agricultural development.

The differential output performance of these various products can be highlighted another way through Table 2.6, which shows their changing percentage shares by value over time. Since this table expresses the relative importance of different products in terms of current value, rather than at constant prices, it reflects both changes in the quantities and the prices of the various commodity groups over time.

The most important observations to be drawn from the table are the major fall in the relative importance of common crops (mainly caused by the declining importance of rice and sweet potatoes)—the share of which fell from 69.5 percent in 1948 to 40.1 percent in 1975, and the increasing relative importance of vegetables and livestock—the respective shares of which rose from 4.8 to 10 percent and 9.9 to 30.1 percent over the same time span.

Table 2.6 also indicates the increase in the share of rice in the current value

14. By far the most important special crops were sugarcane, which represents over half of the total output of this commodity group, and tea and peanuts, which together may represent between a fifth and fourth of the value of this group.

15. Rice represents 80 to 90 percent of the total value of this commodity group; sweet potatoes are the only other significant crop by value.

Table 2.6. Relative Importance of Different Agricultural Products by Current Value (in percentages), in Selected Years, 1948–1975

Year	Common crops		Special crops	Fruits	Vege-tables*	Live-stock	Total
	Common crops	Rice only					
1948	69.5	42.5	11.2	4.6	4.8	9.9	100
1953	62.0	52.8	18.9	2.0	3.2	13.9	100
1958	54.6	41.4	17.0	3.4	5.1	19.9	100
1963	51.6	42.3	15.1	4.5	6.5	22.3	100
1968	44.7	34.7	10.5	8.9	8.3	27.6	100
1971	37.9	29.1	10.2	8.7	11.0	32.2	100
1974	42.1	35.3	11.3	6.3	10.0	30.3	100
1975	40.1	34.0	14.0	5.8	10.0	30.1	100

*Including mushrooms.
Source: Various issues of *Taiwan Agricultural Yearbook.*

of agricultural output in 1974–75 compared to 1971. This phenomenon reflects the sharp increase in the price of rice in recent years, rather than any volume change, and is discussed in detail subsequently.

The above-described changes in the composition of agricultural output reflect a continuing move away from dependence on a few common crops, in particular rice and sweet potatoes, that prevailed in the late 1940s, to a much more balanced and diversified agriculture.

Changes in the Use of Inputs and Technology in Agricultural Production, 1946–1975

In this section, the major changes in the use of inputs and in technology over time are analyzed. Information on the major inputs available each year to produce the agricultural output is consolidated into Table 2.7, which provides various quantitative indicators of agricultural inputs used annually between 1946 and 1975.

Inputs are broken down into five major categories: land, human labor, animal labor, intermediate inputs, and mechanical implements. With respect to land, the key indicators are the amounts of cultivated and crop areas, respectively, the multiple crop index, which is the ratio of the latter to the former, and the area of land under irrigation. An examination of the corresponding input columns in Table 2.7 reveals that the amount of cultivated area remained essentially constant over the period under consideration[16] and that the crop area increased significantly, as reflected in a marked rise in the multiple cropping index. The amount of land under irrigation remained more or less constant over the whole period, while the area of drained land grew

16. Cultivated land area increased by about 10 percent over the period 1946 to 1975 (see column 2, Table 2.7)—most of which occurred by 1952.

Table 2.7. Quantitative Indicators of Agricultural Inputs, 1946-1975

Year (1)	Cultivated area (ha. × 1,000) (2)	Crop area (ha. × 1,000) (3)	Multiple cropping index (× 100) (4)	Actual damaged area by disaster (ha. × 1,000) (5)	Net crop area (ha. × 1,000) (6)	Area of irrigated land (ha. × 1,000) (7)	Area of drained land (ha. × 1,000) (8)	Water pumps (9)	Total number of farm families (× 1,000) (10)	Agricultural population (1,000) (11)	Agricultural workers (1,000) (12)	Total mandays (million days) (13)
1946	832	975	117.2	—	—	—	—	—	527	3,522	1,285	143
1947	834	1,249	149.8	—	—	—	—	—	553	3,578	1,336	166
1948	863	1,383	160.3	—	—	—	—	—	597	3,780	1,373	199
1949	865	1,438	166.2	—	—	—	—	—	621	3,880	1,413	221
1950	871	1,435	164.8	—	—	493	15	—	638	3,998	1,414	225
1951	874	1,502	171.9	—	—	493	15	—	661	4,161	1,419	229
1952	876	1,521	173.6	—	—	471	3	—	680	4,257	1,434	242
1953	873	1,488	170.4	—	—	465	32	—	702	4,382	1,471	247
1954	874	1,501	171.7	112	1,389	466	7	—	717	4,489	1,493	246
1955	873	1,508	172.7	100	1,408	467	20	—	733	4,603	1,489	243
1956	876	1,544	176.3	143	1,401	483	7	—	746	4,699	1,479	252
1957	873	1,566	179.4	14	1,552	484	6	—	759	4,790	1,439	269
1958	884	1,588	179.6	40	1,548	489	6	—	770	4,881	1,454	276
1959	878	1,590	181.1	152	1,438	473	7	—	780	4,975	1,469	275
1960	869	1,600	184.1	74	1,526	549	22	—	786	5,373	1,464	270
1961	872	1,613	185.0	47	1,566	486	9	8,378	801	5,467	1,474	267
1962	872	1,618	185.6	53	1,565	488	4	11,678	810	5,531	1,480	268
1963	872	1,613	185.0	238	1,375	471	24	19,728	825	5,611	1,496	275
1964	882	1,673	189.7	21	1,652	479	29	28,654	835	5,649	1,506	283
1965	890	1,680	188.8	28	1,652	478	47	32,107	847	5,739	1,520	301
1966	896	1,686	188.2	63	1,623	482	8	35,301	854	5,806	1,536	308
1967	902	1,696	188.0	48	1,648	490	54	42,330	869	5,949	1,562	304
1968	900	1,692	188.0	15	1,677	500	54	49,310	877	5,999	1,562	305
1969	915	1,679	183.5	191	1,488	465	70	52,037	877	6,152	1,554	299
1970	905	1,656	183.0	54	1,602	468	67	52,794	880	5,997	1,520	296
1971	903	1,620	179.4	102	1,518	453	43	61,660	879	5,959	1,494	299
1972	899	1,586	176.4	58	1,528	449	114	65,755	880	5,947	1,468*	288*
1973	896	1,567	174.9	30	1,537	441	124	112,998	877	5,868	1,462*	288*
1974	917	1,644	179.3	44	1,600	442	45	119,905	878	5,802	1,527*	285*
1975	917	1,659	180.9	82	1,577	428	105	124,626	868	5,598	1,487*	282*

continued

Table 2.7. continued

| | Human labor | Animal labor | Intermediate inputs | | | | Mechanical implements | | | | | |
| | Mandays per agri. worker (14) | Draft cattle number (1,000) (15) | Consumption of chemical fertilizer (mt 1,000) (16) | Consumption of farm prod. fertilizer (mt 1,000) (17) | Nutrient equivalent | | Power tillers (20) | Tractors (21) | Power sprayers (22) | Power threshers (23) | Rice transplanters (24) | Rice combine (25) |
Year (1)					Chemical fert. (mt 1,000) (18)	Farm fert. (mt 1,000) (19)						
1946	111	268	43	10,348	—	—	—	—	—	—	—	—
1947	124	288	121	9,043	—	—	—	—	—	—	—	—
1948	145	301	188	15,477	—	—	—	—	—	—	—	—
1949	157	348	223	14,118	—	—	—	—	—	—	—	—
1950	159	355	415	13,394	—	—	—	—	—	—	—	—
1951	162	364	400	13,377	—	—	—	—	—	—	—	—
1952	169	382	688	13,650	145	129	—	—	—	—	—	—
1953	168	389	558	13,534	121	128	—	—	—	—	—	—
1954	165	405	522	13,231	104	126	7	—	—	—	—	—
1955	163	410	628	13,535	125	131	9	—	—	—	—	—
1956	170	412	652	14,040	134	135	60	—	—	—	—	—
1957	187	412	674	14,700	163	141	180	—	—	—	—	—
1958	189	426	670	15,005	160	145	600	—	—	—	—	—
1959	187	417	721	14,947	179	145	2,262	—	—	—	—	—
1960	184	417	681	14,135	183	137	3,708	—	—	—	—	—
1961	181	414	704	16,428	186	160	5,313	—	317	—	—	—
1962	181	405	725	17,400	194	168	7,504	—	804	—	—	—
1963	184	389	799	16,766	215	157	9,079	—	1,028	—	—	—

Year												
1964	188	379	805	14,339	221	139	10,201	—	2,949	—	—	—
1965	198	370	767	14,803	205	138	12,213	425	4,489	—	—	—
1966	200	360	805	14,274	229	137	14,272	448	6,123	—	—	—
1967	194	338	805	13,837	214	134	17,240	479	9,734	—	—	—
1968	195	324	945	14,262	247	136	21,153	496	12,901	—	—	—
1969	192	306	959	14,917	257	136	24,640	512	14,791	—	—	—
1970	194	275	743	14,166	188	136	28,292	539	17,820	—	280	20
1971	200	245	939	11,983	237	114	32,030	554	27,038	—	454	75
1972	196*	227	1,004	12,026	255	117	35,222	620	25,309	146	658	154
1973	197*	204	1,161	11,227	282	111	38,393	749	43,176	316	972	329
1974	187*	195	1,011	10,434	243	101	42,123	892	45,399	48,973	1,914	1,127
1975	190*	196	1,389	10,252	329	100	45,470	1,323	37,874	27,558	2,481	1,940

*Provided by Joint Commission on Rural Reconstruction (JCRR).

Source: Columns 2–11, 15, and 17: Various issues of Taiwan Agricultural Yearbook.

Column 16: The consumption figures for the period up to 1965 come from the Taiwan Agricultural Yearbook, based on the sum of domestic production plus import minus imported raw materials minus export (thus excluding inventory changes). From 1966 on, the reporting procedure in the Taiwan Agricultural Yearbook was changed to amounts of fertilizer actually sold or distributed by the Taiwan Sugar Corporation and the Taiwan Provincial Food Bureau, thus excluding fertilizer directly sold by the Kaohsiung Ammonia Corporation and the Taiwan Fertilizer Corporation. Consequently, the series given here was adjusted from 1966 on to include the sales of these last two corporations. One inconsistency that remains in this series is that fertilizer handled by the Provincial Food Bureau before 1969 was not recorded on a calendar-year basis but on a fiscal-year basis from 1970 on. The drastic drop in apparent fertilizer consumption in 1970 as compared to 1969 is due to the reporting shift from a fiscal to calendar-year basis.

Columns 12 and 13: Lee and Chen, pp. 66–67.

Columns 20–25: Data for 1954–69 from Department of Agriculture and Forestry, Provincial Government of Taiwan, Republic of China, as quoted in You-Tsao Wang, "Farm Mechanization in Taiwan: Its Problems and Research Needs," in Herman Southworth, ed., Farm Mechanization in East Asia (1972), p. 221. Data for 1970–75 are from Tien-Song Peng, "Agricultural Mechanization in Taiwan," in Taiwan Agricultural Machinery Guide (Taipei, 1976), pp. 132–59.

Columns 18 and 19 computed by the author. Conversion ratios obtained from Fertilizer Institute, The Fertilizer Handbook, 2d ed. (Washington D.C., January 1976).

Column 19: Conversion ratios obtained from T. H. Shen, Agricultural Development in Taiwan since World War II (Ithaca, N.Y., 1964), p. 141. The nutrient-equivalent estimates depend on the composition of the chemical fertilizers, which varied over time. Since the composition of chemical fertilizers given in column 16 was available only for 80 to 100 percent of the total volume, the figures on nutrient equivalent in column 18 are estimates.

substantially, a phenomenon that is highly correlated with the very large increase in the number of water pumps used (see column 9).

The major indicators with respect to human labor are the total number of agricultural workers (or alternatively the total number of farm families or agricultural population), the total number of man-days of agricultural labor, and the average number of man-days per agricultural worker. The total number of agricultural workers and man-days of agricultural labor rose until about 1968, after which both series started falling. The same trend is noticeable with regard to the average number of man-days per agricultural worker.

The number of head of draft cattle (mainly water buffalo)—reflecting animal labor—rose from 1946 to 1958, when it reached its peak, to fall very substantially thereafter.

The major indicator of intermediate inputs is the consumption of chemical fertilizer, which rose very substantially until around 1952, remained relatively constant until the early 1960s, and then grew unevenly and moderately until 1972 and very sharply thereafter. The best indicator of total fertilizer application (organic and chemical) can be obtained by converting chemical fertilizer and farm fertilizer into comparable nutrient-equivalent terms (see columns 18 and 19 of Table 2.7). In these terms, both chemical and farm fertilizers increased gradually until 1962, after which year chemical fertilizer started replacing farm fertilizer.

The last category of inputs given in Table 2.7 is that of mechanical implements. Farm mechanization is a recent phenomenon which became important in Taiwan only from about the mid-1960s on.

Perhaps a clearer and more concise way of examining the trends in the use of inputs is to compute the growth rates of the major input indicators for the three agricultural development phases that were identified on the basis of output trends. This information is presented in Table 2.8.

Thus, in the recovery period, output increased mainly because of a more intensive use of labor and of land. The former is reflected by the high growth rate of total man-days of agricultural labor (amounting to 6.4 percent annually), while the actual number of workers rose by only 1.6 percent per annum. Likewise, the increase in the intensity of land cultivation is reflected by a relatively high annual rate of growth of crop area of 3.8 percent, in contrast with the cultivated land area which increased only marginally. Furthermore, the use of current inputs (mainly fertilizer) grew substantially from an abnormally low base prevailing in 1946.

In the growth phase between 1954 and 1967, labor inputs in terms of total man-days continued to rise, but at the low rate of 1.7 percent per annum— mainly through a continuing but small increase in the average number of man-days per worker. The growth of current inputs was high in this period, making possible continued gains in labor and land productivities even though the labor and land constraints were being reached.

Table 2.8. Growth Rates of Inputs in Different Phases of Agricultural Development, 1946–1974 (annual percentage rates)

Phases*	Labor			Land			Fixed capital			Current inputs	
	Total man-days (1)	Number of workers (2)	Man-days per worker (3)	Culti-vated area (4)	Crop area (5)	Total value (6)	Machinery horse-power (7)	Total value (8)	Fertilizer in nutrient equivalent	
									chemical (9)	organic (10)
I 1947–53 Recovery	6.4	1.6	4.7	0.6	3.8	4.7	—	26.7	n.a.	n.a.
II 1954–67 Growth	1.7	0.4	1.3	0.2	0.9	3.5	77.0	7.3	5.7	3.3
III 1968–74 Slowdown	−0.9	−0.7	−0.2	0.1	−0.7	5.9†	17.3	16.2†	3.7	1.2
IV 1947–74 Average	2.0	0.4	1.6	0.3	1.1	4.0‡	49.9§	13.0‡	2.5‖	−1.0‖

*The annual growth rates prevailing in each phase have been computed on the basis of three-year averages centered on the first and last year of each period: 1947 = average 1946–48, 1953 = average 1952–54, and so forth.
†Average of 1968–72.
‡Average of 1947–72.
§Average of 1954–74.
‖Average of 1954–74.

Source: The growth rates are computed from information in Table 2.7, except for columns 6 and 8, which are based on Lee and Chen, pp. 66–67, and column 7, which is based on author's estimates (for methodology used see Table 2.11).

Finally, Table 2.8 reveals very clearly that in the slowdown period after 1968, both the labor and land constraints had become effective—as reflected by negative growth rates for total labor inputs and crop area, respectively—which could be relaxed only through a massive effort at mechanization. The fact that mechanical energy had to substitute increasingly for human and animal energy and had to compensate for a leveling off of the total crop area is brought out explicitly in the subsequent analysis.

The changes in the use of inputs over time (in a broad sense, the aggregate agricultural production function) can be illustrated by a simple identity:

(1)
$$\frac{Y}{L} = \frac{Y}{A} \times \frac{A}{L}$$
where Y = agricultural output,
L = number of workers, and
A = area of cultivated land.

This identity expresses output per worker as being equal to the product of output per hectare of cultivated land (that is, the productivity of land) and the amount of cultivated land per worker (that is, the land-man ratio). An even more meaningful extension of the above relationship is:

(2)
$$\frac{Y}{L} = \left\{ \frac{Y}{CA} \times \frac{CA}{A} \right\} \left\{ \frac{MD}{L} \times \frac{A}{MD} \right\}$$
where CA = crop area and
MD = total number of man-days
of labor per year
(other terms as defined above).

Thus, in this formulation, agricultural output per worker is equal to the product of four ratios: the yield per hectare of crop area, the ratio of crop area to cultivated area (that is, the multiple crop index), the average number of man-days per worker, and, finally, the reciprocal of the man-days applied annually per hectare of cultivated area. The use of this decomposition procedure shows the relative importance of different inputs in the development process.[17]

Table 2.9 gives the decomposition of production per worker in agriculture in terms of the four components referred to above, annually, for the period 1946 to 1975. Likewise, Table 2.10 provides, in a consolidated form, the above information for four selected post–World War II periods and three pre–World War II periods in order to permit a historical comparison.

Tables 2.9 and 2.10 reveal clearly that different factors were responsible for the dramatic increase in the output per worker throughout the post–World War II era. In the recovery period (1946–53) land productivity increased because of a combination of substantial rises in yield (column 2 of both tables) and in the multiple cropping index (MCI) (column 3) while labor was more in-

17. T. H. Lee, *Intersectoral Capital Flows*, used the simpler identity (equation 1) in explaining historical changes in output per worker. It appeared more useful, at least for the period after 1946, to decompose labor productivity in terms of the four components given above.

Table 2.9. Decomposition of Production per Worker in Agriculture, 1946–1975*

Year	$\frac{\text{Production}}{\text{Worker}}$ Y/L (N.T.$) (1)	=	$\frac{\text{Production}}{\text{Crop area}}$ Y/CA (N.T.$) (2)	×	$\frac{\text{Crop area}}{\text{Cult. area}}$ CA/A (MCI) (3)	×	$\frac{\text{Mandays}}{\text{Worker}}$ MD/L (number) (4)	×	$\frac{\text{Cult. area}}{\text{Manday}}$ A/MD (ha/MD) (5)	$\left[\frac{\text{Mandays}}{\text{Cult. area}}\right]$† (MD/ha) (6) = 1 ÷ (5)
1946	172		227		117		111		.006	172
1947	201		215		143		124		.005	199
1948	226		224		156		145		.004	230
1949	255		251		166		157		.004	256
1950	286		282		170		159		.004	259
1951	292		276		170		161		.004	262
1952	312		294		172		169		.004	276
1953	339		335		173		168		.004	283
1954	336		335		174		165		.004	282
1955	333		329		171		163		.004	278
1956	365		350		176		170		.003	287
1957	400		367		179		187		.003	308
1958	421		386		180		189		.003	312
1959	417		385		182		187		.003	313
1960	421		385		184		184		.003	310
1961	450		412		186		181		.003	306
1962	455		416		185		181		.003	307
1963	451		418		185		184		.003	315
1964	495		445		188		188		.003	321
1965	531		481		190		198		.003	338
1966	543		495		190		200		.003	343
1967	558		514		187		194		.003	337
1968	589		543		188		195		.003	339
1969	583		540		184		192		.003	326
1970	628		577		183		194		.003	326
1971	651		600		180		200		.003	331
1972	687		636		175		196		.003	320
1973	723		675		175		197		.003	321
1974	706		656		179		187		.003	311
1975	699		626		181		190		.003	308

*For explanation of decomposition, see text.
†Column 6 is the reciprocal of column 5.
Source: The underlying data used to compute the ratios come from Table 2.7. The agricultural production series is that of Lee and Chen, pp. 63–64, based on 1935–37 constant prices. Since that series was not extended beyond 1972, it was assumed that production at 1935–37 prices grew after 1972 at the same rate as the official agricultural output series of the DGBAS given in column 3 of Table 2.4.

tensively used, as reflected by a big jump in the average number of man-days per agricultural worker (column 4). During the same phase, the much more intensive use of the limited cultivated area (column 6) exerted a negative effect on production per worker.[18]

In the growth phase (1954–68), the yield per hectare of crop land continued to rise substantially and the multiple crop index increased slowly, to level off in 1965–66 and then turn downward. Likewise, the average number of man-

18. Column 6 is the reciprocal of column 5 in both Tables 2.9 and 2.10. It is, perhaps, intuitively easier to grasp the concept of man-days per cultivated hectare, which is given in column 6, than its reciprocal in column 5.

Table 2.10. Decomposition of Production per Worker in Agriculture for Selected Periods[*]

Year	$\dfrac{\text{Production}}{\text{Worker}} = $ $\dfrac{Y/L}{\text{N.T.\$}}$ (1)	$\dfrac{\text{Production}}{\text{Crop area}} \times$ $\dfrac{Y/CA}{\text{N.T.\$}}$ (2)	$\dfrac{\text{Crop area}}{\text{Cult. area}} \times$ $\dfrac{CA/A}{\text{MCI}}$ (3)	$\dfrac{\text{Mandays}}{\text{Worker}} \times$ $\dfrac{MD/L}{\text{(number)}}$ (4)	$\dfrac{\text{Cult. area}}{\text{Manday}} \times$ $\dfrac{A/MD}{\text{(ha/}MD\text{)}}$ (5)	$\left[\dfrac{\text{Mandays}}{\text{Cult. area}}\right]$ $[MD/A]$ $MD/\text{ha of land}$ (6)
1911–13	155	213	120	120	.005	199
1922–24	207	250	124	143	.005	213
1936–38	302	362	132	143	.004	226
1946–48	200	227	139	127	.005	200
1952–54	329	320	173	167	.004	280
1966–68	563	516	188	196	.003	339
1973–75	709	652	178	191	.003	313

	$\dfrac{\text{Production}}{\text{Cult. area}}$ $\dfrac{Y}{A}$	$\dfrac{\text{Cult. area}}{\text{Worker}}$ $\dfrac{A}{L}$
1911–13	256	.60
1922–24	310	.67
1936–38	478	.63
1946–48	316	.64
1952–54	554	.60
1966–68	970	.58
1973–75	1,160	.61

[*]For explanation of decomposition, see text.
Source: For prewar periods, computed on the basis of data in Lee and Chen, pp. 62–63. For postwar periods, derived from Table 2.9.

days per worker continued to grow until reaching a peak of two-hundred in 1966. On the other hand, the fact that the total area of cultivated land remained essentially constant led to a sharp drop in cultivated area per man-day of agricultural labor (that is, a rise in the number of man-days worked per hectare).

Finally, during the slowdown phase after 1968, the rise in output per worker was solely caused by a continuing rise in yield which more than compensated for the decline or leveling off of the other three components. In turn, the increase in yield since the mid-1960s was caused by a major substitution of mechanical energy for human and animal energy. This took the form mainly of power tillers, the total number of which tripled between 1966 and 1974 from about 14,000 to 42,000 (see column 20, Table 2.7), and more recently of tractors and combines.

The ratios given in Tables 2.9 and 2.10, as well as the quantitative input indicators in Table 2.7, are very useful in helping to pinpoint some important turning points, particularly the one occurring around 1966–68. For instance, the multiple crop index, which is a measure of the intensity of productive land use, peaked in 1966 at a level of 190 (from 117 in 1946) and gradually declined to around 178 in the mid-1970s (see column 3, Table 2.9). Likewise, the total number of man-days of agricultural labor—which is probably the best measure of total labor input into agriculture—grew from 143 million in 1946 to a peak of 305 million in 1968, to decline thereafter (see column 13, Table 2.7). Similarly, the total number of agricultural workers (column 12, Table 2.7) and the number of man-days per worker (column 14, Table 2.7) kept on rising until 1966 and then leveled off.

At least two other indicators suggest a turning point—the acceleration in the agricultural wage rate around 1966–68 and the worsening terms of trade of agricultural versus nonagricultural income. These indicators will be examined later in the chapter. Clearly, the labor shortage that occurred around this turning point encouraged the adoption of mechanical implements and the increased application of chemical fertilizer to permit a continuation of the rise in the yield per hectare.

To highlight the dramatic move away from an agricultural technology relying mainly on human and animal labor as major sources of energy until the mid-1960s to one gradually substituting mechanical power for human and animal power, I attempted to convert these sources of power to horsepower equivalents so as to make them comparable. Table 2.11 summarizes the results. The procedure used to convert the various sources of energy—human, animal, and mechanical—into equivalent units is complex and subject to a number of assumptions mainly based on agricultural engineering estimates. This procedure is explained in detail in the notes to Table 2.11. In essence, the three sources of energy were converted into equivalent horsepower-days of actual work. Thus, for example, it was assumed on the basis of engineering estimates that ten man-days of human labor were equivalent to one horsepower-day, in terms of actual work performed, and that two man-days of animal labor were equivalent to one horsepower-day. For mechanical labor, the procedure required estimating the total horsepower capacity represented by different types of farm implements, such as power tillers, power sprayers, and tractors, the average number of hours of utilization of each type of machine per year, and the total number of horsepower-days of mechanical power. Because of the difficulty of converting these various sources into a meaningful common denominator and the number of assumptions that had to be made, these results ought to be considered as only suggestive of a trend.

Two major trends are revealed by Table 2.11. First is the tremendous shift in the relative importance of the three types of energy. Hence, whereas in 1952–53, 67 percent of the total energy used in agricultural crop production came from human labor and 33 percent from animal labor, by 1975 human labor represented only about 35 percent of total energy and animal labor 7 percent. On the other hand, mechanical energy, which was practically

Table 2.11. Sources of Human, Animal, and Mechanical Energy in Crop Production in Horsepower-Day Equivalent Units and Percentages of Total, 1952–1975

Year	Human labor in equivalent horsepower-days (million) (1)	Percentage of total energy (2)	Animal labor in equivalent horsepower-days (million) (3)	Percentage of total energy (4)	Mechanical labor in equivalent horsepower-days (million) (5)	Percentage of total energy (6)	Total energy in horsepower-days (million) (7)
1952	24.20	67	11.94	33	—	—	36.14
1953	24.70	67	12.15	33	—	—	36.85
1954	24.60	66	12.64	34	0.01	0	37.25
1955	24.30	65	12.82	35	0.01	0	37.13
1956	25.20	66	12.89	34	0.02	0	38.11
1957	26.90	67	12.89	32	0.07	1	39.86
1958	27.60	67	13.32	32	0.25	1	41.17
1959	27.50	66	13.04	31	0.98	3	41.52
1960	27.00	65	13.04	31	1.76	4	41.80
1961	26.70	63	12.94	30	2.92	7	42.56
1962	26.80	60	12.66	28	5.21	12	44.67
1963	27.50	59	12.17	26	6.58	15	46.25
1964	28.30	59	11.85	25	8.13	16	48.28
1965	30.10	60	11.57	23	8.55	17	50.22
1966	30.80	54	11.26	20	14.84	26	56.90
1967	30.40	56	10.56	19	13.21	25	54.17
1968	30.50	53	10.13	18	17.12	29	57.75
1969	29.90	50	9.57	16	20.35	34	59.82
1970	29.60	47	8.59	14	24.19	39	62.38
1971	29.90	45	7.66	11	29.23	44	66.79
1972	28.80	42	7.10	10	32.45	48	68.35
1973	28.80	39	6.39	9	38.86	52	74.05

1974	28.50	35	6.09	8	46.02	56	80.61
1975	28.20	35	6.12	7	47.37	58	81.69

Sources: Human Labor (column 1) was computed as follows: (1) the total number of man-days of labor input in agriculture was taken from Table 2.7 (column 13); (2) it was assumed that the conversion ratio in terms of actual work was ten man-days of human labor = one horsepower-day. This estimate is based on agricultural engineering estimates contained in Theodore Baumeister, ed., *Mark's Handbook for Mechanical Engineers,* 7th ed. (Willtown Bluff, N.C., 1966) pp. 9-209-10.

Animal Labor (column 3) was computed as follows: (1) the total number of draft animals (buffaloes and yellow cattle) is taken from Table 2.7 (column 15); (2) it was assumed that each animal worked five hundred hours per year on the average. This is based on 1958 survey report results that a buffalo was used for fifty-two days per year and yellow cattle forty-eight days per year (see T. H. Shen and Y. T. Wang, "Technological Adjustments," in T. H. Shen, ed., *Agriculture's Place in the Strategy of Development: The Taiwan Experience* (Taipei, 1974), p. 398); (3) it was assumed that a draft animal is equivalent to half a horsepower in terms of actual work performed (see A. Makhijani and A. Poole, *Energy and Agriculture in the Third World* [Cambridge, Mass., 1975], Table 2.1, footnote d, p. 17).

Mechanical Labor (column 5) was computed as follows: power tillers, tractors, power sprayers, rice transplanters, and power threshers were included. The data on the numbers of machinery of each class were obtained for the years 1964–69 from the Department of Agriculture and Forestry, Provincial Government of Taiwan, Republic of China, as quoted in Wang, p. 221. Data for the years 1970–75 are from Peng, "Agricultural Mechanization," pp. 132–59. Horsepower capacity of each class of machinery was computed on the information given in the above-mentioned sources. Average horsepower per machine of each class was computed by dividing the horsepower capacity by the number of machines by class. To compute the horsepower hours per machine, it was assumed that the utilization rates for the machinery classes would be as follows: 600 hours per year for power tillers, 500 hours per year for tractors, 300 hours per year for power sprayers, 200 hours per year for rice transplanters, and 100 hours per year for power threshers. These assumptions were made on the basis of following studies: Tien-Song Peng, "A Survey on the Utilization of Power Tillers and Mist-Blowers in Taiwan," March 2, 1970, JCRR, mimeo; and Provincial Government of Taiwan, Taiwan Provincial Department of Agriculture and Forestry, Department of Agriculture and Forestry, *Report on the Survey of Power Tiller Use in Taiwan Province* (Taipei, 1966). Based on the above assumptions, horsepower hours per machine per class were obtained by multiplying average horsepower per machine by the utilization rates for each class of machinery. Total number of horsepower hours was obtained by multiplying the horsepower hours per machine of each class of machinery by the number of machines in that class and summing up for the classes. Total number of horsepower days was derived by dividing total number of horsepower hours by eight to convert the data to the same unit as the data on other sources of energy used in the analysis.

nonexistent at the outset, appeared to contribute 58 percent of total energy in crop production in 1975.

Second, total energy applied in agriculture as measured in terms of millions of horsepower-days, particularly after 1968, rose substantially. Thus, the annual growth rate of total energy expressed in horsepower-days (column 7 in Table 2.11) increased at a rate of approximately 3 percent between 1952 and 1968 and at a rate of 5.1 percent between 1968 and 1975.

These facts suggest that a major substitution of mechanical energy for human and animal energy occurred in Taiwan's agriculture during the period under consideration and that mechanical energy is much less efficient[19] than human and perhaps even than animal energy. This inference can be drawn from the fact that the growth rate of total energy—an increasing part of which came from mechanical power—rose markedly in the post–1968 phase and yet yielded a substantially lower growth rate of agricultural output than in the preceding period. Indeed, the great advantage of human labor is that it is highly divisible and usually works fairly close to its capacity level, in contrast with machines, particularly tractors and combines, which are much less divisible and which, even when in use in many agricultural activities, require only a fraction of their total horsepower capacity.[20] This probably explains why the growth rates of horsepower-days accelerated substantially after 1968 without any corresponding growth in crop output.

An alternative procedure for estimating the relative contributions, respectively, of human, animal, and mechanical energy to total energy in Taiwan agriculture was undertaken on the basis of survey data.[21] These surveys provide information on the amount of time each type of labor was used annually per farm family. Because the average size of the family farm is known, these estimates can be converted into man-days of human and animal labor and man-hours of machine time used per hectare. The next step is to multiply animal and human labor per hectare by the total cultivated area in Taiwan and to convert these estimates into horsepower-day equivalents, using the same conversion ratios as in the previous procedure. For mechanical labor, the average number of horsepower per average machine of each type had to be computed for each year and multiplied by the number of machine hours used per hectare, and, finally, by the total number of cultivated hectares in Taiwan to yield the total amount of mechanical energy in horsepower-days (see Table 2.12).

19. The term efficiency here is not used in the economic but in an engineering sense.

20. In addition, mechanical farm implements are used for only limited periods of time (see notes to Table 2.11 for hours of use per year of certain machines), a fact that was allowed for in the estimation procedure, which is based on horsepower-days of actual utilization.

21. Provincial Government of Taiwan, Department of Agriculture and Forestry, *Report of Farm Record-Keeping Families in Taiwan, (Taipei, 1960, 1965, and 1974).*

Table 2.12. Sources of Human, Animal, and Mechanical Energy in Crop Production in Horsepower-Day Equivalent Units and Percentages of Total, Selected Years, 1961–1974

Year	Human labor in equivalent horsepower-days (millions) (1)	As percent of total energy input (2)	Animal labor in equivalent horsepower-days (millions) (3)	As percent of total energy input (4)	Mechanical labor in equivalent horsepower-days (millions) (5)	As percent of total energy input (6)	Total energy in horsepower-days (millions) (7)
1961	34.5	72	12.33	26	1.1	2	47.93
1965	35.0	60	16.73	29	6.9	11	58.63
1970	33.8	59	11.48	20	12.3	21	57.58
1974	25.3	44	8.90	15	23.2	41	57.50

Source and methods: Human Labor (column 1): In the computation of horsepower-day equivalent units of human labor, the total labor input per average farm family was obtained from Provincial Government of Taiwan, Department of Agriculture and Forestry, *Report on Farm Record-Keeping Families in Taiwan*, various issues. Total labor requirement per hectare of cultivated land was obtained by dividing the labor input per average family by average farm size. This figure multiplied by the total cultivated land area gives the total labor input in man-days. To derive the horsepower-day equivalent units, it was assumed that ten man-days were equivalent to one horsepower-day (for reference see Table 2.11). By using this conversion ratio, the horsepower-days of human labor were computed.

Animal Labor (column 3): Total animal input per average family was obtained from the above-mentioned *Reports*. The derivation of horsepower-days equivalent was similar to the above-mentioned procedure. But it was assumed that one horsepower-day was equivalent to two animal labor days, based on the same references given in Table 2.11.

Mechanical Labor: Using the data on number of hours of mechanical labor applied per hectare in the above-mentioned *Reports*, and adopting a similar procedure as for the other two sources of power above, it was possible to derive the total number of hours of mechanical power (MP_h). But for my analytical purpose, it was necessary to derive the total number of machine hp days (M_{hpd}), for which a conversion factor was needed. In the computation of the conversion factor one has to distinguish between the types of machine equipment used, the capacity differences of such equipment, and their utilization rates. The five types of machinery used for Table 2.11 were included. An average of hp per machine for each type was computed by dividing the total hp capacity of each machine type and class by the number of machines of that type and class. As there are different types of machinery, it was necessary to obtain a weighted average hp per machine. To derive the weight, an index was computed to reflect the different type and utilization rates of machinery. The utilization rates were derived on assumptions similar to those made in Table 2.11. The index becomes a ratio of utilization rate of each type of machinery to the total utilization rates of all types of machinery. By multiplying the average hp per machine in each type by the above-mentioned index, to compute the total number of machine hp days (M_{hpd}), a weighted average hp per machine was derived. This figure multiplied by the machine power hours (MP_h) gives the total number of machine hp in hours. This was converted to hp days by dividing by eight to make it comparable to other sources of energy in the analysis.

The resulting estimates of total energy supplied by different sources depend crucially on how representative the sample of family farms was. In any case, these estimates, which are summarized in Table 2.12, show mechanical power increasing from 2 percent of total energy in agriculture in 1961 to 41 percent in 1974; the contribution of human labor drops from 72 to 44 percent and that of animal labor from 26 to 15 percent over the same time span.[22] Clearly, both procedures point to a major substitution of mechanical energy for human and animal labor in the slowdown phase after 1968.

An Interregional Analysis of Agricultural Production, 1952–1974

No systematic interregional analysis of agricultural production in Taiwan has yet been undertaken. Some important insights can be gained by disaggregating interregionally the structure of agricultural production and that of input use. The addition of the spatial dimension helps to throw further light on the interregional shifts in the composition of agricultural output and the distribution of factors of production required to produce the actual output. Such an interregional analysis is particularly useful in understanding better some of the shifts in the commodity composition of output over time which tend, of course, to be correlated with geographical shifts in cropping patterns and use of resources. Furthermore, since labor is a key resource, this type of analysis can be helpful in explaining the pattern of migration that occurred in Taiwan.

Annual agricultural statistics relating to production and to some inputs are available at the prefecture level, hence, any regional classification has to be built up from that level. Given this constraint, seven major regions were identified, mainly on the basis of such criteria as climate, geography, output mix, and cropping patterns. These regions—including in parentheses the prefectures they embrace—are, moving from the North to the Southwest, (1) northern rice region (Taıpei, Yilan, Taoyuan); (2) tea region (Sinchu, Miaoli); (3) central rice region (Taichung, Changwa); (4) banana-pineapple region (Nantou); (5) southwestern rice–sugarcane region (Yunlin, Chiayi, Tainan); (6) southern rice region (Kaohsiung, Pingtung); and finally, on the eastern side, (7) eastern mixed region (Taitung, Hualien).[23]

For purposes of comparison over time, three benchmark years were selected in the present analysis—1952, 1965, and 1974. The interregional analysis is undertaken in three interrelated steps. First, the interregional and

22. The total energy levels in horsepower-days obtained under this method (see Table 2.12) are significantly lower than those obtained under the first procedure (see Table 2.11). The latter estimates are likely to be more accurate, because they rely on more solid evidence.

23. This regional breakdown covers the whole of Taiwan's agriculture except for the small prefecture (island) of Penghu and covers about 99.5 percent of the total value of agricultural output in Taiwan.

commodity composition of total agricultural output is highlighted in relative terms so as to explore over time the changing relative importance of different regions and different commodities. Second, the output performance of different product groups in the seven regions is described for the two periods, 1952-65 and 1965-74, to determine the differential growth performance among regions and commodity groups. Finally, the interregional changes in the use of factors of production (agricultural inputs) are highlighted to show that important shifts have taken place in the regional use of land, labor, and capital, reflecting to a large extent the changes in output and its composition as between products.

Table 2.13 provides in a consolidated form the percentage shares of each agricultural commodity group in each region in the current value of total agricultural output for the three benchmark years. This table suggests first, that the regional distribution of total output in terms of current value (see line 9, Table 2.13) remained relatively more stable than the distribution of total output among commodity groups (see Table 2.13, columns 22-24). In the two northern rice and tea regions shares of total national output dropped fairly significantly from, respectively, 19.2 to 16.4 percent and from 9.0 to 6.8 percent between 1952 and 1974. On the other hand, southwestern rice-sugarcane and southern rice regions gained in relative importance, their shares of total output rising from, respectively, 26.9 to 29.9 percent and from 16.2 to 18.5 percent over the period. Thus a shift in relative production appears to have taken place away from the North to the South. Evidently the southern regions were able to capture a larger share of the rising livestock and vegetable production.

Second, the changing commodity composition of output, described previously and given in the last three columns of Table 2.13, can be analyzed interregionally. As one would expect, regions that were able to convert best from producing commodities such as rice and sweet potatoes—the importance of which was declining—to commodity groups expanding in relative importance, such as livestock, vegetables, and, to some extent, fruits, either retained or increased their relative share of total output. This occurred in the central rice region and the two southern regions.

Another way of examining the changing interregional and intercommodity production performance is to compute the growth rates for each commodity group and for each region for the two subperiods 1952-65 and 1965-1974. This is done in Table 2.14. The two southern regions displayed significantly higher growth rates of total agricultural output in the two subperiods (see columns 5 and 6) than obtained for Taiwan as a whole (see column 8). In contrast—as one would expect—the two northern regions performed much worse than the average for Taiwan (see columns 1 and 2). The growth rates of total

Table 2.13. Interregional and Commodity Composition of Agricultural Output, 1952, 1965, 1974 (percentages of current value of total agricultural output of Taiwan in each of the three benchmark years)

	Northern rice region			Tea region			Central rice region			Banana-pineapple region		
	1952 (1)	1965 (2)	1974 (3)	1952 (4)	1965 (5)	1974 (6)	1952 (7)	1965 (8)	1974 (9)	1952 (10)	1965 (11)	1974 (12)
1. Rice	9.79	6.92	5.05	4.73	2.99	2.89	12.60	9.24	8.81	1.93	1.33	1.37
2. Sweet potatoes	.72	.67	.33	.74	.59	.32	.99	.92	.52	.29	.30	.15
3. Other common crops	.08	.04	.02	.05	.07	.03	.54	.50	.17	.05	.15	.13
4. Sugarcane	.03	.01		.08	.05	.02	1.06	.59	.58	.30	.14	.05
5. Other special crops	1.18	.68	.56	1.26	.80	.62	1.18	1.25	.32	.59	.50	.53
6. Fruits	.34	.58	.39	.31	.41	.40	.78	1.31	1.99	.59	1.11	.62
7. Vegetables/mushrooms	1.20	.85	1.28	.38	.58	.62	.70	1.98	2.30	.20	.19	.43
8. Livestock	5.88	8.38	8.72	1.42	1.90	1.90	2.35	3.77	4.94	.55	.85	.89
9. Total agric. prod.	19.22	18.13	16.35	8.97	7.39	6.80	20.20	19.56	19.63	4.50	4.57	4.17

	Rice-sugarcane region			Southern Rice region			Eastern mixed region			Total Taiwan*		
	1952 (13)	1965 (14)	1974 (15)	1952 (16)	1965 (17)	1974 (18)	1952 (19)	1965 (20)	1974 (21)	1952 (22)	1965 (23)	1974 (24)
1. Rice	10.12	8.35	9.62	8.60	6.39	5.98	1.48	1.74	1.68	49.25	36.96	35.40
2. Sweet potatoes	3.81	3.24	1.68	1.49	.83	.64	.49	.49	.27	8.53	7.04	3.91
3. Other common crops	.92	.69	1.14	.64	1.32	1.04	.17	.27	.23	2.45	3.04	2.76
4. Sugarcane	4.67	4.04	4.15	1.73	1.15	1.20	.34	.43	.43	8.21	6.41	6.43
5. Other special crops	2.97	2.60	1.44	.60	.88	.78	.42	.60	.51	8.20	7.31	4.76
6. Fruits	.44	1.38	1.42	.37	3.45	1.28	.15	.29	.25	2.98	8.53	6.35
7. Vegetables/mushrooms	.76	1.36	3.56	.50	.77	1.54	.24	.26	.34	3.98	5.99	10.07
8. Livestock	3.21	5.34	6.86	2.28	3.46	6.04	.71	.92	.93	16.40	24.62	30.28
9. Total agric. prod.	26.90	27.00	29.87	16.21	18.25	18.50	4.00	5.00	4.64	100.00	100.00	100.00

*The current values of total agricultural production in the three benchmark years were, respectively, in million current N.T.$, 1952 = 5,956; 1965 = 32,059; and 1974 = 89,059.
Source: Computed by the author on the basis of data in *Taiwan Agricultural Yearbooks.*

Table 2.14. Growth Rates of Agricultural Output by Commodity Groups and Regions, 1952-1965 and 1965-1974 (annual growth rates)

	Northern rice region (1)		Tea region (2)		Central rice region (3)		Banana-pineapple region (4)		Rice-sugarcane region (5)		Southern rice region (6)		Eastern mixed region (7)		Total for Taiwan (8)	
	1952-65	1965-74	1952-65	1965-74	1952-65	1965-74	1952-65	1965-74	1952-65	1965-74	1952-65	1965-74	1952-65	1965-74	1952-65	1965-74
1. Rice	2.1	-2.2	1.5	0.3	3.0	0.4	2.5	1.2	4.3	2.3	3.4	0.6	5.5	0.7	3.1	0.5
2. Sweet potatoes	2.5	-3.4	2.8	-1.9	2.7	-3.0	2.3	-2.5	4.0	-1.3	1.2	1.0	4.6	-0.6	3.2	-1.3
3. Other common crops	-0.7	—	7.5	-3.6	4.4	-6.3	11.8	-1.8	2.6	7.9	10.4	1.8	7.1	4.0	6.4	2.7
4. Sugarcane	-3.1	—	3.7	-10.3	2.6	-1.1	1.1	-10.5	6.2	-0.5	4.1	-0.3	9.4	-0.6	5.4	-0.7
5. Other special crops	0.8	0.5	2.0	0.3	5.4	-7.6	3.9	3.1	5.3	-3.7	9.6	2.8	8.1	-2.0	4.8	-1.5
6. Fruits	10.2	7.8	13.4	2.0	8.4	8.2	4.8	4.8	12.3	11.3	20.3	2.4	12.3	5.4	11.9	6.0
7. Vegetables	1.4	3.7	1.1	2.3	6.3	7.4	—	18.0	6.8	16.2	5.8	14.7	4.8	26.2	4.4	11.0
8. Livestock	5.6	5.6	5.1	4.8	5.5	7.9	5.3	5.7	5.9	7.6	5.9	10.4	4.0	4.5	5.6	7.1
Total agricultural production	3.7	2.8	3.1	1.8	4.1	3.0	3.7	3.5	5.2	4.0	5.6	4.7	6.0	2.2	4.5	3.5

Source: Volume figures for the various crops (usually in metric tons) and for the number of head of cattle were obtained for 1952, 1965, and 1974 by prefectures and consolidated into the above seven regions from various issues of *Taiwan Agricultural Yearbook*. The volume figures were then multiplied by the average prices prevailing over the period 1952-75, which were used as weights, and the growth rates were computed for the two periods.

agricultural production and for the major commodity groups for Taiwan as a whole (given in column 8 of Table 2.14) are, on the whole, consistent with those shown in Table 2.5.[24]

Perhaps the most noteworthy regional-cum-commodity developments are the very high growth rates of vegetable, livestock, and, to a somewhat lesser extent, fruit production in the second subperiod in the two southern regions.[25]

After this review of the major interregional and intercommodity shifts, it is important to attempt to correlate these shifts with corresponding changes in the use of agricultural inputs. The question that can be posed is the extent to which changes in the interregional input mix affected the interregional and intercommodity output mix. Table 2.15 provides information on a number of quantitative indicators of agricultural inputs by region for the three benchmark years. It also gives the regional distribution of a number of major inputs. Table 2.15 reveals a relative shift in resources away from the northern rice and the tea regions toward the southwestern rice–sugarcane and southern rice regions–a move that parallels the one already observed on the output side.

Whereas the two northern regions accounted for 25.9 percent of the total number of man-days used in Taiwan's total agricultural production in 1952, this proportion fell to 19.2 percent in 1974. In contrast, the corresponding regional share of total labor inputs in agriculture in the two southern regions rose from 43.4 percent in 1952 to 47.8 percent in 1974 (see Labor, line 4 in Table 2.15). This regional change in the distribution of labor inputs was not paralleled by any significant changes in the regional distribution of the agricultural population. Indeed, as can be seen from line I.2 of Table 2.15, the regional distribution of agricultural population remained very stable over the period under consideration.

This phenomenon suggests that in the northern regions which are close to at least two large metropolitan centers, Taipei and Taichung, a large number of farm family members took jobs outside of agriculture without changing their

24. The growth rates given in Table 2.5 were recomputed to correspond to the subperiods in Table 2.14 that are different from those in Table 2.5. The slight discrepancies between the two series are explained by the use of two different systems of weights. Table 2.5 uses as weights the gross value added per unit of product in 1971, whereas Table 2.14 uses as weights the average product prices prevailing over the period 1952–75. This explains why, for instance, the growth rate of agricultural production for Taiwan as computed in Table 2.14 between 1965 and 1974 is 3.5 percent annually, compared with a 3.0 percent growth rate obtained on the basis of the weighting system used in Table 2.5. More specifically, the higher growth rate obtained in Table 2.14 is caused by a much larger relative weight being given to livestock products in total production which amounted to approximately 34 percent in that period as compared to a weight of 22.1 percent (representing the share of gross value added of livestock products in 1971) used in computing Table 2.5. Since the growth of livestock production was substantially higher than that of most other commodity groups in the period under consideration, if livestock is given a higher relative weight in total production, it pushes up the overall growth rate of agricultural output.

25. The high growth rates of vegetable production in the banana-pineapple region and in the eastern mixed region reflect mainly a very low starting base.

Table 2.15. Quantities and Distribution of Agricultural Inputs by Region, 1952, 1965, and 1974

	Taiwan			Northern rice region (1)			Tea region (2)			Central rice region (3)		
	1952	1965	1974	1952	1965	1974	1952	1965	1974	1952	1965	1974
Labor												
1. Agricultural population (1,000)	4,257.0	5,739.0	5,802.0	579.0	783.0	754.0	412.0	566.0	588.0	816.0	1,036.0	1,099.0
2. Regional ag. population as % of total ag. popn.*	100.0	100.0	100.0	13.6	13.6	13.0	9.7	9.9	10.1	19.2	18.1	18.9
3. Man-days (millions)	250.3	302.1	288.4	39.1	40.4	35.0	25.7	25.4	20.6	42.9	54.8	47.7
4. % of total man-days*	100.0	100.0	100.0	15.6	13.4	12.1	10.3	8.4	7.1	17.1	18.1	16.5
Land												
1. Cultivated area (1,000 ha)*	876.0	890.0	911.0	140.0	135.0	122.0	93.0	84.0	82.0	124.0	125.0	128.0
2. % of cultivated area*	100.0	100.0	100.0	16.0	15.2	13.4	11.1	9.4	9.0	14.2	14.0	14.1
3. Crop area (1,000 ha)	1,495.0	1,676.0	1,636.0	258.0	252.0	226.0	151.0	149.0	133.0	275.0	319.0	292.0
4. % of crop area	100.0	100.0	100.0	17.3	15.0	13.8	10.1	8.9	8.1	18.4	19.0	17.8
5. Multiple cropping index	179.0	196.0	185.0	184.0	187.0	185.0	163.0	177.0	162.0	221.0	256.0	229.0
6. Average farm size (ha)	1.29	1.05	1.05	1.52	1.17	1.10	1.51	1.11	1.01	0.95	0.80	0.79
Other inputs												
1. Chemical fertilizer (1,000 mt)	361.7	637.2	1,000.3	66.2	72.3	139.0	34.6	43.8	91.0	92.9	184.6	218.1
2. Power tillers (numbers)	—	8,488	42,145	—	1,733	11,455	—	333	3,037	—	1,999	8,552
3. % of power tillers	—	100	100	—	20.4	27.2	—	3.9	7.2	—	23.5	20.3
4. Tractors (numbers)	—	—	952	—	—	39	—	—	34	—	—	56
5. % of tractors	—	—	100	—	—	4.1	—	—	3.6	—	—	5.9
6. Power threshers (number)	—	—	49,033	—	—	30,304	—	—	9,274	—	—	2,616
7. % of total	—	—	100	—	—	61.8	—	—	18.9	—	—	5.3
8. Water pumps (number)	—	33,271	119,060	—	2,359	3,955	—	5,319	12,016	—	5,319	23,592
9. % of total	—	100	100	—	7.1	3.3	—	16.0	10.1	—	16.0	19.8
10. Rice combines (number)	—	—	1,127	—	—	44	—	—	39	—	—	377
11. % of total	—	—	100	—	—	3.9	—	—	3.5	—	—	33.5

continued

Table 2.15. continued

	Banana-pineapple region			Rice-sugarcane region			Southern rice region			Eastern mixed region		
	1952	1965 (4)	1974	1952	1965 (5)	1974	1952	1965 (6)	1974	1952	1965 (7)	1974
Labor												
1. Agricultural population (1,000)	226.0	300.0	323.0	1,143.0	1,562.0	1,545.0	609.0	844.0	870.0	200.0	314.0	327.0
2. Regional ag. population as % of total ag. popn.*	5.3	5.2	5.6	26.9	27.2	26.6	14.3	14.7	15.0	4.7	5.5	5.6
3. Man-days (millions)	13.2	15.9	14.5	76.1	90.8	93.4	33.2	45.5	44.3	12.9	21.6	21.4
4. % of total man-days*	5.3	5.3	5.0	30.1	30.1	32.4	13.3	15.1	15.4	5.2	7.2	7.4
Land												
1. Cultivated area (1,000 ha)	42.0	51.0	64.0	257.0	256.0	257.0	129.0	134.0	146.0	50.0	72.0	86.0
2. % of cultivated area*	4.8	5.7	7.0	29.3	28.8	28.2	14.7	15.1	16.0	5.7	8.1	9.4
3. Crop area (1,000 ha)	67.0	77.0	81.0	429.0	471.0	486.0	234.0	286.0	292.0	82.0	123.0	126.0
4. % of crop area	4.5	4.6	5.0	28.7	28.1	29.7	15.6	17.1	17.8	5.4	7.3	7.7
5. Multiple cropping index	159.0	151.0	126.0	167.0	184.0	189.0	181.0	213.0	200.0	164.0	171.0	146.0
6. Average farm size (ha)	1.12	1.12	1.24	1.40	1.09	1.05	1.26	1.05	1.10	1.47	1.35	1.54
Other inputs												
1. Chemical fertilizer (1,000 mt)	12.0	23.4	61.4	81.9	191.9	274.0	60.2	94.8	161.0	13.9	26.3	55.8
2. Power tillers (numbers)	—	288.0	1,282.0	—	1,931.0	9,810	—	1,545.0	4,295.0	—	659.0	2,714.0
3. % of power tillers	—	3.4	3.0	—	22.8	23.3	—	18.2	10.2	—	7.8	6.4
4. Tractors (numbers)	—	—	14.0	—	—	602.0	—	—	120.0	—	—	87.0
5. % of tractors	—	—	1.5	—	—	63.2	—	—	12.6	—	—	9.1
6. Power threshers (number)	—	—	288.0	—	—	1,297.0	—	—	319.0	—	—	4,935.0
7. % of total	—	—	0.6	—	—	2.6	—	—	0.7	—	—	10.1
8. Water pumps (number)	—	392.0	1,492.0	—	9,102.0	51,954.0	—	10,297.0	24,859.0	—	483.0	1,192.0
9. % of total	—	1.2	1.3	—	27.4	43.6	—	30.8	20.9	—	1.5	1.0
10. Rice combines (number)	—	—	11.0	—	—	452.0	—	—	199.0	—	—	5.0
11. % of total	—	—	0.9	—	—	40.1	—	—	17.7	—	—	0.4

*The percentages do not add up to 100 because the island of Penghu and other major urban centers have been excluded in the regional data, but are included in the Taiwan total.

Source: Compiled by the author from various issues of Taiwan Agricultural Yearbook. Labor, line 3 on total man-days and Other Inputs, line 1 on chemical fertilizer were provided by the JCRR. The reliability of the regional estimates of chemical fertilizer consumption given in Other Inputs, line 1 is questionable because these regional fertilizer consumption data include only that handled by the Provincial Food Bureau. The data exclude fertilizer sold directly by the Taiwan Sugar Corporation and the Taiwan Fertilizer Corporation for which regional data are not available.

residence. In fact, this appeared to have taken two forms, part-time work, often of a seasonal nature outside of agriculture, and full-time jobs in industry and services in cities or rural centers, which required commuting to and from the farm.

The changing distribution of crop land followed a shift similar to the one that occurred for labor. Thus, the share of total crop area accounted for by the two northern regions dropped from 27.4 percent in 1952 to 21.9 percent in 1974. Again, the relative importance of the southern regions and the eastern mixed region in the total cropping pattern increased, as shown in line II.4 of Table 2.15. Furthermore, it is highly relevant that the average farm size declined significantly for Taiwan as a whole, mainly in the first subperiod 1952-65 from 1.29 hectare to 1.05—the same level as in 1974.

Perhaps the most significant interregional differences in changing farm size are the very sharp drops in the two northern regions from an average of 1.5 hectare in 1952 to just over one hectare in 1974, and the very low and declining average farm size in the central rice region, which amounted to .79 hectares in 1974. The only two regions that underwent slight increases in average farm sizes are the banana-pineapple region and the eastern mixed region. The southern regions appeared to maintain high MCIs and not to have been subjected to the national trend of increasing MCI over the first subperiod from 1952 to 1965, followed by a decline in the second subperiod.

Finally, an examination of the distribution of mechanical implements and chemical fertilizer reveals that the southern regions received a considerable share of chemical fertilizer and water pumps—inputs that tend to be highly complementary with labor. This helps to explain the increasing share of labor inputs accounted for by these regions. The bulk of the power threshers went to the northern regions, and heavy mechanical implements such as tractors and combines tended to be heavily concentrated in the southern regions—almost 76 percent of the tractors and 58 percent of the combines in 1974.

One important question that must be explored is the seasonal pattern of labor use in agriculture, both at the national and the regional levels. An intrinsic characteristic of agricultural production is that the fluctuations in seasonal labor demands parallel the production calendar. Clearly, a more intensive use of land reflected by the growing of more crops and a corresponding rise in the multiple cropping index may tend to even out seasonal fluctuations in labor requirements. Table 2.16 checks the seasonality of labor demand interregionally and over time in Taiwan. On the basis of survey data, providing monthly labor inputs per farm family, the seasonal variation in labor demand was measured by computing the coefficient of variation obtaining regionally for three years, 1960 (the first year for which this survey information is available), 1965, and 1974.

The most remarkable fact brought out by this table is the relatively balanced

Table 2.16. Coefficient of Variation in Monthly Agricultural Labor Use by Region, 1960, 1965, and 1974

Region	1960		1965		1974	
	Average monthly labor inputs in 1,000 of mandays	Coefficient of variation (percent)	Average monthly labor inputs in 1,000 of mandays	Coefficient of variation (percent)	Average monthly labor inputs in 1,000 of mandays	Coefficient of variation (percent)
Northern rice	3,330	16	3,387	25	2,913	30
Tea	1,969	39	2,121	17	1,720	24
Central rice	4,043	21	4,567	30	3,974	25
Banana-pineapple	1,184	22	1,322	11	1,204	19
Rice-sugarcane	6,880	14	7,567	13	7,784	15
Southern rice	3,775	13	3,792	18	3,690	15
Eastern mixed	1,336	25	1,800	15	1,781	19
Taiwan total	22,616	13	25,174	14	24,034	15

Source: Computed by the author on the basis of monthly labor inputs per farm family (and per hectare) survey data from various issues of *Report of Farm Record-Keeping in Taiwan*.

pattern of labor use in agriculture prevailing in Taiwan over this whole period, as judged by very low levels of the coefficient of variation in these three years—respectively, 13, 14, and 15 percent (see the last line of Table 2.16). In other words, as early as 1960, the previous substantial seasonal underemployment in agriculture had been largely alleviated. This is reflected, for instance, by the fact that the average number of man-days per agricultural worker, which had been 111 in 1946, reached 184 in 1960, and increased only fairly marginally thereafter to a level of about 195 in the mid-1970s (see column 14 in Table 2.7).

Even though the national demand for labor is spread relatively evenly throughout the year, interregional differences in seasonal labor use do exist, as appears clearly from Table 2.16. The two southern regions appear to display a more even seasonal distribution of labor than the other regions, particularly the northern regions.

A final phenomenon that deserves to be explored at this stage is the regional migration pattern that occurred in these two subperiods. Some fairly realistic assumptions can be made to estimate the rates at which agricultural population moved out of agriculture in the seven regions. The procedure used to compute these migration rates was to assume that in each of the two subperiods (1952–65 and 1965–74) the regional agricultural populations would have grown at a rate equal to the observed natural increase in rural population if migration had not taken place. Estimates are obtained of hypothetical regional

Table 2.17. Apparent Migration Rates of Agricultural Population

Region	Annual rate 1952–65	Annual rate 1965–74
Northern rice	.9	2.7
Tea	.8	1.9
Central rice	1.4	1.6
Banana-pineapple	1.1	1.4
Rice-sugarcane	.9	2.4
Southern rice	.8	2.0
Eastern mixed	−.2	1.9
Taiwan	.9	2.1

Source: It was assumed that in the absence of net migration the regional agricultural populations would have grown at the same rate as the observed total increase in rural population in the two subperiods, that is, at 1.53 percent per year in 1952–74 and at 1.23 percent in 1965–74. The differences among the hypothetical regional agricultural populations were obtained by applying these growth rates to the base populations in, respectively, 1952 and 1965, and the actual populations in 1965 and 1974 yield estimates of apparent regional agricultural migration for these two years. These figures are then expressed in annual growth rates for the two subperiods. Actual regional agricultural populations for 1952, 1965, and 1974 come from Table 2.15.

populations for both final years of these two periods, 1965 and 1974, from which the actual regional populations are subtracted to obtain the apparent regional out-migration for the two periods.

Table 2.17 presents these apparent regional migration rates. These rates are net migration rates. As such, they are likely to reflect the net geographical changes because members of family households who commute to work outside of agriculture either on a full-time or part-time basis would continue to be counted as members of the regional agricultural population.

Two relevant trends can be deduced from Table 2.17: (1) the sharp acceleration in out-migration in the second subperiod as compared to the first, and (2) the fact that the highest regional migration rates occurred in the northern rice region and the two southern regions, amounting to, respectively, 2.7, 2.4, and 2.0 percent annually between 1965 and 1974, which in all likelihood reflects the pull of the urban centers in the north (Taipei) and in the south (Kaohsiung and Tainan). The migration pattern will be discussed in detail in the next section.

Phases of Agricultural Development and Contributing Factors and Policies

Before analyzing in detail the three agricultural development phases since World War II, the work of other authors will be reviewed. In general, there is substantial agreement as to turning points, if not actual phases.

T. H. Shen,[26] writing in 1971, places the turning point in Taiwan's agricultural development around 1965. He distinguishes two phases—from 1952 to 1964 and from 1965 to 1968—which was presumably the last year for which data were available. The basic argument is that the factors accounting for the increase in agricultural output were mostly the expansion of the crop area and labor inputs in the first phase. In contrast, intermediate and cash inputs (such as chemical fertilizer and feedstuff) and mechanical implements were instrumental in pushing production upward in the second phase.[27] From a technological standpoint, the first phase was associated with the use of biological innovations (such as improved varieties), chemical fertilizer, and a substantially more intensive utilization of land and labor through the multiple cropping system. Farm mechanization characterized the second phase.

Yu-kang Mao,[28] in a more recent analysis, distinguishes four stages: (1) recovery and rehabilitation, 1946–51; (2) further development after recovery,

26. T. H. Shen, *Agricultural Development on Taiwan since World War II* (Taipei, 1972). See in particular chap. 22, ''Turning Point in Taiwan's Agricultural Development Policy.''

27. It will be seen subsequently that the key role played by intermediate inputs in recent years is reflected by the rising share of working capital (that is, intermediate inputs) in the annual costs of total inputs.

28. Yu-kang Mao, ''Effects of Changes in Agricultural Structure on Farm Management in Taiwan'' (mimeo, JCRR, October 17, 1975).

1951-60; (3) sustained growth, 1960-68; and (4) stagnation under drastic changes in structure after 1968. The binding nature of the labor and land constraints are identified as causing the stagnation stage after 1968.

A final example of an attempt at distinguishing developmental phases is that of John C. H. Fei, Gustav Ranis, and Shirley W. Y. Kuo.[29] These authors, in a general treatment of Taiwan's development process, distinguished between a period of primary import substitution from 1953 to 1961 and one of export substitution from 1961 to 1972. In addition, they identified a phase of growth with distribution extending from 1953 to 1968, which they considered to be largely influenced by changes in agriculture at least until 1964.

Recovery, 1946–1953

The exact determination of when a subperiod begins or ends is bound to be somewhat arbitrary. The major reason for ending this period in 1953 is that it marks the completion of the institutional changes connected with the land reform process, that is, the enactment of the Land-to-the-Tiller Program.[30]

This phase is marked by two essential developments: (1) the recovery of the agricultural sector from the disruption of the war which restored the level of total agricultural production to its prewar level by the early 1950s; and (2) the set of land reform measures which were to have a crucial effect on the future agricultural development of Taiwan. This phase can be considered as establishing initial conditions conducive to an equitable growth path in Taiwan's agriculture. The first step was to regain full use of agriculture's capacity to produce; the second, to undertake drastic changes in the distribution of land and in the resulting factorial and household income distributions.

The extremely high rate of growth of agricultural output over this period of over 10 percent per year reflects the fact that resources were not used to anywhere their fullest capacity. Evidence that both land and labor were used at low levels of intensity is clearly provided by the considerable jumps in, respectively, the multiple crop index from 117 in 1946 to 170 in 1953 and the average number of man-days per agricultural worker from 111 to 168 over the same period (see Table 2.7). Likewise, the growth of current inputs by value was very large, amounting to an annual rate of about 27 percent over this period (see Table 2.8). The level of total agricultural production in 1946 was only slightly over half (52 percent) of its prewar peak in 1939, the 1939 peak was not reached again until 1952.[31]

Three interrelated policy elements played a crucial role in this phase: (1) the

29. John C. H. Fei, Gustav Ranis, and Shirley W. Y. Kuo, "Equity with Growth: The Taiwan Case" (mimeo, prepared under the auspices of the World Bank, 1976), see in particular chap. 2.

30. Actual land redistribution under this program was not completed until 1958.

31. See Lee and Chen, who measure total agricultural production at 1935–37 constant farm prices (pp. 62–63).

establishment of the Chinese-American Joint Commission on Rural Reconstruction (JCRR) in 1948, which became the major institution—comparable to a ministry of agriculture—in planning and helping to carry out Taiwan's agricultural development; (2) U.S. foreign aid, initiated in 1951, which was largely directed toward agriculture at the outset and provided the major resources to the JCRR; and (3) the set of land reform measures. Clearly, this last element had, by far, the greatest impact on the growth and distribution of output. Yet the close complementarity among these three elements made the land reform as successful as it was.

The JCRR was set up as bilateral agency initially on the mainland, before the move to Taiwan. Five principal objectives formulated in its early days have guided its work. They are:

i) to improve the living conditions of the rural people; ii) to increase the production of food and other important crops; iii) to develop the potential power of the rural people to reconstruct their own communities and society at large; iv) to help build up and strengthen related services of government agencies at all levels that are established to carry out measures pertaining to rural reconstruction; and v) to offer liberals [sic], educated youth and other constructive elements opportunities to participate in a program of service.[32]

The JCRR performed a number of functions in a comprehensive and integrated fashion as a de facto superministry of agriculture, such as the formulation of the various agricultural development plans for Taiwan; the actual implementation of a large number of activities and projects dealing with integrated rural development; and acting as the major channel or conduit for U.S. foreign assistance in agriculture.

U.S. foreign aid was first granted to Taiwan in 1951, when the latter found itself in a critical financial and economic position. A total of $267 million was allocated to Taiwan in the three fiscal years 1951–53—about half of which was earmarked for agriculture. The bulk of the aid took the form of commodity-import programs that generated local currency counterpart funds which, in turn, were largely earmarked for agricultural activities to be undertaken by the JCRR.[33] In addition to the actual resources provided in 1951–53, it is probable that the technical assistance that accompanied the aid was another important factor in helping to design and implement the land reform process.

The land reform process itself was undertaken in three steps: (1) the rent reduction program; (2) the sale of public land to cultivators and tenants; and

32. JCRR, *JCRR, Its Organization, Policies and Objectives, and Contributions to the Agricultural Development of Taiwan* (Taipei, 1973), p. 3.

33. U.S. foreign aid to Taiwan spanned the period from 1951 to 1965. Since over four-fifths of the total aid resources were extended in phase from 1954 to 1967, an attempt at evaluating its impact on Taiwan's agricultural development is undertaken in the next section.

Table 2.18. The Extent of Taiwan's Land Reform

	Redistribution of land			
	Public land sale 1948–58	Land-to-the Tiller Program 1953	Total redistri- bution	Rent control 1952
Area affected (chia)*				
Total	71,663	143,568	215,231	256,948
Paddy land	34,089	121,535	155,624	220,029
Dry land	37,524	22,033	59,557	35,305
Other†	50	—	50	1,614
Number of farm households affected	139,688	194,823	334,511	302,277
Number of landlords affected	—	106,049	106,049	—
Cultivated area affected as a percent of total cultivated area‡	8.1	16.4	24.6	29.2
Farm households affected as a percent of total farm households§	20.0	27.9	47.9	43.3

*1 chia = 0.9699 hectare.
†Includes farmhouse sites, ditches, ponds, and the like.
‡Total cultivated area used in this calculation is the average of 1951–55.
§Total number of farm households used in this calculation is the average of 1951–55.
Sources: Calculated by Samuel P. S. Ho, *Economic Development of Taiwan, 1860–1970* (New Haven, 1977), p. 264, from Hui-Sun Tang, *Land Reform in Free China* (Taipei, 1954), pp. 289, 292, and 293; and Cheng Chen, *Land Reform in Taiwan* (Taipei, 1961), p. 311.

(3) the Land-to-the Tiller Program, which limited land ownership of current landlords.[34]

The rent reduction program was initiated in 1949 and limited farm rents to a maximum of 37.5 percent of the annual yield of the major crop. This new rent level was substantially lower than the average farmland rental, which had amounted historically to approximately 50 percent in the more fertile areas.[35] The immediate effects of the rent reduction program were to improve substantially the lot of the tenants, while reducing land values and the asset position of the landlords. As Table 2.18 indicates, the coverage of this program was very broad, affecting by 1952 over 43 percent of the total number of farm households and over 29 percent of the total cultivated area.

The second stage of the reform was the sale of public land that had been acquired after World War II from Japanese nationals. The amount of public land that could be purchased by one farm family was limited to between .5 and 2 chia of paddy land and between 1 and 4 chia of dry land, depending on its

34. Among good accounts of the land reform process in Taiwan are: Hui-Sun Tang, *Land Reform in Free China* (Taipei, 1954); Anthony Y. C. Koo, "Agrarian Reform, Production and Employment in Taiwan," in International Labour Office, *Agrarian Reform and Employment* (Geneva, 1971); and Cheng Chen, *Land Reform in Taiwan* (Taipei, 1961).

35. Koo, p. 166.

quality.[36] Table 2.18 shows that 20 percent of the farm families purchased public land under this program, embracing approximately 8 percent of the total cultivated area.

The last step of the land reform process consisted of the Land-to-the-Tiller Program, promulgated in 1953, which limited land ownership by current landlords to a maximum of 3 chia (2.9 hectares); any land in excess was confiscated by the government and redistributed. This program affected approximately 28 percent of the farm families and over 16 percent of the land area (see Table 2.18). Thus, under these last two steps about 210,000 hectares of land were redistributed, or approximately one-fourth of the total cultivated area in 1951–55.[37] In addition, approximately half (48 percent) of the farm households were affected by land redistribution (see Table 2.18). Clearly, one of the major effects of land reform was to reduce drastically the proportion of tenants and, correspondingly, to convert Taiwan's land-tenancy system into one relying preponderantly on owner-cultivators.[38]

It is not possible to make an exact comparison of the distribution of land by owner-families and size of holding just before and after the reform because the two land-ownership surveys preceding World War II, those made in 1932 and 1939, give the number of owner-families by farm size but not the corresponding total land area in each holding size.

This information is available only in the 1920 survey, which has a number of defects, including an underestimation of the concentration of land ownership. Keeping in mind these limitations, it is nevertheless instructive to compare the 1952 survey with that of 1920, which is probably fairly representative of the prewar land distribution. Thus it appears that in 1920, 572 families (representing .14 percent of all owner families) with holdings above 50 chia owned approximately 120,000 chia (representing 16.6 percent of total cultivated land). In contrast, in 1952, 262 families (representing only .04 percent of farm families) with holdings above 50 chia owned jointly only about 4 percent of the total cultivated land.

Another comparison of these two distributions is provided by taking the shares of total families and cultivated land represented by families owning at least 20 chia in the two benchmark years. Thus in 1920, 25.6 percent of the cultivated land was held by one-third of 1 percent of the owner-families; in

36. One chia is equal to .9699 hectare.

37. As Table 2.18 reveals, two-thirds of the redistributed land came from Taiwanese ownership and one-third from Japanese ownership (expropriated by the government after the war and referred to as public land).

38. The share of tenant farm households to total farm households dropped from 41 percent in 1947 to 21 percent in 1953; that of owner-cultivator households grew from 32 percent to 55 percent over the same period.

1952, 8.7 percent of the land was in the hands of .12 percent of the families.[39] Clearly, the upper tail of the land distribution was practically eliminated following land reform. Together with a widening in the distribution of land ownership, a reduction in the average size of holdings occurred as a result of the land reform program. In contrast with the structure of land ownership in the majority of the developing countries, Taiwan's structure had become unimodal.[40]

Under the Land-to-the-Tiller Act, landlords were compensated for their confiscated land by being offered two types of commodity bonds tied to the purchasing power of rice and sweet potatoes, respectively. These bonds yielded a 4 percent annual interest rate and were to be amortized over a ten-year period. In addition, each landlord received shares of stock in four government enterprises.

Even though it is difficult to show unambiguously that land reform had a significant effect on static efficiency, its effect on income distribution was substantial.[41] Samuel P. S. Ho[42] provides an excellent analysis of the effect of land reform on equity. Its main impact was to reduce substantially the size of the wealth of landlords and, therefore, their future income streams. First, the negative wealth impact resulted from the fact that landlords whose excess land was confiscated under the Tiller Act were compensated only on the basis of 2.5 times the annual yield of the major crop, when in fact it had been esti-

39. See Table A.36 in Ho, *Economic Development*, p. 549. These figures are, at most, suggestive since they contain a number of defects. In particular, the data for 1952 do not include public land confiscated from the Japanese at the end of World War II. Given the purpose of this comparison, which is to obtain some information of the land distribution before and after land reform, the exclusion of public land does not matter because the land was parceled out and redistributed under the public sale program. In addition, the 1920 data underestimate the concentration of land ownership, and the land reform was not completed until the mid-1950s. Hence, the land reform program must have had an even more pronounced effect than is described here. More specifically, it must have eliminated the tail of the distribution consisting of farm holdings above twenty to thirty chia.

40. See Bruce F. Johnston and Peter Kilby, *Agriculture and Structural Transformation, Economic Strategies in Late-Developing Countries* (New York, 1975). A unimodal structure and agricultural development strategy relies on small-scale farms using labor-intensive technologies. Most developing countries display a bimodal agricultural structure consisting of a modern subsector embracing large holdings and using relatively capital-intensive techniques, side by side with a traditional subsector relying on small farms using labor-intensive technologies.

41. With regard to the effects of land redistribution on static economic efficiency, it could be argued that land ownership in contrast with tenancy provides a strong motivation to apply family labor more intensively per unit of land and to invest more in accretionary activities that improve the quality of the land (such as land leveling, small irrigation canals, and better rotational practices). The new owners might have a greater incentive to adopt a more appropriate agricultural technology. The fact that no study appears to have been made confirming the positive effects of land reform on static efficiency in Taiwan means that one can only speculate that there were positive effects.

42. Ho, *Economic Development*.

mated that in the period 1914–43 the average market value of paddy fields was about 4 to 6 times the annual yield of the main crop, namely, rice. Hence, the compensation paid to the landlords fell considerably short of the market value of the appropriated land. On the assumption that true land value was equal to 5 times the annual yield of farm land, Ho calculated that the Tiller Act had a net wealth redistribution effect, measured at 1952 prices, of N.T.$ 2.2 billion, or approximately 13 percent of Taiwan's GDP in 1952.

Second, the government commodity bonds that were given to landlords as a compensation for the confiscated land carried an interest rate of only 4 percent compared to a real market rate ranging between 30 and 50 percent per annum prevailing at that time, thereby further affecting negatively the wealth and income position of landlords before reform. The fact that a large number of landlords unloaded these bonds at a market value substantially lower than the nominal value meant a further redistributive effect.[43]

It is interesting to estimate not only the negative redistributive effects of the land reform on the landlords, but also the positive effects on the tenants who became owner-cultivators as a consequence. In a very careful computation of the effect of land reform on the real income of an average tenant, comparing what would have happened with and without land reform and rent reduction, Ho shows that in the former case, the income of the average tenant would have increased by 107 percent between 1948 and 1959 (after which he would have become an owner-cultivator) compared to only 16 percent had he remained a tenant.[44]

A final phenomenon is that, notwithstanding the fact that this was a recovery period, there was a substantial net capital outflow from agriculture to nonagriculture amounting to about 22 percent of the total value of agricultural production.[45] It would thus appear that even in the recovery period (at least toward the end of it) the agricultural sector performed the crucial function of supplying the rest of the economy with capital resources.

Growth with Equity, 1954–1967

At the outset of this period, the initial conditions were right for a sustained growth in agricultural output and a relatively equal distribution of value added generated in that sector. The extremely high growth rate of output achieved in the previous period could not be maintained because agriculture was now working closer to full capacity. One remaining slack was seasonal underem-

43. Ibid., p. 268.
44. Ibid., pp. 271–74.
45. T. H. Lee, "Strategies for Transferring Agricultural Surplus under Different Agricultural Situations in Taiwan" (JCRR, mimeo, July 1971). This percentage refers to the period 1950–55, which does not correspond exactly to our first phase (1946–53).

ployment of labor, which disappeared, to a large extent, over the course of this phase.

Agricultural output grew at an annual rate of about 4.4 percent during this period—with fruits (14.2 percent) and livestock and vegetables (6.3 and 5.9 percent, respectively) acting as the most dynamic commodity groups (see Table 2.5).

The output growth was made possible mainly through a more intensive use of labor, a somewhat more intensive use of land, a major increase in the use of current inputs, and the beginning of mechanization toward the end of this phase. Thus, total labor input, measured in terms of millions of man-days, increased by 24 percent from 1954 to 1967. This was the combined result of a relatively slight rise in the total number of workers from 1,493 thousand in 1954 to 1,562 thousand in 1967 and a somewhat more pronounced increase in the number of average man-days per worker from 165 to 194 over this period (see Table 2.7).[46]

There was a slight increase in the intensity of land cultivation, as reflected by the multiple crop index moving from 172 to 188 during this phase. The moderate rise in the MCI was almost totally caused by a small increase in the crop area although cultivated area remained essentially fixed. Finally, the signal importance of current inputs, which grew by more than 7 percent a year in value terms during this period, and the beginning of mechanization appear clearly from Table 2.8.

The decomposition procedure explained in the section on changes in the use of inputs is useful in analyzing the effects of different inputs. Thus, Tables 2.9 and 2.10 show that the major factor that contributed to the substantial increase in output per worker during this phase was the continued sharp rise in the yield of land (production per hectare of crop area),[47] which was made possible through improved varieties and higher levels of application of intermediate inputs. The share of current inputs in the total cost of agricultural production was estimated to have risen from 15.4 percent in 1946–50 to 23 percent in 1961–65.[48] The same tables indicate that the more intensive use of land and labor—reflected by the multiple crop index and the average number of man-days per worker—also contributed, although slightly, to the higher labor productivity in agriculture.

From a technological standpoint, perhaps the most interesting changes are the substitution of chemical fertilizer for farm (organic) fertilizer, the substitu-

46. The corresponding growth rates of total mandays, number of workers, and mandays per worker were, respectively, 1.7, 0.4, and 1.3 percent during this phase (see Table 2.8).

47. Thus, for instance, the average yield of rice rose substantially during this phase from 2,271 kgs. per hectare in 1959 to 3,092 kgs. per hectare in 1967.

48. See Lee and Chen, p. 75.

tion of human labor for animal labor, and the beginning of mechanization, particularly through the adoption of power tillers.

During this growth phase, the transformation away from a system based mainly on tenants to one relying on owner-cultivators was completed. Thus, the proportion of farm families consisting of tenants dropped from an already low 21 percent in 1953 (compared to 41 percent in 1947) to 12 percent in 1967, and the share of owner-cultivator households continued to grow from 55 percent to 68 percent over the same time span.[49] Clearly, during this phase, Taiwan's agriculture was in the hands of a large number of very small owners, the average size of a family farm having dropped from 1.29 hectare to 1.05 hectare.

The momentum of industrial development, particularly with the outset of the export-substitution phase at the beginning of the 1960s, provided expanding working opportunities outside of agriculture. As a consequence, an increasing number of members of the agricultural population became commuters, seasonal workers, and long-term employees.[50]

The rising importance of off-farm activities is reflected in different ways. One is the substantial rise in the proportion of part-time farms from 60 percent in 1956 (and only 52 percent in 1961) to 68 percent in 1966 and the corresponding reduction in the proportion of full-time farms.[51] Furthermore, the share of part-time farms to total farms is negatively correlated with the average farm size; for example, 84 percent of the farms below half a chia were part-time farms, but only 51 percent of those above 2 chia were part-time. A second example of off-farm activity was the sharp upward trend in the proportion of nonfarm receipts in total farm family receipts from about 13 percent in 1952 to approximately 25 percent in both 1962 and 1967.[52]

The permanent migration rate out of the agricultural population in all farm activities was relatively low during this period, it was estimated at .9 of 1 percent between 1952 and 1965 (see Table 2.17). Thus the great bulk of the farm family household members who engaged in off-farm activities appears to have been commuters and seasonal workers, who maintained their residence on the farm. This is confirmed by a study based on a sample survey which

49. The residual share, that of part owners, fell from 24 percent in 1953 to 20 percent in 1967.

50. A long-term employee means, in this connection, a person who leaves his farm home and works permanently in the cities or rural centers, but who maintains close connections with his farm home, for instance, through remittance of earnings.

51. See Terry Y. J. Yu, "Economic Analysis of Full-time and Part-time Farms in Taiwan" (based on farm income survey 1968, mimeographed by the Research Institute of Agricultural Economics, Taiwan Provincial Chung Shing University, Taichung, Taiwan, 1969). A full-time farm is defined as a farm yielding the totality of the income accruing to the corresponding farm household. All farms that yield less than the total income of the farm household are considered part-time farms.

52. See JCRR, *Taiwan Farm Income Survey of 1967: With a Brief Comparison with 1952, 1957 and 1962* JCRR Economic Digest Series, no. 20 (Taipei, January 1970), p. 28.

found out that in 1963, 57 percent of those engaged in off-farm activities were seasonal workers, 26 percent commuters, and the remaining 17 percent long-term employees residing away.[53] In addition to releasing labor, agriculture contributed to the economy by continuing the net capital outflow which amounted to roughly 15 percent of total agricultural production throughout this period.[54]

The discussion of changes within agriculture during the development process revealed that some important shifts in the commodity composition and in the regional distribution of agricultural output took place during this phase. Thus the shares of common crops and special crops fell substantially from, respectively, 62 and 19 percent in 1953 to 44.7 and 10.5 percent in 1968 (the share of rice, which is included under common crops, dropped from 52.8 to 34.7 percent over the same period). In contrast, the shares of fruits, vegetables, and livestock increased markedly—the latter from almost 14 to 27.6 percent (see Table 2.6). Clearly, this period is characterized by a trend toward product diversification—particularly toward higher-value crops requiring more labor per unit of output. One measure of product diversification is the so-called diversity index, which rose from 3.18 in 1953 to about 6 in 1967–68.[55]

A number of policy measures had an important impact on the agricultural growth process during this stage. The most important of these, which are discussed below, appear to have been (1) the set of rice price policies and particularly the rice-fertilizer barter program; (2) the continued work of the JCRR in establishing a truly integrated rural development program based on farmers' associations and providing the whole gamut of services needed by farmers; (3) the various agricultural development plans which were largely formulated by and based on the programs of the JCRR, fitted within a national economic context; (4) the level and form of U.S. foreign aid which continued to benefit agriculture; and (5) a very rapid rate of industrial development which was regionally decentralized.

Agricultural pricing policies were perhaps the most important factor contributing to product diversification—mainly by taxing rice directly or indirectly as compared to other commodities—and to the transfer of capital from the agricultural sector to the rest of the economy. The government control of rice was a large source of revenues for the public sector through such mechanisms as land taxes payable in rice, compulsory purchases, the rice-

53. Y. C. Tsui and T. L. Lin, *A Study on Rural Labor Mobility in Relation to Industrialization and Urbanization in Taiwan*, JCRR Economic Digest Series, no. 16 (Taipei, 1964).

54. See Lee, "Strategies," p. 27.

55. See Shirley W. Y. Kuo, "Effects of Land Reform, Agricultural Pricing Policy and Economic Growth on Multiple Crop Diversification in Taiwan," *Philippines Economic Journal* 14, nos. 1 and 2 (1975), 150. The diversity index is defined as the reciprocal of the sum of the squares of the ratio of the value of each product to the value of total product.

fertilizer barter system, and land taxes paid in kind. Since all rice collections were obtained at government purchasing prices, which were considerably lower than market prices, the government extracted through these various mechanisms an amount of taxes equivalent to the difference in these two prices multiplied by the total amount of rice purchased. Shirley W. Y. Kuo coined the term "hidden rice taxes" to embrace this form of taxation.[56]

The most important of these mechanisms was the rice-fertilizer barter program. Since chemical fertilizer was a public monopoly, the government established fixed barter ratios between rice and different types of chemical fertilizers. Throughout this phase, these barter ratios were set at levels that made chemical fertilizers quite expensive in terms of rice. Gradually, the ratios became more favorable to rice before they were abolished in 1973.[57]

The magnitude of this hidden rice tax was very large as judged by the fact that it exceeded the total income tax for the whole economy throughout much of this phase (for example, it was more than 60 percent higher than the income tax in 1955, about equal to it in 1960, and only slightly lower in 1965). By far the most important source of total government rice collection was the rice-fertilizer barter program, which accounted for between 60 and 70 percent of total collection throughout this phase; land tax payment in kind and compulsory rice purchasing accounted for the bulk of the remainder.[58] Another way of assessing the extent of government intervention in the rice market is that the government collected as much as 73 percent of off-farm rice marketing in 1954, which was gradually reduced to about 50 percent in 1966–68.[59]

In addition to collecting taxes indirectly, another subsidiary objective of the government rice program was price stabilization. A low and stable price for rice was considered essential to an anti-inflationary policy. Hence, the government engaged widely in stabilization activities. The Provincial Food Bureau, the agency responsible for administering the rice program, disposed of the rice in a variety of ways, such as rations to armed forces and military dependents, which accounted for approximately 25 percent of total rice disposal in 1966–68, rations to government employees and teachers, accounting

56. Ibid., pp. 159–64.
57. Thus, for example, the ratio for ammonium sulfate was dropped from 1 kg. of paddy to be exchanged for 1 kg. of this type of fertilizer to .90 in 1960–61 and again marginally to .86 in 1965–66. Likewise, the barter rate for calcium ammonitrate fell from 1 in 1955 to .9 in 1956 and .8 in 1960–61; that of urea dropped from 2 to 1.8 in 1960–61 and that of ammonium phosphate from 1.3 to 1.2 in 1960. See H.-Y. Chen, Wen-fu Hsu, and Yu-kang Mao, "Rice Policies of Taiwan" (Paper presented at the Workshop on Political Economy of Rice sponsored by Food Research Institute, Stanford University, Los Banos, Philippines, July 1974), see Annex, Table 8.
58. Ibid., see Annex Table 12.
59. Ibid., see Table 3, p. 17.

for about 17 percent, exports, about 20 percent, and market stabilization sales, about 25 percent.[60]

In an excellent study relying on regression analysis, Shirley W. Y. Kuo concluded that the hidden rice tax was the most significant factor explaining the drop in the share of rice production in 1952–60 and the consequent product diversification trend. The low de facto government rice price was a deterrent to production. In contrast, from 1961 to 1971, the decline in relative rice consumption contributed most to the continued reduction in the share of rice production.[61] The product diversification trend was further enhanced by favorable price policies for major vegetables and fruits; the government offered guaranteed prices for these crops in order to encourage production.[62] Hog production was also encouraged. Besides its effects on diversification, the hidden rice tax was a major mechanism of transferring capital from agriculture to the rest of the economy.

The JCRR was involved in an integral way in the process of agricultural planning in Taiwan as well as in the implementation of a number of agricultural activities. From the outset, the JCRR was given the responsibility for planning agricultural development jointly with the Ministry of Economic Affairs and the Economic Planning Council. Four Four-Year Plans were formulated during this period, for 1953–56, 1957–60, 1961–64, and 1965–68. The planning process was clearly of an indicative type with major and subsidiary objectives being specified to be achieved through a combination of broad policy instruments and specific activities and organizational changes.

Perhaps the most noteworthy feature of agricultural planning in Taiwan has been the attempt at local participation. Starting with the first Plan, government agencies were required to specify goals on a county-by-county basis in consultation with local people and taking local conditions into account.[63] Continuing contacts were maintained between the Economic Stabilization Board (the planning agency) and local leaders so that the annual crop production plans could be worked out jointly between the center and the periphery. The success of agricultural development in Taiwan—if not of agricultural planning—is evidenced by the fact that the actual growth rates of production in agriculture achieved during the first two Plans were substantially higher than those planned. Incidentally, this phenomenon is in contrast with actual GNP growth rates, which corresponded fairly closely to the targeted ones.

60. Ibid., see Annex Table 13. These last two shares fluctuated widely from year to year depending on circumstances.

61. Kuo, pp. 162-64.

62. The phenomenal growth of mushrooms and asparagus during this phase contributed significantly to product diversification.

63. See T. H. Shen, ''The Mechanism for Agricultural Planning,'' in Shen, ed., *Agriculture's Place,* p. 24.

The history of the JCRR has been well recorded and analyzed.[64] The JCRR was actively engaged in a fully integrated program of rural development long before this concept became popular. Its activities included crop and livestock improvement, water resource development, soil conservation, agricultural organization and extension, agricultural financing, rural health improvement, and agricultural research. The JCRR was particularly successful in helping to organize and direct the activities of the farmers' associations. The extent of the growth of these associations is apparent in the fact that the amount of farmers' savings deposited in the credit section of the associations increased from about N.T.$100 million in 1953 to $2.7 billion by the end of 1965.[65]

Table 2.19 shows the cumulative allocation of JCRR funds by major categories as of the end of November 1965. By far the most important funding activity was water use and control, which accounted for about 31 percent of the total amount spent in N.T. dollars. Other important activities were crop production and economic research and agricultural credit, which accounted for, respectively, 10.3 and 9.1 percent of total local currency expenditures. It will be seen subsequently that the great bulk of the JCRR funds—the breakdown of which is given in Table 2.19—came from U.S. foreign aid sources.

This growth phase was the heyday of U.S. foreign aid. Between 1954 and the termination of aid in 1965, total U.S. foreign aid amounted to approximately $1.2 billion (over its whole lifetime, from 1951 to 1965, total U.S. aid obligations amounted to $1.465 billion). It is difficult to determine the exact share of total aid to agriculture because of the multisectoral nature of a number of infrastructure projects and the fact that many of the industry projects were connected with producing inputs for agriculture, such as fertilizer. A rough approximation would be that as much as one-third of the total aid went into agriculture.

As Neil H. Jacoby pointed out, "Clearly, the developmental strategy followed by the Chinese government and AID in Taiwan, was to utilize government aid funds primarily to build an infrastructure and to foster agriculture and human resources, leaving the bulk of industrial development to private enterprise."[66] He also points out the unique character of the JCRR derived from its dual roles as the de facto department of agriculture of the Taiwanese government and the agricultural division of the U.S. AID mission.[67]

64. An excellent source is T. H. Shen, *The Sino-American Joint Commission on Rural Reconstruction: Twenty Years of Cooperation for Agricultural Development* (Ithaca, N.Y., 1970).

65. Wen-fu Hsu, "The Role of Agricultural Organizations in Agricultural Development in Taiwan," in JCRR and Academia Sinica, *Conference on Economic Development in Taiwan* (Taipei, 1967), p. 118.

66. Neil H. Jacoby, *U.S. Aid to Taiwan: A Study of Foreign Aid, Self-help and Development* (New York, 1966), p. 51.

67. Ibid., p. 62.

Table 2.19. Allocation of JCRR Funds to Major Categories (as of November 30, 1965)

Activity	Amount		Percentage	
	1,000 N.T.$	1,000 U.S.$	N.T.$	U.S.$
Crop production	416,696	1,024.4	10.29	14.41
Livestock production	293,516	348.9	7.25	4.91
Water use and control	1,249,714	2,552.4	30.86	35.92
Forestry and soil conservation	216,521	475.9	5.34	6.70
Rural organization and agricultural extension	297,093	88.0	7.33	1.24
Economic research and agricultural credit	369,335	11.4	9.12	0.16
Fisheries	310,791	30.5	7.67	0.43
Land reform	25,812	—	0.64	—
Rural health	143,013	317.5	3.53	4.47
Agricultural research and education	90,643	731.2	2.24	10.29
Rural electrification and communication	53,763	—	1.33	—
Government budget support to local agricultural programs	242,946	1,027.0	6.00	14.45
Miscellaneous projects	153,023	194.5	3.78	2.73
Administration	187,129	304.7	4.62	4.29
Total	4,049,995	7,106.4	100.00	100.00

Source: JCRR, *Sixteenth General Report* (Taipei, 1966), pp. 2, 130.

The crucial role of foreign assistance in agriculture can be gathered from the fact that U.S. capital assistance to that sector amounted to $213 million between 1951 and 1965, which was 22.5 percent of the U.S. total capital assistance to Taiwan. More significantly, however, it represented nearly 59 percent of net domestic capital formation in agriculture.[68] The major form which foreign assistance to agriculture took was through local currency counterpart funds generated through aid-financed imports. The bulk of these funds went through the JCRR, which used them to undertake nearly six thousand projects during the period under consideration. In fact, of the total allocation of JCRR funds given in Table 2.19, it appears that 91 percent of the local currency counterpart funds given in column 1 of that table and amounting to N.T.$4,050 million, came from U.S. aid, while the totality of the dollar aid shown in the second column of Table 2.19 and amounting to U.S. $7.1 million came from U.S. aid.[69]

In retrospect, there can be no doubt that the resource transfer into agriculture generated by U.S. foreign aid played a key role in the agricultural development of Taiwan—as judged, for instance, by the fact that it generated about 59 percent of net domestic capital formation in agriculture. Perhaps even more important than the resource transfer per se is the enlightened form

68. Ibid., p. 180.
69. This presumption is based on a comparison of Table 2.19 and ibid., Table 23.2 on p. 182. As was seen previously in the analysis of Table 2.19, the bulk of U.S. aid to agriculture—which is practically equivalent to the JCRR's expenditures on agriculture—went for water use and control and crop production.

agricultural aid took because it was linked to a semi-independent planning and implementing agency, the JCRR.

A final question that has to be raised is whether income distribution became more equal within agriculture during this phase. There is some evidence based on fairly detailed household surveys of farm families between 1952 and 1967 that this was indeed the case. Fel, Ranis, and Kuo show that the Gini coefficient of farm family incomes stratified by farm size (that is, where farm size is used as a proxy for farm income) shows a substantial drop from .286 in 1952 to .234 in 1957 and to .179 in 1967.[70] The main reason for the greater equality in the overall Gini coefficient of income of farm families over this phase appears to be a direct result of the sharply growing share of wage income from off-farm activities out of total farm family income, which rose from 6 percent in 1952 to 25 percent in 1967. This follows from the fact that this type of income was much more equally distributed than farm income from agricultural activities (from both land and labor) and from property income from rural industry and services.

In addition, the proportion of farm family income derived from nonagricultural sources moved negatively with the size of the farm. Thus, smaller and poorer farmers with between zero and half a chia earned 44 percent of their income from off-farm activities in 1967, while the corresponding share for farmers with between half and one chia was 27 percent, between one and two chia, approximately 18 percent, between two and three chia, 15 percent, and above 3 chia, 10 percent.[71] Clearly, off-farm income was an important family income distribution equalizer because it contributed a larger share of total income for the smaller and poorer farm families. Thus the regionally decentralized nature of industrial development was providing off-farm job opportunities to rural dwellers who could keep their farm residence.

Agricultural Slowdown or Stagnation? (1968–1975)

This period is marked by a sharp drop in the growth rate of agricultural output to 2.3 percent annually between 1968 and 1974 (see Table 2.5).[72] The same table shows that common crops and special crops displayed negative growth rates of − .6 and − .8, respectively, during this phase. Rice production remained essentially constant. On the other hand, the growth performance of vegetables, fruits, and livestock products continued to be remarkably high, accounting for growth rates of 9.7, 6.1, and 5.9 percent, respectively. Hence, this period is marked by the stagnation of common crops and special crops and a continued growth of the other commodity groups.

70. See Fei, Ranis, and Kuo, chap. 2.
71. See JCRR, *Taiwan Farm Income Survey, 1967,* Table 6, p. 12.
72. All output and input growth rates are computed on the basis of three-year averages centered on the beginning and end year of the period under consideration.

Some interesting changes occurred in the relative importance of the various agricultural commodity groups in current value terms. Thus the share of common crops and that of its main component, rice, continued to fall from 1968 to 1971 from 44.7 percent to 37.9 percent and from 34.7 to 29.1 percent, respectively.[73] However, a turnaround occurred subsequently with these two shares reaching 40 and 34 percent in 1975, respectively. Since in volume terms, common crops, in general, and rice, in particular, stagnated, the increasing relative importance of these commodities in terms of current value is a price phenomenon reflecting a discrete jump in the price of rice. Likewise, the surprising relative rise in the share of special crops from 10.5 percent in 1968 to 14 percent in 1975—in the light of a declining volume— represents an almost four-fold increase in the price of first-grade sugar purchased by the Taiwan Sugar Company over the same period. The relative stability of the shares of the other commodity groups is a result of compensating forces—substantially greater than average volume increases but less than average price rises.[74]

From a technological standpoint, the binding constraint to further agricultural growth in this phase was clearly labor, which became superimposed upon the land constraint that had already become effective in the previous growth phase. This phenomenon can be seen from many angles. A first way is to go back to Table 2.8 and notice that all indicators of labor inputs—total man-days, number of workers, and man-days per average worker—fell throughout this period, the former at almost 1 percent per year. Likewise, the crop area and the multiple crop index shrunk slightly as a direct consequence of labor shortages at peak times.

The labor slack that had prevailed during the previous phase had gradually become exhausted and eliminated by the beginning of this third phase. Thus total man-days of labor in agriculture dropped from a peak of about 306 million in 1966–68 to about 285 million in 1973–75, as a combined result of a reduction in the number of man-days per average worker and of the total number of agricultural workers (see Table 2.7). Clearly, an important turning point had been reached, as evidenced by the decline in the size of the absolute population in agriculture, which reached a peak of 6.15 million in 1969 and dropped sharply, particularly between 1974 and 1975, to a level of 5.6 million in that last year.

There is some evidence that as a result of the worsening labor shortage, the agricultural wage rate rose significantly compared to that of factory workers during this phase. In this connection, Table 2.20, which was prepared for me

73. See Table 2.6.
74. It is clear that the relative importance of different agricultural products based on constant prices, rather than current prices, would have shown a further reduction in the shares of common and special crops and further rises in the shares of the other product groups.

Table 2.20. Comparison of Agricultural and Factory Workers' Wage Rates, 1961–1975 (at current and constant 1971 prices)

Year	Daily wage rate at current prices			Deflator		Daily wage rate at 1971 prices		
	Farm worker (1)	Factory worker (2)	Ratio (3) = (1)/(2)	Rural consumer price index (4)	Urban consumer price index (5)	Farm worker (6) = (1)/(4)	Factory worker (7) = (2)/(5)	Ratio (8) = (6)/(7)
1961	35.03	39.54	88.59	76.72	75.01	45.66	52.50	86.97
1962	36.09	41.60	86.75	78.07	77.09	46.23	53.96	85.67
1963	36.53	43.27	84.42	80.47	78.77	45.40	54.93	82.65
1964	37.76	44.18	85.47	82.01	78.63	46.04	56.19	81.94
1965	38.76	47.92	80.88	82.56	78.58	46.95	60.98	76.99
1966	41.26	50.88	81.09	85.50	80.16	48.26	63.49	76.04
1967	43.93	57.68	76.16	87.75	82.85	50.06	69.63	71.90
1968	50.99	64.26	79.35	92.19	89.38	55.31	71.90	76.93
1969	60.60	65.99	91.83	94.09	93.91	64.41	70.27	91.66
1970	67.28	71.43	94.19	97.43	97.26	69.05	73.44	94.02
1971	70.82	83.49	84.82	100.00	100.00	70.82	83.49	84.82
1972	78.13	90.40	86.43	106.40	102.99	73.43	87.78	83.65
1973	101.17	95.55	105.88	127.65	111.42	79.26	85.76	92.42
1974	171.10	144.89	118.09	194.31	164.31	88.06	88.18	99.86
1975	195.26	160.49	121.66	201.68	172.90	96.82	92.82	104.31

Source: Prepared for the author by the Rural Economics Division of the JCRR on the basis of following sources:
Column 1: Male worker, no meal offered. Source: DGBAS, *Commodity-Price Statistics Monthly, Taiwan Province.*
Column 2: Data provided by JCRR.
Column 4: Index of price paid by farmer in Taiwan Province (daily necessities for living only). Source: Same as column 1.
Column 5: General Index of Urban Consumer Price in Taiwan District. Source: DGBAS, *Commodity-Price Statistics Monthly, Taiwan Province,* various issues. The index applied to Taiwan district.

by the JCRR, shows that the ratio of the daily wage rate of farm workers deflated by the rural consumer price index to that of the daily wage rate of factory workers deflated by the urban consumer price index rose from a level of about 75 in 1966–68 to 104 in 1975. The increasing cost of labor was reflected in a sharp rise in the share of labor costs in the total cost of agricultural production from about 39.2 percent in 1966–70 to 44.5 percent in 1971–75.[75]

In essence, the dual labor and land constraints could be relaxed only through mechanization, that is, the substitution of capital and mechanical energy for labor and human energy. Taiwan had reached the almost unique situation of having to switch from an agricultural development strategy based on a small-scale, highly labor- and land-intensive pattern to one requiring mechanization and related changes in the scale and structure of production. Table 2.7 (columns 20 to 25) shows the extent of mechanization that took place during this phase. Thus, for example, the number of power tillers almost tripled from about 17,000 in 1967 to over 45,000 in 1975, and the number of tractors went from fewer than 480 in 1967 to almost 900 in 1974 and about 1,300 in 1975. Other mechanical implements that were previously almost nonexistent, such as combines, rice dryers, and power sprayers, began to be used on an expanding scale.

The substitution of mechanical energy for human and animal energy, described and analyzed in detail above, accelerated substantially during this phase. Hence, it was estimated that the contribution of mechanical energy (in terms of equivalent horsepower-days) to total energy used in crop production might have risen from about one-fourth in 1967 to over half in 1975, with a corresponding decline in the shares of human and animal labor (see Table 2.11).[76]

In addition to widespread mechanization, this phase is also characterized by a more intensive use of current inputs. Feedstuffs and chemical fertilizer accounted for the great bulk of expenditures on total current inputs. The growth of the former was directly correlated with the previously observed rising livestock production. Since the bulk of these feedstuffs had to be imported, this was one of the major factors responsible for the reversal of the positive balance of agricultural trade in recent years.[77] Although the consumption of commercial fertilizer had practically leveled off throughout the period from 1963 to 1967 (at around 800,000 metric tons) a sharp acceleration in

75. Information supplied by Rural Economics Division of the JCRR.
76. The share of mechanical energy to total energy is very likely to have been exaggerated, given the procedure used in the section on changes in the use of inputs and technology. Even allowing for an overestimation of the share of mechanical energy in total crop production in recent years, there is no doubt that this share rose very sharply during this phase.
77. This point is discussed in the section on aggregate performance after World War II.

consumption occurred from 1973 on—a phenomenon that was undoubtedly related to the elimination of the rice-fertilizer barter program and the consequent major drop in the price of fertilizer.[78]

During this phase, the rice-fertilizer barter ratios continued to be reduced before being eliminated in 1973. One major consequence of the elimination of the rice-fertilizer barter program was a substantial drop in the hidden rice tax. This is reflected by a considerable absolute and relative decline in the government collection of total rice marketed off-farm. This last share, which had reached a peak of 73 percent in 1954, as was seen previously, fell to 20 percent in 1973.[79]

The elimination of the rice-fertilizer barter program was one measure, among a number of others, undertaken to improve the relative income position of farmers, vis-à-vis nonfarmers. Another related measure was a sharp increase in the official (current) price of rice, which more than tripled during this stage from approximately N.T.$ 3.5 per kilogram to N.T.$ 11.5 per kilogram in 1975. More specifically, a discrete jump in this official price occurred in June 1974, when this price was moved up from approximately N.T.$7 to 10.[80] This sharp rise in the price of rice compared to other agricultural products accounted for the previously discussed significant jump in the share of rice in the current value of agricultural output from 29 percent in 1971 to 34 percent in 1975. This turning point assumes greater significance when it is recalled that the rice share declined continuously throughout the postwar period.

The discrete jump in the government purchase price of rice in 1974–75 converted a price policy that had been designed to extract a surplus out of farmers (in the form of the hidden rice tax) into a policy that amounted to a price-support program. The official price became the de facto market price. Whereas before 1973 the government purchased rice at an official price corresponding to only 70 to 80 percent of the prevailing market price, the subsequent discrete jump in the official price transformed this policy from a tax measure into price-support program to improve farmers' income. As a result of this new policy, the stock of rice went up significantly, reaching about 975,000 tons in 1976, which represents a new peak as compared with an aver-

78. The consumption of chemical fertilizer, which had averaged about 872 thousand metric tons in 1967–69 grew to over 1 million metric tons in 1974 and almost 1.4 million metric tons in 1975 (see column 16 of Table 2.7).

79. See Chen, Hsu, and Mao, Annex, Table 12.

80. The increase in the rice price relative to other prices can also be seen by looking at the index of urban consumer prices for Taiwan. The price of rice went up from a base of 100 in 1971 to 233 in 1974 and 245 in 1975; the general consumer price index amounted to 168 and 177, respectively, in these two years. (The relative weight of rice in this general index is slightly over 8 percent.)

age stock level of between four and five hundred thousand tons in the earlier part of this phase.

A major implication of the elimination of the barter program and the new price-support policy for rice is that their joint effect must have reduced substantially—if not ended altogehter—the net capital outflow or squeeze out of agriculture that characterized the previous phases. Unfortunately, the excellent historical study by T. H. Lee[81] has not been brought up to date after 1969, but it is most likely that the net outflow in the mid-1970s must be disappearing.

One might speculate what the effect would have been of an earlier liberalization of rice marketing. Clearly, a tradeoff must have existed between continuing to squeeze a surplus out of agriculture, mainly through the rice-collection mechanisms discussed above, on the one hand, and a sacrifice in output caused by lower rice prices and suboptimal application of fertilizer because of its artificially inflated price, on the other hand. Even though this last point is not made in the literature, it appears indirectly in a study that attempted to postulate the changes in the relative weights of rice policy objectives in Taiwan before and after 1970.[82] According to this study, the three most important objectives of rice policy before 1970 were consumers' welfare, government revenue, and economic stability. These objectives were judged to be equally important, each being given a weight of .3, and a final objective, foreign exchange, being given a weight of .1 so that the sum of the weights adds up to unity. After 1970, farmers' income and consumers' welfare were assigned weights of .3 each, while self-sufficiency and economic stability were assigned weights of .2 each. Thus, in fact, according to this subjective evaluation of experts,[83] farmers' income after 1970 had replaced government revenue as a major policy objective.

This phase is characterized by a continuation and significant acceleration of the active and complex migration pattern previously described. The acceleration of the migration process out of agriculture can be judged from the estimates obtained in my interregional analysis of agricultural production (see Table 2.17) indicating that the apparent migration rates out of agriculture during 1965–74 amounted to 2.1 percent annually in contrast with .9 percent annually between 1952 and 1965.

In the Taiwan context, it is useful to distinguish three categories of migrants: (1) the true migrants, who moved from the rural areas to the cities and rural centers; (2) the commuters, who work full time in off-farm activities in the rural areas; and (3) the seasonal migrants or part-time farmers who accept productive work outside of agriculture in the off-peak period. An impression

81. Lee, "Strategies."
82. See Chen, Hsu, and Mao, p. 11.
83. Mao is the present chief of the Rural Economics Division of the JCRR.

of the relative importance of these groups can be gathered from a survey based on 1968 data,[84] which revealed that out of the "moved-out members of farm families" in this sample, 48 percent were commuters, 26 percent seasonal workers, and 26 percent long-term employees.[85] A comparison of this survey with a similar one undertaken in 1963 and described in the Lin-Chen study indicates that the share of commuters had risen from 26 percent to 48 percent and that of long-term employees from 17 to 26 percent, while that of seasonal workers fell markedly from 57 to 26 percent over the same period.

Presumably, these trends can be explained by increasing full-time off-farm job opportunities for commuters, the rising difficulty of true farmers to engage in seasonal off-farm work in the light of the high labor requirements in agriculture,[86] and the rising rural-urban migration that accounts for the larger share of long-term employees in this sample. The occupational breakdown of these three types of commuters is also scrutinized by the Lin-Chen survey in broad regional terms. Hence, the great bulk of the commuters in 1968 were engaged in factory work (31 percent of all commuters but 44 percent of female commuters). Other important job outlets were as public officials and teachers (18 percent), clerks and office workers (16 percent), and maids and servants (8 percent). The interregional differences in the types of jobs taken by commuters were not very significant, except that a much larger proportion of southerners became public officials and teachers as compared to northerners.

The bulk of seasonal workers, as one would expect, went into farming (53 percent), and the remainder were spread evenly among a number of categories. Finally, the occupational pattern of long-term employees revealed that most of them either became factory workers (32 percent) or clerks and office workers (24 percent) in 1968. The same study concludes that the most important factors enhancing labor exodus from rural areas were education, youth, and low farm income.

An analysis of the migration pattern in Taiwan is made difficult not only because the pattern takes different forms, as was seen above, but, in addition, because the geographical rural-to-urban migration may not be permanent, as indicated, for instance, by the return flow of labor—mainly female—in 1974 during the recession period in industry.

Hence, according to the *Quarterly Report on the Labor Force Survey in Taiwan,* employment in primary industry increased by seventy-three thousand from 1973 to 1974, thereby reversing a long-time trend. The first three quarterly surveys in 1975, however, revealed that average employment in primary

---

84. T. L. Lin and H. H. Chen, "Rural Labor Mobility in Taiwan," *Journal of Agricultural Economics* 9 (June 1971), 123–47.

85. Ibid., p. 127.

86. The average number of mandays per worker had reached about 200 by the late 1960s.

industry dropped by sixty-nine thousand from the levels in the comparable period the previous year—reflecting a return flow to industry after it began to recover.[87] Clearly, the return flow to agriculture during the recession and some possible reluctance on the part of the former city dwellers to go back to the cities must reflect, among other reasons, the very high marginal productivity of labor in agriculture.

To understand the migration pattern in Taiwan, it is essential to distinguish the geographical migration from the intersectoral one. As was shown previously, the bulk of the migration out of agriculture is not an actual geographical migration into the cities because many members of farm families commute daily from their residences on the farm to work and back. This intersectoral labor transfer without physical movement undoubtedly contributed greatly to the developmental success of Taiwan. This migration pattern is integrally related to the process of rural industrial decentralization as one transferable element of the Taiwan developmental strategy. As a corollary to the increasing off-farm job opportunities, the proportion of part-time farmers continued to increase substantially during this phase.

The trend toward a more equal distribution of personal income among farm households apparently continued during this later phase. S. P. S. Ho, in a thorough study of the rural nonfarm sector in Taiwan, concluded that the increased employment opportunities outside of agriculture not only helped to raise the income earned by farm households but contributed to a more equal income distribution.[88] Ho shows that the distribution of personal income of farm households in 1974, as compared to 1966, based on the DGBAS *Report on the Survey of Family Income and Expenditure in Taiwan,* displayed a significantly more even Lorenz curve than that for 1966.

One key policy question connected with this third phase is the emergence of new forms of farm management. The government started to recognize that the labor constraint (added to an already very tight land constraint) in the late 1960s was threatening the existence of small-scale farming in Taiwan. Consequently, the government, and more specifically the JCRR, encouraged some important institutional changes including joint decision making in specific operations; joint management and contract farming; and the promotion of

87. Minister Y. S. Sun states that "in the spring of 1975, when export conditions became favorable, many industries wanted to call back their old workers. They found most of them were not willing to leave their home in the rural area . . . and, the improved rural economy in Taiwan served well during periods of economic slowdown but it also has unfavorable effects for a speedy industrial recovery" (quoted in JCRR, "Some Observations on Intersectoral Labor Mobility in Taiwan" [mimeo, January 1976]).

88. Samuel P. S. Ho, "The Rural Non-farm Sector in Taiwan," World Bank Studies in Employment and Rural Development, no. 32 (mimeo, Washington, D.C., September 1976), see pp. 51–52.

specialized production areas.[89] Whereas cooperatives to buy inputs and sell products existed on a large-scale basis, the establishment of cooperation in actual management of production activities to raise the efficiency of small farmers was relatively unknown and very difficult to institute. The intent was to organize farmers to manage jointly such specific operations as plowing or harvesting, or a combination of operations from land preparation to harvesting, on adjacent fields and thereby to be able to own and use jointly expensive machinery. This new form of farm management could best be implemented in practice by bringing together twenty to twenty-five farmers having an area of ten to fifteen hectares located in one block. Such farmers, particularly if related by blood ties, could organize themselves more easily than when farm lands were fragmented and scattered, which, unfortunately, might well be the rule rather than the exception.

The second form of organization—joint management and contract farming—entailed joint responsibility for such specific enterprises as the growing of mushrooms or poultry raising; or an agreement with other farmers or corporations to manage part or all of the land and share the profits or losses. A crucial aspect of this form of organization is that the decision-making authority is relinquished by the owner in favor of the user of the contracted land.

The final new farm management form, which the government tried to establish in 1973, consisted of specialized production areas as one of the measures under the so-called Accelerated Rural Development Program.[90] Under this program, all similar farms in a locality were urged to form a specialized agricultural production area (feed corn production, for example) and jointly to perform operations (such as land preparation, harvesting, and storage and marketing of products). By mid-1975, a total of 510 such projects had been implemented, embracing a variety of products.[91]

Serious obstacles appear to stand in the way of expanding the scope and coverage of these new management forms. These include (1) the individualistic nature of the Taiwanese farmer, who is reluctant to give up even part of his decision-making authority over the use of his land; (2) the highly fragmented nature of land ownership, with even very small farmers owning noncontigu-

---

89. Yu-Kang Mao, "Effects of Changes in Agricultural Structure on Farm Management in Taiwan" (mimeo, JCRR, 1975), contains a good discussion of these new forms of farm management.

90. Under this program nine new measures were recommended: (1) abolition of the rice-fertilizer-barter system; (2) abolition of the educational surtax on farm land tax; (3) easing of the terms of agricultural credit; (4) improvement of agricultural marketing; (5) strengthening of rural infrastructure; (6) acceleration of the extension of integrated use of improved cultural techniques; (7) establishment of specialized agricultural production areas; (8) strengthening of agricultural research and extension; and (9) encouraging the establishment of new industries in rural areas.

91. For a discussion of concrete examples of joint management farms and specialized production areas, see T. H. Shen, "Taiwan's Family Farm during Transitional Economic Growth" (JCRR mimeo, 1976).

ous sublots and the consequent problem of achieving true land consolidation; and (3) the difficulty in achieving an efficient division of labor, either on a geographical basis through an appropriate selection of specialized production areas or in terms of specific operations to be undertaken within the context of a consolidated set of individual farms. New forms of management have not yet had any significant effect on agricultural output. These organizational changes have not spread extensively; for example, as of 1975, about fifty-seven thousand farmers participated in joint operations covering a total land area of only thirty thousand hectares.

Taiwan's Agricultural Development: Quo Vadis?

The role of agriculture in Taiwan's economic development appears to be switching from that of a supporting sector providing important resources to the rest of the economy to that of a dependent and protected sector.[92] A strong case can be made that if land and labor constraints are binding, the increased application of capital inputs, including both current intermediate inputs and farm machinery, yields diminishing returns—at least in an institutional setting of extremely small farms. Because of the setting and the difficulties involved in implementing schemes such as joint operations and management, which would amount to de facto land consolidation, mechanization appears to have been relatively unsuccessful in replacing human labor as a major source of energy, as judged by the deceleration in the growth rate of agricultural output since 1968.

Indeed, in addition to the organizational and administrative problems of bringing fifteen to twenty farmers together to cultivate fifteen hectares, which appears to be the norm for a typical joint operation, the consolidated block of land may still be too small to use farm machinery efficiently in a technological sense. It was argued in the analysis undertaken in the section on changes in the use of inputs that mechanical energy applied to relatively small holdings is less efficient than human energy because of its relative indivisibility and tendency to be underutilized in terms of its total horsepower capacity. The clear advantage of human labor is its almost complete divisibility and the fact that it is utilized fairly close to its capacity level.

Clearly, the current major objective in Taiwan's agricultural development is to converge on an institutional setting and a technology that would permit output to grow at a rate substantially higher than that of population growth in the light of a continuing dwindling labor input. This problem is particularly complex because the government perceives that farm income has worsened

92. Walter P. Falcon talks about agriculture's change from a "supporting" to a "sustaining" sector in his perceptive analysis, "Lessons and Issues in Taiwan's Development," in Shen, ed., pp. 269-84. I believe that the term "dependent" used in the text above is probably more representative of the recent change in the position of agriculture than the term "sustaining."

relative to nonfarm income, thereby creating political pressures from farmers. Even though it is difficult to document unambiguously that such a relative worsening in farm income did, in fact, occur, some indicators might tend to confirm that the relative income position of farmers did not improve vis-à-vis that of nonfarmers.[93]

The key question as Taiwan proceeds to move rapidly from a developing to a developed country is whether its agriculture, which had previously been squeezed, should now be helped, as almost all developed countries have done through price-support programs and various subsidies and other measures. There is general agreement that Taiwan's agriculture is at a crossroad. It is likely that the two objectives of increasing agricultural output and improving the relative income standards of the farmers, given the present institutional setting, may well be in conflict.

At the present level of per capita income in Taiwan, the income elasticity of demand for most common crops (in particular, rice) is bound to be very low, if not negative, as already happened for sweet potatoes. On the other hand, livestock and dairy products, which face the highest income elasticity, require very large imports of feedstuffs that cannot be economically produced in Taiwan.[94] The prospects for identifying new successful export products such as asparagus and mushrooms which were successful in the last decade appear slim. It is clear that, given the new demand situation, a deceleration in the growth of agricultural output and a continuing shift in the composition of output is needed. In the light of increasingly inelastic price and income elasticities of demand, as per capita income continues to rise, high growth rates of agricultural production, in particular of rice,[95] might well be counterproductive in terms of farmers' income—at least under a regime of relatively free prices. Alternatively, a continuation of the present price-support policy for rice in the face of bleak export prospects and limited internal demand is bound to result in a regime of large rice surpluses (these stocks reached almost one million metric tons in 1976).

The real question appears to be whether Taiwan can continue to provide enough food—the composition of which is changing—to a still expanding

---

93. Thus, a comparison of the ratio of per capita farm income to that nonfarm income between 1966 and 1975 yields the following series:

| 1966 .65 | 1970 .60 | 1972 .64 | 1974 .58 |
| 1968 .56 | 1971 .64 | 1973 .53 | |

This ratio, which was prepared by the Rural Economics Division of the JCRR, seems to indicate that the relative position of farm income dropped sharply in 1966–70 and in 1972–74 in real terms.

94. Presently, Taiwan's annual feed corn production is about 140,000 metric tons, which can provide only about one-tenth of the requirement of the booming livestock industry. See Shen, "Taiwan's Family Farm," p. 12.

95. The export prospects for rice appear very bleak in view of the high price of Taiwanese rice and the existence of such other competitive exporters as the United States and Thailand.

population without affecting negatively the relative income position of farmers. There is a real risk that under the present institutional setting (very small farms and increasing mechanization and use of intermediate inputs) and the maintenance of a market economy (freely determined prices) the farmers would be subjected to a double squeeze. Any success on their part to increase output of rice and other crops facing inelastic price and income elasticities would result in lower prices for these commodities, while on the input side, the necessity of adopting an increasingly capital-intensive technology would continue to increase their costs of production.[96] On the other hand, shifting from rice production to higher-valued crops for which demand is expanding, such as vegetables, fruit, and livestock, is difficult beyond a certain point and could be undertaken only at rising costs of production. It might be suggested that, subject to the constraints faced by the government, products for which demand is expanding should be protected instead of rice. The constraints in following such a policy are the desire for self-sufficiency in rice and the overwhelming importance of rice as a cash crop that has a major effect on most farmers' income. Supporting the price of rice is the closest the government can come to a nonselective income-support policy in agriculture.

The government has apparently not undertaken a systematic analysis of the costs and benefits of alternative agricultural policies on the major objectives (growth, improved income situation for farm households relative to nonfarm households, and self-sufficiency). Thus, for example, the type of question to explore relates to the weighing of the budgetary costs of the rice price-support policies and resulting increased storage costs as against the benefits in terms of improved farm income and self-sufficiency. It is conceivable that alternative agricultural policies of supporting products that face a stronger growth in demand than rice—such as livestock, dairy products, fruits, and vegetables—might achieve greater benefit-costs ratios in terms of growth and relative improvements in farmers' incomes and yet not be inconsistent with a strong desire for self-sufficiency in rice. This would be the case once stocks have been built up so as to take care of any emergency situation that could occur as a result of, for example, a severe drought. Once stocks have reached such a level, any further rice accumulation might be clearly counterproductive, and production should be scaled down to meet domestic consumption needs. Judging from the present size of stocks, Taiwan appears to have reached the point where any further increase in rice production should be discouraged and, consequently, where equity objectives with regard to farm

---

96. There is evidence that gross farm family income per hectare per rice crop in Taiwan dropped substantially between 1961 and 1972 because of a greater proportional increase in paid-out costs than that in yield per hectare. See L. Y. Shi Tsai and Robert W. Herdt, "Economic Changes in Typical Rice Farms in Taiwan, 1895–1976" (International Rice Research Institute, Los Banos, mimeo, March 1976), pp. 5–6.

income could be achieved better through means other than a price-support program for rice.

In trying to reconcile the apparent conflict between the output objective and that of improving the relative income position of the farmers, it is essential to explore how the structure of the whole agricultural sector could be rationalized. Three alternative models have been suggested, mainly with respect to the farm size, which might be considered in the future development of the country:[97] (1) at one extreme would be the U.S. approach which would require wide-scale land consolidation and the adoption of even more capital-intensive techniques than at present in order to increase labor productivity; (2) at a polar extreme would be the Japanese model which can be characterized as a system of part-time farmers; and (3) an intermediate position would separate ownership from management and land operation and, either as an alternative or as an additional element, involve a concomitant significant increase in the average farm size.

The first alternative would have major implications by causing a massive exodus out of agriculture and consequent urbanization. Nor is it likely to be acceptable to the Taiwanese farmers—and therefore feasible—given their very strong attachment to and identification with their own land. The process of land consolidation in the narrow sense of combining together adjacent landholdings of different owners into a larger land unit has not taken place in Taiwan. Rather, the term "land consolidation" in the Taiwanese context applies at best to the consolidation process of different scattered landholdings of the same owner and a variety of measures to provide more efficient drainage and irrigation facilities, land leveling and filling, and the improvement of the road system.[98]

The second alternative, the Japanese model, appears to be the easiest one to follow from an institutional standpoint because it would presumably emerge gradually from the present system. But, it may, in the process, entail major inefficiencies if the farmers are heavily protected or create a real farm income problem if they are not.

The third model appears to be the most reasonable one from an economic standpoint, but would require tremendous innovative thinking as to how ownership can actually be divorced from operation within the realities of Taiwan agriculture and, alternatively or additionally, how the average farm can be raised to a more efficient size. The new structures and forms of farm management discussed previously, such as joint operations, joint management, and specialized production areas, are attempts to effect a separation between

97. These models are presented in Falcon, p. 282; he tries to summarize the results of a conference on agricultural development in Taiwan. The three models given in the text differ somewhat from that typology.

98. The various elements of land consolidation in the Taiwanese context are defined in Chen, pp. 101–2.

ownership and operation. It is probably fair to say that so far this attempt has met with only limited success. The total number of farmers affected is still quite small (on the order of less than 10 percent of the total number of farm households) and is likely to be very difficult to spread more widely in the future.

With regard to the average size farm, T. H. Shen argues that "it is generally accepted that the ideal size of a family farm in Taiwan should be about three hectares, with which it would be able to buy a power tiller and other farm machines for its use."[99] Since the average size of the farm at the present time is about one hectare, the total number of farm families would have to be reduced by two-thirds to achieve this target. In other words, agricultural population would have to decline from its present level of approximately 5.6 million to 1.87 million—entailing a physical migration to the cities and rural centers of more than 3.7 million people. Such a transformation is not conceivable in less than a couple of decades.[100] Thus, realistically, an increase in the average size of the family farm can be expected to occur gradually over at least the next two decades. In the meantime, imaginative new structures may have to be conceived and designed which would allow for a de facto, if not de jure, significant increase in the operating land unit. The average age of farmers in Taiwan has gone up, however, and with the ultimate retirement of this cohort land consolidation should meet with less resistance and mechanization might spread more rapidly.

The new agricultural policy tries to walk a tightrope between the objectives of continued efficient agricultural growth, increasing the farmers' relative income, and self-sufficiency (particularly in the case of rice). In this connection, most of the nine new measures listed by the government in its Accelerated Rural and Agricultural Development Program in 1972 appeared to favor these last two objectives[101] through the elimination of the rice-fertilizer barter program and a reduction in the land tax. In contrast, the new Six-Year Plan for Economic Development, 1976–81, appears to emphasize efficiency relatively more than improvement in farmers' relative income,[102] probably because measures to achieve the latter had already been implemented.

99. Shen, "Taiwan's Family Farm," p. 16.

100. Even then such a drastic reduction in the size of the agricultural population would imply an annual migration rate of 2.6 percent, to which should be added the natural rate of increase in the agricultural population over the next twenty years, say, 1 percent a year, yielding a total rural-to-urban migration rate of 3.6 percent.

101. See Footnote 90.

102. The Six-Year Plan for Economic Development, 1976–81, specifies the following policy measures to be undertaken in agriculture: "i) encourage joint farming to make for economies of scale; ii) promote mechanization; iii) introduce technological and institutional innovations (such as to insure self-sufficiency in rice production); iv) develop higher value crops for exports; v) improve the marketing system for greater efficiency; and vi) promote the development of rural communities; improve farm housing, country roads, and environmental sanitation." See Economic Planning Council, "Six-Year Plan: An Outline" (mimeo, Taipei, 1976), p. 6.

I have argued that there appears to be a limit as to how far joint operations and joint management can be pushed, particularly in the light of the highly fragmented and scattered nature of holdings and the consequent difficulty of bringing together farmers to cultivate jointly a larger unit. A prior step to the expansion of joint operations and management probably should consist of land consolidation at both the intrafarm and interfarm levels. At the intrafarm level, this would necessitate trading scattered lots in different locations until all the fragmented holdings had become one unit. At the interfarm level, the objective would be to work out exchanges among farmers so as to create adjacent pieces of land that could be cultivated as a larger common unit. Both of these exchange processes are extremely difficult to implement because farmers are reluctant to trade their holdings for others in different locations. Unless progress takes place on both of these fronts, however, a continuation of the present trend toward part-time farming would entail high efficiency costs resulting from two factors: (1) the use of suboptimal mechanical technology on extremely small farms because of the difficulty of consolidating land into larger units; and (2) the consequent need for subsidizing agricultural income to retain a minimal number of farmers on the land at farm income levels not drastically different from those obtained outside that sector.

Evaluation of Taiwan's Agricultural Development Strategy and Transferable and Nontransferable Elements

To understand and evaluate Taiwan's agricultural development strategy, it is useful to compare it to other possible alternative strategies. One useful typology of agricultural development strategies distinguishes the following four alternatives: (1) unimodal strategy; (2) bimodal (dual) strategy; (3) "industrialization-first" strategy, that is, discrimination against agriculture and the rural sector; and (4) collectivization or socialization of rural areas.[103] The choice of a strategy depends on a combination of historical factors, the political orientation of the regime, the policy makers' preference function, and other initial conditions.

A unimodal strategy is based on the progressive modernization of agriculture from the bottom up. In contrast with the bimodal strategy, which encourages the growth of the modern commercial, large-scale, relatively capital-intensive subsector of agriculture along with a traditional subsistence subsector, the unimodal approach relies on the widespread application of labor-intensive technology to the whole of agriculture. Through a combination of agricultural research, land redistribution, the provision of rural in-

103. The distinction between a unimodal and a bimodal strategy was first proposed by Bruce F. Johnston and Peter Kilby in their excellent and seminal study, see particularly chap. 4. Subsequently, I expanded this dual classification into the four types indicated in the text (see Erik Thorbecke and Gunars Dambe, *Agricultural Development and Employment Performance and Planning: A Comparative Analysis,* FAO, Agricultural Planning Studies, no. 18 [Rome, 1974]).

frastructure, the growth of rural institutions, and other measures, agricultural development is spread relatively evenly over the mass of the people.[104]

The bimodal structure and strategy is based on the promotion of a commercial, modern subsector that provides the bulk of agricultural output to satisfy the domestic and export demand for food and other agricultural products. The remainder of agriculture is confined to a traditional subsistence sector that has practically no claims on public resources.[105]

The "industrialization-first" strategy is based on the belief that industrialization is the key to development and that the industrial sector, as the advanced and dynamic sector, is to pull behind it the backward agricultural sector. The strategy as it was pursued in the 1950s and 1960s entailed, inter alia, discriminating against agriculture through such measures as turning the terms of trade against it, promoting import-substituting industries through high protection, allocating only a minimal share of public resources to agriculture, and not encouraging the development of rural institutions.[106]

Finally, the socialization and collectivization of agriculture usually takes the form of collective or cooperative farms involving the elimination of land ownership; the consolidation of land and other assets into communes or collectives which are run jointly and where the benefits are shared among members; and the undertaking of both farm and nonfarm activities.[107]

The success of an agricultural development strategy must be judged according to its effect on the major policy objectives—growth, income distribution, and employment—as well as according to such more specific subobjectives as those relating to farmers' income vis-à-vis nonfarmers' income, agriculture's role in earning foreign exchange and achieving self-sufficiency in food production, and satisfying the urban consumption and raw material demand adequately so as to help maintain low food prices and overall price stability. Clearly, these objectives and subobjectives might be in conflict, thus necessitating hard choices with respect to the package of policy measures, that is, the strategy which is adopted. The sources cited in note 103 have cogently argued that, if the prevailing structure and development strategy is unimodal in nature, no conflict between the output and distributional objectives need arise if the strategy is well conceived.[108]

104. Japan in the Meiji period, South Korea, and Taiwan are prototype examples of systems based on a unimodal strategy.

105. Mexico and Colombia are examples of countries that followed this bimodal strategy.

106. India and Pakistan in the 1950s and 1960s were prototype examples of this strategy.

107. A number of Eastern European countries, Tanzania, and to some extent mainland China, followed this strategy.

108. In addition to the two previously cited comparative analyses by Johnston and Kilby and by Thorbecke and Dambe, see also Graham Pyatt and Erik Thorbecke, *Planning Techniques for a Better Future* (Geneva, 1976), in particular, pt. III, which analyzes in detail the impact of a unimodal agricultural development strategy on growth and distribution within a general equilibrium consistency framework and upon which my review of the typology of agricultural development strategies is based.

Taiwan is clearly the best contemporary example of a developing country that followed a unimodal strategy with considerable success in achieving multiple objectives, at least up to 1968. Thus, the previous parts of this chapter have highlighted explicitly the outstanding agricultural output performance of Taiwan, by international standards, until 1968, the tendency for the income distribution to become more even among farm families, and the fact that full employment had been reached by the end of the second phase in the sense that the labor slack and seasonal underemployment had been replaced by a labor shortage. With regard to the subsidiary objectives, agriculture contributed in a major way to export earnings until the mid-1960s and to the maintenance of self-sufficiency in the major food crops and consequent low food prices and price stability. The Taiwanese strategy was least successful only with regard to a possible worsening of the income position of farmers vis-à-vis nonfarmers. In general, the agricultural strategy was conducive to the major and rapid structural transformation that moved the center of gravity in terms of the composition of output and the labor force away from agriculture toward the rest of the economy.

Because it was a successful prototype case of a unimodal strategy, the question arises whether the Taiwanese model can be followed and duplicated in other developing countries with initial conditions fairly similar to those of Taiwan at the outset of its development process. More specifically, the key question is which components of Taiwan's agricultural development strategy may or may not be transferable to other developing countries.

Five elements of the Taiwanese rural development strategy can be identified as having been crucial and potentially transferable within limits. These elements are (1) the land reform program; (2) the integrated and comprehensive nature in which rural development was planned, coordinated, and implemented, mainly through the activities of the JCRR; (3) a choice of agricultural technology that encouraged an efficient use of available resources and crop diversification; (4) the set of policies and taxes that were used to transfer capital resources from the agricultural sector to the rest of the economy; and (5) the regional and rural decentralization of industrial development. Since these elements were reviewed and analyzed in detail in the section on phases of agricultural development, only their major characteristics are sketched here.

A number of characteristics of the land reform process in Taiwan proved to be very effective and might, consequently, be transferable. First, the land reform program was implemented in gradual stages—rent reduction, public land sales, and the Land-to-the-Tiller Program—which followed one another in quick succession so that the whole process was effectively completed in less than eight years (1948–56). Second, the land reform process was all-embracing, affecting around half of the total number of farm families in Taiwan. This had the result of converting the agricultural sector from a tenant-

or landlord-dominated agriculture to an owner-cultivator-dominated sector in a very short period. Third, land redistribution was truly unimodal in the sense that very few farmers could own more than three chia. Clearly, given the limited amount of land available and the large agricultural population, the average family farm size had to be very small. In essence, even though some variance continued to exist in terms of the farm size, practically every rural family was granted some land.

Taiwan was blessed at the outset of the land reform process by not having a large number of landless workers, which is not typical of the situation in many developing countries today. A unimodal distribution of land—relying on small holdings—would alleviate the problem of these densely populated countries. In certain countries, however, the size of the agricultural population compared to the area under cultivation (the man-land ratio) is so high that it would be impossible to transform every landless worker and tenant into an owner-cultivator because the resulting farm size would be suboptimal.

A fourth important characteristic of the Taiwanese land reform process was that the asset position of the prereform landlord was only gradually and not drastically affected.[109] The rent reduction program, which limited rent to 37.5 percent of the yield of the major crop, was the first step in reducing the market value of land and the asset position of the landlords. The next step occurred under the Land-to-the-Tiller Program, which led to the confiscation of excess holdings above three chia at compensation rates that further undervalued land. The form of compensation—government commodity bonds and shares in public enterprises—was innovative in two senses: it did not impose a burden on current Taiwanese budget expenditures, and it provided a hedge against inflation to the former landlords The gradual nature of the process whereby land values fell and the form of compensation might have made land expropriation more palatable to the landlords. Yet it had a major wealth redistributional consequence which was estimated as being equivalent to about 13 percent of Taiwan's GNP in 1952. In turn, wealth redistribution was a crucial factor in generating a more equal income distribution within agriculture after 1953.

A final essential characteristic of the land reform process was the immediate implementation of a set of complementary policy measures including inter alia, the provision of credit, extension services, and strong organizational support in strengthening farmers' associations and continued public investment in traditional agriculture. The availability of these complementary services, provided mainly by the JCRR, must be considered as a crucial element that permitted output growth to continue during the transitional redistribution. Indeed, there are many counterexamples of countries where a land

109. This means that they received some compensation for their land.

redistribution scheme not accompanied by such complementary measures led to serious reductions in production and consequent failures.

The second transferable element is connected with the JCRR. The concept of the JCRR was organizationally innovative and imaginative. From a potential transferability standpoint, the following characteristics should be highlighted. First, it was established as a semipublic institution—initially to help allocate and channel U.S. foreign assistance—which provided it some independence from the government. This independence was greater in that, at the outset, the JCRR was almost totally financed through U.S. aid funds. The JCRR could take a longer-run view of the agricultural development process because it was insulated from the daily political and bureaucratic pressures of, say, a typical agricultural ministry.

Clearly, it is unrealistic to expect present developing countries to have access to the same level of foreign aid as Taiwan received. On the other hand, a mechanism similar to the JCRR might be explored in present-day developing countries to channel in an integrated fashion bilateral and multilateral aid to agriculture.

A second and related characteristic of the JCRR is that it combined the planning function with the actual implementation of research, extension, irrigation, and the revitalization and strengthening of farmers' associations. Responsibility for carrying out these activities was concentrated in only one agency, thus allowing these activities to be implemented in an integrated fashion. It is typical in the developing world for these functions to be conducted by different agencies in an uncoordinated and, therefore, inefficient way. It is no great exaggeration to speculate that the JCRR was involved in integrated rural development long before the concept had been coined in the literature and espoused by such development agencies as the World Bank. The fact that the same individuals were responsible for the planning and the actual carrying out of agricultural development added an important element of realism to the planning process. Instead of being an academic exercise, planning became a means of conducting a dialogue with the actors (for example, the farmers) regarding general objectives and specific targets and the best means of achieving them at the local level. A final essential characteristic of the JCRR is its effectiveness in operating at the local level in a decentralized fashion, thereby circumventing what might otherwise have been a cumbersome bureaucracy. By involving local farmers in the planning and implementation process, the planning objectives could more easily be translated into specific local actions.

A third key element in the Taiwanese strategy was the design of an agricultural technology and a complementary set of institutions that were admirably suited to the underlying resource endowment. Because at the end of World War II labor was, by far, the most abundant factor of production, while land

and capital were scarce, it was correctly perceived that agricultural technology should be based, as much as possible, on labor. Hence, until the labor constraint became truly binding in the late 1960s, Taiwan relied on an agricultural technology that maximized utilization of the available labor. The form this technology took was package approach, using inputs which were highly correlated with labor, such as high-yielding varieties of seeds adapted to the local circumstances, chemical fertilizer, irrigation and improved drainage (which required water pumps), and some selective mechanization in the form of power tillers which, at the outset, were not competitive with labor. In a sense, Taiwan was having its own green revolution before it appeared elsewhere.

In retrospect, it is ironical that it was the very real success of this technology in utilizing to its fullest the labor resources available that led to the serious labor shortage after 1968 and required a major switch toward mechanization and the use of capital as a substitute for labor.[110] Also, by pushing on different fronts, agricultural research encouraged product diversification.

The next transferable element is the efficient, yet delicate, mechanism through which capital resources were transferred from the agricultural sector to the rest of the economy. The two remarkable features of this intersectoral transfer process are its magnitude and its form. Repeated references have already been made to the size of this net transfer as a proportion of total agricultural production, which fluctuated between 20 and 30 percent before World War II, amounted to 22 percent in 1950–55, and around 15 percent between 1956 and 1969.[111] The magnitude of this transfer is the best evidence of the key role Taiwan's agriculture performed in providing capital resources to other sectors in the process of economic development.

The first and major observation regarding the form this transfer took is that it was very much a *net* rather than a *gross* transfer. By this is meant that throughout its history, Taiwan's agricultural sector received *gross* resources from nonagriculture in a variety of ways that by increasing its productivity allowed it to provide a *net* transfer to the rest of the economy. Therefore an essential lesson many developing countries can learn from the Taiwan experience is that "the goose cannot be starved before it has laid a golden egg." The major specific mechanisms through which the transfer was effectuated were (1) agricultural exports in the prewar period which amounted to roughly

---

110. To the extent that "labor shortage" reflects the full and efficient employment of the labor force it is, of course, a desirable objective. What is suggested here is that the switchover from a labor-intensive technology relying on intermediate inputs to mechanization was quite abrupt.

111. These figures are based on the excellent study by T. H. Lee, "Strategies," based on his book *Intersectoral Capital Flows,* which has become the classic treatment of intersectoral capital flows in the process of economic development. It is based on a very detailed accounting procedure that measures the various outflows of agricultural products and funds and the various inflows of nonagricultural products and funds into agriculture. As a consequence, the net outflow of funds can be computed for different historical periods.

one-fourth of total agricultural production in the 1930s; (2) the various taxes and fees, particularly the hidden rice tax, which amounted to about 10 percent of total agricultural production between 1950 and 1955 and 5 to 6 percent between 1956 and 1969; and (3) a transfer of funds through financial institutions, particularly in the 1960s, which grew from an insignificant 1 to 3 percent in the 1950s to 12.3 percent in 1961–65 and over 17 percent of agricultural production in 1966–69. This last element is truly remarkable in revealing the role rural savings performed in effectuating this transfer and providing capital for the economy as a whole.[112]

The final noteworthy element that influenced Taiwan's rural development is the process of regional and rural decentralization of industrial development which occurred at least from the mid-1950s on. A great advantage of this process was to provide a productive way to absorb rural labor either on a full-time or a part-time (seasonal) basis and thereby improve the income position of particularly the smaller and poorer farmers. At the same time, it reduced significantly the actual physical rural-to-urban migration because most of the farm family members engaged in off-farm activities tended to be commuters or part-time employees who maintained their residence on the farm. This intersectoral rather than geographical migration pattern appears to have been a key to the success of Taiwan in achieving the multiple objectives of output growth, full employment, and a more equal income distribution. In speculating about the potential transferability of this process, one has to recall the topography of the island. The existence of a long and very narrow north-south strip served by a major railroad line and highway must have greatly facilitated this regional industrial decentralization. Nevertheless, the fact that the implementation of this kind of process might be more difficult in countries displaying different topographies does not reduce its potential importance.

In addition to the potentially transferable elements, Taiwan was blessed with a number of factors conducive to its development since World War II that may not be transferable. The most important among these factors appear to have been, first, the large-scale immigration of approximately 600 to 735,000 highly skilled individuals between 1947 and 1956 and representing over 10 percent of the population in 1946.[113] This major influx relaxed almost completely the skill constraint typical of developing countries and, in addition, brought a group of people to Taiwan who had a relatively clear conception of the form agricultural development should take and no vested interest vis-à-vis the political and economic balance of power as between rural and urban groups or between different rural groups such as landlords and tenants.

A second clearly nontransferable element was the extremely high level of

---

112. These figures are based on Lee, "Strategies."
113. See Simon Kuznets, Chapter 1 of this volume, Table 1.6. The great bulk of these migrants came in the three-year period 1947–49.

U.S. foreign assistance Taiwan received over the period 1951–65, which amounted to about $1.4 billion.[114] The level of this aid, expressed on the per capita basis, is almost unique by international standards and extremely unlikely to be repeated elsewhere. Political factors must have played an important role in facilitating the strong convergence in the goals of the U.S. AID mission and the provincial government with respect to agricultural development. Whereas it might be unrealistic to expect the same level of aid to be available to other developing countries, the previous analysis made it clear that its form through some JCRR-type agency, for example, might be transferable.

A final success factor in Taiwan's development experience that may not be transferable—at least to the same degree—is the tremendous growth of the industrial sector based on export substitution and the availability of entrepreneurial talent and markets. The point here is that very few developing countries can hope to succeed in competing for limited foreign markets, and the very success of what Ian Little in Chapter 7 calls The Four (Taiwan, South Korea, Hong Kong, and Singapore) may well have preempted many export markets for other developing countries. However, even if access to markets in the industrialized countries were limited, there exists a scope for trade among developing countries in labor-intensive manufactures.

The importance of these nontransferable elements should not be underestimated. There can be no doubt that they contributed significantly to Taiwan's development. Yet it would be hard to argue that they were a sine qua non of Taiwan's success. Without these factors, Taiwan's development would have been less spectacular. Nevertheless, some unique features of Taiwan's experience in agriculture should be seriously studied and considered by the developing world for possible adoption—with appropriate modifications—in the design of an agricultural development strategy.

114. Expressed on an annual per capita basis, U.S. foreign aid represented approximately $8 per capita per year for fourteen consecutive years.

3 | Industrial Development

GUSTAV RANIS

This chapter traces the development of Taiwan's industrial sector during the two and one half decades from 1952 to the present. At the beginning of this period, Taiwan's industrial sector was small, both absolutely and relative to the rest of the economy. Some modern industrial capacity existed, primarily under government control, and most private production was of traditional products. Only a small portion of total industrial output was exported, mostly processed agricultural goods.

Over these two and a half decades all of these characteristics were dramatically altered. A few indicators of this change are presented in Table 3.1. Between 1952 and 1975, industrial output, for example, increased more than twentyfold. The shares of industry in net domestic product (NDP) and employment rose from 17.9 to 36.3 percent and from 9.3 to 23.5 percent, respectively. At the same time, public-sector ownership of manufacturing industries fell from over half of the total to less than a sixth, and the share of industrial products in total exports rose from 8 to 84 percent. Within this prodigious growth of industrial activity, equally dramatic compositional changes occurred. For example, between 1954 and 1971, the combined shares of mining and food processing in total industrial production fell from 28.6 to 10.7 percent, while textiles, metal machinery, and electrical machinery combined rose from 24.0 to 38.1 percent.

This chapter will attempt to trace the causes of these far-reaching sets of changes in the industrial sector over these more than two decades, paying

I wish to express my special gratitude for the advice of Chen Sun of the Economic Planning Council and the research assistance of Chi-yuan Liang of National Taiwan University and Gunnar Knapp of Yale University.

Table 3.1. Selected Indicators of Major Changes in Taiwan's Industrial Sector, 1952–1975

	1952	1975
Industrial output index (1952 = 100)	100	2059
Share of industry in NDP	17.9	36.3
Share of industry in total employment*	9.3	23.5
Percentage of public ownership in total industrial production	56.2	15.4
Share of industrial products in total exports	7.8	83.6
Output of selected industrial products:		
Electric power (million kwh)	1,420	22,894
Fertilizer (1,000 million tons)	148	1,529
Cement (1,000 million tons)	446	6,796
General machinery (million tons)	6,115	253,321
Television sets (1,000 units)	0	4,036

	1954	1971
Selected shares in industrial production:		
Mining	10.2	3.5
Food processing	18.4	7.2
Textiles	18.4	20.8
Chemicals, petroleum, and rubber products	10.8	22.3
Metal machinery and electrical machinery	5.6	17.3

*1952 figure for age twelve and over; 1975 figure for age fifteen and over.
Source: Economic Planning Council (EPC), *Taiwan Statistical Data Book, 1976* (Taipei, 1976); Directorate-General of Budget, Accounting, and Statistics (DGBAS), *Statistical Yearbook of the Republic of China, 1975* (Taipei, 1975).

attention as well to significant subphases of development that emerge from the analysis. The behavior of this sector over time can be really understood—instead of merely described—only in terms of the role it played within the context of the economic system as a whole; thus an occasional brief foray into the realm of intersectoral relations and the structure and performance of the economy as a whole is unavoidable. Moreover, the historical period under scrutiny can be satisfactorily analyzed only in relation to what went before—during the Japanese colonial period—and what seems to be happening most recently, with the help of a brief glance into an always misty future.

Accordingly, this chapter has been organized as follows: the first section presents a brief review of the industrial sector during the colonial period, 1895–1945, as well as the impact of the momentous politicoeconomic events immediately following, both with an eye to an accurate assessment of the initial conditions affecting independent industrial development in the two decades to follow. The next two sections trace the development and discuss the role of the industrial sector during the decade of the 1950s (approximately 1953 to 1962) and that of the 1960s (approximately 1963 to 1972). The final section assesses the more recent period and the probable future position of Taiwan's industrial sector from the vantage point of the historical perspective achieved.

Japanese Colonialism and the Initial Conditions for Independent Industrial Growth

The generally accepted view of Taiwan's economy under colonial rule (1895–1945) is that of a principally agricultural appendage to the Japanese economy—with government policy focused mainly on increasing agricultural productivity—via both organizational and infrastructural investments. The colonial goods required by the mother country from Taiwan were sugar and rice; Taiwan, in turn, was expected to accept Japanese industrial goods. This overall outline of the late colonial period, while generally correct, is misleading in certain important respects. First, although the traditional colonial exchange of rice and sugar for textiles and fertilizer represented the predominant flow, food processing within Taiwan, mostly in sugar refining but also in the preliminary processing of rice and pineapples, became increasingly important. Fiscal incentives and, after 1911, tariff protection, were provided to encourage the growth of privately owned (by Japanese) sugar mills on the island. By 1930, it is estimated that close to 20 percent of national income on the island was generated within industry, with food processing responsible for the lion's share, accounting for 67 percent of all registered factories, 75 percent of total industrial product, and 55 percent of industrial employment.[1] By 1940 there were twenty-three pineapple canning plants and forty-two sugar refineries on the island and a variety of other miscellaneous processing operations, including sugar-processing by-products, lychees, bamboo shoots, tomatoes, papayas, and fruit juices. Textiles and other nondurable consumer goods, plus bicycles, rounded out the picture.

Second, and less well appreciated, during the 1930s, as international tensions grew in the Pacific area, Japan increasingly came to realize the strategic importance of Taiwan's location and began to invest more heavily in such nonagricultural infrastructure as power and transport as well as in some basic industries, including cement, chemicals, pulp and paper, fertilizer, petroleum refining, and metallurgy. Some of these, such as cement, may be viewed as resulting from the natural comparative advantage occasioned by raw material availability and location, but the same is not true of activities that required a Japanese government subsidy. Therefore a pattern of secondary import-substitution industrialization, mainly in producer goods and in public hands, was initiated quite early. Manufacturing output grew at 6 percent annually during the 1930s. By 1941, taking 1937 as a base, the production index for metal and metal products stood at 449, chemicals at 145, and textiles at 132.

Finally, and perhaps most important in creating the initial conditions for later industrialization, the transport network, both road and narrow-gauge rail, as well as all electrification works, were, from the beginning, directed not to

1. Samuel P. S. Ho, *Economic Development of Taiwan, 1860–1970* (New Haven, 1977).

the narrow purpose of the extraction and export of some primary raw material or mineral—as is typical of many colonial situations—but to the purpose of a broad agricultural mobilization, especially on the fertile West Coast of Taiwan. The typically Japanese attention to rural organization and surveys provided the necessary ingredients for the farmers' association structure and for land reform in later years.

In industry, on the other hand, Japanese policy was expressly directed against the participation of Taiwanese entrepreneurs, especially in the larger-scale activities, including food processing and the intermediate goods industries. By 1940, the number of Japanese residents on Taiwan had risen to more than 310,000 from 180,000 in 1925. Although opportunities for Taiwanese to learn by doing were thus limited, nevertheless, during these years a substantial and important increase in the island's human capital stock took place, reflected in remarkable health and, especially, educational improvements. Between 1905 and 1936, for example, the death rate fell from 40 to 20 per 1,000 and the percentage of school-age children attending primary school increased from approximately 10 to almost 70.

World War II and its political aftermath provided a series of major shocks to Taiwan's economy. Early on, the interruption of shipping plus other strategic considerations gave the island new importance to the Japanese and led them to locate shipbuilding, machinery, and additional petroleum refining capacity there. Allied bombings caused substantial destruction of both industrial plant and infrastructure, putting three-quarters of industrial capacity, two-thirds of power, and one-half of the transport network out of commission by 1945. About thirty thousand Japanese technicians, administrators, and professionals, the bulk of the large-scale industrial and public-sector human capital resources, left Taiwan in 1945. Given these facts, it is surprising that industrial output was able to recover its prewar levels as early as 1951.

But more important than the question of physical destruction and the time required to rebuild was the impact of two additional major shocks. These were the retrocession of Taiwan to China in 1945, followed shortly thereafter by civil war and the evacuation of the Nationalist Chinese government and its armed forces to Taiwan. In rapid succession, Taiwan's industry was forced to shift its export markets—mainly processed foods, but also including cement, paper, and aluminum—from Japanese to (internal) Chinese markets, and then once again to Japanese and/or other (international) markets. At the same time, the rupture of the colonial links with Japan obliged Taiwan to begin producing domestically such essential consumer items as textiles, leather goods, soaps, and oils.

A full analysis of the whole array of political and administrative problems caused by these two body blows to the economic system is beyond the scope of this study. Few developing economies face a similar convergence of crises

Table 3.2. Change in Output and Export Orientation 1937–1951 (million yen)

Year	Value of total output (excluding services) (1)	Total exports (2)	Export ratio (percent) (3)	Total mfg. value added (4)	Mfg. value added excl. sugar refining (5)	Nonsugar refining mfg. ratio (6)
1937	887	400	44	182	72	40%
1951	847	74	9	133	111	80%

Sources: Columns 1 and 2 from Ching-Yuan Lin, *Industrialization in Taiwan, 1946–72* (New York, 1973), p. 37. Columns 4 and 5 from DGBAS, "The National Product and National Income of the Republic of China/Taiwan, 1955."

at a time of their initial economic independence effort. It is small wonder that the 1946–49 period has been characterized as an era of confusion, neglect, and mismanagement by the Central Chinese government, combined with the repercussions of severe inflation on the mainland. Only when the Nationalist government had established itself firmly on Taiwan in 1949 could a series of policy reforms be introduced to permit the system to adjust to the new domestic and international situation. These included a package of monetary reforms accompanied by the imposition of exchange and import controls that, buttressed by U.S. aid, managed to cut the rate of inflation from a runaway 3,400 percent in 1949 to 9 percent by 1953. This achievement of relative stabilization was not accomplished overnight, and it required continuing efforts throughout the 1950s; but these early reforms did bring the economy a giant step closer to the reestablishment of properly functioning markets.

Even then the purely economic problems to be overcome were formidable. As Table 3.2 indicates, Taiwan's export ratio in 1937 was extremely high and, even though total output had recovered by 1951, it fell precipitously in the early postwar period. The relative importance of processed sugar exports also sharply declined. In 1937, 64 percent of Taiwan's textiles and wearing apparel and 57 percent of its wood products and furniture supplies had been imported. By 1954, these figures were 5.6 and 7.3 percent, respectively.[2] The process of primary import substitution, measured in terms of the declining proportion of consumer goods imports in total imports, got under way in the 1930s.

Taiwan's ability to pull herself together in relatively short order—in spite of these formidable challenges—was based in large part on the substantial replenishment of the human capital lost during the war, as a by-product of the evacuation from the Chinese mainland. Between 1946 and 1950, the arrival of more than a million civilians plus members of the armed forces filled large public- and private-sector managerial and entrepreneurial gaps in a population

2. Ching-Yuan Lin, *Industrialization in Taiwan, 1946–72* (New York, 1973), Table 4-2.

that only totaled seven million at the time. Given the precipitous departure of the Japanese and the effects of their policies that caused the relative isolation of the Taiwanese population, this injection was essential to create the minimum administrative and private entrepreneurial conditions underlying resumed growth.

In summary, substantial industrialization and import substitution had begun in Taiwan well before 1953, when the curtain of analysis is usually opened. At the outset inflation was rampant and defense requirements unusually high. Nevertheless, in spite of a number of traumatic shocks that had to be absorbed during the decade of the 1940s, the conditions on which to base further industrial progress in the early 1950s were by no means totally unfavorable— certainly not compared to other less developed countries (LDCs). In 1953, Taiwan had a total population of approximately eight million, almost 15 percent of them migrants from the mainland, a per capita income of less than $100, but a sound human and physical infrastructural base from which to pursue her transition to modern growth.

Primary Import Substitution and the Transition to Export Substitution, 1953-1962

The decade 1953–62 was one of generally rapid, if occasionally erratic, growth for Taiwan's industrial sector. Agricultural output increased by 59 percent, industrial output more than tripled, and the weight of industry in gross national product (GNP) rose steadily by about 1 percent per year. This was reflected in the increasing importance of such consumer goods industries as textiles, apparel, wood and leather products, and bicycles. As is typical for developing countries, Taiwan's initial industrial spurt in the 1950s was largely based on primary import substitution. Between 1952 and 1957, the share of consumer goods in total imports fell from 19.8 to 6.6 percent, (see Table 3.3, column 4). Imports of consumer goods as a percentage of total domestic supply of consumer goods, another indicator of this process, were at approximately 5 percent by the late 1950s. After a few years, as the domestic market for consumer goods became more and more saturated, Taiwan began an unusually early shift toward export substitution. Exports as a fraction of GDP rose only slightly between 1952 and 1957, from 8.0 to 9.5 percent; by 1962 this share had risen to 13 percent. More important, within this still relatively low share of exports industrial products were becoming increasingly important by the end of the decade.

The initial resort to primary or consumer goods import substitution after independence was a natural phenomenon. Not unlike most newly independent developing economies, Taiwan was confronted by the need to focus her attention and resources on the expansion of consumer goods industries to

Table 3.3. Industrial Growth and Changes in the Structure of Trade, 1952–1975

	Industrial production index (1)	Annual growth rate of industry (2)	Share of industry in NDP (3)	Share of consumption goods in imports (4)	Share of exports in GDP (5)	Share of industrial products in exports (6)
1952	100		17.4	19.8	8.0	7.8
1953	124.7	24.7	17.6	17.2	8.6	8.6
1954	132.9	6.6	22.0	12.7	6.5	10.8
1955	149.3	12.3	20.9	9.0	8.2	10.6
1956	154.8	3.7	22.2	7.7	9.0	17.0
1957	174.0	12.4	23.6	6.6	9.5	12.8
1958	189.0	8.6	23.7	6.6	11.5	14.1
1959	212.3	12.3	25.4	7.4	12.4	23.6
1960	242.5	14.2	24.6	8.1	11.2	32.3
1961	279.5	15.3	24.7	9.9	12.8	41.0
1962	302.7	8.3	25.5	8.2	13.0	50.5
1963	328.8	8.6	27.8	6.4	17.6	41.0
1964	398.6	21.2	28.0	6.1	18.7	42.5
1965	464.4	16.5	28.1	5.2	18.3	46.0
1966	537.0	15.6	28.4	5.0	20.6	55.0
1967	626.0	16.6	30.3	4.7	21.6	61.6
1968	765.8	22.3	31.9	4.7	23.6	68.5
1969	917.8	19.9	33.8	4.5	26.3	74.0
1970	1104.1	20.3	34.1	4.9	29.5	78.7
1971	1369.9	24.1	36.5	5.1	35.1	80.9
1972	1657.5	21.0	38.9	5.7	42.7	83.3
1973	1975.3	19.2	40.1	5.6	49.1	84.6
1974	1946.6	−1.5	38.4	6.1	45.4	84.5
1975	2059.5	5.8	36.3	6.8	40.7	83.6

Source: EPC, *Taiwan Statistical Data Book, 1976.*

supply the domestic market. The pressures were made even more powerful by the sudden threat to her traditional primary and processed agricultural export markets as well as to her sources of supply of imported industrial consumer goods, combined with the unusually heavy import requirements of military preparedness. Although, as already noted, import substitution in Taiwan had begun much earlier and had not been restricted to industrial consumer goods, this process was substantially accelerated as a consequence of the policies adopted between 1949 and 1951, primarily in response to inflation and balance-of-payments pressures.

The array of policies that were employed to push import substitution during this period beyond its more natural beginnings is familiar to most observers of development. The customary mix of exchange controls, import licensing, protective tariffs, and multiple exchange rates, combined with some deficit financing, inflation, and an increasingly overvalued currency was in evidence. More unusual was the substantial size of the producer goods industries taken over from the Japanese (for example, chemicals, fertilizer, and petroleum products) in the public sector, amounting to more than 50 percent of total industrial production (see Table 3.1). These government corporations were intended to stand on their own feet but, in fact, received substantial official help in the form of direct subsidies and interest rate differentials. The basic purpose of the total policy syndrome was to capture the foreign exchange resources for purposes of public-sector overhead construction, to maintain existing industry, and to expand consumer goods industries by providing protection for and driving profits into the hands of a relatively inexperienced private industrial entrepreneurial class.

Import substitution customarily begins with heavy emphasis on the replacement of nondurable consumer goods imports by domestic production. This is the so-called primary or ''easy'' import-substitution subphase, since it requires less capital and technology than secondary import-substitution and is consequently closer to the initial endowment conditions of the typical developing economy. The Taiwan case, as indicated, was somewhat more mixed for good historical reasons. Total industrial production, which only regained its 1940 peak by 1951, doubled between 1951 and 1954. Using the Chenery decomposition formula for assessing the sources of total market demand, Ching-Yuan Lin[3] found import substitution responsible for more than 90 percent of the total between 1937 and 1954. Some of this growth, however, consisted of the expansion of producer and consumer durable industries inherited from the Japanese era. Nevertheless, the quantitatively major brunt of the industrial expansion of the early 1950s was borne by nondurable consumer goods, especially textiles, apparel, wood, and leather products.

Primary import substitution was a process that began in the colonial period, accelerated in the early 1950s, and was already showing signs of running out of steam—as a consequence of the gradual exhaustion of the protected domestic market—by the mid- or late 1950s. This exhaustion at the aggregate level exhibited itself by the bottoming out of the percentage of the total supply of nondurable consumer goods still being imported, a decline of the growth rate of industrial output (nonfood processing manufacturing fell from annual rates of 22 to 10 percent between 1953 and 1958), and, at the micro level—for example, in the textile industry—by a record of falling prices, increased competitiveness, and businessmen's pressure for cartelization and other government action to avoid bankruptcy.

Such action over the longer term can take one of two forms: one, directed toward the maintenance of growth in the more labor-intensive nondurable consumer goods industries, to facilitate the shift from domestic to export markets; the other, directed toward a further expansion of the more capital- and technology-intensive durable consumer and capital goods industries, to induce secondary import substitution in other areas of the domestic market. Taiwan's policy makers seem to have hesitated for a time between these two

3. Ibid.

solutions before finally embracing the industrial export-oriented alternative by the early 1960s.

I will examine the features of primary import substitution, paying special attention to the important differences that mark off this case from the more "normal" LDC pattern. It is these differences, I believe, that were of utmost importance for the success of the overall industrialization and development effort on the island.

Among the more important differential features of primary import-substitution industrialization in Taiwan are those focusing on its relation with the preponderant agricultural sector. Domestic agriculture is frequently the sector that is severely discriminated against during this phase, but an examination of the intersectoral terms of trade indicates that the customary severe deterioration of the agricultural terms of trade did not occur here; the relative stability of these series over two and a half decades of rapid development represents a remarkable example of intersectoral balance.[4] Agriculture was certainly "squeezed," in the sense of providing the bulk of the domestic capital to finance nonagricultural growth, but this coincided with the implementation of a major three-step program of land reform and other technology- and credit-related efforts to ensure the simultaneous vigorous growth of agricultural productivity. Though this part of the story is primarily the subject of Chapter 2 in this volume, its influence on the rate and direction of industrial progress was substantial. First, the non-neglect of domestic agriculture provided ample wage goods to keep industrial wages from rising prematurely, that is, before the natural exhaustion of rural surplus labor; second, it assured a relatively strong domestic market for the expanding consumer goods industries; and third, the precise nature of the land reform measures (especially the important final step, the Land-to-the-Tiller Program) ensured a relatively wide participation of former landlords in private industrial activity.[5]

To this must be added the, I believe, crucial point that the inherited good rural physical and institutional infrastructure was not only maintained but further improved during the 1950s; rural transportation and communication networks were expanded, as were investments in education and in transformed farmers' associations. All these measures supported agriculture, but also proved extremely important for the development of a relatively decentralized rural-oriented industrial sector in Taiwan. This early reasonable approximation to balanced growth—or, in Chinese terminology, "developing agriculture by means of industry and fostering industry by virtue of

---

4. According to unpublished data provided by the Joint Commission on Rural Reconstruction (JCRR), the index of prices received over prices paid by farmers (1971 = 100) stood at 96.8 in 1952, at 101.2 in 1960, at 98.4 in 1970, and at 103.6 in 1976.

5. Thirty percent of landlord compensation was in the form of shares in large public-sector (previously Japanese-owned) enterprises.

agriculture''—was crucial in permitting the particular industrialization path described in this chapter to be followed in both its quantitative and qualitative dimensions.

Other features of the primary import-substitution subphase in Taiwan that distinguish it as a much milder version of the normal stereotype include the relatively (again by LDC standards) lower levels of protection (via tariffs and quantitative restrictions [QRs]).[6] Also, Taiwan's monetary policies were from the outset much more favorable to the establishment of a relatively more competitive and efficient industrial sector. For example, interest rates were pegged relatively high, by LDC standards, though, given the real rate of return to capital and the customary annual rate of inflation, still by no means at realistic levels.[7] Again by way of contrast, there was a fairly general disinclination to resort at will to the whole range of direct allocative devices, for example, in the areas of steel, cement, fertilizer, and so forth, often in evidence during primary import-substitution regimes.

Additional important direct government actions were crucial to the emerging pattern of industrial development. The most important of these undoubtedly were the aforementioned efforts in rural transportation and power, taking up where the colonial government had left off. Highway density measured in meters per square kilometer of area was high and rising throughout the 1950s, with rural highways making up approximately two-thirds of the total (see Table 3.4). The same was true for the railway system, whose density was, and remains, second only to Japan's in all of Asia. With respect to power, government policy in the 1950s, supported by U.S. project aid allocations, was to maintain capacity well ahead of demand, to distribute it throughout the island, and, perhaps most important, to aim for realistic (that is, no profit, no subsidy) overall pricing levels while maintaining a uniform set of rates as between rural and urban locations.

Finally, although their impact is difficult to assess, the government established a number of industry-oriented technology and investment institutes (examples are the China Productivity and Trade Center, the Food Industry Research and Development Institute, the China Development Corporation, and the Industrial Development and Investment Center) to provide management training and technical assistance along with credit for industrial entrepreneurs. While the effort to provide such packages is a common phenomenon in developing countries, the concentration on usefulness to the private sector in areas of expanding activity compares favorably with the "search for major breakthroughs" approach to technology financed by government subsidies

6. See T. H. Lee, Kuo-shu Liang, Chi Schive, and Ryh-sang Yeh, "The Structure of Effective Protection and Subsidy in Taiwan," *Economic Essays* 6 (November 1975), 55–176.

7. Interest rates on time deposits fluctuated from 10 to 16 percent between 1953 and 1957. Lending rates were above 20 percent for secured and higher for unsecured loans.

Table 3.4. Transport Network

Year (1)	Total highway length (kms.) (2)	Paved highway length (kms.) (3)	Paved (percent) (3) ÷ (2) (4)	Rural highway length (kms.) (5)	Rural highway (percent) (5) ÷ (2) (6)	Highway density Meters per sq. km. (7)	Highway density Meters per 1,000 persons (8)	Railway density Meters per sq. km. (9)	Railway density Meters per 1,000 persons (10)
1952	15.6	1.0	6.7	10.6	67.6	434	1,922	170	751
1953	15.7	1.2	7.6	10.6	67.2	435	1,855	167	711
1954	15.7	1.4	8.9	10.6	67.1	436	1,792	159	652
1955	15.7	1.4	9.2	10.5	66.9	436	1,727	156	617
1956	15.7	1.5	9.3	10.5	66.9	436	1,670	159	607
1957	15.7	1.6	10.1	10.5	66.6	436	1,620	156	578
1958	16.0	1.9	12.0	10.4	64.7	446	1,598	156	558
1959	16.2	2.2	13.6	10.4	64.4	450	1,553	159	546
1960	16.2	2.5	15.3	10.4	64.3	451	1,504	156	519
1961	16.3	2.7	16.8	10.4	64.0	453	1,461	156	502
1962*	14.5	2.7	18.9	9.6	65.9	403	1,260	156	486
1963	14.6	3.1	21.1	9.6	66.1	406	1,229	150	454
1964	14.7	3.5	23.5	9.7	65.7	409	1,200	150	441
1965	14.8	3.9	26.5	9.7	65.5	413	1,175	153	436
1966	15.0	4.4	29.2	9.8	64.9	418	1,158	153	423
1967	15.3	4.9	31.9	10.0	65.1	426	1,151	153	414
1968	15.5	5.5	35.4	10.0	64.5	430	1,132	153	403
1969	15.5	6.1	39.1	10.0	64.6	431	1,082	153	384
1970	15.6	6.8	43.5	10.0	64.3	434	1,064	156	382
1971	15.7	7.4	47.3	10.1	64.4	438	1,050	156	373
1972	15.4	7.9	49.8	10.2	63.4	442	1,040	156	366
1973	16.1	8.3	51.7	10.3	63.9	448	1,036	153	353
1974	16.2	8.8	54.6	n.a.	n.a.	450	1,022	153	347
1975	16.2	8.8	54.6	n.a.	n.a.	450	1,182	153	311

*Urban roads excluded since 1962.
Source: Columns 1–3, 7–10, EPC, *Taiwan Statistical Data Book, 1976;* columns 5–6, *Taiwan Highway Bureau Statistics.*

frequently encountered elsewhere. In general, the government avoided the splashy ''white elephant'' route and seemed more interested in enhancing the capacity of the infant entrepreneur to stand on his own feet—presumably the basic purpose of erecting the primary import-substitution hothouse in the first place—rather than to force-feed him continuously into the need for permanent protection from foreign and domestic competition.

The overall consequences of the primary import-substitution subphase of development in Taiwan can be summarized from several vantage points. For one, the overall trade orientation of the economy declined sharply from the prewar period and remained at relatively low levels during the 1950s (see Figure 3.1). For another, within manufacturing industry there was a dramatic change from the complete dominance of food processing (73 percent of total manufacturing in 1936–40) for export to Japan to such primarily import-

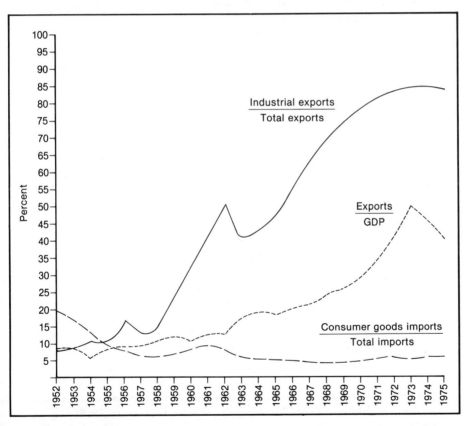

Figure 3.1. From import to export substitution. Source: Economic Planning Council, *Taiwan Statistical Data Book, 1976.*

Table 3.5. Annual Rate of Growth of the Industrial Sector (in percentages)

	I sector	Manufacturing	Food processing	Textiles and leather goods
1953-58	8.9	8.9	4.4	4.4
1958-63	12.1	12.6	3.7	13.4
1963-68	18.4	19.7	6.9	24.3
1968-72	21.2	23.1	6.9	26.4
1972-75	7.5	7.1	0.0	12.3

Source: EPC, Executive Yuan, "Taiwan Economic Statistics," *Industry of Free China.*

replacing industries as textiles, rubber and leather goods, wood products, and bicycles, which amounted to 66 percent of total manufacturing production by 1954.[8] Table 3.5 indicates the shifts in the direction of manufacturing growth over time. There was also a gradual shift from concentration on textiles, to wood products, to leather and rubber products, in terms of the changes in the imported portion of total domestic supply in these industries (see Table 3.6).

Although the Taiwan version of import substitution was relatively mild and flexible, some of the well-known negative consequences associated with this policy regime could not be avoided. Inevitably, a package of policies that shifts profits to a new industrial class via import licenses and credit rationing tends to favor the relatively large-scale and the relatively capital-intensive. But "relatively" remains terribly important; it is intended to convey a contrast with the later, more export- and market-oriented growth phases; compared to other developing countries in a similar (primary import-substitution) sub-phase, Taiwan's manufacturing sector was already unusually labor-intensive and decentralized, growing at respectable annual rates of output (10 percent) and employment (6 percent) for the 1950s as a whole.

The well-known problem with primary import substitution, however, is that it is bound to run out of steam. The growth rates of industrial output for the second half of the 1950s, for example, declined to 11 percent, employment to less than 5 percent. Once domestic markets for nondurable consumer goods become exhausted, there are essentially two paths open to the system: to continue (and probably intensify) the existing policy regime by moving into secondary import substitution, that is, the increased domestic production of previously imported capital goods and durable consumer goods, and the domestic processing of intermediate goods; or to increase the relative concentration on the manufacture of nondurable consumer goods, but now directed into international markets, that is, export substitution.

Most observers (including this one) have tended to characterize the transition path of Taiwan as one of a relatively smooth progression from primary import substitution in the 1950s to export substitution in the 1960s. However,

8. C. Y. Lin, Appendix Tables A-19, A-20.

Table 3.6. Imports as a Percentage of Total Supply (individual industries)

	1954	1961	1966
Textiles	3.8	5.8	9.5
Wood and wood products	3.9	0.3	0.5
Paper, paper products, and printing	12.3	9.9	11.9
Leather and leather products	44.6	36.9	44.4
Rubber products	37.6	27.5	22.2

Sources: Inspectorate General of Customs, *The Trade of China* (Taiwan, issues published in 1955, 1962, 1967); Industrial and Commercial Census of Taiwan (ICCT), *Industrial and Commercial Census of Taiwan* (Taipei, 1954, 1961, 1966).

a closer look at the record indicates that, in fact, the period between 1954 and 1958 was characterized by a good deal of backing and filling and indecision on this score. As "easy" domestic markets for nondurable consumer goods were gradually exhausted in the late 1950s, industrial surveys indicate increasing excess capacity in textiles, paper, rubber goods, and soap. Pressures for a change in the direction of the system accordingly mounted. Some of the responses took the form of the organization of domestic cartels to resist price cutting; others, the granting of export subsidies via tax rebates and the like on top of a basically unchanged policy structure as a way of at least partially redressing the discrimination against exports. At the same time, there resulted an increasingly frantic search for new (and the expansion of old) secondary import-substituting industries, including chemicals, rayon fiber, urea fertilizer, prevulcanized plastics, and compact cars. Not until about 1958 did the small size of the market, the continuing pressure of surplus labor, and the obviously steeply rising costs associated with the expansion of these more capital- and skill-intensive industries shift the balance of private and public opinion in favor of the export-substitution path.

The shift, when it did occur, did not come overnight—nor was it accomplished in line with an overall design or master plan. Nevertheless, looking back, the outlines of a more or less systematic package of policy changes can be discerned which facilitated the transition to a basically different orientation of the economy. Between 1958 and 1963, for example, the following major changes may be quickly recorded.[9] First, the multiple exchange rate system, a response to the currency overvaluation endemic to a controlled economy still experiencing substantial inflation (at an annual rate of 11 percent during the 1950s), was gradually dismantled and displaced by an effectively devalued unitary rate. With inflation now more or less under control, this rate could be maintained at fairly realistic levels. Second, a substantial liberalization of the

9. For a fuller analysis, see Chapter 5. Also M. Hsing, "Taiwan: Industrialization and Trade Policies," in *Taiwan and the Philippines: Industrialization and Trade Policies* (Oxford, 1970).

foreign exchange allocation system via a link system for would-be exporters and a drastic reduction (from twenty to two) in the number of import licensing categories was undertaken. Also helpful was the introduction of a less than 25 percent price differential requirement before an item could be placed on the import control list. At the same time, though the QRs represented the really effective constraint, tariffs on finished goods were moved downward slightly, toward greater uniformity with the relatively high level of duties on primary and intermediate goods, thus somewhat lowering effective protection levels. Third, tax rebates for industrial exports were liberalized and generalized, and a marketable foreign exchange entitlement or linkage system at 100 percent of export earnings was instituted. Fourth, a large multifaceted package of fiscal incentives for both domestic and foreign investors was put in place.[10]

Unfortunately, there are no studies using a consistent methodology that would permit one to trace, in a precise quantitative fashion, the sum total of the changes in the bias from import substitution to production for exports over time.[11] With respect to tariffs and import controls, one important study says that the "commodity categories containing all items subject to import control and with average tariff rates higher than 30 percent have shown a decreasing tendency since 1956"[12] and that by the mid-1960s effective protection on manufacturing was lower in Taiwan than in any other developing country examined, with the exception of Mexico.[13] There is also evidence of the decreasing importance of exchange entitlements, tax and tariff rebates, interest rate differentials, and outright export subsidies, in addition to the continuing maintenance of a more realistic exchange rate in the 1960s. And, finally, more very helpful calculations by Lin[14] demonstrate, by way of example, the relative attractiveness of import substitution in cotton yarn in 1953—showing a 42 percent premium of the implicit over the official exchange rate—in sharp contrast with the 1966 premium of 30 percent in favor of foreign over domestic sales.

There can be little doubt that the long list of modifications in the foreign exchange, fiscal, and monetary spheres at the end of the 1950s and early 1960s added up to a massive change in the overall policy package, inducing, or, better, accommodating, the required major adjustment in the structure of the economy, especially its industrial sector. This adjustment in the total

10. These represented a major strengthening of investment incentives first promulgated in 1954–55.

11. We have only the work of Fu-Chi Lin for 1966, "The Effective Protection Rates under the Existing Tariff Structure in Taiwan" (Research Report of Tax Reform Commission, January 1970), which was utilized by M. Hsing in his Organization for Economic Cooperation and Development (OECD) study, and the current but still incomplete effort by Lee et al. for 1969.

12. Lee et al., p. 3.

13. Hsing, p. 244.

14. C. Y. Lin, pp. 113–14.

environment permitted the economy to shift from an essentially domestic raw materials or land-based to an imported raw materials and labor-based pattern of production and exports. In this way, the still relatively abundant supplies of labor could be increasingly combined with an enhanced entrepreneurial capacity to concentrate on the penetration of foreign markets with the products of Taiwan's labor-intensive consumer goods industries.

Primary Export Substitution and the Gradual Exhaustion of the Labor Surplus, 1963-1972

The decade of the 1960s was characterized by the extremely rapid overall growth of the economy. Per capita income growth rates more than doubled, from 2.7 percent annually in the 1950s to 5.8 percent in the 1960s, with (gross) savings rates spurting from 12 to 26 percent. An integral part of this picture—and of the explanation—was the changing and expanded role of the industrial sector. Table 3.5 indicates the acceleration of industrial-sector growth, from 10 percent annually in the 1950s to 20 percent in the 1960s. As a consequence, the relative position of industry was rapidly displacing that of agriculture in terms of their relative quantitative importance over time.

The changes were just as significant within the I sector, as participation in world trade increased rapidly and new export-substituting industries gained dramatically in importance. As shown in Table 3.3, between 1962 and 1972 exports of goods and services rose from 13 to nearly 43 percent of GDP and the share of industrial products—primarily nondurable consumer goods—in these exports increased from 50 to 83 percent (also see Figure 3.1). By the end of the decade, Taiwan's export ratio was one of the highest on record, and the shift in the composition of exports certainly one of the most spectacular. During this period, imported raw-material-based industries (such as textiles, leather, and wood products) dramatically increased their importance relative to domestic raw-material-based industries—in spite of the boost received by the latter from the boom in mushrooms and asparagus tips of the mid-1960s.

The obvious sine qua non for a successful transition from import substitution to export substitution is the ability of domestic entrepreneurs to stand on their own feet as windfall profits are gradually withdrawn and to compete successfully in international markets. During the primary import-substitution subphase of transition growth, a substantial portion of industrialists' profits is typically derived from windfalls resulting from government interventions designed to shift profits from agriculture-based surpluses in their direction. During export substitution, industrialists' profits are based more on entrepreneurial efficiency and competitiveness in international markets. With the veil between endowments and relative prices in factor and commodity markets having been partially lifted, the test of success becomes more nearly market-oriented. An industrial entrepreneurial class is required that is not only able to withstand the rigors of having the temperature in the industrial hothouse turned down (or off) but can also take on the problem of trying to conquer unfamiliar foreign markets.

A second necessary condition for successful export substitution is whether or not the infrastructural ground has been prepared to ensure the sustained contribution of a substantially dynamic agricultural sector. In the absence of continuous agricultural productivity increase, not only would the cheap supply of labor to the expanding industrial sector be threatened, but a whole variety of dynamic linkages between agriculture and nonagricultural production—both of the input-output and of the incentives variety[15]—would be weakened. As already noted, given the relatively mild version of the prior primary import-substitution subphase in Taiwan, especially the unusually favorable conditions of rural infrastructure, a vigorous, more or less balanced advance in agriculture and industry became possible. During the 1960s, the policy and technological environment for agricultural growth (see Chapter 2) was ever more propitious, with annual growth rates in excess of 5 percent recorded.

Whereas the agricultural sector—and agricultural raw-materials-based industry—provided the main engine of economic, and, in particular, industrial, growth in the 1950s, in the 1960s this role was gradually taken over by imported raw-materials-based industries, adding value chiefly in the form of unskilled labor. In fact, the rate of growth of industrial employment, approximately 6 percent annually in the 1950s and comfortably ahead of population growth, rose to a spectacular 10 percent annually in the 1960s. As a consequence, by the end of the 1960s, the economy had mopped up much of its surplus agricultural labor, and unskilled real wages that had been rising only slowly in the 1950s showed substantial increases.

In probing more fully into this spectacular spurt of industry in the 1960s, some decomposition of the manufacturing sector, both in terms of the regional or spatial dimension and of a somewhat closer look at some of the important component industries, may be helpful. I contend that the relatively dispersed rural character of Taiwan's industrialization effort represents a key to its successful growth and export-substitution performance. We know, for example (see Tables 3.7 and 3.8), that the proportion of industrial establishments in the five largest cities was only 34 percent of the total in 1951 and remained virtually unchanged by 1971—and that the proportion of persons employed in manufacturing in the cities actually declined (from 43 to 37 percent) between 1956 and 1966. This particular spatial characteristic of industrialization, way out of line by contemporary LDC standards, was responsible in large part for the maintenance of a fairly labor-intensive growth pattern, for minimizing the

---

15. Including the impact of industrial growth back on agriculture, as emphasized by Tang, Nicholls, and others of the Vanderbilt "contact" school.

Table 3.7. Regional Growth and Distribution of Industrial Establishments, 1951–1971*

	1951 Number of establishments (1)	Growth of establishments 1951 = 100 (2)	Percent share of establishments			
			1951 (3)	1961 (4)	1968 (5)	1971 (6)
Cities						
Taipei	1,849	2,692.7	15.1	14.1	15.4	17.8
Taichung	544	2,038.1	4.5	3.4	3.5	4.0
Kaohsiung	566	1,991.7	4.6	3.7	3.8	4.0
Subtotal	2,959	2,438.3	24.2	21.5	22.8	25.8
Semiurban cities						
Keelung	408	1,601.0	3.3	2.4	2.5	2.3
Tainan	827	2,278.0	6.7	6.0	6.1	6.7
Subtotal	1,235	2,054.3	10.1	8.5	8.6	9.1
Semiurban prefectures						
Taipei	860	2,527.8	7.0	7.5	7.1	7.8
Yilan	373	2,125.5	3.1	2.8	3.0	2.8
Miaoli	576	2,313.9	4.7	4.1	3.5	3.1
Taichung	594	2,303.7	4.9	5.4	5.1	4.9
Yunlin	473	2,558.4	3.9	4.6	5.0	4.3
Subtotal	2,876	2,228.2	23.6	24.4	23.7	22.9
Rural prefectures						
Taoyuan	323	3,513.0	2.6	3.7	3.9	4.1
Nantou	375	2,379.5	3.1	3.7	3.6	3.2
Chiayi	515	2,470.9	4.2	4.8	4.8	4.6
Tainan	700	2,320.0	5.7	6.7	6.5	5.8
Pingtung	616	1,998.2	5.1	5.0	5.0	4.4
Taitung	95	5,411.6	0.8	1.7	2.0	1.8
Subtotal	2,024	2,541.4	21.5	25.6	25.7	23.9
Mixed urban, semiurban, rural prefectures						
Hsinchu	560	1,965.2	4.6	4.4	3.9	3.9
Changhua	956	2,043.0	7.8	6.6	6.7	6.6
Kaohsiung	618	2,003.1	5.1	5.4	5.1	4.4
Hualien	299	2,145.8	2.4	2.4	2.4	2.3
Penghu	84	3,225.0	0.7	1.1	1.0	1.0
Subtotal	2,517	2,029.5	20.6	20.0	19.2	18.3
All Taiwan	12,211	2,287.8	100.0	100.0	100.0	100.0

*By number in operation at end of the year.
Source: Executive Group of ICCT, *General Report, 1971 Industrial and Commercial Census of Taiwan and Fukien Area* (Taipei, 1971), I, Table 6.

inevitably high costs of urbanization, and for avoiding a deterioration of the size distribution of income in Taiwan during this initial period of accelerated growth.[16]

Among the reasons for the relative dispersion of industries in Taiwan are

16. For a thorough analysis underlying this latter point, which is treated more fully in Chapter 1, also see John C. H. Fei, Gustav Ranis, and Shirley W. Y. Kuo, "Growth with Equity: The Taiwan Case" (mimeo, prepared under the auspices of the World Bank, 1976), and as well as Fei, Ranis, Kuo, "Growth and the Family Distribution of Income by Factor Components," *Quarterly Journal of Economics* 92, no. 1 (February 1978), 17–53.

Table 3.8. Distribution of Employed Persons by Locality (in percentages)

	1956			1966		
	Cities	Towns	Rural	Cities	Towns	Rural
Total*	21.59	5.54	72.89	23.68	6.73	69.58
Agriculture, forestry, fishery, hunting	4.78	2.42	92.81	4.38	2.38	93.25
Mining	18.90	0.88	80.22	19.04	1.55	79.41
Manufacturing	42.68	10.06	47.26	37.02	10.80	52.18
Food	24.11	8.51	67.38	23.50	9.83	66.67
Textile and apparel	34.10	14.40	51.50	27.87	13.65	58.48
Production of wood, stalk, bamboo	31.29	8.16	60.55	40.06	6.63	53.31
Furniture and fixtures	32.00	9.71	58.29	32.07	9.28	58.65
Chemicals	57.53	9.68	32.79	42.48	10.92	46.60
Nonmetallic products	31.84	6.70	61.46	25.85	6.12	68.03
Metal products	52.32	12.58	35.10	49.90	12.37	37.73
Machinery and equipment	62.60	8.66	28.74	54.94	6.10	38.96
Transport equipment	60.32	5.82	33.86	48.58	7.55	43.87
Others	57.10	9.27	33.63	42.90	12.50	44.60
Construction	44.84	11.45	43.71	43.92	12.27	43.81
Utilities	51.30	9.74	38.96	47.25	9.89	42.86
Commerce	44.36	9.98	45.66	42.34	10.56	47.10
Trade	42.77	9.92	47.30	38.78	10.83	50.39
Bank, insurance, etc.	65.47	10.79	23.74	65.12	8.83	26.05
Transport and communication	54.27	8.92	36.81	50.74	9.50	39.76
Services	41.16	9.73	49.11	34.44	9.38	56.17
Public service*	50.27	10.45	39.28	32.63	9.97	57.41
Education	36.81	8.79	54.40	36.53	9.50	53.98
Personal service	34.06	9.76	56.18	33.14	7.88	58.98
Others	39.85	8.89	51.26	43.48	8.86	47.67
Not elsewhere classified	31.35	3.24	65.41	16.78	5.35	77.87

*In 1956, excludes military personnel living on military bases.

Source: Table 4 in Samuel P. S. Ho, "The Rural Non-Farm Sector in Taiwan," World Bank Studies in Employment and Rural Development, no. 32 (Washington, D.C., September 1976). Underlying data from the 1956 and 1966 population censuses. Cities includes the seven largest Cities; Towns, the nine largest towns; Rural, the rest.

the special topographical features of the island. High mountains make up about two-thirds of the total land area and divide the island into three main zones. Both agricultural productivity and related industrial output are highest in the fertile plains areas of the West Coast. The narrow East Coast, on the other hand, which encompasses 23 percent of the total land area but only 7 percent of the cultivable area, shows manufacturing production at a miniscule 2 percent of the national total and per capita income at only 67 percent of the national average for 1969.[17] A smaller, but topographically favored area, mainly because of port facilities, is the South. The concentration of population and arable land in the West and South would naturally tend to favor the balanced growth of agricultural and nonagricultural output in these areas. Second, as Table 3.4 indicated, the excellent road and rail network inherited from the Japanese period was not only maintained but continuously and sub-

17. Hua Fei, "Introduction to the Overall Development Planning of Taiwan, Republic of China," *Industry of Free China*, 37, no. 4 (April 1972).

stantially improved. Especially noteworthy is the rapidly increasing proportion of paved rural roads. To provide some points of reference on the unusual infrastructural preparation of Taiwan for dispersed industrial development, Table 3.9 presents some Asian comparisons, in terms both of the spatial and the population density of the transportation network.

Third, the internal transport network was extremely well articulated with the main ports, Kaohsiung, Keelung, and Hwalien. This not only facilitated the heavy export of domestic raw-material-intensive products in the 1950s and early 1960s but was of substantial importance in enhancing the system's export-substitution potential once the overall policy environment had shifted. When industrial production became more and more domestic labor- and imported raw-materials-oriented, the ability to attract labor to the proximity of the port cities and/or to locate industries rurally—either the entire operation or subcontracted units—became even more important. It made it feasible for much urban industrial labor to bicycle in for the day, returning to the rural household at night, and for both domestic (for example, sugar refining, later mushrooms and asparagus canning) and imported raw-materials-intensive industries (for example, textiles) to be located near the main sources of rural labor supply.

Fourth, beginning in 1965, bonded factories for export and Export Processing Zones, with the express purpose of facilitating the new mode of export-oriented industrial production, were established and gradually expanded. Bonded establishments were more footloose in their location throughout the island, and the Export Processing Zones were located in the port cities to

Table 3.9. Transport Density in Selected Asian Countries 1973–1974

				Density			
	Paved highway (percent)	Population 1974 (millions)	Area (1,000 sq. km.)	Meters per square kms.		Meters per 1,000 persons	
Country				Railway	Highway	Railway	Highway
Taiwan	51.7	15.9	36	153.0	457.6	353	1,036
Burma	27.1	31.2	680	5.7	36.8	124	802
Sri Lanka	38.4	14.0	66	30.5	963.0	144	4,540
India	18.3	620.7	2,960	36.6	434.7	175	2,073
Indonesia	49.1	134.7	1,514	5.2	23.5	59	264
Iran	27.8	34.1	1,630	3.2	26.6	155	1,273
Iraq	31.2	11.4	303	8.4	68.6	222	1,824
Japan	25.2	112.3	381	171.0	2755.9	581	9,350
Malaysia	87.2	12.4	334	6.6	54.2	178	1,460
Pakistan	56.5	72.5	877	14.5	38.7	176	468
Philippines	20.5	44.0	298	4.4	332.2	30	2,250
South Korea	6.1	34.8	98	55.4	355.1	156	1,000
Thailand	51.3	43.3	515	8.6	56.0	102	666

Source: Henry Sampson, ed., *Jane's World Railways* (New York, 1974); Ministry of Communications, *Statistical Abstracts of Transport and Communications, 1974* (Taipei, 1975).

facilitate the application of various fiscal and investment incentives via a reduction to "one stop" of a cumbersome set of official procedures. With raw or processed raw materials coming into these zones, value was added in the form mainly of unskilled labor, and the more fully processed or finished goods reexported (thus also gaining an advantage under the U.S. tariff code).[18] The export processing zone schema was a perfect representation of the new pattern of export-oriented industrial growth based on imported raw materials. But although it grew rapidly and captured the imagination and, incidentally, a good deal of foreign private capital, it remained quantitatively of less importance than the quiet kind of export-oriented production activity going on throughout the island during the 1960s.[19]

Finally, the importance of an active program of rural electrification and a policy of maintaining equality between urban and rural power rates, as well as fuel prices, has already been mentioned. In terms, once again, of international comparisons, a marked effort was made to avoid providing additional advantages above and beyond the normal benefits of industrial agglomeration to the urban location of industry. Through the 1960s, the government increasingly invested in rural industrial estates, providing the essential physical overheads for private industry in a substantial number of rural locations.[20] Such assistance also extended to the technical side. The Joint Commission on Rural Reconstruction (JCRR), for example, financed research and development efforts in support of fish canning at Kaohsiung; farmers' associations were encouraged to include rural transport and the promotion of rural industries among the services offered; such institutions as the Forestry Research Institute, Agricultural Experiment Stations, and the Food Industry Research and Development Institute were set up to provide for additional strengthening of the linkages between the agricultural and nonagricultural sectors.

This combination of a gradual change in the economy's endowment and capacities with a more rapid change in the policy environment that permitted these changes to be reflected in the economy's production structure resulted in a remarkable shift in the pattern of industrial development on the island. It is useful to distinguish among the various crucial, if mutually interrelated, dimensions of that performance: the extraordinary rate of growth of industry during the export-substitution decade; its unusually pronounced rural orientation; and its relatively large contribution to the generation of employment.

First, with respect to the overall rate of growth of industry, and, more

18. This code provides for import tariffs to be levied only on the value added of processing zone exports.

19. By 1972, for example, booming processing zone exports still amounted to only 8 percent of total exports.

20. Seventeen such industrial districts comprising almost 1,600 hectares were established before 1966. The government provided the necessary infrastructure and then sold the pieces to private interests.

specifically, manufacturing, I have already noted the enhanced performance of the 1960s, in contrast with the respectable if more modest growth of the 1950s. The shift from domestic raw-materials-based industries to imported raw-materials-based industries is dwarfed by the shift from home demand and import substitution to exports as a source of demand for industrial output. Table 3.10 captures both these trends. Based on the Chenery decomposition technique—with all its well-known shortcomings—it indicates how substantial a portion of the rapid industrial growth of the 1960s is attributable to the increased international competitiveness, especially in labor-intensive nondurable consumer goods.

What is usually less well understood in the discussion of import substitution versus export expansion is the only gradually diminishing absolute importance of the growing domestic market, which continued to be sustained and fed by the simultaneous growth in agricultural income. The elements of industrial decentralization and labor-intensity are crucially tied up with both the achievement of international cost-effectiveness and the successful strengthening of agricultural/nonagricultural linkages, from both the technical and market incentives points of view.

The unique spatial characteristic of Taiwan's industrialization pattern can

Table 3.10. Sources of Demand for Manufacturing Output Growth (percent)

	Import substitution	Exports	Home demand
1937–1954			
Nonfood manufacturing	91.1	−13.4	22.3
1953–1955			
Total manufacturing	9.0	−8.7	99.6
Food, beverages, and tobacco	20.6	−56.4	135.8
Nondurable consumer goods	22.4	2.5	75.2
1955–1960			
Total manufacturing	−8.1	16.5	91.7
Food, beverages, and tobacco	1.4	34.8	63.8
Nondurable consumer goods	−5.7	21.2	84.5
1960–1965			
Total manufacturing	3.6	13.8	82.5
Food, beverages, and tobacco	1.5	9.4	89.0
Nondurable consumer goods	−2.2	27.5	74.7
1965–1970			
Total manufacturing	−7.3	31.2	76.1
Food, beverages, and tobacco	0.2	7.3	92.4
Nondurable consumer goods	−6.3	74.2	32.1
1970–1972			
Total manufacturing	0.1	20.9	79.1
Food, beverages, and tobacco	−14.1	12.9	101.2
Nondurable consumer goods	−13.1	59.6	53.5

Sources: The data for 1937–54 are from C. Y. Lin, Table 4-3, p. 68; other data from Kuo-shu Liang and Ching-ing Hou Liang, "Exports and Employment in Taiwan," in Institute of Economics, Academia Sinica, *Conference on Population and Economic Development in Taiwan* (Taipei, 1976), p. 37.

be examined further with the help of both the population and industrial censuses of Taiwan. A recent paper by Samuel Ho[21] presents impressive evidence on the extent of rural industrialization by use of the population census. Dividing Taiwan into an urban sector (its seven largest cities containing 25 percent of the total population in 1966), a town sector (the nine largest towns with 7 percent of the population), and a rural sector (the rest), he shows (see Table 8) a remarkable relative decline in the urban proportion of total industrial and manufacturing employment, with the most pronounced increase (for example, from 47 to 52 percent of total manufacturing employment) occurring in the rural areas. This relative shift from cities to rural areas, with the towns more or less holding their own, seems to be a representative phenomenon occurring in virtually all branches of manufacturing, as well as in other parts of the nonagricultural sector, like services. As late as the mid-1960s, more than half of Taiwan's rapidly growing manufacturing labor force was employed outside of the seven largest cities and nine largest towns; for commerce and services, the equivalent figures are 47 and 56 percent, respectively (see Table 3.8). During the 1956–66 decade, the share of rural manufacturing employment in total rural employment rose from 7.9 to 10.8 percent, that of rural commerce from 4.7 to 5.4 percent, and that of rural services from 10.6 to 20.4 percent.[22] Thus, while the whole of Taiwan and the nonagricultural sectors in particular were booming, the relative role of rural industry and services,[23] at least from the point of view of employment, was substantially enhanced. It is doubtful that many other developing countries have a similar record.

The industrial censuses of 1951, 1961, 1968, and 1971 yield similar conclusions, as already noted. When Taiwan is divided into a somewhat more refined set of gradations between the most urban and the most rural (see Table 3.7), the number of establishments in the three biggest cities are shown to have grown at a lower rate over the two decades than in the most rural prefectures.[24]

An important factor contributing to this relatively rural location of industry and services is the dualistic nature of many households referred to in Chapter 2 of this volume. In 1960, for example, less than 50 percent of Taiwan's farm families were fully engaged in farming, 31 percent had nonagricultural sidelines, and 20 percent viewed agriculture as their sideline.[25] In 1964,

21. "The Rural Non-Farm Sector in Taiwan," World Bank Studies in Employment and Rural Development, no. 32 (Washington, D.C., September 1976).

22. Ibid., Table 2.

23. The lion's share of the increase was in rural services, from 10.6 to 20.4 percent; rural manufacturing went from 7.8 to 10.8 percent.

24. Since many repair establishments, included in earlier industrial censuses, are excluded from the 1971 census, and such establishments are probably more important in rural areas, the evidence is probably understated.

25. Ho, *Economic Development*, p. 254.

nonagricultural income made up an amazing 32 percent of total farm family income; by 1972, the proportion was in excess of 50 percent.[26] This clearly could be accomplished only via the rural location of industry and/or easy physical access to urban industry. For 1963, for instance, a JCRR survey indicates that of workers leaving the soil, only 24 percent of the females and 16 percent of the males actually migrated to urban employment; commuting to work (for example, by bicycle to the Export Processing Zones) was the method of industrial participation for 24 percent of the males and 35 percent of the females moving out; and seasonal participation in nonagriculture was the method for 61 percent of the males and 41 percent of the females.[27]

For some industries, such as food processing, the rural location of industry was dictated in large part by the location of the domestic raw material; in others, like textiles, that import their raw materials and do not require large plants, by closeness to the relatively large pool of cheap labor; and in still others, like electronics, that also import their raw materials, but require large plants, by the advantages of the urban Export Processing Zones that could be enjoyed without sacrificing access to cheap rural labor. In all these cases, the presence or absence of economies of scale and the relative labor-intensity of the production process was and remains an important feature in determining location. Table 3.11 shows that when manufacturing is divided into consumer and producer goods for a later year—1971—61 percent of consumer goods production, as opposed to 39 percent of producer goods production, still took place outside of the five large cities.[28] Within industrial subsectors, there also were continuing shifts into relatively more labor-intensive activities, for example, from sugar to mushroom and asparagus processing. This ability to continuously reflect an abundant labor supply in its industrial production structure—both in terms of technology and output mixes—provided the cutting edge for the export-substitution growth phase after the 1958–63 reforms.

Table 3.12 gives urban and rural capital-labor ratios for the main census years between 1954 and 1971 for all of nonagriculture, the Kuznets I sector, manufacturing, and a number of individual manufacturing industries. Several points are important. First, with the important exception of the food processing industry, in 1954 and 1961, the urban industrial capital-labor ratio is invariably larger than the rural at every level. Moreover, excluding sugar processing—which is characterized by the continued presence of Japanese-built, large, capital-intensive mills in the rural areas of Taiwan—food process-

26. From household surveys conducted by the Directorate-General of Budget, Accounting, and Statistics.

27. Y. C. Tsui and T. C. Lin, "A Study on Rural Labor Mobility in Relation to Industrialization and Urbanization in Taiwan," JCRR Economic Digest Series, no. 16, (Taipei, 1964).

28. As before, the five major cities are classified as urban, the rest of the country as rural. In the 1966 and 1971 censuses, only total assets, instead of fixed assets, are available.

Table 3.11. Composition of Manufacturing Production by Region, 1971 (unit: million N.T.$)

Region	Total value of production	Consumer goods*		Producer goods†	
		Value	Percent	Value	Percent
City of Taipei	24,551	16,200	65.98	8,351	34.01
City of Kaohsiung	33,452	7,300	21.82	26,152	78.18
City of Taichung	5,255	2,874	54.69	2,381	45.31
City of Tainan	6,439	3,348	51.99	3,091	48.01
City of Keelung	5,059	2,125	42.00	2,935	58.00
Taipei Hsien	38,503	19,624	50.97	18,879	49.04
Taoyuan Hsien	15,228	10,194	66.94	5,035	33.06
Hsinchu Hsien	9,448	3,197	33.83	6,252	66.17
Miaoli Hsien	5,737	2,726	47.53	3,010	52.48
Taichung Hsien	13,384	9,611	71.81	3,773	28.19
Changhua Hsien	9,662	8,100	82.81	1,661	17.19
Nantou Hsien	1,134	716	63.09	419	36.91
Yunlin Hsien	2,897	2,635	90.95	262	9.05
Chiayi Hsien	3,631	2,482	68.37	1,149	31.64
Tainan Hsien	7,005	5,544	79.14	1,462	20.86
Kaohsiung Hsien	5,306	2,792	52.26	2,514	47.38
Pingtung Hsien	1,663	1,531	92.07	132	7.93
Hualien Hsien	1,335	1,120	83.91	215	16.09
Taitung Hsien	702	680	96.89	212	3.12
Yilan Hsien	3,106	1,641	52.83	1,465	47.17
Penghu Hsien	18	11	61.29	7	38.71
Urban	74,750	31,846	42.60	42,910	57.40
Rural	118,758	72,503	61.05	46,255	38.95
Total	193,515	104,350	53.92	89,165	46.08

*Consumer goods include food, beverages, tobacco, textiles, wearing apparel, leather products, wood products, furniture, paper products, printing, rubber, and miscellaneous products.

†Producer goods include chemicals, petroleum, nonmetallic minerals, basic metallics, metal products, machinery equipment, transportation equipment, and electrical machinery.

Source: Sen-hsun Yen, "On the Regional Category of Industrialization in Taiwan" (in Chinese), *Industry of Free China,* 44 (July 1975), p. 7. Cities are classified as urban, hsien as rural.

ing follows the same pattern.[29] Second, Table 3.12 shows that, while capital-labor ratios seem to be generally growing, the growth is much more marked in the case of urban industry, that is, the rural/urban technology gap seems to be growing. Third, although the more reliable fixed capital data are unfortunately not available for 1971, all the data indicate overall increases in industrial capital-intensity during the import-substitution subphase, with some reversal—largely caused by output mix changes—thereafter. Finally, Table 3.13 also points out that capital-intensity is not highly correlated with labor productivity levels across industries. Food canning and electrical machinery, for example, had especially large contributions from total factor productivity. The observed relatively low levels of the capital-labor ratio in the machinery

29. This is further illustrated by Table 3.13, which contrasts the overall fixed capital-labor ratios for food processing (which includes sugar) and food canning (which does not), for 1961. Given the declining relative importance of food processing over time, it should be noted that the capital-intensity of rural manufacturing as a whole declined below that of urban manufacturing.

Table 3.12. Capital-Labor Ratios in Urban and Rural Areas* (unit: N.T.$ per worker)

	Urban and rural fixed capital-labor ratios						Urban and rural total assets-labor ratios								
	1954			1961			1954			1966			1971		
	Urban	Rural	Urban/rural	Urban	Rural	Urban/rural	Urban	Rural	Urban/rural	Urban	Rural	Urban/rural	Urban	Rural	Urban/rural
Nonagricultural (Including food processing)	15.907	20.535	0.775	62.161	37.723	1.648	44.463	30.573	1.454	303.071	49.198	6.160	464.176	93.834	4.947
(Excluding food processing)	n.a.	n.a.	n.a.	62.909	32.325	1.946	n.a.	n.a.	n.a.	295.536	49.207	6.006	n.a.	n.a.	n.a.
I sector (Including food processing)	20.225	27.318	0.740	53.377	44.835	1.191	46.505	38.425	1.210	202.734	51.194	3.960	258.175	102.304	2.520
(Excluding food processing)	n.a.	n.a.	n.a.	54.237	37.673	1.440	n.a.	n.a.	n.a.	n.a.	n.a.	n.a.	n.a.	n.a.	n.a.
Manufacturing (Including food processing)	12.590	11.750	1.071	45.126	50.010	0.902	36.476	22.876	1.595	374.943	45.904	8.168	242.007	115.757	2.090
(Excluding food processing)	n.a.	n.a.	n.a.	45.680	39.373	1.160	n.a.	n.a.	n.a.	348.242	41.999	8.292	n.a.	n.a.	n.a.
Food processing	11.551	16.201	0.713	39.354	80.984	0.486	46.026	31.996	1.439	626.610	53.749	11.658	n.a.	n.a.	n.a.
Textiles	16.893	9.571	1.765	70.216	39.105	1.796	53.821	17.115	3.145	830.698	41.341	20.094	n.a.	n.a.	n.a.
Nonelectrical machinery	8.875	7.405	1.199	24.633	17.298	1.424	20.061	11.860	1.692	68.163	29.417	2.317	n.a.	n.a.	n.a.

*All *cities* are classified as urban. All *hsien* are classified as rural. Fixed assets consist of plant, equipment, and land. Total assets also include inventories and cash.
Source: Executive Group of ICCT, *General Report, Industrial and Commercial Census of Taiwan.*

Table 3.13. Capital-Labor Ratios and Labor Productivity in Manufacturing, 1961

	Employees (persons) (1)	Fixed capital (N.T. $1,000) (2)	Value added (N.T. $1,000) (3)	Fixed capital/labor ratio (2) ÷ (1) (N.T. $1,000) (4)	Labor productivity (3) ÷ (1) (N.T. $1,000) (5)
Food processing	88,498	6,614,853.3	3,940,750.6	74.75	44.53
Canning of food products	11,494	208,993.2	476,541.4	18.18	41.45
Textile industries	70,612	3,140,714.9	1,962,529.0	44.48	27.79
Machinery	16,528	354,491.8	444,416.5	21.45	26.88
General industrial machinery	4,711	95,686.2	132,873.1	20.31	28.20
Electrical machinery	13,039	340,821.9	463,134.6	26.14	35.51
Electronics	1,853	48,470.6	57,872.7	26.13	31.23

Source: Executive Group of ICCT, *General Report 1961, Industrial and Commercial Census of Taiwan,* III, 750, 751.

industries generally provide support to the work of Howard Pack and Michael Todaro.[30]

Other corroborative evidence of the general point—given reasonably "well-behaved" production functions—may be marshaled in the form of a comparison of the relative shares in urban and rural nonagricultural activities (see Table 3.14). All the ratios are substantially above 1, that is, labor's relative share is consistently and usually substantially above .5; moreover, and more to the point, rural industry and services are consistently more labor-intensive than urban ones are.[31] An international comparison of relative labor shares in some of the industries specifically of interest tends to confirm the impression that the industrial sector in Taiwan was unusually labor-intensive and its rural subsectors even more so.[32]

I have already noted that export substitution clearly gave a new lease on life to an industrial sector that had been running out of steam. The rest of the sector's rapid growth in the 1960s was caused by an increase in the domestic demand, fed by growth in per capita income. The relatively labor-intensive character of the overall expansion path can also be demonstrated by the fact that industrial employment rose by 10 percent annually in the 1960s compared

30. Howard Pack and Michael Todaro, "Technological Transfer, Labour Absorption and Economic Development," *Oxford Economic Papers* 21 (November 1969), 395–403.

31. With labor-intensity measured in this indirect way generally increasing, moreover, either as a function of changes in output mix or technology; this is an indication that the relationship between capital-labor ratios and relative shares holds only under normal production function assumptions.

32. For textiles, for example, the wage share for 1965–68 in Taiwan was 51.3, for West Pakistan, 34.6. For metal products, the comparison is 60.7 versus 31.1 (see Hsing).

Table 3.14. Relative Shares for Nonagricultural Activity (wage/property income)

	1964	1966	1968	1970	1972
All	1.80	1.86	1.82	2.14	2.25
Rural	1.91	2.02	3.25	3.50	3.95
Urban	1.78	1.84	1.67	2.00	2.13

Source: DGBAS, *Report on the Survey of Family Income and Expenditure* and *Study of Personal Income Distribution in Taiwan* (Taipei, 1964, 1966, 1968, 1970, 1972).

to 6 percent annually in the 1950s; increases in labor productivity amounted to less than 50 percent of the larger industrial output growth in the 1960s and to more than 50 percent of the smaller output growth in the 1950s.

Turning to the decomposition of the total employment generated in Taiwan during the 1960s, use of the 1961, 1966, and 1971 input-output tables indicates (see Table 3.15) that exports were responsible for 15 percent of the employment generated by the I sector in 1961, for 28 percent in 1966, and for 38 percent in 1971; for manufacturing only, the equivalent figures are an even more dramatic 19, 36 and 47 percent, respectively. The importance of the new export orientation for both generation of output and the gradual exhaustion of the labor surplus condition is clear even if the defects of this method of racking up the direct and indirect employment effects of exports are acknowledged.

One especially interesting feature of industrialization in Taiwan is the relationship between labor-intensity and output cum export growth over the longer term, using the censuses of 1954, 1961, and 1971. Ranking industries by their total capital-labor ratios for these years (see Table 3.16), with some notable exceptions, such as the position of textiles,[33] the lineup is about as expected—it moves from nondurables to durables and intermediate goods. This meshes well—though not perfectly—with the order of the quantitative importance of the various industries at the outset in 1954. Moreover, the relative growth rates of output and of employment by industry seem to be somewhat related in the sense that the relative gap between these two is generally smaller for the faster growing industries. For the entire 1954–71 period, for example, the highest output growth rate registered was in electrical machinery (27 percent), which also registered the highest employment growth rate (21 percent), or a gap of only 20 percent. Especially comparing the growth rates of industrial Gross Domestic Product (GDP) for 1961–66 and 1966–71, the export-substitution decade, with those of industrial employment, it is clear that industries that had relatively more success in absorbing

33. Which, at this level of aggregation, includes both intermediate and finished goods.

Table 3.15. Sources of Employment Generation

Industries	Employment source (1,000 persons)		
	Final demand (domestic final demand plus exports) (1)	Exports (2)	Percent (3) = (2) ÷ (1)
1961			
1. Agriculture	1,565	143	9.1
2. Manufacturing	466	92	19.7
3. Services	1,056	84	8.0
4. I Sector	732	113	15.4
1966			
1. Agriculture	1,624	298	18.3
2. Manufacturing	605	208	34.4
3. Services	1,224	167	13.6
4. I Sector	883	249	28.2
1971			
1. Agriculture	1,677	285	17.0
2. Manufacturing	1,095	518	47.3
3. Services	1,637	304	18.6
4. I Sector	1,432	549	38.3

Classification by sector of input-output tables, prepared by Shirley W. Y. Kuo.
1. Agricultural sectors (01-03)
2. Manufacturing sectors (09-46)
3. Service sectors (51-54)
4. I Sectors (04-50)
Source: Shirley W. Y. Kuo, "Labor Absorption in Taiwan, 1954-1971," in *Economic Essays* (November 1977), 144.

labor at the margin (that is, where relatively less of the output increase was attributable to labor productivity gains) also did relatively well in terms of output growth.

The same, of course, is true for export performance. Kuo-shu Liang and Ching-ing Hou Liang, using the 1966 and 1971 input-output tables, found that export industries had weighted capital-labor ratios of N.T.$52.68 in 1966 and N.T.$105.35 in 1971, compared to N.T.$75.05 and N.T.$280.69, respectively, for import-competing industries.[34]

Of the industries that had the largest GDP weight initially—food, textiles, and chemicals in 1954—textiles and chemicals performed relatively strongly in terms of both output and employment growth during the entire 1954-71 period. Electrical machinery and petroleum and coal products, on the other hand, trivially small in 1954, also experienced substantial growth rates in GDP; only the former, however, also exhibited a high rate of growth of employment (during the 1966-71 period, the rate of growth of employment in

34. Taking account of embodied capital in the form of skilled labor as well, they found that a very similar comparative relationship holds. See Kuo-shu Liang and Ching-ing Hou Liang, "Exports and Employment in Taiwan," in *Population and Economic Development in Taiwan*, Institute of Economics, Academia Sinica, (Taipei, 1976), p. 27.

Table 3.16. Annual Growth Rates of GDP and Employment by Industries

Industries	Industry ranking 1954-71 avg. total assets-labor ratio (N.T. $1,000)	Annual growth rates (percent) GDP (at 1971 constant prices)				Employees			
		1954-61	1961-66	1966-71	1954-71	1954-61	1961-66	1966-71	1954-71
Furniture and fixtures	35.64	13.7	13.1	17.7	14.7	9.4	-17.4	15.5	2.3
Miscellaneous manufacturing industries	42.99	0.9	23.2	18.9	11.5	-0.7	0.6	33.2	8.7
Metal products	49.89	21.8	14.5	8.5	15.6	5.0	2.3	15.0	7.0
Printing, publishing, and allied industries	54.14	13.8	3.3	12.1	10.1	3.2	-0.2	6.6	3.2
Machinery (except electrical machinery)	56.26	19.4	21.1	12.4	17.8	3.4	13.3	14.6	9.5
Leather and leather products, except footwear	63.83	8.5	10.1	15.5	4.9	0	-4.5	38.1	8.5
Rubber products	75.69	13.3	8.9	19.9	13.9	3.2	8.6	16.2	8.5
Chemicals and chemical products	87.06	0.6	18.2	10.4	10.8	5.2	14.3	20.6	12.2
Electrical machinery apparatus, appliances and supplies	94.18	16.8	37.8	31.0	26.8	14.1	20.1	31.4	20.7
Beverages	98.42	15.1	19.8	18.3	17.4	12.5	-19.5	5.8	0.1
Wood and cork products, except furniture	98.68	14.1	8.0	10.4	10.5	5.7	4.0	17.9	8.6
Textiles, footwear, and wearing apparel	105.28	1.4	14.7	22.5	11.2	4.6	4.5	21.1	9.2
Nonmetallic mineral products	109.12	13.8	11.3	7.4	11.2	4.0	3.3	6.5	4.5
Food	119.68	8.6	4.9	7.4	7.1	5.7	6.9	1.3	4.7
Transport equipment	121.09	16.8	25.4	16.1	19.0	6.3	-3.4	11.1	4.7
Paper and paper products	132.87	14.1	11.7	15.6	13.8	10.9	5.2	14.2	10.2
Basic metal industries	201.23	21.4	1.6	15.6	13.5	8.0	9.7	11.7	9.6
Tobacco	408.41	3.0	15.4	16.4	7.7	1.4	16.3	-2.1	4.5
Products of petroleum and coal	504.04	17.1	19.8	18.8	18.4	7.2	15.0	7.3	9.4

Source: Executive Group of ICCT, *General Reports, 1954, 1961, 1966, 1971, Industrial and Commercial Census of Taiwan* (Taipei, 1955, 1962, 1967, 1972).

Table 3.17. Capital-Labor Ratios of Exports to Selected
Countries, 1966 and 1971

	Capital-labor ratio	
Area and country	1966	1971
Developed areas	41.56	104.30
United States	45.11	105.55
Japan	44.36	105.22
European Economic Community	20.02	88.28
Other developed countries	48.83	117.10
Developing areas	68.90	154.42
Hong Kong	61.48	150.85
Viet Nam	82.41	251.45
Other developing countries	75.06	138.60

Source: Liang and Liang, p. 28.

electrical machinery was marginally higher than that of value added, an unusual occurrence). By 1971, textiles still accounted for 21 percent of the
industrial GDP as compared with 11.6 percent for electrical machinery. In
other words, and with few exceptions, the most labor-absorbing industries,
regardless of their initial size, also exhibited the relatively fastest output
growth rates.

The main reason that such initially relatively large industries as textiles
could keep up with a very rapid rate of overall industrial growth was, of
course, the increasingly pronounced export orientation of Taiwan's industrial
sector. Moreover, the bulk of the expansion of labor-intensive industrial consumer goods exports (such as apparel and plywood) was directed toward the
developed countries (DC), whereas the expansion of intermediate and capital
goods exports (such as petroleum and chemical products, paper, and pulp)
was directed toward other developing countries in the region.[35] This is demonstrated in Table 3.17. Lin, using a finer Standard International Trade
Classification (SITC) classification of industries for 1968, derives roughly
similar results, presented in Table 3.18;[36] the level of detail sharpens the
contrast as, for example, between textile yarn and fabrics, an intermediate
good, exported mainly to developing countries, and apparel, a final good,
exported mainly to developed countries.[37]

This trend is very much in keeping with the theory of comparative advantage, including its dynamic product cycle variant. Taiwan's greatest advan-

35. C. Y. Lin, p. 133, estimates the value of gross fixed assets per employee at N.T.$46,000
for manufactures exported to developed countries and at N.T.$105,000 for exports to less de-
veloped countries.

36. Ibid., Table 6-6, p. 130.

37. Using fixed assets–employee ratios for 1968, Lin finds the production of intermediate
textile goods to be in the N.T.$51,000–N.T.$100,000 range, with apparel production in the
below N.T.$50,000 range.

Table 3.18. Capital-Intensity and Export Orientation, 1968

Industries (ranked in ascending order of capital-intensity as per Table 3.16)	Percentage of total exports to	
	LDCs	DCs
Leather manufactures	34	66
Chemical products	89	11
Wood products	8	92
Apparel	5	95
Footwear	8	92
Textile yarn and fabrics	75	25
Paper and paper products	100	0
Petroleum products	67	33

Source: C. Y. Lin, Table 6-6, p. 130.

tage relative to the advanced countries was her relatively cheap, but efficient, supply of labor, and the labor-intensive industrial consumer goods exports grew the fastest during most of the 1960s. On the other hand, the more capital-intensive intermediate and producer goods, the consequence of early (Japanese period) and later (1955 to 1963) secondary import-substitution efforts, sold better in neighboring LDCs, given the advantage of lower transport costs (compared to potential DC suppliers) and the greater availability of skilled labor (compared to internal LDC producer). With reference to the product cycle, Taiwan would be expected, on a global basis, to gradually move from the export of labor-intensive industrial consumer goods to, first, the production at home, and then the exportation of the more technology- and capital-intensive durable consumer and producer goods categories. Already in several cross-sectional slices Taiwan's LDC customers were somewhat ahead of her DC customers.

The one important class of goods that does not fit too well, in temporal terms, either the product cycle or the related Linder "representative demand" explanation for trade[38] is the assembly and export of intermediate goods, especially in the area of electronics, which were an important component of Taiwan's exports to the DCs even in the mid-1960s. But this phenomenon probably should not be viewed as a jump in the product cycle or as a serious refutation of the representative demand theory; rather, it is a phenomenon based on the very special circumstances of the Export Processing Zones as early transition devices. These zones, established after 1965, substantially facilitated (and thus lowered the costs of) obtaining all the locational and fiscal benefits required to promote the reexport of intermediate goods after the addition of at least 20 percent domestic value added in the form of (mainly)

38. The Linder explanation is that to become competitive in international markets for a good a nation must first "cut its teeth" in the domestic market.

Table 3.19. Imports and Exports of Export Processing Zones

	Imports						Exports					
	Total		From abroad		From domestic		Total		To abroad		To domestic	
Year	Value (U.S. $1,000)	Percent	Value (U.S. $1,000)	Percent	Value (U.S. $1,000)	Percent	Value (U.S. $1,000)	Percent	Value (U.S. $1,000)	Percent	Value (U.S. $1,000)	Percent
1966	2,024	100	2,024	100.00	0	0.00	272	100	272	100.00	0	0.00
1967	13,896	100	13,607	97.92	289	2.08	7,970	100	7,970	100.00	0	0.00
1968	31,061	100	29,597	95.29	1,464	4.71	26,685	100	26,685	100.00	0	0.00
1969	58,475	100	54,380	93.00	4,095	7.00	63,077	100	62,181	98.58	896	1.42
1970	94,976	100	87,916	92.57	7,060	7.43	111,742	100	109,338	97.85	2,404	2.15
1971	124,345	100	110,349	88.74	13,996	11.26	167,721	100	163,475	97.47	4,246	2.53
1972	189,005	100	165,755	87.70	23,250	12.30	249,048	100	241,021	96.78	8,027	3.22
1973	348,105	100	299,791	86.12	48,314	13.88	423,554	100	404,681	95.54	18,873	4.46
1974	360,046	100	309,903	86.07	50,143	13.93	531,021	100	511,323	96.29	19,498	3.71

Source: Taken from pamphlets put out by Export Processing Zones Administration, Republic of China.

Table 3.20. Selected Indices of Production (1971 = 100)

	Food processing	Textiles	Telecommunications equipment	Machinery
1952	26.6	3.7	—	6.6
1953	39.1	5.9	—	7.7
1954	34.4	6.8	—	9.0
1955	40.6	7.1	—	10.4
1956	41.7	7.7	—	10.3
1957	49.7	7.5	—	13.3
1958	48.6	7.3	—	13.2
1959	48.9	8.9	—	16.3
1960	54.2	9.9	—	19.3
1961	59.3	11.7	0.4	16.8
1962	54.8	13.2	0.7	19.2
1963	58.3	13.7	0.6	23.3
1964	71.4	15.8	3.0	30.3
1965	80.5	17.9	5.9	34.4
1966	78.8	22.2	8.3	38.9
1967	80.1	29.2	14.2	47.9
1968	82.4	38.7	36.3	55.8
1969	83.8	52.3	47.3	64.7
1970	92.7	73.1	67.4	81.4
1971	100.0	100.0	100.0	100.0
1972	107.4	105.6	171.5	124.1
1973	112.8	115.4	238.4	145.0
1974	113.1	113.7	226.1	121.5
1975	107.5	146.7	172.3	96.8

Sources: DGBAS, *Statistical Yearbook of the Republic of China, 1976* (Taipei, 1976), pp. 120, 121; Ministry of Economic Affairs, *Taiwan Industrial Production Statistics Monthly* 89 (February 1977), 21.

unskilled labor. DC customers, such as the United States, in turn, by permitting the waiver of tariffs upon reentry on all but the value added portion of the product, provided additional encouragement for this new form of international subcontracting by process. Moreover, multinational companies became heavily (though not exclusively) involved in this type of industrial activity and thus, given the enhanced flexibility for intrafirm pricing and profit location decisions, provided it with additional cost-reducing advantages. The value of exports from the three Export Processing Zones[39] grew rapidly, from U.S.$272,000 in 1966 to U.S.$511,000,000 in 1974, but domestic value added achieved major significance only around 1970 (see Table 3.19).

A brief look at four industries at a more micro level with the help of Tables 3.20, 3.21, and 3.22 may illustrate these general points. Table 3.20 shows the growth pattern of these industries over time; Table 3.21 indicates their changing share in the composition of total industrial production; and Table 3.22 indicates their share in total exports.[40] Food processing represents the rela-

39. Kaohsiung in the South was established in 1965; Nantze and Taichung on the West Coast were established in 1969.
40. The industry groupings in Table 3.22 do not coincide fully with those of Tables 3.20 and 3.21.

Table 3.21. Percentage Shares of Selected Industries and Products in Industrial Production

	1954	1961	1966	1971
Food processing	18.42	17.44	11.14	7.19
Canned foods	0.68	1.91	3.14	1.88
Wheat flour	2.31	2.78	0.96	0.44
Refined sugar	9.98	9.74	4.37	2.54
Textiles	18.26	10.86	11.65	17.51
Cotton textiles	11.19	5.88	6.09	5.98
Artificial and synthetic textiles	0.51	0.49	1.76	4.40
Electronics	—	0.07	1.03	3.53
Television sets	—	—	0.55	2.53
Machinery	1.40	2.26	2.40	3.10

Sources: Ministry of Economic Affairs, *Taiwan Production Statistics Monthly* (December 1962), p. 47 (July 1965), p. 69; Ministry of Economic Affairs, *Taiwan Industrial Production Statistics Monthly* (January 1969), p. 235; Executive Group of ICCT, *General Report, 1971, Industrial and Commercial Census of Taiwan.*

tively land- and domestic raw-materials-intensive type of industry that was very important early on and provided much of the export fuel during the primary import-substitution phase of development in the 1950s.

Textiles, mainly based on raw material imports, grew more slowly in the 1950s when the domestic market was constrained, but were very important in

Table 3.22. Selected Shares in Total Exports (percentages)

	Processed agricultural products	Textiles, leather wood, paper, and related products	Electrical machinery and apparatus	Other machinery
1952	69.8	0.9	—	—
1953	77.3	1.5	—	—
1954	76.3	1.1	—	—
1955	61.8	2.4	—	—
1956	64.4	4.2	—	—
1957	71.6	4.1	—	—
1958	62.2	4.5	—	—
1959	52.8	12.7	—	—
1960	55.5	17.1	0.6	—
1961	44.1	22.1	1.0	0.5
1962	37.6	29.8	0.9	0.5
1963	45.5	22.6	0.9	0.6
1964	42.5	24.7	1.2	1.2
1965	30.4	26.2	2.7	1.3
1966	25.2	29.7	4.9	2.2
1967	23.2	34.2	6.1	2.3
1968	20.4	38.7	9.8	2.8
1969	16.7	40.7	11.2	3.1
1970	12.8	42.2	12.3	3.2
1971	11.2	45.1	12.9	3.2
1972	9.9	42.6	16.3	3.2
1973	7.9	37.6	17.2	3.3
1974	10.7	35.6	17.6	4.4
1975	10.8	37.6	14.0	4.4

Source: EPC, *Taiwan Statistical Data Book, 1976*, pp. 180–82.

the export-substitution drive of the 1960s. Table 3.21 shows that the relative importance of the more sophisticated artificial and synthetic textiles branch has gained strength relative to the more unskilled labor-based cotton textile branch of the industry since the mid-1960s.

The electronics industry, based almost exclusively on imported inter-mediate goods, has been almost entirely export-oriented from the outset. Its rate of growth has been prodigious; between 1964 and 1973 there was no year in which it did not grow by at least 40 percent. Within the industry a shift in the product mix can be discerned, among transistor radios, phonographs, tele-vision sets, tape recorders, and calculators, toward the more skilled labor and technology-intensive end of the spectrum. The growth of this industry has from the beginning been very largely (84 percent of the total in 1976) based on foreign investment seeking a cheap and dependable labor supply, and on within-firm, as opposed to arm's length, export markets that account for more than 80 percent of the total.[41]

Taiwan's machinery industry, finally, serves as an example of a late-starting secondary import-substitution type of activity. Although machinery output in 1973 was more than twenty times as large as in 1952, this growth was from a very small base, and the industry's share in total industrial produc-tion remained at a mere 3.1 percent in 1971. Various import-substitution policies have encouraged the growth of the machinery industry from the production of a limited range of simple products, such as electric fans and sewing machines, to a much larger spectrum of advanced products. Some of the simpler items, like sewing machines, have been exported in great quan-tity, giving rise to the beginnings of secondary export substitution, but total imports still considerably exceed overall production in this industry. With the coming of relative scarcity of unskilled labor, Taiwan's businessmen and planners have increasingly recognized the need to direct future growth toward these more capital- and skill-intensive industries serving both the domestic and foreign markets.

The decade of the 1960s was thus characterized by the very rapid growth of manufacturing and of the I sector generally, made possible in large part by Taiwan's increased international competitiveness. Figure 3.1 demonstrated the marked changes over time in the export ratio as well as in the proportion of industrial exports to total exports.[42] Other aggregate indicators of enhanced growth may be cited: a gross saving rate rising from 12 percent in 1960 to

41. Industrial Development Bureau, Ministry of Economic Affairs; information obtained in a conversation. The overall role of foreign capital in Taiwan's industrialization effort is discussed later in the chapter.

42. In recent years, the export ratio has reached 50 percent of GDP, one of the highest in the world, and the proportion of exports that are industrial in nature 95 percent (of which only about 10 percent are processed agricultural goods).

Table 3.23. Composition of Economic Activity (percentage of total net domestic product)

Year	A sector	I sector	S sector
1952	35.7	17.9	46.4
1953	38.0	17.6	44.4
1954	31.5	22.0	46.5
1955	32.5	20.9	46.6
1956	31.2	22.2	46.7
1957	31.3	23.6	45.1
1958	30.8	23.7	45.2
1959	30.1	25.4	44.2
1960	32.4	24.6	42.8
1961	31.1	24.7	43.8
1962	28.8	25.5	43.6
1963	26.4	27.8	45.4
1964	27.6	28.0	44.1
1965	26.8	28.1	44.8
1966	25.5	28.4	45.7
1967	23.2	30.3	46.4
1968	21.5	31.9	46.5
1969	18.5	33.8	47.7
1970	17.6	34.1	48.3
1971	15.3	36.5	48.2
1972	14.9	38.9	46.2
1973	15.0	40.1	44.9
1974	15.7	38.4	45.9
1975*	16.3	36.3	47.4

*Estimate.
Source: EPC, *Taiwan Statistical Data Book, 1976*, p. 32.

almost 26 percent in 1970 and real per capita income rising at an average rate of 5.8 percent during the decade, compared to 2.7 percent annually between 1953 and 1960. By the end of the 1960s, as indicated in Table 3.23, the structure of the economy had undergone a marked change, with the M sector and the A sector changing their relative position of importance and the S sector maintaining its important position with relatively little change.

Little can be said about services. It is, of course, a labor-intensive sector, relative to manufacturing, accounting for 30 percent of employment in 1952 and 46 percent of Net Domestic Product, when contrasted with industry, which accounted for 9 percent of employment and 18 percent of Net Domestic Product.[43] Disaggregating the sector by activity (see Table 3.24) provides some additional clues on its changing role in the course of development. The share of wholesale and retail trade, restaurants, and hotels in the total, for example, fell from 40.6 percent to 25.3 percent between 1952 and 1975. Meanwhile, other subsectors, especially transport and communications, finance, insurance, real estate, and other business services, increased substan-

43. For 1975 the relevant numbers are as follows: services account for 40 percent of the employment and for 47 percent of the NDP; industry for 23.5 percent of employment and 36 percent of NDP.

Table 3.24. Percentage Share of Service Activities in Total Services (NDP)

Year	Wholesale and retail trade, restaurants, and hotels	Transport, storage, and communications	Finance, insurance, real estate, and business services	Community social and personal services	Public administration and defense
1952	40.6	9.1	18.7	11.5	20.0
1956	39.2	9.1	18.9	10.6	22.2
1960	36.7	10.9	18.4	10.5	23.5
1964	34.0	11.7	19.4	11.8	23.1
1968	31.5	13.3	19.8	11.0	24.3
1972	26.5	14.3	21.6	13.6	23.9
1975	25.3	14.1	23.0	14.0	23.5

Source: DGBAS, *Statistical Yearbook, 1976*, p. 350.

tially in relative importance. This permits the expected conclusion that the relatively "soft" or labor-supply-pushed components of services declined in importance relative to the more "hard" or rest-of-the-economy-pulled components. Especially in the light of the modest overall relative growth of the services sector in total Net Domestic Product these trends are clear. Wholesale and retail trade, for example, declined from 18.7 percent of Net Domestic Product to 11.3 percent between 1952 and 1975, while the share of the services sector as a whole was growing.[44]

The acceleration of industrial and overall growth during the 1960s was, of course, intimately tied up with, and dependent upon, the continuation of the remarkably sustained steady advances in the agricultural sector analyzed in Chapter 2—thus avoiding premature rises in the price of wage goods and/or the need to divert foreign exchange to the importation of food. On the contrary, agricultural (net) exports, though less important relatively, continued to support rather than inhibit sustained growth of the nonagricultural sector. As Lin put it, "The competitiveness of Taiwan's labor supply is the . . . result largely of successful agricultural development, which made the 'unlimited' supply of labor a reality.'"[45] Both the remarkable steadiness of the domestic terms of trade (see Chapter 2) and the maintenance of a positive trade balance in basic foods provide ample evidence of this important feature of growth.[46]

Another important dimension of this overall successful growth performance is represented by Taiwan's relatively generous access to international capital flows throughout the two and a half decades under observation. The relevance of Taiwan's experience for other developing countries is often questioned on the basis of such favored access to capital, especially from the United States.

44. Economic Planning Council, *Taiwan Statistical Data Book, 1976* (Taipei, 1976), p. 32.
45. C. Y. Lin, p. 158.
46. Food exports as a percentage of domestic consumption remained in the 10 to 15 percent region until the late 1960s (for a fuller discussion see John C. H. Fei and Gustav Ranis, "A Model of Growth and Employment in the Open Dualistic Economy: The Cases of Korea and Taiwan," *Journal of Development Studies* 2, no. 2 [January 1975] 49).

Taking the period as a whole, foreign capital commitments to Taiwan averaged U.S.$116.4 million annually between 1952 and 1975 (see Table 3.25). Two distinct subphases can be discerned, not unrelated to the import- and export-substitution subphases—the almost exclusive reliance on (mostly U.S.) foreign aid prior to the mid-1960s and the shift to foreign private capital (mostly U.S., Japanese, and overseas Chinese in origin) thereafter. Taiwan was, and remains, one of the most famous cases of successful graduation from concessional to nonconcessional capital inflows as the internal economic conditions on the island permitted a change from prime concentration on a relatively narrow domestic to participation in large international markets. The overall levels of foreign aid commitments dropped sharply during the transition period, but the substantial opportunities for private capital participation in the later phases of export substitution soon brought total inflows to higher levels than ever.

The U.S. aid program to Taiwan was initiated in the early 1950s largely in connection with the communist takeover on the mainland and was stepped up considerably in the wake of the Korean War. Almost U.S.$1.5 billion of economic aid—including Public Law 480 food aid—was appropriated over the seventeen-year period from 1951 to 1968; these amounts do not include

Table 3.25. Foreign Capital Commitments (unit: U.S.$ million)

	U.S. aid obligations	Percent U.S. aid	Private foreign investment	Percent private foreign investment	Total foreign capital commitments
1952–1954					
average	93.8	97.6	2.3	2.4	96.1
1955	132.0	96.6	4.6	3.4	136.6
1956	101.6	96.7	3.5	3.3	105.1
1957	108.1	98.5	1.6	1.5	109.7
1958	81.6	97.0	2.5	3.0	84.1
1959	128.9	99.2	1.0	.8	129.9
1960	101.1	86.7	15.5	13.3	116.6
1961	94.2	86.8	14.3	13.2	108.5
1962	65.9	92.7	5.2	7.3	71.1
1963	115.3	86.4	18.1	13.6	133.4
1964	83.9	80.8	19.9	19.2	103.8
1965	56.5	57.6	41.6	42.4	98.1
1966	4.2	12.5	29.3	87.5	33.5
1967	4.4	7.2	57.0	92.8	61.4
1968	29.3	24.6	89.9	75.4	119.2
1969	0	0	109.4	100	109.4
1970	0	0	138.9	100	138.9
1971	0	0	162.9	100	162.9
1972	0	0	126.7	100	126.7
1973	0	0	248.9	100	248.9
1974	0	0	189.4	100	189.4
1975	0	0	118.2	100	118.2

Source: EPC, *Taiwan Statistical Data Book, 1976*, pp. 217, 230.

the military assistance program, whose economic impact—especially the net effect of complementary domestic defense expenditures[47]—is difficult to analyze.

Considering, admittedly somewhat artificially, the economic impact of the foreign aid program, its major early contribution was in the form of commodity imports, budget support, and the resulting curbing of inflation. Large government deficits occasioned by the multiple security and reconstruction tasks faced by the new government on Taiwan had led, as noted earlier, to runaway inflation in the early 1950s. By 1954–55 substantial injections of aid—almost $10 per capita annually—had relieved pressing essential commodity shortages and reduced the need for deficit financing. Only when the essential prerequisite of stabilization had been met could private-sector markets begin to function effectively and aid be directed to longer-term development objectives represented by infrastructural and industrial projects (also see Chapter 5).

A further important shift in the quality, rather than the quantity, of concessional capital inflows occurred between 1959 and 1961. This consisted of a return from project to nonproject (or program) assistance, dovetailing this time, however, with the economy's move from import to export substitution and the satisfaction of the associated import requirements of private-sector entrepreneurs.[48] It is also generally accepted that the combination of advice and reassurance provided by the U.S. aid mission to Taiwan played an important role in the overall liberalization package (including the famous Nineteen Points) adopted by the Taiwan government during this period.[49]

Given the inherent fungibility of an economy's total foreign exchange resources, it is hazardous to attempt to tag foreign aid inflows in terms of their precise sectoral or even project impact, but official allocations, which reveal something about donor intentions, show approximately 37 percent of the total assigned to infrastructure, 26 percent to human resource imports, and the rest to agricultural and industrial requirements over the 1951–65 period.[50] One may similarly be skeptical with respect to some of the claims made as to the quantitative overall impact of aid flows on growth, based on oversimple models that customarily understate both the extent of substitution between domestic and foreign saving and the importance of the timeliness of aid arrivals at critical moments of decision making with respect first to stabiliza-

47. Estimated at 11 percent of GNP in 1951.
48. During 1951–55, 78 percent of U.S. aid was of the nonproject type. This fell to 63 percent in 1956–60 and was back up to 79 percent for 1961–65. See Hsing, pp. 192–94.
49. For a full statement of the role of U.S. aid during this transition period see Neil H. Jacoby, *U.S. Aid to Taiwan: A Study of Foreign Aid, Self-help, and Development* (New York, 1966). The adoption of the nineteen-point reform program, for example, was at least facilitated by the offer of an additional $20–30 million loan conditional on prompt implementation.
50. See Ibid., p. 50.

tion and then to liberalization policies.[51] There can be little doubt that the transition to export substitution and the related entry of foreign commercial capital would not have been possible in the absence of the aid contribution. In sheer quantitative terms, however, a 47 percent share in gross capital formation in 1951–55 fell to 17 percent in 1961–65 and to negligible amounts thereafter.

Foreign private investors were reluctant during the 1950s because of the relatively narrow domestic market orientation of the system and its still precarious prospects. Once the policy changes of the late 1950s and early 1960s were in place, however, and the economy was responding well to the altered set of signals and opportunities, foreign investment began to take up the slack left by the termination of U.S. aid.[52] As Table 3.26 indicates, the overseas Chinese (mostly Hong Kong and other Southeast Asian) and U.S. investors were the most important contributors, with the Japanese and others (mostly European) increasing their participation after 1965.

These dramatic increases in private capital inflows resulted from a combination of factors. By the 1960s not only had Taiwan's political situation stabilized, but the containment of domestic inflation followed by the liberalization of the foreign exchange regime made participation in the industrial export drive look more attractive to outside investors. The package provided a large variety of incentives, including a "five-year exemption from corporate income tax for new investors, or acceleration of asset depreciation; a maximum of 25 percent corporation income tax after the completion of the five-year tax holiday, exemption or deferment of payment of customs duties on imported machinery and equipment; exemption or reduction on stamp, deed and business taxes for export transactions; and acquisition of plant sites in government-designated industrial land or industrial districts."[53] At the same time, rapid wage increases in the United States, Europe, and especially Japan induced manufacturers to take advantage of Taiwan's cheap and abundant labor that was virtually free of disputes and strikes. Good levels of health and education, adequate transportation, and cheap electric power were the other advantages noted by foreign investors.

A further stimulus to foreign investment was provided by the establishment of the Kaohsiung Export Processing Zone (EPZ) in 1965 and the two other zones, in Nantze and Taichung, in 1969. These zones were set up with the primary purpose of increasing exports by attracting foreign investment. As of

51. Jacoby (pp. 151–52), for example, sees aid as having more than doubled the annual rate of growth of GNP, but the causation mechanism is not at all clear.
52. The United States needed a successful aid graduate for its own reasons, but Taiwan government officials, were understandably apprehensive and pleasantly surprised by the foreign private-investor response. The continuation of military and some economic (food) aid after 1965 helped ease the transition.
53. Jacoby, p. 129.

Table 3.26. Foreign Investment Commitments by Year and Origin, 1952–1974 (amount: U.S.$ million)

Year	Total	United States		Japan		Other countries		Overseas Chinese	
		Amount	Percent of total	Amount	Percent of total	Amount	Percent of total	Amount	Percent of total
Total	1,287.1	428.9	33.3	192.6	15.0	302.5	23.5	363.1	28.2
1952–59	20.2	9.5	46.9	1.4	6.8	.1	0.2	9.3	46.4
1960–64	72.9	38.0	52.1	6.4	8.8	1.7	2.3	26.8	36.8
1965–69	327.9	126.9	38.8	52.7	16.1	50.4	15.4	97.1	29.7
1970–74	866.7	254.5	29.4	132.2	15.2	250.3	28.9	229.8	26.5

Source: Shou-Eng Koo, "Foreign Investment and Industrialization in Taiwan," *Academia Economic Papers* 4, no. 1 (March 1976), 128.

August 1976, they had accumulated U.S.$195.4 million in investments, of which $139.8 million, or 81.8 percent, was in foreign hands (also see Chapter 5). The simplification and "one-stop" access to all the liberalization-related incentives provided in this fashion were of particular value to the foreign investor.

As Table 3.27 demonstrates, the preponderance of the foreign investment flows was directed toward these export-oriented activities, with electronics and electric appliances accounting for the lion's share of the total, and the remainder reasonably well distributed among chemicals, metal products, textiles, and trade.

The distribution of investment differed considerably by national origin of the investor. For example, the investment in electronics accounted for almost 60 percent of the U.S. total (and nearly one-third of all foreign private investment). Chemicals accounted for another 15 percent of total U.S. investment. Electronics and chemicals were also the major targets for Japanese investors (with 37.2 and 14.3 percent of the total, respectively), but for them textiles and machinery also had considerable weight (13.2 and 9.6 percent). A different pattern emerges with respect to the overseas Chinese investors, who, outside of textiles, concentrated heavily on trade and other services, presumably where their particular knowledge of local market conditions gave them the biggest advantage.

Another important dimension of foreign investment is, of course, represented by differences in average size and institutional quality. U.S. investors, for example, not surprisingly, tended to invest in larger chunks.[54] But, perhaps of greater substantive relevance is the decided preference of the U.S. investor, here as elsewhere, for the wholly owned subsidiary form; his Japanese counterpart was much more interested in engaging in joint ventures. Globally, 71 percent of U.S. foreign investment is in the 95–100 percent parent-ownership category, compared to 27 percent for Japan, a sharp contrast that applies to Taiwan as well.[55] As a consequence, it can be asserted that the technological "spread" effects, such as via the ability to involve small domestic subcontractors, were substantially larger for the equivalent amount of Japanese foreign investment.[56]

The problem of assessing the economic effects of the foreign investment flows on the performance of the economic system is one of considerable

54. According to Shou-Eng Koo ("Foreign Investment and Industrialization in Taiwan," *Academia Economic Papers,* 4 [March 1976], p. 133), the average size of U.S. investments was $1.78 million, that of Japanese $.34 million, and that of the overseas Chinese $.31 million.

55. See Yoshihiro Tsurumi, "The Multinational Spread of Japanese Firms and Asian Neighbor Reactions," in *The Multinational Corporation and Social Change,* David Apter and Louis Goodman, eds. (New York, 1976).

56. See Gustav Ranis, "The Multinational Corporation as an Instrument of Development," in ibid.

Table 3.27. Foreign Investment Commitments by Industry and Origin, 1952–1974* (amounts in U.S.$ million)

Industry	Total		United States		Japan		Other countries		Overseas Chinese	
	Amount	Percent	Amount	Percent	Amount	Percent	Amount	Percent	Amount	Percent
Agriculture, forestry, fishery, and animal husbandry	9.4	.7	.6	.1			1.0	.3	7.8	2.1
Food and beverage processing	27.4	2.1	4.6	1.0	3.7	1.9	1.3	.4	17.9	4.9
Textiles, garments, and footwear	86.1	6.7	4.4	1.0	25.4	13.2	5.8	1.9	50.4	13.9
Lumber, bamboo, pulp, and paper products	22.2	1.7	1.1	.3	4.3	2.2	.4	.1	16.3	4.5
Plastic and rubber products	34.2	2.7	8.0	1.9	9.6	5.0	1.0	.3	15.6	4.3
Chemicals	138.2	10.7	64.4	15.0	27.6	14.3	33.2	11.0	13.0	3.6
Nonmetallic minerals	76.8	6.0	4.8	1.1	5.3	2.6	19.8	6.5	47.0	12.9
Basic metals and metal products	105.8	8.2	10.1	2.3	17.3	9.0	68.2	22.5	10.2	2.8
Machinery, equipment, and instruments	109.3	8.5	8.6	2.0	18.4	9.6	77.4	25.6	4.8	1.3
Electronics and electric appliances	419.4	32.6	253.8	59.2	71.6	37.2	82.1	27.1	12.0	3.3
Construction	50.7	3.9	8.3	1.9	1.1	.6	0.3	0.1	41.0	11.3
Trade, banking, insurance, and transportation	92.0	7.1	35.4	8.3	0.6	0.3	7.3	2.7	48.7	13.4
Services	76.6	5.6	14.9	3.5	1.5	0.8	2.1	6.9	58.2	16.0
Others	39.0	3.0	10.0	2.3	6.2	3.2	2.6	0.9	20.2	5.5
Total	1,287.1	100.0	428.9	100.0	192.6	100.0	302.5	100.0	363.1	100.0

*Refers to the amount officially approved. The actual arrival amount may be different.
Source: Koo.

analytical difficulty and controversy. The same problem arises as in the case of concessional capital inflows discussed earlier. Given the fungibility of foreign exchange resources and our inability to know just how the economy would have behaved (what domestic saving rates or export competitiveness would have been) in the absence of the particular inflow, it is hazardous to make precise quantitative claims. It is, nevertheless, highly likely that, taking the quantitative dimension first, direct foreign investment has substantially increased the total volume of investment on Taiwan. Gross domestic capital formation (GDCF) and foreign investment rates are shown in Table 3.28. Private foreign investment remained a very small fraction of GDCF during the 1950s, but grew in importance to over 11 percent of GDCF by 1971 (representing over 19 percent of GDCF in industry overall and, of course, substantially more in such industries as electronics, in which foreign investment was concentrated). The Export Processing Zone phenomenon, in particular, was

Table 3.28. Capital Formation and Foreign Investment (unit: N.T.$ million)

	Gross domestic capital formation (GDCF)	Private foreign investment		U.S. aid, foreign capital, and loans	
		Amount	Percent of GDCF	Amount	Percent of GDCF
1952	2,643	14	.5	1,057	40.0
1953	3,224	53	1.6	1,190	36.9
1954	4,041	35	.9	2,111	52.2
1955	3,998	72	1.8	1,298	32.5
1956	5,524	87	1.6	2,366	42.8
1957	6,355	40	.6	2,111	33.2
1958	7,898	62	.8	3,487	44.2
1959	9,768	35	.4	4,473	45.8
1960	12,587	562	4.5	4,698	37.3
1961	13,887	573	4.1	4,952	35.7
1962	14,554	708	4.9	5,048	34.7
1963	15,459	723	4.7	621	4.0
1964	19,647	798	4.0	−233	−1.2
1965	25,995	1,664	6.4	4,016	15.5
1966	29,308	1,171	4.0	1,299	4.4
1967	37,014	2,280	6.2	3,198	8.7
1968	45,319	3,596	7.9	5,290	11.6
1969	49,229	4,377	8.9	1,671	3.4
1970	58,946	5,556	9.4	526	0.9
1971	67,565	6,518	11.3	−6,364	−9.4
1972	72,815	5,066	7.0	−19,811	−27.2
1973	106,552	9,486	8.9	−21,648	−20.3
1974	200,812	7,206	3.6	42,758	21.3
1952–60	56,038	960	1.7	22,791	40.7
1961–68	201,183	11,513	5.7	24,191	12.0
1969–74	555,919	38,209	6.9	−2,868	−0.5
Total, 1952–74	813,140	50,682	6.2	44,114	5.4

Source: EPC, *Taiwan Statistical Data Book, 1976*, pp. 45, 46, and 230. Exchange rates used to convert private foreign investment from U.S.$ to N.T.$ were those given for imports in Scott's chapter, Table 5.3.

heavily tied to attracting additional foreign investment. In more recent years the net contribution of foreign investment has been sharply reduced through the repatriation of profits and the repayment of loans (see Table 3.28). The cumulative contribution of private foreign investment during the 1952-74 period comes to only about 6 percent of total capital formation. When foreign aid is added, the figure approaches a still modest 12 percent. What is clearly more important than total amounts is the timing and the quality, that is, the impact of foreign capital flows on the performance of the domestic economy.

Foreign investment has contributed significantly to the expansion of Taiwan's foreign trade, for example. As Table 3.29 indicates, foreign investors' participation in the export-substitution phase of development was important in nearly every major industry. Fully 48 percent of the export proceeds overall of the enterprises surveyed in Table 3.29 were used in the import of raw materials and component parts. The import intensity of these enterprises varies greatly; as expected, it is lowest in such industries as food processing and highest in such industries as pulp and paper products. But even in industries where domestic value added is relatively small, without the marketing channels of multinational corporations, especially in intermediate goods, these export earnings would not have been available in the absence of the foreign investor. Foreign investment also made a substantial contribution to overall employment levels; in 1973, for example, almost 13 percent of the total organized industrial labor force was employed by foreign enterprises.[57] There is no consensus, however, on the impact of foreign investment on technology choice in Taiwan.[58]

The most important, if difficult to assess, contribution of foreign investment surely resides, finally, in the area of linkage and learning processes as far as the domestic industrial sector is concerned. This includes purchases of locally made raw materials, introduction of new manufacturing and marketing techniques, and training of local skilled labor and management. These impacts have not been significant in Taiwan in the past because foreign, especially U.S., firms have remained relatively insulated from domestic firms. Most foreign firms import raw materials and components from abroad rather than contract for them locally. The extreme case, of course, is represented by the Export Processing Zone where local sources supplied less than 14 percent of the machinery, equipment, and raw materials between 1966 and 1974.[59] The greater tendency of U.S. companies to retain 100 percent ownership and hire their own nationals for upper-level management posts must be contrasted with the greater willingness of Japanese firms to license technology imports.

57. Koo, p. 142.
58. See, for example, Benjamin Cohen, *Multinational Firms and Asian Exports.* (New Haven, 1975).
59. Koo, p. 148.

Table 3.29. Export Proceeds and Imports of Raw Materials and Components Parts by Foreign Investment Industry: 1973 (unit: N.T.$ million)

	Gross revenue	Export proceeds		Imports of raw materials and component parts		
		Amount	Percent of gross revenue	Amount	Percent of gross revenue	Percent of exports proceeds
Food and beverage processing	4,161	1,601	38.5	433	10.4	27.0
Textile, garment, and footwear	11,726	9,595	81.8	3,834	32.7	40.0
Lumber, bamboo, pulp, and paper products	997	631	63.3	571	57.3	90.5
Plastic and rubber products	2,246	1,862	82.9	415	18.5	22.3
Chemicals	10,805	5,671	52.5	2,106	19.5	37.1
Nonmetallic minerals	4,675	423	90.4	388	8.3	91.8
Basic metals and metal products	1,984	952	48.0	826	41.6	86.8
Machinery, equipment, and instruments	1,309	735	56.1	346	26.4	47.0
Electronic and electric appliances	28,635	19,773	69.1	10,985	38.4	55.6
Construction	265	—	—	8	3.1	—
Services	1,902	—	—	59	3.1	—
Others	1,771	1,233	69.6	366	20.7	29.7
Total	70,474	42,476	60.3	20,338	28.9	47.9

Source: A survey of 449 foreign enterprises by the Foreign Investment Commission, Ministry of Economic Affairs, China, *An Analysis of the Operations and Economic Effects of Foreign Enterprises in Taiwan* (in Chinese) (Taipei, June 1975).

Of 837 technical cooperation projects approved between 1952 and 1974, 615 (or 73 percent) were between Japanese and indigenous companies—indicating that in this area Japanese investment has probably been the more beneficial.[60]

In summary, the burden of proof is on those who reject the relevance of the successful Taiwan development experience because of the unusually high levels of foreign capital inflows. Even in the early 1950s, U.S. aid constituted only 6 percent of all GDP, and Taiwan's military budget amounted to 10 percent of GDP (and 85 percent of the budget). The quantitative contribution of foreign capital to overall capital formation during the two decades was clearly important but by no means overwhelming. Other developing countries have received large capital inflows that were not associated with successful industrialization and development efforts. There can be little doubt, on the other hand, as to the important strategic and qualitative significance of foreign capital. Without timely concessional flows in the 1950s, Taiwan might have remained locked in a hyperinflationary morass; and without the program lending and gentle persuasion of the early 1960s the transition from primary import to export substitution certainly would have been much more painful, if not aborted. The flow of private capital since then undoubtedly made a significant contribution to industrial-sector growth, especially to exports and employment. But the potentially important spillover effects of foreign investment—backward and forward linkages to domestic industry and associated technology transfers—were limited and are only now gradually being realized. These linkages are likely to assume greater importance as industry shifts from unskilled, labor-intensive export substitution to the more technology- and capital-intensive output and export mixes.

By the end of the 1960s, pursuit of a balanced growth path, fueled at first almost exclusively by agricultural surpluses, then aided materially by the labor-intensive export boom, had gradually led to a tightening of the labor market. The combined effects of 9 percent annual rates of industrial-sector labor absorption with a reduction in population growth (from 3.8 percent annually in the early 1950s to around 2 percent annually in the late 1960s) were helping to end the phase of unlimited labor supply.

Much qualitative evidence is available in this respect—mostly based on the increasing volume of industrialist complaints concerning the unavailability of labor. There is also the quantitative evidence of the response to the increasing relative labor shortage via higher female participation rates, from 27 percent in 1965 to 31 percent in 1969. But the most convincing argument in support of the appearance of such a second important turning point is derived from an examination of real wage patterns. In the absence of an unskilled wage series, Figure 3.2 presents real wage indices for all manufacturing, for textiles, and

---

60. Ibid., p. 140.

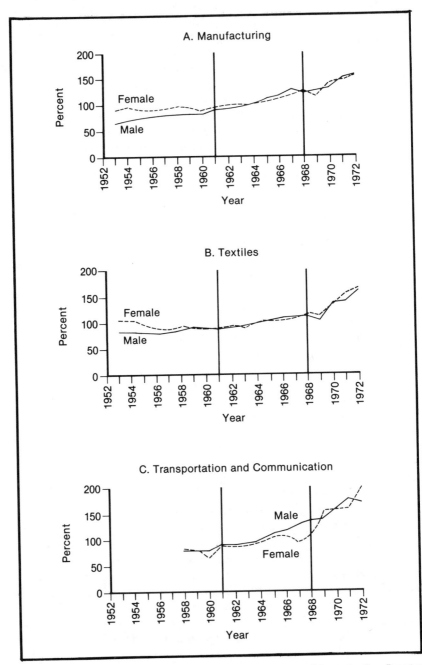

Figure 3.2. Index of real wages (1964 = 100). Source: Department of Reconstruction, *Report of Taiwan Labor Statistics* (Taipei, 1958, 1963, 1969, 1973).

for the transportation and communications sector, separately for male and female workers. All three series indicate the increased relative scarcity, first of male, then of female workers, near the end of the 1960s—a feature of Taiwanese labor markets much commented upon in qualitative discussions. Moreover, the wage series for female workers in textiles and in transport and communications—which come closest to replicating an unskilled real wage series—show the beginnings of a marked upward trend by the end of the decade. The unskilled industrial wage had been rising throughout the 1960s as rapid agricultural productivity increases affected the agricultural real wage on which it is based. But there can be little doubt that the combined cumulative effect, over the years, of a balanced push out of agriculture with the pull of increased nonagricultural demand had led to a perceptible shift from relative unskilled labor surplus to scarcity by the end of the decade.[61] These are not absolute but relative price-related concepts, and the shift is gradual. But there is a difference between a labor market in which all the unskilled labor needed is available at a given wage at a given point in time—even though that wage may be rising from year to year—and a market in which higher wages must be paid this year to attract more such labor. New policies have been instituted since the late 1960s to keep the price of unskilled labor from rising too much via land consolidation and mechanization. This, in fact, confirms the basic notion that around the end of the last decade the old combination of a well-developed entrepreneurial capacity with an ample supply of unskilled labor began to give way to a new type of industrial growth regime increasingly based on skilled labor, labor-saving technology, and capital.

Industrialization in the 1970s and beyond in Historical Perspective

The period 1972–75 was one of drastic shocks to the world economy. These shocks were felt strongly in Taiwan, a small trade-oriented economy, reversing the steady growth in per capita income, industrial production, exports, and imports that had been more or less uninterrupted since 1952 and causing the highest inflation rates since the early 1950s. Taiwan demonstrated notable resilience in meeting these shocks. In fact, her ability to respond as she did represents a prime indicator of the increasing maturity of the economic system.

More specifically, the international monetary crises of 1971 and 1973 led to small (5 percent) devaluations of the New Taiwan dollar, which helped to improve the trade balance with Japan but constituted a revaluation relative to the U.S. dollar (see Chapter 5). Increasing inflationary pressures were at first addressed by a tightening of credit. During 1973, however, Taiwan was hard hit by severe increases in the price of such key commodities as corn, wheat,

---

61. Virtually all observers of the Taiwan case seem to be in agreement on this phenomenon. See, for example, the work of Shirley W. Y. Kuo, ''Labor Absorption in Taiwan, 1954–1971,'' *Economic Essays* (1977); Ho; and C. Y. Lin.

soybeans, petroleum products, petrochemical raw materials, and shipping, yielding a 23 percent rise in wholesale prices and an 8 percent rise in consumer prices.[62] These inflationary shocks were worsened by the growing labor shortage that was bringing about sustained wage increases in manufacturing.

To combat inflation, the government further restricted credit, introduced various energy conservation measures, and attempted to increase supply by reducing import restrictions. By 1974, however, these measures combined with the worldwide recession to halt growth entirely. The Economic Stabilization Program undertaken in January 1974 to combat inflation cooled the economy effectively. The one-time large increase in the controlled prices of petroleum products and other public-sector goods, designed to allow prices to adjust to costs while curbing inflationary expectations, had a similar effect. A further sharp increase in interest rates brought about shortages of working capital and an excessive inventory buildup. Meanwhile, export orders dwindled because of the worldwide slump and the efforts of industrial countries to reduce their own oil deficits. In addition, Taiwan's effective revaluation vis-à-vis the United States and the rise in prices and wages reduced the competitiveness of her manufactures. These shocks to the export sector in particular caused the share of industry in Net Domestic Product to drop in 1974 for the first time since 1955. Industrial production declined by 1.5 percent and real per capita income fell by 3.0 percent, as shown in Table 3.30. The balance of payments went into deficit for the first time since 1970, when the value of imports rose by 82 percent, compared with a 25 percent rise in the value of exports. Taiwan's international terms of trade worsened dramatically.

Beginning in September 1974, the government began to reverse itself by easing credit. Prices had stabilized, but the economy remained in deep recession. By the second half of 1975, however, most indicators had once more begun to rise. The resumption of a modest (5.8 percent) growth in industrial production in 1975 can be primarily attributed to strengthening domestic demand as the value of exports in both constant and current dollars continued to fall. Thus increased domestic demand came not only in the form of private and government consumption, but also in additional government investment—in particular the "ten great projects." By 1976, Taiwan's economic recovery was in full swing, with exports and industrial production rising rapidly, as foreign demand grew with general, if slow, world economic recovery. Excess capacity in some industries persisted. Labor markets seemed to have undergone a shift to a situation reminiscent of mature economies—a reluctance of rural labor, particularly young women, to leave their farms for urban factory work even when cyclical unemployment abated.

---

62. Wholesale prices of all imports rose by an average of 55 percent ("Taiwan Economic Statistics," *Industry of Free China* [March 1974], p. 5).

Table 3.30. Growth Rates of Selected Economic Indicators, 1969-1975 (percentages)

	1969	1970	1971	1972	1973	1974	1975
Industrial production	19.4	20.3	24.1	21.0	19.2	−1.5	5.8
Gross domestic product							
(constant dollars)	8.5	10.9	11.5	11.9	12.0	0.6	2.9
Real per capita income	4.4	8.7	9.1	7.7	7.8	−3.0	−1.4
Exports (constant dollars)	25.1	25.9	33.5	32.6	23.8	−7.9	−12.6
Imports	15.9	22.1	22.2	18.4	23.3	17.2	−25.8
Consumer price index	5.1	3.6	2.8	3.0	8.2	47.5	5.2
Share of industry in NDP	33.8	34.1	36.5	38.9	40.1	38.4	36.3
Net barter terms of trade	101.8	103.2	100.0	100.0	93.5	83.3	81.8

Source: EPC, *Taiwan Statistical Data Book, 1976.*

Taiwan has had to, and may continue to have to, adjust to other, exogenous changes of a longer-term nature. These include a shift in political as well as, if to a lesser extent, trade and investment relations between many of Taiwan's traditional postwar partners and the mainland; they also include a perceptible trend toward a more protectionist attitude in the United States, Europe, and Japan that has exhibited itself mainly in increases in nontariff, often informal, barriers to entry, especially in such fields as apparel, leather goods, and electronics, areas of Taiwan's greatest demonstrated comparative advantage in recent years. Here again Taiwan's economy has shown considerable resilience, responding to quotas, for example, by adjusting the precise export mix or investing so-called "quota capital" in neighboring countries' facilities. The spillover of changes in political ties to trade and investment relations has been by and large avoided; in many cases economic relations seem to have been strengthened in the wake of political estrangement. This very flexibility and adaptability represents a measure of the state of development that has been reached on Taiwan—and her importance to her trading partners as a matter of mutual economic self-interest. The dominant role of trade in the total GNP is little short of remarkable. Taiwan's continued capacity to "ride with the punches" in such a flexible, pragmatic fashion is likely to be crucial to her future and depends in large part on the current health and adjustability of her industrial sector.

Viewed in the historical perspective hopefully provided by this chapter, Taiwan's industrial development pattern in the past can thus, broadly speaking, be defined as an early primary import-substitution subphase, followed by a primary export-substitution subphase. I say "broadly speaking" because of the presence of intermediate and processing industries during the Japanese colonial period and of the growth of, for example, the chemical and petroleum industries during the 1960s. The real world is never neat and clear-cut; nor, since I believe, with Alfred Marshall, in the gradualness of nature, do I take the dates of transition between any two subphases too seriously. Nevertheless, given all such cautionary footnotes, the burden of the empirical evidence presented is clear: a principally domestic raw-materials-fueled consumer goods or primary import-substitution period was followed by a principally unskilled-labor-fueled primary export-substitution period, followed by the gradual exhaustion of the unlimited supply of unskilled labor.

Events of the past few years clearly indicate that the industrial sector is gradually entering a new era, that of secondary import substitution. The evidence for this shift under the overall impact of increasing relative labor shortage takes a number of forms. For one, there has been a gradual increase in the relative size of domestic intermediate and capital goods industries. For example, in electronics assembly there has been a notable shift, both forward and backward, in the processing activities undertaken in Taiwan. The relatively more capital-intensive electrical machinery industry, to cite another example, is now showing faster growth rates than nonelectrical machinery, and consumer durable goods are experiencing the most rapid growth. Taiwan's industrial sector remains labor-intensive by international standards—so-called light industry still comprises more than 40 percent of the total—but this is down from 51 percent in 1966,[63] and there is evidence of a perceptible shift toward production requiring more embodied education and capital. Industrial capital-labor ratios, both in terms of the choice of technology for given industries and of the aforementioned change in output mix, are undergoing much more rapid increases in recent years than earlier.

Another piece of evidence of the advent of a new subphase is the behavior of the Export Processing Zones. These zones were established on the principle that all raw materials are imported, only domestic labor is added, and the product is 100 percent reexported. As indicated in Table 3.19, however, there has been an increasing use of two kinds of exemptions from this general rule: one has to do with the use of domestic raw materials—which in 1974 had reached 14 percent of the total; the other with the export (after payment of import duties) to the rest of Taiwan—which had reached about 4 percent of the total. These are relatively small magnitudes, but they indicate that the raison d'être of the export processing zone based mainly on the supply of cheap, unskilled labor is gradually being weakened by labor shortage. Thus it has become profitable to use some domestic raw materials—which means loss of, for example, the U.S. tariff advantage, and to sell some of the output within Taiwan—which means loss of the Taiwan tariff advantage. As unskilled real wages continue to rise at a faster clip, the advantages of the export processing zone device, useful during the export-substitution subphase, can be expected to continue to diminish.

A third and final piece of evidence may be derived from the changing role

---

63. Figures from *Industrial and Commercial Census of Taiwan* (Taipei, 1966 and 1971).

Table 3.31. Distribution of Industrial Production by Ownership (percent)

	Total		Manufacturing	
	Private	Public	Private	Public
1953	44.1	55.9	44.1	55.9
1958	50.0	50.0	52.8	47.2
1963	55.2	44.8	59.4	40.6
1968	68.9	31.1	75.3	24.7
1972	79.4	20.6	86.9	13.1
1975	77.3	22.7	84.6	15.4

Source: EPC, *Taiwan Statistical Data Book, 1976.*

of the public sector. As pointed out in Table 3.1, the government's role in directly productive activities, both in industrial and manufacturing output, was surprisingly substantial in the early 1950s because of the large volume of government-held former Japanese assets, as well as the relatively large weight of heavy intermediate goods industries in the total.[64] In 1954, as part of the Land-to-the-Tiller Program, which provided 30 percent of landlord compensation in the form of shares of government corporations, cement, pulp and paper, and a variety of the enterprises included in the Taiwan Industry and Mining Corporation and the Taiwan Agriculture and Forestry Development Corporation were sold to the private sector.[65] The effect of policies relatively favoring the private sector over time, especially during the 1960s, is demonstrated in Table 3.31.[66]

Table 3.31 also shows a shift in recent years back toward the public sector as a consequence both of renewed emphasis on infrastructure and a greater government role in directly productive activities. In the early 1970s, the government announced plans to invest U.S.$6 billion (at 1974 prices) in ten major public-sector projects. Six of these projects are addressed to Taiwan's major transportation infrastructure, which, though already extensive, has been increasingly tested by the rapid expansion of traffic. The North-South Freeway, running from Keelung to Kaohsiung, is intended to relieve chronic traffic tieups on existing highways as well as to ease the railroads' passenger and freight burden. Electrification of the mainline West Coast railroad is expected to save on fuel imports and to increase the carrying capacity of the railroad. Two new ports, at Suau and Taichung, will relieve the present

64. Smaller consumer goods industries initially in private Japanese hands were transferred directly by auction into private Taiwanese hands between 1946 and 1949.

65. What essentially remained in the public sector was power, sugar, chemical fertilizer, aluminum, petroleum refining, and wine and tobacco (government fiscal monopolies). Reserved for mixed enterprises were shipbuilding, iron and steel, petrochemicals, and heavy machinery.

66. It may nevertheless surprise those who view Taiwan as the complete private enterprise model that between 1953 and 1972 public-sector output grew at 10.8 percent a year contrasted with 18.6 percent for the private sector.

overcrowding at Keelung and Kaohsiung and further encourage regionally balanced growth. The Suao-Hualien railroad spur is intended to end the relative isolation of Taiwan's East Coast, which has thus far lagged behind in development. Other infrastructure projects include a new international airport near Taipei and several nuclear power plants. The three remaining projects involve directly productive activities: an integrated steel mill, a large shipyard, and several petrochemical plants.

These well-publicized ten major projects are really the public relations top of an even larger iceberg of heavier government involvement anticipated in the future. The reasons for this reversal in trend seem clear: secondary import-substitution activities exhibit economies of scale, are more capital-, skill-, and technology-intensive, and require more externalities in the form of public-sector investments—plus a longer time horizon—than the still inadequate private capital markets can muster.[67] Although this reversal in the long-standing policy of increased reliance on private industry is of recent origin, current public policy pronouncements indicate that the trend will probably continue and accelerate. These pronouncements deal not only with project planning but also with the increased need for government to concern itself with higher and technical education,[68] with investments in science and technology infrastructure, and, for the longer run, with the restructuring of still very inadequate domestic financial markets.

In the future, the relative success in monetary policy and in the construction of new financial intermediation networks probably will determine the relative size of the public sector required and thus the probable efficiency of future industrial activity. But regardless of the outcome on this particular score, the underlying resource endowment and growth pattern permits a number of predictions to be made with some degree of confidence.

First, we can expect secondary export substitution to follow much more closely on the heels of secondary import substitution than was the case with the earlier primary import/export substitution sequence. This is partly because the domestic market for producer goods is more quickly saturated than that for consumer goods and partly because of the relatively high import cost of this new kind of import substitution. Thus, if conditions are good, we may expect only a short-lived decline in Taiwan's unusually high export ratios in the years ahead.

67. On a relatively small island, the possibility of the validity of natural monopolies, not only too large but also too socially risky to be handled by a private company, also arises. There is, moreover, the military component of secondary import substitution, with rising political content—for example, in the assembly of jet interceptors (jointly with Grumman) and in the production of rifles, machine guns, mortars, howitzers, trucks, and jeeps.

68. In 1968 compulsory education was extended from six to nine years. In 1972 a vocational training fund to which employers must contribute 1.5 percent of the total wage bill was established. See also Chapter 6.

Second, the volume of indirect interventions by government will probably increase. This prediction is based on the fact that, although we do not expect a return to the whole panoply of import-substitution devices of the 1950s, the demand by domestic producer goods industries for some protection for Taiwanese entrepreneurs (public or private) in these relatively new areas will undoubtedly intensify. The precise forms these interventions will take are hard to predict, but early indications are that they will likely take the form of interest rate differentials favoring capital-intensive industries and increased export subsidies. The trick, as before, will be to maintain this regime as flexibly as possible to avoid overheating the system, as, for example, in the recent history of Korean exports, and to keep a firm eye from the outset on the time period for which a given industry is extended special assistance.

Just as the transition from land- to unskilled-labor-based industrial production and exports in Taiwan was gradual from year to year, yet dramatic looking back over time, we can expect the current transition to a skilled-labor- and capital-based pattern of industry to follow a similar pattern. The labor-intensive industrial exports that have recently been so important will continue to have substantial weight for some years to come. Current government efforts to encourage joint farming, to induce more agricultural mechanization generally,[69] to provide day care centers, among others, indicate an awareness that such measures can ease the transition to a higher wage regime. Nevertheless, we can expect an acceleration of the capital-deepening trend—within given industries as well as in terms of the industrial output mix. Moreover, as capital-labor ratio gaps change, we can, in accordance with our earlier analysis, expect some relative shift in favor of the current export basket to other LDCs—with such countries in the area that still have a labor surplus, as Indonesia, Malaysia, and the Philippines, having a chance to take up the slack with respect to labor-intensive consumer goods exports to the developed countries.

In this context I must comment on the note of apprehension and gloom that seems to dominate current internal discussion, official and private, on the future of Taiwan's industrial sector. Practitioners of the dismal science are, of course, accustomed to the fact that "the" economic problem is never really "solved" but that each phase brings with it its own peculiar set of difficulties that need to be addressed and overcome. Two points seem to be obvious. One is that the shift from one subphase of growth to another is always difficult and painful for all the parties concerned—mainly because it is not always easy to achieve the necessary historical perspective when one's short-run ox is being gored and when the longer-run benefits of a new set of policies and conditions

---

69. The idea is to increase the average cultivating unit from around one to between eight and ten hectares over time. By the end of 1971 there were already thirty-two thousand power tillers in use, almost 90 percent of which, thanks to secondary import substitution, were locally manufactured.

are not yet clear. The record of the late 1950s, the earlier major transition period, shows similarities in the tone of despondency and the apparent inability of industrialists and officials to see a way out. Then the exhaustion of the domestic market for consumer goods preoccupied businessmen and planners; today the shortage of human skills and technology seems to lie at the heart of the common belief that a cul de sac has been reached. Historical and cross-sectional analysis may be cold comfort to those faced with the task of adjusting to a new set of endowments and relative prices. But it may nevertheless be helpful to remind them of the almost uniquely flexible and successful response—compared with almost any other contemporary LDC—of Taiwan's industrialization effort over the past several decades.

The second point is that the pattern of industrialization I have attempted to trace corresponds unusually well to what might be called a textbook description of industry following its course of dynamic comparative advantage. Such an approximation required, in the first instance, a government willing and able to let the changing endowment be heard in terms of changes in relative output and factor prices and, in the second, sufficient public and private entrepreneurial capacity to take the necessary economic actions to help it along. As in any real world situation, the path taken was neither smooth nor monotonic; there were uncertainties, mixed strategies, errors, and backsliding. Nevertheless, building on the favorable heritage left by Japanese colonialism, Taiwan's economy has moved resolutely from a period of initial infrastructure construction and entrepreneurial ripening in the 1950s through an open labor-intensive industrial export-oriented system in the 1960s, and is now entering the postcommercialization era of adjustment to relative labor scarcity. More than anything else, I believe the decentralized and labor-intensive character of her industrial sector, growing rapidly in balance with a dynamic agriculture, was the key to the sustained growth of output and employment registered. Not only were the complementarities between industrial output and employment growth maximized in this fashion and full employment achieved but, via the impact of this industrialization pattern on the relative shares, both the level and trend of the size distribution of income were favorably affected.[70] Taiwan's per capita income today is more than $800 and life expectancy hovers above seventy—a far cry from the conditions of the early postwar period. In spite of the inevitable blemishes and "special case" arguments, it all adds up to quite an achievement.

70. See Chapter 1 as well as Fei, Ranis, and Kuo, "Growth with Equity."

4 | Fiscal and Monetary Policies

ERIK LUNDBERG

The main emphasis in this book is on the long-term development and transformation of the Taiwan economy. Long-term growth trends in production, foreign trade, capital formation, and consumption in Taiwan subsume a certain stability in short-term changes from year to year and over cycles. Short-term deviations from the trends are not independent of the trends and may have an impact on them.

Development trends should therefore be studied with regard to short-term deviation or disturbances. These may include business cycles with periods of recession and stagnation, balance-of-payments disturbances, and high and varying rates of inflation. In Taiwan, storms, floods, and droughts have also had an important impact on production and prices from year to year.

Short-term variations in production, employment, and prices partly depend on the structural sensitivity of the economy to internal or external disturbances. The current stabilization policies of the Taiwanese authorities also have an important influence on the behavior of the economy. This chapter deals with fiscal and monetary policies from this point of view.

Fiscal and monetary policies not only affect the short-term performance of the economy. The long-term rate of inflation, the shares of savings and investment, and the balance-of-payments developments are also influenced by current policy changes. Therefore this chapter considers both short-term stabilization issues and longer-term aspects, with special reference to inflation and to problems of monetary expansion. In many less developed countries (LDCs), strong and varying rates of inflation have led to serious disturbances and caused difficulty in attaining balanced growth. The Taiwanese experience of periods of strong inflation as well as of remarkable price stability therefore merits serious study. Attention is also given to such other related policy issues as capital formation and balance-of-payments fluctuations.

In this chapter I first search out and present the main problems that the Taiwan experience seems to offer in the field of monetary and fiscal development. Policy attitudes are presented as a background to the ensuing discussion of actual fiscal and monetary policies. Because I place a good deal of emphasis on inflation, Taiwan's experience is studied against an international background, comparing Taiwan's achievements and failures with those of other LDCs. A short account is then given of some relevant features of the financial system from the point of view of how various policy measures may affect the working of the system. The role of monetary policy, of money supply, and interest rates is considered next. Before dealing with issues of fiscal policy—taxation, government expenditure, and finance—general conditions affecting the relations between savings and investment in the Taiwan economy are discussed: balance of payments and exchange rates, wage and productivity growth as influencing prices, income distribution, and savings. Finally, fiscal policy measures as methods of influencing capital formation are dealt with.

General Survey of the Problem

Fiscal and monetary policy issues generally fall into two broad, but interrelated, categories: (1) short-term stabilization problems such as business cycles, balance-of-payments disturbances, inflation, and unemployment; and (2) longer-term issues of growth, with emphasis on development of investment and supply of savings as well as the financing of government expenditures and private investments. Business cycles and the rate of gross national product (GNP) growth are related in various ways. Inflation and unemployment or underemployment may be both short-term and long-term phenomena. Stabilization policies also have longer-term effects. Methods of arranging investment incentives or mobilizing savings may have effects on the short-term stability of the economy. In spite of these interrelations, I prefer to consider these two types of problems as separately as possible.

No clear cyclical movements can be observed in the general pattern of the development of production, prices, and employment in Taiwan. There are numerous sharp irregularities in the indices of real GNP and still more in industrial and agricultural production. Some weaknesses in the growth pattern occurred around 1956, 1960, 1966, and 1974, but no real recession occurred prior to the extreme shocks of 1973–74. Storms, floods, and typhoons cause interruptions in the series of high yearly growth rates. Outstanding peaks in the growth rates occurred in 1954, 1964, and 1972–73, but again there are no significant traces of cycles that could be coupled to international or U.S. cycles. There was much wider, irregular fluctuation in the growth rates of industrial production and the export volume than in GNP.

The only years that could be regarded as cyclical are 1973–75. The extreme boom of 1973 with big increases in production and exports and a rapid price and wage inflation was followed in 1974 by the first real recession, characterized by a decline in industrial production and export volume, stagnation of GNP, and a big deficit in the current balance of payments. The rapid recovery during 1975 is a remarkable feature of Taiwanese development.

This apparent absence of cyclical movements of production and trade up to 1973 raise the question of whether stabilization policy played any part or whether the force of rapid economic growth implied resistance to recessionary impulses. In the 1950s, the urgent need to rebuild the economy and the excess demand for both investment and consumption created the type of stability characteristic of a demand pressure economy. The rate of inflation tended downward in the 1950s in spite of demand pressures. As noted in Chapter 5, internal demand weakened at the end of the 1950s in some important sectors of manufacturing, as easy import substitution came to an end. The stability of growth prevailing during the 1950s required a continued expansive monetary and fiscal policy. The concomitant high rate of inflation may have been a necessary condition of the absence of business cycles during this period.

The greater stability of the more rapid growth process during the 1960s is another problem. The growth process of the 1960s was predominantly led by exports, the volume of which rose at an average of about 25 percent per year. The variability was tremendous, however: from a maximum of over 50 percent to a minimum of 4 percent. These large year-to-year fluctuations in export volume are not clearly related to American or international business cycles; even more paradoxically, they do not seem to have had any significant impact on the growth of GNP or on domestic industrial production. In contrast to the 1950s, the absence (or lower level) of excess demand and the corresponding surprisingly high stability of the price level (GNP deflator rising on the average by 3 percent a year during the period 1962–72) should further stable growth combined with declining rates of under- and unemployment. Again the role of monetary and fiscal policy in this remarkable achievement raises the question whether the very lack of ambitious efforts to achieve stabilization were responsible. Taiwan seems to have escaped the results of "stop-go" policies.

The surprising instability of Taiwan's economy in the 1970s, in contrast to the 1960s, remains a dramatic issue. The inflationary boom of 1973, the big impact of the oil shock, and the subsequent recession were new experiences. The subsequent quick revival during 1975 is in sharp contrast to the drawn-out recession in most other countries and may have resulted from the stabilization policies followed by the government. But the question is raised whether the Taiwanese economy, after having reached the present stage of development, has become more sensitive to business-cycle shocks than was the case in the 1950s and 1960s.

The postwar period began with the consumer price index rising about tenfold a year during 1946–49 and about 500 percent in 1949–50. By 1950–51, the rate of inflation was still out of control (80 to 100 percent a year). It is of great interest to determine how this very rapid inflation was dampened so quickly and brought down to manageable proportions by 1952 without a depression or a severe break in economic growth. To understand how this happened, we have to look at the interrelations of monetary and fiscal policies, particularly the development of the money supply and government deficit financing, with special attention to the role of interest rates. Acceptance of very high interest rates during these years seems to be an outstanding feature of Taiwan's monetary history.

Another central issue is Taiwan's success in bringing down the relatively high rate of inflation during 1952–60 (7 to 8 percent a year) to a remarkably stable value of money—the GNP deflator rising by 2 to 3 percent annually during 1960–72—and with a minimum of fluctuations. This achievement cannot be explained solely by prudent monetary and fiscal policies. As shown in other chapters of this book, there was a fundamental shift in policy attitudes, as well as in actual policies, around 1959–60, including liberalization of foreign trade, abolition of the multiexchange rate system, and tying the N.T. dollar to the U.S. dollar. All this implied a shift of the economy from the path of import substitution to that of growth led by exports. This was not an abrupt change of development strategy, but took place gradually during the years 1958–62. The apparent success of monetary and fiscal policy during the following period must be related to a fundamental change in the economic climate, in the conditions of balanced economic growth, and in general policy. Perhaps the most remarkable accomplishment was the fact that the absence of or errors in stabilization policies did not significantly disturb the process of stable economic growth during the long period 1960–72.

In a developed country, wage determination and wage policies would have to be emphasized to explain inflation and long-term price stability. But these problems are very different in the LDCs. Taiwan did not have active trade unions and during most of the period had a relatively elastic supply of labor, so that wages were mainly market-determined.

General demand conditions may be influenced by current monetary and fiscal policies, but how and to what extent can never be precisely ascertained. Supply and cost conditions were heavily influenced by the rapid growth of labor productivity that implied slowly rising or even falling labor costs per unit of production and must have been an important condition for the stable, almost noninflationary period from 1960 to 1972. But favorable productivity growth will never in itself be sufficient for attaining price stability, as the inflations of the 1950s and 1972–74 demonstrated. Repeated devaluations of the N.T. dollar had an inflationary impact during the earlier period and world inflation and the oil shock during the second period. In the 1970s, wages and labor costs may have become more of an inflationary factor.

In a Keynesian model the inflation issue is often studied against the background of the balance between savings and investments. This approach may be fruitful in studying changes in the demand pressure on prices and wages that seems to have occurred during the period discussed here. And these changes may in many ways be related to the shifts in monetary and fiscal policies.

The deficient supply of internal savings in relation to the actual investment needs during the 1950s, and especially during the first period of high inflation rates, appeared ex post in the form of large deficits in the current balance of payments. The low supply of internal savings could partly be accounted for by observing the large budget deficits of the government that were not sufficiently covered by private savings. Money from the U.S. Agency for International Development (AID) covered most of the savings gap during the 1950s and early 1960s. One challenging problem was how to increase and mobilize internal savings from households, agriculture, and enterprises, as well as from the public sector, to cover the gap and attain the rise in capital formation needed for rapid growth.

Trying to explain how the Chinese succeeded in bringing up the gross savings ratio to GNP from 5 to 10 percent in the first half of the 1950s to about 30 percent in the years around 1970 is an interesting problem. Not only was the savings gap closed, but a net surplus in the current balance of payments was attained. Determination of the role of fiscal and monetary policies in this remarkable achievement is difficult. There was a shift from reliance on forced savings in the public sector and agriculture in the 1950s to an increasing dominance of private, voluntary savings during the 1960s and 1970s.

The growth process, involving a rapidly increasing savings ratio, has been accompanied by a remarkable monetization of the economy, mainly in the form of a tremendous rise of bank deposits. The growth and accompanying radical transformation of the Taiwan economy has implied large and rising transfers of excess savings from some sectors, especially industry. These problems, and how economic policy can influence the process, must be studied with regard to the functioning of the entire financial system.

It is always doubtful to single out specific policy measures as being especially important—for example, tax incentives or the high interest rates (in real terms) on savings deposits prevailing during the 1960s—because the validity of such assertions can never be adequately confirmed. Much of the explanation of the rapid growth of private savings probably had its source in the favorable economic climate of the free private enterprise system that appeared by 1960. This was partly a function of government policy or, rather, the effects of abolishing a number of the economic regulations that prevailed during most of the 1950s. But here there are difficult problems of mutual causation. The shift in economic policy around the years 1958–62 was not an autonomous, sudden change in attitudes and actual determination of policy.

These changes were to a large extent a function of the economic developments during the 1950s and can therefore be explained, at least in part. Savings and investment as items in the national accounts are not independent of one another. The combination of the generous stimulus to private investment in industry by means of low taxes on profits and various forms of tax incentives, with a rapidly expanding export market and high rates of productivity growth, implied high and rising profits and large savings out of profits. But the possibility of analyzing these questions and testing plausible hypotheses is limited in part by lack of the necessary statistical evidence.

Policy Attitudes and Aims

The official declarations of policy targets must be considered in studying the development of fiscal and monetary policy. Although declarations of policy aims may not necessarily be very useful in explaining the actual policies pursued, there is always some relation between declared aims and policy attitudes. And an understanding of attitudes might be helpful in explaining actual decisions. The application of various measures at different times may be interpreted as implying certain policy targets. Even if these are not specifically referred to by the government, they may indicate policy preferences.

There is first the question of how and to what extent the political and social background may have had an impact on the setting of policy goals. The Chinese officials apparently had a genuine anti-inflationary attitude, partly based on a belief that the downfall of the Nationalist regime on mainland China was related to the hyperinflation (as well as to excessive concentration of land ownership). This anti-inflationary attitude was probably strengthened by Taiwan's own inflationary experience during the years 1946-60. One can read off a high sensitivity to each inflation impulse during subsequent years of high rise of the price level: 1959-60, 1968, and 1973, when restrictive monetary and fiscal policy measures were pursued.

Apparently the U.S. AID advisers and missions had an impact on policy attitudes as well as on actual measures that were introduced during the period of active aid (1950-65). The U.S. agencies strongly supported the anti-inflationary attitudes of the Chinese authorities, but there seem to have been some differences of opinion on how to curb inflationary tendencies. The Chinese originally believed in rigid regulation of the economy. The American advisers, with their credo of a free enterprise system, strongly urged successive liberalization of production and trade, gradual abolition of import and exchange control, and elimination of subsidies. As important conditions for the effective functioning of a freer economic system with a minimum of inflation, the government budget deficits had to be reduced and controlled. Less credit rationing and more general control of the money supply were needed.

These were the recommendations of U.S. advisers and International Monetary Fund (IMF) missions. It is impossible to judge to what extent this advice helped bring about the shift in economic policy that took place at the beginning of the 1960s. The U.S. agencies did have a strong position. On several occasions they made further aid conditional on the adoption of desired changes in policy.

The shift in policy attitudes was expressed in the Nineteen-Point Program of Economic and Financial Reform of 1960. This program included a number of measures designed to encourage saving and private investment, to remove subsidies, to raise public utility rates, to liberalize trade regulations, and to unify the multiple exchange rate system. But the change of policy attitudes revealed by the program, as well as the actual policies followed, were not as abrupt as they might have seemed and did not result solely from the urgings of U.S. advisers. Success in killing the rapid inflation of 1951 and the remarkable growth and relative stability achieved from year to year in the 1950s created the material basis for liberalization and other policy changes. A most important condition for this change in policy attitudes was the confidence in the viability of the Taiwanese economy that was built up during the 1950s. This political confidence was strengthened by successful resistance to military attacks from Red China on the offshore islands.

The policy aims contained in government declarations do not show much quantitative precision. Price stability targets are mostly given in the negative form of the necessity of bringing down current rates of inflation. In later years, however, some precision appears in the four-year plans. Employment does not appear explicitly as a stabilization target. The very uncertain unemployment figures are never referred to. Production aims are presented in the four-year plans and can be compared with actual results. The degree of underestimation of the possibilities of growth is remarkable. The four-year plans contain many declarations as to targets for increasing investment and exports. The incentive schemes of taxation and subsidies for stimulating private investment and improving the investment climate imply clear policy aims.

Policy targets refer not only to ultimate aims such as price stability, high growth rates, and investment shares, but also to what we usually regard as means of policy. It is not always easy to distinguish between aims and means of economic policy. One of the government aims in the 1950s was to bring down or eliminate the large budget deficits, which was also continually recommended by the U.S. missions. The derived policy intention implied the aim of cutting down the rate of money creation and ultimately dampening the rate of inflation. The necessary rise of tax rates or limitation of government expenditures would also result in more resources for investment and export and thereby would have positive effects on economic growth.

Monetary and fiscal policies usually have a complex aim reference basis, as well as conflicts of targets. Besides the ordinary goals of inflation control and investment allocation there are secondary targets of the level and stability of interest rates. The discussions as well as actual policy performance indicate opposing crosscurrents. On the one hand, there was a strong desire to bring down and keep down the high interest rates of the early 1950s. This could be a goal in itself, as well as a means of bringing down production costs. On the other hand, high real rates of interest were considered an important means of stimulating private savings as well as imports of private capital. This contradiction of attitudes as to the function of the interest rate seems to explain some of the ambivalent policy during the 1950s. When prices were stabilized in the 1960s, the level of nominal interest rates was brought down and the real rate of interest reached a remarkably high level.

One very curious feature of the Bank of Taiwan's policy attitude refers to the supply of bank notes. The highest denomination is still the N.T.$100 note. This limitation causes considerable difficulty with wage and salary payments, as well as other types of payments. The refusal of the Central Bank to accommodate the need for an efficient payment system is based on the superstitious belief, inherited from the past, that use of higher denominations would result in more inflation. Those who opposed the issuance of notes of large denomination—even the introduction of the N.T.$100 note—cited close relationship between inflation and large denominations during and after World War II.

As already stated, the U.S. AID and IMF economists played a crucial role in persuading the Chinese to reduce the scope of direct control measures and to rely more on the functioning of a relatively free enterprise and free market system. In the 1960s, the basic policy aims were thus to create the necessary conditions for the effective functioning of a private enterprise system, including appropriate fiscal and monetary policies.

Inflation and Money: Some International Comparisons

Comparisons of Taiwan's experience with inflation and monetary expansion with those of other countries may be useful. In other chapters of this book, such comparisons with other LDCs are made with regard to economic growth, capital formation, foreign trade, and the transformation of the economy from an agricultural to an industrial base. The rapid growth and the drastic transformation of the economy from the early 1950s to the mid-1970s were accompanied by an increase of the share of exports in industrial output matched by few countries. But it was not a continuous process: the beginnings in 1949–52 were difficult, and progress went slowly in the 1950s.

These achievements were based upon relatively favorable monetary and financial conditions—serious monetary disequilibria in the form of inflation, recessions, and balance-of-payments disturbances could have interrupted or

Table 4.1. Rate of Inflation (Consumer Price Index) and Money Expansion (M_1), for Selected Countries (average rate per annum)

	1952–61	1962–72	1973–76
Taiwan			
Inflation	12.3	2.9	16.1
Money expansion	23.0	20.9	25.2
South Korea			
Inflation	33.9	13.6	17.2
Money expansion	54.2	29.0	34.0
Thailand			
Inflation	3.1	2.3	11.1
Money expansion	8.4	7.1	14.0
*Asian countries** (average)			
Inflation	3.6	8.2	12.9
Money expansion	8.1	11.5	16.7
*Latin American countries**			
Inflation	21.4†	21.0	48.9
Money expansion	22.5†	27.6	52.0
Industrial countries			
Inflation	1.9	3.7	9.6
Money expansion	4.4	7.5	8.4

*Except OPEC countries and China.
†1958–61.
Source: International Monetary Fund (IMF), *International Financial Statistics,* 1977 Supplement (Washington, D.C., March 1977).

retarded the growth process. Many such disturbances were common in a number of LDCs during the postwar period, but apparently were not equally serious in Taiwan.

There appears to be no clear relation between rate of growth and rate of inflation. Plotting growth and inflation rates by country in a diagram will show a very wide scatter; to get an acceptable regression line, the choice of countries must be biased.[1] In such a diagram Taiwan would take a unique position, with a very high rate of growth and relatively slow rate of general price increase, especially for the period 1962 to 1972, when Taiwan's achievement in combining high growth rates and price stability is almost unique among LDCs (only Thailand and Japan can compete). Some comparisons of rates of inflation and money expansion are presented in Table 4.1.

During the 1950s as well as the 1970s Taiwan had a higher rate of price rise than the average for Asian countries, but a much better record than the Latin American countries (this average contains a tremendous dispersion of inflation rates), although the averages for 1973–76 provide poor information about the actual course of developments. The combination of the world inflationary boom of 1973–74 and the oil price shock led in some countries (especially in Latin America) to a new acceleration of inflation during the years 1973–76. In

---

1. See, for example, Everett E. Hagen, *The Economics of Development* (Homewood, Ill., 1975), fig. 14-3, p. 367.

some Asian countries, especially Taiwan, Thailand, and the Philippines, the rate of price increase was brought down to the preinflation rate by 1975.

The combination of high growth rates, including the rapid growth of total employment and consequent reduction of the rate of underemployment, and a relatively slow rate of inflation may be taken as success in attaining policy targets. From this perspective Taiwan's achievement is outstanding, especially during the period 1962–72, though not as good in the 1950s and after 1972. Inflation rates were extremely high in 1949–51 as well as the single year 1973–74 (48 percent).

One common cause of inflation is large government budget deficits, affecting total demand as well as the supply of money. Such deficits may result from rapidly rising military expenditures, overambitious industrial investment programs, or expanding social expenditures, all combined with weak taxation systems. A number of Latin American countries, as well as some Asian and African ones, have gotten inflation dynamite from large and rising budget deficits. In this respect Taiwan has been relatively fortunate. The United States helped substantially with the financing of military expenditures. The very stable government that Taiwan has had since 1949 has shown a respectable conservatism as to government expenditures. But certainly at times, as in the 1950s, budget deficits did create problems of monetary disequilibrium.

Another important common cause of inflation in LDCs is supply disturbances, especially from bad harvests and general food shortage. Rising food prices with strong repercussions on wages and other prices are common experiences in most LDCS. In Taiwan, especially in the 1950s and in the beginning of the 1960s, storms, floods, and droughts caused substantial price increases for food products. These impulses to inflation were accidental phenomena and did not imply cumulative price spirals. An essential background to the Taiwan experience of relative price stability was the high productivity growth in the agricultural sector and the ample supply of basic food. As shown in Chapter 2, the Chinese government gave high priority to the agricultural sector from the beginning. The moderate price rise of agricultural products was a strategic condition for Taiwan's relative success in preventing general price inflation. This condition differed from that in many other LDCs.

In many LDCs social and political unrest in the form of strikes, controversy about income distribution, and wage inflation, partly as results of profit inflation and large capital gains, have resulted in acceleration of price inflation. Expectations of continued rapid inflation have been built into the system. High inflation rates have in turn provoked more social strain and political unrest. Weak and rapidly changing governments have made matters worse. Several Latin American countries offer examples of this type of inflation fever. Except for the few years of hyperinflation, Taiwan has been nearly completely free from tendencies of this kind.

Taiwan's anti-inflationary tendency has also been furthered by a stable government with complete authority, disciplined labor conditions (no militant trade unions and no right to strike), and therefore hardly any independent wage inflation and a minimum of social strife over income distribution. These very important stability conditions are not just embodied in the system. They are also consequences of the high growth rate of real income, the expanding employment opportunities, and the relatively low rate of inflation.

Serious and repeated balance-of-payments deficits have directly and indirectly caused inflationary impulses in a number of LDCs. Balance-of-payments difficulties are interrelated with the other sources of disturbances, but the ways of dealing with the deficits usually have inflationary consequences. Import controls and trade regulations may be expected to create scarcities and price increases via import-substitution production and investment. Recurring devaluations have been a common cause of cumulative waves of inflation in a number of countries. Taiwan had serious balance-of-payments problems during the 1950s, and devaluations during this period aggravated the internal inflation. Few countries, however, have been as fortunate as Taiwan in getting strong U.S. assistance to fill most of the balance-of-payments gap during the years 1951–64. Without this support there probably would have been larger devaluations, more import controls, and a more rapid inflation.

After the substantial devaluations of the 1950s, the N.T. dollar was fixed at a stable exchange rate with the U.S. dollar during the decades of the 1960s and the 1970s, except for a 5 percent devaluation in 1973. Because Taiwan was a very open economy, with relatively free foreign trade during this period, its attachment to the U.S. dollar implied a close long-run relationship between U.S. price developments and those of Taiwan. But monetary and fiscal policies had somehow to be geared to this exchange rate policy. The fixed exchange rate meant that the stable development of import and export prices helped create stability in the internal price level, but it meant also that disturbances from the world inflation in the 1970s were transmitted to the Taiwan economy. In fact, the price-wage development in Taiwan showed a stronger sensitivity than in any other LDC to the oil shock and accompanying wave of rising world market prices in 1973–74. Few countries, however, matched Taiwan's record in quickly interrupting this burst of inflation during 1974 and reestablishing the same low rate of price rise as before 1973.

I have already noted the unique constellation in Taiwan of rapid economic growth and slow general price rise during a large part of the postwar period. It is an established truth, confirmed by any number of econometric price equations, that under favorable monetary conditions the growth of production and productivity is negatively correlated with the rate of inflation, that is, it has a dampening effect. For Taiwan this effect came not only from agricultural production. The remarkable yearly rise in labor productivity within industry implied, at more or less market-determined wage levels, that labor costs per unit of production were stable or rising only slowly during long periods. This is clearly a most important explanatory factor of price stability. But this result should never be taken as given or self-evident. Monetary disturbances and financial disorder could have reduced or eliminated the potential possibilities of such productivity effects on the rate of inflation, as shown by the example of many LDCs. The case of Taiwan in the 1950s also demonstrates this point.

The statement that certain favorable monetary and financial conditions are necessary to keep down the inflation rate has several connotations. First, there are certain short-term stability conditions. Large government budget deficits financed by the central bank may start a wave of inflation owing to the accompanying money creation. Reckless financing of industrial development by credit expansion may have the same effect. When a strong inflation has started, money and credit may have to be created by the monetary authorities in order to maintain employment and production, with the result that inflation continues. This pattern, found in many LDCs during the postwar period, also existed in Taiwan, especially during the early part of the period. All such cases of temporary inflation were accompanied by increases of the money supply that might have had causal significance or might be regarded as having been a necessary condition for accommodating expansion.

An important aspect of monetary disturbance lies in the effects of restrictive policies by the central bank in efforts to combat an outburst of inflation. There are many examples of how deflationary measures have created industrial recession and stagnation. Success in bringing down the rate of inflation, usually accompanied by a reduction in the money/GNP ratio, has occurred at the expense of a contraction of output and an increased rate of unemployment. Thus inflation may cause serious disturbances to balanced growth owing to destabilizing anti-inflationary policies. During most of the years since the early 1960s there seems to have been none or very little of this type of monetary disturbance in Taiwan. No recession was created by sharp anti-inflationary policies.

A third aspect of monetary and financial conditions involves long-term and structural questions. Table 4.1 shows a surprisingly rapid expansion rate of money supply (M_1), even during a period of relative price stability (1962–72), when the money supply was rising at an average of more than 20 percent per year and consumer prices by only 3 percent. This type of relatively strong expansion of the money supply is found in most LDCs (see Table 4.1) and

Table 4.2. Money and GNP in Taiwan (N.T.$ billions)

	1955	1965	1975
1. Money and deposits (M_2)	2.6	33.3	313
2. GNP	30.0	113.0	556.0
3. Line 1 as percentage of			
line 2	9	30	56

Source: IMF, *International Financial Statistics,* 1977 Supp.

may in part be considered to be an indicator of the continuing process of monetization of the economies. But this tendency was, as Table 4.1 shows, much stronger in Taiwan than in the other LDCs.

This question of monetization is further clarified by including in money supply all kinds of "quasi-money" (M_2) and comparing this total with GNP. Table 4.2 demonstrates the exceptional monetary development of Taiwan. These figures indicate a tremendous expansion of the banking system. Within two decades Taiwan almost reached the degree of monetization of Japan. A few comparisons with other countries are made in Table 4.3. This very rapid expansion of money and bank deposits in Taiwan is apparently connected with a remarkable augmentation in the ratio of gross savings and capital formation to GNP (from 10 percent in the mid-1950s to more than 30 percent in the 1970s). As Ronald McKinnon has argued, such a monetary expansion as Table 4.2 demonstrates implies a strong reduction of financial repression by mobilizing savings to an increasing extent in the form of bank deposits.[2]

When—as should be the case in Taiwan—this strong monetary expansion is largely determined by a growth in demand for money (in this wide sense), the expansion of the money supply will not have a corresponding impact on the rate of inflation, but rather will tend to satisfy the rising demand for holding cash and deposits. It is plausible that this growth of demand should be determined to a considerable extent by the high nominal (and real) interest rates on deposits maintained in Taiwan most of the time. Taiwan was a pioneer among LDCs in setting interest rates at very high nominal levels in the beginning of the period and keeping them high enough above the rate of inflation. A few countries, like South Korea, later followed the example of Taiwan.

It can be argued that the Taiwanese monetary policy, with high and flexible interest rates, contributed to the result of restraining effective demand for goods and services in boom periods, thus preventing the economy from attaining positions of excess demand and overheating. The rise in the savings ratio, interrelated with rapid growth, increasing profits, and high real interest rates, seems to have dampened booms without need for strong contractive policies that frequently provoked recessions in other LDCs.

2. Ronald McKinnon, *Money and Capital in Economic Development* (Washington, D.C., 1973).

Table 4.3. Relation between Total Money Supply (M_2) and GNP
(in percent)

	1955	1965	1975
Philippines	17	22	17
Thailand	20	25	35
Taiwan	9	30	56
Japan	60	79	68

Source: IMF, International Financial Statistics, 1977 Supp.

It is difficult to judge the precise importance of the rapid rate of monetization for capital formation and growth with moderate inflation in Taiwan. We may refer to such concepts as "money's increasing usefulness as a financial instrument"; the extent that savings have been induced by a portfolio effect of increased money holdings; and the complementarity between money holdings and physical capital—types of effects that McKinnon stresses.[3]

The high interest rates and, since the 1950s, the rising confidence in the banking and financial system should have contributed to monetization, stimulating savings and improving the allocation of investment in the direction of projects with relatively high yields.

The high mobility of resources necessary for the rapid transformation and growth processes of the Taiwan economy, especially since the end of the 1950s, must have been based upon relatively efficient operation of the money and credit system. Availability of finance is an important condition for dynamic changes, for financing of production initiatives, and for expanding and transferring resources. The figures in Tables 4.1 to 4.3 indicate that Taiwan's monetary expansion in this respect, in addition to all the others mentioned in this section, provided favorable conditions for stable and rapid growth.

Problems in the Functioning of the Financial System

Economists have a penchant for combining monetary policy with inflation issues and fiscal policy with production and employment goals. There is some validity to this dichotomy. But it is evident that certain aspects of fiscal policy (for example, the financing of budget deficits) and exchange policy will have to be considered when discussing effects of monetary and credit policies. These effects can be understood only against the background of some knowledge about how the whole financial system is functioning and through which means the government and the central bank can have an impact on its opera-

3. See especially chaps. 4 and 8 in ibid. Without doubt there were positive effects of this kind. The monetization of the Taiwan economy—as illustrated by the tables—has also implied a successive improvement in the functioning of the credit and financial markets.

tion. In a rapidly developing country like Taiwan, the financial system may be seen as an instrument for development on which the government can play for attaining various policy goals: shifts of resources, changes in income distribution, size and allocation of savings and investment, and changing rates of inflation.

The growth of money and bank deposits in Taiwan in relation to GNP that was exceptionally rapid during this period may be taken as an indication of several underlying changes: (1) The structural development of the financial system implied an increasing rate of monetization. There was a combination of financial growth and diversification, whereby the institutional structure of financial intermediation developed. (2) Total savings were stimulated and mobilized, then transmitted by the banking system and other financial intermediaries to agencies of production, trade, and the like. The long-term effects on capital formation, structural change, and growth must have been strongly conditioned by the development of the financial system. But certainly there is a mutual causation. Rapid growth and structural change created strong demands on the financial system that were partially met. (3) From another point of view, monetary expansion can be regarded as a process of rapid money creation closely related to changes of interest rates and expansive fiscal and monetary policies. These policies, including changes of interest rates, have had short- and long-term effects on the rate and distribution of savings and investment as well as on prices. (4) Money creation and interest rate changes, as well as changing relations between savings and investment during short-term fluctuations in activity, have had an impact on the rate of inflation. And the changing rate of inflation has had important repercussions back upon the stability of the economy and on the growth process.

Inflation and the savings-investment process are closely interrelated both in the short and the long term. The very rapid but variable rate of increase of deposits in the banking system over the decades is thus related both to the growth of savings and to the rate of inflation. The functioning of the banking system, together with other financial institutions, determines in what directions and how efficiently savings are being transformed into investments. Interest rates may play an important role in the allocation process. By means of monetary and fiscal policies, the government influences this process and thereby also determines how much inflation will accompany different phases of development.

These very cursory observations on the problems involved are presented as a reminder that all these processes are extremely complicated and the various parts closely interrelated. This must be borne in mind when I now make some sharp divisions of the issues: first, I treat the inflation problem with emphasis on the supply of and demand for money, and then pass on to the wider issues of relations between income formation, financial flows, and the determination of savings and investments. The binding link is how these relationships have been affected by monetary and fiscal policy.

For the following analysis it is not necessary to go deeply into the institutional setting of the financial system in Taiwan and its development since 1949, but some remarks may be needed to clarify the operation of monetary and fiscal policy.

As compared with most LDCs, Taiwan inherited a relatively advanced banking system. At the end of the 1950s there were a growing number of other financial institutions. In the middle of the 1960s there were ten commercial banks, most of them government-owned (or with dominant government ownership). Branch offices were spread all over the island. In addition, there were savings and loan companies and credit cooperatives. In rural areas there were credit departments of farmers' associations and post offices handling postal remittances and savings deposits. A number of newly established or reactivated institutions appeared from 1959 on. Most important of these were the Central Bank of China (from July 1961) and the China Development Corporation. In the 1960s, some insurance companies and a few foreign banks were established.

Taiwan had no formal central bank during the period 1949 to 1961. The functions of the old Central Bank of China (established in 1928) were suspended and not reactivated until July 1, 1961. In the interim, the largest commercial bank, the Bank of Taiwan, performed most of the functions of a central bank: issuing notes, handling the banking business of the government and the treasuries of the municipal and local governments, and maintaining custody of foreign exchange assets.

The means of monetary policy available to the government and the central bank were the standard ones, but their effectiveness was doubtful in many respects. The main tool was the control of official bank interest rates on deposits and loans. The discount rate of the central bank (or Bank of Taiwan) was not strategic. The government's direct control of the bank interest rates and rate structure was more or less complete thanks to perfect social discipline within the banking system. But lending and borrowing outside the banking system has—as in all LDCs—been substantial, and the rates on these ''black'' or ''gray'' credit markets have only to a limited extent been influenced by official interest rate policy. The declining differential between the official and the unofficial interest rates from the 1950s to the end of the 1960s may be taken as an indicator of the improvement of the efficiency of the financial system.

The central bank has certain controls over the expansion of the volume of bank credit and deposits. Government control of exchange rates and the bank's buying and selling of foreign exchange have affected the cash reserves of commercial banks and thereby, indirectly, their lending capacity. In the 1950s, the requirement of marginal deposits for foreign exchange applications by importers had a restrictive effect on money supply. Bank reserve requirements could be adjusted, and the central bank had power over rediscounts, call loans, and advances to the commercial banks. The banks have consistently been in large debt to the central bank.

There has not been much of a functioning market for government bonds and other securities. The commercial banks have held relatively small amounts and were thus immune from price variations. Therefore, there has been no recourse to open market operations as a tool of monetary policy.

Securities markets and financing by means of stock issues have been relatively underdeveloped. The Taiwan Stock Exchange Corporation started in 1962, but only a very limited number of companies issue securities for public subscription. Most corporations are family ventures or partnerships and corporations only in name.

The institutional setup of the financial system as well as the financing pattern of economic development, especially with regard to the tremendous growth of industry and foreign trade, must have had important implications for current financial policy. The transfer of surplus savings from households, agriculture, and government sources to sectors with large savings deficits caused by high and growing investments has occurred mainly with the banks as intermediaries. There has been a heavy reliance by the private sector on the commercial banks for both short- and long-term credit needs.

When trying to judge the functioning of the system and the operation of financial policies, it is important to point out the deficiencies. The supply of bank credit was consistently inadequate, even though relatively high real interest rates prevailed most of the time. There must have been a lot of credit rationing with varying degrees of restrictiveness. Credit availability has varied, with big corporations being favored, partly because of conservative collateral rules. High priority seems to have been given to loans to public companies, especially during the 1950s, when the Bank of Taiwan was the main supplier. Low rates of interest were applied from the beginning of the 1960s to finance exports.

The shortage of credit supply was most serious in long-term financing of fixed investments. Short-term bank credits were apparently used extensively for this purpose. The central bank provided refinancing facilities for the long-term loans granted by the banks. The China Development Corporation has been able to fill a small though important part of this demand, getting its resources from U.S. AID counterpart funds and World Bank loans. Inadequate financing resources, especially for medium-sized and small family enterprises, have been supplemented by borrowing from friends and relatives and by employee deposits. Uncertainty as to availability of finance is expressed in the holding of large amounts of financial assets (especially bank deposits) by the firms.

In spite of all these shortcomings, however, the financial system worked well enough so that the impressive growth process could continue without serious interruption and during most of the time with moderate inflation. The financial system as a whole must have contained enough resilience and elasticity to meet the most urgent needs of a rapidly growing economy involved in a great transformation process.

A very important condition for financing the extraordinary yearly increase in private investment has been the existence of sufficient profits for self-financing. Financing out of profits has played a significant role in the expansion process.

My attempt to present a general picture of the operation of the financial system should be supplemented with some observations about changes over the period involved. The operation of the system changed a good deal over time because of changing demands. These problems will be more fully discussed in the following sections in connection with specific policy issues. The functioning of the financial system was different when large government deficits had to be taken care of by the banking system, as in the beginning of the period, compared with the situation in the 1960s and 1970s, when this task had disappeared and the current balance of payments had shifted from deficit to surplus.

The content of the financial system was also transformed by the shift of the growth process from import substitution during the 1950s to growth led by exports thereafter. The financial difficulties experienced by a number of firms when production growth for import substitution was coming to an end in the late 1950s resulted in bankruptcies and a high frequency of default of private loans. This stimulated a shift of savings toward bank deposits and financing by means of bank credits, resulting in a relative decline in the unofficial credit market. These examples illustrate the point that the financial system adapted itself to the new growth conditions beginning in the 1960s.

The Control of Money Supply and Inflation

Under certain circumstances changes in money supply may be used as an indicator of the intentions and results of monetary policy. One problem is to what extent the authorities really control changes in the quantity of money in the short and long run, that is, whether they have the effective instruments to do it and really try to do it. Another question is if, how, and to what extent such changes in the supply of money affect economic activity and the price level. That will also depend on the partly independent trend in the demand for money.

Table 4.4 presents the year-to-year changes (in percent) in money supply (M_1), high-powered money (notes and currency held by the public plus bank reserves) compared with price changes. A confused picture emerges of relations between changes in money supply and prices. A neat relationship over longer periods of time (see Table 4.7 below), to be discussed in the next section, is not reflected in the year-to-year fluctuations. Only during periods of sharp price increases, 1949–51 and 1972–74, are there corresponding increases in the money supply. The sudden bursts of money growth in 1958, 1963, and 1964 were not accompanied or followed by similar increases in prices, but the 1967 increase in money supply was followed by some acceleration in the rate of inflation. The notably large increases in money supply

Table 4.4. Annual Changes in Money and Prices (percent)

Year	Money supply (1)	High-powered money (2)	GNP deflator (3)	Consumer price index (4)	Import prices (5)	Export prices (6)
1950	99*	90†	—	384‡	—	—
1951	61*	53†	—	30‡	—	—
1952	42*	68†	—	29‡	—	—
1953	26	17	23	19	−12	−10
1954	27	25	1	2	14	6
1955	20	22	11	10	3	7
1956	25	29	9	11	58	58
1957	18	17	9	8	2	8
1958	35	29	6	1	4	−15
1959	9	4	8	11	36	59
1960	10	7	14	18	16	7
1961	20	16	5	8	10	27
1962	8	11	3	2	−6	−2
1963	28	24	4	2	3	23
1964	32	27	5	0	4	0
1965	11	14	0	0	2	−9
1966	16	12	3	2	6	−1
1967	29	32	5	3	1	3
1968	13	14	8	8	0	0
1969	16	10	5	5	0	4
1970	21	19	5	4	2	3
1971	19	29	3	3	6	3
1972	35	26	5	3	12	9
1973	47	46	13	8	23	19
1974	7	12	34	48	47	39
1975	26	29	2	5	−4	−6

*Figures for 1950–52 taken from Fu-Chi Liu, "Demand for Money in Taiwan," Appendix Table A-1, *Academia Economic Papers* (1970).

†Figures for 1950–52 taken from ibid., Appendix Table C.

‡Figures for 1950–52 taken from Kowie Chang, ed., *Economic Development of Taiwan* (Taipei, 1968), Table 8-8.

Source: Columns 1, 2: *Taiwan Financial Statistics Monthly,* December 1976; column 3: Economic Planning Council (EPC), *National Income of the Republic of China* (Taipei, 1976); columns 4,5,6: EPC, *Taiwan Statistical Data Book, 1976* (Taipei, 1976).

during 1972 and 1973 and the following burst of inflation will be discussed below.

On the other hand, there were discontinuities in the price series, such as in 1954 and 1960, that have no correspondence in money supply. The specific reasons for these discontinuities were nonmonetary, such as the previous year's decline in international prices in 1953 and storms and floods in 1959 that led to a rise in farm prices.

From the point of view of stabilization policy, the main observation is that monetary (and fiscal) policies during the long period 1952–72 did not significantly disturb economic activity and prices. Nor did an accidental price rise build into a cumulation spiral. Apparently the big increases in money supply were easily absorbed, with a minimum of fluctuation in the interest rate. The question is which factors controlled the short- and long-term changes in money supply and how much conscious central bank control occurred.

The supply of money has been affected mainly by four categories of factors: (1) balance-of-payments transactions, (2) government finance policies, (3) U.S. AID operations, and (4) interest rate policies. During the period of rapid inflation (1949–51) government deficit financing dominated the money-creation process. This was a continuation of the hyperinflation that exploded in 1947 on mainland China. Despite a rapid appreciation of the local currency (the "taipi") in relation to the "yuan," the Taiwan authorities did not succeed in neutralizing the inflation impact from the mainland.[4]

A monetary reform was announced in June 1949, involving a new currency named the New Taiwan dollar (N.T.\$) with 100 percent reserves in gold and foreign exchange (and export commodities) and with the exchange rate pegged at 20 percent of the United States dollar. A maximum amount of currency permitted to be in circulation was established. But, in fact, monetary policy became completely passive because the Bank of Taiwan financed the government budget deficits as well as the investment expenditures of public enterprises. The tremendous rise of public expenditures (80 percent for military purposes) was not and could not be matched by increased taxes. The inflation effect of the monetary expansion was aggravated by the serious deficiencies of supplies because production in 1947–48 was reduced to 40–50 percent below the prewar level.

The quantitative limit on the note issue had to be abolished. Inflation was accompanied and supported by a rapid devaluation of the external value of the currency, reaching less than 10 percent of the U.S. dollar in July 1950. Efforts were made in the first half of 1950 to stabilize the exchange rate and strengthen the confidence in the value of money by means of a gold savings deposit program and the free sale of gold and foreign exchange. The inflation

4. See Fu-Chi Liu, "Taiwan's Experience of Transition from Inflation to Stability," Academia *Economic Papers* (1970), p. 2.

of 1949–51 was a classic illustration of a money-propelled price rise under a system of relatively free exchange rates. The exchange rate of the currency was partly determined by market values of foreign exchange certificates. A feature in common with Latin American inflation was that the rate of price increase was much higher than the rate of monetary expansion, indicating a rapid rise in the income velocity of money (from about 4 in 1937 to 10 in 1947 and around 20 in 1949–52). However, the major problem was how this inflation could be kept from accelerating and turned into a stable retardation process after 1951.

Because of the exhaustion of foreign assets in 1951, the Bank of Taiwan was forced to abandon its passive and cheap monetary policy and introduce restrictive policy measures. Some direct controls were established, including rationing of some basic commodities. A foreign exchange reform of 1952 established multiple exchange rates and control of trade proceeds, supported by selective import controls. The supply of money was constrained by an import deposit scheme introduced in 1952 and abolished in 1953, the raising of interest rates on time and savings deposits, and the absorption of funds into U.S. counterpart deposits.

This last factor was of special importance in the stabilization process. When U.S. AID was reinstated in July 1950, the old agreement between China and the United States that Chinese currency equivalent to the sales value of aid commodities delivered should be deposited in the Bank of Taiwan was reestablished. The stabilizing effects of U.S. aid worked both on the demand and the supply sides. The increase of counterpart fund deposits reduced the availability of high-powered money from the central bank. These AID deposits, which in 1952 corresponded to about one-fifth to one-fourth of the total liabilities of the Bank of Taiwan, were used to finance public investment and to cover the government budget deficit. But, given these expenditures, the absorption of the AID funds had a contractive effect on the supply of money and on total demand. At the same time, the increased supplies of raw materials and investment goods flowing from U.S. AID released the pressure on the supply side.

It is neither possible nor necessary to make exact calculations about the effects on money supply of these various factors. We can merely observe the dampening effect on the rate of money expansion in Table 4.4 and the accompanying retardation of the rate of inflation. Of fundamental importance for the successful stabilization after 1951 was the simultaneous improvement in production and productivity. Confidence in the new currency in Taiwan rose, further consolidating success in stopping the previous high rate of inflation.

The gross monetary expansion during the following years is presented in broad categories in Table 4.5. The periods are selected arbitrarily to give a rough indication of the changing patterns.

Table 4.5. Expansion of the Monetary System (changes between years in N.T.$ 1,000 million)

Year	Net foreign assets	Claims on government and government enterprises	Claims on private enterprises	Total assets	Annual rate of change in Total assets	Annual rate of change in Money supply
1952–56	0.6	4.7		5.3		
Shares	(10%)	(89%)		(100%)	27	25
1956–60	2.6	2.9	5.4	10.9		
Shares	(24%)	(27%)	(49%)	(100%)	23	18
1960–64	9.2	5.6	13.4	28.2		
Shares	(83%)	(20%)	(47%)	(100%)	25	22
1964–68	3.9	10.8	28.7	43.4		
Shares	(9%)	(25%)	(66%)	(100%)	18	17
1968–71	18.6	6.6	42.5	67.7		
Shares	(27%)	(10%)	(63%)	(100%)	20	18
1971–73	36.1	10.2	84.1	130.4		
Shares	(28%)	(8%)	(64%)	(100%)	35	40
1973–75	−1.8	46.2	116.0	160		
Shares		(29%)	(72%)	(100%)	25	17

Source: Taiwan Financial Statistics, passim, estimates made at the EPC.

The financing of the expenditures of government and government enterprises still played a dominant role during the period 1952–56. Thereafter, and especially during the first half of the 1960s, the increasing exchange reserves became a more important source of money creation. But with the tremendous expansion of the private enterprise sector from the beginning of the 1960s, most of the asset expansion of the monetary system came from demand for credit from this sector. The monetary expansion during the boom of 1971–73, led by a vigorous expansion of exports, was to a considerable extent generated by the purchase of foreign exchange. By contrast, during the recession of 1974–75 the small loss of exchange reserves was counteracted by accelerated debt financing of the public sector.

It is not possible to judge from Table 4.5 the effect of an active monetary policy in attaining some autonomous control over the rate of monetary expansion. The purchase of foreign exchange by the central bank was largely a passive response. A considerable part of the rise in exchange reserves during the 1950s, however, was caused by repeated devaluations of the N.T. dollar (in particular the 65 percent devaluation in 1958).

It is difficult to judge, from the point of view of monetary control, the character of the tremendous expansion of private loans after 1960. This expansion was largely a reflection of credit demand related to the very high growth rate of investment, production, and trade within the private sector. No one can judge to what extent such automatic demand expansion was influenced or controlled by interest rates and various forms of credit rationing by the banks. There were, however, steady complaints about the lack of response of bank credit supply to the rising demand.

One way to test the degree of autonomy of the central bank's control of monetary supply is to study changes in the quantity of high-powered money. This type of money is created by the Central Bank in correspondence with its monetary liabilities and stands in some variable multiplier relation to the entire money supply. The yearly changes in high-powered money are shown in Table 4.4. It seems clear that the fluctuations in the two kinds of money supply are generally quite close. On the average, over a longer period changes in high-powered money accounted for 93 percent of the variations in the money stock.[5] Part of the explanation for this conformity is that the Bank of Taiwan both in the 1950s and after the reform of 1961 behaved like a commercial bank and considerably increased loans to private enterprises.

But there were some considerable deviations in the rates of increase of the two kinds of money stock in various years, implying corresponding changes in the reserve and currency ratios. Table 4.4 shows some specific years of large monetary expansion. The strong upsurge in 1957–58 was to a considerable extent related to a military crisis, accompanied by a burst of government expenditures and deficit financing by the Bank of Taiwan. The big jumps in 1961 and again in 1963–64 were mainly caused by large accumulations of net foreign assets. A very large rise in the price of sugar (connected with the Cuban crisis) is the main explanation of the increase in the export price index and of exchange reserves. Again, the abrupt rise of central bank money supply in 1967 (by 32 percent) was mainly caused by a combination of increased foreign reserves, loans to the private sector, and a decline in U.S. AID deposits. And the largest inflationary impulse in 1972–73 (rise of high-powered money by 45 percent) came from the boom demand for credits by the industrial sector, reflecting a big increase of bank borrowing from the central bank and accompanying increasing foreign reserves.

Effects of changes in the supply of central bank money on the total stock of money can in principle be controlled by legal reserve requirements that were in effect during the entire survey period. Variations in requirements for demand and time deposits have been applied in a countercyclical fashion. Thus, requirements were successively lowered during 1953–58 to the lowest possible level (10 percent against demand deposits) and quickly raised again during 1959 to the highest allowed level (15 percent). After having lowered these reserve requirements to the minimum in 1966, the central bank tried to counteract the inflationary rise of the money supply in 1967 by again raising the reserve requirements to 15 percent. The new inflation disturbance in 1972–73 was met by raising the requirement to the upper limit, followed by rapid reduction in the fall of 1974.

There is no evidence that this type of reserve policy was really effective in

5. Fu-Chi Liu, ''The Supply of Money,'' p. 10.

controlling the money supply and credit availability. Most of the time, especially during the 1950s, the commercial banks had ample excess reserves so that changes in reserve requirements primarily served as policy signals. The effectiveness of this instrument was greatly weakened by the narrow limits of allowed variation; the upper limit (15 percent on demand deposits) was quickly reached.[6] Furthermore, potential effects of these reserve changes were largely neutralized by generous possibilities of getting extra reserves by borrowing from the central bank.

These changes in reserve requirements were as a rule accompanied by movements in discount rates and other interest rates, as shown in Table 4.6. The surprisingly successful monetary restriction of 1974 and the expansion of 1975 and 1976 must be viewed against the background of the extremely strong monetary expansion of 1972 and 1973, when money supply increased by 35 and 47 percent, respectively. The accompanying credit expansion helped finance the investment boom of 1973-74, with a record increase in imports of machinery and a fantastic rise of inventories, amounting to N.T.$48 billion (corresponding to 25 percent of total capital formation). The ensuing combination of a rise in the level of interest rates by about 50 percent from 9.5 to 14 percent (see Table 4.6) and a reduction of the rate of expansion of the money stock from 47 percent (1972-73) to 7 percent (1973-74) is certainly a remarkable achievement. Immediately following, the inflation rate dropped. In 1974 there was apparently a credit squeeze toward private borrowers from banks; although loans and discounts by all banks expanded by 35 percent in 1974, there might have been a decline in real terms (to be compared with an annual ratio of credit expansion in real terms of about 20-25 percent in average for the period 1967-72). The credit restriction might have contributed to the killing of the tremendous inventory boom of 1974.

Again this very restrictive monetary policy was partly automatic. As already noted, the expansionary force of the balance-of-payments surpluses in 1971-73 was reversed as an automatic result of the large import surplus. The expansionary impact on money supply of rapidly rising loan financing of public expenditures (see Table 4.5) was apparently reduced by means of the interest-rate effect on savings deposits. Time and savings deposits expanded at a record rate in 1973-74, by N.T.$43 billion, corresponding to 50 percent of the money supply, measured as M_1. Again, as in the 1950s, the question arises of the extent to which this shift from M_1 to M_2 can be taken as an indicator of monetary contraction.

Table 4.4 showed that the high rate of money expansion in 1972-73 provided monetary space for the high rate of inflation. Most of the price rise

6. In the revised bank law of 1975, the instrument of reserve requirements was simplified and sharpened by the introduction of much wider margins of variation (for example, between 15 and 40 percent for checking accounts).

Table 4.6. Major Changes in Rates on Bank Loans

Effective date of change	Central bank rediscount rate	Commercial banks	
		Unsecured loans	Secured overdrafts
		Percent per month	
July 1961	1.20	1.56	1.35
January 1962	1.08	1.56	1.20
July 1963	0.96	1.38	1.08
May 1967	0.90	1.17	1.02
		Percent per annum	
December 1970	9.80	13.20	11.40
March 1971	9.80	12.50	10.75
July 1972	8.50	11.75	10.00
July 1973	9.50	12.50	10.50
October 1973	10.75	13.75	11.75
January 1974	14.00	17.50	15.00
September 1974	12.50	16.00	13.75
December 1974	12.00	15.50	13.25
December 1975	10.75		

Source: Directorate-General of Budget, Accounting, and Statistics (DGBAS), *Statistical Yearbook of the Republic of China, 1975* (Taipei, 1976).

occurred in the beginning of 1974. Apparently part of the government's economic stabilization program was to take the unavoidable price increases emanating from the oil shock and rising import prices "at one shot," and then to stabilize. The government let the prices of rice and wheat increase substantially at the beginning of 1974 by lowering subsidies. This active inflation policy seemed to squeeze out tendencies of excess demand and eliminate most speculative price rises. Restrictive monetary policy should have contributed to the effective dampening of the price rise in the second half of 1974. The stabilization and even decline of import prices was an important factor behind this achievement.

The Taiwan economy picked up remarkably well in 1975, after two years of relative stagnation, so that the growth in real GNP reached the high rate of 12 percent in 1975–76. The expansion of exports was the main determining factor, but certainly the return to a more expansive monetary policy provided favorable conditions for the successful revival. The remarkable fact was that this could happen so quickly after the price inflation had been brought down to preinflation rates.

Interest Rates and the Demand for Money

The preceding discussion of the possible effects of money supply changes has assumed some kind of money demand equivalent. This need not necessarily be given explicitly in the form of a demand function, but our understanding of the monetary problems can be improved by looking at the demand side.

I will first look at the trend periods and discuss the differences in underlying conditions that might explain the remarkable shift in the rates of inflation from the 1950s to the 1960s. It would not be easy for a monetarist to account for the difference between the two periods. Fu-Chi Liu has determined a demand function for money covering the period 1947–68.[7] According to his analysis, the real demand for money is determined mainly by real GNP, with interest rates and the general price rise playing insignificant roles. He estimated that the income elasticity of demand was about 1.5 for M_1 and 1.8 for M_2 (see Table 4.7).[8]

Table 4.7. Average Annual Rates of Change of Prices, Money Supply and GNP (percent)

	Consumer price level	Money supply (M_1)	GNP (in 1971 prices)
1952–60	10.0	21	6.4
1961–72	3.3	20	9.4

Source: From Table 4.4 above.

These elasticities imply a steady decline in the income velocities as shown in Table 4.8.

Table 4.8. Income Velocity of Money (averages per period)

	Y/M_1	Y/M_2
1951–54	16.7	11.5
1955–59	11.6	7.5
1960–64	10.4	4.5
1965–68	8.0	3.5
1969–73	7.0	2.8
1974–75	6.2	2.2

Source: Taiwan Financial Statistics Monthly, National Income of the Republic of China. Estimates made at the Economic Planning Council.

There was a remarkable trend rise in the demand for money and bank deposits in Taiwan over this period, implying a strong, fairly regular decline in the

7. Fu-Chi Liu, ''Demand for Money in Taiwan,'' *Academia Economic Papers* (1970), pp. 4–10.

8. The following regression equations refer to the period 1951–75:

$$\ln \left(\frac{M}{P}\right)_1 = -8.6 + 1.5 \ln\frac{Y}{P} + 0.5 \ln (r) - 0.4 \ln\frac{dP}{P}$$
$$R^2 = 0.99$$
$$\ln \left(\frac{M}{P}\right)_2 = -9.75 + 1.8\frac{Y}{P} - 0.18 \ln (r) - 0.04 \ln\frac{dP}{P}$$
$$R^2 = 0.99$$

M_1 includes only cash and net demand deposits. M_2 also covers time and savings deposits. Y/P is GNP in constant prices, r is interest rates charged by private moneylenders, dP/P refers to the rise of the wholesale price index. The calculations have been made in the Economic Planning Council, Executive Yuan, Taipei.

income velocity of circulation. There are different alternatives for explaining this phenomenon. One can consider monetization of the economy, progressing from the more primitive state of the early 1950s to a modern business economy with a need for bank accounts and services in the 1970s. This trend includes a reflection of an increasing confidence in the value of money. The demand function of money and bank deposits should thus contain a strong structural trend factor. Other forms of the demand function can be used to account for the unusually high elasticities.

S. C. Tsiang has tried to take into account the effects of Taiwan's rapidly rising international trade.[9] The value of foreign trade (exports plus imports) increased from about 25 percent of the gross national product at the beginning of the 1950s to between 80 and 90 percent in the 1970s. Tsiang argues that import and export transactions create an extra demand for balances that is not taken care of by the national income variable. He secures the following regression equation:

$$\text{In } M_1 = 0.10 + 0.83 \text{ In } y + 0.70\frac{T}{y} - 0.32 \text{ In } r$$

where M_1 is in real terms, y is real GNP, T the volume of international trade, and r the interest rate.

The result of including the new variable (T/y) is to bring down the income elasticity of money demand below one and to raise the correlation coefficient somewhat. The time period covered is 1953–72.

Whatever money demand function we might prefer, its stability makes possible a monetarist type of explanation for the trend rise in prices (in this case the gross domestic product [GDP] deflator). Money supply increased at an annual rate of 21 percent during the period 1952–68. The rate of real growth of GDP was 9 percent, and using the Fu-Chi Liu demand function for money (in real terms), the demand should have increased by about 14 percent per annum. The gap between the rise of the nominal supply of money and real demand, equal to 7 percent per year, corresponds quite closely to the average actual rate of inflation.[10]

This type of analysis may satisfy the simplest needs of a Friedmanian approach. We all know the limitations, especially as to the causal interpretation. Money supply is not independent of demand; there are many interrelations between the supply and demand variables, working through bank lending, government deficits, U.S. AID counterpart funds, and balance-of-payments changes. However, a simple quantity theory may be useful or suggestive. Under ruling conditions the observed rate of money expansion (of 20 percent)

9. S. C. Tsiang, "The Monetary Theoretical Foundation of the Modern Monetary Approach to the Balance of Payments" (unpublished).
10. See Liu, "Demand," pp. 37–41.

was a necessary condition for the actual long-term inflation. This simple approach may help to explain the shorter-term variations in the rate of inflation.

Comparing the two periods 1952–60 and 1961–72, it seems paradoxical that the average rate of monetary expansion (M_1) should be about the same (around 20 percent per year) and yet the difference in the inflation rate so large (10 and 3 percent, respectively). The higher growth rate of GNP after 1960 seems to explain only about half of this difference. Figure 4.1 shows actual and estimated income velocity of money from 1951–75. The estimated series is based on the regression equations presented in note 8.[11]

There was considerable variation in the velocities (referring to M_1) during the 1950s, with high figures at the beginning of the decade and a large deviation from the estimated values. The trend rate of monetary expansion was raised in a nonsignificant way compared with developments during the 1960s. The corresponding curves for M_2 (including savings and time deposits) give the impression that the irregularities of the early 1950s were evened out.

Cash balances were shifted to time and savings deposits in 1950–52 thanks to an active interest rate policy. The Chinese authorities, during the years of high inflation or persistent danger of price increases, used extraordinarily high interest rates as an anti-inflationary measure. When confronted with postwar inflation, most governments, in LDCs as well as in the developed countries, have been slow to adjust interest rates to current inflation rates and to expectations of future price rise. In this respect the Chinese authorities were admirably bold and unorthodox. Reed J. Irvine and Robert F. Emery note, ''The Chinese, however, managed to break through this psychological barrier to the adoption of realistic interest rates.''[12]

The scheme introduced in the spring of 1950—preferential interest deposits (PIR)—meant that even during the high rate of inflation of 1950 and 1951 people could earn a positive real interest on their savings. In 1951 the rate of inflation was about 50 percent per year, but a nominal interest rate of about 4 percent per month (it had been 7–9 percent per month in the spring of 1951) meant that the real return on a one-month preferential deposit was as high as 12 percent a year. As the inflation rate was reduced after 1951, these preferential rates were lowered successively from 4 percent per month to about 20 percent per year at the end of 1953. But still the real rate could be kept high and positive; on one-year deposits in 1958 the real return was as high as 17 percent.

The essence of the anti-inflationary monetary policy was the absorption of excessive liquidity created by the deficit budgets in the early 1950s. The rapid

11. Cf. the corresponding Chart 3 in Liu, ''Demand,'' p. 23. The period has been extended to 1975 using Liu's equations for the period 1951–68.

12. Reed J. Irvine and Robert F. Emery, ''Interest Rates an Anti-Inflationary Instrument in Taiwan'' *National Banking Review* (September 1966), p. 2.

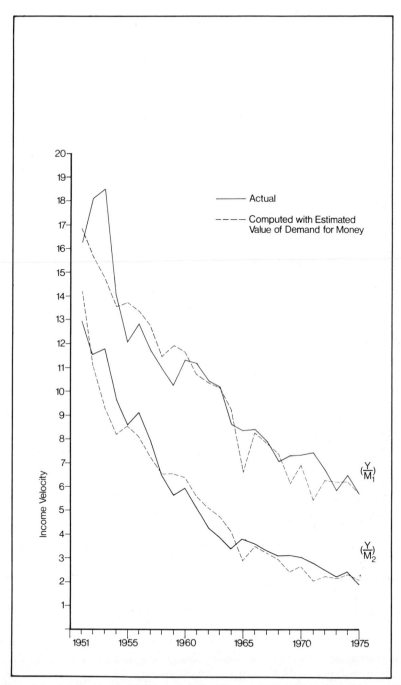

Figure 4.1. Actual and estimated income velocity of money, 1951–1975; Y, national income; M, money. Sources, actual: *Taiwan Financial Statistics Monthly; Economic Planning Council, National Income of the Republic of China* (Taipei, 1976); and estimates of the Economic Planning Council.

rise in these preferential deposits resulted in a dampening effect on money supply (M_1) under given supply conditions. The PIR deposits, as a share of money supply, increased from 9 percent in the spring of 1951 to more than 50 percent from June 1952 to September 1953. At the same time, by manipulating the PIR interest rates the authorities succeeded in switching the deposits into longer maturities—six months at first and later one- and even two-year deposits. Under this policy the commercial banks received more money in preferential deposits than they could lend to their customers under the prevailing conservative credit standards. The rising excess deposits were increasingly redeposited with the Bank of Taiwan.

In a way, the introduction of the PIR deposits, with high real returns, worked like a kind of open market operation policy. Excess liquidity was absorbed and put into less liquid form. To what extent such a policy effectively contributed to the dampening of demand and an increase in monetary savings is an open question.

The policy of relatively high interest rates seems to have been maintained during subsequent periods of more stable prices, although the nominal rates were reduced continuously with the retardation of the general price rise. Thus the interest rate on one-year savings deposits was lowered from 1.65 percent per month at the end of the 1950s to .8 percent at the end of the 1960s. Yet because of the stability in the price level, the reduced level of interest rates corresponded with a high real rate of about 7 percent per year. The lending and discount rates of the commercial banks were reduced at about the same tempo, but have also been kept on a high real level. As Irvine and Emery pointed out, Taiwan also pioneered in interest rate policy by issuing high-interest government and corporation bonds. In 1959, 18 to 20 percent bonds were sold to the nonbank public, and government bonds were exempt from income taxes.

These high official interest rates, in real terms, could be regarded as much too low for creating equilibrium. The supply of loans provided by commercial banks at these officially controlled rates were generally insufficient to satisfy demand during the entire period. There was a significant shortage of loanable funds for covering the needs of the private sector, as can be seen most clearly from the free market rates outside the banks. These rates of interest on unsecured loans from private moneylenders in Taipei were as high as 10 to 15 percent per month in 1950 and 1951, 3 to 4 percent in the second half of the 1950s, and still close to 2 percent at the end of the 1960s. However, the gap between official and market rates was reduced from three times to about twice the official bank lending rates during this period. The risk premia for such loans were high, partly because of antiusury laws.

The situation on the credit markets implied credit rationing by the banks. The imperfections of the credit market were supported in part by the government's selective credit policies. Thus in 1957 a special export loan program was initiated, and favorable interest rates for export financing have been available since then. Schemes were also devised for providing cheap loans to farmers and public enterprises.

At this point, as in many other countries, the persistent argument was made for the lowest possible interest rates in order to keep down costs of production and prices (for example, to keep down electric power rates). During the entire period the official interest rates, although relatively high, were below the natural rate that would clear the market. The credit market was functioning badly, with distortions from the point of view of an optimal allocation of available loan funds and savings. The wide discrepancies between the interest costs for subsidized public enterprises and the cost of marginal credit supplies to the private sector were tremendous in the 1950s. As an anti-inflation policy, it is more than doubtful whether these efforts to subsidize interest costs in preferred markets really helped. Certainly, the prices of electric power, cement, sugar, and some other basic commodities could be kept lower than otherwise would have been the case. But, on the other hand, the distorted loan markets, with much rationing, entailed much higher average costs and great risks of borrowing on the black money market. These high costs should have contributed to raising prices. But it is impossible to judge the relevance of this type of argument because so many other market distortions, especially during the 1950s, were caused by import controls and the overvalued currency with multiple exchange rates.

These conditions were changed drastically at the beginning of the 1960s. The N.T. dollar was devalued and the exchange rates unified, foreign trade liberalized, and the range of subsidized capital costs reduced. More of the savings became concentrated to the banking system. Table 4.9 shows the rapid growth of bank deposits beginning in 1959.

This development may be regarded as indicating a significant improvement in the functioning of the economy of Taiwan as a market system. As already pointed out, the tremendous growth of bank deposits meant a monetization of the economy, a transfer of savings resources from black markets and self-financing activities to the banking credit market, as well as to other financial institutions. The extraordinary expansion of deposits of individuals and others—their share of total deposits increased from 36 to 60 percent—is especially noteworthy. This category of deposits contains much of the savings from farms and small unincorporated firms.

Monetization provided increasing possibilities for monetary policy. The rising dependence of the private sector on outside finance gave the central bank more power to control financial flows. The level of interest rates, under these conditions, became an important control instrument, both for the allocation of savings resources and for the regulation of the total demand and supply

Table 4.9. Total Bank Deposits, 1959–1975 (N.T.$ 1,000 million)

Year	Total	Government and public enterprises	Private enterprises	Individuals and others	Counterpart fund and U.S. agencies
1959	9.6	2.6	1.7	3.5	1.8
	(100%)	(27%)	(18%)	(36%)	(19%)
1964	30.7	5.6	4.0	15.5	5.6
	(100%)	(18%)	(13%)	(51%)	(18%)
1968	59.7	15.0	10.0	32.9	1.8
	(100%)	(25%)	(17%)	(55%)	(3%)
1973	197.0	51.0	32.9	111.4	1.7
	(100%)	(26%)	(17%)	(56%)	(1%)
1975	307.5	75.4	46.1	185.1	0.9
	(100%)	(25%)	(15%)	(60%)	(0%)

Source: Taiwan Financial Statistics, passim.

of money. The process of transferring funds from surplus to deficit savings must have been working better and better. Funds could be allocated on the basis of profitability criteria. But the transfers of savings to the banking system in the 1960s did not bring the system close to a perfect market. The banking system has preserved much of its conservative style, and the capital markets for bonds and shares have remained underdeveloped.

The improvement in the functioning of the financial markets was closely related to the general liberalization of the economy and its integration into world markets through a single rate of exchange that was realistic and well adjusted to some norm of purchasing power parity. There must have been a process of mutual causation, though it is impossible to be precise about the direction. Loan fund markets functioned more effectively, and this together with liberalized and more competitive markets for goods and services contributed to greater flexibility and improved allocation of resources, leading in turn to greater productivity growth. All this helped to bring about a stable growth pattern and to reduce the rate of inflation. Confidence in the viability of the Taiwanese economy supported the trend. But the positive outcome of this combination of vigorous expansion and transformation also depended on the absence of disturbances caused by monetary and fiscal policies. There were inflationary episodes, but, on the whole, there was smooth adjustment between supply and demand factors, preventing major interruptions to the growth process. The 1974–75 recession was a unique case that clearly demonstrated the viability of the Taiwan economy and the nondisturbing flexibility of monetary policy.

An isolated account of monetary policy, as I have presented it, is only part of the story. More insight can be gained from examination of some of the general conditions of policy that are relevant to the distribution and flow of savings funds in the Taiwan economy.

Some General Policy Problems: Exchange Rates, Wages, and Profits

During the 1950s, strong devaluation of the N.T. dollar, from N.T.$5 to N.T.$40 per U.S. dollar, gave a strong upward push to import and export prices and indirectly to the internal inflation rate. The multiple exchange rates ruling during this period, together with exchange and import controls, created a very complex system of price formation. During the 1960s and up to the beginning of the 1970s, the unified N.T. dollar rate, pegged to the U.S. dollar, was a strategic condition for price stability. But the inflationary impact increased when the U.S. dollar was devalued at the end of 1971 and the Taiwan dollar followed it down. The international inflation that began in 1972 was neutralized only to an insignificant extent by an appreciation of the N.T. dollar in relation to the U.S. dollar, by about 5 percent. A considerable part of the 1972–74 inflation in Taiwan can therefore be explained by the world inflation because it led to an increase in import and export prices. As already noted, however, the reaction to inflation of the Taiwan price level during 1973–74 was surprisingly strong.

The conditions of competition determined to what extent international price changes affected price and wage formation in Taiwan. During the 1950s, an intricate system of import and exchange controls and an overvalued currency created independent price movements and high profits in the protected markets. This situation changed with the new policy orientation beginning in the 1960s. One can argue that the relaxation of import controls in 1964, alongside the direct impact on prices, indirectly served as a kind of instrument of monetary policy. The subsequent rapid increase in import volume also put a brake on the previous excessive accumulation of exchange reserves and thereby dampened the growth of money supply.

Another strategic set of factors influencing the price level has to do with the determination of wage costs. In Taiwan there existed no, or very little, active wage push or wage policy as an independent factor in the inflation process. Without active trade unions and with a relatively elastic supply of labor, at least up to the 1970s, the price of labor can be regarded as a passive factor, adjusting to market conditions, including changes in prices and productivity.

Some attempts have been made to relate wage changes to the unemployment rate as well as to prices and productivity, but they must be regarded with skepticism. Wage statistics (mainly monthly wages in industry) are deficient, particularly before 1966. Unemployment figures, as for all developing countries, are not reliable indicators of changes in labor market conditions. Regression analysis, using available statistics, seems to indicate some pattern of regularity of a Phillips curve type.[13] Thus the relatively high unemployment

13. See Yu-Chu Hsu and Chi-Ming Hou, *Manpower Utilization in Taiwan* (Taipei, 1975).

rates around 1964 were accompanied by low wage rate increases (about 4 to 6 percent per year), and the significantly lower unemployment rate in 1968 was accompanied by a 12 percent money wage rise. The lower unemployment rates and the apparently tighter labor market in the 1970s were accompanied by an increased rate of wage inflation.

There is also some correlation between price and wage changes. Table 4.10 shows that in the first decade, years with large nominal wage increases (1957, 1960, 1961) followed upon large price increases, with a time lag of one to two years. The result was wide fluctuation in real wage changes, between −8 and +13 percent. This relationship disappeared between 1961 and 1973. The trend became much smoother, with no discernible lag relations, and a steady

Table 4.10. Annual Changes in Wages, Prices, Productivity, and Labor Costs (percent)

Year	Money wages*	Prices	Real wages†	Output per man‡	Unit labor costs§
1953		4.5		39.5	
1954	10.0	0.3	9.7	2.0	8.0
1955	5.6	14.1	−7.5	−3.1	8.7
1956	12.1	10.4	1.5	−8.3	20.3
1957	14.2	6.1	7.6	6.2	8.0
1958	5.3	3.2	2.1	0.4	4.9
1959	6.1	10.6	−4.1	5.2	0.9
1960	17.0	21.4	−1.2	11.1	5.9
1961	20.9	7.8	12.1	11.2	9.7
1962	6.4	2.4	3.9	2.5	3.9
1963	3.9	2.2	1.7	3.8	0.1
1964	3.0	−0.2	3.2	13.5	−10.5
1965	10.1	−0.1	10.2	7.0	3.1
1966	6.0	2.0	4.0	5.9	0.1
1967	12.5	3.4	8.8	9.4	3.1
1968	11.5	6.3	5.0	13.9	−2.4
1969	6.6	5.1	1.4	15.2	−8.6
1970	7.6	3.5	3.8	5.7	1.9
1971	15.9	0.8	15.0	17.2	−1.3
1972	9.8	4.9	4.7	8.0	1.8
1973	22.8	13.1	8.0	4.4	18.4
1974	43.2	47.5	−2.3	−1.8	45.0
1975	15.8	5.2	10.0	1.1	14.7

*Weighted average money wages per hour in mining, manufacturing, and public utilities computed by dividing daily (or monthly) wages by working hours per day (or per month). Wages include salary, overtime pay, bonus, and cash value of pay in kind. To calculate the average wage for the three sectors, employment in each in 1966 was used as weights (mining, .12; manufacturing, .86; and public utilities, .02).

†Money wages divided by the index of urban consumer prices.

‡Value of output in 1966 as weights (mining, .04; manufacturing, .91; and public utilities, .05). Output per man year is calculated by dividing an output index by the corresponding employment index.

§Difference between rate of change of money wage and rate of change of output per man hour.

Sources: Money wages: for 1951–72 figures, Department of Reconstruction, Taiwan Provincial Government, *Report of Taiwan Labor Statistics;* for 1973–75 figures, DGBAS, *Monthly Bulletin of Labor Statistics.* Prices: DGBAS, *Commodity-price Statistics Monthly, Taiwan District.* Output: Ministry of Economic Affairs, *Taiwan Industrial Production Statistics Monthly.* Employment: for 1951–72 figures, Council of International Economic Cooperation and Development, *Revised Estimates of Population, Labor Force and Industrial Distribution of Employment,* December 1972; for 1972–73, *Monthly Bulletin of Labor Statistics.*

annual rise in real wages of about 6 percent. Unexplained is the large increase in nominal wages in 1971 without any earlier price inflation and with no apparent increased stringency in the labor market. Again, the pattern was reversed during 1972 to 1975.

The changes in labor productivity and unit wage costs shown in Table 4.10 should be taken with strong reservations. The underlying statistics of prices and production and the weighting and deflating procedures are shaky. There is, however, both logic and some consistency in the time series in Table 4.10. Thus it would appear that in a few cases, an acceleration in the rise of labor productivity helps to explain abnormal increases in nominal wages in the same or the following year (look at 1960 and 1961, 1967 and 1968, as well as 1971). It would seem that high actual or potential profits during these years made entrepreneurs more willing to pay higher wages.

The most interesting feature of the figures in Table 4.10 lies in the longer-term aspects, particularly the differences between the two eras. Table 4.11 demonstrates the significance of these differences in the average rates of change.

Table 4.11. Long-Run Changes in Wages, Productivity, and Labor Costs (annual rate of change)

	1951–61	1961–73	1973–75
Money wages	11.4	9.7	29.5
Labor productivity	4.2	10.8	6.0
Unit labor cost	7.2	−1.2	23.5

Source: Table 4.10.

The outstanding feature of this constellation is that the substantial acceleration in the growth of labor productivity between the first two periods (from about 4 to 11 percent per year) was accompanied by a slight retardation in the rate of wage rise, so that unit labor costs even declined during the period 1961–73. This is the background of the competitiveness of Taiwanese export industries, as well as of the stability of the price level from 1961 to 1972.

The wage and productivity trends provide a partial explanation of the remarkable stability achieved during the years 1961–72. The apparent passive adjustment of wages and salaries to market conditions is indicated by the space for wage increases as determined by price and productivity changes. But this result was certainly not automatic. As argued above, a more expansive monetary and fiscal policy could have disrupted the equilibrium development, for example, by causing a higher rate of price increase eventually followed by devaluation of the currency. Then the rise of wages and wage costs would have been more rapid. This possibility was illustrated by the events of 1973 to 1975, when an excess monetary expansion in 1972 and 1973 was followed by strong inflationary impulses from abroad.

The rapid rise of labor productivity, particularly since the beginning of the 1960s, was not an autonomous factor. The acceleration in productivity growth can be explained by the shift in the development pattern from import substitution to growth led by exports, by the very rapid rise in the volume of investment, and by increased technical efficiency, especially in manufacturing. Again, in this interdependent system of determination, the high rate of investment was dependent on such variables as the rapid growth of markets and high profits, which implied strong incentives for investment and possibilities of self-financing.

During the period 1954–73, nominal wages in manufacturing and mining rose by 9.2 percent per year and unit labor costs by 2.2 percent, while the industrial wholesale price index increased by 4.1 percent.[14] It is thus likely that the growth of productivity and the relatively slow rise in wages, especially during the 1960s, resulted in rapidly rising profits, but such assertions cannot be directly verified because of the lack of reliable profit statistics. It seems likely that during most of the period, real wages were rising more slowly than labor productivity.[15] This seems to be true on average for the entire period 1954–73, and the gap shows a rising trend (see Table 4.11). There are wide fluctuations from year to year, but the trend seems convincing. From the point of view of Western economies, this is a perplexing phenomenon and may be regarded as part of the remarkable growth achievement of Taiwan.

Chinese economists have questioned whether this type of development has come to a close in the 1970s. Labor is getting scarcer, and the rate of productivity growth may be reduced for various reasons. The data for 1973–75 could indicate new trends. Nominal wages rose by about 30 percent per year. Import costs increased still more, and productivity growth fell. The result was probably some squeeze of profit margins.

Another indication of relatively large profits and high profitability within the private economy refers to the high level and rapid expansion of investment. The annual rate of growth of private investment (excluding housing) was about 20 percent a year during the period 1962–75 (about 15 percent in real terms). Within manufacturing, the relation of gross fixed investments to value added increased from about 25 percent at the beginning of the 1960s to about 35 percent in the 1970s. About 20 percent has to be added to value of fixed investment to include inventory investment and to get an approximate notion of the order of magnitude of the capital formation ratio.

14. See Chi-Ming Hou and Yu-Chu Hsu, "The Supply of Labor in Taiwan," Institute of Economics, Academia Sinica, *Conference on Population and Economic Development in Taiwan* (Taipei, 1976), p. 347.
15. See Chen Sun, "The Trend of Economic Development and Productivity in Taiwan," *Conference on Population and Economic Development,* pp. 109 ff.

There is no reliable information on the degree of self-financing and the nature of balance sheets of all firms and corporations in the private sector. We do not know to what extent investment has been financed by profits. But discussion in Taiwan about imperfect credit and capital markets, implying difficulty in financing long-term fixed investments, suggests a relatively high share of self-financing, particularly for the great number of small and medium-sized firms in manufacturing and trade.

It may be possible to draw some inference about high profitability from the rapid growth of industrial production and investment. Maurice Scott has made some courageous estimates based on assumptions that are difficult to test and has concluded that net profitability on the average must have been relatively very high, as compared with the United States.[16] Similar conclusions may be reached by looking at some stylized facts relating to the growth pattern of the manufacturing industry. During the period 1961–73, the volume of manufacturing production increased at an average annual rate of about 20 percent. Under the assumption that the capital-output ratio was about constant (real investment increased at nearly the same rate), average profitability (the rate of profits in relation to capital) would have to be of the order of 20 percent, if the degree of self-financing was unchanged over the period. Based on the same type of reasoning, production for exports should show still higher profitability, since export volume expanded at a higher rate than total manufacturing production.

The conclusion to be drawn from these exercises is that the rapid expansion of production in the private sector, accompanied by the high level and rapid growth of investment, has had as a necessary condition high gross profit ratios and generally high profitability. The trends in productivity and wages, as discussed above, made such profits possible. The dispersion in profitability must have been large, with very high profitability for the branches of industry and firms that expanded the most.

The phenomenal rise in the gross domestic savings ratio from 8 to 10 percent at the beginning of the 1950s to more than 30 percent in the 1970s could to a considerable extent be explained by the high and rising share of gross profits in the national income. The propensity to save out of profits and entrepreneurial income is much higher than that out of other incomes. This refers both to corporate profits and to the surpluses of private firms. The incentives to invest in the rapidly expanding economy of Taiwan must have been strong in most branches of activity at the same time as the propensity to finance the investment expenditures out of current income (or profits) was high.

It can be argued that the necessary rate of profit for this investment to occur

16. See Chapter 5.

was achieved under quite different conditions before and after the early 1960s. In the 1950s, with a considerable degree of government regulation, imperfect competition, and import-substitution investment, prices could be raised to attain sufficiently high profits. After that, during the period of a relatively stable growth pattern with more or less given export and import price trends, the profitability conditions were to a larger extent attained by means of productivity gains from new investments and technical innovations. But, as emphasized above, all these were conditioned by current monetary and fiscal policies.

Fiscal Policies and Capital Formation

Fiscal policy aimed at stimulating capital formation and influencing its allocation can employ a wide variety of instruments. Government savings can be raised by higher tax rates and holding back expenditures for current consumption. The government may directly increase its investment expenditure. Private savings can be encouraged by means of such instruments as tax incentives and subsidies. Private investment can be stimulated by lowering profit taxes, introducing generous write-off rules, and direct and indirect forms of investment subsidy. Foreign investors may be given favorable treatment. All these policy measures have been applied in Taiwan since the middle of the 1950s, when the income tax laws were revised, but in varying combinations.

Since the beginning of the 1950s, the government has adopted fiscal policy measures intended to encourage and enforce an increasing ratio of savings and to stimulate investment. A favorable climate for capital formation exists in Taiwan, with a minimum of concern for the distribution of income and wealth.

These measures can be discussed under two headings: (1) the trend of government revenues and expenditures, with special regard to the position and share of government savings and investment; (2) policies aimed at stimulating private savings and investment. It should be clear that even if policy results could be ascertained under each of these headings, the net result on capital formation is not the sum of the two because the effects are closely interrelated.

Table 4.12 sets out the relevant data on the composition of gross savings. Foreign savings, corresponding to the deficit or surplus of the current balance of payments, consist mainly of U.S. aid in the 1950s. This large item, corresponding to 40 percent of gross domestic capital formation, meant that the gross investment ratio during this period could be kept about 67 percent above the domestic savings supply.

A question that has been discussed but can never be answered is whether and to what extent the U.S. aid portion of foreign savings may have depressed

Table 4.12. Composition of Savings (percentage of gross domestic capital formation)

	1952–55	1956–60	1961–65	1966–70	1971–74
Foreign savings	40.4	40.7	17.7	5.8	−8.9
Gross national savings	59.6	59.3	82.2	94.2	109.0
Capital consumption	33.3	33.7	31.9	25.5	26.2
Net national savings	26.3	25.6	50.3	68.7	82.8
General government*	−4.1	−4.5	0.6	12.6	22.4
Public corporation and government enterprises	3.9	6.8	7.4	8.7	7.0
Private savings	26.5	23.3	42.3	47.4	53.4
Statistical discrepancy	0	0	0.1	0	−0.1

*General government includes the two levels of local governments. Local government expenditures amounted to about 30 percent of total (general) government expenditures.
Source: EPC, *Taiwan Statistical Data Book, 1976.*

the supply of domestic savings.[17] This might have been the case; for example, without the U.S. aid that helped finance government investment expenditures, the government might have been forced to raise taxes or reduce other expenditures, thereby increasing government budget savings. The supply of foreign savings fell drastically during the 1960s, with the reduction and disappearance of foreign aid. The net import of capital borrowing abroad and direct investment has been important for development but of limited magnitude. During the years 1971–73, there even appeared a net surplus on current account, but this turned negative again in 1974.[18]

As shown in Table 4.12, the decline in the supply of foreign savings has been more than compensated by the rapidly increasing share of private savings and, to some extent, of government savings. However, this observation cannot very well be used as an argument for the case that earlier foreign aid really had depressed the supply of domestic savings. Too many other factors were at work.

In the national accounts, government savings include part of the U.S. aid payments to Taiwan. The central government financed its deficits by means of the counterpart funds. Calculated in that way, government savings (excluding public corporations) amounted to about one-third of total gross savings in the period 1951–55 and 20 percent in 1956–60. Table 4.12 shows that the total government budget excluding U.S. aid contributions but including investment expenditures was in considerable deficit during the 1950s. The improvement

17. See H. T. Lin, "U.S. Aid and Taiwan's Economic Development," *Conference on Population and Economic Development in Taiwan,* pp. 305–6. Lin bases his conclusion that U.S. aid actually depressed internal savings on a hazardous comparison between the potential trade and savings gaps, the former assumed to be the larger.

18. The supply of foreign savings in Table 4.12 is underestimated (and domestic savings overestimated), since information on undistributed earnings of foreign companies in Taiwan is included in that for private savings.

in government finances on all three levels was achieved both by holding back the rate of growth of expenditures and by improvements on the revenue side.

It is remarkable that although general government expenditures in real terms (1966 prices) increased by five times from 1952 to 1974, their share in GNP declined from 38 to 25 percent.[19] The distribution of government expenditures appears in Table 4.13.

Defense has been the major expenditure item, around 60 percent of the central government budget in the 1950s and about 30 percent in recent years. Government consumption expenditure and transfer payments take a surprisingly modest share. Public consumption as a share of GNP has declined steadily from 25 percent during 1956-60 to 14 percent during 1970-73, a more drastic decline than in private consumption (from 67 percent to 52 percent). On the other hand, government outlays on capital investment, physical and human capital, have shown an increasing share, although on a relatively modest scale.

Table 4.13. Distribution of Government Expenditures (percentage of total)

	1951–55	1956–60	1961–65	1966–70	1971–73
Administration and defense	66.5	66.8	67.8	58.2	52.2
Development expenditures	13.5	20.8	19.3	22.5	23.8
Education and research	6.9	12.8	12.3	15.0	16.4
Public health	1.5	2.0	2.0	1.7	1.7
Economic reconstruction	2.8	3.8	2.8	4.0	4.4
Transport and communication	2.3	2.2	2.2	1.8	1.3
Other consumption	20.0	12.4	12.9	19.3	24.0

Source: DGBAS, *National Income of the Republic of China, December 1976* (Taipei, December 1976).

One can argue that part of the success of fiscal policy in creating a savings surplus lay in the ability to hold back current expenditures. Compared with Western countries, it is remarkable how low the social and health budget and pension payments have been kept. In Taiwan the family is still a strategic social unit, taking care of these needs. Private household savings have been brought up to a relatively high level because of the lack of a developed public social system.

On the revenue side, the main source is indirect taxes, comprising 70 to 80 percent of total government revenue, and this relation has scarcely improved, as shown in Table 4.14.

The share of total tax revenue of GNP is rather constant at around 14 to 15 percent. The stated goal of fiscal policy—to increase government revenues and raise the level of public savings—was offset by the desire to improve

19. See Samuel Ho, *Consumption and Investment in Postwar Taiwan,* chap. 11. Note the intricate problems involved in measuring shares of government expenditures in GNP in real and nominal terms.

Table 4.14. Structure of Tax Revenues (percentage of total taxes)

Fiscal year	Direct taxes			Indirect taxes				Total taxes as percentage of GNP
	Total	Income*	Property†	Total	Monopoly revenue	Domestic products‡	Imports§	
1952	31.2	13.5	17.7	68.8	17.8	26.7	24.3	13.7
1956	21.6	9.2	12.4	78.4	22.6	33.1	22.7	15.7
1961	21.6	11.9	9.7	78.4	23.9	33.1	21.4	14.4
1966	18.7	7.5	11.2	81.3	21.4	33.1	26.8	14.4
1971	26.3	13.5	12.8	73.7	15.8	32.3	25.6	16.7
1975	29.7	19.5	10.2	70.3	13.4	28.1	28.8	18.2

*Includes land value increment tax, consolidated income tax, business income tax.
†Includes license tax, deeds tax, mining-lot tax, estate tax, house tax, rural tax, land value tax.
‡Includes amusement tax, salt tax, securities transfer tax, commodity tax, business tax, stamp tax, slaughter tax, feast tax.
§Includes customs duties and harbor fees.
Source: Ministry of Finance, Year Book of Financial Statistics of the Republic of China (Taipei, 1976).

conditions of production and capital formation in the private sector. There apparently was a conflict of aims. Import tariffs, although still high and uneven, were reduced in the process of trade liberalization. Otherwise, tariff revenue would have risen much more than in proportion to GNP. The dependence on commodity taxes remained high because of the modest yield of income taxes. The return from direct income (and profit) taxes was kept low by means of low rates and tax rebates, partly with the intention of stimulating private savings and investment. The commodity taxes consist of a mixture of special taxes (around thirty items with tax rates in 1975 varying between 5 and 100 percent) and excise taxes on raw materials and on luxury goods. There is a general belief that this complicated system of commodity taxes is inefficient, carrying negative allocation effects, and is largely regressive.

The impact of government tax and expenditure policies on government savings and investments is only one—and the most easily observable—effect of fiscal policy. The more important but more complicated problem is how savings and investments in the private sector may have been affected by these policies.

A much-discussed feature of the Taiwan art of mobilizing resources for investment has to do with agriculture. The government, especially in the 1950s, relied heavily on the agricultural sector for its tax revenue, but also encouraged agricultural development. The system of land taxes is very complicated—a progressive tax (partly collected in kind), based on the estimated produce of land assessed as far back as the Japanese occupation.[20] More important, there is a specific burden on agriculture in the form of hidden taxes—compulsory government purchases of rice at below-market prices and the rice-fertilizer barter system. According to estimates by Frederick Chow, the total in 1957–61 amounted to about 8 to 10 percent of government revenues both from taxes and from monopoly profits on fertilizers. This figure declined to 2 percent by the end of the 1960s. The system was abolished in 1973–74, when sharp increases in the official price of rice were put into effect.

Chow concludes that the total tax burden of agriculture, including the hidden taxes, was significantly higher than that for the nonagricultural sectors. The calculated tax-income ratios for the years 1957–61 were about 25 percent for farm income and 19 percent for nonagricultural income.

This differential tax burden was partly the result of the slightly regressive tendency of the total tax system that was due to the heavy weight of indirect consumption taxes; the income per household of the farm population was

20. Most of the information on agricultural taxation comes from a manuscript by Frederick Chow, ''The Role of Taxation in Economic Development: A Case Study of Taiwan, 1957-1970'' (unpublished).

significantly lower than that of the rest of the economy, but the difference was caused mainly by the specific land tax and the hidden tax.

A number of assumptions must be made to reach conclusions as to the effects on capital formation of this differential tax burden on agriculture. Chow tries to show that the extra tax burden on farmers came mainly at the expense of their consumption and that the government used the extra resources for increasing investment. In that way the maximum effect on capital formation is attained; other more plausible alternatives imply much lower or no effects. The analysis made by Rong-I Wu seems to support Chow's maximum effect hypothesis. He reaches the conclusion that "the agricultural sector provided directly and indirectly a massive investment fund for industrialization."[21] In any event, a considerable part of the increase in agricultural productivity was transferred in these ways to the government and the nonagricultural sectors.

The general statement can be made that the tax policy of the government from the beginning was very generous toward private savings and capital formation. Not only have average tax rates been kept low over the entire period, but specific tax rebates and exemptions favored savings by private individuals as well as by firms and corporations. Most households do not pay any personal income taxes. Tax rates have been kept moderate except for rather high incomes (the maximum marginal rate, including surcharges, is 60 percent at present, previously 80 percent). But such high rates are mostly theoretical because there are many loopholes and apparently a good deal of tax evasion.[22] Business income taxes were low but progressive, ranging from 5 percent to 25 percent during most of the period, rising to 35 percent after 1974. Family firms as well as corporations have generally been able to keep their profit taxes at very low levels, partly by using insufficient auditing procedures.

The general situation is a favorable tax climate, stimulating capital formation. But a number of special measures to reduce income taxes were introduced, mainly in the 1961 fiscal and monetary reform bill, to encourage investment. Among these are:[23] (1) Two percent of the total export revenue could be deducted from taxable income. (2) A five-year tax holiday or tax reduction was given by means of accelerated depreciation of fixed assets for established enterprises and for firms increasing their capital for expansion pur-

21. Rong-I Wu, *The Strategy of Economic Development: A Case Study of Taiwan* (Louvain, 1971), p. 191.

22. See Ching-Sheng Shih, "Recent Development in Public Finance in Taiwan," *Conference on Economic Development of Taiwan* (Taipei, June 1967).

23. Yu-Chu Hsu and Chi-Ming Hou, *Economic Effects of Business Income Tax Reduction due to the Encouragement of Investment*, Commission of Taxation, Ministry of Finance (Taipei, March 1973).

poses. (3) Retained earnings used for investment could be deducted from taxable income. (4) Dividends from some forms of new investment were exempted from income tax. (5) Tax rebates were given for raw materials used for manufacturing export goods. (6) Tax exemptions were allowed for interest on certain kinds of savings deposits. The tax incentives also include foreign investment, which has been expanding rapidly since the early 1960s. Ownership and earnings on foreign investment are treated generously.

It is impossible to determine, even approximately, the costs and benefits of all these measures. Here we are interested in their effects on capital formation. Estimates of the order of magnitude of taxes paid and tax rebates and concessions may provide a basis for informed guesses. The Commission of Taxation has made an effort to do this. The yearly loss of profit tax revenue could be as large as N.T.$12 billion, compared with the sum of business taxes actually paid of about N.T.$4 billion in 1972 (direct taxes on households amounted to N.T.$5.5 billion the same year and total tax revenue to N.T.$74 billion). Fixed capital formation of private enterprise amounted to N.T.$34 billion in 1972, so that this type of tax relief could have had a considerable positive effect on the financing of private investment.

K. T. Li maintains that fiscal measures were successful in stimulating capital formation. But he asserts that the incentives have been excessive and unnecessarily generous considering the heavy costs and the disadvantages of the system of tax rebates and concessions.[24] The substantial loss of government tax revenue may have resulted in underdevelopment of government investment in various lines of infrastructure. The lag in this type of development in relation to the rapid growth of private capital accumulation (especially in manufacturing) could have implied an imbalance in the capital structure of the Taiwan economy. The rapid growth of manufacturing production (and productivity), from this point of view, took place at the expense of infrastructure development (for example, in communication, public utilities, and housing). The new Six-Year Plan, with greater emphasis on various types of long-term investment, could be taken as evidence of the existence of this kind of imbalance. K. T. Li also mentions the negative effects on income and wealth distribution that must have been a result of a generous tax relief system favoring owners of business property.

Fiscal policy has been used only to an insignificant extent for stabilization purposes. The tax structure is not well adapted to these purposes, and the expenditure side is too rigid. But the need for an active fiscal policy for stabilization has thus far not appeared urgent. Government budget deficits, except in the early 1950s, have not been serious obstacles to an anti-inflation policy.

24. K. T. Li, *A Decade of Accelerated Economic Development through Taxation Policy* (Taipei, 1972), p. 17.

The framework of government taxes and expenditures has had long-term development aims. The low effective tax rates have created a stimulating savings and investment climate, while at the same time the growth of government expenditures has been kept down to provide government savings.

From the point of view of capital formation, the fiscal policies pursued, especially since the beginning of the 1960s, have mainly been in harmony with monetary policy. The policy of keeping relatively high interest rates (in real terms) as a stimulus to private savings and enforcing economy in the use of financial resources has not been affected by a too rapidly rising government debt. Since the middle 1950s, government debt has not been a serious obstacle to a sound monetary policy.

There are some black spots in the picture. The tax system is primitive, relying too much on indirect taxes and with quite a low efficiency. Considerable distortion, of unknown overall importance, must be the result of the very uneven rates of customs and commodity taxes. Similar distortion effects result from the imperfect functioning of the credit and capital markets. A great deal of room remains for improvement and reform of the fiscal and financial system of Taiwan.

5 | Foreign Trade

MAURICE SCOTT

The growth in Taiwan's trade since World War II has been phenomenal. In 1952, three years after the civil war on the mainland had ended, inflation was subsiding and U.S. aid had got under way. Taking that year as a base, the average rate of growth of the volume of exports was 17 percent per annum and of imports 13 percent per annum, until they were checked by the oil crisis after 1973 (see Figure 5.1). Few other countries can equal that record of sustained—and, indeed, accelerating—growth over twenty-one years.[1] This growth has made Taiwan one of the biggest markets in Asia for other countries' exports. In 1974, only Japan's and Singapore's imports were larger, although Hong Kong's and South Korea's (both formidable competitors) were nearly as large. Taiwan's population was only sixteen million, but its imports were then 40 percent greater than India's (596 million population), 80 percent greater than Indonesia's (128 million population), and 300 percent greater than Pakistan's (68 million population).

1. The volume of Japan's exports, for example, grew by 16 percent per annum from 1952 to 1973 and that of her imports by 14 percent per annum. For West Germany the corresponding figures are 11 and 12 percent per annum, and for Italy they are 13 and 11 percent per annum. For South Korea, the U.N. series start in 1963 (before which exports were very small). From 1963 the volume of exports grew by 38 percent per annum and of imports by 19 percent per annum, which is even faster than Taiwan's 25 and 20 percent per annum over the same period, but is partly a reflection of the later date at which South Korea's recovery began. These figures are derived from United Nations, *Yearbook of International Trade Statistics,* various issues.

I have relied heavily on many others who have measured, described, and analyzed Taiwan's economy and to whom reference is made. In addition, I greatly benefited from my visit in 1976 when I met many people, both in government and private business, who patiently answered questions, allowed me to see around enterprises, and gave me the benefit of their experience and knowledge. There are too many to mention all by name. I owe special thanks to K-S. Liang, both for introducing me to most of the others and for several lengthy discussions and for comments on the first draft of the chapter. I learned much from W. Kuo, T. H. Lee, K. T. Li, C. Sun, S. C. Tsiang, T. K. Tsui, and T-S. Yu. The data provided by C. M. Wang, C-H. Yang, W. A. Yeh, and T-L. Yu were invaluable. C. Schive, R-S. Yeh and T. M. F. Yeh helped with data and personally conducted me on many visits. T. Y. Oh efficiently combined research and secretarial assistance. I gained much from the advice and comments of my fellow authors, and especially from Walter Galenson. Finally, I must thank my wife for her support during my visit and while the chapter was being written.

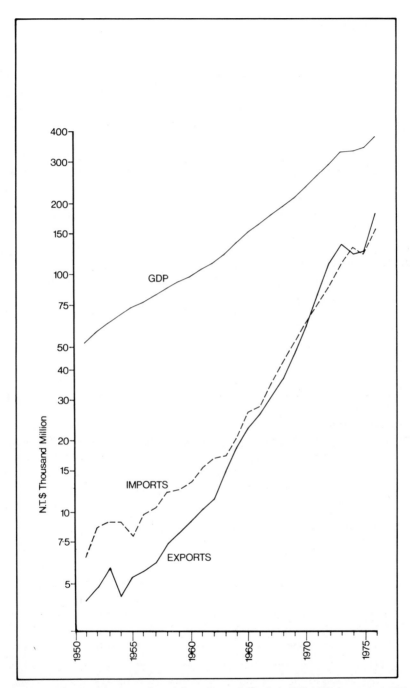

Figure 5.1. Volume of foreign trade and Gross Domestic Product, 1951-1976, in constant 1971 prices. Source: Economic Planning Council, *National Income of the Republic of China,* December 1975.

At the start of our period, as before the war, Taiwan was an importer of manufactures and an exporter of primary products, mainly sugar and rice. She has transformed her situation by becoming an exporter of manufactured goods. In 1953 her exports of manufactures were a negligible 0.017 percent of exports of manufactures of the twelve leading exporting countries. By 1976 her share had climbed to 1.6 percent (Figure 5.2).

The growth in exports transformed an initially very weak balance-of-payments position into a strong one. Throughout the 1950s Taiwan relied heavily on U.S. aid to pay for, typically, a third of her imports of goods and services (Figure 5.3). From 1970 to 1976 her exports of goods and services financed, typically, all her imports of goods and services. She has a very small debt-service ratio because of the generous terms on which U.S. aid was given, and her foreign exchange reserves at the end of 1976 were nearly U.S.\$3 billion (Table 5.10).

This chapter seeks to describe this unusual trading record, to analyze it, and, finally, to explain it. The first section is a brief history of events, especially of government measures that affected trade. In the second section, I consider the very high ratio of Taiwan's trade to total product, a ratio that increased remarkably over the period, and how the commodity composition of trade has changed and its relation to Taiwan's comparative advantage. In the third section I look for explanations of her export success—the emphasis here is placed on those factors that made exporting very profitable and led to such a strong response by Taiwan's exporters. I also consider the role of U.S. aid (which, I believe, was of great importance). I ask whether the initial phase of strict import controls and resulting import substitution in the 1950s was a precondition of the subsequent export success (I do not believe it was, with some qualifications). In a brief concluding section, I review a few of the problems now confronting economic policy makers.

A Survey of the Period

The Immediate Postwar Years

In the 1930s, Taiwan's trade was mainly with Japan, whose colony she was.[2] Exports consisted overwhelmingly of foodstuffs, mostly sugar and rice. Around 90 percent of exports went to Japan, and nearly as large a proportion of imports came from there. The most important other trading partner was mainland China, but it accounted only for a modest proportion of trade. The value of exports of merchandise exceeded that of imports by a large margin in

2. The following description is based mainly on Samuel P. S. Ho, *Economic Development of Taiwan, 1860-1970* (New Haven, 1977).

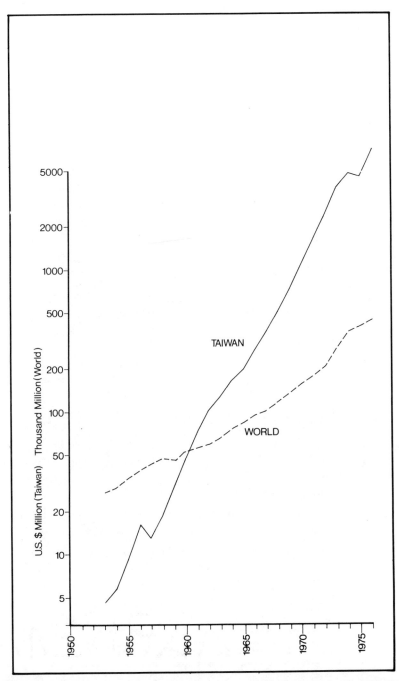

Figure 5.2. Exports of manufactures from Taiwan and twelve leading countries (world), 1953-1976, in current prices. Source, Taiwan: R. S. Yeh, National Taiwan University. Source, world: National Institute of Economic and Social Research, *National Institute Economic Review*, 1965, 1966, 1970, 1973, 1976.

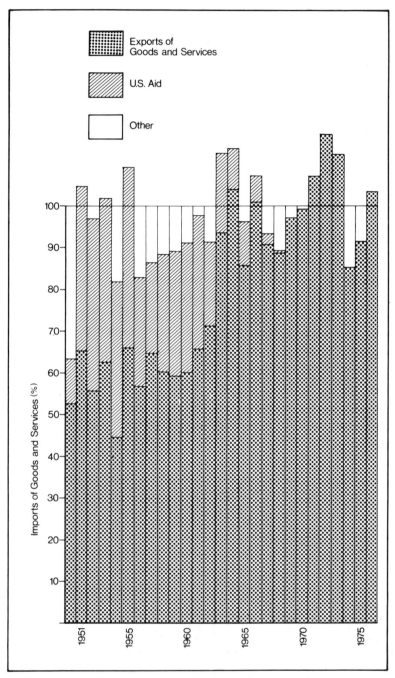

Figure 5.3. Paying for imports of goods and services, 1950-1976. Source: Central Bank of China.

every year, the surplus covering a deficit on invisibles and, apparently,[3] an outflow of capital. Taiwan was heavily dependent on trade in this period. Combining S. C. Hsieh and T. H. Lee's estimates of net national product[4] with Samuel P. S. Ho's estimates of trade,[5] we find that in 1935–37 exports of merchandise amounted to about 50 percent of the net national product and that imports were nearly 40 percent. Not until the 1970s were these very high ratios regained.

Taiwan was restored to China in October 1945. As a result of the war her trade had fallen very considerably and, in the next five years, recovered only very slowly for a number of reasons.[6] She was cut off, by an edict of the U.S. military government there, from her former main trading partner, Japan. Nearly all her trade in 1946–48 was thus with mainland China, but that country's civil war caused a rapid inflation that spread to Taiwan. Prices rose about tenfold in each of the years 1945–48, and their rate of increase accelerated in 1949. Small wonder, then, that exports and imports had, by 1948, recovered to around only a quarter or less of their prewar volume.

The fall of Shanghai in May 1949 ended economic relations with the mainland, and Taiwan's main trading relationship was once more destroyed. As Ching-yuan Lin remarks, "Deprived of protected markets in Japan and China for its exports, the economy of Taiwan was left to reestablish itself as an independent economy for the first time in its history."[7] The ending of the civil war on the mainland also ended U.S. aid to the Nationalist government of China, and it was not resumed until the outbreak of the Korean War in June 1950.[8] Despite these several disasters and the tremendous acceleration of

3. Ho's estimates of the balance of payments in the 1930s show a surplus on goods and services in every year. Errors and omissions, however, are shown as a deficit item in all years and larger than the surplus on goods and services in some. This might imply unrecorded capital outflow, or, possibly, errors and omissions in the current account which, if allowed for, would reduce or eliminate the surplus there.

4. S. C. Hsieh and T. H. Lee, *Agricultural Development and Its Contribution to Economic Growth in Taiwan*, JCRR Economic Digest Series, no. 17 (Taipei, April 1966). Mo-huan Hsing, *Taiwan: Industrialization and Trade Policies* (London, 1971), p. 152n, states that their estimates "imply a much higher national income (and hence income per head and per person employed) for 1936–40 than the estimates made by this writer, which are in fact higher than virtually all others for the same years." However, this remark presumably applies to the change in real income from prewar to postwar rather than to the level of income at 1935–37 prices prewar, as given by Hsieh and Lee. Hsing's own estimate (p. 153) of income per head at 1935–37 prices in 1935–36 [sic] is 139.5 yen, which, when multiplied by a population of 5.45 million, gives a national income of about 760 million. This is close to Hsieh and Lee's estimates of 706 million for 1931–35 and 797 million for 1936–40.

5. Ho, Table A 67.

6. The following material is based on Ching-yuan Lin, *Industrialization in Taiwan, 1946–72* (New York, 1973), ch. 2.

7. Ibid., p. 39.

8. Neil H. Jacoby, *U.S. Aid to Taiwan: A Study of Foreign Aid, Self-Help, and Development* (New York, 1966), p. 30n.

inflation, in 1949 the government began to take measures that were to propel the Taiwanese economy forward at a rate few other countries have ever matched.

The land reform, currency reform, credit policies, and reconstruction of industry are described in other chapters in this volume. My concern is with foreign trade and the balance-of-payments, and the most important development here was the resumption of U.S. aid in June 1950. This took a year or so to build up to a rate of about U.S.$90 million a year, when it financed about 40 percent of Taiwan's imports of goods and services (Figure 5.3). Apart from U.S. aid, no very effective measures were taken to deal with the foreign exchange situation until April 1951.[9] The large balance-of-payments deficit nearly exhausted the government's gold and foreign exchange reserves,[10] and no stringent and effective system of exchange control was put into force until 1951. By that time the exchange rate, which had been initially fixed at N.T.$5 = U.S.$1 when the New Taiwan dollar was introduced in June 1949, had become N.T.$10.30 = U.S.$1 for certain official transactions and N.T.$15.65 for imports by private enterprises.

Strict Import Controls, 1951–1957

The strict import controls imposed in April 1951 were accompanied, as the figures given above imply, by a multiple exchange rate system. Changes were made in the system from time to time, with the exchange rates being repeatedly devalued. Broadly speaking,[11] the effect of these measures was to give a much stronger financial inducement to import substitution than to exporting. This was not, in the main, a result of the multiple rate system because the rates applicable to most imports (U.S. aid imports, imports by government enterprises, and imports of raw materials and equipment by end users) were usually much the same as those applicable to exports by private enterprises (see Table 5.3). The bulk of exports—sugar and rice—often received a more unfavorable exchange rate, but because sugar was manufactured and exported by a public enterprise (the Taiwan Sugar Corporation) and rice exports were also controlled by the government, this could be regarded as merely a bookkeeping transaction. The ''export tax'' on sugar and rice either transferred revenue from the Taiwan Sugar Corporation to the government or

9. There were import restrictions already in 1949, but imports were, apparently, licensed fairly liberally. See Lin, pp. 43–48, and also C. T. Chien, ''The Problem of Foreign Exchange in the Economic Development of Taiwan,'' *Industry of Free China,* November 1957, p. 4, who states that the period June 1949 to April 1951 ''may be considered as a period of free imports.''

10. The net foreign assets of the banking system are estimated at only U.S.$15 million at the end of 1950, equal to one or two months' imports. See Table 5.10.

11. What follows is only a brief summary of a complicated series of measures. For details, the reader may refer to Chien; Hsing, chap. 5; Lin, chap. 3; and K. T. Li, ''A Resume of Foreign Exchange Control in Taiwan, 1949–58,'' *Industry of Free China,* May 1959.

formed part of the government's system of taxing the farmers (through the rice-fertilizer barter system; see Chapter 2). The only important exception was the higher rate of exchange applied to other imports by private enterprises, on which there was, in effect, a substantial import tax. Apart from this, there were high tariffs on a great many imports (Table 5.2), and importers were required to make advance payments for imports equivalent to their full value for most items until 1965.[12] Last, but probably most important, imports were severely restricted by license. According to data cited by Lin,[13] the premiums over import costs (including duties) of many commodities, both industrial materials and consumer goods, were substantial. For example, in 1953, wheat flour commanded a premium of 48 percent, cotton yarn 33 percent, cotton piece goods, poplin, about 150 percent, woolen yarn 350 percent, soda ash 275 percent, and ammonium sulphate about 100 percent.

These measures undoubtedly increased the profitability of import substitution and must have been partly responsible for the doubling of manufacturing production between 1952 and 1958. K. Y. Yin, the vice-chairman of the Taiwan Production Board from 1951 to 1954 and minister of economic affairs in 1955, has been widely credited with the promotion of the plastics, artificial fibre, glass, cement, fertilizer, plywood, and many other industries in this period, but, above all, of the textile industries. The measures taken (apart from the restriction of imports, especially of finished manufactures) included making loans on favorable terms, allocating imported materials directly to manufacturers, and imposing penalties on producers of poor-quality products to encourage the improvement of quality.[14]

However, the import-substitution strategy had some adverse effects. As Yin himself pointed out as early as 1954:

1. ... the quantitative restriction placed on imports due to the limited amount of foreign exchange available has resulted in a big difference between the market price and actual cost of imported commodities. The profiteers, with their eyes glued on profits yielded by this disparity and in the name of factories they have founded with negligible capital and symbolic or make-believe equipments, scramble for the privilege of obtaining foreign currency allocation or import quota.[15]

12. See Lin, p. 105. The 100 percent deposit was reduced to 50 percent in 1965 and to 25 percent in 1969. See Council of International Economic Cooperation and Development (CIECD), *Annual Report on Taiwan's Economy 1969* (October 1970), p. 14.

13. Lin, pp. 50–51.

14. In 1954 Yin was dissatisfied with the quality of electric light bulbs produced in Taiwan. He ordered the destruction of twenty thousand of these in Taipei New Park and threatened to liberalize imports if the quality did not improve in three months. The quality improved, and the threat did not need to be implemented. See *Industry of Free China*, January 1955, p. 33, and February 1963, p. 10.

15. K. Y. Yin, "Adverse Trend in Taiwan's Industrial Development," *Industry of Free China*, August 1954. This article was originally published in Chinese in the *Central Daily News*, April 18, 1954.

Their profits were often at the expense of firms (to which the imports were resold) actually using the imported materials to manufacture import substitutes. Furthermore, the incentive to acquire licenses led to overexpansion of capacity. Finally, more than two thousand firms were engaged as importers, although forty or fifty would have been sufficient to handle all the business. There was thus a loss of economies of scale in trading. C. T. Chien states that toward the end of 1953, 3,729 applications for import licenses were being made each week by 2,226 merchants, despite a margin deposit requirement of 100 percent by the Bank of Taiwan.[16] As only about 7 percent of the amounts of foreign exchange applied for could be allocated, the average application received a mere U.S.$400–500.

2. Inefficient and high-cost manufacturers were able to survive. They were protected from foreign competition by import restrictions, and they were protected from new entrants by government reluctance to license additional capacity, since existing capacity was already often excessive.

3. Efficient manufacturers were able to make high profits, but did not, as a result, seek to expand and drive out the inefficient firms. Instead, they formed monopolistic agreements to keep up prices and made little attempt to improve quality or cut costs.

Most of Yin's proposed remedies for this situation were subsequently put into practice in one way or another: (1) Restrictions on the establishment of new factories should be lifted, but some minimum standards in regard to size and quality should be enforced, both for new and existing factories. (2) Imported raw materials should be auctioned or, if this should prove impractical, allocation should be made preferentially to factories producing high-quality products and selling at low prices. (3) The period of protection by import restriction for any industry should be specified, although subsequent protection by tariffs should be allowed. (4) An antitrust law should be promulgated and, until this was done, liberalization of imports should be used to counteract local monopolistic arrangements.

By the early 1970s, nearly all industries were free of licensing restrictions on capacity (apart from requirements relating to town planning, safety, and the like), and nearly all products could be imported freely (but subject to import duty). Hence the substance of the first three of Yin's proposals had been implemented, although not in exactly the way he had originally proposed. Thus there was never any system for auctioning imports or import licenses. Nevertheless, once licenses were freely granted, the market mechanism produced a similar effect. Protected industries were set explicit deadlines in 1964, but it was not so much this as the progressive removal of all controls that really mattered.

16. Chien, p. 5.

No antitrust law was promulgated,[17] but here again one could argue that, at least regarding traded goods, such a law was unnecessary once imports were liberalized and especially after the economy had become as export-orientated as it did in the early 1970s. However, the high tariff rates on some items still made possible the formation of local cartels.

Although Yin put forward these remedies in 1954, and although he became minister of economic affairs in 1955, the remedies were not adopted until some years later, and then only gradually. In July 1955, Yin resigned as minister because of a court case involving a firm that had been lent money by the Central Trust of China (of which Yin was then director) and that subsequently defaulted on the loan. In September 1956 the court cleared him of any blame, and in August 1957 he returned, not as minister of economic affairs, but as member of the Council for U.S. Aid; he was subsequently promoted to other high posts in economic affairs.[18] His unfortunate absence from official duties for two years[19] probably explains why more was not done sooner to remedy the "adverse trend in Taiwan's industrial development" (the title of Yin's 1954 article). In an article in *Industry of Free China* in May 1959, "A Retrospect on 'Adverse Trend in Taiwan's Industrial Development,'" Yin wrote,

A review of this article in the light of subsequent developments in the intervening five years has led me to realize the inherent difficulties in a nation's effort toward economic progress and the general resistance to change in certain concepts. Five years is not a short period of time. Yet, it is quite unexpected that that article written five years ago calling for a reversal of the adverse trend is found today still valid in many respects without the necessity for any major modification.

A critic might, nonetheless, ask why Yin should consider that the trend had been adverse. After all, manufacturing production doubled from 1952 to 1958, an average rate of growth of 12.7 percent per annum. Over the same period the real gross domestic product (GDP) grew at a healthy 7.1 percent per annum. The inflation rate had come down, and employment and real wages were rising. Nevertheless, there were some worrying features.

17. In September 1954, the Ministry of Economic Affairs circulated a draft nineteen-article "Statute for Suppression of Unfair Competition in Industry and Commerce," aimed at outlawing such business practices as the collusive fixing of prices, quantities or qualities of output, and market sharing. Many objections were raised against this draft statute, and it was never promulgated. See *Industry of Free China,* December 1954, pp. 26–31.

18. Secretary-general and member of the Economic Stabilization Board, 1958; vice-chairman of the Council for U.S. Aid, 1959–63; chairman of the Foreign Exchange and Trade Control Commission, 1959–63; chairman of the Bank of Taiwan, 1959–63. He died in 1963, too early to see many of the results of the reforms he had effected.

19. It is an interesting reflection on both the man and Chinese culture that Yin is reported to have spent most of his time during the enforced absence from official duties in preparing a bibliography on a Chinese scholar of the Ching dynasty.

First, the balance of payments on current account remained heavily in deficit, with exports of goods and services typically financing only 60 percent of imports of goods and services throughout this period (see Figure 5.3). Of course, a deficit was to be expected as a result of U.S. aid, but it showed no sign of coming down, and the heavy aid program could not last indefinitely. Because imports were already severely restricted, the main hope lay in a growth of exports. Their volume had grown as fast as GDP from 1952 to 1958 (Figure 5.1), and their ratio to GDP at current prices had changed little (Table 5.12). This, however, was not good enough. Exports were only 8 to 9 percent of GDP, whereas imports were 13 to 14 percent, with the latter percentage showing no inclination to fall, despite the import-substitution strategy. At some point, when aid was reduced, exports would have to rise faster if an even more severe cutback on imports was to be avoided. Furthermore, the faster rise in exports had to come from a very rapid increase in exports of manufactures (Figure 5.4). Sugar and rice still formed 69 percent of total exports in 1958, but sugar exports were limited by quota under the International Sugar Agreement, and sugar production competed with other agricultural crops (especially rice) for scarce land. Rice exports were also limited by the availability of land, and because of the fast-growing population exports would have to fall (as, in fact, they did, rice forming less than 1 percent of total exports after 1968).

Second, the growth rate of the GDP was decelerating (Figure 5.1), and there had been a pronounced decline in the absolute amount of private-sector gross investment after 1954.[20] Although investment by public enterprises and general government had continued to grow, private-sector investment was stagnating.

Neil H. Jacoby attributes this stagnation to "the 1954 Communist Chinese attack on Tachen, an offshore island north of Quemoy. This attack raised a spectre of continued insecurity that frightened the investor at a time when Taiwan's investment opportunities were not clear. Only after Chinese Communist forces were decisively repulsed in the attack on Quemoy in 1958 was apprehension dispelled."[21]

Other reasons were the limited size of the domestic market and the failure to make a decisive break into foreign markets. Thus General P. Kiang, then minister of economic affairs, in a speech in September 1956, remarked:

---

20. Shirley W. Y. Kuo, "Economic Development of Taiwan—An Overall Analysis," in *Economic Development in Taiwan,* ed. Kowie Chang (Taipei, 1968), pp. 80–81, gives figures derived from the Directorate-General of Budget, Accounting, and Statistics (DGBAS) that show that private-sector gross investment reached a peak of N.T.$3.9 billion at 1964 prices in 1954, but was lower than this in each of the following years until 1958, when it was N.T.$3.6 billion at 1964 prices. Its share of total gross investment at current prices fell from 56 percent in 1954 to 41 percent in 1958.

21. Jacoby, p. 89.

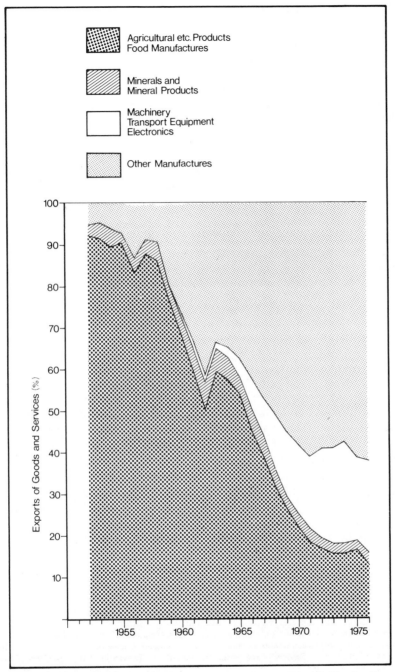

Figure 5.4. Commodity composition of exports, 1952-1976. Source: Economic Planning Council, *Taiwan Statistical Data Book, 1976.*

Although both agricultural and industrial production has been increasing year by year, yet the rate of increase has somewhat slowed down in recent years. On the agricultural side, the slowdown is attributable to the limited area of cultivated land. . . . On the industrial side the decline was because of the limited market. Both the production and consumption of the existing industrial products are almost in a state of saturation. If the output of such products further increases, they will be congested in the domestic market, while it is hard to gain access to foreign markets.[22]

A similar point was made by K. T. Li, then secretary-general of the Council of U.S. Aid,[23] who, in a review of the economic situation in 1958, explained the falling off in investment partly in terms of a lack of investment opportunities:

As to the lack of investment opportunities, it is because productive sectors with handsome returns but involving little risk have been developed more or less to a saturation point and can no longer absorb more investment. Investment opportunities that are now open generally involve considerably more hazards and more efforts by way of opening up new markets abroad. Naturally more investors are becoming reluctant to come forward. In the foreseeable future, the lack of investment opportunities will probably constitute a serious obstacle to the continuing economic development of Taiwan, an obstacle far greater than the lack of investment capital.[24]

Lin points out that the growth of output of some important sectors of manufacturing (textiles, wood products, and rubber goods especially) slowed down after the early 1950s as "easy" import substitution came to an end, and this led to a slowing down in the growth of manufacturing production as a whole. Competition on the home market intensified, and in 1957 and 1958 several sectors' output prices fell.[25] In January 1958 the "Topic of the Month" in *Industry of Free China* was an article on "Competition at Home," which drew attention to an appeal by the Taiwan Provincial Council of Industries to the Ministry of Economic Affairs "to take preventive measures against the runaway competition in the home market." Li, in his review of 1958, says, "A price decline took place during June–July 1958 when there was a wave of business failures."[26]

Thus by 1958 there were many indications of a need for measures to promote private investment and exports of manufactures. The government,

22. The quotation is from the English translation of the speech published in *Industry of Free China*, October 1956, pp. 2, 3.

23. The Council of U.S. Aid (CUSA) was succeeded by the Council for International Economic Cooperation and Development (CIECD) in 1964, of which K. T. Li was also secretary-general, then vice-chairman and minister of economic affairs (1965–67) and finally minister of finance (1968–76), when he retired because of ill health and became minister without portfolio.

24. K. T. Li, "A Review of the Economic Situation in Taiwan in 1958," *Industry of Free China*, March 1959.

25. Lin, pp. 68–70.

26. Li, "Review," p. 9.

and notably C. K. Yen, vice-chairman of the Council for U.S. Aid and of the Economic Stabilization Board and minister of finance from 1959 to 1963 (president of the Republic at the time of writing), and K. Y. Yin (see footnote 18), responded with a series of reforms designed for both purposes.

The 1958–1960 Reforms and Some Earlier Ones

The 1958–60 reforms were preceded by two important sets of measures, most of them taken in 1955. The 1958–60 reforms permitted the "fuel" to flow into the tanks without which exports could never have taken off in the way they did. The 1955 measures, however, made the "fuel," crew, and other costs cheap enough for the flight to be a worthwhile proposition. This elliptical metaphor must be explained.

Taiwan has very few mineral resources and strictly limited agricultural resources. It could only prosper, and has in fact prospered, by exporting what effectively are labor and capital services. These services, however, have mainly taken the form of adding value to imported materials rather than being services pure and simple (as are tourism, banking, transportation, and the like). Thus the most important single condition for an export "take-off" was access by manufacturers to imported materials, components, and capital equipment at world prices. For a typical manufacturer in one of Taiwan's export industries, as is shown in Table 5.15, materials account for around 65 to 70 percent of the selling value of output, capital altogether receives a further 5 to 12 percent of selling value, and, of this, over half can be attributed to costs of plant machinery, vehicles, and stocks of materials. Hence, the total percentage of selling value represented by the cost of materials or equipment might be around 70 to 75 percent or even more for a typical exporter. If his exports are sold at world prices, without benefit of any subsidy, he must be able to buy these materials and equipment at or close to world prices if the export is to be profitable. A 40 percent tax on materials and equipment would wipe out, not merely all potential profit, but also all potential wages, fuel costs, or payment for other bought-in services (advertising and other selling costs, rent of buildings and land, and so forth), and a much smaller tax, say 10 percent, would make many exports totally unprofitable.

Unfortunately, the system of import duties and commodity taxes that had existed for many years on the mainland and was taken over to Taiwan after the war meant that taxes were often substantially in excess of 10 percent on essential materials, components, or equipment. This can be seen from Tables 5.1 and 5.2. For example, in 1954 the commodity tax, which applied to both domestically produced and imported goods, was levied at 15 percent on cotton yarn and rayon staple fiber yarn, 20 percent on artificial filament yarn, and 30 percent on woolen yarn. These taxes alone were probably enough to knock out most exports of yarn or cloth *unless they were rebated on exports*. Likewise,

Table 5.1. Rates of Commodity Tax, 1946–1974* (percent ad valorem)

Commodity	1946	1947	1948	1949	1950	1952	1954	1958	1962	1965	1968	1971	1972
Sugar													
Centrifugal	25			35			60		60				
Brown	25			35			48						
Other													
Saccharine													40
Soft drinks	20		30					25	30–36				
Monosodium glutamate									29				20
Cotton yarn	5	7	10	15		5	15						20
Hemp yarn									10				20
Woolen yarn			15										
Woolen thread			15										
Artificial filament							30						
Artificial-fiber spun yarn							20		20				
Synthetic spun yarn									25			20	
Leather	15												
Plastics									17		23		
Rubber tires	15						20		17		20		
Cement							15		24		30		
Lumber							20						
Paper								15					
Sheet glass								15	23			5	
Petroleum products and natural gas									10–48		10–55		
Cosmetics	45				100	150	20–100						
Matches	20					10	20						
Light bulbs							20						
Refrigerators										15			
Television sets										10			
Air conditioners										15			
Radios, electric fans, sewing machines											10		
Steel products											10		
Electric meters											15		
Automobiles											15		
Motorcycles											20		

*Only years in which the tax rates were changed are shown.
Source: Ministry of Finance, direct communication to the author.

Table 5.2. Tariff Rates for Certain Commodities,* 1948–1976 (percent ad valorem)

Commodity	1948	1955	1960	1965	1971	1976
Cotton yarn	5	17	30	30	33	33
Cotton piece goods	20–30	40	51	51	55	55
Artificial fibers	100	140	96	48	52	52
Synthetic fibers	100	140	60	48	52	52
Iron ore and concentrates	5	5	6	6	0	0
Pig iron; blocks of iron; spiegeleisen	35	15	12	12	13	13
Agricultural machinery and its parts	7½	7½	12	12	7	7
Steam engines and their parts	10	10	12	12	32	32
Shuttles, bobbins	10	15	30	30	26	26
Lathes	7½	7½	9	9	13	13
Sedan cars (incl. taxis)	60	60	72	60	75	75
Chassis of vehicles	25–60	60	60	42	46	46
Motorcycles	60	60	42	42	65	65
Parts and accessories of motorcycles	30	30	24	42	55	55
Bicycles	45	45	36	36	46	46
Air-conditioning machines		60	60	42	46	45
Mustard flour and prepared mustard	60	60	96	96	104	104
Milk powder	40	25	24	24	22	22
Sugar (including raw sugar)	100	100	120	120	130	130
Cigarettes	100	160	192	120	130	130
Alcoholic beverages	200	160	192	120	130	130
Soaps and compounded detergents	40–50	40–50	60	60	65	65
Diesel oil	18	18	21	21	23	23
Crude oil for refining purposes	7½	7½	9	9	10	10
Chemical wood pulp, mechanical wood pulp	10	10	12	12	13	13
Common printing paper	15–20	25	30	30	33	33
Hide of buffalo or cattle tanned	15	15	18	18	13	13
Furniture	50	50	60	60	65	65
Plywood	35	35	42	42	46	46
Cement	70	70	84	6	7	7
Perfumery, cosmetics, and toilet preparations	120	120	144	144	156	156
Domestic refrigerators	150	100	60	42	46	45
Commercial window glass	40	40	48	48	52	52
Soda ash	25	25	30	42	46	40

*Including defense surcharge or temporary tax.
Source: Ministry of Finance, direct communication.

the 15 percent commodity tax on lumber was enough to knock out exports of plywood. But this was only a beginning. *Imported* materials were subject to additional duties that were often very high. Thus in 1955 duties on cotton piece goods were 40 percent, on manmade fibers 140 percent, on pig iron 15 percent, and on soda ash 25 percent. Domestically produced materials did not have to bear these duties, but domestic producers' prices could not be much below the import costs, inclusive of duty, at least in the early stages of industrialization. Hence, whether he relied on imports or on domestic products for his supply of materials, the manufacturer had to pay substantially above world prices. Unless these taxes were rebated, he could not possibly export.

It should be emphasized that this conclusion is quite independent of the exchange rate (provided it is a *unitary* exchange rate—I return to the question of multiple rates presently). Devaluation can help only by reducing the cost of *nontraded* inputs in relation to the selling value of exports. For materials or equipment that are traded, devaluation is no help at all, since their prices go up in the same proportion as the selling value of exports. Hence, if taxes on inputs take away all or nearly all the margin between input costs and selling value, one cannot hope to make exporting profitable by reducing the other, nontraded, elements of costs. Devaluation has nothing (or too little) to bite on. If, however, a reasonable margin is left, devaluation can help by enlarging the share of profits in that margin, which it will do mainly by reducing the share of wages.

Prior to 1955 there was no general system of rebating either import duties or commodity taxes for exports. As an article in *Industry of Free China* remarked, "Fragmentary measures had been taken in the past to refund tax to raw materials used in producing export products. But they were disorganized and not well coordinated."[27] Accordingly, the "Regulations for Rebate of Taxes on Export Products" passed by the Executive Yuan in July 1955 were widely welcomed. They provided for the rebate of commodity tax, import duty, and defense tax.[28] In fact, exporters did not need to pay the first two

27. *Industry of Free China,* August 1955, p. 20. See pp. 34–36 for the regulations, and the issues of January 1959 and November 1962 for revisions to them. According to Lin, p. 101, the system of tax rebates was extended in July 1954 so as to cover customs duties on all exports. The 1955 regulations extended the rebates to commodity tax and defense surtax. Lin describes subsequent extensions and improvements in detail.

28. Defense tax was introduced in September 1953 at a rate of 20 percent on all imports other than industrial raw materials, aid-financed imports, and public-sector imports. In January 1954 it was extended to all imports except those financed by aid. In April 1958 it was converted into a 20 percent surcharge on import duty (that is, the rate of import duty was effectively raised by one-fifth). In July 1969 the 20 percent surcharge was maintained for materials used in manufacturing export goods (rebateable at the time of export), but higher rates were introduced: 26 percent on plant and equipment, instruments, and certain daily essentials, and 30 percent on all other goods. For a period of fourteen months from May 1962 to June 1963 an additional surcharge of 20 percent of the import duty was levied on certain consumption goods (see Lin, pp. 88, 198). Finally, in 1971 the defense surcharge (then called the "temporary tax") was consolidated with the import duty.

taxes at all, merely giving an undertaking that they would be paid if the materials concerned were not used for making exports, this bond being redeemed at the time of exportation.

The rates of commodity tax and import duty mentioned above and given in Tables 5.1 and 5.2 are one demonstration of the importance of this measure. Another very striking demonstration is provided by the following estimates.[29]

For the average manufacturing establishment engaged in producing exports, rebates of import duty, commodity tax, and other indirect taxes on exports in 1971 equaled nearly three-quarters of its estimated value-added and were more than double its estimated operating surplus (that is, trading profits net of depreciation, but before deducting income tax or interest payments). These estimates may somewhat exaggerate the importance of the rebates, since they do not allow for the fact that rebates can be passed back to suppliers of materials who have themselves manufactured these items from imported materials. Thus my estimates assume, in effect, that a garment maker receives all the rebate of taxes on the cloth he has used, whereas in fact he may pass back some of them to a weaver who has supplied him with cloth made from imported yarn. Despite this, it seems clear that, given the high rates of tax levied on raw materials and semimanufactures, very few exports would have been profitable unless these taxes had been rebated.

The second important measure taken in 1955 was the devaluation of the exchange rate applicable to private-sector exports of manufactures from N.T.$15.55 to around N.T.$25 per U.S. dollar,[30] which, by reducing the cost of nontraded inputs (chiefly wages) in exportable products, increased the potential profitability of exporting (see Table 5.3).

The profitability, to a great extent, however, remained only *potential* for two reasons. First, the tax rebate system needed to be improved. Any such system is complicated, since it requires that estimates be made of the quantities of hundreds or thousands of inputs needed to manufacture hundreds or thousands of outputs, and products and processes change all the time.[31] There is an inevitable conflict between the objective of promoting exports, which is best achieved by a relaxed system of administration that does not worry unduly if wastage rates are generous and some revenue is lost, and the objectives of obtaining revenue or protecting the domestic market, which are best achieved by a tight system of administration. There may be (and there were)

29. The estimates were made as follows: total commodity taxes and import duties rebated to exporters in 1971 were compared with "value-added in export" in that year. The latter was estimated from Economic Planning Council, *Taiwan Input-Output Tables, Republic of China, 1971* (June 1974), Table IV, in the way described in the note to Table 5.14. "Operating surplus in export" was estimated using the same method.

30. See Table 5.3. The exchange rate depended on the rate for exchange certificates, which fluctuated over the period March 1955 to April 1958, the effective exchange rate for exports ranging from N.T.$20.43 to N.T.$28.99 per U.S. dollar.

31. See Lin, p. 102, who states that by 1968 there were more than seven thousand different input-output coefficients approved by the relevant official committee.

Table 5.3. Exchange Rates, 1952-1976 (N.T.$ per U.S.$)

	Exports			Imports		
	'Average'	'Trade'	'National income'	'Average'	'Trade'	'National income'
1952	14.93	12.60	10.30	12.98	13.53	10.30
1953	15.55	15.55	15.55	15.65	14.37	15.55
1954	15.55	15.55	15.55	17.35	15.63	15.55
1955	23.18	15.55	15.55	23.78	15.65	15.55
1956	24.71	24.78	24.78	24.78	24.78	24.78
1957	25.53	24.78	24.78	24.78	24.78	24.78
1958	34.14	24.78	24.78	33.90	24.78	24.78
1959	39.38	36.38	36.38	39.53	36.38	36.38
1960	39.73	36.38	36.38	39.73	36.38	36.38
1961	39.83	40.03	40.00	39.83	40.03	40.00
1962	39.83	40.03	40.00	39.83	40.03	40.00
1963	39.87	40.05	40.00	39.89	40.05	40.00
1964	40.00	40.10	40.00	40.10	40.10	40.00
1965-72	40.00	40.00	40.00	40.10	40.10	40.00
1973	38.16	38.08	38.25	38.35	38.25	38.25
1974	37.90	37.90	38.00	38.10	38.10	38.00
1975	37.95	37.95	38.00	38.05	38.05	38.00
1976	37.95	37.95	38.00	38.05	38.05	38.00

Sources: 'Average'. These were derived from the table in the Directorate-General of Budget, Accounting, and Statistics (DGBAS), *Statistical Yearbook of the Republic of China, 1975* (Taipei, 1976), pp. 226-27 (a similar table is in Mo-huan Hsing, *Taiwan: Industrialization and Trade Policies* [London, 1971], pp. 226-29). The figures given there were averaged simply in proportion to the periods for which the different rates were in force. Where the rates fluctuated over a period, the mean of the range given was taken. The rate for exports for the period up to April 14, 1958, is that applicable to exports by private enterprises. Thereafter, until September 30, 1963, it is the rate applicable to all exports other than a few commodities (for example, sugar, rice, salt, bananas) for which lower rates applied. After September 30, 1963, the same rate applied to all exports. The rate for imports up to April 14, 1958, is that applicable to ordinary commerical procurements of U.S. aid-financed imports (prior to July 1952 it is the only rate given for U.S. aid imports). The same rate usually applied to the bulk of imports. From April 14, 1958, until the unification of all import rates on September 30, 1963, the rate is that applicable to other imports.
'Trade'. These are the exchange rates used by the Department of Statistics, Ministry of Finance, to convert customs figures of exports and imports in U.S. dollars into N.T. dollars. The rates are implicit in the series for exports and imports in both currencies given in Ministry of France, *Monthly Statistics of Exports and Imports, the Republic of China*. See, for example, the issue for June 1976, pp. 15, 16.
'National income'. These are the exchange rates used by the DGBAS to convert balance-of-payments statistics in U.S. dollars into N.T. dollars for national accounts estimates.

long delays in negotiating the input-output coefficients or in getting back duties that had been paid at the time of importation. Even when the duties were not so paid, fees had to be paid to banks to provide guarantees to cover the duty outstanding. The system was, however, steadily improved. One test of this is the attraction of the Export Processing Zones for manufacturers wishing to export. When they were initiated in 1965, there was still much to be gained by locating within a zone since all the formalities connected with obtaining tax rebates on exports could thereby be avoided. By the time I visited Taiwan in 1976, however, this advantage no longer appeared to be very substantial. The implication was that the administrative costs of the tax rebate system had been substantially reduced.[32]

The second reason why exporting was only *potentially* very profitable was more important. This was the existence of quantitative import restrictions and the way they were allocated. As the quotations from Yin given above show, the allocation system was highly inefficient. The costs of imported materials for a potential exporter were raised both by the small lots in which imports were purchased and by the need in many cases to pay the license holder a premium. The quotas for some commodities might be quite inadequate, while for others there was no effective restriction at all. The uncertainties and delays of the allocation system compounded the normal uncertainties and delays of obtaining supplies from abroad.

The reforms initiated in April 1958, and spread out over the next two years, made three important changes.[33]

First, and in my view by far the most important change, quantitative restrictions on imports were removed in many cases and the allocation system was much improved in others. It was this freeing of imports (especially materials) from control that I characterized as "allowing the fuel to enter the tanks."

Second, the multiple exchange rate system was gradually collapsed into a single rate system. This could have been a very important measure if the multiple rate system had, in effect, imposed an import duty on industrial materials that was not rebateable. To some extent it did indeed do this. Thus, from March 1955 to June 1957, imports by private enterprises, other than raw materials and equipment for end users, could be obtained at an exchange rate that fluctuated between N.T.$24.88 and N.T.$38.58 per U.S. dollar, which was higher than the rate of N.T.$20.43 to N.T.$28.99 applicable to exports by private enterprises. The premium (in effect, an import duty) on imports thus varied over this period from 22 percent to 33 percent, which was substantial and was not rebateable. However, although this category of imports probably included some semimanufactures, parts or components that could

32. Some other factors were relevant to the decisions whether to locate inside a zone or not. Inside a zone, one could import all one's capital equipment and replacements and parts duty-free. Outside a zone, even if one had a bonded factory (which therefore paid no duty on imported materials), one was entitled to import capital equipment duty-free only if one's investment project was approved for this privilege. And even if it was approved, one could not import replacement parts duty-free. The attractiveness of being inside a zone will be reduced in the future if commodity taxes and import duties on materials and semimanufactures are reduced or eliminated. This is the present direction of policy; a start was made when the import duty on raw cotton was reduced from 16 percent to 1.28 percent (with rebating no longer permitted) and import duties were abolished on timber, industrial salt, and iron ore.

33. For a more detailed account, see K. Y. Yin, "A Review of Existing Foreign Exchange and Trade Control Policy and Technique," *Industry of Free China*, November 1959; Hsing, chap. 5; Lin, chaps. 4 and 5.

have been used for exports, the bulk of materials and equipment came in at a rate of N.T.$24.78, which was close to the mean of the range of rates applicable to exports by private enterprises.[34] Consequently, the replacement of the multiple rate system by a single rate, which was gradually achieved by 1960, probably did not provide a substantial inducement to export. Nevertheless, by simplifying the administration of foreign exchange and by removing a hidden import duty on some imports of semimanufactures, components, or parts, it undoubtedly helped.

Third, the exchange rate applicable to the bulk of imports and to exports by private enterprises was devalued from around N.T.$25 to close to N.T.$40 per U.S. dollar. As may be seen from Figure 5.5, this resulted in a sharp fall in manufacturing wage costs per unit of output, measured in U.S. dollars, at a time when similar costs in the United States, Japan, or Germany were stationary or rising. However, the increased profitability of exporting thereby gained was eroded by inflation and rising money wages in 1960–61. How far was this inflation the direct consequence of the devaluation itself?

In view of the disastrous inflation of the early postwar years, the authorities were understandably anxious to avoid any action that might aggravate it. T. C. Liu and S. C. Tsiang had pointed out, when they served on an important mission to the Chinese government from the International Monetary Fund (IMF) in 1954, that devaluation *accompanied by import liberalization* need not be inflationary. For the rise in the c.i.f. price of imports could then be offset by a fall in the profit margins received by import licenseholders, so that prices of imports on domestic markets need not rise. K. Y. Yin was aware of this point, as is shown by his analysis of price changes following the 1958 reforms.[35]

The first changes in exchange rates were made in April 1958, but not until November was the exchange rate for "essential" imports raised. Until then, wholesale prices in Taipei on average increased very little. Even after November, price increases were moderate until August 1959, when there was a disastrous flood. This was followed by a drought in the first half of 1960 and then by a bad typhoon in August 1960. Wholesale prices rose by 1.4 percent (2.4 percent per annum) from March to October 1959, by 8.5 percent (11.4 percent per annum) from October 1958 to July 1959, and by 20.3 percent (16.2 percent per annum) from July 1959 to October 1960. Thereafter they

34. According to Li, "Resume," p. 14, the rate of N.T.$24.78 applied to 85.4 percent of imports in 1957. Furthermore, as long as the "certificate rate" was above a certain minimum figure, exporters actually received more than N.T.$24.78 per U.S. dollar so that there was, in effect, a hidden export subsidy. From July 8, 1957, until April 1958, for example, when the "certificate rate" was fixed by the authorities, the export rate was N.T.$26.35.

35. Yin, "Review," pp. 8–13. Yin's analysis on page 9 is apparently in terms of import prices, whereas what is required is an analysis in terms of the domestic market prices of importables.

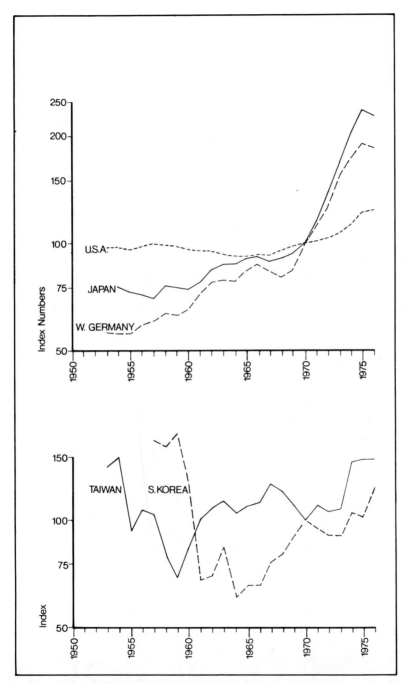

Figure 5.5. Index of wage costs per unit of output for Taiwan and other countries, in U.S. dollars (1970 = 100). Sources: Economic Planning Council, *Taiwan Statistical Data Book, 1976;* National Institute of Economic and Social Research, *National Institute Economic Review,* 1965-1976.

increased very slowly for more than a decade. Hence, while the devaluation probably had some impact on the price level, it was greatly aggravated by natural calamities together with increased government expenditure for relief and reconstruction.[36]

Apart from the three main sets of measures discussed above, the 1958–60 reforms assisted exports by removing export controls from more than two hundred items, simplifying the procedure for tax rebates, waiving the 2 percent harbor dues on exports, and providing easier credit terms for exporters.[37]

The tremendous growth of exports following the 1958–60 reforms is shown in Figure 5.1. Until 1974 there was no check to the expansion. In what follows, I review some further measures affecting trade and payments which were taken in this period of remarkable growth.

Import Liberalization

Import Restrictions. It is not easy to assess the changes in the retrictiveness of the import licensing system. There is no easily obtainable number, like the rate of import duty, to measure their effect. Data on price comparisons are not readily available.[38] We must therefore fall back on less satisfactory indicators.

One such indicator is provided by Table 5.4, which shows the number of imported items classified as being "prohibited," "controlled," or "permissible" from 1968 to 1976. A short explanation of the last two categories is given at the foot of the table. The figures seem to suggest that there was a substantial freeing of imports after 1970, as the numbers included in both the "prohibited" and "controlled" categories were then drastically reduced. Lin gives similar figures to show that from 1957 to 1969 not many more items were shifted from the "controlled" to the "permissible" category than were shifted the other way—although the balance definitely was in favor of liberalization from 1964 onward following the very favorable balance of payments achieved in 1963 as a result of a doubling of the sugar price in that year.[39] The main conclusions these figures suggest are that liberalization did not really get under way until about 1964, that most controls were not swept away until after 1970, and that, by 1976, few remained. Although this probably is the broad picture, it is not altogether accurate.

In the first place, as was mentioned above, the restrictions on imports of materials and, to only a slightly lesser extent, equipment, for manufacturers

36. There was also increased defense expenditure following the gun battles in Kinman offshore island in August 1958.
37. See Yin, "Review," p. 7.
38. But see footnote 41.
39. Lin, p. 93. From 1957 to 1963 inclusive, 251 items were placed under control and 214 items were freed. From 1964 to 1969 inclusive, the corresponding figures were 34 and 201. Lin shows 1,056 items as being freed in 1970.

Table 5.4. Numbers of Imported Commodities According to Their Status Under Import Control, 1968-1976

	Prohibited	Controlled	Permissible	Total
1968 (Dec.)	209	4,551	6,240	11,000
1970 (July)	208	4,780	6,431	11,419
1972 (July)	5	2,822	12,531	15,358
1974 (Feb.)	4	453	14,605	15,062
1976 (June)	13	531	14,822	15,366

Source: Ministry of Economic Affairs, Board of Foreign Trade, *Classification of Import and Export Commodities of the Republic of China,* various issues. "Controlled" means that import licenses are given only if comparable goods are not produced, or cannot be supplied, domestically. "Permissible" means that import licenses are, in general, automatically granted, although there may be restrictions on particular sources of origin.

who wanted to export were very substantially eased from 1958 onward. The items concerned were not formally decontrolled,[40] but in practice exporters could get what materials they wanted. In fact, the allowances were deliberately generous so as to provide an incentive to export. The exporters were, in effect, subsidized through their ability to sell surplus foreign exchange entitlements to other manufacturers, such sale being legally permitted. This system lasted throughout the 1960s, but became redundant in the early 1970s, when nearly all items were liberalized, and partly because of this and partly because it was in conflict with the principle of a unified exchange rate, it was abolished in January 1971.[41]

Second, even for nonexporters there was some liberalization during the 1960s as the criteria used to justify the banning of imports of a commodity were progressively tightened. In 1960 domestic manufacturers seeking protection had to show that the quantity and quality of their products were adequate to satisfy domestic demand and that their prices did not exceed the prices of comparable imports (inclusive of all duties) by more than 25 percent. In 1964 this was reduced to 15 percent and in 1968 to 10 percent. In 1964 a time limit of three years was set for restricted items.[42] These rules were probably not applied strictly—to do so would have required the collection of a great deal of data on price comparisons every year. Nevertheless, their existence helped the

40. On the contrary, according to Lin, p. 100, the authorities deliberately placed certain materials under control in 1959 in order to create the scarcity conditions that would enable exporters' foreign exchange entitlements to command a premium.

41. For a detailed description, see Lin, pp. 97-100. The system actually began in August 1956, but apparently was not liberally interpreted until 1958. Lin gives estimates of the premiums earned by manufacturers who sold their entitlements to other firms in 1968. Although most of these are small (1 to 3 percent), their existence testifies to the fact that import restrictions on materials and semimanufactures were still having some effect at that date. Earlier on, the premiums were probably much greater.

42. Ibid., p. 92.

import liberalization lobby and made the task of those seeking protection more difficult.

The above two qualifications show that there was more liberalization in the 1960s than the numbers in Table 5.4 suggest. Three further qualifications show that the degree of liberalization finally achieved by 1976 was not as complete as that table makes it appear. First, the fall in the number of "prohibited" or "controlled" items was partly caused by a change in the method of classification. Thus in the 1960s, imports of alcoholic drinks and tobacco products were classified as "prohibited," whereas in 1976 they were not so classified and were not even classified as "controlled," but their status was just the same, that is, they could be imported only by the state monopolies.

Second, although the items remaining "prohibited" or "controlled" in 1976 were nearly all in these categories for reasons that clearly had nothing to do with protection and little to do with saving foreign exchange (at least on current account),[43] there were other items, subject to control over their origin, for which protection remained an important motive. Thus, most garments (apart from military uniforms) were not classified as "prohibited" or "controlled" and are, therefore, counted in Table 5.4 as "permissible." Yet they could be imported only from Europe or America, thus effectively excluding the most competitive sources of such products—Hong Kong, Japan, and South Korea. The same was true of some yarns, artificial fibers, and fabrics, with the further restriction that only approved manufacturing plants could import many of the yarns and artificial fibers. Some manufactured foodstuffs, chemicals, toilet preparations, machinery, and electrical apparatus were subject to similar restrictions. Imports of ordinary passenger cars, with few exceptions,[44] were banned, although no mention of this fact is made in the Board of Foreign Trade's *Classification of Import and Export Commodities.*

Many of these restrictions (including the ban on imported cars) were aimed at Japan, and here the reason was not just protection. Taiwan had a large bilateral trade deficit with Japan. In a rational world this would not matter since the deficit could be offset by surpluses in trade with other countries. Unfortunately, the world is not so rational. Taiwan was under pressure from her other trading partners to reduce her bilateral surpluses with them by importing more from them or by restricting her exports to them. She in turn was therefore under some compulsion to transmit this pressure to Japan, since a reduction in her surpluses with other countries would necessitate a reduction

43. In 1976, most "prohibited" items were narcotics, and most "controlled" items were defense-related (for example, arms and ammunition) or related to nuclear energy or could have been used as a means of evading controls over capital movements abroad (antiques, jewelry, precious stones) or were connected with mainland China (Chinese medicines).

44. For example, foreign diplomats and foreign investors could import cars.

Table 5.5. Products Manufactured in Taiwan and Subject to Minimum Percentages of Domestic Content in 1976

Products	Minimum percentages in 1976*
Black and white television sets	90
Color television sets	50
Telephones	90
Switch exchangers: manual and step by step	80
Automobiles†	60
Motorcycles	90
Power tillers	90
Crossbar exchanger components	85
Crossbar exchanger frames	90
Crossbar exchanger switches	70
Crossbar exchanger wire spring relays	60
Registers	50
CR-7 terminal boards	100
CR-6 terminal boards	90

*The minimum percentages refer to: $\dfrac{\text{Total costs} - \text{imported components}}{\text{Total costs}}$ "Imported components" means those *directly* imported by the manufacturer. The import content of inputs bought from other manufacturers is ignored.

†Automobile manufacturers must choose to make at least one of the following six parts in their own factories: engine body, cylinder head, piston connecting pin and rod, camshaft, crankshaft, main spring.

Source: Industrial Development Bureau, Ministry of Economic Affairs, direct communication.

in her deficit with Japan. A further reason sometimes given for restricting imports from Japan was that it was alleged that Japanese exporters were sometimes dumping, although this was difficult to prove.

As a third and final qualification, the regulations governing the manufacture of certain products laid down minimum percentages of total costs that must consist either of value-added within the factory itself or of inputs produced in Taiwan.[45] The objective was to encourage the formation of "backward linkages," and the regulations usually required a progressively increasing percentage of "domestic content." New manufacturers had to meet the same requirements as those who had started earlier, so that there was no "unfair" advantage. This meant that the government was under pressure from two different directions. Some manufacturers had more than satisfied the minimum percentages and wanted them raised to squeeze out their competitors; others who had not wanted them lowered. Table 5.5 shows the products affected in 1976 and the relevant percentages.

Tariffs. Although the tariff system was revised in 1955, 1959, 1965, and 1968 (when the Brussels Tariff Nomenclature was adopted), there was apparently no marked change in the general incidence of duties until 1973, when

45. See the formula at the foot of Table 5.5.

Table 5.6. Ratio of Customs Revenues to Imports, 1950 to 1975-1976 (percent)

Year*	Net revenues (1)	Gross revenues (incl. rebates) (2)	Year	Net revenues (1)	Gross revenues (incl. rebates) (2)
1950	22	22	1963-64	17	24
1951	20	20	1964-65	18	23
1952	21	21	1965-66	17	23
1953	21	21	1966-67	16	22
			1967-68	17	23
1954-55	31†	31†	1968-69	17	23
1955-56	28†	28†	1969-70	16	23
1956-57	24	25	1970-71	13	23
1957-58	30†	31†	1971-72	13	23
1958-59	22	23	1972-73	12	20
1959-60	17	19	1973-74	12	17
1960-61	15	18	1974-75	10	15
1961-62	16	19	1975-76	11	16
1962-63	17	20			

*Calendar years 1950-53, financial years beginning July 1, 1954-55 to 1975-76.
†See footnote 47 for discussion of these high rates.
Sources: Net revenues from DGBAS *Statistical Yearbook of the Republic of China, 1975*, pp. 240-42, for years 1950-73-74. Later years and rebates to give gross revenues from Ministry of Finance. Revenues from import duty and defense surcharge (see footnote 28) are included, but not harbor dues (which were levied at 2 percent on the value of imports until November 1958 when the rate was raised to 3 percent, and then to 3.75 percent in August 1967; see Lin, p. 88). Imports from 1954-75 on are two-year moving averages except for 1973-74 to 1975-76, which are actuals, derived from *Monthly Statistics of Exports and Imports*, Ministry of Finance (June 1976), for 1952-76, and *Industry of Free China*, May 1959, for 1950 and 1951.

they were appreciably reduced. Table 5.6 shows the ratio of tariff revenues to imports, and, although this is not a good measure of the average degree of protection provided by the tariff system, it is the best available.[46] Both of the series shown in Table 5.6 are of interest. Column 2, which is the ratio of duties including those rebated to exporters to total imports, is the better measure of the average height of the tariff schedule. It is, of course, affected by the changing composition of imports, but it is not affected, as is the ratio in

46. Estimates of the level of effective protection (that is, protection to value added) in 1966 are given in Hsing, chap. 6, and in T. H. Lee and K. S. Liang, "The Structure of Protection in Taiwan," in *Economic Essays* (November 1971).

The former estimates the average rate of effective protection in manufacturing at 43.8 percent, and the latter, for manufacturing, agriculture, forestry, fishing, mining, and energy, at 43.5 percent. Both of these estimates allow for exports (for example, Hsing assumed that export production received zero protection). Protection for production sold on the home market was considerably higher. (Lee and Liang put it at 116.5 percent for their industries. Hsing put it at 125.7 percent for consumption goods, 47.7 percent for intermediate goods, and 31.9 percent for capital goods.) Lee and Liang assumed that domestic prices were raised by 15 percent over c.i.f. prices plus duties by quantitative import restrictions, but neither they nor Hsing were able to make direct price comparisons. A much more thorough investigation of effective protection for a more recent year that does make use of direct price comparisons is currently being undertaken by Liang, but the results are not yet available.

column 1, by the increasing share of imports used to manufacture exports, which were thus exempted from duty. Apart from some freakishly high ratios in 1954–55, 1955–56, and 1957–58, which may be more statistical than real,[47] the ratio in column 2 shows no obvious trend up or down until 1972–73, after which it definitely falls. The ratio in column 1, on the other hand, shows the influence of rising imported materials for export manufacture to a marked extent after 1958–59. In one sense this does show a decline in the average level of protection, as more and more of industry consisted of production for export which received little or no protection.

Table 5.6 gives a summary picture, while Table 5.2 is an attempt to provide detail. It is very inadequate because tariff rates are given for only some thirty-four items. Nevertheless, it suggests certain conclusions. Comparing 1948 or 1955 with 1971 we find twice as many increases as decreases, while comparing 1971 with 1976 there is scarcely any change. This suggests that tariff rates tended to rise in the 1950s and 1960s and that there is no sign that they have fallen in the 1970s. The apparent conflict with Table 5.6 may be due to the unrepresentativeness of the very limited sample of rates given in Table 5.2. Alternatively, rates may indeed have risen in this way, but customs revenues may not have benefited because of a shift to imports at lower rates of duty. Further investigation seems necessary.

A more solidly based conclusion is that there were many high rates throughout the period and that many could be brought down drastically without any loss of revenue, and, indeed, with revenue increasing in some cases. Thus the 33 percent duty on cotton yarn and 55 percent duty on cotton piece goods, when Taiwan is a substantial exporter of both products, serves only to exclude imports of most types altogether.[48] Lowering rates of duty would increase both imports and tariff revenues. Furthermore, by encouraging greater specialization and longer runs it would lower costs. It is worth noting in this connection that, whereas Taiwan is a net exporter of cotton yarns and piece-goods, Hong Kong is a net importer, with consequent benefits to her

---

47. In Table 5.6 customs revenues for fiscal years 1954–55 (starting July 1), for example, have been related to the averages of imports in the years 1954 and 1955. The customs revenues are given in N.T. dollars; the customs figures of imports are also expressed in N.T. dollars. However, the latter are converted from U.S. dollar figures using rates which, it seems likely, do not properly reflect the values on which the duties were originally based. Thus for 1954–55 the average exchange rate used by customs to convert imports from U.S. dollars to N.T. dollars is N.T.$15.6375 per U.S. dollar, whereas the average exchange rate applicable to the bulk of imports was probably N.T.$20.78. Likewise, in 1955–56 the average exchange rate used by customs is N.T.$20.215, whereas the one applicable to the bulk of imports was probably N.T.$24.78. If appropriate corrections are made to the ratios for 1954–55 and 1955–56 in column 2, they become 24 percent (instead of 31 percent) and 23 percent (instead of 28 percent). No such correction seems necessary for the 1957–58 ratios, whose height I am unable to explain.

48. Apart, that is, from imports to be used in the production of exports, on which duty would not have to be paid.

garment industry where she exports far more than Taiwan despite a much smaller population and a higher level of wages.[49]

This conclusion is strengthened by the contrast between an average rate of duty for 1975–76 in Table 5.6 of 16 percent (gross of rebates) and the typically much higher rates shown in Table 5.2. It seems that very few imports at the higher rates of duty are coming in.[50] The advantages of reducing rates of duty are appreciated by many officials, but it has been difficult to reduce them because of the cumbersome procedures that have had to be followed. Recently, however, power has been given to vary the rates of duty up or down by half without reference to the Legislative Yuan, and this should enable reductions to be made more quickly.

Export Promotion

Exports were promoted following the 1958–60 reforms by the setting up of Export Processing Zones and bonded factories, cheap credit for exporters, some private schemes, and a group of miscellaneous measures.[51]

Export Processing Zones and Bonded Factories and Warehouses. The original idea for setting up export processing zones in Taiwan was put forward by the Economic Stabilization Board in 1956.[52] Establishment of such zones was also recommended in 1958 by an American port expert when reviewing the Kaohsiung Harbor extension plan (partly financed by U.S. aid) and was investigated in connection with the drafting of the Statute for Encouragement

---

49. The contrast is striking. Thus, for 1972, in U.S.$ million, we have, for Standard International Trade Classification (SITC) 65 (textiles) and 84 (clothing):

	Hong Kong		Taiwan	
	65	84	65	84
Exports	384	1079	346	494
Imports	650	87	102	1
Balance	−266	992	244	493

In principle, the Taiwan garment exporter should be on a level with that of Hong Kong because of the rebate system. Nevertheless, there are still some costs in obtaining rebates, and, as it is ceteris paribus more convenient and cheaper to buy locally than to import, higher cost domestic cloth does reduce the competitiveness of garment exports.

50. According to Lin, p. 89, the rates of duty expressed as percentages of c.i.f. values are in reality about one-fifth higher than appears in Table 5.2. This is the result of the system of valuation for customs purposes, which adds 20 percent to the c.i.f. value before calculating the value on which the duty is based. The reason for this is historical and is explained by Lin. That being so, the contrast mentioned in the text becomes even more marked. See also "Import Tariff Provisional Rules," *Industry of Free China*, March 1956, pp. 29–32, especially p. 32.

51. See also Hsing, pp. 213–16 and 232–33; Lin, pp. 103–15.

52. The story of the establishment of the Kaohsiung Export Processing Zone is given in *Industry of Free China*, January 1967, pp. 2–30.

of Investment in 1963. Finally, a special law was promulgated in January 1965. The Kaohsiung Export Processing Zone was formally opened in December 1966, although exporting from the zone had begun before. Subsequently, in 1969, as applications from investors to set up in the zone flooded in in excess of the space available, the government decided to set up two more zones: one in Nantze, which is also in Kaohsiung City, and a smaller one in Taichung. Table 5.7 gives some data on all three zones. Exports from them in 1975 amounted to U.S.$459 million and imports to $271 million, some 8.6 percent and 4.6 percent, respectively, of Taiwan's total exports and imports. Employment in the zones accounted for 6 percent of total employment in manufacturing.

Although there had been free trade zones elsewhere in the world, the idea of combining in one place the advantages of a free trade zone, an industrial estate, and all the relevant administrative offices of the government was a new one and has received the compliment of many imitators since. Much impor-

Table 5.7. Statistics for the Three* Export Processing Zones in Taiwan

Products	Cumulative exports, September 1966 to August 1976 (U.S.$ millions)	Number of employees,† August 1976
Electronic	1,312	40,248
Garments	311	10,912
Plastic	143	4,512
Leather	112	2,965
Knitted and woven	94	4,071
Metal	86	3,221
Handicraft	58	3,045
Other	233	9,212
Total	2,349	78,186

Cumulative imports, September 1966 to August 1976 (U.S. $ millions)	
From abroad	1,489
(of which, machinery and equipment)	(110)
From Taiwan	236

Sources of capital,‡ cumulative to August 1976 (U.S.$ millions)	
Domestic	35.6
Hong Kong	24.5
Other Overseas Chinese	3.6
Japan	78.8
United States	27.5
Europe	25.1
Other	0.4
Total	195.4

*Kaohsiung, Nantze, and Taichung.
†In addition, there were 1,405 employees of government agencies.
‡Total approved projected investment less withdrawals. Total investment arrived was U.S. $134.8 million at August 1976.
Source: Export Processing Zone Administration, Ministry of Economic Affairs, *Export Processing Zones Essential Statistics,* August 1976.

tance was attached to cutting red tape so that investors could start their projects quickly and could run them with minimal bureaucratic fuss. Indeed, one of the principal advantages of locating in a zone was precisely to avoid the administrative costs of obtaining rebates of taxes on inputs or outputs. In view of the success of the zones in attracting investors, especially foreign investors (for whom the problems of dealing with bureaucracy would seem more formidable), one must conclude that these costs were important outside the zones and were successfully reduced within them. The situation seems to have changed since the zones were set up, however, especially as a result of the establishment of bonded factories and warehouses. The government deliberately encouraged these from October 1965, and they give the investor the advantage of a wider choice of location. Partly because of this, and partly because of the world recession after 1973, applications to set up in the zones fell off. Since there is still plenty of room in the Nantze Export Processing Zone, there are currently no plans to set up more zones elsewhere.

The first zone at Kaohsiung was set up with the view that it should be located as close as possible to the harbor because all the output and most of the input of the factories would go to or come from abroad. Land reclaimed from the harbor formed the site. Experience has shown, however, that proximity to a harbor is not as important as proximity to a supply of labor. For one thing, many of the goods (especially electronic products) have gone by air and have had to be taken to the international airport at Taipei. For another, it is much cheaper to transport goods a few miles in a lorry than to transport workers the same distance back and forth every day. There was considerable congestion initially at Kaohsiung, since only one road gave access to the zone. One businessman told me in 1967 that transport costs of workers added 25 percent to his labor costs. The position has since improved, but some firms there have their own fleets of buses to bring their workers in. For these reasons, the next two zones were not sited near a harbor, but, instead, nearer to their labor supply.

Another change since the first zone was established is in the emphasis given to employment as an objective. In 1972 and 1973, when demand for labor in Taiwan was particularly strong, the government stopped giving tax holidays to labor-intensive investments. No doubt partly because of this, investment per employee in the Nantze and Taichung zones has averaged between two and six times the average of the Kaohsiung zone.[53] The government has preferred to encourage more "technology-intensive" industries.

I have never been very clear as to what exactly constitutes this kind of industry (a tour of almost any factory leaves me amazed at the complexity, ingenuity, and skill on display), but some of the products made in the zones

---

53. K. J. Wong, "Critical Review on Costs and Benefits of Establishing and Operating Export Processing Zone in the Republic of China" (mimeographed, undated), p. 37.

undoubtedly require a high degree of engineering and manual skills to produce. The foreign firms that have come in have not merely trained their operatives—over 80 percent of whom are women, about half of them in their teens—but also managers and technicians, some of whom are sent abroad for this purpose. The American firms in particular seem to prefer Chinese managers and technicians. They are much cheaper and have no language problems. The Japanese firms, for whom these advantages are probably smaller, tend to retain more of their own management. The managers and technicians who are trained in this way earn higher salaries as a result and since there is a certain turnover of jobs, often subsequently work for Chinese firms. Apart from training labor, there is some transfer of technology as a result of foreign firms purchasing materials from Taiwan. As can be seen from Table 5.7, such "backward linkages" have amounted to about 10 percent of the value of exports.[54]

One reason for the preference for "technology-intensive" firms has been the desire to avoid competition with Taiwan's existing export industries. This is a particularly important consideration for exports that are limited by quota, and it was for this reason that no manufacturers of cotton textiles or cotton garments were allowed into the zones.

Have the zones benefited Taiwan? I cannot attempt a proper social cost-benefit analysis here although it should not be too difficult to undertake one.[55] There have been criticisms of the tax holidays given to foreign investors (five years initially, with four years for subsequent investments), of the high import content of exports (63 percent, see Table 5.7), of the inflationary effects resulting from the increased demand for labor, and of the alleged dearth of "technology-intensive" industries. Some of these criticisms are mutually inconsistent, irrelevant, or unsubstantiated.

The main benefit from the zones has probably been that they provided employment at higher wages and better working conditions. The wages of each worker are, in effect, paid in foreign exchange; the worker's expenditure from any *extra* he or she earns may be partly saved (which is socially benefi-

54. That is, U.S.$236 million of imports from Taiwan compared to U.S.$2,349 million of exports.

55. Since such a large part of the output and input are directly exported or imported, it would be a good case for the application of the method devised by I. M. D. Little and J. A. Mirrlees, *Project Appraisal and Planning for Developing Countries* (London, 1974), and applied to assess the net social benefit of private investment (foreign and domestic) by, for example, D. Lal, *Appraising Foreign Investment in Developing Countries* (London, 1975); D. M. G. Newbery, "The Social Value of Private Investment in Kenya," in *Using Shadow Prices*, ed. I. M. D. Little and M. FG. Scott (London, 1976); and M.FG. Scott, "A Set of Accounting Prices for Kenya," in M. FG. Scott et al., *Project Appraisal in Practice*, (London, 1976), chap. 6. A social cost-benefit analysis of the Kaohsiung Zone was undertaken in 1969, which concluded that the ratio of benefit to costs was 3.6 if only government and local private investment was considered and 2.4 if investment from overseas Chinese and foreign enterprises was included. However, this study is not regarded as very reliable, and I did not examine it. See Wong, pp. 26–27.

cial) or, insofar as it is consumed, bears tax. Furthermore, some workers might otherwise have been employed in import-substituting industries where their wages would exceed their marginal products measured in foreign exchange. Alternatively, they might have been employed in export industries that were subsidized (for example, by the foreign exchange retention schemes or by subsidized credit), with the same result.[56] Hence the social cost of each worker, expressed in terms of foreign exchange, is appreciably less than the foreign exchange he (or more often she) earns. To express the same point in another way, as a result of setting up the zones, the pattern of employment and output has been altered in such a way as to provide some workers with higher wages and better working conditions than they would otherwise have had and also to provide the government with more tax revenue. The latter has accrued partly from taxes on the additional consumption of the workers and partly from higher import duties (because of less output by import-substituting industries) and lower export subsidies (because subsidized export industries elsewhere have produced less). Apart from this the government (including the local governments) benefits from rents and from some taxes levied directly on the enterprises, and some of the services provided to firms in the zones run at a good profit. The direct government investment required to secure these benefits has been quite small—K. J. Wong puts it at only U.S.\$12 million. Since annual value-added in 1975, net of remittance of profits and so forth, abroad, was of the order of U.S.\$150 million, of which perhaps a tenth or more might have been social profit in the form of extra taxes, the social value of higher wages, and the like, the social rate of return was probably very high.[57]

Cheap Loans for Exporters. In July 1957, the Bank of Taiwan initiated an Export Loan Program under which short-term loans were extended to finance the materials and work in progress of exporting firms.[58] The interest rate was fixed at 0.99 percent per month for loans repayable in N.T. dollars (and at 0.5 percent per month if repayable in foreign currencies). This was appreciably less than the rate the Bank of Taiwan (and other banks) then charged on secured loans to private enterprises, which was 1.65 percent per month, or than the 3.0 percent per month charged by private moneylenders. A favorable margin has been preserved ever since, although it narrowed appre-

56. Some of the workers might otherwise have been unemployed, in which case the social benefits of employing them would have been even greater. This was an important consideration when the zones were first set up, but in more recent years, with full or fuller employment, it was probably much less so. A social cost-benefit analysis should focus on the long-run average and not on the situation in a few years, which may be untypical.

57. Some of the enterprise investment cost should be considered as part of the social investment cost. Some of the foreign investment might have come in without the zones. Some of it was financed locally (for example, by mortgages on buildings and loans for working capital) and some was provided by domestic investors who might otherwise have invested elsewhere in Taiwan. Even so, I would guess that the social return was probably very high.

58. See *Industry of Free China*, July 1957, pp. 33–36, for details. See also Lin, pp. 105–7.

ciably at the peak of the export boom in 1973–74. In April 1977 the rate on export loans was 6.5 percent per annum compared with the lowest rate of 11.0 percent per annum for secured bank loans and 1.75 percent per month (equivalent to 23.1 percent per annum) for the cheapest loans in the unorganized money market in Taipei.[59]

The value of this "export subsidy" obviously varies from firm to firm, depending on the extent of its borrowing and on whether the alternative would be bank loans, unorganized money market loans, or (if the firm is a net lender rather than borrower) deposits with a bank. However, the "subsidy" clearly could be appreciable.[60] It could be justified on the grounds that many other countries also subsidize credit for exporters.

Private Schemes to Promote Exports. An interesting aspect of Taiwan's experience is that private firms, and not just the government, have acted to promote each others' exports. These schemes, described by Mohuan Hsing and Ching-yuan Lin,[61] amount to private levies on domestic sales or on materials used to manufacture domestic sales, with corresponding bounties on exports or on materials used for export. The industries concerned (cotton textiles,[62] paper, steel products, rubber manufactures, monosodium glutamate, cement, and woolen textiles) have thus acted collectively as discriminatory monopolists, as the effect of these measures is to reduce the pressure of competition on the domestic market and keep up prices there in relation to export prices. In principle, everyone can gain, including domestic consumers, if higher production leads to sufficiently large economies of scale.

Other Export-Promotion Measures and Import Restrictions by Foreign Countries. Many other export-promotion measures were undertaken by the government and its agencies. As far back as 1953, the Taiwan Provincial Government (TPG) took steps to inspect the quality of goods produced in Taiwan, especially export goods.[63] Subsequently, this inspection has been handled by the Controls Bureau of Standards of the Ministry of Economic Affairs working with the Bureau of Commodity Inspection and Quarantine of the TPG. It is perhaps especially important for such exports as canned foodstuffs, where there are numerous producers, and where poor quality on the part of some may adversely affect exports by all. Financial incentives provided for export included exemption of income tax amounting to 2 percent of the total export exchange settlements of a manufacturer or trader, and total

59. See *Taiwan Financial Statistics Monthly,* May 1977, pp. 72–74. Export loans are now denominated in foreign currencies.

60. Thus, if an exporter's loans equaled half the annual value of his exports, and if the subsidy is taken as 6 percent per annum on the loan, it is equivalent to 3 percent on the value of his exports.

61. Hsing, pp. 215–16; Lin, pp. 108–10.

62. The cotton textiles scheme ended in 1972.

63. See "Inspection of Industrial Products," *Industry of Free China,* December 1955, pp. 33–40.

exemption of income tax for a corporation whose product was categorized as "encouraged" and whose exports exceeded 50 percent of annual production.[64] Export insurance was improved and cheapened and, starting in 1969, special awards were made to successful exporters. Cash awards were also made to enterprises in the machinery industries for the development of new products and expansion of exports.

Initially, overseas representation and the provision of information were secured through economic counselors from the Ministry of Economic Affairs stationed in many countries, as well as through the branch offices of the Central Trust of China.[65] However, following the admission of mainland China to the United Nations in October 1971 and as diplomatic relations with more and more countries were broken off, including with Japan in September 1972, a new approach had to be found. Overseas representation was undertaken by Far East Trade Services, Incorporated, which worked in conjunction with the China External Trade Development Council, set up in July 1970. Arrangements continued to be made to participate in trade fairs, to send trade missions overseas, and to provide displays of Taiwan's export products. The facilities of the World Trade Centre Association, of which Taiwan is a member, were used. Many foreign governments (including Japan) continued to give Taiwan most-favored-nation treatment, no doubt bearing in mind that it was one of the largest markets for imports in Asia.[66] Taiwan did not, however, benefit under the scheme for Generalized Special Preferences, approved at the United Nations Conference on Trade, Aid, and Development (UNCTAD) in 1968, under which tariff preferences were eventually accorded to many of her competitors, including Hong Kong, Singapore, and South Korea.

Before considering the restrictions imposed on Taiwan's exports by foreign countries, it is useful to review their country and commodity composition, as shown in Tables 5.8 and 5.9. Table 5.8 shows that the United States has become much the most important market, with Japan in second place. Together these two countries account for nearly half of Taiwan's total exports, as they did in 1953, but Japan was then much more important because it bought so much of Taiwan's sugar and rice. Apart from these two countries, Taiwan exports substantial amounts to Hong Kong and Singapore (where restrictions are relatively minor or absent altogether), to West Germany, Canada, the United Kingdom, and the Netherlands (where tariffs are generally low, but where quantitative restrictions are important for some of Taiwan's products),

64. See "Export Promotion in the Republic of China," *Industry of Free China*, January 1968, p. 36.

65. Hsing, p. 216.

66. Taiwan left the General Agreement on Tariff and Trade (GATT) in May 1950 and hence was not covered by its provisions, although it benefited from the most-favored-nation clauses in its trade agreements with other countries.

Table 5.8. Percentages of Taiwan's Exports Going to Different Countries, 1953 and 1975

	1953	1975
United States	4.2	34.3
Japan	45.6	13.1
Hong Kong	8.2	6.8
West Germany	0.8	6.0
Canada	0.1	3.4
Indonesia	—*	3.3*
Singapore	—	2.7
United Kingdom	6.6	2.6
Netherlands	—*	2.6*
Australia	0.1	2.4
South Korea	1.3	2.3
Saudi Arabia	0.0	2.2
Philippines	0.2	1.5
Thailand	0.5	1.3
Nigeria	0.0	1.2
Other	32.4*	14.3*
Total	100.0	100.0

*No figures for Indonesia and the Netherlands are given in the first source. The 1975 figures have therefore been taken from the second, but the 1953 figures in that source do not appear to be comparable, and so they are included in "other."

Source: Economic Planning Council (EPC), *Taiwan Statistical Data Book, 1976* (June 1976), and Ministry of Finance, *Monthly Statistics of Exports and Imports* (June 1976).

and to a number of developing countries where both high tariffs and severe import restrictions are common.

Table 5.9 shows Taiwan's share in Organization for Economic Cooperation and Development (OECD) countries' imports of products for which that share was at all sizable in 1973. These were, therefore, the products most sensitive to protectionist lobbying. As the last line of the table shows, Taiwan's share in all imports was tiny, less than 1 percent for all OECD countries taken together. But for the items shown, which accounted for nearly 70 percent of all Taiwan's exports to these countries, her share was quite important in many countries and very important in some. Thus, to take the most important, she accounted for 44 percent of radio broadcast receivers imported into Japan, 41 percent of television broadcast receivers imported into the United States, 38 percent of vegetables preserved or prepared not elsewhere specified (n.e.s.), 27 percent of the footwear, and 20 percent of the clothing imported into Japan. For European countries, her share was usually small, apart from vegetables preserved (these were canned mushrooms and asparagus) imported by West Germany, where she provided 17 percent of the total.

Cotton textiles were an early victim of protectionism. Following the Long-term Arrangement on Cotton Textiles (LTA) negotiated under the auspices of the General Agreement on Tariffs and Trade (GATT), which started in 1962,

Table 5.9. Imports of Organization for Economic Cooperation and Development Countries from Taiwan in 1973 (percentage of imports from Taiwan)

	Standard International Trade Classification commodity group	United States	Japan	Canada	European Economic Community	West Germany	United Kingdom	OECD	Value of imports from Taiwan U.S.$ millions
03	Fish and fish preparations	1.8	9.2	0.9	1.0	1.0	0.3	3.1	135
0555	Vegetables preserved or prepared n.e.s.	18.0	37.5	12.8	11.0	17.1	2.1	13.8	128
631	Veneers, plywood, etc.	16.0	15.8	22.8	1.8	0.8	2.5	8.2	203
65	Textiles yarns, fabrics, etc.	1.6	7.4	0.6	1.1	0.7	1.1	1.5	221
7241	Television broadcast receivers	41.2	0	5.7	0.9	0.7	0.9	13.7	238
7242	Radio broadcast receivers	10.8	44.4	7.4	3.6	7.4	4.1	7.4	118
7249	Telecommunications eqpt. n.e.s.	11.3	7.8	2.0	0.4	0.4	0.5	3.3	105
7293	Thermionic valves, tubes, transistors, etc.	8.9	11.1	0.8	0.5	0.6	1.2	3.2	96
841	Clothing, except fur	17.1	20.2	14.2	2.4	2.4	5.7	6.6	664
851	Footwear	13.3	26.8	15.5	2.6	2.8	2.4	7.7	212
89111	Gramophones, tape recorders, etc.	5.6	4.5	1.9	1.3	1.2	1.4	3.3	53
893	Articles of artificial plastic material	18.4	10.8	2.4	0.6	1.9	0.7	4.2	79
8942	Toys, indoor games, etc.	13.9	10.1	5.5	2.1	3.1	1.5	5.8	74
899	Manufactured articles n.e.s.	8.1	13.5	1.7	1.4	2.3	0.9	4.0	55
	Total all imports	2.6	2.3	0.7	0.3	0.4	0.3	0.9	3,453

Source: "Trade by Commodities, Market Summaries: Imports," OECD Foreign Trade Statistics, Series C, January–December 1973. The figures are derived from OECD member countries' statistics of imports. The originals were rounded to the nearest $1 million before calculation of percentages, which are therefore subject to rounding errors.

Taiwan's exports of cotton textiles to the United States were restricted by quota and other countries (such as Canada and the European Economic Community) followed suit. In 1974 the LTA was replaced by the Multi-fiber Agreement (MFA), which widened its coverage by including products made largely from manmade fibers and wool. Taiwan has not been a member of the GATT since 1950 and took no part in the negotiations of the MFA (although she had been a member of the LTA). However, she agreed to abide by the MFA and has been allocated quotas in importing member countries (although, for example, in the case of the European Economic Community, these were fixed unilaterally by the importers).

Taiwan's exports of canned foodstuffs, especially mushrooms and asparagus, reached such a dominating position in some markets that they also encountered restrictions in the 1960s and 1970s. Some other foodstuffs (eels, oranges, bananas) have been restricted as well, sometimes allegedly for health reasons. Exports of electronics products to developed countries have, by contrast, been almost wholly free of restriction.

Despite all the restrictions, Taiwan's exports have grown and will probably continue to do so in the future. Nevertheless, the restrictions have hampered that growth and will doubtless continue to do so. Not only is this unfortunate for Taiwan, but it also harms consumers in developed countries, who have to pay higher prices and who find their choice restricted. As with any quota arrangement, the resulting gap between supply and demand produces a rent or premium for someone. It may go to the developed country importer, but the government in Taiwan is naturally anxious that as much as possible should accrue to Taiwan and has therefore devised systems for allocating export quotas to manufacturers so as to raise export prices. For example, while part of the quota for a particular product is allocated in accordance with past performance, part is allocated to those manufacturers whose bids to fulfill export orders are at the highest prices compatible with securing the orders.

Another method of countering, or forestalling, import restrictions has been the formation of export associations. By keeping up prices and restricting export quantities, these have offset the bargaining power of importers (to whom import licenses have been allocated) or have prevented restrictions being imposed at all. Once again, the chief loser has been the consumer in the importing country.

Developments in the Balance of Payments, 1960–1976

The growth of the volume of exports, especially of industrial goods, accelerated following the 1958–60 reforms and averaged 23 percent per annum from 1960 to the peak in 1973. Thereafter they fell, touching bottom in early 1975, and then recovering briskly. The volume of imports rose more slowly, 18 percent per annum, from 1960 to a peak in 1974, and then fell and recovered as had exports (see Figure 5.1).

Table 5.10. Net Foreign Assets of the Banking System

Year	Value at end of year U.S.$ million	As percentage imports goods and services of year	Year	Value at end of year U.S.$ million	As percentage imports goods and services of year
1950	15	8	1963	245	59
1951	49	32	4	321	67
1952	45	20	5	306	49
1953	54	25	6	371	56
1954	42	18	7	449	51
1955	67	32	8	418	36
1956	70	28	9	509	37
1957	78	29	1970	703	40
1958	83	27	1	882	40
1959	91	30	2	1,458	50
1960	102	32	3	1,878	41
1961	138	37	4	1,854	24
1962	122	33	5	1,830	27
			6	2,890	32

Source: Central Bank, direct communication.

Because exports rose faster than imports, the balance on goods and services improved. Exports of goods and services, which had financed only around 60 percent of imports of goods and services during the 1950s, financed successively higher percentages after 1960, reaching 93 percent in 1963 and 104 percent in 1964 (Figure 5.3). The gain in these two years owed much to a doubling of the price of sugar in 1963, following the fall in Cuban sugar production. The improvement in the current balance of payments led to a sharp rise in foreign exchange reserves. By the end of 1964 they had doubled their ratio to imports (Table 5.10).

In 1962, before the sugar boom, the U.S. Agency for International Development (AID) decided that concessional aid to Taiwan should be ended as soon as possible.[67] In early 1963, the AID mission estimated the rate of growth that could be sustained without aid and concluded that it would be 6 to 7 percent per annum from 1965 to 1972 (in fact, 10 percent per annum was achieved). This led to the decision to end assistance by 1968, but no public announcement was made. Then, during 1963, the AID administrator, David Bell, stated that Taiwan's progress had been so great that U.S. aid could end "in three to five years." In May 1964, however, the administrator announced that no further economic aid would be committed after June 20, 1965, except for a limited amount of surplus agricultural commodities. The decision to bring forward the termination date was taken because of Taiwan's very favorable balance of payments and because AID wanted a "success story" as ammunition in their battle with the U.S. Congress for the current aid appropriation. As can be seen from Figure 5.3., U.S. aid was financing only 10

67. See Jacoby, pp. 228–30, on which the following account is based.

percent of Taiwan's imports of goods and services in 1964, and by 1969 this had dwindled away to nothing, aid received after 1965 mainly reflecting the backlog of commitments made earlier.

Although some were uneasy when the crutches were removed that had helped to sustain them for some fifteen years, the Chinese government remained confident. The strong balance of payments in 1963–64 encouraged it to liberalize more imports. Measures had already been taken to attract private foreign investment and, according to Jacoby,[68] more was now done to welcome such investment from Japan. Loans were obtained from the Japanese government, from the World Bank, and from the U.S. Export-Import Bank. Although these were all very helpful, much the most important growing source of foreign exchange was Taiwan's own exports of industrial products. Thus, from 1965 to 1976 inclusive, private long-term capital inflow financed on average only 7 percent of total imports of goods and services, and the loans mentioned from 1965 to 1972 inclusive financed only 4 percent. Meanwhile, exports of goods and services financed on average 99 percent of imports of goods and services from 1965 to 1976 inclusive.[69] Hence, over this period Taiwan was on average paying its own way virtually completely, the surplus foreign exchange resulting from the inflow of capital being used, for the most part, to build up her foreign exchange reserves—which even so, because of the very rapid growth in trade, failed to keep pace with imports (see Table 5.10).

In fact, after 1963–64, the authorities were never seriously worried about the balance of payments. Imports were liberalized and, although this was not a smooth and continuous process, but tended to follow periods when the balance of payments was unusually strong (1963–64 and 1970–73), this was probably more because of a desire to counter the inflationary effects of the surplus than the result of any lessening of concern with the balance of payments. The situation was very different from that during the 1950s.

Foreign exchange reserves rose in nearly every year from 1966 to 1973 (Table 5.10), and, even if they could not keep up with the growth in imports, the underlying situation was very healthy. Exports were becoming increas-

68. Jacoby, p. 230.

69. See Figure 5.3. The data for the loans are from successive issues of CIECD, *Annual Report on Taiwan's Economy,* and data beyond 1972 are not given. It is sometimes alleged that Taiwan's exports benefited greatly from the Vietnam War during this period. Exports to Vietnam rose from 2 percent of total exports in 1960 to 6 percent in 1961, 10 percent in 1962, where they more or less remained until 1966, when they climbed to a temporary peak of 16 percent. Thereafter, with the deescalation of the war, they fell back rapidly to under 5 percent in 1970 and under 1 percent in 1973. Hence, although the war undoubtedly boosted exports to begin with, it played no direct part in their continuing rapid growth after 1966. By providing a market for the output of some "heavy" industries (cement, metals, chemicals, transport equipment, machinery, paper) at an early stage, it may have indirectly helped their subsequent development and export to other markets.

ingly diversified, and so the balance of payments was less vulnerable to the vagaries of the world sugar market, and Taiwan's credit-worthiness steadily improved. Both these factors reduced the need for reserves.

Taiwan benefited greatly from the generous terms on which U.S. aid had been given. As a result, she did not emerge from the years of heavy aid with a debt-servicing problem. Eighty-four percent of all the economic aid she had received was in the form of grants, and the remaining 16 percent consisted of loans at low interest rates and with long periods of repayment. Some interest rates were as low as 0.75 percent per annum and none was higher than 4.0 percent per annum. Repayment periods ranged up to thirty-six years. Inflation has further reduced the burden of repayment. Consequently, Taiwan's debt service ratio as calculated by the World Bank is among the lowest of the developing countries and shows no tendency to rise.[70]

The exchange rate, for all practical purposes, remained fixed at N.T.$40 per U.S. dollar from 1960 to 1972 inclusive. When the U.S. dollar was devalued in December 1971, the Taiwan dollar followed it down, and this increased the competitiveness of Taiwan's exports and contributed to the large surplus on goods and services in 1972. In February 1973, however, when the U.S. dollar weakened further, the Taiwan dollar was slightly upvalued against it to a rate of N.T.$38 per U.S. dollar, where it still remains. This upvaluation against the U.S. dollar meant that on average the Taiwan dollar remained more or less unchanged against the currencies of its trading partners during 1973. Subsequent changes in this "effective" exchange rate during 1974 and 1975 were also quite small.[71]

The surplus on goods and services increased further in 1973, as Taiwan responded to the surge in world demand. However, these large surpluses in 1972 and 1973, and the rapid rise in world prices, eventually had their effect, and inflation accelerated in 1973. In 1974 the volume of exports fell, largely because of Taiwan's reduced competitiveness (see Figure 5.5 and Table 5.16). The strong upward trend in Taiwan's share of world exports of manufactures was reversed for the first time since 1957 (Figure 5.2). The volume of imports, however, still reflecting the boom of 1972–73, continued to rise. The terms of trade, which had deteriorated appreciably since 1970, continued to worsen (Table 5.11). The combined result was a very large deficit on goods and services in 1974, financed almost entirely by an inflow of private capital,

70. The ratio of service payments on external public debt to exports of goods and nonfactor services for Taiwan in 1974 was only 2.7 percent, compared with 3.2 percent in 1967. Many other developing countries had much higher ratios in 1974, for example: South Korea 10.5 percent; Philippines 5.3 percent; India 15.9 percent; Pakistan (including Bangladesh) 15.3 percent; Sri Lanka 11.2 percent; Argentina 16.2 percent; Brazil 15.2 percent; Mexico 18.4 percent. See *World Bank Annual Report 1976* (Washington, D.C., 1976), pp. 104–5.

71. In December 1974, the Korean won was devalued from 399 to 484 won per U.S. dollar. For a time, this worsened Taiwan's competitive position, but in a few months the effect was canceled out by inflation in Korea and falling prices in Taiwan.

Table 5.11. Terms of Trade, 1951–1976 (export prices divided by import prices, 1971 = 100)

Year	Index	Year	Index	Year	Index
1950	...	1960	88	1970	102
1951	106	1961	93	1971	100
1952	106	1962	99	1972	97
1953	104	1963	112	1973	93
1954	100	1964	117	1974	89
1955	103	1965	97	1975	89
1956	103	1966	96	1976	91
1957	109	1967	99		
1958	98	1968	101		
1959	95	1969	102		

Source: DGBAS, *National Income of the Republic of China, December 1976* (Taipei, December 1976), pp. 138–41, implicit price deflators for exports and imports of merchandise, freight, and insurance. These figures differ markedly (and especially before 1959) from the terms of trade estimated for exports of merchandise f.o.b. and imports c.i.f. as in Ministry of Finance, *Monthly Statistics of Exports and Imports* (June 1976), for reasons which are unclear, although it is believed that the series given here is preferable. For 1952, for example, the corresponding Ministry of Finance figure is 83, as compared with 106 above.

mostly short-term. The government measures described in Chapter 4 (subsequently reinforced by the fall in exports and the balance-of-payments deficit) brought inflation to a halt early in 1974. Later in the year, however, the world recession gathered momentum, and Taiwan's exports continued to fall into 1975, but by now the volume of imports was falling very sharply, and so the deficit on goods and services was reduced. Later in 1975, exports recovered, and they rose strongly in 1976. Imports rose less rapidly, and in 1976 a surplus on goods and services was once again achieved.

Some Aspects of Taiwan's Trade

Trade in Relation to Total Product

Taiwan's trade has risen much faster than her GDP since World War II, as indicated in Figure 5.1 and Table 5.12. An increasing ratio of trade to income has been a worldwide phenomenon, but the increase for Taiwan is particularly striking, the ratio having nearly quadrupled between the early 1950s and the mid-1970s. Why has this occurred? Does it represent a return to a normal state, or is Taiwan's ratio now abnormally high?

Prewar figures suggest that there has been a return to normal—if the prewar situation *was* normal (which it probably was not). In 1935–37, exports were about 44 percent of GDP and imports 33 percent, the average for both together being 38 percent.[72] There was also an average of 38 percent in 1975. The

72. See footnote 4 for sources used. Hsieh and Lee's estimates of net national product have been adjusted upward by 17 percent to give an estimate of GDP, this being the ratio in 1951. This probably understates GDP, however, inasmuch as net factor income paid abroad before the war was quite sizable. Hence the true ratio with GDP could well have been lower than 38 percent.

Table 5.12. Ratios of Exports and Imports to GDP, 1951–1976 (percent)

Year	Export ratio	Import ratio	Year	Export ratio	Import ratio
1951	8.8	13.7	1964	16.9	16.7
1952	8.5	14.7	1965	15.8	19.6
1953	8.6	12.0	1966	16.9	19.7
1954	5.8	13.1	1967	17.5	22.1
1955	6.4	10.5	1968	18.4	21.1
1956	8.5	13.9	1969	21.4	24.8
1957	9.1	13.0	1970	26.1	26.9
1958	8.6	12.5	1971	31.5	28.3
1959	11.0	16.2	1972	38.9	32.8
1960	9.5	17.2	1973	43.9	37.3
1961	11.1	18.3	1974	40.7	50.6
1962	11.3	15.7	1975	36.0	40.4
1963	15.1	16.5	1976	47.2	44.1

*The ratios in the early years depend upon which of the multiple rates (or what combination of them) is used to convert U.S. dollars into N.T. dollars. The rates used by the customs, which are those underlying the figures given above, are the 'Trade' ones in Table 5.3. Alternative rates are also given there.

Sources: Exports (f.o.b) and imports (c.i.f.) in N.T. dollars from EPC, *Taiwan Statistical Data Book, 1976,* p. 177, for 1952–75. 1951 figures from *Industry of Free China,* May 1959, pp. 89–93. 1976 from Ministry of Finance, *Monthly Statistics of Export and Imports, The Republic of China,* March 1977, no. 91, June 10, 1977, p. 15. GDP at market prices from DGBAS, *National Income of the Republic of China, December 1976,* p. 11.

ratios for 1973 (41 percent), 1974 (46 percent), and 1976 (46 percent) were, perhaps, abnormally high, but, on this way of looking at the matter, 1975 was "normal."

The prewar ratio could have been abnormally high because Taiwan was a colony of Japan, dependent on her for most manufactures and supplying her with foodstuffs. Hence it seems worthwhile to compare Taiwan's current ratio with that of other countries. Excluding small countries (population less than seven million) as being liable to be particularly affected by "special factors," Taiwan's ratio in 1973 (before the oil crisis had time to show its effects) appears to have been the fourth highest (after Belgium, Malaysia, and the Netherlands) out of forty-three countries for which the data were available. Let us now consider what factors might account for this very high ratio.

First, it is well known that small countries have higher ratios than large ones. Size can be measured either by population or by GNP. I have followed Hans Linnemann's *An Econometric Study of International Trade Flows* in taking population as the most relevant measure and have used his adjustment factor (based on a cross-section study of some eighty countries' trade in 1958–60) to correct for size.[73]

73. H. Linnemann, *An Econometric Study of International Trade Flows* (Amsterdam, 1966), p. 206. Linnemann's adjustment consists of multiplying the trade ratio of Country A by the ratio of its population to that of Country B, raised to the power of 0.25, in order to make A's ratio comparable to B's. Thus, a country with sixteen times Taiwan's population would have its trade ratio doubled to make it comparable to Taiwan's on account of this factor.

I also used his estimates to correct for a second relevant factor, distance. The more remote a country is from its trading partners, the smaller one would expect its trade ratio to be.[74] Despite corrections for both factors, Taiwan's trade ratio remains abnormally high. In fact, it becomes the second highest (after Malaysia) of the forty-three countries.

I have no means of correcting for other relevant factors, and so can only list them. A third factor is the existence of restrictions on trade, and it seems likely that Taiwan's relatively liberal trade regime accounts to some extent both for her high ratio in 1973 and (as a result of increasing liberalization) for the increase in the ratio since World War II.

A fourth factor is the commodity composition of trade. Countries with a strong comparative advantage in a few primary products often have high ratios, and this may help to explain Taiwan's high prewar ratio. It can no longer do so, but another factor has taken its place. Exports of sugar and rice have given way to exports based on imported materials: clothing, textiles, electronics, plywood, and others. The direct import content of electronics exports is especially high.

A final factor, mentioned by Linnemann,[75] is the tendency for official exchange rates to understate the real GNPs of poorer countries relative to richer ones. It has been estimated, for example, that India's GDP would be increased by a factor of three and a half relative to that of the United States in 1970 if an exchange rate based on direct price comparisons were used rather than the official exchange rate.[76] Since trade figures require no adjustment on this account, the ratios of trade to GNP for poorer countries would be reduced if their GNPs were increased on this account. This is unlikely to be an important explanation of Taiwan's high trade ratio in 1973 because its per capita GNP (using official exchange rates) was close to the median of the forty-three countries considered.[77]

The Commodity Composition of Trade and Taiwan's Comparative Advantage

The changing composition of exports and imports and of net exports is shown in Table 5.13. Comparing 1952–54 with 1973–75, we see that the

74. Ibid., pp. 26–30, 70–71, 184–87. The nature of the adjustment cannot be summarized briefly.

75. Ibid., pp. 203–9, discusses most of the factors considered here.

76. See I. B. Kravis et al., *A System of International Comparisons of Gross Product and Purchasing Power* (Baltimore, 1975), p. 8.

77. This also makes it unlikely that differences in per capita GNP could account for Taiwan's high ratio in 1973. Linnemann does not believe that such differences affect trade ratios (apart from the exchange rate point mentioned in the text). Thus, according to Linnemann, if two countries have the same population, but different incomes, their trade ratios will be the same (ignoring such other factors as distance and tariff preferences). Simon Kuznets, "Quantitative Aspects of the Economic Growth of Nations: IX. Level and Structure of Foreign Trade: Comparisons for Recent Years," *Economic Development and Cultural Change* 13, no. 1, pt. 2 (October 1964), 1–106, however, argues that the evidence shows that the country with the higher per capita income will have a higher trade ratio, a conclusion which Linnemann disputes (p. 14).

Table 5.13. Changes in the Commodity Composition of Trade

Item	1952–54			1973–75		
	Exports	Imports	Balance	Exports	Imports	Balance
	U.S.$ millions per annum					
Agriculture, forestry, fishing, food, beverages, and tobacco	102	51	51	812	963	−151
Minerals (mainly fuels)	4	12	−8	119	687	−568
Machinery and transport equipment*	0	29	−29	1164	1858	−694
Other manu-factures	6	104	−98	3043	1985	1058
Total†	112	197	−85	5144	5570	−426
	Percentages of total					
Agriculture, forestry, fishing, food, beverages, and tobacco	91	26		16	17	
Minerals (mainly fuels)	4	6		2	12	
Machinery and transport equipment*	0	15		23	33	
Other manu-factures	5	53		59	36	
Total†	100	100		100	100	

*Includes electrical machinery and apparatus.
†Includes commodities not classifiable into above sections.
Source: EPC, *Taiwan Statistical Data Book, 1976,* pp. 180–81.

share of unprocessed and processed foodstuffs (line 1, which also includes beverages, a little timber, and some manufactured tobacco) in exports has fallen drastically and that the corresponding share in imports has fallen much less. Taiwan has moved from a net exporter of these products (which was always her position before the war) to a net importer. The obvious explanation is her limited land resources and rapidly growing population. There has also apparently been a shift in demand from rice (home produced) to wheat (imported),[78] although it is not evident that this has reduced the export surplus because, by freeing land and labor devoted to rice, it could have allowed exports of other foodstuffs to increase.

The counterpart of the fall in the share of foodstuffs in total exports has

78. See W. Wou and B. C. Liu, "Wheat and Rice: An Investigation of Taiwan's Export and Import Problems," *Industry of Free China,* November 1974, who use statistical regression analysis to estimate income elasticities of demand for rice and wheat in Taiwan. They conclude that the income elasticity of demand for rice is negative, while that for wheat is positive.

been the rise in that of exports of industrial products, as is shown in Figure 5.4. The big shift in composition started after 1958, when the main foreign exchange reforms were introduced. Although this was to some extent caused by a fall in the price of sugar from a peak in 1957 to a trough in 1961, the main explanation is the combination of factors that led to the take-off of exports of industrial products. However, the recovery in the share of foodstuffs in 1963 and 1964 was caused by the doubling of the sugar price between 1962 and 1963–64.

Table 5.13 brings out three other important shifts. First, there was a big increase in net imports of fuels, exacerbated by the rise in oil prices after 1973. Second, despite the tremendous growth in exports of machinery (mainly electronics), imports increased by even more, so that Taiwan remained a big net importer. This was partly because of the high import content of electronic exports and partly because of the need to import machinery and equipment for investment in a rapidly growing economy. Third, the deficits in all the other categories of trade were, in a sense, financed by the surplus in "other" manufactures. This statement should not be misinterpreted—for example, electronic exports earned a surplus that was just as real as that of clothing exports. All it means is that exports of "other" manufactures grew by much more than did imports, unlike the first three categories of goods distinguished in the table. This suggests that Taiwan's comparative advantage mainly resided (and developed) in the "other" group of goods: textiles, clothing, travel goods, footwear, plywood, furniture, and a host of miscellaneous manufactures. However, since the four categories are very big, it is not surprising to find within the first three many important examples of goods in which Taiwan clearly had (or developed) a comparative advantage, including fishing products, certain canned foodstuffs, bananas, and electronic goods.

On what did this comparative advantage depend? No single answer can comprehend the complexity of the situation. Perhaps the most important ingredients were human skills and know-how, cheap labor, climate and soils, geographical location, and historical ties. Econometric attempts to explain comparative advantage have generally shown that many different hypotheses explain part of it.[79] It is multifaceted or multidimensional. Nevertheless, it is interesting to consider one hypothesis which is of long standing and lends itself to relatively easy statistical measurement, namely, that a low-wage country like Taiwan should export relatively labor-intensive goods and import relatively capital-intensive ones.

79. See G. C. Hufbauer, "The Impact of National Characteristics and Technology on the Commodity Composition of Trade in Manufactured Goods," in *The Technology Factor in International Trade*, ed. R. Vernon (New York, 1970), and also the review by R. M. Stern, "Testing Trade Theories," in *International Trade and Finance*, ed. P. B. Kenen (Cambridge, England, 1975).

Both Kuo-shu Liang and Ching-ing Hou Liang and Lin[80] have investigated the relation between factor-intensity and trade for Taiwan. The Liangs take four indicators: the ratio of fixed assets[81] per worker for 1966 and 1971, the ratio of the number of skilled and semiskilled[82] workers to the total number of workers for 1966 and 1971, value-added per employee at domestic market prices for 1969, and the same at world market prices.[83] For fixed assets per worker and the skill ratio, the indirect as well as the direct requirements for each industry are added together, making the usual assumption of constant returns to scale. The Liangs show that fixed assets per worker, the skill ratio, and value-added per employee at world market prices give similar rankings of industries.[84] Industries are divided into four categories: (1) export industries— those exporting more than one-tenth of their gross output and importing less than one-tenth of domestic consumption; (2) import industries—those importing more than one-tenth of domestic consumption and exporting less than one-tenth of gross output; (3) export-and-import-competing industries—those both exporting more than one-tenth of their gross output and importing more than one-tenth of their domestic consumption; and (4) other industries, which may be called "nontraded goods industries." The Liangs give weighted averages of fixed assets per worker and the skill ratio for these groups, using production weights. They also give value-added per employee for each. Export industries appear to have significantly lower ratios of fixed assets per worker than import industries, and their skill ratio is on average somewhat lower. At domestic prices their value-added per employee is lower, but at world market prices it is higher, according to these estimates.

The Liangs also compute fixed assets per worker and skill ratios for exports to different areas. Exports to developed areas have markedly lower fixed assets per worker ratios and also somewhat lower skill ratios. These are very interesting results, which suggest that factor-intensities play a part in deter-

---

80. Kuo-shu Liang and Ching-ing Hou Liang, "Exports and Employment in Taiwan," in Institute of Economics, Academia Sinica, *Conference on Population and Economic Development in Taiwan* (Taipei, 1976). K-S. Liang also discussed the relation between factor-intensity and trade in K-S. Liang, "Taiwan's Industrial Development and Foreign Trade in Manufactures," in National Taiwan University, *Economic Essays* 1 (November 1970), and in K-S. Liang, "Trade and Employment in Taiwan," in *Sino-American Conference on Manpower in Taiwan* (Taipei, 1972). Lin, pp. 131–37; also Ken C. Y. Lin, "Industrial Development and Changes in the Structure of Foreign Trade: The Experience of the Republic of China in Taiwan, 1946–66," International Monetary Fund, *Staff Papers* (July 1968).

81. These were derived from industrial census data for most industries; they exclude land and are presumably book values, although this is not stated in the source.

82. Most of the data are from the industrial censuses. Skilled and semiskilled workers include skilled workers, technicians and managerial and assistant personnel.

83. Estimates of effective protection were made for 731 commodities, allowing for tariffs and various forms of export subsidy. Apparently 150 direct price comparisons were made.

84. The Liangs do not give the rank correlation coefficients relating value added per employee at domestic market prices to the other indicators.

mining the structure of trade.[85] They are in agreement with the results reported by Lin.

I undertook an analysis on rather different lines than those reported above. I used only one of the Liangs' four indicators, namely, value-added at domestic prices per employee, but this is related to *net* exports or imports by industries, not just to gross exports or imports, and I considered trade in natural-resource-dominated goods separately. Both of these differences are important, as is shown below. The reasons for choosing value-added per employee are those given by Hal Lary, who pioneered this approach. This indicator combines both physical and human capital in one measure and also measures their contributions correctly in flow terms. In other words, industries with relatively high value-added per employee in Taiwan are those for which either gross profits per employee are relatively high (so physical capital per employee is relatively high) or wages per employee are relatively high (so the workers are relatively highly skilled on average), or both, "relatively" in all cases referring to other industries in Taiwan. The hypothesis tested is that exports come from industries for which physical or human capital per employee is relatively low, whereas imports substitute for the output of industries that, in Taiwan, require relatively much physical or human capital per employee.

The other measures of capital- or skill-intensity suffer from various disadvantages. Thus fixed assets per worker omits human capital and inventories and does not distinguish between longer- or shorter-lived capital.[86] In addition, estimates of fixed assets are particularly unreliable. The skill ratio ignores physical capital and relies on classifications that probably are not uniform and are in any case crude.[87] On the other hand, value-added per employee also has defects. Similar factors may receive different rewards in different industries because of market imperfections, and these, rather than differences in quantities of human or physical capital, could account for some of the differences observed. I am not persuaded that value-added for this purpose should be measured at world prices, rather than at domestic prices.[88]

85. Both the Liangs and Lin recognize that other factors are important. The greater capital-intensity of exports to developing countries, for example, might be partly caused by the fact that heavy transport costs for cement and refined petroleum, both very capital-intensive, limit their markets, for the most part, to countries fairly close to Taiwan. Also, developing countries tend to impose very severe import restrictions on labor-intensive goods, such as garments, in order to protect their own industries.

86. The same net present value of capital (or book value, insofar as that is a good approximation to it) may earn very different quasi-rents (gross profits) depending on its rate of depreciation.

87. Workers must be classified either as skilled or unskilled, whereas there is in reality a spectrum of skills (and earnings).

88. If domestic markets were perfect, value-added at domestic, not world, prices would correctly measure the quantities of factor inputs, weighted by their common prices. Value-added at world prices is, however, of interest in making international comparisons.

Table 5.14. Value-Added Per Employee in 1971 (N.T.$ thousands)

Industry group	Total (1)	Exports (2)	Imports (3)	Export surplus (4)	Import surplus (5)
Primary products	21.8	25.2	27.5	24.1	27.4
Food, drink, and tobacco manufactures	44.0	32.6	66.2	29.5	47.5*
Other manufactures	49.6	41.2	54.7	37.1	62.2
Total all commodities	33.0	36.7	38.4	32.5	36.7

*This figure is particularly uncertain as net imports were very small.
Source: Economic Planning Council, *Taiwan Input-Output Tables, Republic of China, 1971* (June 1974), Table IV. 'Value-added' is rows 77–79 less 'Government', row 79. 'Value-added in export' is 'export share' multiplied by 'value-added'. 'Export share' is column 80 'export' divided by 'total input', row 01–79, less 'Government'. 'Employment in export' is 'Employees', row 80, multiplied by 'export share'. 'Value-added per employee in export' is 'value-added in export' divided by 'employment in export.' 'Import share' is 'import', column 85, plus 'net import duty', column 86, all divided by 'domestic product', column 83. The calculation of 'value-added in import' and 'employment in import' then proceeds as for export, but using 'import share' instead of 'export share'. 'Export surplus' equals 'value-added in export' less 'value-added in import', if this is positive. If it is negative, it equals 'import surplus'. Corresponding employment figures are obtained by taking the difference between 'employment in export' and 'employment in import'.

In any case, no estimates of the former were available for the year chosen (1971). The main results are summarized in Table 5.14.

In order to explain the table, consider the last line in it. The first entry, N.T.$33.0 thousand, shows value-added (excluding indirect taxes) per employee in all commodity-producing industries in 1971. The next entry, N.T.$36.7 thousand, shows the same ratio, but this now refers to export production only. The figure has been arrived at by assuming that the proportion of value-added, or employees, devoted to export production in each of the sixty-one commodity-producing industries in the source was equal to the ratio of exports from that industry to gross production of the industry (total sales, including increases in stocks and intraindustry sales, but excluding indirect taxes). The next entry, N.T.$38.4 thousand, is similarly constructed, under the assumption that the proportion of value-added or employees "saved" by imports was equal to the ratio of imports inclusive of duties to gross production of the industry inclusive of indirect taxes. We thus have estimates of value-added and numbers of employees *directly*[89] devoted to exports or saved by imports. Taking the differences for each of the sixty-one industries yields either an export surplus or an import surplus for each. The entry in column 4 shows the sum for the industries with an export surplus; that for column 5

89. Indirect inputs have been ignored throughout. These are frequently taken into account in studies of this kind (see the Liangs' study referred to above, and, of course, Leontief's pioneering study of U.S. trade). However, particularly in a very open economy like that of Taiwan, it is by no means clear that they should be, since many of the indirect requirements are imported and their prices are determined in world markets and cost structures are not determined by domestic factor endowments. It seemed best, therefore, to focus attention on the cost structures of the activities directly involved in exporting or import substitution.

shows the sum for the industries with an import surplus. The other lines in the table are just the same, but refer to particular groups of industries.

What does Table 5.14 show? The last line does indicate a slightly higher figure for value-added per employee in imports than in exports, and the difference is slightly increased if we consider import-surplus industries versus export-surplus ones. But these differences are rather small, and might be attributable to inevitable inaccuracies in the basic data. However, if we look at the other three lines, we can see at once that the smallness of the differences is entirely due to the inclusion of primary products among the industries. One would expect that value-added per employee would not provide a good explanation for trade in primary products. The availability of arable land, forests, and mineral resources and the climate are all of the first importance here and are not measured by our indicator. I had thought that the same might have been true for processed foodstuffs, since the location of these industries is heavily dependent on the availability of primary products close at hand. However, the table does show a marked difference between value-added per employee in exports and imports here.[90] The difference is also pronounced for all other manufactures, especially for export-surplus and import-surplus industries. Hence we may conclude that Taiwan has tended to export products that use relatively little human or physical capital and to import those that use relatively much of both.

This conclusion is further reinforced by the fact that the assumption on which the estimates in Table 5.14 are constructed is that each industry's products are homogeneous and require the same amount of labor and nonlabor inputs. In reality, many of the imports would require much more human or physical capital per dollar (if they had to be made in Taiwan) than those products actually made there. Indeed, some imports could hardly be made at all. Consequently, there is little doubt that Taiwan's trade has enabled her to economize very greatly on her scarce supplies of human and physical capital and probably also on land.

The Reasons for Taiwan's Export Success

Costs, Prices, and Profitability

My approach to answering the question, "Why did Taiwan's exports grow so fast?" is to look for reasons that made exporting very profitable and then to discuss why high profitability in turn encouraged rapid growth.

Profitability can be high if costs are low relative to prices. The relative importance of different costs in three major categories of Taiwan's exports—

---

90. The entry for import-surplus industries of N.T.$47.5 thousand is particularly unreliable because the category is very small.

Table 5.15. The Structure of Costs in Textiles, Apparel and Electronics in Taiwan, 1971 and the United States, 1967 (percentages of gross output)

Country and industry	Traded inputs (1)	Nontraded inputs (excl. value-added) (2)	Wages (3)	Indirect taxes (4)	Gross profits (5)	Total (6)
A. Taiwan						
1. Textiles	70.1	7.8	8.3	2.3	11.6	100.0
2. Apparel	70.1	8.4	16.2	0.6	4.7	100.0
3. Communication equipment	65.7	8.5	11.3	3.8	10.8	100.0
B. United States						
4. Textiles	58.8	11.3	21.2	0.5	8.4	100.0
5. Apparel	53.8	9.2	30.2	0.4	6.4	100.0
6. Radio, television communication equipt.	40.5	14.5	36.4	0.6	8.1	100.0
7. Electronic components and accessories	40.7	14.6	38.3	0.6	5.9	100.0

Sources: A: Economic Planning Council, *Taiwan Input-Output Tables, Republic of China, 1971* (June 1974), pp. 124, 134, 137. 'Textiles' is the sum of 'artificial fibres', 'artificial fabrics', 'cotton fabrics', and 'woolen and worsted fabrics'. 'Apparel' is miscellaneous fabrics and apparel, accessories'. 'Traded inputs' includes inputs from agriculture, forestry, fishing, mining, and manufacturing (lines 01 to 61 in the source). 'Indirect taxes' is line 79 in the source and includes other government revenues. 'Gross profits' is the sum of 'operating surplus' and 'depreciation'.
B: U.S. Department of Commerce, "Input-Output Structure of the U.S. Economy: 1967," *Survey of Current Business* (February 1974), pp. 45–46. 'Textiles' is 'broad and narrow fabrics, yarn, and thread mills' (industry no. 16 in the source) and excludes 'miscellaneous textile goods and floor coverings' and also 'miscellaneous fabricated textile products'. 'Traded inputs' include those from industries no. 1 to 64, similar to Taiwan.

textiles, apparel, and electronics[91]—are shown in Table 5.15, where a comparison is made with the structure of costs for similar industries in her principal export market, the United States.

The overwhelming importance of traded materials and components in total costs in Taiwan is clear. Exportation is possible only if these inputs can be purchased by the export manufacturer at a price close to or below those paid by his main competitors. Any appreciable taxes on these inputs or any premiums resulting from import controls (assuming the manufacturer must buy or can sell at premium-inclusive prices) are likely to make exporting unprofitable. Thus for the industries shown in Table 5.15, a tax or premium of only 17 percent on all traded imports would eliminate the average gross profit margin on all three industries, assuming that prices could not be increased nor other cost elements reduced. Since the gross profit margin must cover the rent of land and depreciation before it starts contributing to interest and profit, a much smaller tax or premium would knock out most exports of these products. This underlines the importance of the tax rebate system and of the free availability of imported materials and components to would-be exporters.

91. Radio, television, other communications equipment, and electronic components and accessories are all in the category of "electronics."

Transport costs could also be important. Although these may add only a few percentage points to the cost of imported materials,[92] that is still a large proportion of the available profit margin. There is thus a real advantage in being able to buy locally, if local producers' costs are as low as those of an overseas supplier (f.o.b.). As Taiwan's industrial base widened and as costs came down, the scope for local purchase at competitive prices increased. Increasing competitiveness in one sector therefore helped to increase it in others.

The share of traded inputs in total costs is much higher in Taiwan than in the United States, perhaps because of differences in the product mix, but probably at least partly because of lower ex-factory prices for the same goods in Taiwan than in the United States. Indeed, unless those prices were lower, it is difficult to see how exports could have increased so fast. It was precisely because Taiwan's goods were cheaper that U.S. buyers switched to them in preference to U.S. goods. Furthermore, ex-factory prices of exports in Taiwan had to be lower to bear the transport costs to the United States. If one makes the bold assumptions that prices of traded inputs for export goods were the same in Taiwan as in the United States, that the cost structures in Table 5.15, which in reality are for the whole of production, apply to that part of it destined for export, and, finally, that the same quantities of traded inputs per unit of output were needed in both countries, then it follows that prices in Taiwan were about 16 percent lower for textiles, 23 percent lower for apparel, and 38 percent lower for electronics.[93]

After traded inputs, the next largest category of costs is wages, and here the contrast between Taiwan and the United States is even more striking. The proportion of wages in total costs is only half or a third as high in Taiwan as in the United States. Using the same assumptions as in the last paragraph, and so allowing for lower prices in Taiwan, wage costs per unit of output in Taiwan work out at from 18 percent (for electronics) to 41 percent (for apparel) of their levels in the United States. *Wage-rates,* however, are a good deal lower than this. I reviewed the available evidence on hourly earnings in Taiwan, the United States, and some other countries in 1972.[94] Such comparisons are difficult to make, and the results are correspondingly uncertain. The follow-

92. For a discussion and some estimates of the ratio of transport costs to the values of some exports from developing countries see I. M. D. Little, T. Scitovsky and M. FG. Scott, *Industry and Trade in Some Developing Countries* (London, 1970), pp. 305–11.

93. On the assumptions stated, the ratio of output prices is inversely proportional to the ratio of the traded input coefficients. For example, textile prices in Taiwan: textile prices in United States = 58.8:70.1 = 0.84. If the prices of traded inputs were lower in Taiwan than in the United States, the ratio of output prices in Taiwan would be even smaller.

94. The main sources used were the *Yearbooks of Labor Statistics* of the International Labor Office for 1971 and 1975, and an article on the "General Characteristics of the Electronics Broad Industry Group in Taiwan," Ministry of Economic Affairs, *Economic Review* (March–April 1974).

ing figures give the orders of magnitude for typical hourly earnings, including fringe benefits, for workers in textiles and electronics in 1972 (since then all the other countries' wages have risen relative to those of the United States):

	U.S.$/hour
United States	2.75
Germany	1.90
Japan	1.20
South Korea	0.22
Taiwan	0.20

Thus wage rates were perhaps only 7 percent as high in Taiwan as in the United States in 1972. The difference between relative wage rates and wage costs per unit of output presumably reflects higher productivity resulting from better skills and more and better equipment in the United States, but undoubtedly in some particular processes the productivity of Chinese workers was just as high as that of U.S. workers. In some electronics operations, for example, it does not pay to design and build expensive equipment to save labor because the technology is changing so fast that such equipment would be obsolete before it had recouped its cost. Consequently, for these processes the cost advantage in undertaking them in Taiwan, rather than in the United States, is equivalent to virtually the whole of the wage-rate difference. There are then substantial profits to be earned by shifting such processes to Taiwan, as many U.S., Japanese, and other electronics companies have done. More generally, Taiwan's low wage rates gave her a comparative advantage in labor-intensive products and processes, with the result that she specialized in the production and export of these goods.

Another relevant factor regarding labor costs is hours and intensity of work. Obviously, the harder one works for a given hourly wage, the lower is one's labor cost. A survey of electronics firms undertaken in 1972 concluded that, in the judgment of the industrialists operating factories in various Asian countries and the United States, labor efficiency ("the time required to manufacture a specific product") was highest in Japan and Hong Kong and next highest in Taiwan, which ranked above the United States and South Korea. The Philippines, Singapore, Indonesia, Malaysia, and Thailand were placed lower still.[95] Taiwan's laborers work long hours, especially by comparison with those in North American and European countries. While this does not reduce hourly labor costs, it does reduce average capital costs per unit of output because it permits fuller utilization of capacity.

Two other categories of costs on which some comments may be given are

95. See "General Characteristics of the Electronics Broad Industry Group in Taiwan," p. 13.

nontraded inputs and capital.[96] The lower share of the former in Taiwan than in the United States may mainly reflect lower wages, since most of these costs consist of services (such as wholesaling) with a big wage element. The availability of power and water was, of course, essential, but their relative prices were probably not important because they represented a small fraction of costs for these industries.[97]

Capital is a more complicated problem. A distinction must be made between the cost of physical capital goods (machinery, equipment, buildings, and the like) and interest rates. As regards the former, building costs were certainly lower, but imported machinery would cost more, even if duties were exempted (as they were for "approved" projects or in the Export Processing Zones). On balance, these costs were probably a bit lower in Taiwan than in the United States, but there is no hard evidence.

I would also classify as capital costs, on a par with the costs of physical capital, all other costs of *change*,[98] including, for example, costs of migration and training of workers. The youthfulness of the Taiwan labor force and its good standard of education must have increased its adaptability and speed of learning and kept these costs low. Furthermore, the expansion of exports was heavily concentrated in particular industries where the techniques soon became familiar—clothing, textiles, canned foodstuffs, and plywood, for example. This concentration, in effect, reduced the cost of change since businessmen, managers, and technicians did not have to learn new and unfamiliar techniques—it was a case of "more of the same." In the electronics industries, where the techniques were new, the knowledge was to a great extent supplied by foreign investors, and so the cost of learning (and discovering) was not borne by the Taiwan economy. All this is an exemplification of the gains from specialization made possible by foreign trade. Had an inward-looking strategy been pursued, such specialization would not have been possible, and the capital costs of growth (properly defined to include both physical capital and all other costs of change) would have been much higher.

Interest rates were, of course, much higher in Taiwan than in the United States or Europe, but this should be regarded as a reflection of the generally high rate of return to investment and not a subtraction from it. A business that

96. I have nothing useful to add on indirect taxes beyond the remarks already made above. Their share was generally higher in Taiwan than in the United States (Table 5.15, column 4), but this may not have been true for exports; the figures in the table include output for the domestic market.

97. Thus electricity represented only 0.7 percent of total costs for apparel in 1971 and 0.6 percent for communications equipment (electronics). However, it was as much as 1.8 percent for artificial fibers and for cotton fabrics.

98. M. FG. Scott, "Investment and Growth," *Oxford Economic Papers*, 28, no. 3 (November 1976), 317–63.

was entirely self-financed would receive the whole of the "interest" as part of the return on its investment, and there seems no reason to suppose that a business that could borrow would earn any less on that part of the capital it had subscribed itself. Indeed, given the high average real rate of return, "gearing" of this kind would generally increase the owner's return.

Study of the relative costs of inputs in Taiwan and the United States thus makes it appear that they either cost about the same or else were cheaper in Taiwan—and very substantially so for direct and indirect labor. Of course, we are not treating the rate of return on capital as a cost here but rather are subtracting all other costs from revenues in order to deduce something about that rate of return. The entrepreneur is not merely someone who combines all other inputs, including capital, which he hires, and who receives "pure" profit as a result. He is an investor as well as an organizer, and I am trying to explain the return on his investment.

Changes in Relative Costs and Prices

Thus far we have considered relative costs and prices at a point in time, around 1967–72. We now review their development over time in relation to costs and prices in other countries—see Table 5.16 and Figure 5.5. Table 5.16 shows that export prices (measured in U.S. dollars) of manufactures from Taiwan moved quite closely in line with those of other countries over the period 1961[99] to 1973. They lagged a bit behind in 1972 but caught up in 1973 and outpaced world prices in 1974 (when, as Figure 5.2 shows, Taiwan's export share declined for the first time since 1957). However, in 1975 they seem to have fallen sharply, whereas world prices went on rising, so that Taiwan's competitive position must have strengthened considerably. After a lag, Taiwan's exports surged up, and her share rose once more in 1976 (Figure 5.2).

Bearing in mind that the index numbers in Table 5.16 refer to different bundles of goods and may also be constructed according to different systems of weighting, it is remarkable how closely the movements parallel each other from 1961 to 1971. Since then, exchange rate changes and the oil crisis have apparently led to large relative price movements, whose effects have yet to work their way through the system. The table suggests, however, that for Taiwan, until the last few years, export prices kept a more or less constant relation with those of her competitors.

Figure 5.5 shows wage costs per unit of output in manufacturing,[100] measured in U.S. dollars, for Taiwan, the United States, West Germany, Japan, and South Korea. There is a good deal of uncertainty about the figures, since

99. No data are available for Taiwan before 1961.

100. Index of wage costs per unit of output = index of hourly earnings divided by index of output per man hour, so far as data permit.

Table 5.16. Index Numbers of Export Prices of Manufactures in U.S. Dollars 1961–1976

	Twelve leading countries (1)	Taiwan (2)	South Korea (3)
1961	86	84.8	—
1962	86	86.4	—
1963	86	86.2	80.7
1964	87	90.6	82.5
1965	89	89.5	85.7
1966	90	91.3	93.5
1967	91	95.5	97.8
1968	91	96.4	100.8
1969	92	97.6	95.8
1970	100	100.0	100.0
1971	105	103.7	98.8
1972	113	104.4	99.9
1973	133	137.0	126.5
1974	162	177.8	160.2
1975	182	155.4	148.4
1976	183	165.9	164.5

Sources: Column 1: *National Institute Economic Review,* National Institute of Economic and Social Research, London, various issues. Column 2: Price indices for five groups of exports were obtained from Ministry of Finance, *Monthly Statistics of Exports and Imports, The Republic of China,* June 1976 and March 1977, pp. 9–10. The five groups were numbers 3, 5, 6, 7, and 8 of the Chinese Customs Classification: products of textile, leather, wood, paper, and related products; chemicals and chemical and pharmaceutical products; basic metals, metal products; miscellaneous manufactured products. It is believed that, in total, these correspond closely to SITC 5–8. The five price indices were combined using a Laspeyres price index, the values for the base period being exports of each group in 1971 as given in the *Statistical Yearbook of the Republic of China, 1975,* p. 147 (1971 was the base year for the price indices in the original source). The resulting index was then rebased to 1970 = 100 to make it comparable with the index number in column 1 and was converted into U.S. dollars using the exchange rate implicit in the figures of exports in terms of U.S. dollars and N.T. dollars as given in the source used for the price indices. This exchange rate is given in Table 5.3. Column 3: Unit value of total exports in U.S. dollars from Bank of Korea, *Monthly Economic Statistics,* various issues. In 1968 about 75 percent of total exports consisted of manufactures and in 1974 about 85 percent. However, in 1963 only about one-half were exports of manufactures. Consequently, in the earlier years this index is less comparable with those in columns 1 and 2.

different index numbers of earnings, manufacturing output, and employment can yield very different estimates of the rate of growth of wage costs per unit of output for Taiwan over this period (I have used what are thought to be the most reliable estimates). From 1953 to 1958, Taiwan's wage costs per unit of output fell markedly in relation to those of the United States, Germany, and Japan, mainly because of the devaluations of the N.T. dollar in 1955 and 1958. This must have increased Taiwan's potential profit margin on exports over this period very considerably. Some of this gain in competitiveness was eroded by inflation in Taiwan from 1958 to 1961, but, taking the whole span of years 1953 to 1971, there was a substantial fall in Taiwan's wage costs, especially vis-à-vis Japan and West Germany. After 1971 changes were more mixed. To begin with, Taiwan's costs remained stable, as did those of the United States, while those of Germany and Japan shot up when their currencies were revalued against the U.S. dollar. Then in 1974 it was the turn of

Taiwan's costs to shoot up. From 1974 to 1976 they remained remarkably stable, thus recovering some of the ground lost in 1974 vis-à-vis the three large countries.

Figure 5.5 also shows South Korea's wage costs; these are interesting both because of similarities in her experience to that of Taiwan and because she is a close competitor. Like Taiwan, South Korea secured a big decline in her wage costs as the result of devaluation; only she did so in 1961, later than in Taiwan. Since then her inflation has been more rapid, but she has resorted to further devaluations to prevent her costs in U.S. dollar terms from rising too fast.

No figures are available to illustrate the movement of material costs, but it is reasonable to assume that for traded goods these would have changed in line with material costs elsewhere apart from the question of taxes and premiums resulting from import control. These were greatly reduced as a result of the tax rebating system and liberalization of imports of materials at the end of the 1950s.

In sum, during the 1950s, as a result of the devaluations in 1955 and 1958, the introduction of tax rebates for exports in 1955, and the liberalization of imports of materials for exports in 1958–60, costs in Taiwan relative to costs abroad fell dramatically. The result was a very big increase in the potential profitability of exporting. From 1961 to 1971 the situation tended to improve further so that, at the outset of the world boom in 1972–73, profit margins on exports should have been very high. Since then the position has become more mixed, with profit margins on exports to the United States probably much reduced, those on exports to Japan possibly increased,[101] and profits (as opposed to margins) reduced by the fall in the volume of exports in 1974 and 1975, but recovering with their subsequent increase.

The Average Rate of Return

Can we say anything about the actual rates of return earned? This would be difficult for any country because accounting data for profits and assets are difficult to interpret, especially with inflation. For Taiwan, such data are not generally available. In default of anything better, national accounts data have been used to provide an average rate of profit for all enterprises in the economy, excluding household enterprises, where it is difficult to distinguish between profits and what are, essentially, payments for management or labor (for example, for farmers and very small businesses). This measure is based on the idea that profits, net of depreciation properly defined, should be ex-

---

101. This is suggested by the relative movements of costs in Japan and Taiwan. However, competition between exporters from Taiwan, with their profits being squeezed in their main export market in the United States, might have lowered profit margins even on sales to Japan. A similar result might have occurred because of competition between Taiwan and South Korea.

pected to grow in real terms only as a result of net investment.[102] If gross investment is equal to depreciation, net profits should be that amount the owner of a firm can take out of it, by way of dividends, and still expect to achieve the same real net profits in future years. If gross investment exceeds depreciation, so that there is positive net investment, net profits should be expected to grow in real terms. In a period of steady growth, we can then relate the increase in real net profits to the rate of net investment by the equation:

$$rI = \frac{dP}{dt}$$

where r is the rate of return, I is the rate of net investment, and dP/dt is the rate of increase of real net profits. Dividing through by P and rearranging gives:

$$r = \frac{P}{I} \cdot \frac{1}{P} \cdot \frac{dP}{dt}$$

or, in words, the rate of return equals the ratio of net profits to net investment, multiplied by the proportionate rate of growth of real net profits, which we will call g.

Estimation of the rate of return by this method thus requires estimates of the ratio of net profits to net investment and of g. In order to abstract from fluctuations due to numerous causes and to approximate more closely to the steady growth assumptions, averages over several years were grouped together. Net profits were deflated by the price index for private consumers' expenditure, as this seemed to give the most meaningful "real" profit figure with which a business should be concerned. The results for Taiwan and the United States (for comparative purposes) are in Table 5.17.

The figures show a much higher average rate of return in Taiwan than in the United States, especially before the oil crisis. The Taiwan figures include government enterprises (but not the income of government monopolies which are treated as indirect taxes), and it is possible that, if these could have been excluded, the rate of return of private enterprises would have been higher still. Whether rates of return in exporting would have been higher or lower than these averages is difficult to say. The rates of return are before deduction of corporation tax or income tax. Rates of return after taxes are difficult to estimate, but it is virtually certain that the differential between the Taiwan and U.S. figures would have been wider if taxes had been deducted.

The higher rate of return in Taiwan than in the United States was entirely due to the higher rate of growth. The ratio of profits to investment was lower;

102. For further discussion of the approach taken here, see Scott, "Investment and Growth."

Table 5.17. Average Rate of Return in Taiwan and the United States

Period	P/I	g % p.a.	r % p.a.
Taiwan			
1958–61 to 1964–67	1.4	13.3	18.0
1964–67 to 1971–74	1.2	11.6	13.9
1958–61 to 1971–74	1.3	12.4	15.8
United States			
1960–63 to 1969–72	2.4	4.3	10.1

Sources: DGBAS, *National Income of the Republic of China* (Taipei, December 1975), pp. 106–9, 112–13, 128–29; United Nations, *Yearbook of National Accounts Statistics,* various issues, 1970–74; U.S. Department of Commerce, *Business Statistics, 1973 Edition,* p. 8.

P/I is the average of the annual ratios of net profits to net investment, excluding households, for the period shown.

g is the average rate of growth of net profits, deflated by the price index for private consumers' expenditure, from the initial to the final group of years of the period shown.

$r = g \cdot P/I$ is the estimated average real rate of return (before tax).

in other words, firms there invested much more, in relation to their profits, than those in the United States. The uncertain quality of the figures, however, must be borne in mind. The figures of depreciation are especially uncertain and may not correspond well with the theoretical definition necessary for my formula to hold. The Taiwan figures are apparently based on firms' own accounts, without adjustment. In periods of rapid inflation, this will generally result in an understatement of true depreciation, and, if so, my estimates of the rate of return for Taiwan are probably too small.[103] Against this, firms may avail themselves of provisions for accelerated depreciation so as to reduce their tax bills. Another possibility is that gross profits are understated to avoid tax, which would result in an understatement of the rate of return.[104]

The above all refers to the private rate of return, not the social rate of return. High private rates of return are compatible with low social ones because the former can result from subsidies or other devices that shift income from the rest of the community to the profit receiver. But where that happens, high private rates of return are unlikely to lead to sustained high rates of growth for the whole economy. There is then no large social surplus that can be ploughed back to generate further growth. In the case of Taiwan, it seems

103. Since *P/I* is greater than one, if the same absolute amount is deducted from *P* as from *I*, to correct for the understatement of depreciation, the ratio *P/I* will be increased, and so therefore will *r* (assuming that the correction does not affect *g* to any appreciable extent).

104. The officially estimated national accounts contain no residual error, so cannot be used as evidence for the probable understatement of profits. Stock appreciation (inventory valuation adjustment) is deducted from profits, although no estimates of its magnitude are given. See DGBAS, *National Income of the Republic of China, 1975* Taipei, December 1975), pp. 182–83.

very likely that high private rates of return in exporting corresponded to high social rates as well. The reasons for this are similar to those given above in relation to the social profitabi;ity of the Export Processing Zones. The result was that high private rates of profit in exporting generated a sustained and rapid rate of growth.

Some Other Factors

The evidence indicates that prices and costs created profit opportunities and that high rates of profit were actually earned. The further conditions necessary for this may be listed as know-how, finance, confidence, and response.

Know-how may be subdivided into that relating to production and that relating to marketing, of which only the latter is discussed here. Knowledge of and contacts with foreign markets were to a great extent provided by the Japanese *shosha* (large trading houses) in the early 1960s. I was told that about 60 percent of Taiwan's textile exports were being marketed by the *shosha* at that time. They had trading relations with many countries, provided knowledge of customers and their requirements and trade finance, arranged shipping, handled documentation, and also took many of the risks. Unlike U.S. importers, who tended to specialize in a few products and to sell only in the United States, the Japanese dealt in many products and markets. Later in the 1960s and early 1970s, foreign buyers from the United States and Europe, including representatives of big chain stores, set up offices in Taiwan and dealt directly with the Chinese manufacturers, even with firms employing as few as a hundred workers. Each office might handle fifty or one hundred visits a year by buyers from the parent company expert in particular lines of business. They would specify their requirements and designs (for example, for garments) and obtain samples from different manufacturers, ordering from the cheapest, though considering also quality and continuity. A manufacturer who had been a good supplier would be told if his price quotations were getting out of line, so as to give him the opportunity to lower them.

If the manufacturer in Taiwan was a subsidiary of a foreign company, the parent company would generally provide the marketing service. This was true, for example, of many electronic companies that would both have their main components supplied by the parent and return the processed and assembled goods to that parent.

Not all marketing abroad was done by foreigners. At least one large Chinese trading company was set up, and Chinese engineering companies, for example, sent their own representatives abroad to get orders and provide after-sales servicing. Export associations (as for canned goods) dealt directly with buyers in overseas markets.

Finance and capital markets are dealt with in Chapter 4. It is obvious that high rates of profit are both a source of finance and a means of attracting outside funds because they provide cover against risk as well as enabling high rates of interest to be paid. It is a case of "to him that hath shall be given." Experience shows that faster growing firms tend to make more use of outside finance, and the importance of the latter should not be underestimated for Taiwan. Foreigners were probably not a very important source of finance except in the 1950s when U.S. aid (mostly lent to private firms out of counterpart funds) was important.[105]

Confidence is a factor frequently mentioned by businessmen, not susceptible to measurement, but no less important because of that. Investment depends on expectations of future profit. Businessmen must feel reasonably confident of political stability, of being allowed to keep most of the profits they succeed in earning, and, of course, of the economic situation itself developing in such a way as to enable them to earn a profit. In the 1950s, this confidence was weak, partly because of the uncertain political situation and partly because of the recently experienced high rates of inflation. Private investment faltered toward the end of the 1950s, but confidence was restored by the improvement in both the political and economic situation, and the prolonged boom in exports and investment followed. The world economic environment was very favorable, with rates of growth in most of the big countries that were high by historical standards and with world trade expanding faster than output. Confidence probably became excessive in 1973, when very large amounts of capital equipment were ordered, much from overseas, resulting in a 60 percent rise in the volume of imports of metal products in 1974 and excess capacity in several industries. The subsequent recession and profits squeeze must have shaken it severely.

Finally, given all the other factors, the pace at which change took place and exports and production grew depended on the response of businessmen and managers. Hard work by workers has been mentioned; there was also hard work by businessmen.

Some interesting parallels can be drawn between Taiwan and South Korea. In both, an initial sharp fall in wage costs per unit of output created the

---

105. According to balance sheet data compiled by the Central Bank for 945 firms with capital in excess of N.T.$1 million, in 1974 only 34 percent of total liabilities represented internal funds, the rest being external. The proportions were much the same for public as for private industries and for firms with capital under N.T.$10 million as for larger firms. In 1959, for a smaller sample of 286 firms with capital over N.T.$1 million, internal funds represented 42 percent of total liabilities. The data are, however, of uncertain reliability. The value of internal funds is, presumably, a residual between the total value of the firm and the value of external liabilities, and the former could easily be understated in the balance sheet. In 1974, foreign loans accounted for only 9 percent of all loans for the 945 firms surveyed, and all loans represented 33 percent of total liabilities. In 1959 U.S. aid loans accounted for 54 percent of all loans for the 286 firms surveyed, and all loans represented 39 percent of total liabilities.

Table 5.18. U.S. Economic Aid* to Taiwan, 1950–1968 (U.S.$ millions)

Year	Grants to public sector	Grants to private sector‡	Loans†	Total
1950	20.48	—	—	20.48
1951	61.60	—	—	61.60
1952	92.55	—	—	92.55
1953	84.32	—	—	84.32
1954	88.40	—	—	88.40
1955	90.40	—	—	90.40
1956	65.15	—	—	65.15
1957	58.47	—	—	58.47
1958	82.00	4.92	—	86.92
1959	67.97	8.27	13.24	89.48
1960	84.78	4.38	11.47	100.63
1961	84.43	10.08	23.21	117.72
1962	42.40	13.36	18.08	73.84
1963	36.62	9.52	33.40	79.54
1964	16.74	7.47	23.40	47.61
1965	18.37	7.72	39.67	65.76
1966	6.91	4.99	30.58	42.48
1967	0.09	4.61	18.95	23.65
1968	4.90	1.84	—	6.74
Total	1006.58	77.16	212.00	1295.74

*Excluding direct forces support. See note to Table 5.19.
†Including program loans, development loans, and imports under PL 480-IV and part of PL 480-I.
‡Mainly unrequited transfers under PL 480 II and III.
Source: Central Bank, direct communication.

potential for highly profitable production of manufactures for export (Figure 5.5). In both, measures were taken that enabled manufacturers to buy imported materials at (or close to) world prices. In both, the political situation stabilized or became more secure. Finally, in both, a marked response by businessmen led to tremendous export growth.

The Role of U.S. Aid

In the 1950s and early 1960s, Taiwan received considerably more aid per head than the average population of the developing countries.[106] Table 5.18 shows the amounts received, and Table 5.19 shows that, during the eleven

106. Thus, taking the average of 1962 and 1963 (when aid to Taiwan was already beginning to decline), Taiwan received about 56 percent more net loan and grant aid (and about 100 percent more grant aid) per head from OECD and multilateral sources than did the average population of all developing countries, according to I. M. D. Little and J. M. Clifford, *International Aid* (London, 1965), Table 13, p. 66 (derived from the figures of net lending, grants, and population there given). Other measures of the importance of aid also show that Taiwan received much more than the main large developing countries (see, for example, the figures of aid in relation to imports in 1955–60, compared with Argentina, Brazil, Mexico, India, and Pakistan in Little, Scitovsky, and Scott, p. 53), but there were many small countries (and some not so small, including South Korea) that received more aid.

Table 5.19. U.S. Aid in Relation to GNP, Investment and Imports, 1951–1968 (percent)

Year	Aid/GNP at market prices (1)	Aid/Gross investment (2)	Aid/Imports of goods and services (3)
1951	5.1	35.6	39.6
1952	6.7	45.5	41.2
1953	5.7	41.0	39.3
1954	6.1	37.9	37.4
1955	7.1	53.8	43.4
1956	4.7	29.2	26.2
1957	3.6	22.8	21.8
1958	6.5	37.3	28.2
1959	6.8	36.2	30.0
1960	6.4	31.8	31.0
1961	6.7	33.8	32.0
1962	3.8	20.2	20.2
1963	3.6	20.5	19.1
1964	1.9	9.7	9.9
1965	2.3	10.1	10.6
1966	1.3	5.8	6.4
1967	0.6	2.6	2.7
1968	0.2	0.6	0.6
Average 1951–61	6.0	36.8	33.6

Source: Aid figures are from the Central Bank and are for calendar years, derived from the balance-of-payments accounts. They are gross receipts of economic aid (both gifts and loans) and do not include 'direct forces support', which was used for military construction and to purchase commodities and materials that were directly consumed by the military. It could be argued that this should be included in economic aid because, given the government's commitment to military expenditure, its effect was really to increase expenditure on economic development—and for this reason Neil H. Jacoby included it in economic aid (*U.S. Aid to Taiwan: A Study of Foreign Aid, Self-Help, and Development* [New York, 1966], pp. 42, 122). Over the whole period it accounted for only 8.5 percent of total economic aid (including itself). Aid figures in U.S. dollars have been converted into N.T. dollars for comparison with GNP and gross investment using the 'average' exchange rates for imports given in Table 5.3. For comparison with imports of goods and services no such conversion was necessary, as U.S. dollar figures from the balance of payments were used for both. GNP and gross investment are from DGBAS, *National Income of the Republic of China* (December 1975), pp. 13, 15.

years 1951–61, aid was typically 6 percent of GNP at market prices, 37 percent of gross investment,[107] and 34 percent of imports of goods and services (for the latter, see also Figure 5.2). After 1961, it tailed off. How important was it in explaining Taiwan's economic success?

Some answer this question by attributing most, or all, of Taiwan's, and for that matter South Korea's, rapid growth to the large amount of aid they

107. As is pointed out by Hsing, pp. 196, 198, these ratios understate the importance of aid inasmuch as the exchange rates used to convert it from U.S. dollars to N.T. dollars understate its market value very considerably. Thus, the differences between c.i.f. and domestic market prices for imported goods in 1953 given in Lin, p. 51, some of which I quoted above, could justify an exchange rate perhaps 50 percent greater in the early 1950s.

received. Their example, it is said, cannot be followed because the aid that was essential to them is not available to the same extent to other developing countries. Others take a diametrically opposite view and regard aid as unimportant or as positively harmful. We consider some of the arguments on both sides in what follows. My own view, for what it is worth, is that aid played a very important role in helping to control inflation in the early 1950s, and that this may have been essential for political stability. In addition, aid at least enabled the economy to recover and set off on its growth path substantially sooner than would otherwise have been possible. It may have done more than this by influencing the choice of economic policies at a crucial time, although the extent it did so is difficult for an outsider to judge. If it did, then, given the importance of that choice (on which see especially Chapter 7), its effects on economic growth were very substantial. Nonetheless, it was far from being both a necessary and sufficient explanation of Taiwan's economic success. Other heavily aided countries have not performed nearly as well, and some countries have performed well with less aid. In short, the truth lies between the extreme views: aid was important, but so were other factors.

In 1951, when military forces equaled 7.6 percent of Taiwan's civilian population and around 20 percent of the civilian labor force and the government's military expenditures equaled some 11 percent of GNP, the problem of balancing the budget without U.S. aid would have been acute. It was, indeed, this problem which had largely caused runaway inflation in the 1940s. The government had been able to finance itself and the balance-of-payments deficit to some extent by running down its gold reserve, but by the end of 1950 there was little left to run down (see Table 5.10). Inflation was reduced in 1950 from the astronomical levels of 1946–49, but, if aid had not started to flow in again, it is questionable whether the government would have remained in control of the situation. Thus, Jacoby says, "Without aid rapid inflation would have continued, and domestic savings would have been reduced to a point that would have made economic growth almost impossible. Indeed, without massive U.S. assistance the very survival of the Republic of China as an independent country was doubtful."[108] And K. Y. Yin says, "The timely arrival of U.S. aid was no less than a shot of stimulant to a dying patient. . . . The import in three years [i.e., three financial years ending 30 June 1953] of U.S.$150 million of daily necessities financed with aid funds greatly contributed to economic stabilization. This may be illustrated by the fact that while the Taipei wholesale index shot up by 3,400 percent in 1949, it rose by only about 300 percent in 1950, 66 percent in 1951 and 23 percent in 1952. Granted that other factors also contributed to this achievement in stabilization, it was evident that the main factor has been the arrival of substantial aid and its

108. Jacoby, pp. 118, 274, 151.

proper utilization.'' Hsing, after reviewing figures similar to those in Table 5.19, concluded, ''It can hardly be imagined that, in an economy devastated by war and with ensuing large trade deficits, any significant progress could have been made without foreign aid. This is not only true for Taiwan but also largely true for postwar Western Europe and Japan.''[109]

It seems fair to conclude that aid played a crucial role in helping to control inflation. Very high rates of inflation have not generally been consistent with political stability and had not been so in mainland China. Hence it must remain doubtful, as the quotation from Jacoby states, whether the Republic of China would have survived as such without aid.

Some countries, of course, suffered losses as great or greater than Taiwan in World War II and managed to recover and grow without aid. The Soviet Union is the leading case, but its situation was in some respects very different. It had a strongly entrenched and ruthless government that had just emerged victorious in a major war, instead of a government that had just suffered a major military defeat. It was not, like Taiwan, an open economy, normally reliant to an unusually large extent on foreign trade. Its population had not been suddenly swollen by immigrants speaking a different dialect (or dialects), many of whom were not directly productive because they were in the army. Finally, it did not have very rapid inflation. Hence, while economic and political stability might have been secured without aid, little imagination is needed to see that they might not.

Disregarding the question of inflation, let us assume that some solution could have been found without aid through heavier taxes combined with some cuts in defense expenditure and that despite such measures political stability could have been maintained. Comparing the actual outcome with some such hypothetical alternative, what would have been the difference in economic performance? Several authors have attempted to answer this difficult question, and their conclusions are interesting, although they should be regarded with a good deal of skepticism. All the quantitative estimates point to aid having had a large beneficial effect.

In the autumn of 1964, Neil H. Jacoby, then dean of the Graduate School of Business Administration at the University of California, Los Angeles, was invited by the administrator of the United States Agency for International Development to evaluate the effects of U.S. economic assistance on the development of the Republic of China over the period 1951 to 1965. He agreed on condition that he would have a free hand in formulating and carrying out the evaluation and that AID would permit publication of a book based on his research. Both conditions were accepted, and the book was published

---

109. K. Y. Yin, ''A Decade of U.S. Economic Aid and Economic Development in Taiwan,'' *Industry of Free China,* June 1961, pp. 16–17; Hsing, p. 198.

in 1966. It is the most careful study available of the question posed above, which he examined from several different aspects. We shall return to some of the qualitative conclusions he came to later, but our immediate concern is with his quantitative estimates of the effect of aid on economic growth, which are based on a simplified model of the Taiwan economy.

For the period 1951–64, Jacoby puts the actual growth rate of GNP at 7.9 percent per annum, and his "probable" estimate of the rate of growth without economic aid is 3.5 percent per annum, barely more than the 3.3 percent per annum increase in population. The level of GNP in real terms in 1964, assuming no economic aid, is put at 58 percent of its actual level. He thus estimates that, without economic aid, per capita GNP would more or less have stagnated, but not because of inflation or a breakdown in government because these are explicitly assumed away. The main reason is that Jacoby estimates that there would not have been enough foreign exchange to pay for more than a fraction of actual imports of capital goods. Most of the foreign exchange earned by exports, which he assumes would have grown at 7.5 percent per annum, as in 1951–56,[110] would have been needed to pay for imported materials and also (to a small extent) for some consumer goods. This is true despite assuming a fall in the ratios of both categories of imports to GNP as compared with their actual levels. Consequently, the brunt of the cut in imports would have had to fall on imports of capital goods which, in turn, would have reduced the investment ratio from the actual average of 18.4 percent to 7 percent. Since Jacoby assumes that the marginal capital-output ratio (2:1) would have been lower than its actual average level (2.5:1), the growth rate would not have fallen by as much as this cut in the share of investment.[111]

Other estimates have been made on similar lines and with similar results.[112] The basic approach is the "two-gap" model, with growth constrained either

110. Jacoby puts the actual growth in exports, 1951–62 (at constant prices), at 9.75 percent per annum. However, he points out that exports accelerated after 1956, when rehabilitation and stabilization had been achieved. With slower growth, this stage would not have been reached until about 1964, so he puts the "no-aid" growth rate of exports at 7.5 percent per annum, the rate achieved in 1951–56 (Jacoby, pp. 323–28).

111. The above account of Jacoby's "Probable Effect No-Aid Growth Model" is based on his Appendix E. Unfortunately, he does not make all his assumptions explicit. In particular, the precise relationship between imports of capital goods and gross domestic investment is unclear, although this is a key assumption.

112. Thus Kuo, p. 112, gives estimates of Net National Product (NNP) with no aid, showing a growth rate of 4.1 percent per annum, 1951–64. H. T. Lin, "U.S. Aid and Taiwan's Economic Development," in *Conference on Economic Development of Taiwan* (Taipei, June 1967), p. 306, put the no-aid growth rate as low as 2.8 percent per annum, 1951–65. A. M. Tang and K-S. Liang, "Agricultural Trade in the Economic Development of Taiwan," in *Trade, Agriculture and Development*, ed. G. S. Tolley and P. A. Zadrozny (Cambridge, Mass., 1974), adopt a similar "two-gap" approach and argue that Taiwan's growth would have been severely constrained by foreign exchange availabilities without U.S. aid, but do not estimate "no-aid" growth rates.

by a shortage of foreign exchange or by a shortage of domestic savings. For Taiwan, the former is held to be relevant over this period. Since U.S. aid financed around a third of Taiwan's imports (Table 5.19), the bulk of which consisted of materials necessary to support production or else capital goods to make it grow, it is hardly surprising that application of the "two-gap" approach leads to the conclusion that aid had a big effect on growth.

I am not sympathetic to the "two-gap" model if it is used, as it sometimes is, to predict growth or to argue that a certain quantity of aid is necessary to achieve a given rate of growth in a normal situation. The assumptions that have to be made (that exports cannot be increased beyond certain levels, that the ratio of domestic investment to imports of capital goods is fixed, and the like) are then unrealistic. Concerning the situation confronting Taiwan in 1950–51, however, there is some virtue in the approach. The structural changes that had to be made to cope with the influx of population from the mainland and the very heavy military expenditures would have made it very difficult to raise either exports or domestic investment without aid. Jacoby believes that, even if aid had been cut, the government would not have cut military expenditure.[113] And even if they had, since the bulk of it went to pay the armed forces, the result might have been to increase unemployment or underemployment.[114] Without complementary imported materials, domestic output of some industries would have suffered. In this situation, even supposing that political stability could have been maintained, it is doubtful whether private investors would have wanted to invest very much. Confidence would have been totally lacking. Hence, without wishing to name a precise figure, I believe that aid probably made a big difference to the performance of the economy in those years. This is the opinion of a great many people who lived through them and also of those who have studied the situation since, and it seems right.

However, there are those who disagree with this view, and we now turn to consider some of their arguments. Quite a number of people have become disillusioned by aid or have always been skeptical of its effects on economic development. Because Taiwan is one of the most frequently cited cases of a successful aid recipient, it is important to see whether it is really a case that can withstand a critical analysis.

One of the main points made by the aid critics has been that aid tends to

113. Jacoby, p. 122. He points out that "the U.S. repeatedly, and unsuccessfully, tried to persuade the Chinese government to reduce military spending during the latter half of the aid period."

114. Ibid., pp. 124–25. He estimates that if both aid and military expenditure had been eliminated, the growth rate for 1951–65 would have been 5.2 percent per annum—still much lower than what was achieved, although aid was a smaller fraction of GNP than was military expenditure.

reduce domestic savings and therefore the rate of growth.[115] Regarding Taiwan, this view might appear to derive support from the fact that the ratio of domestic savings to GNP rose markedly in the 1960s, just when aid declined. But there is no reason to suppose that the main cause of the rise in the domestic savings ratio was the fall in U.S. aid. The rate of growth of GNP started to accelerate in the early 1960s, which is also when the domestic savings ratio started to rise. Several studies suggest that savings ratios depend upon the rate of growth of income; therefore it is plausible to suppose that the rise in the savings ratio in the 1960s was at least partly caused by that acceleration. Another factor was probably the reduction of inflationary expectations, which would have increased the real rate of return expected on savings denominated in terms of money. Admittedly, government savings (net of transfers received from abroad) also increased markedly, and here the ending of aid was undoubtedly a factor. However, the major part of the increase in savings in the 1960s was private.[116]

It has been argued that, if aid had been lower, defense expenditure would have been cut, so that aid in effect increased defense expenditure rather than investment.[117] Opposed to this is Jacoby's view that defense expenditure would not have been cut. Defense expenditure would have been difficult to cut by much because there was considerable military activity in the offshore islands and there would have been difficulty finding alternative employment for the soldiers.

115. Several articles produce evidence of an association between high aid and low domestic savings ratios, which has led some of the authors to conclude that the former has caused the latter. See, for example, M. Anisur Rahman, "Foreign Capital and Domestic Savings: A Test of Haavelmo's Hypothesis with Cross-Country Data," *Review of Economics and Statistics* 50 (February 1968), 137–38; K. B. Griffin and J. L. Enos, "Foreign Assistance: Objectives and Consequences," *Economic Development and Cultural Change* 18, no. 3 (April 1970) 313–27; K. B. Griffin, "Foreign Capital, Domestic Savings and Economic Development," *Bulletin Oxford University Institute of Economics and Statistics* 32, no. 2 (May 1970), 99–112; H. B. Chenery and P. Eckstein, "Development Alternatives for Latin America," *Journal of Political Economy* 78, no. 4 (July–August 1970), 966–1006; and T. Weisskopf, "The Impact of Foreign Capital Inflow on Domestic Savings in Underdeveloped Countries," *Journal of International Economics* 2, no. 1 (February 1972), 25–38; G. F. Papanek, "The Effect of Aid and Other Resource Transfers on Savings and Growth in Less Developed Countries," *Economic Journal* 82, no. 327 (September 1972), 934–50, has argued that the regressions do not prove that high aid has caused low savings ratios. While agreeing that it is reasonable to expect that some aid would be used to increase consumption, he points out that the critics of aid go further and assert that their statistical association shows that each dollar of aid has increased consumption by more than one dollar. He gives many examples to show that, in fact, the statistical association could be due to third factors causing both low domestic savings and large balance-of-payments deficits (frequently taken as a measure of "aid"), and/or high aid receipts. Taiwan, as is shown subsequently in the text, is one such example.

116. Statistics on savings are given in DGBAS, *National Income of the Republic of China, 1975*, pp. 54–55.

117. K. B. Griffin, *Land Concentration and Rural Poverty* (London, 1976), pp. 260–61.

It has also been argued that "the minority Nationalist Chinese regime believed that it was essential for the ordinary consumption of the local population to be maintained at a reasonable level . . . most of the aid in the early period had to be directed into consumption."[118] This betrays some confusion. The more essential consumption was deemed to be, the less likely is it that it would have been cut in the absence of aid. However, if there had been less aid, I would agree that, in fact, consumption (and investment) would probably have been lower. But this does not constitute a strong criticism of aid because in the early years inflation was very high and the political situation uncertain. Hence, if aid did increase consumption, then that was a highly productive use for it.

As well as considering the effect of aid on the total quantity of savings and investment, we must ask how it affected the composition of investment. Even if we accept that total investment was increased, the influence of the aid donors on the allocation of investment could have been so unfavorable as to have actually reduced growth. The critics of aid have sometimes asserted that this has happened and, in the case of Taiwan, that Jacoby's study provides evidence of serious misallocation.[119]

Certainly Jacoby criticized the choice of investments in several sectors as being less than optimal. He was especially critical of investment in the electric power industry, where he concluded that "faulty investment criteria and evaluation methods resulted in a large waste of aid." He thought too much was invested in hydroelectric schemes and not enough in thermal, despite the much lower capital costs of the latter. This mistake resulted from the use of too low an interest rate and from a desire to save the foreign exchange costs of imported fuel. Jacoby also criticized "the largest single project in the Taiwan aid program—the Shihman Dam and Reservoir" because a postevaluation by the U.S. Aid mission showed it to have a rate of return of only 1.5 percent per annum.[120]

These criticisms were certainly made,[121] but one must point out that Jacoby himself thought that the choice of investments was highly productive in other cases.[122] He concluded, "By a rough calculation, an *ideal* selection of proj-

118. Ibid.
119. Ibid., p. 261.
120. Jacoby, pp. 196, 198.
121. How far they were justified is another matter. Jacoby was writing in 1965–66. Since then there has been an enormous increase in the cost of oil, which must have improved the yield on hydroelectrical generation compared to thermal. The U.S. AID mission's estimate of the yield of the Shihman Dam was not accepted by the Shihman Development Commmission (as Jacoby points out, p. 198).
122. For example: "Despite some failures, U.S. aid to transportation had a large, overall multiplier effect and was highly productive" (Jacoby, p. 179). "Although criticism can be made of individual projects and of the proliferation of small-scale projects, in the aggregate, U.S. aid to Taiwan's agricultural sector was highly productive" (p. 183). "A major aid investment was made

ects might have added something like 10 percent to developmental results. Alternatively, it might have enabled Taiwan to attain the same growth with around 10 percent less U.S. assistance.''[123] Hence, Jacoby believed that misallocation, compared with the *ideal,* resulted in U.S. aid having only 90 percent of the benefit it might have had. It seems somewhat extreme to conclude from this evidence that aid actually *reduced* growth.[124]

Nor is this all. There were some other effects of aid which Jacoby believed were beneficial and which it is important to mention. He points out that the U.S. AID mission "often played the role of 'whipping boy' for the development-minded officials of the Joint Commission and the Council [for U.S. AID]. These officials could argue for economic reforms within the Chinese government on the grounds that they were under pressure by the U.S. government. The U.S. AID Mission had a strong, persistent, and generally beneficient influence upon the formation of Chinese economic policies. This is the consensus of Chinese officials, and is amply buttressed by the record.'' He cites the Nineteen-Point Program of Economic and Financial Reform of 1960 and the push toward liberalization of economic policies and believes that "By far the most important consequence of U.S. influence was the creation in Taiwan of a booming private enterprise system. . . . AID made the private sector flower both by financing projects that created external economies for the private investor, and by putting steady pressure on the Chinese government to improve the climate for private investment.''[125]

It is very difficult to know how far the economic reforms of 1958–60 and the generally favorable attitude of the Chinese government to private enterprise were indeed attributable to pressures exerted by U.S. AID. The view taken in Chapter 7 is that the latter was not the main factor, but that the credit was due rather to the Chinese themselves, both economic ministers and visiting Chinese economists. Even if this is right, aid may still have been an important factor by making it easier to embark on what many must have regarded as a risky venture. Without aid, the temptation to retreat inside the walls of a siege economy would have been powerful.

---

in Taiwan's public health and sanitation. . . . The high productivity of these investments can be measured by the fact that Taiwan in 1965 had one of the lowest annual death rates of any country in the world—6.5 per 1,000 population—and a notably healthy, vigorous, and mobile work force'' (p. 188).

123. Ibid., p. 204 (italics added).

124. It is, in any case, difficult to pin responsibility for the choice of specific projects on U.S. AID as opposed to the Chinese authorities. As Jacoby points out, "Total foreign exchange resources—U.S. and Chinese—were, from the first, treated as a fungible pool of assets. The amount and composition of aid-financed and other imports were jointly controlled in the interests of economic stabilization and, later, of development'' (p. 60). Consequently, to show that *aid* resulted in a serious misallocation of investment one would need to show that the U.S. influence was strongly perverse. As the initiative for most projects came from the Chinese (p. 202), this would be difficult to demonstrate, and it is certainly not Jacoby's thesis.

125. Ibid., pp. 131–32, 138.

My general conclusion was given at the beginning of this section. I think aid was an important factor in Taiwan's successful economic performance. To avoid misunderstanding, I repeat that I certainly do not think it was the only, or even the main, important factor. Some of the others were mentioned in earlier sections, and all the main ones are to be found in other chapters of this book. The following quotation from Shirley W. Y. Kuo sums up the position succinctly:

U.S. aid was really an indispensable key factor in the economic development of Taiwan. However, such financial injection was only to be a "necessary but not sufficient" factor. That U.S. aid could have helped bringing such tremendous achievements in Taiwan is greatly due to the foundations laid by the Japanese during their occupation of the island, the diligent and economical character of the Chinese, political stability, and the efficient policies implemented by the government.[126]

Was the Initial Phase of Import Substitution Really Necessary?

It is frequently asserted that all countries that have successfully industrialized have made use of protection in the early stages of the process. Even the United Kingdom, which might be regarded as having started the fashion, protected itself against hand-loom cloth from India. Military metaphors are pressed into service. Manufacturers need a secure home base before they can venture out to attack world export markets. Does Taiwan's experience support or refute this view?

The stringent import restrictions that were imposed in 1951 were (as in many other countries) a natural reaction to the drain on foreign exchange reserves, which had reduced them to a very low level. As we have already seen, K. Y. Yin was well aware of the unsatisfactory features of such restrictions. Some of his remarks seem to imply that their main purpose was not to protect domestic industry, but (presumably) to save foreign exchange.[127] On the other hand, other of his statements clearly favor "reasonable" protection (both by tariffs and by controls) as a means of encouraging domestic industry.[128] Perhaps these two views can be reconciled as follows. Yin accepted the

---

126. Kuo, p. 112.

127. "Foreign exchange control and the protection policy are by far the most complicated problem, and they have been adopted for other important reasons than industrial development" (Yin, "Adverse Trend," p. 3). "If any relaxation were shown in the enforcement of protective or restrictive regulations, the old manufacturers would voice their protest in unison to keep up their rights and interests which they thought they had lawfully acquired. Thus, it seems that they take such protection and restriction as vested privilege, while overlooking the real intent of the government in enforcing such regulations which were in fact made under exigencies and as such are in the nature of a makeshift only" (K. Y. Yin, "A Retrospect on 'Adverse Trend in Taiwan's Industrial Development'," *Industry of Free China*, May 1959, p. 6).

128. "So far as the extent of protection is concerned, it should not be excessive; and so far as time is concerned, its duration should not be too long. The longer the period of protection, the greater will be the losses incurred by the consumers, which cannot be beneficial to the nation as a

infant industry argument for protection. He frequently stressed that protection should be temporary and indeed recommended that periods should be specified after which it should end. He also seems to have accepted the necessity for import controls as the best available way to cope with the foreign exchange situation in the early 1950s. He was opposed to such controls as a permanent feature, but he evidently thought they were necessary in the initial phase. Tariff changes had to have the approval of the legislature, whereas import controls did not, so that, until this situation could be changed (as it has been to some extent), this constituted an additional argument for controls.

Lin's views seem similar. He asks, "Is it not possible for Taiwan and countries similarly situated to start outright with manufacturing for export (as did Hong Kong) without infant industry protection?" The question could hardly be more clearly put, and it is also clear that Lin's answer is that it is not possible. Unfortunately, his reasons are far from clear. The gist of it seems to be that industrialization requires taxation of the primary sector in order to subsidize the secondary sector. Because of underdeveloped fiscal systems and monetary institutions, however,

the reallocation of resources needed for new industrialization efforts was rarely done through direct fiscal methods. Instead of receiving cash subsidies the new industrial activity was encouraged by the expectation of reaping large profits through the exclusion of foreign competition, the allocation of foreign exchange, bank credits, and essential inputs at preferential rates; and the remission of major taxes and duties. Conversely, instead of paying more taxes in cash, the traditional export activity was often discouraged by unfavorable exchange rates for its products and by land reform measures and agricultural pricing policies that kept the domestic prices of agricultural goods low relative to those of the new industrial goods.[129]

Lin admits that these policies may have reduced economic efficiency, but he seems to believe that they nonetheless stimulated economic growth. Only at a later stage in the growth process, he believes, would efficiency considerations have to be brought back into the picture.

The protectionist policies not only reduced efficiency, they also hampered exports of manufactured goods made from imported materials. At the time, however, few can have believed that Taiwan's exports of manufactures could

---

whole because it merely enriches a few entrepreneurs and is incompatible with the original purpose of protection.

In the enforcement of the policy of protection, tariff and the control of imports are methods which should both be used at the same time. A protection tariff itself lacks elasticity and cannot fully attain the objective for protection. The control of imports is more flexible in its operation because it can be readjusted from time to time in accordance with the actual requirement" (K. Y. Yin, "A Discussion on Industrial Policy for Taiwan," *Industry of Free China*, May 1954, pp. 7–8).

129. Lin, pp. 162–65.

ever have grown as fast as they did. K. T. Li told me that, in the early 1950s, most people thought of Taiwan only as an exporter of traditional products, sugar, rice, and the like. When in 1954 he was arguing the case for rebating taxes on materials used in the manufacture of exports, there was skepticism about the effects this would have. He was asked, ironically, "Do you want to turn Taiwan into another Lancashire?"

It is clear now that the skeptics were wrong. When the hindrances were removed in 1958-60, exports responded dramatically. Why could the controls not have been removed sooner? Why was it not possible to give infant industry promotion that was neutral as between production for the home market and production for export?[130] Lin alleges that underdeveloped fiscal systems and monetary institutions were a reason for using a battery of controls, multiple exchange rates, and a complicated indirect tax structure. It is not clear that the actual system was easier to administer than a more neutral one would have been. Of course, time was required to learn production methods and to make contacts with foreign buyers—but the Japanese *shosha* were, so to speak, waiting in the wings for their cue to enter, and the cue could have been given some years sooner than it was. Lin's other point that traditional exports should be taxed to provide finance for industrialization is also easily dealt with. The export taxes on sugar and rice that were levied in Taiwan were perfectly compatible with a more neutral system for manufactured goods.

The idea that a long period of production for the domestic market is a necessary prelude to exporting is not borne out by Taiwan's experience. Some industries (plywood, some canned foodstuffs, some electronics, for example) have depended on export markets for nearly all their sales from almost their very beginnings. Some of the firms concerned were foreign, especially in electronics, and some were established by businessmen from the mainland, but some were founded by Chinese born in Taiwan. The success of the Export Processing Zones and bonded factories shows that firms can be established which export 100 percent of their output from the start, although admittedly most of these were foreign or overseas Chinese.

But even if a period of selling on the domestic market was the normal prelude to exporting, as it undoubtedly was for many manufacturers, that does not mean that the firms would never have started without a protected home market. All that was needed was a profitable opportunity, and that depended on the structure of costs and prices. Taiwan's costs were relatively high in the early 1950s (for labor costs, see Figure 5.5) and were brought down by the devaluation of 1955, although still not sufficiently to compete with foreign manufactures because of import controls and indirect taxes. The remedies for this situation, therefore, lay in the hand of the government. Protection was the reason for lack of competitiveness, not a remedy for it.

130. See Little, Scitovsky, and Scott, especially chaps. 4 and 9.

There remains the question as to whether import controls were the best available way to handle the foreign exchange crisis in the early 1950s. Presumably they were preferred to the alternative of devaluation because it was believed that they were less inflationary, and inflation was an acute problem at the time. Against this one can argue that, since prices could not be controlled directly, devaluation accompanied by liberalization of controls would not have raised the domestic market prices of imports.[131] It would merely have shifted abnormal profits from licenseholders to the government or to exporters (where, if they were traditional exports, the extra profits would have been taxed away).

Other reasons may have justified import controls in the early 1950s, such as the need to control capital movements abroad and the tying of U.S. aid to U.S. goods. Given time, however, more liberal systems of control to deal with these problems could have been devised. After 1953, inflation was fairly moderate and U.S. aid was substantial. Whatever the justification of controls as a crisis measure in earlier years, I believe that a serious start on their elimination could have been made then, with beneficial results.

To return to the question posed at the beginning of this section, I must admit that Taiwan's experience does not enable an absolutely clear-cut answer to be made. It could be, and has been, interpreted as showing the need for infant-industry protection and import controls to deal with a balance-of-payments crisis. My own view is that, on the contrary, other methods of promoting industry would have been preferable and that, by comparison, controls and tariffs were inefficient. If that view is accepted, it is not merely of historical interest. Some controls and many high tariffs remain. There is still scope for further improvement.

Conclusion

The world economic recession that followed the oil crisis in 1973 has left its mark on Taiwan. Although exports rose strongly in 1976 to an all-time high, and although the economy grew by close to 12 percent in real terms, it does not seem, at the time of writing (summer 1977), that these rates of growth were being maintained in 1977, even before the disastrous typhoons, which further slowed recovery.

The world environment is less favorable than in the twenty years that ended in 1973. The real cost of energy has increased, and some estimates suggest that this alone will slow down world growth appreciably in the coming decades. The problem of inflation has become more acute in many countries, and that has made their governments more cautious in expanding demand and

---

131. This was, in fact, pointed out by T. C. Liu and S. C. Tsiang during their mission to Taiwan in 1954.

more tolerant of higher levels of unemployment. Not surprisingly, this situation has strengthened protectionist lobbies, so that countries as dependent on trade as Taiwan, and outside the major trade blocs, feel more vulnerable.

Taiwan's export growth has hitherto rested heavily on labor-intensive manufactures. With rising real wages and with poorer countries (such as India) increasing their exports, can this be expected to continue? Taiwan is heavily dependent on United States and Japanese markets for outlets for about half of its exports (Table 5.8). Is it safe to let this persist? Taiwan has become a net food importer (Table 5.13). In a world in which population doubles every thirty-five years, this may cause concern.

The government is naturally worried about several of these developments, and, in consequence, feels that it must do something about them. The problem is to know in what ways government action can help and to avoid well-meaning action that is really a hindrance. It is doubtful, for example, whether the government as such can do much to develop new exports or to diversify markets. An examination of the record shows that a continual succession of new products has been developed largely by private enterprise. In some cases (especially with such agriculture-based commodities as bananas, canned mushrooms, and asparagus) government-sponsored research has been important, and government regulation of quality and of competition between exports has been found desirable. But in the main it has been private enterprise which has discovered the profitable export opportunities, and businessmen have been quick to imitate successful pioneers. The Taiwan economy has, in fact, been extraordinarily resilient. Exports of particular commodities have grown at a tremendous rate, have reached a peak, and have then declined, sometimes quite sharply, but their place has been taken by something else. Other wood manufactures have succeeded plywood. Clothing has followed and surpassed textiles and been followed in turn by travel goods. Canned asparagus followed canned mushrooms and has been followed by bamboo shoots and tomato products. Banana exports grew very rapidly in the mid-1960s and then collapsed, but exports of fish were still growing rapidly in 1976. Different types of electronic products have succeeded each other.

This succession of success stories can be expected to go on without any special government help, provided conditions similar to those discussed above are satisfied relating mainly to the development of costs, prices, and profitability. Export profitability suffered in the recession, but is recovering and will continue to do so as long as inflation in Taiwan lags behind that in the United States, Japan, and her chief competitors among the less developed countries. Real wages may, and should, increase, but with productivity rising as well, wage costs need not rise unduly, and they do not seem to have done so since 1974 (Figure 5.5). The government's chief role will be to control fiscal and monetary policy and the exchange rate so as to maintain an adequate level of competitiveness. Apart from that, however, costs can be lowered by reducing import duties, many of which are unnecessarily high, even from the point of view of maximizing revenue.

What of diversification of markets and protectionism abroad? The United States and Japan are both enormous markets, and it is doubtful whether there is much to worry about in being dependent on them rather than on some other countries. Would Taiwan be safer if it exported more to Africa, Latin America, Southeast Asia, or even Europe? The government has an important part to play in seeing that the case for liberal (or more liberal) treatment of Taiwan's exports is not allowed to go by default. The interest groups most likely to be sympathetic to that case, which should include consumer organizations as well as foreign firms that buy from Taiwan or have invested there, must be consulted and informed. Measures to promote foreign investment in Taiwan have the benefit, in addition to the ones usually mentioned, of strengthening these interests.

The government may also have a part to play in securing supplies of some essential commodities, including wheat, oil, and logs. There may be a place for long-term contracts, especially if they can be negotiated at a time when they look to be unnecessary!

Until 1974, Taiwan's growth was both spectacular and, seemingly, impervious to fluctuations in the rest of the world. The fact that it suffered then in the recession should not make one forget the previous record. Its exports are still very small in relation to world exports, and even more so in relation to total sales in its main markets, so that there is still plenty of scope for further expansion. Even if the world economy does slow down, Taiwan should be able to continue to grow fast provided its policies remain as sensible and well adapted to the unfolding situation as they have been hitherto.

6 | The Labor Force, Wages, and Living Standards

WALTER GALENSON

The Labor Force

Long-Term Trends

The number of people available for work in a given population depends upon the age structure of the population and upon the numerous factors that determine the propensity of various groups in the community to engage in productive labor. Data on the labor force of Taiwan from 1953 to 1975 are presented in Table 6.1. Reference to the separate participation rates for men and women indicates that beneath the remarkable stability of the overall rate, substantial changes occurred that are to be ascribed to social and economic factors.

Although the labor force grew fairly steadily throughout the entire period,[1] the rate of change between the early and later portions differed markedly. During the thirteen years 1953 to 1966, the labor force grew by 27 percent; in the following nine years, the increase was 48 percent. This growth spurt in the later period occurred even though the population of working age rose by 42 percent from 1953 to 1966, compared with 37 percent for the period 1966 to 1975.[2] The answer to the discrepancy lies in the behavior of the participa-

1. A small decline is shown from 1964 to 1966. Whether this was a real phenomenon or a statistical artifact is not clear. Alternative series (see Table 6.1, *footnote) suggest that there was actually an increase during the period. The most reliable of these alternative sets indicates an increase of .4 percent between 1964 and 1966 (*Quarterly Report on the Labor Force Survey in Taiwan,* no. 50 [1976], p. 29). In either case, not much change occurred during these years.

2. The population data for 1953 and 1966 are from Institute of Economics, Academia Sinica, *Conference on Population and Economic Development in Taiwan* (Taipei, 1976), p. 114. The 1975 data were supplied by the Economic Planning Council. In comparing these rates, it should be kept in mind that the first covers a period of thirteen years, the second only nine years. The average annual increase in the population of working age was clearly higher in the first than in the second period.

tion rates, which fell substantially from 1953 to a low point in 1966 and rose thereafter.

The determinants of labor force participation rates are particularly complicated during the course of rapid economic development. Trends in female participation rates are considered in a later section of the chapter; here, I will examine those of males. The data in columns 3 and 4 of Table 6.1 are from different sources and are difficult to reconcile on the basis of available information. Perhaps the most important difference relates to the inclusion of military personnel among the gainfully employed, beginning in 1969, in the series in column 3, whereas column 4 relates only to the civilian population. Differences in the treatment of the unemployed may also have contributed to the divergence between the two series.

The data indicate a fairly steady decline in the male labor force participation rates from 1953 to 1967. Thereafter, one series shows yearly fluctuation but no trend; the second shows a continuing decline, but at a considerably slower rate than previously. Increased years of schooling appear to have been the major explanatory factor. For 1956 (the earliest year for which relevant data are available), 8.5 percent of all males in the age groups fifteen to twenty-four years were in secondary or higher schools. The proportion rose to 21.9 percent by 1967 and then more moderately to 23.6 percent in 1973.[3]

Although the growth of the labor force in Taiwan was rapid, even for the more recent period, the growth rates by themselves tell us nothing about their significance for promoting economic development. A rapidly increasing labor force can be an impediment to development if unaccompanied by a corresponding increase in the demand for labor and can result either in unemployment or in a reduction in labor force participation.[4] If matching opportunities for productive employment become available, labor force growth can be a powerful engine for economic growth.

Sectoral Distribution

The sectoral employment series are divided into two time periods for reasons of data availability. Table 6.2 contains estimates for the period 1952–66, based on census and household survey data. Table 6.3, covering the years

3. Calculated from data in Directorate-General of Budget, Accounting, and Statistics (DGBAS), *Statistical Yearbook of the Republic of China, 1975* (Taipei, 1976), pp. 6–7, and DGBAS, *Statistical Abstract of the Republic of China, 1975* (Taipei), pp. 522–29.

4. It is usually difficult to distinguish between the two in less developed countries. In the common situation of gross underemployment, whether or not a person is available for work is not an operational statistical concept. In the absence of an unemployment support system, all able-bodied persons of working age, except those at school and women with small children, are presumably available for work if there is any to be done. Work sharing and low-productivity employment are also facets of unemployment commonly found in less developed countries.

Table 6.1. The Labor Force and Participation Rates in Taiwan, 1953–1975

	Total labor force* (thousands) (1)	Participation rates				
		Total† (percent) (2)	Male		Female	
			Household registers‡ (3)	Labor force survey§ (4)	Household registers‡ (5)	Labor force survey§ (6)
1953	3,062	57.8	91.6	—	29.2	—
1954	3,102	57.1	91.1	—	27.7	—
1955	3,122	55.9	89.5	—	27.0	—
1956	3,105	54.1	87.2	—	26.3	—
1957	3,209	54.4	88.1	—	26.1	—
1958	3,286	54.2	88.0	—	25.2	—
1959	3,390	54.5	87.3	—	25.1	—
1960	3,471	54.6	87.3	—	25.0	—
1961	3,565	55.0	87.2	—	24.9	—
1962	3,649	55.1	86.7	—	24.6	—
1963	3,788	55.6	86.0	—	24.8	—
1964	3,908	55.7	85.0	83.7	24.4	34.0
1965	3,904	53.8	82.7	82.6	23.5	31.2
1966	3,883	51.6	81.6	81.4	23.0	28.7
1967	4,162	53.4	80.0	80.4	27.9	33.4
1968	4,345	53.9	80.3	80.2	28.6	34.4
1969	4,590	54.8	81.4	79.9	30.9	35.8
1970	4,718	54.3	80.4	78.9	30.2	35.5
1971	4,885	54.2	80.8	78.4	34.5	35.4
1972	5,089	54.5	81.2	77.2	38.5	37.1
1973	5,449	56.5	81.3	77.1	40.5	41.5
1974	5,636	56.6	80.8	78.2	40.3	40.2
1975	5,734	55.8	80.8	77.6	40.7	38.6

*Institute of Economics, Academia Sinica, *Conference on Population and Economic Development in Taiwan* (Taipei, 1976), p. 114. Military personnel are not included in the totals. This series is based upon Taiwan Provincial Labor Force Survey and Research Institute, *Quarterly Report on the Labor Force Survey in Taiwan* (Taipei, various issues), adjusted by the Manpower Group of the Economic Planning Council. The labor force survey was first undertaken in October 1963. Data for the years 1953–63 were estimated by the Manpower Group from statistics derived from household registers. The household register series may be found in Directorate-General of Budget, Accounting, and Statistics (DGBAS), *Statistical Yearbook of the Republic of China, 1976* (Taipei, 1976), p. 20. These data are regarded as less reliable than those based upon the labor force survey. See W. A. Yeh and P. C. Chang, "A Review and Evaluation of the Demographic and Manpower Statistics of the Republic of China," Institute of Economics, Academia Sinica, *Conference on Population and Economic Development in Taiwan,* p. 127. The unadjusted labor force data are to be found in Taiwan Provincial Labor Force Survey, *Quarterly Report on the Labor Force Survey in Taiwan.*

†This is the ratio of the civilian labor force to the total population aged fifteen and over. Inclusion of the military in the labor force raises the participation rate between 3 and 4 percentage points for individual years.

‡These figures represent the ratio of persons gainfully employed to the total population fifteen years of age and over. To the extent that they exclude persons who were available for work but unable to find it, they understate the labor force participation rate. Beginning in 1969, the employment figures include the armed forces; prior to that year, they were excluded.

§These figures represent the ratio of the civilian population fifteen years of age and over and who are able and willing to work to the total civilian population aged fifteen and over.

Sources: Columns 1 and 2: Institute of Economics, Academia Sinica, *Conference on Population and Economic Development in Taiwan,* pp. 114–15; columns 3 and 5: DGBAS, *Statistical Yearbook of the Republic of China, 1976,* pp. 14–15, 20–23; columns 4 and 6: *Quarterly Report on the Labor Force Survey in Taiwan,* no. 50 (1976), p. 33.

Table 6.2. Sectoral Distribution of Employment (thousands of persons and percentage of total employment)

	Agriculture* (thousands)	Industry† (thousands)	Services‡ (thousands)	Agriculture* (percent)	Industry† (percent)	Services‡ (percent)
1952	1,528	465	532	60.5	18.4	21.1
1953	1,569	489	548	60.2	18.8	21.0
1954	1,594	513	563	59.7	19.2	21.1
1955	1,610	547	579	58.8	20.0	21.2
1956	1,619	589	596	57.7	21.0	21.3
1957	1,592	643	621	55.8	22.5	21.7
1958	1,606	690	635	54.8	23.5	21.7
1959	1,628	736	659	53.9	24.3	21.8
1960	1,641	786	687	52.7	25.2	22.1
1961	1,653	841	711	51.6	26.2	22.2
1962	1,659	884	747	50.4	26.9	22.7
1963	1,675	928	778	49.6	27.4	23.0
1964	1,683	980	811	48.5	28.2	23.3
1965	1,688	1,041	873	46.9	28.9	24.2
1966	1,709	1,113	927	45.6	29.7	24.7

*Includes agriculture, forestry, and fishing.

†Includes mining; manufacturing; construction; electricity, gas, and water; and transport and communication.

‡Includes commerce and other services. Military personnel are excluded from both total employment and employment in services because of lack of data.

Source: T. S. Yu, "Taiwan Employment and Productivity Trends since 1953," *Sino-American Conference on Manpower in Taiwan* (Taipei, 1972), p. 123.

1966–75, emanates from more reliable quarterly surveys of the labor force.[5]

The dramatic structural change in the labor force mirrors the character of economic growth in Taiwan. In most less developed countries characterized by rapid population growth, the labor force has tended to move directly from agriculture into the service sector. In Taiwan, however, the rapid growth of industry made it possible to avoid the buildup of a large, low-productivity, urban service sector that has become one of the major problems of the developing world. Taiwan did not completely escape unemployment or low-productivity employment, but the magnitude of the problem it faced was relatively smaller.

By 1975, Taiwan had achieved a labor force distribution closer to that of a developed than of a developing country. Its proportion of agricultural employment had fallen to a level equal to or lower than the 1970 ratios for such European countries as Greece, Ireland, and Spain. If it is true that the bulk of the poverty population in the less developed nations of the world is to be found in the countryside, the manner in which Taiwan was able to halve its

5. A comparison of the figures for the year 1966, shown in both tables, indicates that although total employment does not differ by much from one series to the other, the earlier series tends to overstate agricultural and industrial employment at the expense of the services. The principal reason is probably the fact that the household surveys, on which the earlier data are based, often registered all members of a farm household as farm workers, even though some of them might actually have been engaged in nonfarm work.

Table 6.3. Sectoral Distribution of Employment, 1966-1975 (thousands of persons and percentage of total employment)

	Agriculture* (thousands)	Industry† (thousands)	Services‡ (thousands)	Agriculture* (percent)	Industry† (percent)	Services‡ (percent)
1966	1,617	1,050	1,055	43.5	28.2	28.3
1967	1,723	1,207	1,093	42.8	30.0	27.2
1968	1,676	1,266	1,283	39.7	30.0	30.3
1969	1,726	1,383	1,324	38.9	31.2	29.9
1970	1,681	1,543	1,352	36.8	33.7	29.5
1971	1,665	1,685	1,389	35.1	35.6	29.3
1972	1,632	1,847	1,469	33.0	37.3	29.7
1973	1,624	2,106	1,598	30.5	39.5	30.0
1974	1,697	2,185	1,604	30.9	39.9	29.2
1975	1,652	2,276	1,593	29.9	41.2	28.9

*Includes agriculture, forestry, and fishing.
†Includes mining; manufacturing; construction; electricity, gas, and water; and transport and communication.
‡Includes all other industries.
Source: Quarterly Report on the Labor Force Survey in Taiwan, no. 50 (1976), p. 38. Only the civilian population is included.

agricultural employment share within two decades should be of great interest to those presently concerned with the poverty problem.

Manufacturing

The particular manufacturing industries that absorbed labor rapidly in Taiwan in the latter half of the 1960s can be seen from the data in Table 6.4.[6] Between 1966 and 1975, some 75 percent of the net increase in manufacturing employment was in four industries: food, textiles and apparel, chemicals, and electrical machinery. All of these are heterogeneous industries, and some subgroups within them were the main employment gainers. In food, canning and sugar gained; in textiles, the large increases were in cotton textiles, synthetic fibers, knit goods, and clothing; in chemicals, plastics showed the most gain; and in electrical machinery, it was communications equipment and apparatus—the electronics industry.[7]

Countries at stages of economic development characterized by an abundance of labor and a shortage of capital are often advised, if they wish to maximize employment opportunities without sacrificing economic growth possibilities, to adopt some mix of the following industrial policies: (1) Accord priority to new industries that are labor-intensive in nature, that is, industries that tend to employ relatively more labor than capital. (2) For all industries, adopt so-called intermediate technologies, that is, technological

6. Comparable data are not available for years prior to 1966.
7. Detailed employment data for the period December 1973 to January 1976, by industrial subgroup, can be found in DGBAS, Statistical Yearbook of the Republic of China, 1976 (Taipei, 1976), Table 16.

processes that permit the economic use of a large amount of labor. They should eschew the advanced technology of developed industrial nations, which is designed to economize on labor, and either devise new technology or use older technology discarded by the developed nations because it was too labor-consuming. (3) Preserve handicrafts and small-scale industry, which tend to be labor-intensive. The practice by large Japanese enterprises of subcontracting to small firms is sometimes cited as a successful application of this policy.[8]

To what extent did Taiwan follow the prescribed course? A recent study of the industrial history of Taiwan provides a partial answer to this question. (1) The rapid growth of capital was positively correlated with the rate of labor absorption. After 1960, a large proportion of foreign investment went into electrical machinery, chemicals, and textiles. (2) For the first half of the 1960s, the employment effect of heavy investment was somewhat dampened by the adoption of capital-intensive technologies. During the second half, however, technological advance proceeded more slowly despite a very large increase in capital investment, with the result that labor was absorbed at a very rapid rate. (3) The expansion of the labor-absorbing industries was made possible to a large extent by export growth. This was not true of the food industry, but it was true of many others.[9]

The first policy prescription, encouragement to inherently labor-intensive manufactures, was clearly followed in Taiwan. Knit goods, plastic rainwear and sportswear, and radio and television sets are among the products in this category that have had an enormous output expansion. Much of this was due not to the result of conscious choice on the part of the Taiwan authorities, but rather to the desire of foreign firms to take advantage of Taiwan's supply of highly productive, low-cost labor. The decision of the government to operate an open economy rather than to rely on import substitution was crucial. To quote the conclusions reached in another study of the subject: "Taiwan has made the best of its comparative advantage by exporting commodities with relatively low capital intensity to the developed countries. . . . Economic development in Taiwan is a successful demonstration of a comparative advantage approach as the development strategy. It makes possible output growth and employment growth not in conflict even in the short run."[10]

Whether intermediate technology played a role in furthering employment is a question that is difficult to answer in the absence of relevant studies. There

8. See, for example, Hugh Patrick and Henry Rosovsky, eds., *Asia's New Giant* (Washington, D.C., 1976), pp. 508–16.

9. Shirley W. Y. Kuo, "A Study of Factors Contributing to Labor Absorption in Taiwan, 1954–1971," in Institute of Economics, Academia Sinica, *Conference on Population and Economic Development in Taiwan*, p. 449.

10. K. S. Liang, "Trade and Employment in Taiwan," National Taiwan University, *Economic Essays* 3 (1972), 254.

Table 6.4. Employment in Manufacturing Industries, 1966–1975 (thousands of persons)

	Total manufacturing*	Food, beverages, and tobacco	Textiles and apparel	Leather and leather products	Wood and wood products	Paper and paper products
1966	634.6	80.7	130.4	6.0	38.2	23.7
1967	774.9	88.6	162.5	12.3	48.2	22.3
1968	799.2	93.4	164.0	8.1	48.0	26.8
1969	877.9	97.8	179.3	10.2	51.4	27.3
1970	898.2	100.5	189.4	10.4	52.5	29.4
1971	1,064.3	106.8	234.6	9.8	64.1	32.7
1972	1,157.8	106.7	243.5	10.9	70.9	32.0
1973	1,245.8	126.4	255.5	11.8	72.1	32.9
1974	1,214.4	123.1	294.0	9.6	68.1	33.6
1975	1,107.4	112.1	271.7	7.3	60.0	31.9

*Individual industries do not add up to total manufacturing employment because of omission of basic nonmetallic mineral products and basic metal products in the source.
Sources: 1966–67: Estimated by applying index numbers in P. C. Chang and S. M. Chao Chen,

is some evidence that Chinese entrepreneurs were ingenious in making do with a minimum of capital. According to K. K. Fung, "More frequent maintenance and more extensive repairs prolonged the service from machines. Recycling sometimes even through salvaging from garbage dumps constituted another source of capital. Capital resources could also be enlarged by using substitutes which could be produced without resorting to capital that was most scarce."[11]

Taiwan's entrepreneurs also seem to be aware of the problem. On several occasions, when I visited factories, I queried plant managers about labor-intensive operations for which more modern machinery is used in the United States and Japan. They remarked that it might become profitable to introduce such machinery if labor costs in Taiwan were to exceed specified levels. The feeling that only the latest in manufacturing technology will do, which is common in developing countries, does not appear to be prevalent in Taiwan.

Although small-scale industry declined considerably over time, it has persisted to some extent. In 1961, out of 51,600 manufacturing enterprises, 67 percent had three or less employees, and an additional 23 percent had from four to six employees. By 1971, the total number of enterprises had fallen to 42,700, with corresponding small size percentages of 12 and 22.[12] The manager of an automobile-producing firm informed me when I visited his plant that he normally secured parts from more than a hundred independent local subcontractors.

11. K. K. Fung, "Maximum Labor Participation and Economic Growth," Institute of Economics, *Academia Economic Papers,* 1 (March 1973), 98.
12. The data are from the *Industrial and Commercial Census of Taiwan* (Taipei, 1961), Vol. IV, Table 6; and ibid. (Taipei, 1971), Vol. I, Table 6.

Printing	Chemicals	Rubber products	Metal products	Machinery	Electrical machines	Transport equipment	Miscellaneous manufacturing
12.0	74.1	9.1	36.1	33.2	32.2	25.9	38.7
16.3	95.3	11.0	35.4	42.8	45.6	27.0	42.6
16.4	96.8	14.7	36.5	43.6	65.1	32.7	42.4
16.4	100.2	15.6	41.2	47.0	84.7	35.0	48.9
16.4	99.9	16.1	35.8	44.6	95.1	34.0	47.2
16.1	119.5	21.8	45.1	50.5	115.1	39.3	49.2
16.7	129.2	27.1	46.2	56.0	142.5	39.9	51.8
17.0	146.5	27.8	50.9	63.9	174.0	45.6	55.7
18.2	154.2	29.5	43.8	69.0	172.0	49.4	50.8
17.9	151.8	27.4	39.4	65.6	138.4	44.9	47.2

"Productivity Index of the Manufacturing Sector in the Republic of China," July 1975 (mimeographed), to the data for 1968. 1968-75: Data provided by the Manpower Group of the Economic Planning Council.

Services

Service-sector employment grew only moderately in Taiwan, partly because of the rapid expansion of manufacturing employment. The only disaggregated time series available for service-sector employment is that shown in Table 6.5. For the years prior to 1972, the distinction is between employment in commerce and in all other services, including government. The data indicate only that commercial employment, often the dumping ground for displaced farmers in the developing countries, grew less rapidly than total nonagricultural employment in Taiwan.

Age Structure

Data on the evolution of the age structure of Taiwan's labor force over a twenty-year period together with a projection to 1980 are contained in Table 6.6. The changes resulted from a complex of interacting factors: changes in the demographic structure of the population, years of schooling, economic opportunity, and, not least, the female participation rate. Whatever the specific cause for particular years, the long-run trend is toward an increase in the average age. The labor force of Taiwan is still relatively young, compared with most developed nations, though the much smaller population cohorts born in the 1970s will begin to have a severe impact on the labor force by the middle of the 1980s.

The Role of Women

Women workers have played a major part in the economic development of Taiwan. Fluctuations in the overall female participation rate were shown in Table 6.1. In this section, I consider the factors that led to an apparent decline in the rate from 1953 to 1966 and a sharp rise thereafter.

Table 6.5. Employment in Services, 1966–1975 (thousands of persons)

	Total services	Commerce	Finance and insurance	Services	Other
1966	1056	446	—	566	44
1967	1093	503	—	569	21
1968	1283	614	—	654	15
1969	1325	628	—	678	19
1970	1352	671	—	671	10
1971	1389	685	—	700	4
1972	1470	661	91	718	—
1973	1598	737	95	766	—
1974	1604	753	101	750	—
1975	1593	737	118	738	—

Source: Quarterly Report on the Labor Force Survey in Taiwan, no. 50 (1976), p. 38.

The large differences in the participation rates shown in columns 5 and 6 of Table 6.1 make the data for the earlier years suspect, since the latter series (column 6) is generally regarded as the more reliable one. Differences in concept—gainfully employed versus the civilian labor force—would not account for much of the divergence. During the 1950s, the bulk of the female labor force was in agriculture—78 percent in 1953 and 75 percent in 1960—most as unpaid family workers, a category for which it is notoriously difficult to determine labor force status. Most farm women would have devoted some time to field work.

The picture changed drastically in the 1960s, with the large-scale entrance of women into manufacturing occupations. Although the absolute number of women engaged in agriculture remained fairly constant (Table 6.7), the relative share declined sharply. The number of women in service occupations almost doubled in the decade 1965–75; in manufacturing, it rose by a factor of three.

Table 6.6. Age Distribution of the Labor Force (percent of total)

Age group	1956*	1966	1970	1975	1980 (estimated)
15–19	20.4	16.8	19.5	16.0	14.7
20–24	14.0	10.2	10.5	14.5†	15.6
25–34	27.9	27.4	25.2	23.6	27.8
35–44	21.0	24.3	23.8	22.8‡	18.6
45–54	12.2	15.2	14.6	15.9§	15.4
55–64	3.9	5.3	5.8	6.5	7.2
65+	0.6	0.8	0.6	0.7	0.7

*Refers to the economically active population.
†The 1980 projection source shows 17.1 percent for this age group for 1975.
‡The 1980 projection source shows 19.1 percent for this age group in 1975.
§The 1980 projection source shows 16.8 percent for this age group in 1975.
Sources: 1956: DGBAS, *Statistical Yearbook of the Republic of China, 1975* (Taipei, 1976), p. 18; 1966–75: *Quarterly Report on the Labor Force Survey in Taiwan,* no. 50 (1976), p. 35; 1980: Economic Planning Council (EPC), "Six Year Plan" (mimeographed).

Table 6.7. Sectoral Distribution of the Female Labor Force, 1965–1975 (thousands of persons and percent of total)

	Agriculture (thousands)	Mining, manufacturing, utilities, construction, transport, and communication (thousands)	Services (thousands)	Agriculture (percent)	Mining, manufacturing, utilities, construction, transport, and communication (percent)	Services (percent)
1965	570	209	313	52.2	19.1	28.7
1966	485	220	329	46.9	21.3	31.8
1967	611	275	383	48.2	21.7	30.1
1968	559	279	418	44.5	22.2	33.3
1969	593	314	409	46.1	23.9	30.0
1970	578	364	482	40.6	25.6	33.8
1971	556	435	500	37.3	29.2	33.5
1972	567	505	537	35.3	31.4	33.3
1973	576	638	629	31.3	34.7	34.0
1974	599	623	591	33.0	34.4	32.6
1975	552	648	569	31.2	36.6	32.2

Sources: 1965–74: Yen Hwa, "The Female Labor Force of Taiwan," Institute of Economics, Academia Sinica, *Conference on Population and Labor Force in Taiwan* (1976), p. 378; 1975: *Quarterly Report on the Labor Force Survey in Taiwan*, no. 49 (1976), passim. The data are for October.

To a considerable extent, the new female recruits to industrial occupations were unskilled and in the fifteen- to 24-year age group. In 1975, for example, 46 percent of women workers were in this age group, compared with 22 percent of men.[13] They went predominantly into such processing industries as canning, textiles, and electronics. In January 1976, 57.3 percent of all women employed in manufacturing were in these three industries, compared with 27.5 percent of the men.[14] Even more striking is the fact that although women constituted only 30.8 percent of the nation's total labor force in that month, their share of the manufacturing labor force was 46.6 percent.[15] The Export Processing Zones at Kaoshiung and Taichung, important elements in Taiwan's growth, have employed mostly women.[16]

The number of females employed in services increased considerably, though not as much as in manufacturing. The number of women in commercial activities rose from 121,000 in 1965 to 235,000 in January 1976. About 75 percent of the latter were engaged in retail trade and most of the rest in restaurants and hotels.

A woman's decision to seek paid work depends on her family obligations,

13. *Quarterly Report on the Labor Force Survey in Taiwan,* no. 50 (1976), pp. 36–37.
14. *Monthly Bulletin of Labor Statistics,* no. 30 (1976), Table 1–3.
15. Ibid.
16. In May 1976, 82.5 percent of the employees at Taiwan's three Export Processing Zones were women (Ministry of Economic Affairs, *Export Processing Zones, Essential Statistics* [Taipei, May 1976], p. 20).

the wages being offered, and the location of the workplace, among other factors. Married women in Taiwan do not participate in the labor market to the same extent as unmarried women, but the growth of employment opportunities nevertheless pulled substantial numbers of them into paid jobs. In 1965, the labor force participation rate for unmarried women was 44 percent, that for married women 20 percent. The corresponding figures for 1974 were 61 and 34 percent.[17]

Wage incentives for women will be dealt with in the section on incomes. The third factor, the locational pattern of industry, has been an important element in inducing women to work. A good deal of the industry that employs young women has been located in cities other than Taipei or in small towns, thus enabling women in farm areas to commute to work and facilitating the tapping of labor resources that might otherwise not have been available.

A 1975 study of the two Export Processing Zones in Kaohsiung makes this point very clearly.[18] About half of all the women employed in these zones whose families were living in rural areas commuted to work daily. A third of this total used company buses, another third motorcycles or bicycles, the rest public transportation. The company buses were particularly important for outlying areas:

At a given level of salary, transportation facilities, and socio-economic structure, the most feasible method for a company to solve the problem of a labor shortage would be to operate a company bus service. And it is very interesting to note that the time span of bus operation (or distance) changed proportionately with the quantity of labor demanded. If a company required more labor, it might extend its bus service farther in order to recruit the needed laborers at the same wages. Or, on the contrary, a company might curtail the number of or distance traveled by buses when it required fewer laborers.[19]

When the women were asked why they preferred to commute rather than to move into the city, one-third stated that living costs were cheaper at home and another 21 percent gave parental desires as the principal reason. A substantial majority of the rural dwellers continued to help with farm work on weekends and holidays, and absenteeism rose in the peak agricultural seasons. The latter pattern is not unusual in developing nations, where the labor force is not fully committed to industry, but daily commuting to the farm is much less common.

The pattern of industrialization followed by Taiwan would not have been possible without the deployment of its female labor reserves. The net increase

17. Yen Hwa, "The Female Labor Force of Taiwan," Institute of Economics, Academia Sinica, *Conference on Population and Economic Development in Taiwan*, p. 369.

18. Rong-I Wu, "Urbanization and Industrialization in Taiwan," *Conference on Population and Economic Development in Taiwan*, p. 593.

19. Ibid., pp. 598–99.

of almost four hundred thousand in the number of young women working in manufacturing in the decade 1965 to 1975 facilitated the rise of much of the new export-oriented industry that is associated with the nation's development. The importance of the female contribution is evidenced by the fact that during the same decade, the entire manufacturing labor force increased by less than nine hundred thousand workers.[20] The flow of relatively cheap labor that attracted foreign investors to Taiwan would have come to an end much sooner had women decided to remain at home.

Occupational Structure

The data available for Taiwan reveal what happens to the occupational structure of the labor force during rapid industrialization. There are counterforces at work. The expansion of the labor-intensive sector of the economy tends to reduce the proportion of professional and technical personnel. On the other hand, the growing complexity of the economy would seem to require an increasing proportion of this type of high-level manpower. The data in Table 6.8 suggest that the rapid growth of labor-intensive manufacturing was the stronger force for most of the period, but that emergent technology-intensive industries became more important at the very end of the decade.

The proportion of administrative and managerial personnel declined by almost one-half during the decade. This suggests the existence of substantial economies of scale in the employment of this category of manpower.

Education

Much attention has been paid in recent years to the role of education—or, to use a more fashionable term, the creation of human capital—in the development process, but none of the work is conclusive. Education is just one of a number of variables contributing to economic growth, and it is by no means the most important. Its value is difficult to quantify because of great variation in quality. There is no obvious relationship between the content of an educational program and its potential contribution to development. For example, many of the talented government administrators who directed the course of the economy of Taiwan for the past twenty-five years were trained in the physical sciences, yet the decisions they were called upon to make were mainly within the domain of the social sciences.

I shall present only available data on the improvement in the educational level of Taiwan's labor force, including both academic and vocational education. This improvement clearly raised the productivity of the labor force, but I will make no effort to determine by how much. Those concerned

20. *Quarterly Report on the Labor Force Survey in Taiwan,* no. 50 (1976), p. 38. The precise increase from October 1965 to October 1975 was 897,000 for all workers and 386,000 females.

Table 6.8. Occupational Structure of the Nonagricultural Labor Force, 1964–1975 (percent of total)

	Professional and technical	Administrative, managerial, and executive	Clerical	Sales	Service	Craftsmen and operatives in production and transportation
1964	8.2	5.2	10.2	20.3	11.0	45.1
1965	7.5	4.5	11.5	20.2	9.9	46.4
1966	9.0	6.7	12.9	19.5	10.8	41.1
1967	8.8	6.9	12.5	19.6	10.2	42.0
1968	8.3	5.5	11.2	21.0	10.0	44.0
1969	7.2	5.3	10.3	20.0	9.4	47.8
1970	6.5	4.9	10.5	20.5	9.2	48.4
1971	6.3	4.7	10.2	18.9	8.3	51.6
1972	6.8	2.9	12.1	18.5	9.0	50.7
1973	6.6	3.4	12.4	18.0	8.0	51.6
1974	6.3	2.6	12.1	18.6	7.9	52.5
1975	7.0	2.8	12.5	17.4	8.0	52.3

Source: *Quarterly Report on the Labor Force Survey in Taiwan*, no. 50 (1976), p. 40.

with educational aspects of development will be interested to see the magnitudes of educational advance that were consistent with the rapid growth of Taiwan's economy. More or less investment in education may have been optimal, in some sense, but the policies adopted worked.

Statistics on the educational level of Taiwan's labor force are shown in Table 6.9. Most notable is the doubling of the proportion of senior high school and college-level education over the decade 1964–75. The illiterate and self-educated group had been reduced to a relatively small proportion of the labor force by 1975, and the proportion with only a primary education was declining rapidly toward the end of the period.

From 1953 to 1967, when the government made six years of primary

Table 6.9. Educational Status of the Labor Force, 1965–1975 (percent of total labor force)

Year*	Illiterate and self-educated	Primary school	Junior high and vocational schools	Senior high and vocational schools	Colleges and universities
1965	26.0	54.3	9.0	7.5	3.1
1966	22.5	54.1	10.5	9.0	3.9
1967	21.7	53.8	11.5	9.1	3.9
1968	20.9	52.7	12.0	10.2	4.3
1969	22.3	53.0	11.7	9.4	3.7
1970	20.7	52.7	12.1	10.5	3.9
1971	20.1	53.1	12.4	10.5	3.9
1972	19.2	52.3	12.8	11.4	4.3
1973	18.9	50.0	13.7	12.3	5.2
1974	17.9	50.4	14.5	12.5	4.7
1975	15.9	47.9	15.4	14.7	6.1

*From 1965 to 1968, includes persons twelve years of age and older; after 1968, persons fifteen years and older.
Source: *Quarterly Report on the Labor Force Survey*, various issues.

schooling compulsory, school attendance of children in the six- to twelve-year age bracket rose from 88 percent to 98 percent. Beginning in 1968, an additional three years of free education were made available, though not compulsory. The result was an increase in the enrollment ratio of the twelve- to seventeen-year-old age group: from 49 to 71.5 percent for males and 32 to 60 percent for females.[21]

The educational status of the labor force, by category of employee, as of January 1976, can be seen from the data in Table 6.10. The bulk of the uneducated were either unpaid family workers, most of them probably engaged in farming, and the self-employed. Employees in both the private and government sectors had a much higher educational status; the government alone employed 50 percent of all those above the high school level.

Enrollment in universities, colleges, and junior colleges increased from 44,000 in 1962 to 282,000 in 1974. The distribution by field of specialization is shown in Table 6.11. The increase in the proportion of students in engineering was clearly in line with the manpower requirements of an industrializing economy, but the decline in percentage in natural science was not. However, it cannot be assumed that people chose fields of specialization primarily in response to economic requirements. Particularly in the best universities, rigid departmental quotas tended to steer students into disciplines for which there was little demand.[22]

The lack of manpower skills has often been considered a serious obstacle to economic development. With respect to high-level manpower, a recent study concluded that "Taiwan is no exception to the general pattern that in all modernizing countries there is a likely shortage of high-level and subprofessional manpower such as scientists, engineers, technicians, craftsmen, doctors, nurses, managers, administrators, teachers, accountants."[23] But the difficulty with this and most other similar work is that the demand side of the labor market is not taken into account. As we have seen, a declining ratio of professional and managerial personnel to the total labor force may be perfectly consistent with labor requirements at particular stages of development, especially where labor-intensive processing industries are growing.

There are similar problems with arguments on the other side, that the educational system of Taiwan may have created a surplus of highly educated manpower, a situation that is not uncommon in developing countries, particularly in Asia. In support of this view is the fact that unemployment rates

21. Economic Planning Council (EPC), *Social Welfare Indicators, Republic of China* (Taipei, 1976), p. 49. The period covered was the school years 1967–68 to 1975–76.

22. See Chien-sheng Shih, "High Level Manpower and Higher Education in Taiwan," *Sino-American Conference on Manpower in Taiwan* (Taipei, 1972), p. 205.

23. Chi-ming Hou and Yu-chu Hsu, "The Supply of Labor in Taiwan," *Conference on Population and Economic Development in Taiwan,* p. 355.

Table 6.10. Educational Status of the Labor Force by Category of Employee, January 1976 (thousands of persons)

Educational level	Total	Employers	Own-account workers	Unpaid family workers	Paid employees, private	Paid employees, government
Total	5,475	153	1,345	772	2,540	666
Illiterate	581	4	223	161	172	21
Self-educated	228	4	108	33	68	15
Primary school	2,613	66	802	378	1,231	136
Junior high school*	873	25	128	125	518	77
Senior high school	266	14	28	22	125	77
Senior vocational school†	544	22	37	45	283	157
Junior college, university, graduate school	369	19	18	8	142	183

*Includes junior vocational school.
†Includes normal school.
Source: EPC, "Taiwan Regional Manpower Utilization Survey Report" (preliminary computer printout, 1976), Table 2.

Table 6.11. Enrollment in Schools of Higher Education, by Specialization, 1962–1974 (percent of total)

	1962	1966	1970	1974
Humanities	15.4	10.7	9.5	9.7
Education	7.8	6.8	6.8	8.4
Fine arts	2.6	3.1	2.7	2.7
Law	3.4	1.7	1.4	1.2
Social sciences	26.6	38.9	34.1	31.9
Natural sciences	9.5	5.6	5.1	5.1
Engineering	17.7	18.0	24.5	29.9
Medical sciences	8.7	8.9	10.2	7.4
Agriculture	8.2	6.4	5.6	3.7
Total (numbers of persons)	44,314	113,855	203,473	282,168

Source: Ministry of Education, *Education and Manpower Planning in the Republic of China* (Taipei, 1975), Table 27.

among graduates of higher educational institutions have been relatively high.[24] Formal rates of unemployment, however, do not tell us enough about the actual operation of the labor market. College graduates are more prone than members of other skill groups to remain in the labor force when they lose their jobs and are also less likely to accept employment that they consider beneath their skills. Moreover, easy access to highly trained manpower may have been an important element in facilitating the rapid expansion of industrial enterprises in Taiwan. Visits to factories give the impression that engineering and scientific personnel are used lavishly.

No firm conclusions can be reached about the economic efficacy of Taiwan's educational effort. Taiwan has invested fairly heavily in education, but whether the amount and the allocation of the investment provide an appropriate model for other developing countries is not clear. Additional work could be of great value in this area.

Vocational Training[25]

The available statistics relevant to vocational training for manual skills in Taiwan are contained in Table 6.12. These figures tell only part of the story, since they do not include on-the-job training. Many vocational school graduates receive further training in the factory, and some individuals go directly from academic schools to jobs, receiving all their skill training on the job. Shipbuilding trainees, for example, typically spend three years at a vocational school, followed by six months in a special shipbuilding vocational training center run by the government in cooperation with an enterprise. The final step in the process is a six-month training period on the job.[26]

24. See, for example, Charles H. C. Kao, "Education and High-Level Manpower Utilization: The Case of Taiwan" (October 1975, mimeographed).

25. For a detailed description of the various vocational training programs in Taiwan, see T. K. Djang, *Industry and Labor in Taiwan* (Taipei, 1976), ch. 9.

26. Interview with manpower specialists of the Economic Planning Agency.

Table 6.12. Number of Vocational Trainees, by Sponsoring Organization, 1966–1974 (thousands of persons)

Year	Total	Public enterprise	Private enterprise	Government agencies	Schools*	Civic organizations and others
1966	54	20	7	9	10	7
1967	88	28	19	16	15	8
1968	124	38	30	21	16	19
1969	144	36	28	19	20	41
1970	170	30	30	23	31	55
1971	201	32	35	29	20	84
1972	184	32	31	32	23	66
1973	234	33	72	36	21	71
1974	339	40	144	51	19	84

*Nonvocational institutions.
Source: Ministry of Interior, *Vocational Training in the Republic of China* (Taipei, 1975), Table 1.

Apart from the rapid growth in the number of trainees, particularly since 1972, the increase in the share of training done by private enterprises is the most interesting aspect of Table 6.12. This increase was due primarily to the establishment in 1972 of a National Vocational Training Fund, financed by a payroll tax of 1.5 percent. A good deal of this money went to private enterprises for approved training programs, often in cooperation with vocational schools. During 1973 and 1974, 47 percent of the total sum collected was disbursed for this purpose.[27]

One participant in the program, the Tung Yuan Electrical Works, set up an apprenticeship training program in 1958 providing both theoretical and practical training, but did not establish a formal training center until July 1973. It obtained the approval of the Vocational Training Fund for programs in nineteen job categories and now employs seven training officers, fifty-seven instructors, and eight assistant instructors.[28] The Yue Loong Motor Company, the largest automobile producer in Taiwan, is the site of a vocational training center in the metal trades and holds six-month courses for about two hundred participants. In addition to receiving compensation from government funds, the company benefits because it has first pick of the graduates.[29]

The diversity of vocational training sponsorship is exemplified by the fact that of the total of 562 training institutes in existence in 1974, 42 were operated by government agencies, 80 by public enterprises, 133 by private enterprises, 78 by universities and technical colleges, and 229 by private organizations.[30] In view of the difficulties that most countries have had with

27. Ministry of the Interior, *Vocational Training in the Republic of China* (Taipei, 1975), Tables 12, 13.
28. Djang, p. 165.
29. Interview with the plant manager of the Yue Loong Motor Company.
30. Djang, p. 147.

public vocational schools, the Taiwan sponsorship scheme has probably made for a more effective program.

Because vocational training is closely geared to the private sector, one would presume that it reflected the demand for skills. From 1966 to 1974, the nonagricultural labor force increased by 80 percent, and the number of vocational trainees rose more than sixfold. There is no question that this expansion of skill training was of critical importance to the nation's economic progress. Whether it was of sufficient magnitude to prevent the emergence of production bottlenecks is more difficult to determine.

The ten major construction projects inaugurated by the government in 1973 did not have much effect on the skilled labor market. There was some fear of skill shortages, particularly in construction and the metal trades, but the problem had not become acute by the summer of 1977.[31]

A few conclusions can be drawn from this brief review of manpower training in Taiwan. (1) There does not appear to have been an insufficiency of either high-level or manual skills during the course of Taiwan's development. It would be difficult to support the conclusion that economic growth had been impeded by a lack of skilled labor resources. The training programs that were undertaken appear to have achieved their purposes. (2) A large increase in the supply of professional, technical, and skilled manual labor was achieved within a short period through the nation's own resources, with little assistance from the outside. (3) The pattern of vocational training adopted by Taiwan, a pragmatic mixture of government- and private enterprise-sponsored institutes, plus a substantial addition of on-the-job training, seems to have worked well.

The Brain Drain

The movement of highly trained professionals from less developed to developed nations has been a subject of controversy in international development circles. On one side are those who condemn it as an unfair advantage taken by rich countries at the expense of the poor; the latter have borne the cost of educating people, often through the college level, only to have them leave when they become productive. The skills involved—medicine, engineering, natural sciences—may be in short supply in the sending countries and essential for development. Proposals for remedies range from compensation to be paid by the receiving countries to outright prohibition of movement.

Those who defend migration argue that it occurs because the migrants cannot find satisfactory employment at their skills in their native countries, and if they were not free to leave they might simply join the ranks of the

31. Indeed, the Manpower Group of the Economic Planning Council recommended relaxing controls over sending skilled manpower abroad in connection with construction contracts in order to stimulate the export of building materials and to provide additional job opportunities for the expanding labor force.

educated unemployed. Their remittances home are often an important source of foreign exchange. More generally, the defenders argue that the right to emigrate is a human right.

Taiwan has followed a consistent policy with respect to emigration: anyone who wanted to leave could do so without impairing his right to return. The result has been a substantial loss of people going abroad for study, as well as of already trained professionals.

The number of those studying abroad averaged 558 a year from 1952 to 1961 and rose from 1,833 in 1962 to 2,285 in 1974. In 1974, about half were getting degrees in the natural sciences and engineering and another 10 percent in agriculture. This might have been an important source of high-level skills, since many were receiving training superior to that provided by all but the top Taiwan universities, were it not for the fact that relatively few students returned. In 1962, for example, those returning constituted only 3.4 percent of the total studying abroad in that year. This ratio increased in the course of time, but in 1974 it was still only 21.3 percent.[32]

For the period 1960–67, approximately 11,500 students from Taiwan went to the United States for further training, about one-sixth of all college graduates. Two-thirds of them were in science and engineering. Only 4.5 percent returned to Taiwan.[33] The number of returnees increased sharply in 1973 and 1974, because of a combination of deteriorating job prospects in the United States and rising real income in Taiwan.

For a sample period of five years, the major skill-exporting nations of Asia-India, the Philippines, Hong Kong, Korea, and Taiwan sent eight thousand scientists, engineers, and physicians to the United States, of whom 15 percent came from Taiwan. On a per capita basis, the contribution of Taiwan was the greatest.[34]

The magnitude of the loss to the economy of Taiwan from migration can be determined only by a careful analysis, but none has yet been made. It is easy enough to estimate the lifetime earnings of the emigrants and put the total on the loss side of the equation, but to make an accurate judgment would require knowledge of the relative quality of the group that remained away and those who returned. The fields of study, and even the subfields, are important. Income alone would not adequately serve as a weighting system for, say, returned nuclear, electronic, and chemical engineers versus home economists and nutritionists—all of these included in the general categories of engineering and science. An additional variable that is often neglected is visits to

32. EPC *Taiwan Statistical Data Book, 1975* (Taipei), pp. 243–44.

33. Charles H. C. Kao, *Brain Drain: A Case Study of China* (Taipei, 1971), passim.

34. Charles H. C. Kao, "A Preliminary Analysis of the Republic of China's 'Brain Drain' into the United States," *Industry of Free China*, September 1969, p. 29.

Taiwan for long or short periods by eminent emigrant professionals as consultants and teachers, key people whose quality and cost would be difficult to match from among non-Chinese.[35] A final factor, not measurable but nonetheless of great importance, is the value to Taiwan of having former citizens occupying important positions in government, industry, and universities in the United States. Special circumstances may make this factor of greater value to Taiwan than it would be to other countries, but it should not be left out of the equation for any.

In sum, Taiwan has been a large exporter of trained individuals during the years of its rapid economic growth. The magnitude of the loss, if indeed there was a net loss, has not been determined. It is difficult, however, to find anyone in Taiwan who regards the policy of permitting people to move freely across national borders to have been a mistake.

Unemployment and Underemployment

The magnitude of the unemployment problem in most of the underdeveloped world makes the relevant experience of Taiwan of great interest. The idea that economic growth, unaccompanied by radical government measures to redistribute income and wealth, cannot solve the closely related problems of lack of productive work and poverty has gained widespread acceptance and is being promoted by influential international agencies, among them the World Bank and the International Labour Organization.[36]

Taiwan provides a good case study. Until the mid-1960s, its pattern of population growth was typically Asian. Its agricultural resources are limited, and it would not have progressed very far as a predominantly agricultural nation. It has few natural resources, no fuel or metals. Although it received economic aid from the United States, its main resources were a population accustomed to hard, steady work, if they could find work; an ability to organize; and a pragmatic rather than an ideological approach to economic problems.

Estimates of unemployment from different sources are not in agreement; they are shown in Table 6.13. The data for years prior to the labor force survey in 1964 are not reliable, but they suggest that a higher level of unemployment prevailed from 1953 to 1965 than subsequently. The estimates in column 2 of Table 6.13 include persons willing to work but not actively seeking work, who are excluded from the official count in column 1, but who

35. A case in point is Ta-Chung Liu, to whom this volume is dedicated. A leading American econometrician, he served frequently as adviser to the government of the Republic of China and was largely responsible for a major reform of its tax system.

36. See, for example, Hollis Chenery et al., *Redistribution with Growth* (London, 1974); International Labour Organization, *Employment, Growth and Basic Needs* (Geneva, 1976).

Table 6.13. Estimates of Unemployment (percent of labor force)

	Labor force survey (1)	W. Y. Kuo (2)	Census of population (3)
1953		6.3	
1954		6.0	
1955		6.0	
1956		5.6	6.3
1957		5.7	
1958		5.9	
1959		6.0	
1960		6.1	
1961		6.2	
1962		6.3	
1963		6.4	
1964	4.3	6.4	
1965	3.3	5.2	
1966	3.1	4.2	6.1
1967	2.3	3.4	
1968	1.7	2.8	
1969	1.9	3.4	
1970	1.7	3.0	4.6
1971	1.7	3.0	
1972	1.5	2.8	
1973	1.3	2.2	
1974	1.5	2.7	
1975	2.4	3.7	

Sources: Column 1: *Quarterly Report on the Labor Force Survey in Taiwan,* no. 50 (1976), p. 45; columns 2 and 3: Shirley W. Y. Kuo, "A Study of Factors Contributing to Labor Absorption in Taiwan, 1954–1971," *Conference on Population and Economic Development in Taiwan,* p. 482.

should realistically be considered as unemployed because "in rural areas, the unemployed usually do not know whom to contact, nor where to find jobs."[37]

The recorded unemployment statistics for Taiwan, as well as for virtually every other developing country, provide only a partial picture of the true unemployment problem. The labor force participation rates of females suggest that a good deal of additional hidden unemployment existed in the past. The female labor force participation rates for industrial nations tend to be about 35 to 40 percent, although there are exceptions.[38] Given the propensity of Chinese women to work, it was probably true that many women were not actively in the labor force simply because there was no work to be had. But this situation changed after 1966, as evidenced by the figures in Table 6.1.

Another locus of hidden unemployment, or more accurately, underemployment, is the so-called dual or traditional sector in both industry and the

37. Kuo, p. 481. Kuo is vice-chairman of the Economic Planning Council, and her estimates reflect the best present judgment of the council.

38. In 1970, for example, the rate for Italy was 27 percent; for the Netherlands, 26 percent; for Norway, 28 percent (World Bank, *World Tables 1976* [Washington, 1976], p. 517).

services. Although some people in these occupations earn fairly good incomes, many others are engaged in low-productivity trades that yield a marginal existence. The street merchants, small shopkeepers, lottery ticket salesmen, and others who are part of the urban scene in most developing countries are examples of the latter, but they are difficult to count. Part of the problem is conceptual. What level of productivity or earnings is the cutoff point? The problem is further complicated by the fact that people with low earnings often work long hours at physically difficult tasks, so that they are anything but idle.

Although precise estimates of this kind of under employment cannot be made, the Taiwan data lend themselves to evaluation of trends over time. In 1961, there were 34,700 manufacturing enterprises with three or less employees, engaging a total of 73,000 persons.[39] By 1971, the number had fallen considerably.[40] Presumably many of these small enterprises were marginal, and their decline marked progress toward fuller employment.

Unpaid family workers constitute another category in which underemployment is common. The data in column 2 of Table 6.14 illustrate the decline in the number of such workers for the years 1964 to 1975. Most of these were in agriculture, where the decline was from 45 percent in 1965 to 36 percent in January 1976.[41] In manufacturing, the drop was from 7 percent in 1966 to 3 percent in January 1976. The figure for commerce has remained fairly constant at about 7 percent.[42] As of January 1976, some 7.6 percent of all male employees and 28.8 percent of female employees were working without pay in family enterprises, and while by no means all of them are underemployed, they are a reservoir of manpower that could be drawn upon for more productive work.

Another possible area of underemployment is among those working on their own account (Table 6.14, column 1). There has been a gradual decline in the number of persons in this group, but they still constitute about one-quarter of the total labor force. Almost 60 percent of these are independent farmers, who are not underemployed, for the most part, although many engage in sideline activities during slack seasons. Most of the rest are in commerce (25 percent)

39. *Industrial and Commercial Census of Taiwan* (1961), Vol. III, Table 8.

40. The 1971 census lists 15,200 manufacturing enterprises with 31,400 employees. Unlike the 1961 census, however, only those enterprises that were required to apply for factory registration were included in manufacturing. Some small processing and repair shops were included among wholesale and retail enterprises. The figure of 15,200 enterprises would have to be adjusted upward, but there is no doubt that a substantial reduction in the total number occurred. See *Industrial and Commercial Census of Taiwan* (1971), Vol. 1, Table 13.

41. *Quarterly Report on the Labor Force Survey in Taiwan,* no. 50 (1976), Table 8–8. They constituted 73 percent of all unpaid family workers in January 1976.

42. Ibid., and Chi-ming Hou, *Manpower Utilization and Labor Mobility in Taiwan* (Taipei, July 1975), p. 13.

Table 6.14. Indicators of Underemployment, 1964–1975 (percent of all employees)

	Own account workers (1)	Unpaid family workers (2)
1964	29.8	28.5
1965	28.8	23.4
1966	28.9	22.5
1967	27.1	23.9
1968	26.9	22.5
1969	26.4	21.5
1970	26.2	20.1
1971	25.9	18.5
1972	25.4	16.8
1973	25.1	16.2
1974	25.0	16.7
1975	24.3	15.9

Sources: DGBAS, *Statistical Yearbook of the Republic of China, 1975*, p. 48; *Quarterly Report on the Labor Force Survey in Taiwan*, no. 50 (1976), p. 43.

and personal services (6 percent).[43] The commerce category, mainly the small shops prevalent in Taiwan, provides an additional potential group of workers if appropriate opportunities arise.

Some statistics on underemployment are defined in terms of working hours. Paid workers who are employed for more than one hour but less than thirty-six hours per week, or unpaid family workers who work between fifteen and thirty-six hours a week and who wish to work longer, are defined as underemployed for this purpose. The ratio of underemployed to total employment fell from 3.2 percent in 1965 to .6 percent in January 1976.[44] This has clearly ceased to be a problem.

These indicators point to the conclusion that rapid economic growth has indeed led to a marked improvement in Taiwan's employment situation. Full employment has not been achieved in Taiwan, any more than it has in the industrial market economies. But Taiwan has clearly left the stage of massive unemployment and underemployment that still characterizes most of the developing world.

An insight into the nature of the employment problem that remains in Taiwan can be gained from a special labor force survey conducted in January 1976. The official rate of unemployment during that month was 1.6 percent. Some 77 percent of the unemployed could not find jobs, but the rest had rejected work, mainly because the pay was too low or the location was bad. Young people under the age of twenty-five constituted 71 percent of the total

43. *Quarterly Report on the Labor Force Survey in Taiwan,* no. 50 (1976), Table B-8.
44. Hou and Hsu, p. 329.

unemployed,[45] with another 13 percent in the twenty-five- to twenty-nine-year age bracket. There were few older people among the unemployed.

The young people could afford to look around, even without unemployment compensation, because they were being taken care of by their families: 86 percent listed families as their source of support. Some 79 percent of all unemployed were single, and among females, 96 percent. Married women who wanted employment but could not find suitable jobs presumably withdrew from the labor market.[46]

Working Time

No consistent data exist on working hours prior to 1969, nor does there appear to have been any marked trend since then, the changes primarily reflecting cyclical forces.[47] The labor code provides for a basic eight-hour day, with overtime at one and one-third the basic rate for the first two additional hours and one and two-thirds thereafter. In December 1975, production workers in manufacturing were averaging 230 hours and 25.9 days per month, that is, eight to nine hours a day.[48]

In 1974, 30 percent of factories were working overtime when visited by factory inspectors; the figure was almost 50 percent for factories employing thirty or more workers.[49] The managers of large, modern enterprises who were interviewed in the summer of 1976 stated almost uniformly that they were working an eight-hour day, forty-eight-hour week, with little if any overtime. It is apparently not uncommon, however, for plants to operate on a nine-hour day,[50] without always abiding by the overtime pay provision of the law because of a lack of adequate enforcement machinery.

The law also stipulates one day of rest in every seven and six days off annually for national holidays. However, 37 percent of the enterprises visited in 1973 by factory inspectors were allowing only one day of rest every fourteen days, although almost all observed holidays.[51]

The larger firms tend to provide paid annual vacations. A leading au-

45. Many of these were actually preparing themselves for taking college entrance examinations and were looking for jobs that allowed them ample time to study.

46. The data are from EPC, "Taiwan Regional Manpower Utilization Survey Report" (computer printout, 1976).

47. See EPC, *Social Welfare Indicators 1976*, p. 65.

48. *Monthly Bulletin of Labor Statistics*, no. 30 (April 1976), pp. 28, 32.

49. Ministry of the Interior, *Annual Report of Factory and Mining Inspection* (Taipei, 1974), Table 32.

50. In a special 1973 survey of the Kaoshiung-Pingtung area, the average number of weekly working hours in manufacturing were 51.6; in construction, 51.9; in commerce, 54.2; and in transportation, 56.8. For men, the hours were longer—53.3 in manufacturing and 56.3 in commerce. EPC, *Report on Experimental Survey for Measurement of Work Force Utilization in Kaoshiung-Pingtung Area* (Taipei, 1975), Table 61.

51. Ministry of the Interior, *Annual Report of Factory and Mining Inspection*, Table 35.

tomobile manufacturer, for example, gives its employees one week off after three years with the firm, rising to a maximum of one month with additional seniority. A producer of motorcycles allows seven days of annual vacation after one year at the plant; ten days after three years; two weeks after five years; and thirty days after ten years. How typical this practice is of manufacturing generally cannot be determined from available data.

The industrial workers of Taiwan are still some distance from the point at which they begin to prefer leisure to added income. Their basic working week exceeds that of the United States and Western Europe by about eight hours, and the disparity increases if overtime is taken into account.

Labor Mobility

Labor can move in several ways: between major sectors of the economy, within sectors, and among firms within an industry or a local labor market. In this section the mobility experience of Taiwan is examined.

Some of the most difficult problems faced by developing nations stem from large-scale migration from rural areas to cities, from the agricultural to the industrial or service sectors. Many of the people who move find low-productivity jobs, if they find any at all, and live in squatter settlements that proliferate wherever there is vacant space. Inadequate water and sewage systems create health problems. A large group of semi-idle, low-income people is created, and they become a menace to political stability. Apart from the communist countries, which employ police methods to prevent migration into cities and to deport the excess urban population (deportation has been done systematically and on a large scale in Communist China, and Cambodia provides a particularly horrible example), few countries have found adequate solutions to the problem.

Taiwan has managed to keep this problem under reasonable control by a combination of rapid economic growth and good industrial location. A recent study concluded:

With a few exceptions, rural-to-urban migration in Taiwan can be viewed as a rational response to changing economic conditions. The growing rural population has adjusted to the pressure of population on limited resources by sending to the major cities those members of the rural population who are best qualified for urban employment. The migrants have been drawn disproportionately from the young adults, from the more highly educated, from those working most recently in nonagricultural employment, and from the larger farms.[52]

This does not mean that Taiwan has remained a rural nation. On the contrary, if urban areas are defined as those with five hundred thousand or more

52. Alden Speare, Jr., "Urbanization and Migration in Taiwan," *Economic Development and Cultural Change,* 22 (January 1974), 319.

Table 6.15. Labor Turnover Rates,* 1972–1975 (month of December) (percent of total employment)

	1972	1973	1974	1975
All manufacturing				
Accessions	4.1	1.6	1.7	2.7
Separations	1.8	1.6	2.7	1.8
Textiles and apparel				
Accessions	3.8	1.0	0.9	1.4
Separations	2.1	2.7	2.3	1.9
Communications equipment				
Accessions	—	2.7	0.2	2.9
Separations	—	2.0	7.7	2.3
Services				
Accessions	1.8	2.2	2.3	1.5
Separations	1.4	2.2	2.5	1.8

*These rates are defined as the ratio of accessions or separations in a given month to total employment at the end of that month.
Source: *Monthly Bulletin of Labor Statistics,* no. 30 (April 1976), Tables 4-5, 4-6, 4-7.

inhabitants, Taiwan is more urbanized than Canada or New Zealand and not far behind the United States.[53] But much new manufacturing industry was located in smaller towns and in the countryside, attracted by cheap land, by the availability of labor, and by industrial sites and infrastructure provided by the government at low cost or entirely free. Service employment tended to increase more rapidly in large cities, but fortunately, the increase in absolute terms was not so great as to overwhelm them.[54]

Job mobility rates have been moderate, on the whole, as shown in Table 6.15. Separation rates rose sharply with the 1974 recession, particularly in electronics. Some subsectors of the service industries, primarily restaurants, hotels, and tailor shops, experienced high turnover rates in the recession years, and this was probably true of retailing as well.

Labor turnover increased unexpectedly in 1976, despite the recovery in business conditions, leading to speculation about the onset of a labor shortage. Particularly affected were the industries employing large numbers of unskilled females. In cotton textiles, for example, the separation rate in February 1976 was 5.8 percent, higher than in any comparable month for which data are available. For the same month, the separation rate was 5.9 percent for knit goods, 4.3 percent for clothing, 7.3 percent for electrical equipment, and 7.2 percent for communications equipment.[55] A major manufacturer of electronic parts reported, in an interview in June 1976, a turnover rate of 12 percent a month; it was hiring one thousand new employees each month in order to

53. Paul K. C. Liu, "Relationships between Urbanization and Socio-Economic Development in Taiwan," *Conference on Population and Economic Development in Taiwan,* p. 623.
54. Ibid., p. 631.
55. *Monthly Bulletin of Labor Statistics,* no. 30 (April 1976), Table 4-3.

maintain a labor force of eight thousand. Smaller companies that relied mainly on adult males were able to keep their turnover down to 3 to 4 percent a month.

The special labor force survey of January 1976 provides some explanation of the recent labor mobility trends. Only about 10 percent of those sampled appear to have ever changed jobs. Thirteen percent of the job changers were under twenty years of age; 18 percent were between twenty and twenty-four years old; and another 19 percent were between twenty-five and twenty-nine. Thus, half were under thirty, a not unexpected finding. Seventy percent of all the job changers had only a primary or junior high school education. Among manufacturing workers, 80 percent of the moves were voluntary, and the main reasons cited were better pay (37 percent), better location (16 percent), better working environment (5 percent), and improved future opportunities (3 percent). Voluntary change was considerably lower in commerce (53 percent), with unsatisfactory pay again the main cause. For all industries, long working hours, night work, lack of job guarantees, poor training, and poor relationships with fellow workers accounted for a relatively small portion of separations.[56]

Data regarding frequency of job change by individuals are contained in Table 6.16, which indicates that drifting has not been a common occurrence. Even among those who shifted their employment, most had made only one change and very few more than two.

If all these figures are to be credited, Taiwan has a remarkably stable labor force. Once employees have settled down, they tend to remain with the same employer. A number of possible reasons can be cited: the relatively short labor market experience of a young labor force; rapid growth, opening up opportunities within enterprises; and the labor practices of employers.

It is not yet clear whether the increase in turnover rates that began in 1976, particularly in industries employing large numbers of unskilled workers, marks a new phase in Taiwan's labor mobility history or whether it was the result of increased competition for available labor because of rapid recovery of the economy. An evaluation of the future prospects for labor supply and demand may help throw some light on the matter.

The Future

A good supply of relatively cheap and well-qualified labor was undoubtedly a major factor in fueling Taiwan's industrialization drive. Questions are being raised in Taiwan[57] as to whether this era may be drawing to a close and will result in real wages rising more rapidly and the mass-processing indus-

---

56: EPC, ''Taiwan Regional Manpower Utilization Survey Report,'' Tables 29, 32, 33.
57. And not only in Taiwan; see also ''Labor Shortage Is Hurting Taiwan Firms But May Aid Long-Term Industrialization,'' *Wall Street Journal*, September 2, 1976, p. 26.

Table 6.16. Frequency of Job Changes for Individuals Changing Jobs in January 1976 (percent of total job changers)

Year present job began	Number of job changes per individual				
	One	Two	Three	Four	Five and over
Before 1971	56.9	27.9	9.5	2.6	3.1
1971	57.6	29.1	9.0	1.7	2.7
1972	68.2	18.3	7.8	3.1	2.6
1973	65.3	25.2	7.1	0.4	1.9
1974	80.6	14.0	3.6	0.3	1.4
1975	85.2	11.0	1.9	0	2.0

Source: EPC, "Taiwan Regional Manpower Utilization Survey Report," Table 34.

tries giving way to more capital-intensive ones. One of Taiwan's leading economists remarked that the "labor shortage has been increasingly felt in recent years which, I think, does give reason for us to worry about the long-run competitiveness of Taiwan's exports."[58]

The data in Table 6.17 provide some grounds for concern. The estimated annual rate of labor force increase over the six-year-plan period 1975–81 is substantially below that for the years 1970–75. The difference is due primarily to the decline in the rate of increase of the female labor force because of the relatively high female labor force participation rates already prevailing in 1975.

The very large increase in both the male and female twenty- to twenty-four-year age cohort that took place during 1970–75 is reflected in the change in the twenty-five- to thirty-four-year age group from 1975 to 1981. But there will be no comparable replacement for the twenty- to twenty-four-year group; their estimated growth is very low. For those under twenty, an increase in schooling plus demographic events had already brought the increase down to zero for 1970–75, and this will change but little during the following six years.

The 3.0 percent labor force increase projected for 1975–81 is by no means negligible. Between 1960 and 1970, for example, the labor force of the United States rose at an annual rate of 1.8 percent, the largest increase of any of the major Organization for Economic Cooperation and Development (OECD) countries for the same decade. Japan had an increase of only 1.3 percent, which was not incompatible with high rates of economic growth.[59] The important point is how the extra people are used.

The data in Table 6.18 indicate what may happen to the labor force in the

58. M. H. Hsing, in *Conference on Population and Economic Development in Taiwan*, p. 445.

59. Organization for Economic Cooperation and Development, *Labour Force Statistics, 1959–1970* (Paris, 1972), pp. 69, 81.

Table 6.17. Average Annual Change in the Labor Force, 1970–1975, and Estimated, 1975–1981, by Age and Sex

Age group	Total*		Male		Female	
	1970–75	1975–81	1970–75†	1975–81*	1970–75†	1975–81*
15–19	0	0.5	−1.1	0.7	0.5	0.4
20–24	13.5	0.9	11.6	0.8	14.4	0.9
25–34	2.7	7.9	1.9	7.3	4.3	9.4
35–44	3.3	2.2	2.6	2.0	5.3	2.7
45–54	6.5	1.0	5.5	0.2	10.4	4.1
55–64	7.5	4.6	6.7	4.8	12.3	3.2
65 and over	7.1	6.1	6.4	5.9	6.5	8.3
Average	4.3	3.0	3.4	3.0	5.8	3.2

*Total labor force.
†Employment.
Sources: 1970–75: Quarterly Report on the Labor Force Survey in Taiwan, no. 50 (1976), Tables A-6, A-8; 1976–81: EPC, "Six Year Plan."

major industrial sectors during the six-year-plan period compared to what actually happened in 1970–75. Agriculture continues with approximately the same size labor force; services get a larger proportionate share of the new entrants than in the previous five years. The growth of manufacturing employment is greatly diminished; the net increase falls from 568,000 during 1970–75 to 353,000 from 1976 to 1981.

The estimates suggest that the manufacturing sector is not likely to have the manpower bonanza of the past, but it can count upon a continuing flow of new recruits. Particularly in view of the greatly reduced rate of increase in the supply of young women, however, the labor-intensive processing industries will not be able to expand nearly as rapidly as they have in the past.

The eventual state of the labor market can be determined only by comparing labor demand and supply schedules, and the former are not available. Demand estimates are implicit in the estimates contained in Tables 6.17 and 6.18, but changes in the underlying trends on which they are based could produce

Table 6.18. Average Annual Change in Employment, by Industry, 1970–1975, and Estimated, 1975–1981 (percent per annum)

Industry	1970–1975	1975–1981
Agriculture	0	−0.7
Mining	−6.6	−3.0
Manufacturing	12.2	3.9
Construction	10.8	5.3
Public utilities	−1.0	2.2
Transport and communication	4.2	3.5
Services	3.6	6.2
Total	4.1	3.2

Sources: 1970–75: Quarterly Report on the Labor Force Survey in Taiwan, no. 50 (1976), Table A-9; 1976–81: EPC, "Six Year Plan."

substantial demand shifts. If, for example, there were to be a movement of electronics processing out of Taiwan, lack of work for young women could develop quickly. A decline in textile export markets would produce the same result.

On the supply side, the labor force still seems to have substantial reserves for the expansion of higher productivity industries with commensurate wage scales. Agriculture, with 30 percent of the total labor force, contains the major reserve. Whether it will be drawn upon depends in part upon relative incomes; workers in Taiwan have responded quickly to economic incentive. It is generally believed in Taiwan that the rapid rise in farm incomes after 1973, combined with reduced manufacturing vacancies, persuaded many young people to return to or remain on the farm. Employers report that it is much more difficult to recruit in the countryside than at the beginning of the 1970s. The manager of a large enterprise stated in an interview that the New Year vacation, when many people return to their towns and villages, is the most dangerous time. To reduce attrition, he had adopted the policy of sending private buses to bring the employees back. Higher wages could accomplish the same result, but would be more costly.

The employment slice of the service sector is relatively modest, and the indications are that it will increase. But it still has substantial reserves in the form of low-productivity pockets that could be utilized if there were an appropriate demand. For example, many young women employed in retailing receive wages that are often lower than they could earn in manufacturing. They prefer the conditions of work where they are, even though they frequently work very long hours, but they might be attracted by more highly paid white-collar jobs. In addition, many people engaged in small enterprises, often self-employed, could be induced to move if there were more attractive opportunities.

A recent survey of people of working age who are not in the labor force indicates that 380,000, about 10 percent of the total, would be willing to work if they found the right combination of wage and type of job; 300,000 of these were women.[60] Many of the women are not young—almost half are over thirty years of age—and might not be suitable for such industries as electronics.

The labor supply will be reduced by the probable future curtailment of working hours. As incomes rise, the present working day of almost nine hours in manufacturing is bound to come down, as is the working week. Civil servants already enjoy a five- and-a-half-day, forty-four-hour working week, and it is not inconceivable that this will become the norm for modern industry within the decade.

60. EPC, ''Taiwan Regional Manpower Utilization Survey Report,'' Table 62.

On balance, unless there is an unexpectedly large increase in the rate of economic and industrial growth, particularly in labor-intensive industries, Taiwan does not seem to be facing any serious labor stringency for the remainder of the 1970s and even beyond. The era of abundant unskilled labor is drawing to a close, but it is difficult to envision a reasonable pattern of industrial growth that would face serious labor constraints. Shortages of particular skills may arise, but the human resource base that has enabled Taiwan to develop in the past is far from depleted.

The Level and Structure of Wages

Taiwan differs from most less developed countries in that wages have been determined with little government intervention. Trade union impact on wages has been minimal. The development process has been so rapid and compressed that even relatively short time series are useful indicators of what happens to wages as industrial structure changes. The relevant data are not complete, but they are good compared to those available for the generality of less developed countries.

Changes over time in money and real wages in manufacturing are shown in Table 6.19. There are no consistent series for the entire nonagricultural economy.[61] The data for years prior to 1971 are not considered to be as reliable as those for subsequent years. Several attempts have been made to secure better estimates for the period before 1973,[62] but none is yet regarded as completely satisfactory.

Table 6.19 shows that over the twenty-two-year period covered, money earnings rose tenfold, with most of the increase coming in the last decade. This is by no means a model record of wage inflation, by international standards, but it is far from the worst. During the immediate preinflation decade 1962–72, for example, Taiwan's money wage index stood at 216 (1972 based on 1962). Of the major industrial nations, only the United States (159) was lower, whereas Japan (384) and Germany (224) had substantially larger increases.[63] After 1973, Taiwan was caught up in the worldwide inflation and experienced a money wage increase of almost 60 percent in two years.

61. Series are available for public utilities and for transportation and communications.
62. The Manpower Group of the Economic Planning Council prepared a series for the entire period since 1953, and the Bureau of Statistics made estimates for the years 1966–71. The index based upon the Manpower Group data differs from that in Table 6.19 only for years after 1967. The Bureau of Statistics data show a somewhat slower rise in wages for 1966–71 than given in Table 6.19. The Manpower Group data are available in *Conference on Population and Economic Development in Taiwan*, p. 115.
63. Data are from the International Labour Office, *Year Book of Labour Statistics* (Geneva, 1973), Table 19A.

Table 6.19. Trends in Money and Real Earnings in Manufacturing, 1953–1975

	Monthly earnings (N.T.$) (1)	Index of monthly earnings (1953 = 100) (2)	Consumer price index (1953 = 100) (3)	Index of real monthly earnings in manufacturing (1953 = 100) (4)
1953	405	100	100	100
1954	458	113	102	111
1955	511	126	112	113
1956	583	144	124	116
1957	637	157	133	118
1958	669	165	134	123
1959	724	179	149	120
1960	842	208	176	118
1961	1,024	253	190	133
1962	1,077	266	194	137
1963	1,121	277	199	139
1964	1,158	286	198	144
1965	1,256	308	198	155
1966	1,338	330	202	163
1967	1,517	375	209	179
1968	1,677	414	225	184
1969	1,703	420	237	177
1970	1,850	457	245	187
1971	2,162	534	252	212
1972	2,323	574	260	221
1973	2,538*	627	281	223
1974	3,405	841	414	203
1975	4,028	995	436	228

*The method of calculation and the agency responsible for preparation of the data were changed in 1973. The pre-1973 data are not considered to be as reliable as those for subsequent years.
Sources: Column 1: DGBAS, *Statistical Yearbook of the Republic of China, 1975,* Table 171; *Monthly Bulletin of Labor Statistics,* April 1976, Table 3-3; column 2: Column 1 in index form; column 3: EPC, *Taiwan Statistical Data Book* (Taipei, 1975), p. 157; column 4: Column 2 divided by column 3.

The real wage data in column 4 of Table 6.19 are of greater relvance in judging the economic impact of the wage increases.[64] They show a fairly slow but steady rise in real wages from 1953 to 1964; a higher tempo of increase from 1964 to 1967; a deceleration from 1967 to 1970; two years of large increases, 1971–72; and then a large drop during the 1974 inflation, followed by recoupment in 1975. If the entire twenty-two-year period covered in the table is divided into two equal periods of eleven years each, the average

64. The figures for average monthly earnings in all manufacturing represent an average of earnings in seventeen manufacturing industries (nine after 1972), weighted by employment. They are thus affected by the great changes in the structure of industrial employment that took place during the period and particularly by the increase in female employment, mainly at below-average wages. This should be borne in mind in imputing welfare consequences from the real wage trends, since wage rates rose probably more rapidly than earnings for the majority of employees. Thus, for ten out of the original seventeen industries covered, average earnings rose more than the all-manufacturing average, some by very substantial amounts. Of the remaining seven industries, in only three were the earnings increases substantially below the all-industry level.

annual percentage rise is clearly higher in the latter, 5.3 percent compared with 4.0 percent in the former.

If real wage trends were to be taken as a measure of the tightness of the labor market, it would be difficult to read out of either the annual or the long-run trends any sudden changes in labor scarcity. The concept of an unlimited labor supply that has sometimes been used to characterize the labor market of developing economies apparently had little relevance to Taiwan during the growth period.

Wage Differentials

The historical experience of the developed countries leads to the presumption that wage differentials will tend to diminish during the course of development. The spread of education increases the relative supply of skilled workers; fuller employment increases the opportunities available for females; the growing scarcity of unskilled labor obliges low-wage industries and occupations to pay more if they are to preserve their manpower.

The experience of Taiwan calls for at least a refinement of the hypothesis. Table 6.20 presents data for skilled-unskilled and male-female wage differentials from 1953 to 1972.[65] Skill and sex differentials appear to have increased over time, although individual years show sharp reversals of this trend (the year 1970 stands out particularly sharply as a deviant). Unskilled workers did relatively well from 1965 to 1970, but women did not.

Some difficulties arise in interpreting these data. Most women employed in manufacturing were unskilled, so that the sharp rise in the female participation rate that began in 1967 undoubtedly contributed to the maintenance of substantial male-female skill differentials. The same would be true of changes in industrial structure: a relative rise in the processing industries, requiring mainly unskilled labor, would tend to understate the relative increase of unskilled wages within each industry.

Because of the unavailability of data, it is impossible further to disaggregate manufacturing wages by skill and by sex. It is possible to standardize in part for these factors by examining skill differentials in selected industries in which female participation has been low and sex differentials in industries in which female participation has been traditionally high. In printing and in the manufacture of paper products, for example, women accounted for 23 percent of the total labor force in January 1976. They constituted 70 percent of the labor force in textiles and 65 percent in leather products during the same month.

Table 6.21 suggests that the premium for skill may have declined over the

---

65. The series upon which these data are based were discontinued after 1972.

Table 6.20. Trends in Wage Differentials in Manufacturing, 1953–1972 (N.T.$ per day)

	Skilled versus unskilled			Male versus female		
	Skilled earnings	Unskilled earnings	Unskilled as a percentage of skilled earnings	Male earnings	Female earnings	Female as a percentage of male earnings
1953	16.62	13.91	83.7	16.36	13.50	82.5
1954	18.72	15.31	81.8	18.39	14.52	79.0
1955	21.44	16.20	75.6	21.17	15.11	71.4
1956	24.44	18.12	74.1	24.17	16.41	67.9
1957	26.82	20.03	74.7	26.47	18.05	68.2
1958	28.33	21.57	76.1	27.85	19.49	70.0
1959	30.55	23.26	75.1	30.14	20.83	69.1
1960	36.32	26.74	73.6	35.83	23.30	65.0
1961	46.35	31.40	67.7	44.02	26.61	60.4
1962	47.62	33.92	71.2	46.05	23.47	51.0
1963	49.60	34.84	70.2	48.01	28.79	60.0
1964	51.24	35.55	69.4	50.72	29.34	57.8
1965	56.38	37.25	66.1	55.40	30.81	55.6
1966	58.07	41.04	70.7	58.88	32.59	55.3
1967	65.11	45.50	69.9	67.29	35.55	52.8
1968	71.22	51.89	72.9	69.41	40.98	59.0
1969	72.91	53.30	73.1	75.78	42.60	56.2
1970	76.29	62.22	81.6	80.80	49.73	61.5
1971	93.78	63.43	67.6	95.69	54.76	57.3
1972	103.23	67.18	65.1	103.08	59.55	57.8

Source: Report of Taiwan Labor Statistics, various issues.

entire period, although the finding is not unambiguous.[66] In the manufacture of paper products, the skill differential fluctuated in a narrow range until 1972, when it declined sharply. For printing, there was a decrease in the skill premium in the middle of the period, but an increase at the end. The wage differentials by sex (Table 6.22) in textiles and leather goods actually increased from 1953 to 1972, though there was some diminution at the very end of the period.

No statistics for skill differentials have been published since 1972, but the January 1976 labor market survey provides information on average monthly earnings based on years of schooling, which might serve as a rough proxy for skill (figures are in N.T.$):[67]

Primary school	3,940
Junior high school (including junior vocational school)	3,748
High school	5,194

66. It is difficult to believe the 1970 figure for printing, which indicates higher average earnings for unskilled than for skilled workers. Whether this is an error or a sampling aberration cannot be determined from the source.

67. EPC, "Taiwan Regional Manpower Utilization Survey Report," Table 41.

Table 6.21. Trends in Wage Differentials in the Manufacture of Printing and Paper Products, by Skill, Selected Years (N.T.$ per day)

	Printing			Paper products		
	Skilled earnings	Unskilled earnings	Unskilled as a percentage of skilled earnings	Skilled earnings	Unskilled earnings	Unskilled as a percentage of skilled earnings
1953	25.11	15.84	63.1	14.00	11.41	81.5
1955	26.82	19.51	72.7	23.86	19.68	82.5
1960	41.68	30.13	72.3	36.34	28.45	78.3
1965	50.10	43.90	87.6	48.62	38.64	79.5
1970	72.77	78.85	108.4	73.20	56.35	76.0
1972	75.92	58.90	77.6	85.13	77.58	91.1

Source: *Report of Taiwan Labor Statistics,* various issues.

Vocational and normal school	4,730
Colleges and universities	6,814

If a vocational school training is taken to be the equivalent of "skill" and primary school graduates are regarded as unskilled, unskilled earnings were 83 percent of skilled. The reason for the lower junior high school and junior vocational earnings, as compared with earnings for primary school graduates, is that the average age and length of work experience was greater for the latter group. This, in turn, was caused by the substantial extension in length of education that began in 1968 and by the fact that the lower vocational schools were mainly established beginning in the second half of the 1960s.

As for sex differentials, women in manufacturing were reported as earning only 50 percent of the male level in January 1976.[68] Although this figure is not directly comparable with those in Table 6.20, it suggests that sex differentials have not narrowed since 1972.

No definitive conclusion can be reached on the history of wage differentials based on skill and sex without a much more exhaustive investigation than has been possible here. However, the behavior of the various indicators point to the possibility that in the initial stages of rapid industrialization both types of differential tend to widen, the skill differential because of a shortage of skills, the sex differential because of a relatively large increase in the supply of female workers.[69] As the supply of skilled workers grows because of increased schooling resulting from greater affluence, the skill differential should narrow, and this point may have been reached in Taiwan by 1976.

The large number of women entering the labor market in the years after 1966 might have been expected to result in a widening of average male-female

68. Ibid., Table 42.
69. This is not necessarily true for wage differentials of skilled females as compared with skilled males.

Table 6.22. Trends in Wage Differentials in the Manufacture of Textiles and Leather Goods, by Sex, Selected Years (N.T.$ per day)

	Textiles			Leather goods		
	Male earnings	Female earnings	Female as a percentage of male earnings	Male earnings	Female earnings	Female as a percentage of male earnings
1953	18.02	14.66	81.4	14.07	11.43	81.2
1955	18.30	15.13	82.7	16.58	13.46	81.2
1960	33.21	21.49	64.7	29.92	15.18	50.7
1965	42.75	28.10	55.7	42.73	23.62	55.3
1970	70.11	45.51	64.9	69.94	38.23	54.7
1972	86.40	58.56	67.8	79.23	49.93	63.0

Source: *Report of Taiwan Labor Statistics,* various issues.

wage differentials, but in fact, between 1966 and 1972, there was little net change. When a 40 percent participation rate was reached in 1973, the differential should have begun to narrow, but this may have been forestalled by the economic recession that began in 1974. If the industries that employ large numbers of women experience a relative expansion in the future, the wage gap should narrow.

The variability of the manufacturing wage structure has been remarkably stable over time, as the following coefficients of variation for seventeen manufacturing industries indicate:[70]

1953	20.22
1960	21.87
1966	22.87
1972	21.50

There was considerable shift in industry ranking, however; the coefficient of rank correlation between the years 1953 and 1972 was only .14,[71] which is normal in a dynamic economy. Industries with rapidly changing technology would tend to move to the top of the ranking, and those that were relatively stagnant would fall to the bottom.

Low-Wage Groups

A minimum wage law has been in effect in Taiwan since 1956, but it has generally been too low to have much effect on actual rates paid. In 1956, the initial minimum was N.T.$10 a day for adult workers; the average daily rate for manufacturing was N.T.$22.17. The minimum was raised to N.T.$15 a day in 1964 against average wages paid of N.T.$50.72 and to N.T.$20 in

70. Computed from *Report of Taiwan Labor Statistics,* various years.
71. Ibid.

Table 6.23. Employed Persons by Income Category, January 1976*

	Average monthly income (N.T.$)	Percentage of all employed persons with incomes	
		Less than 50 percent of N.T.$4,204†	Less than 33 percent of N.T.$4,204‡
Total economy	4,204	12.6	4.8
Agriculture	3,173	17.3	6.5
Manufacturing	3,758	17.2	5.8
Public utilities	5,465	1.3	0
Construction	4,607	6.6	2.9
Commerce	4,900	13.1	3.9
Transport and communications	5,738	1.9	0.9
Finance	6,359	2.9	0.8
Social services	4,623	11.7	6.2

*Excludes employers and self-employed. Preliminary data.
†These figures are slightly understated because they include workers in wage brackets up to N.T.$2,000, as against the true 50 percent average of N.T.$2,102.
‡These figures are overstated because they include workers in wage brackets up to N.T.$1,500 a month as against the true 33 percent average of N.T.$1,300 a month.
Source: EPC, "Taiwan Regional Manpower Utilization Survey Report," Table 35.

1968 against actual rates of N.T.$64.26.[72] The minimum has not been raised since 1968, which means that it was only 10 percent of the average manufacturing wage in 1976. The government has considered increasing the minimum; the Labor Department of the Ministry of the Interior would like to see it raised to N.T.$1,800 a month (the January 1976 average for all manufacturing was N.T.$5,500 a month), indexed to the cost of living.

The data in Table 6.23 indicate that low-income groups exist that would derive protection from a realistic minimum wage. A minimum of N.T.$1,800 a month would affect all of the workers represented in column 3 and most of those in column 2. Even a minimum of N.T.$1,200 would help almost 5 percent of all those employed. To a considerable degree, however, very low wages are associated with youth. About 65 percent of all persons earning under N.T.$1,500 a month during January 1976 were under twenty years of age.[73]

The government has been cautious about the minimum wage issue, fearing, at different times, a disemployment or an inflationary impact. The case for an effective minimum has been put as follows:

There are areas where the demand for labor schedule is kinked, or where monopoly power is exercised, a rise in the wage rate within a certain range would not necessarily

72. Chen Sun, "Wage Structure and Wage Policy in Taiwan," *Sino-American Conference on Manpower in Taiwan,* p. 282.
73. EPC, "Taiwan Regional Manpower Utilization Survey Report," Table 38.

affect employment. . . . Instead of a general or overall minimum wage rate, minimum wages can be set separately for different industries in the light of the production function and market conditions. Thus, it is believed that a carefully designed minimum wage regulation could help improve the economic welfare of the workers without retarding employment growth.[74]

Supplements to Basic Wages[75]

As is the case in most developing nations, the wage structure in Taiwan includes a great many fringe benefits. As a consequence of the inflation of 1974, many firms are attempting to provide more welfare services to their employees as an alternative to large increases in money wages.

Private enterprises offer very little in the way of housing assistance, mainly dormitories for single persons, particularly young women. Government enterprises are more generous; the tobacco monopoly, for example, provides fifteen-year, 4 percent loans up to 40 percent of the cost of a house for its employees.

The fringe benefits most commonly given are subsidized meals[76] and work clothing. Bonuses are also fairly common, depending upon profits. Several firms reported paying out the equivalent of from two to four months pay in 1975, plus additional payments at the time of three annual festivals.[77] Among other benefits provided by individual firms were educational subsidies for children of workers,[78] recreational facilities, and low-cost canteens. Dismissal pay is given occasionally, but private pension schemes do not exist.

There are no published surveys of wages that include fringe benefits, but a private survey gives a good picture of the situation in April 1976. The data in Tables 6.24 and 6.25 refer to assembly workers in the major Taiwan electronics firms, among them such large multinationals as Phillips, Admiral, Arvin, ITT, Philco, Timex, RCA, General Instruments, Texas Instruments, and Zenith.

Table 6.24 shows the monthly cash wage progression for new employees, mostly young women. There was a shortage of this type of labor at the time of the survey, so that many of the firms were paying small monthly increments to discourage turnover.

---

74. Sun, pp. 282–83.

75. Much of the material in this section is based on interviews conducted in Taiwan in June and July 1975.

76. Government agencies are also generous in this respect. I secured an excellent lunch in the cafeteria of the Economic Planning Commission for the equivalent of 25 cents in U.S. currency.

77. In one large firm, these payments amounted to from N.T.$300 to 500 per person, with N.T.$600 or more for the New Year. This same firm paid a regular annual bonus of two months' salary to anyone with more than ten years' seniority, allocating about 10 percent of total profits for this purpose.

78. In one firm, the stipulated educational benefits were doubled if the student maintained an A grade average—an incentive scheme with a vengeance.

Table 6.24. Cash Wages of Assemblers in Electronics Enterprises, April 1976 (paid after stipulated length of service, N.T.$ per month)

Company	Start	First month	Second month	Third month	Sixth month	One year
Taipei Area						
A	1,500	1,500	1,550	1,550	1,600	1,650
B	1,850	1,850	1,900	1,950	2,000	2,000
C	1,700	1,700	1,700	1,700	1,800	1,900
D	1,526	1,626	1,626	1,626	1,776	1,826
E	1,725	1,775	1,775	1,825	1,875	1,925
F	1,558	1,558	1,649	1,649	1,649	1,714
G	1,700	1,790	1,790	1,860	1,860	1,860
H	1,700	1,750	1,750	1,800	1,850	1,900
Other Areas						
A	1,475	1,500	1,550	1,550	1,600	1,675
B	1,820	1,910	1,910	1,910	1,990	2,060
C	1,550	1,600	1,650	1,650	1,800	1,900
D	1,550	1,600	1,600	1,600	1,650	1,700
E	1,600	1,600	1,635	1,670	1,700	1,760
F	1,750	1,750	1,750	1,750	2,000	2,100
G	1,600	1,600	1,640	1,640	1,720	1,760
H	1,900	2,030	2,030	2,030	2,030	2,160
I	1,525	1,600	1,700	1,700	1,700	1,800
J	1,700	1,700	1,700	1,800	1,800	1,900
K	1,760	1,830	1,880	1,930	1,970	2,010
L	1,700	1,800	1,800	1,800	1,850	1,900

Source: A private survey.

Fringe benefits are shown in Table 6.25. All firms provided subsidized meals and either company transportation or cash in lieu thereof. About half the firms had dormitory facilities, all firms paid monthly bonuses for full attendance, and annual bonuses equal to two months' pay were the norm. In the Taipei area, the fringes added about 25 percent to cash wage cost for most firms; outside Taipei, the range of additional cost was much wider, from 10 to almost 40 percent.

The results of another survey, also conducted in April 1976 and including unskilled workers in textile as well as electronics firms, are shown in Table 6.26. In general, textile manufacturers offered higher wages than did electronics plants. Within the textile group, the range of cash wages was only about 10 percent, and the fringe benefits were similar from company to company. For the large electronics employers, the wage range was somewhat greater; this is consistent with the data in Tables 6.24 and 6.25. The reason for so large a spread is not clear; convenience of location and conditions of work may have been factors in producing the differences.

These wage surveys show that employers have good information about competitive wages and fringe benefits and that a considerable degree of standardization prevails, despite the absence of any significant trade union influence. Statistics cited earlier on turnover rates and causes of job change suggest

Table 6.25. Fringe Benefits Paid to Assemblers in Electronics Enterprises, April 1976

Company	Meals (N.T.$ per month)	Transportation (N.T.$ per month)*	Cost to employee of dormitory accommodations (N.T.$ per month)	Full attendance bonus (N.T.$ per month)	Annual bonuses (months of pay)	Average total wage and fringes cost (N.T.$ per month)
Taipei Area						
A	180	200	None	200	2	2,080
B	475	300	None	200	2	2,825
C	260†	†	50	100	2	2,360
D	215	300	Free	200	2	2,231
E	240	300	None	150	2	2,415
F	270	180	None	100	1–2	2,108
G	215	300	None	5%	2	2,300
H	350	150	50	150	2	2,350
Other Areas						
A	208	360	None	250	2	2,293
B	225	125	None	280	2	2,450
C	290	50	Free	200	2	2,090
D	336	285	Free	200	2	2,371
E	240	400	50	200	2	2,440
F	390	240‡	‡	75	2	2,450
G	150	195	Free	100	1–2	2,420
H	200	200	None	180	2	2,480
I	225	225	50	125	2	2,100
J	435	400	30	n.a.	2	2,535
K	300	125†	‡	50	2	2,235
L	250	10§	n.a.	250	2	2,400

*Cash payment or cost of service provided.
†Meals and transportation.
‡Transportation and dormitory accomodations.
§Per day worked.
Source: A private survey.

Table 6.26. Wages and Fringe Benefits Paid to Assemblers in Textile and Electronic Enterprises, April 1976

Company	Location	Employment (number)	Starting cash package* (N.T.$ per month)	Annual bonus (months)	Other benefits
Tatung Engineering	Taipei	1,400	3,785	2	Free dormitories
Eastern Electronics	Kwei Shen	340	3,080	2	Free dorm, meal subsidy $176
Ta Hsing Fiber	Yang Mei	1,200	3,005	1	Free dorm and transportation, meal subsidy $550
Lien Fu Garment	Taoyuan	1,800	2,850	1–2	Free dorm and transport
Hsin Kong Fiber	Chung Li	1,200	2,826	1–4	Free dorm, meal subsidy $450
Ta Ming Fiber	Kwei Shan	840	2,800	1–3	Free dorm, meal subsidy $300
Kuen Ching Textile	Chung Li	900	2,744	1	Free dorm
Fu Hsin Textile	Taoyuan	1,400	2,600	2	Free dorm and transport, meal subsidy $200
Sharp	Tu Chen	2,500	2,580	3.5	Dorm charge $90, meal subsidy $150
Matsushita	Tu Chen	3,285	2,520	3.5	Dorm charge $80
TI	Taipei	2,500	2,505	2	Housing allowance $500 for third shift workers
TDK	Yang Mei	2,500	2,450	2	Dorm charge $30, meal subsidy $312
Sony	Tu Chen	350	2,430	3–9	Dorm charge $90, meal subsidy $312
OAK	Pan Chao	720	2,375	2	Meal subsidy $240
Compeq	Taoyuan	200	2,300	1	Meal subsidy $360
Timex	Nei Li	1,200	2,260	2	Free dorm and transport
Arvin	Nei Li	700	2,225	2	Meal subsidy $225
Zenith	Nei Li	1,300	2,220	2	Meal subsidy $200
RCA	Taoyuan	6,000	2,100	2	Dorm charge $50, transport charge $180
Ampex	Taoyuan	1,270	2,085	2	Meal subsidy $208

*Excludes free meals, transportation, or dormitories. Any charges made for these services have not been deducted from the starting package. Includes cash wages and bonuses.

Source: A private survey.

that workers actively seek improvement both in their wages and in job quality, including location. An employer paying below the market rate is likely to have difficulty in recruiting and holding workers. Several employers stated in interviews that they tried to stay slightly above the average wage rate in order to retain better workers, but they all felt that an attempt to corner the top-quality labor would bring about a competitive reaction that would be self-defeating.

Institutions and Operation of the Labor Market

There is a dearth of published information on how the labor market operates in Taiwan. There are descriptions of relevant legal codes and of the relevant institutions, but little about how they actually work. This lack is usual for developing nations. Apart from a few exceptional cases—India is an outstanding one—such problems as the details of the wage determination process, the handling of worker grievances, recruitment procedures, the manner in which promotion and discharge are effectuated, all of great concern to the individual worker, have not been subject to analysis. Much of the material that follows is based upon interviews with government officials, enterprise managers, and worker representatives.

Trade Unionism

The Chinese Federation of Labor (CFL), which had moved to Taiwan from the mainland in 1950, was almost moribund until it was restructured in 1975. It had held no national congress in that entire period, and no new appointments had been made to its executive bodies. In 1975, the eleven national federations that constituted the CFL conducted delegate elections, and a congress was held in March 1976 at which the executive organs were reconstituted in full strength. The Chinese Federation of Labor has thus been reestablished as the main body of organized labor.

The union situation is complicated because coexisting with the CFL is the Taiwan Provincial Federation of Labor, an organization that has been active all through the postwar period and that numbers among its affiliates twenty city and district general unions, two industrial unions, and a number of craft federations. The Provincial Federation has been nominally affiliated with the CFL, but in fact it has operated independently.

Below the two federations are a variety of national, district, city, and enterprise units. There are, first, a number of national industrial federations, the major ones catering to seamen, railway workers, postal workers, mine workers, and employees in the Export Processing Zones. Some are affiliated with the CFL, others with the Taiwan Provincial Federation.

The revitalization of the Chinese Federation of Labor in 1976 clearly indicates that it will play a more important role in the future than it has in the past. The CFL is affiliated with the International Confederation of Free Trade Unions, which held an Asian regional economic conference in Taipei in 1974. It maintains fraternal relations with a number of foreign labor movements, including the AFL-CIO.[79] Perhaps of greater significance is the fact that a number of national unions in Taiwan belong to international trade federations, including those in transportation, postal and telegraph services, and the chemicals and metal-working industries.

Many officers of the CFL and of major national unions are members of the national legislature and may have had some influence in promoting labor legislation. The enactment of legislation on vocational training, mine safety, and factory safety and health has been credited to the lobbying efforts of these officials. There is no organic connection between the trade unions and the Kuomintang, Taiwan's only political party, but party members among workers tend to be the activists who are frequently elected to union office. There are no official statistics on the proportion of party members among union leaders, but an informed observer put the figure at slightly over 50 percent.[80]

Functionally, there are two basic types of trade unions in Taiwan: industrial unions and craft or occupational unions established on a geographic basis. According to the law governing trade unions, a minimum of fifty workers in an industrial enterprise may organize a union (the figure is thirty for craft unions). Only one union is permitted per plant. All workers are legally required to join plant unions once they are formed, but in fact, many do not. The checkoff of union dues is common, and this applies to the craft unions as well. The number of plant unions has been growing, but some large companies are not organized, as a survey undertaken in November 1976 showed (Table 6.27). Most unions are of recent origin. It is estimated that about 30 percent of employees in industrial enterprises of all sizes were unionized by 1976.

Craft unions in all major cities cover such occupational groups as taxi and truck drivers, tailors, barbers, cooks, and waiters. An estimated 70 percent of the workers in these categories belong to unions. Part-time or temporary employees are generally not unionized.

Organizational progress has been slow because of employer opposition and

79. On the occasion of the 1976 Congress of the CFL, George Meany, president of the AFL-CIO, sent the following message: "As you know, the AFL-CIO has traditionally supported a democratic Republic of China and a free Chinese Federation of Labor. Knowing that you have struggled for many years to achieve democracy and freedom, and that since the capture of Mainland China by communist forces you have had to devote much of the national income to the defense of the Chinese people resident in Taiwan, it is our hope that in the months and years ahead the Republic of China will prosper and democratize and that the trade union movement can grow in freedom and liberty." Fraternal greetings were also received from the heads of the labor movements in Japan (Domei), Germany, France (FO), Turkey, the Philippines, Singapore, New Zealand, Malaysia, and Sri Lanka.

80. Much of the information in the foregoing paragraphs is based on Djang, chap. 13.

Table 6.27. Trade Union Status in Large Industrial
Enterprises, November 1976

Company	Union status
Admiral	Organized 1973
Ampex	Organizing
Arvin	No union
Bettes	No union
Capetronic	Organized 1975
Clinton	No union
Compeq	No union
Digital	Organized 1975
Ford Lio-Ho	Organized 1972
GIT	Organized 1970
Goodyear	Organized 1975
ITT	Organized 1974
OAK	No union
PGC	Organized 1974
Philco	Organized 1970
Philips	Organized 1974
RCA	Organized 1967
TDK	Organized 1970
Texas Instruments	Organized 1975
TMX	Organized 1976
TRW	Organized 1972
Zenith	No union

Source: EPC, untitled typed document.

workers' lack of knowledge and leadership. During the past few years, perhaps because of diminishing unemployment and the spread of education, interest in unionism has increased, but employer opposition persists. Another obstacle is the prohibition against formation of industrial unions on a local area basis, a form that is permitted to crafts but not to factory workers.

Union officers are generally elected for three-year terms, with the right of reelection. Until a few years ago, long tenure in office was common, but a generational shift and the entrance of many young people into the labor market are altering this pattern. Voting is by secret ballot. The participation rate in union elections tends to be high among industrial workers, where the balloting is held in the plant, but lower in the craft unions, where it is difficult to get members together. The larger national and area unions have full-time officers, though rarely at the plant level. The chairmen of plant unions can usually get time off for union work, and some devote full time to the union at company expense.

Dues are set by law at a maximum of 2 percent of earnings, but in fact, they are generally lower, particularly in factories. In a large machinery plant, for example, with a starting wage of N.T.$3,000 per month, the dues were only N.T.$8 per month; in a tire company, with the same starting wage, the dues were N.T.$5 a month. The Teamsters' Union in Taipei collected N.T.$12 a month and the National Chinese Seamen's Union, .5 percent of earnings.

There is no simple answer to what the trade unions do and how much power they have, particularly at the present time, when trade union status is changing. Both functional patterns and degree of authority vary from one union to another. The best that can be done is to present a few cases occupying different points along the spectrum of union authority.

One of the few generalizations true of all trade unions in Taiwan is that they do not enjoy the right to strike and thus are deprived of what Western trade unions consider to be their ultimate bargaining weapon. That the de facto or even legal right to strike has been disappearing in one developing country after another does not alter the fact that unions operating under such circumstances suffer a severe handicap. There have been a few incidents of sit-downs or collective illness notices in Taiwan, but they were settled before the government found it necessary to intervene.

Taiwan's trade unions, however, are not powerless. The National Chinese Seamen's Union, for example, functions very much like its counterparts in the West. With about five thousand members working on Chinese ships and twenty thousand on Chinese-owned ships flying flags of convenience, it has over fifty full-time staff members in Taipei and in the major ports of Taiwan. The annual budget of the union is about N.T.$10 million, 90 percent coming from dues and the balance from initiation fees.

The Seamen's Union enters into collective agreements with employers, specifying wages and other conditions of labor in some detail. Final arbitration of wage disputes is by the Ministry of Communications. Welfare activities are conducted at three centers around the country. Each of these employs ten female college students as social workers to assist the dependents of members, many of whom have special problems because of the long absence of seamen from home.[81] The union does not engage in strikes, but it appears to have substantial influence on labor conditions in the industry.

The Teamsters' Union of Taipei, which includes drivers of taxis, trucks, and buses, seems to exercise a good deal of authority. With forty-two thousand members, it is the largest local area union in the country, employing twenty-three full-time staff members. There is no national drivers' union, but the Taipei local is affiliated with the Taipei City Labor Federation, to which it pays dues of N.T.$150,000 a year.

An employer association exists for each branch of the transport industry, but there are no written collective agreements. If an individual employer pays wages that are considered to be below the market rate for the job, the union may discuss the matter with his employer association or with him. Strikes are forbidden, but an employer can be put on an unofficial blacklist and may have trouble getting labor. If disputes arise about working conditions other than

81. Information supplied by officers of the National Chinese Seamen's Union.

wages, discussions are held between the union and the employer associations; if agreement cannot be reached, the Taipei city government may be called in to arbitrate.

Among the grievances the Teamsters' Union has taken up in the recent past are license revocations for drivers involved in accidents. The union feels that the police are too strict and the damages assessed against drivers too heavy. It is endeavoring to have the law changed. Some benefits are offered by the union, including welfare relief, educational fellowships to children of members, a union-sponsored medical insurance scheme, and a consumer cooperative.

Election to the union's executive committee is for a three-year term, with the possibility of reelection for one additional term. The officers believe that the maximum term of office is too brief to permit the carrying out of long-run objectives. All incumbent officials at the time of the interview had been drivers and expected either to return to their trade or to establish their own enterprises when their terms of office expired.[82]

Apart from the strike ban, this union operates very much as would its counterpart in the United States. It appears to be efficient and effective, and whether the result of its efforts or of market demand, its members earn good incomes: between N.T.$13,000 and 18,000 a month for over-the-road truckers, N.T.$10,000 a month for construction and oil truck drivers, and N.T.$7,000 for bus drivers.

Among the other well-financed craft unions are those of dock workers and printers. Most of the other crafts are less well established and have occasionally been obliged to secure government subsidy to keep going. They do little in the way of collective bargaining or welfare work.[83]

All factories, regardless of union status, are supposed to establish bipartite factory councils; if there is a union, it selects the worker members of the council. The council's main function is to discuss problems of plant welfare, including occupational safety and health, and it is usually kept informed of pending personnel actions. Councils are required by law to hold monthly meetings, but in fact they do not meet that frequently. In some plants, the councils carry on a wide range of welfare activities, including the maintenance of a library and a canteen, the provision of entertainment and recreational facilities, and occasional tourism. These are financed by worker and employer contributions.

Supplementing the factory councils are small group organizations. For example, the government tobacco monopoly plant in Taipei, with fifteen hundred employees, has sixty-five such groups. Average group membership

82. Information supplied by officers of the Teamsters' Union of Taipei.
83. Djang, p. 255.

varies between ten and thirty members. In the Taiwan Fertilizer Company, also a government enterprise, the functions of the small groups were described as follows:

There are 72 small groups in the Hsinchu Ferilizer Workers' Union with one group leader for each group. Small group meetings are held from time to time in which members may make suggestions or proposals which if they were adopted by the small group by a majority vote will be submitted to the General Council [of the union] for discussion. An average of 250 proposals are thrown out and discussed in the small groups each year. Perhaps 10 percent of the proposals will see light and be submitted to general council meetings.[84]

Plant unions are entitled to enter into collective agreements with management covering conditions of labor other than wages. In 1976, however, only about 250 written agreements were in effect, many of them with large multinational firms. A good many were copies of model agreements that had little to do with the particular circumstances of the enterprises involved.

More important are the informal agreements and frequent discussions that prevail in situations where unions are well established. The unions convey to management the views of their members on various issues, including wages. In the case of a large electronics enterprise that was obliged to reduce staff in 1974, the union was consulted about the layoff list and the amount of the termination allowance to be paid. The union had no formal authority to act, but the firm's failure to consult it might have led to union refusal to cooperate on other matters. Members of the trade union committee in a tire factory stated that they had weekly meetings with management and took credit for an 8 percent wage increase in 1975 and two cost-of-living increases in 1976, despite low profits.

One of the major functions of Western trade unions is to handle individual grievances. Almost every collective agreement in the United States, for example, provides for a grievance procedure, with private compulsory arbitration as the final step. A formal grievance mechanism is not customary in Taiwan, but aggrieved individuals normally go to the union for help in securing redress, although some prefer to take the cases up directly with their supervisors. If settlement cannot be achieved by discussion, the grievance can be taken to local government arbitration boards for final adjudication. To cite an example, a recent grievance in an automobile plant arose over holiday pay. The company had laid down the policy that if a man worked on a holiday, he could take a compensatory day off. The workers preferred extra pay, and when the issue could not be resolved by discussion, it went to the arbitration board. The board delayed making a decision because of the absence of any

84. Ibid., p. 255.

relevant legislation on which to base one, and eventually the company's policy was accepted.

For the decade 1964-74, some 909 disputes were submitted to compulsory arbitration by government boards. The incidence was increasing, however; 72 percent of them occurred in the three years 1972-74. This increase may have been caused by the economic recession since almost 60 percent involved discharges. Wage matters and work injuries were the other main issues. In the discharge cases, 25 percent were upheld, 58 percent were upheld but with severance pay, and the rest led to reinstatement.[85]

There are some interesting parallels between Taiwan and Japan in handling grievances. In Japan, as in Taiwan, formal grievance procedures are rarely resorted to. Disputes are resolved mainly by informal discussion between the worker and his supervisor, usually without intermediation by the enterprise union. The Japanese usually ascribe this to harmonious attitudes imparted by the nation's culture. The same view is to be found among employers in Taiwan; indeed, one of them, in an interview, expressed the belief that the Japanese practice had been borrowed from the Chinese. Another interpretation is that in both countries unions are relatively weak. In Taiwan they cannot strike, and in Japan they do not, for a variety of reasons.[86] Japanese unions, however, are more powerful than those in Taiwan, and are directly involved in wage questions, whereas in Taiwan the unions have only an indirect, if any, influence in this key area.

The ultimate question that would have to be answered before any final evaluation of the trade union movement of Taiwan could be made is the extent to which unions are dominated or influenced by employers or government. There is some reason to believe that employer domination of factory unions is a reality. When a union is organized, the employer often takes the initiative and selects the leadership. All officials of the plant union must be company employees. It is customary for everyone in the plant except the top management to belong to the union, and supervisory officials are often elected to union office. The union is usually provided with office facilities and secretarial services in the plant. Elected union officers are sometimes given special jobs, such as manager of the plant cafeteria, the welfare society, or the canteen, which are desirable from the point of view of pay and work. All of these add up to a pattern which in the United States would create a strong presumption of employer domination. None of these strictures applies to the stronger craft unions; they seem to have a good deal of independence.

85. Ibid., p. 287. By law, ten to thirty days' notice of discharge is required, depending upon length of service. Severance pay is set at one month's wage for each of the first three years of uninterrupted service with the same employer and ten days for each additional year of service.
86. See Walter Galenson, "The Japanese Labor Market," in Patrick and Rosovsky, pp. 648-51.

In the final analysis, however, the government, not employers, will decide the future of the trade union movement in Taiwan. Several nonunion employers stated that the government was pressing them to permit the establishment of unions, and current government policy seems to be to ensure that unions exist in all plants of any substantial size. In the past, the government of the Republic of China has been ambivalent about unionism, influenced by the history of communist infiltration of trade unions on the mainland when the Kuomintang was in power there. As memories of the past fade, this becomes a less important consideration, particularly since there appears to be little communist sentiment among the workers.

At an earlier stage of industrialization, at the beginning of the 1960s, potential foreign investors were guaranteed that there would be no labor problems. This policy is also undergoing modification. When the union question was raised in a discussion with the foreign manager of a large multinational firm, the answer given was that they had few alternatives to locating in Taiwan because of low wage costs, labor availability and quality, political stability, and the existence of essential infrastructure.

In my discussions with government officials, there was no suggestion that the ban on strikes would be lifted in the near future. The Chinese Federation of Labor appears to be gaining prestige, not least because of the importance of its contacts with the International Confederation of Free Trade Unions and the AFL-CIO. Predictions are difficult to make, for the existence and authority of unions are as much political as economic matters.

In any event, the widely held view that trade unions are an impediment to economic development might have had some validity a decade ago but can no longer be applied to Taiwan. In most developing nations, unions represent a small proportion of the labor force, and it can be argued that in advancing the parochial interests of their members, they are acting contrary to the interests of the majority of the population who are engaged in subsistence agriculture and low-productivity services. Taiwan has now reached the point at which unions represent a large proportion of all employees, and the arguments for and against the growth of union authority are much the same as those used in the developed industrial nations.

Personnel Policies

1. Recruitment of labor.   Taiwan is very much a market economy in terms of the manner in which job placement is done. A public employment service was established in 1963, but it has been slow in gaining acceptance. Its principal success has been with graduates of junior high schools who are seeking their first jobs.

When unemployed workers were asked in January 1976 how they went about finding jobs, only 12 percent said they used the public employment service. Assistance from friends and relatives and newspaper advertisements were the avenues used by the great majority of the respondents; private employment agencies were used less than the public one.[87] Employed individuals were asked how they had found their current jobs, and again, the public employment service was very low, with only 4 percent of the total; relatives, friends, and newspaper ads were the principal sources of information. The only groups that used the public service to any significant extent were professional, technical, and clerical workers.[88]

Employers cited a diversity of means by which they found prospective recruits. One of the major sources was recommendation by employees. Foremen, particularly those who still had ties with the countryside, located many new employees. The plant manager of a textile firm told of a visit to Hwalien County, a rural area that had seven hundred and thirty female high school graduates in the particular school year discussed. Although he was in competition with a hundred other firms, he signed on two hundred and fifty of them by dint of exhaustive interviewing and persuasion. Vocational school students who are receiving practical training at an enterprise often stay on. Newspaper ads are frequently used. T. K. Djang writes, "We see two full pages (4 or more pages on Saturdays and Sundays) of small announcements and advertisement columns of all vernacular newspapers in Taipei, over 80 percent of which were inserted by job-offerers and job-seekers. They prefer to try their luck in 'do-it-yourself' fashion. It is only when all doors are closed that they will finally bring their cases to the Public Employment Centers.'"[89]

Bidding employees away from other companies seems to be a fairly common practice, although some informal antipirating agreements apparently exist. The manager of an enterprise in an industrial suburb of Taipei said in an interview that the personnel directors of the twenty factories in the area met for lunch once a month to discuss mutual problems. They agreed upon starting wage rates and that they would not attempt to hire one anothers' employees. American firms are said not to pirate from one another, an arrangement worked out through the local U.S. Chamber of Commerce. As a generalization, it seems to be true that the larger companies prefer not to hire actively from other firms, but small enterprises hire whom they can.

2. Wage determination. When asked how they fixed starting wage rates, the standard reply given by company managers was either that they consulted with other firms in the area or that they paid the prevailing rate in the area, as determined by wage surveys. Wage administration varied a great deal; some had formal systems, others operated informally. The following accounts are

---

87. EPC, "Taiwan Regional Manpower Utilization Survey Report," Table 46.
88. Ibid., Table 21.
89. Djang, p. 138.

for Chinese-managed firms, since the multinationals tend to import their wage administration schemes.

Supervisors in a large tire manufacturing firm grade each employee from A to D each year, with wage increases depending upon the grade. A medium-sized machine tool manufacturer had established a management committee of five to review the work of each employee and gave half-yearly wage increases based solely on merit. An enterprise engaged in metal fabrication gave each employee an annual wage increase, the amount determined by his supervisor, considering both seniority and merit. It also paid merit bonuses for superior work, but these were creating problems because workers on the same production line were receiving substantially different amounts of pay.

In general, merit appears to be the primary consideration in allocating wage increases among employees, although firms are beginning to pay more attention to seniority in order to retain their skilled workers. In no case was there mention of any trade union input into the internal wage determination process. It was taken for granted that this is the sole prerogative of management.

3. Tenure of employment. A surprising finding was that apart from the electronics industry, no firm interviewed had ever dismissed an employee except for disciplinary reasons. During the 1974 recession, normal attrition and shifting people to other jobs took care of overmanning. This does not seem to be the result of any such practice as the Japanese system of permanent employment commitment, but rather a reflection of the rapid growth of most firms in Taiwan. Whatever the cause, an employee who turned in a reasonable performance could count on keeping his job permanently. This was undoubtedly an important morale factor and a contributor to productivity, particularly in the past when employment was harder to find. The normal age of retirement is sixty years, but this is not formalized and has not yet become a problem because of the low average age of the labor force.

Larger firms appear to have fairly formal disciplinary and promotion systems. One such firm reported that breaches of working discipline could lead to major or minor reprimands, with three major reprimands constituting cause for discharge. Rewards for good work consisted of money premia, certificates of merit, and notations on the personnel card that could lead to promotion. In this firm, the plant union was consulted in cases of discharge or promotion to forestall friction.

The impression gained from a small sampling of firms is that Taiwan management follows practices that do not differ greatly from those of industrialized nations. Apart from dormitory facilities for young workers recruited from the countryside, there does not seem to be the paternalism that is often encountered in developing countries. One reason is that the goods and services provided by enterprises to their employees in developing nations—free rice or bread, housing, medical and dental care for themselves and their families, transportation, and low-priced consumer goods of various kinds—can be purchased in the market in Taiwan.

Answers to queries about the reasons for various labor market practices were rarely given in cliches about cultural influences. And indeed, it is difficult to find anything in this area that might be described as peculiarly Chinese. The dominant motive appeared to be simply the pursuit of profit—economic reasons were generally advanced to account for particular labor market practices.

Living Standards

The final question to be addressed is that of the impact of economic growth on the welfare of the people who created it. Have the rates of growth in national product that have characterized Taiwan's recent history led to significant improvements in the nation's living standards? Have the fruits of growth benefited working people or have they inured mainly to the wealthier groups in society?

National income statistics provide a first step toward an answer. Between 1953 and 1974, real private consumption increased at an annual rate of 7.4 percent. On the other hand, private consumption expenditures as a percentage of the gross domestic product fell from 62.8 percent in 1953 to 53.2 percent in 1974.[90]

The distribution of expenditures on private consumption, as shown in Table 6.28, shows that Engel's law was operating in Taiwan. Particularly notable is the rapid rise in the share of transportation and communication, with the consecutive introduction of the bicycle, the motorcycle, and the automobile.

A more concrete picture of the significance of the aggregates for living standards in Taiwan can be obtained from examination of the components of consumption. The consumption indicators presented were chosen on the basis of their availability and their comparability with data for other countries collected by international agencies.

Selected for comparison with Taiwan are countries that share with it at least one characteristic: rapid growth of the national product between 1960 and 1970. These countries are part of a set of the twenty countries that achieved at least a 7 percent average annual increase in gross domestic product (that is, they doubled their national products) over the decade.[91] Several members of the set had to be omitted because of lack of detailed data (Albania, Hong Kong, North Korea); others were left out because they were at very different stages of economic development from Taiwan in 1960 (Greece, Israel, Spain);

90. DGBAS, *Statistical Yearbook of the Republic of China, 1975*, pp. 194–95.
91. The source of these data is World Bank, *World Tables 1976*, Table 1. Excluded are several countries that achieved their growth primarily by exporting oil.

Private Consumption Expenditures, by Major Category, Selected Years (percent of total in expenditures)

Category of expenditure	1953	1960	1965	1970	1974
..u, beverage, tobacco	66.2	60.9	55.5	50.5	47.2
Clothing and footwear	3.8	4.2	4.6	5.3	5.2
Gross rent, fuel, power	{15.9	17.0{	14.6	15.8	17.3
Furnishings and household operation			3.4	4.4	4.4
Medical and health	4.4	5.2	7.0	5.9	5.6
Transport and communications	1.1	1.3	2.1	2.7	3.9
Recreation and entertainment	2.5	3.0	3.2	3.8	4.4
Miscellaneous*	6.1	8.4	9.6	11.6	12.0

*Includes education and cultural services.
Source: DGBAS, *Statistical Yearbook of the Republic of China, 1975,* pp. 208-9.

Pakistan was eliminated because of the unique domestic problems it faced. Japan is included despite its status as a developed industrial nation because of its special relationship with Taiwan.

It should be emphasized that the experience of Taiwan is being compared to that of the countries that were the most successful in achieving high rates of economic growth during the 1960s. Any other set would tend to show the achievements of Taiwan in a more favorable light.

Food

The first set of indicators, relating to overall consumption and to food availability, is shown on Table 6.29. The index of per capita consumption growth shows two countries substantially above Taiwan in this respect. Taiwan is in a group of six countries with about a 50 percent increase in total consumption during the decade. With respect to the quantity of food consumed, as represented by daily caloric intake, Taiwan started the decade relatively well endowed, but showed little change over the period.[92] In protein consumption, which can be regarded as a proxy for food quality, the data show that Taiwan improved over the decade more than any other country except South Korea and had relatively high absolute standards at the end of the decade.

A visitor to Taiwan must be impressed by the abundance, quality, variety, and relative cheapness of food. At the present time, its food situation is at least equal to if not better than that of any Asian country, with the possible exception of Japan. The number of food service establishments, ranging from elegant restaurants to street stalls, is very large. Most factories provide their employees with nutritious lunches (and dinners, for overtime workers) at low cost. The Taiwanese worker certainly eats well. This is a tribute to the nation's agriculture and to its distributive system.

92. The World Bank figure for 1970 is not consonant with the official Taiwan data, which show a substantial improvement for 1960 to 1970. See the footnote to Table 6.29.

Table 6.29. Index of Consumption and Availability of Food, Selected Countries, 1960–1970

Country	Total per capita consumption index (1960 = 100) 1970	Per capita daily consumption of calories		Per capita daily consumption of proteins (grams)	
		1960	1970	1960	1970
Taiwan*	149	2,350	2,360	59	68
Gabon	181	2,180	2,210	51	56
Ivory Coast	148	2,170	2,490	52	60
Japan	204	2,340	2,510	72	76
Mauritania	133	1,970	1,970	73	75
Mexico	139	2,500	2,580	65	65
Nicaragua	137	2,100	2,450	68	70
Panama	145	2,560	2,580	59	61
Singapore	153	n.a.	n.a.	n.a.	63
South Korea	152	1,990	2,350	53	65
Syria	n.a.	2,350	2,650	74	70
Thailand	152	2,120	2,220	47	52
Togo	140	2,040	2,160	48	51

*The following data are presented in an official publication of the Republic of China.

	Caloric consumption	Protein consumption
1953	2,283	53.4
1960	2,390	57.1
1970	2,662	72.1
1975	2,727	74.5

Source: EPC, *Social Welfare Indicators, Republic of China* (Taipei, 1976), p. 53. To maintain comparability with other countries, the figures listed in the table are taken from the World Bank source. The reasons for the divergence between the two sources are not clear.
Source: World Bank, *World Tables 1976* (Washington, D.C., 1976), pp. 518–21, 480–87.

Housing[93]

Comparative data for housing are shown in Table 6.30. They are not sufficiently complete to make any judgments about relative progress. The most that can be concluded from this table is that Taiwan's housing standards are relatively good compared with the other countries for which data are available.

The average worker in Taiwan would be likely to put housing improvement as his first priority. There has been considerable progress over time, as the data in Table 6.31 indicate, particularly in electrification. But a relatively small proportion of the national product has been devoted to investment in housing, and the average dwelling still contains only about one hundred square feet of living space per capita.

Housing programs have been sponsored by both the national and local

93. The information for this section came mainly from interviews at the Housing Office of the City of Taipei and from visits to housing projects.

Table 6.30. Quantitative and Qualitative Indicators of the Housing Supply, Selected Countries, 1960–1970

Country	Average number of persons per room (urban)		Percent of occupied dwellings without piped water		Percent of rural dwellings connected to electricity	
	1960	1970	1960	1970	1960	1970
Taiwan	—	1.6	—	51	—	88
Gabon	—	—	—	—	—	20
Ivory Coast	2.5	—	—	—	—	—
Japan	1.2	1.0	—	5	—	—
Mauritania	—	—	—	—	—	—
Mexico	2.6	2.5	68	61	—	—
Nicaragua	2.2	—	79	—	4	—
Panama	2.1	2.5	—	74	11	16
Singapore	—	2.9	—	20	—	—
South Korea	2.8	2.7	88	80	12	30
Syria	2.1	—	58	—	11	—
Thailand	—	—	31	—	—	13
Togo	—	—	—	—	—	—

Source: World Bank, *World Tables 1976*, pp. 524–27.

governments, but the number of units completed is far below the demand. The city of Taipei, for example, has been operating a program called Subsidized Housing for the Citizen since 1961. About 9,300 units have been completed; in 1975, there were 60,000 applicants for the thousand units available for sale. The selection was by lot. Under the program, loans are made up to 80 percent of construction costs for a fifteen-year term at an interest rate of 9 percent, of which the city pays 4 percent. Additional units were built under a special program for public servants and teachers, a favored group.

The bulk of the city's efforts, however, have been devoted to relief and resettlement dwellings for people who lose their homes because of slum clearance and other construction. From 1966 to 1975, about eleven thousand resettlement accommodations were built. The units are small, ranging in size from twenty-six to forty square meters, but they are modern, and their occupants show considerable ingenuity in using the available space. The problem is not quality, but quantity. The demand far exceeds the supply.

Most new housing was built privately, but such construction has been hampered by the difficulty of securing money and by the price of land. Private mortgage loans are available only up to a maximum of 30 percent of value, for seven years, at an interest rate of 13 percent. Contractors often insist upon being paid, at least in part, before construction begins. A good deal of land is being held for speculation, a practice that is facilitated by assessing it for tax purposes at less than half its value. The city does not have the right of eminent domain for housing purposes, and a good deal of public housing has been built

Table 6.31. Housing Standards in Taiwan, 1953–1975

	Electric lighting			Piped water		Housing investment as percent of GNP
	Kilowatt hours per capita	Percent of families served	Living space per capita (ping)*	Liters per capita†	Percent of families served	
1953	28	35.3	—	163	28.2	1.1
1960	44	56.8	—	208	29.7	2.3
1965	76	72.6	2.2	219	38.3	1.6
1970	163	86.5	2.7	238	43.7	2.1
1975	273	99.3‡	3.8‡	249	50.3	2.9‡

*One ping = 36 square feet.
†Figures up to 1970 are based on designed capacity, that for 1975 on actual water supplied.
‡1974.
Source: EPC, Social Welfare Indicators, 1976, pp. 54–57.

on government-owned land. Luxury housing is readily available; an apartment of two thousand square feet can be purchased for about U.S.$50,000.

The national government initiated a worker housing program in 1975. Under this scheme, if a house or an apartment were to cost, say, N.T.$300,000, the worker can borrow two-thirds from the government at a rate of 8 percent, with the balance of the financing provided by the enterprise and the worker in equal shares. To be eligible, the worker must have lived in the urban area for half a year without owning a house. How large this program will become is not yet clear.

Given the huge backlog of demand, the current housing shortage can be alleviated only through vigorous positive government action. This need not necessarily take the form of either city or national government construction. It will require the decision that housing for lower-income groups should be allocated a considerably larger share of total investment than it has been given in the past and the provision of adequate financing. Government employees can now secure twenty-year home mortgages at subsidized interest rates of 3 percent, and some extension of this scheme might be in order.

Education

Comparative data on education appear in Table 6.32. Taiwan is among the countries that had already achieved universal primary school enrollment in 1960. Its secondary school enrollment ratio was exceeded only by that of

Table 6.32. Indicators of the Availability of Education, Selected Countries, 1960–1970

| | Adjusted school enrollment ratios* | | | | Adult literacy rate (percent) | |
| | Primary | | Secondary | | | |
	1960	1970	1960	1970	1960	1970
Taiwan	102	98	29	50	54	73
Gabon	95	168	5	16	13	30
Ivory Coast	46	77	2	11	9	20
Japan	102	100	79	90	98	99
Mauritania	8	15	0.4	2	—	—
Mexico	81	104	9	23	62	84
Nicaragua	62	80	7	13	51	57
Panama	97	110	29	42	78	82
Singapore	111	105	32	47	50	75
South Korea	96	104	27	41	—	91
Syria	65	88	16	39	36	40
Thailand	79	90	12	13	—	—
Togo	44	56	2	7	—	—

*For countries with universal education, the enrollment may exceed 100 percent because some students are below or above the official school age, that is, the school age population on which the ratio is based may be smaller than the enrollment.
Source: World Bank, World Tables 1976, pp. 522–23.

Table 6.33. Indicators of Educational Standards, Taiwan, 1953–1975

School year	Ratio of educational to total government expenditure (percent)	Enrollment rates			
		Secondary (12–17 years)		Higher (18–24 years)	
		Male	Female	Male	Female
1953–54	6.8	19.5	8.2	1.7	0.2
1960–61	12.6	39.1	21.3	4.9	1.3
1965–66	14.4	45.9	29.2	9.8	3.5
1970–71	16.0	63.5	44.7	10.2	6.4
1975–76	16.9	71.5	59.8	11.5	7.0

Source: EPC, *Social Welfare Indicators, 1976*, pp. 47–49.

Japan in 1970, although a residue of illiteracy remained. Taiwan clearly ranks high among developing nations in educational efforts.

Additional data on the growth of the educational system in Taiwan appear in Table 6.33. The enrollment ratios suggest that by the school year 1974–75, a very substantial proportion of working-class children must have been entering secondary schools, particularly the males. Tuition fees are charged beyond the junior high school level, but they are relatively small and within the financial means of the average family.[94]

Consumer and Cultural Goods and Services

Comparative indicators for the availability of cultural goods, as represented by radio receivers and newspapers, appear in Table 6.34. Taiwan's performance during the 1960s in these respects was average for the group of thirteen countries compared.

A better perception of the changes that have taken place in everyday living in Taiwan can be gained from the data in Table 6.35. The television age came very rapidly, as might be expected of a country that is producing a good share of the world output of television receivers. Sets are well within the reach of workers, and many have them. Telephones are also in good supply, though most worker families do not yet have them.

Transportation has undergone an equally rapid transformation. In the mid-1960s, the bicycle was the worker's only alternative to crowded public buses or trains. The motorcycle is now the favored mode of commuting for younger workers in particular, both male and female.[95] The private automobile is still a luxury; before it can become a vehicle for the common man, Taiwan will have

94. The tuition fee for colleges and universities is U.S.$50–70 for public institutions and $80–120 for private ones. Loans at very low rates of interest are available up to the full amount of tuition and fees.

95. Anyone who was in Italy in the 1950s will recall the age of the Vespa. This same machine is now being manufactured in Taiwan under license.

Table 6.34. Indicators of Availability of Consumer and Cultural Goods, 1960–1970

	Radio receivers per 1,000 population		Newsprint consumption (kilograms per year per capita)	
	1960	1970	1960	1970
Taiwan	43	103	0.9	1.7
Gabon	48	124	—	—
Ivory Coast	17	17	0.1	0.2
Japan	133	550	10.0	18.9
Mauritania	16	47	—	—
Mexico	95	276	2.8	3.1
Nicaragua	53	55	0.9	1.9
Panama	159	157	2.2	4.0
Singapore	—	134	5.6	10.4
South Korea	32	126	1.8	3.4
Syria	57	224	0.2	0.2
Thailand	6	78	0.7	1.2
Togo	—	22	—	0.1

Source: World Bank, World Tables 1976, pp. 524–27.

to make a large investment in roads and other facilities and do a great deal more city planning than is now under way.[96]

Medical facilities in Taiwan compare favorably, on the whole, with those of other developing countries. The 1974 figure of population per physician in Taiwan, 1,075, is considerably lower than for many Latin American countries and for most African and Asian countries. Taiwan is relatively less well endowed with hospital facilities, however. In general, access to medical care does not appear to be a difficult problem in the cities, though it may be in the countryside.

One is constantly struck, in walking about Taipei and other major cities, by the volume and variety of consumer goods that are offered for sale. Clothing shops are ubiquitous and relatively cheap by Taiwan's income standards. Consumer durables, particularly small refrigerators, are finding their way into workers' apartments; the output in 1975 was 433,000 units, most of them for domestic consumption.

Social Insurance

Taiwan has not yet moved very far toward becoming a welfare state. In this area the Chinese worker lags furthest behind his Western counterpart.

The major social insurance scheme now in effect is so-called Labor Insurance. It covers all industrial enterprises and commercial firms with more than

96. One of the ten major construction projects now being built is a North-South freeway, which will greatly help to alleviate highway congestion, but do little for urban traffic problems.

Table 6.35. Availability of Transportation and Communications Facilities, Taiwan, 1953–1975

	Telephones per 1,000 population	Television sets per 1,000 population	Automobiles per 1,000 population	Motorcycles per 1,000 population	Letters posted per capita
1953	4.3	—	1.1	0.5	9.1
1960	8.8	—	2.0	2.4	32.1
1965	12.9	4.8	2.9	5.3	29.4
1970	27.7	35.1	7.1	48.2	38.0
1975	69.7	56.9	17.0	106.2	50.1

Source: EPC, Social Welfare Indicators, 1976, pp. 58–59.

ten employees, as well as manual workers in the government employ. The number of insured has grown rapidly, from half a million in 1960 to 854,000 in 1970 and 1.6 million in June 1976.[97] About 50 percent of all paid employees were covered by the middle of 1976.

The scheme is financed by an 8 percent payroll tax, 20 percent of which is paid by the worker and 80 percent by the employer.[98] There are five categories of benefits: (1) *Maternity benefits* equal to two months' wages for an insured woman or half a month's wages for the wife of an insured man. (2) *Injury*. If job-related, the compensation is 70 percent of the wage for six months and 50 percent for the next six, with a maximum duration of a year. If the injury is not related to the job, the compensation is 50 percent for nine months. (3) *Disability*. Payment is made equal to from one to forty months of wages, depending upon the degree of disability. (4) *Old Age*. There is a lump-sum payment of up to forty-five months of wages upon retirement at age sixty, depending upon years of coverage. (5) *Death*. There are varying lump-sum payments for death of the insured or his immediate family, plus survivors' benefits that may run up to thirty-seven months' pay if death was related to occupational disease or injury.

The proportion of total benefit payments for each of the programs was as follows, for the year 1974:[99]

Maternity benefits	18.5
Injury benefits	3.7
Disability benefits	11.8
Old age benefits	28.6
Death benefits	37.4

In addition, the Labor Insurance system provides medical and hospital services to insured individuals. Medical care and drugs are free, as is the first month of hospitalization. Thereafter, the insured is charged for half the cost of meals. Most of the physicians in the system are on a part-time basis and practice privately as well. There are 4,000 hospitals and clinics in Taiwan, but only 1,100 are within the Labor Insurance scheme, having been selected by a medical advisory board.

Apart from the lump-sum Labor Insurance payment, there are neither state nor private old-age pension schemes in Taiwan. Workers must either save for retirement or rely on traditional extended family support. Nor is there a system of unemployment compensation.

97. Bureau of Labor Insurance, *Statistical Data for Taiwan-Fukien Labor Insurance,* (Taipei, 1975), p. 82, and interviews at the Department of Labor Insurance.

98. In the case of craft workers with no single employer, 30 percent is paid by the government and the balance by the worker.

99. Bureau of Labor Insurance, *Statistical Data,* Table 46.

There is currently much discussion in Taiwan about improving the social insurance system. Government officials in charge of Labor Insurance have indicated that they would like to see the following changes implemented in the near future: (1) extension of coverage to employers with between five and ten employees; (2) an increase in the present maximum fine of N.T.$9,000 for nonreporting of wages, in order to tighten up payments by employers; (3) separating out of the payroll tax the portion relating to workmen's compensation and varying the amount depending upon the accident experience of each employer; (4) increasing the average death benefit from three to five months' wages; (5) payment of cash benefits to workers who are ill. The present system covers only those who are disabled because of injuries.[100]

The existing social insurance system is by no means a negligible achievement for a country that has so recently emerged from an Asian standard of living. Labor Insurance expenditures as a percentage of GNP rose from .07 percent in 1953 to .16 percent in 1960 and to .23 percent in 1975.[101] In view of the nation's level of economic development, however, the time would seem to be ripe for further expansion of the system, especially to provide pensions and unemployment compensation. But employers remain opposed to any increase in the payroll tax, and the present disposition of the government appears to be to continue to rely on the extended family to take care of the aged and the unemployed.

Protective Labor Legislation

The most important protective legislation relates to working safety and health. There is a factory inspectorate, and plant trade unions often play an important role in backing up the government inspectors. Although injury rates have been declining, they are still high. Moreover, the compliance record both with respect to safety and health regulations has worsened in the last few years. Even when noncompliers are brought to court, the fines levied are too low to constitute an effective deterrent.

A recent study group appointed by the government to look into the matter came up with a number of suggestions aimed at improving administration and enforcement. It recommended a substantial increase in the number of factory inspectors—there are now only about 150 for the entire country—and an increase in their salaries. To supplement their work, the study group recommended self-inspection by workers and employers, with more technical training provided for those who were thus engaged.[102]

The experience of the industrialized nations suggests that although government regulation and inspection help, the most effective pressure is generated

100. Interviews with officials of the Bureau of Labor Insurance.
101. *Social Welfare Indicators, 1976*, p. 36.
102. Djang, pp. 209-11.

by workers themselves. If they refuse to work under dangerous conditions, employers will have to make improvements. Without such pressure, it is often more profitable to continue violation of the regulations and pay any fine assessed. In the absence of some form of worker organization in the factories with authority, either by contract or by law, to stop work that has been declared in violation of safety and health regulations, conditions are not likely to improve rapidly.

The Poverty Program

A program designed to help families that cannot support themselves has been in operation for almost a decade. The aim is to provide families with no wage earners, or those with very low earnings, with a minimum income. For example, a family without a potential wage earner would have received in 1976 a monthly payment of N.T.$400 for the household plus N.T.$150 for each person under twelve or over sixty years of age.

In 1975, some 104,000 people in 25,700 households were classified as below the poverty line.[103] This represented a very substantial decline from the 390,000 persons and 75,000 households considered poor in 1971, even though the poverty line has risen with living costs. The program both provides income maintenance and attempts to assist families in becoming self-supporting. The self-employed can borrow up to N.T.$20,000 to help them get started, but in that case, they receive no other financial assistance.

A program designed to assist children supplements the poverty program. Poor families can secure children's allowances of N.T.$300 a month for the first child, plus N.T.$100 for each additional child. There are two thousand child care centers, three hundred in Taipei alone, at which working mothers can leave their children. Ten centers have been established to help train disabled children.

Summary

A few general observations may be made about labor conditions in the Republic of China during the course of two decades of rapid growth. The working men and women in Taiwan do not yet earn an income sufficient to buy what would be regarded in the United States as a minimum decency standard of living. Housing conditions are still poor both in quantity and quality. Hours of work are long, and safety conditions leave a great deal to be desired. There is little protection from the risk of unemployment or the vicissitudes of old age. Taiwan has taken only the first steps on the road toward becoming a modern welfare state.

103. There were 2.9 million households in Taiwan in mid-1974. The poverty households under current definitions thus constituted less than 1 percent of the total number of households.

But in comparison with most other developing nations, particularly those of Asia, workers in Taiwan have made great progress. The gross underemployment that characterizes the less developed nations of the world at the present time has virtually disappeared in Taiwan. Employment is generally available at wages that permit a worker to feed, clothe, and house his family and send his children to school. The increase in the availability of consumer goods has been steady and substantial. The experience of Taiwan confirms the view that the creation of a sufficient volume of economically productive employment is a key factor in the attainment of adequate levels of welfare for all groups in society.

7 | An Economic Reconnaissance

IAN M. D. LITTLE

Taiwan's Growth in a World Context

Taiwan has a good claim to be ranked as the most successful of the developing countries. From 1951, when national income figures begin, to 1975, national income per head has grown at 4.4 percent per annum. It has thus trebled, without benefit from mineral exports and despite a worsening of the terms of trade.[1] The quality of growth has also been admirable. Admittedly poor intertemporal figures, but probably better than those of any other developing country, suggest that income distribution has improved, so that the real incomes of the poorer people may have more than trebled.[2] Real wages have risen throughout, and very rapidly in the 1970s, implying that full employment has been reached. Inflation has been moderate, at 8.4 percent per annum throughout, reducing from about 12 percent in the 1950s to 4 percent in the 1960s, but accelerating in the early 1970s before being brought to near zero in 1975.[3]

Income per head rose every year except 1974, but there was a marked change in the tempo in 1963 and again in 1973. From 1951 to 1962 the rate of growth of per capita income was 3.1 percent; from 1962 to 1973 it was 7.3 percent; from 1973 to 1975 it fell slightly, largely as a result of world events. Rapid growth was resumed in 1976 (8.9 percent per capita). This pattern of experience was not altogether unique. During the 1960s, Korea,[4] Taiwan, Hong Kong, and Singapore (citing them by latitude) became recognized as the new miracle economies of the Far East, joining Japan, which achieved this

1. Real net national product per head rose at 4.7 percent.
2. This claim is examined further, below.
3. Figures refer to the GNP deflator.
4. Korea refers throughout to the Republic of Korea (South Korea), except in a few sentences where the context makes it clear that the whole of Korea is relevant.

status a decade earlier.[5] Korea, Taiwan, and Singapore had all by 1973 sustained a growth of over 10 percent per annum in gross domestic product (GDP) for ten years. Hong Kong just missed this target, with a growth rate of 8.9 percent from 1963 to 1973, but her growth in per capita income for the long period 1950–73 was over 5 percent per annum,[6] higher than either Korea's or Taiwan's. It is also useful to include Japan in our comparisons. Although now an "industrialized" or "developed" country, she was not so regarded in the early 1950s. Japan achieved a growth rate of over 10 percent for the twenty-year period 1953–73. Moreover, Japan never experienced a population explosion, whether from immigration or natural growth. In the twenty-year period her population grew at only 1.1 percent per annum, so that the growth rate of per capita income was an amazing 9 percent per annum.

This performance is unique, both historically and among developing countries in the postwar period. A few other developing countries have recorded as high rates of growth as a result of mineral exports, for example, Botswana, Libya, Iran, Saudi Arabia, and the Arab Emirates. Somewhat more comparable are Israel and Brazil, where income growth has not been dominated by minerals. Israel achieved a growth rate of 10 percent per annum in the 1950s and has done almost as well since. But her growth has been sustained throughout the period by a very heavy inflow of foreign resources, which among The Five has been true only of Korea. Also, of course, Israel started from a far higher level of income per head and human expertise. Brazil, with greater land and mineral resources, reached 10 percent per annum for the six-year period 1967–73. But the quality of the growth does not compare well with Korea's or Taiwan's. Income is far less equally distributed, and it probably worsened during the period, whereas inflation averaged over 20 percent. No country before the 1950s ever came within striking distance of these rates of growth. The performance of The Four remains unique among the developing countries as now designated.

Exogenous Explanations of Far Eastern Growth

Those interested in development tend to believe that these economies have been lucky in their circumstances or to ascribe their success to heavy aid (though this is in conflict with the increasingly popular view that aid deters healthy growth). This belief does not stand up well to examination.

The Four, like Japan, are poor in minerals. From 1963 to 1970 mining

5. I shall refer to Korea, Taiwan, Hong Kong, and Singapore, as "The Four"; and when Japan is included as "The Five." Apart from The Five, Far Eastern growth has been no better than the average of developing countries. Excluding large countries with less than a million people, only Thailand, Malaysia, and Papua New Guinea have achieved since 1960 above average rates of growth of per capita income—in the range of 4–4.5 percent.

6. As estimated from World Bank, *World Tables 1976* (Washington, D.C., 1976).

accounted for 1.6 percent of Taiwan's gross national product (GNP), and it was less than this in Korea, negligible in Hong Kong, and nonexistent in Singapore. Mineral exports are insignificant. This contrasts with the average developing country. Even excluding oil-exporting countries, the average contribution of minerals to exports was almost 20 percent in 1973. The Five are heavily dependent on imported energy. Taiwan, by 1975, was importing over two-thirds of the energy she used.

Apart from a few city states (including Hong Kong and Singapore), Taiwan and Korea together with Japan have the highest population densities in relation to cultivable land of any country in the world, higher even than Egypt and Bangladesh and about four times as high as India. The average farm size in Taiwan is just under one hectare, about the same as in Korea. Obviously, the people in such countries can become well off only through industrialization. Not only this, as they get richer they are likely to become more and more dependent on imported materials, even food. They can become rich, therefore, only through increasing trade in manufactures.

Lack of land may be interpreted as an advantage. It is very rare for agriculture to grow faster than 5 percent per annum in any country where agriculture is an important part of the economy. Therefore, the less important is agriculture, the easier it is to strike up very high growth rates of GDP. This is what people have in mind when they dismiss Hong Kong and Singapore as irrelevant. But the argument does not apply initially to Taiwan or Korea, nor to Japan. In the mid-1950s, one-third of Taiwan's output was from agriculture and about one-half of Korea's; these figures are typical of low- and very low-income countries. The proportions reduced to 23 percent and 28 percent, respectively, by 1973. Japan, in 1953, was already more industrialized; 21 percent of her output was from agriculture, although 42 percent of employment was still there.[7]

It could be argued that it is more appropriate to compare Taiwan's and Korea's industrial growth rates with those of Hong Kong and Singapore. This cannot easily be done. No such figures are available for Hong Kong and Singapore. Nor can one sensibly compare Korea's and Taiwan's industrial growth with the total growth of Hong Kong and Singapore; the latter countries suffered from a relative decline of entrepot trade, and therefore industrial growth has probably been faster than total growth. Also, it can be argued that Korea's and Taiwan's industry had, like most of Asia until recently, the advantage of (almost) unlimited supplies of labor from agriculture.[8] This is a partly countervailing advantage for industrial growth. In other words, growth

7. Figures from K. Ohkawa and H. Rosovsky, *Japanese Economic Growth* (Stanford, 1973).
8. Probably the supply of labor from agriculture to industry is seldom perfectly elastic. Given the free labor markets of Korea and Taiwan, the fact that real industrial wages were slowly rising during the 1950s and early 1960s is evidence of this.

of GDP is slowed down by a large agricultural sector insofar as the latter never achieves the growth that industry can. But industrial growth may, in turn, be speeded so that the presence of a large agricultural sector may not slow total growth as much as it otherwise would. On the other hand, during the 1950s, Hong Kong probably did have a perfectly elastic supply of labor because of immigration from the mainland. It is odd that Hong Kong, with its own tiny agricultural hinterland, was, during the 1950s, perhaps the clearest example one can find of Arthur Lewis's famous concept of growth with unlimited supplies of labor, which came from the mainland. The supply of labor turned inelastic in the early 1960s.[9]

Small size, in numbers, may be reckoned an advantage if the country discovers or can develop some natural wealth or asset whose proceeds are then shared among few people. This, of course, is the explanation of the growth and wealth of countries like Libya or Kuwait. Although none of The Four has significant mineral wealth, Hong Kong and Singapore, with populations of 4.2 million and 2.2 million, respectively, have fine well-placed ports, which have undoubtedly to some extent contributed to their relatively high incomes per head. Korea and Taiwan have no similar locational advantages. Taiwan, indeed, is notably lacking in good harbor sites. Nor are these two countries very small. Korea is the twelfth largest developing country with a population of 33 million. Taiwan, with its 15.4 million people, is from a human point of view considerably larger than Australia and ranks in population with such developing countries as Afghanistan, Morocco, and Peru. Japan is, of course, a giant with 108 million people.[10]

Size in terms of total GNP is also of some importance, for it is a crude indicator of the possibilities of realizing economies of scale in manufacturing for the home market. In 1974, Korean GNP was 126 percent of that of Taiwan, Hong Kong's 54 percent, and Singapore's 39 percent. These proportions have not changed much in the past twenty-years. Comparing with other countries, Taiwan's GNP is very close to that of Thailand, a little less than New Zealand and Portugal, rather more than Colombia or Peru, and more than any African developing country except Nigeria. Twenty years ago her GNP would have been considerably less than that of any of the countries named.

---

9. It is estimated that 1.3 million people entered from 1945 to 1949. Restrictions then slowed the flow, but it remained high because the population rose at 4.9 percent per annum in the 1950s. During this period the average money wage of the unskilled rose 29 percent (and that of the very lowest paid probably not at all), while that of the semiskilled and skilled rose respectively by 48 and 100 percent. Something like full employment was achieved in the early 1960s. During the 1960s, when the population growth rate was greatly reduced, the widening of differentials was reversed. From 1961 to 1971, the average unskilled money wage rose by 141 percent and that of the semiskilled and skilled rose by 125 percent and 79 percent, respectively. See J. England and J. Rear, *Chinese Labour under British Rule* (Hong Kong, 1975), pp. 29-30.

10. These population figures are all as of 1973.

All these countries are islands or peninsulas. It is not wholly a coincidence that relatively small islands and peninsulas tend to do well. Nowhere is very far from the sea, and there are economies of national transport. It is not just that people can fish, like the Icelanders; these are naturally open economies, and they can benefit more easily from foreign trade than very large or land-locked countries. But having a long coastline per square kilometer is of little help if the countries' policies offset the natural openness which their shape determines; one has only to cite the poverty of Sri Lanka as an example. Chile, too, is a strip of a country which derives little advantage from its natural openness; nor does Cuba grow. Indonesia and the Philippines are also not specially successful; perhaps their insularity is overdone. The climatic theory of wealth also gets little support from The Four. Singapore is on the Equator; Seoul freezes hard in the winter months; Taipei in the summer can be as hot and humid as Bombay.

The initial position, that of the early 1950s, requires some discussion. It should not be thought that there is any precise set of preconditions of rapid growth, or any level of income per head which is a sine qua non. Neverthe-less, there is some evidence that countries starting from a very low level of development—as crudely measured by income per head—find it harder to grow fast. In the last decade, for example, the "middle-income" developing countries (with income per head between $200 and $1,000 in 1973 prices) have managed to grow significantly faster than the poorest. In 1973, Singa-pore, Hong Kong, Taiwan, and Korea had national incomes per head of $1,830, $1,430, $660, and $400, respectively. While this now makes Singa-pore the richest developing country apart from the smaller oil exporters, in 1960 her income per head was about $440 in then current dollars, well below that of Chile, for example. Although the city states started in the early 1950s with greater wealth than the great majority of developing countries, this was less true of Taiwan or Korea. Working growth rates backward from 1973 estimated levels, one arrives at a net per capita income, in terms of 1973 dollars, of $222 and $145, respectively, for Taiwan and Korea in 1953. This would have put Korea on a par with Thailand, South Vietnam, and the Philippines. Taiwan was better off than these, though well below Malaysia, which on the same reckoning had an income per head of $360. In terms of other parts of the world, the initial per capita income of these former Japanese colonies was higher than that of South Asia and Africa south of the Sahara, but below the level of the countries which border the Mediterranean and well below any South American country. Japan's 1953 income per head in terms of 1973 dollars was about $680.

The initial position cannot be adequately described in terms of income per head alone. Indeed, it is only a proxy for wealth, that is, the physical and human assets which are the potential sources of income. I have already discussed the nonreproducible physical assets, the land and minerals, the geographical situation, the relation to the size of the population. I turn now to the man-made infrastructure and the human resources.

All of The Five except Korea suffered severely from World War II; but Korea suffered in 1950–53 from one of the most savage wars fought in recent times, losing 1.3 million people and receiving severe physical damage. All except Japan experienced a very heavy influx of population after 1945. These facts set them apart from the vast majority of developing countries. I cannot here make any comparative study of this aspect of their histories. The effects on subsequent development would in any case be likely to remain obscure. But it seems that, with the exception of Burma, all those countries which were defeated or suffered severe physical damage in World War II subsequently did well, not merely during a period of recovery, when their underutilized stock of physical and human capital was put to work again, but for longer.

I will give only a few historical highlights. The Taiwan economy was by no means stagnant under Japanese rule, especially from 1911 to 1940. The Japanese concentrated on agriculture, communications, and power. They introduced irrigation, fertilizers, new seed varieties, and cooperative institutions in agriculture, and they built ports and railways. Apart from sugar and cement, there was little manufacturing, but agricultural outputs and productivity grew rapidly at about 4.5 percent and 3 percent per annum, respectively. By the late 1930s, Taiwan was far ahead of mainland China and most of Asia in agricultural technique. But even with the traditional practices of the time, land productivity in Taiwan in 1895 was comparable to that of most Asian countries in 1960.[11] Although Taiwan's cultivable land is very limited, the climate makes it naturally productive: there is, for instance, much more possibility of double-cropping than in Korea.

In the early years of colonial rule, 1895–1911, the Japanese invested in Taiwan, which had a balance-of-payments deficit. But after 1911 they creamed off 10 percent or more of the GNP.[12] Nevertheless, consumption per head rose, and death rates fell significantly.

Turning to human resources, the Japanese concentrated on primary education in Taiwan (as in Korea) and gave the Taiwanese little opportunity to enter secondary and higher education. At the end of the Japanese occupation about three-quarters of the relevant age groups were enrolled in primary schools

11. See Teng-hui Lee, *Intersectoral Capital Flows in the Economic Development of Taiwan, 1895–1960* (Ithaca, N.Y., 1971), chap. 3.

12. Far more, for instance, than the British abstracted from India. Angus Maddison estimates that the "drain" from India in the period 1921–38 was 1.5 percent of the national income and was probably a little larger before that. See A. Maddison, *Class Structure and Economic Growth, India and Pakistan since the Moghals* (London, 1969), pp. 63–66. But some observers believe that Japanese colonialism was in other respects more favorable to economic growth than British colonialism. See also Chapter 1 in this volume.

(about nine hundred thousand students), but there were only about sixty-five thousand in secondary schools and less than two thousand in college. Illiteracy was still widespread. Of the population aged twelve and over, 40 percent of males and 70 percent of females were reckoned to be illiterate.[13] However, the gaps left by the deficiencies in secondary and higher education were largely filled by immigration from the mainland in the late 1940s. The gaps were, in any case, far less serious than in most of the other newly independent countries.

Taiwan suffered severely during the war. The supply of chemical fertilizers dried up, and irrigation facilities and communications were not maintained. Agricultural production at the end of the war was probably back to the level of 1910. There was heavy bombing in 1944. Ports, electricity supply, and communications were damaged, and it is reckoned that three-quarters of Taiwan's industrial capacity was destroyed.[14] But Taiwan received no reparations from Japan, unlike Burma, Malaysia, the Philippines, and Indonesia.

During the recovery period, the salient feature was the move of the Kuomintang government and its military forces to the island in 1949. This created a totally new situation. The departure of the Japanese in 1945 had left a vacuum because under colonial rule the Taiwanese had not been permitted to occupy any senior government or managerial positions, and there was little education above the primary level. The vacuum, which resulted in chaotic conditions in the immediate postwar period, was filled by the mainlanders, who became responsible for government and for the economic policies that followed. About one and a half million mainlanders arrived, increasing the population by 25 percent from the 1945 level, a large part of this influx coming in 1947–49; of these, six to seven hundred thousand were military. Thus the Taiwan economy suddenly acquired not only an effective administration, but also a very large army in relation to her size. As a result, although the total domestic product had recovered to the 1937 level by 1950, on a per capita basis it probably did not achieve the prewar level until 1953.[15] It seems reasonable to take this year as the end of the recovery period and hence as a year from which long-run growth trends can be projected.

The Korean experience makes her development, until the 1960s, incomparable with that of Taiwan. Korea had a shorter period of development as a Japanese colony from 1910 to 1945. The Korean climate makes agriculture less naturally productive, and the Japanese appear to have paid less attention to it. There was rather more industrial development than in Taiwan, but more than half of this, and a very high proportion of heavy industry and electricity

13. Figures from DGBAS, *Taiwan Statistical Yearbook, 1975.*
14. See Kowie Chang, ed., *Economic Development in Taiwan* (Taipei, 1968), chaps. 3, 4, and 5.
15. For this view and more detail of the transition period, see Chapter 1.

generation, was in the North. Although Korea did not suffer physically during the war, the departure of the Japanese and partition caused a very severe economic setback for the South. The Japanese owned and managed most of the medium and large industrial establishments. As in Taiwan, the Japanese had concentrated on primary education. Unlike Taiwan, few came to fill the resulting gaps. Partition was highly damaging, especially as a result of the crippling lack of electricity and the South's immediate inability to earn foreign currency to buy the material inputs which previously came from the North. It is reckoned that industrial production in 1948 was only about a fifth of what it was in 1940.[16] A flood of refugees came from the North, and some Korean exiles returned, so that total population rose from about 16 to 20 million between 1945 and 1948.[17] The North invaded in 1950, overrunning the whole country except for the Pusan perimeter. About 1.3 million Koreans were killed, and physical damage was of the order of one and a half to two years' GNP.[18] Although the fighting stabilized after 1950, and reconstruction could begin well before the armistice of 1953, it is clear that the year 1953, when official national income figures start, is not a year from which one can date any process of long-term growth. Indeed, industrial production was probably not much more than a third of the level of 1940.[19] It seems likely that reconstruction and recovery were not complete before 1958.[20] Moreover, when Korea's period of "miraculous" growth started in 1963, she was taking off from a lower level of income than that of Taiwan. (In terms of 1973 dollars, her per capita income in 1963 was $214, whereas that of Taiwan in 1953 was $222.) There seems to be no reason to suppose that any superiority in her material or human endowment compensated for this.

Hong Kong was derelict when the Japanese surrendered in August 1945. As a result of mass deportation and flight, the population was 600,000 compared with 1.6 million in 1939. Hong Kong's entrepot trade and commercial services were, of course, totally disrupted. The recovery through 1950 was remarkable. Former residents came back, and there was a massive influx of refugees as a result of communist advances on the mainland. The population trebled in two and a half years, and the entrepot trade was reestablished. Her income per head in 1950 in terms of 1973 dollars was probably about $435.[21]

---

16. Bank of Korea, *Economic Statistics Yearbook 1949*, quoted in Charles Frank, L. Kim, and Lawrence Westphal, *Foreign Trade and Economic Development* (New York, 1975).

17. D. C. Cole and P. N. Lyman, *Korean Development—the Interplay of Politics and Economics* (Cambridge, Mass., 1971).

18. Cole and Lyman and Frank, Kim, and Westphal refer to estimates of $2 and $3 billion, respectively.

19. Frank, Kim, and Westphal, p. 9.

20. The year given by Cole and Lyman as the end of postwar recovery.

21. Deduced from World Bank, *World Tables 1976*, using the same method as for Taiwan, Korea, and Japan.

The recovery can probably be said to have been complete by then, but the special impetus of the influx of skills from the mainland may have lasted longer. There was a fresh blow in 1951 as U.N. embargoes on trade with China were imposed when the latter entered the Korean War. Exports fell 34 percent between 1951 and 1952. The start of industrialization preceded this shock by a few years, assisted by refugee businessmen and capital from Shanghai; but the decline and subsequent stagnation of entrepot trade through the 1950s set Hong Kong, with its pure free trade policy that came earlier than in any other developing country, on a course of rapid industrialization through manufactured exports. This example did not go unremarked in our other three countries.

No income figures for Singapore exist before 1960, but it is clear that it was the richest spot in Asia, after Japan, before World War II. There was little physical damage during the war, and, like Hong Kong, she rapidly restored her entrepot trade afterward. But from the early 1950s to the 1960s her growth was sluggish, and unemployment was a growing problem. Entrepot trade suffered from the emergency in Malaya and the confrontation with Indonesia—for instance, the value of total exports grew at only 3 percent per annum from 1953 to 1962.[22] In the expectation of becoming a permanent member of the Malaysian Federation, the government started promoting import-substitution industries in 1959. Growth was erratic from then to 1965, the period of juncture and disjuncture with the Federation. Only in 1965, when the government switched horses from import substitution to exports of manufactures, did uninterrupted rapid growth begin.[23]

Japan was, of course, devastated by World War II. She also lost her colonial empire in Korea and Taiwan, but this clearly did not have the long-run debilitating effect which some attribute to the United Kingdom's loss of empire. An estimated one-quarter of her material domestic capital was destroyed.[24] Agricultural production, in spite of increased numbers on the land, regained prewar levels only by about 1950. Relief shipments of food were received, but inflation was almost explosive. Industrial production in the 1940s remained far below the level of the 1930s. During the period of the American occupation that ended in April 1952, there were important economic reforms, including land reform. The Americans tried to create in their own image a well-functioning capitalist economy—which included, as in Germany, the initiation of trade unions. Some of this stuck. Experts put the

22. See T. Geiger and F. M. Geiger, *Development Progress of Hong-Kong and Singapore* (London, 1975), from which much of my brief account of the early postwar period in Hong Kong and Singapore is taken.
23. The growth of real income from 1960 to 1964 was 5.8 percent per annum; from 1964 to 1973 it was 12.2 percent per annum. See World Bank, *World Tables 1976*.
24. S. Tsuru, *Essays on the Japanese Economy* (Tokyo, 1958).

end of the period of recovery, which was considerably assisted by the Korean War, in 1952, 1953, or 1954. Prices had been stabilized by 1952. The first year in which GNP exceeded the prewar level was probably 1953, though industrial production was still below the wartime peak.[25] This is not to say that Japan's prewar economy, the war, and the American occupation did not cast their shadows further ahead and support the rapid rate of growth for a longer time. Japan's recovery period may have been longer than in the other countries dealt with simply because there was a greater gap between performance and potential in the first postwar decade than elsewhere. Hugh Patrick and Henry Rosovsky list these features supporting this view:

1. A highly educated and skilled labour force—in a sense overeducated relative to the static needs of the economy;
2. Widespread dualism in labour use, in that there existed great differentials in productivity and wages in various sectors . . . ; and
3. Substantial managerial, organizational, scientific, and engineering skills capable of rapidly absorbing and adapting the best foreign technology.[26]

It is clear from the broad industrial base already established before 1945, and from Japan's technical and organizational achievements during the war, that she had a far higher base level for advance in 1953 (which, for convenience, I take as the base year from which to date her postrecovery performance) than the other countries discussed, higher perhaps than one would judge to be the case from the figure of $650–$700 (1973 dollars per head) as estimated above.

Both Taiwan and Korea were heavily aided in the 1950s and early 1960s. Both, like Japan, also received relief aid in the late 1940s. Heavy aid coincided roughly with their periods of relatively slow growth, and they became "miracle" economies only when aid dwindled away. Any conclusion drawn from this fact alone would be very naive.

The main program of United States economic aid to Taiwan began in 1951, and new commitments ceased at the end of 1964. Aid in the pipeline continued to be disbursed through 1967. Aid from other countries was negligible. During this whole period U.S. economic aid totaled $1.5 billion,[27] averaging about $90 million per annum and around $6 per capita per annum. Almost all of this was in the form of grants or soft loans repayable in local currency. In the 1950s the level of aid, over $10 per head, was far above the average received by developing countries. But by the early 1960s there was not much

25. See, for example, Edward F. Denison and William K. Chung in Chapter 2 of Hugh Patrick and Henry Rosovsky, eds., *Asia's New Giant* (Washington, D.C., 1976), pp. 72–73; and Ohkawa and Rosovsky, pp. 23–24.

26. Ibid., p. 12.

27. Figure from Neil H. Jacoby, *U.S. Aid to Taiwan: A Study of Foreign Aid, Self-Help, and Development,* (New York, 1966). Maurice Scott gives $1.3 billion, which excludes "direct forces support" (see Chapter 5, Table 5.18, footnote).

difference. For instance, for the average of 1962 and 1963, Taiwan was receiving $6.3 per head against an (unweighted) average of $5.4 for all developing countries.[28] By this time several countries larger than Taiwan were receiving more economic aid per head; these included South Vietnam, Korea, Zaire, Turkey, Yugoslavia, and Egypt. It is well known that aid per head is strongly related to numbers, and many smaller countries received far more— notably French Overseas Departments and France's colonies or former colonies in Africa, but also Cyprus, Israel, and Jordan.

Heavy military assistance, amounting to $2.5 billion of military equipment grants, was given over the same period. Taiwan was maintaining a large military force of six hundred thousand men or more, which cost over half of all government outlays and over 10 percent of GNP.[29] If she had maintained such an establishment alone and had had to purchase the equipment supplied by the United States (which would have been patently impossible), the cost would have been almost doubled.[30]

Some part of economic aid may be said to have permitted Taiwan to maintain her military establishment rather than contributing to economic development. To put it another way, Taiwan could have grown as fast and have consolidated her economic infrastructure for further growth as well as she did if she had had less aid but a smaller defense budget. But the real economic costs and benefits of a large military establishment defy quantification. I shall not attempt to pursue this question, limiting myself to describing the actual dependence on aid, taking her level of defense expenditure as a datum. A detailed assessment of the value of aid to Taiwan has been made by Neil Jacoby, and is also discussed in Chapter 5.

There is no doubt that Taiwan relied heavily on U.S. aid from 1951 through 1962. Her total current deficit over this period was about $1.3 billion. This was covered as to about $1.1 billion by U.S. aid, and about $.2 billion by private capital inflows. Other loans and transfers were very small.

The position from 1963 through 1973 was very different. There was about $370 million of U.S. aid in the pipeline. Total Overseas Development Assistance (ODA) and multilateral loans at concessional rates remained at a level of about $5 per capita until 1968.[31] After 1968, as repayments were made, such

28. Little and Clifford, *International Aid* (London, 1965), Table 13: figures from Organization for Economic Cooperation and Development (OECD), ''Flow of Financial Resources.''

29. Samuel P. S. Ho, *Economic Development of Taiwan 1860–1970* (New Haven, 1977), ch. 7, estimates that in the 1950s, and in most years in the 1960s, Taiwan's military establishment absorbed about 12 percent of GNP and about 65 percent of government current expenditures (including all levels of government).

30. See Jacoby.

31. OECD, *Development Cooperation,* various series. Of course, because GNP was rapidly rising, aid as a proportion of GNP was rapidly falling. U.S. aid fell from 6–7 percent of GNP in the years 1958–61 to almost nothing in 1968.

loans became negligible or negative. Net capital transfers, however, went to build up Taiwan's reserves, for the current account was in substantial surplus over the whole period 1963–73 to the tune of about $900 million.

I will discuss the overall degree to which The Four relied on foreign savings (whether through grants, subsidized loans, or commercial loans) in the course of their development after looking at the aid picture in Korea. Korea has been much more heavily aided than Taiwan. From 1953 to 1960, she received $1.9 billion from the United Nations Korean Reconstruction Agency and the U.S. Agency for International Development (AID), a level of about $10 per head.[32] Of course, dollars were becoming gradually less valuable, and the terms of "aid" were hardening; but this applied to Taiwan also. Like Taiwan, Korea has received heavy military assistance, declining from well over 10 percent of GNP in the late 1950s to under 5 percent in the second half of the 1960s. But Korea's own expenditure on defense averaged only 5 percent from 1957 to 1968, less than half that of Taiwan.[33]

Of the city states, aid to Hong Kong has been negligible throughout, but Singapore has been heavily assisted, though mostly in the form of fairly hard loans.[34] ODA and multilateral loans on concessional terms were running at a level of about $12 per capita from 1969 to 1973. But the net result was largely to build up Singapore's foreign assets rather than to increase domestic investment. Like Japan, the city states spend very little on defense.

The extent to which a country can and does use foreign resources is partly outside its control, but partly a matter of policy. The aid I have been considering falls mainly in the former category. But the possibility of commercial borrowing, including to a lesser extent borrowing from the International Bank for Resettlement and Development (IBRD) and the Asian Development Bank (ADB), depends largely on foreign confidence in political and hence economic stability and on the growth of exports—and hence largely on success itself. Since the question here is the extent to which the performance of these countries is to be attributed to forces outside their control, that is, to "luck," it could thus be argued that their total reliance on external savings is irrelevant at this juncture. Nevertheless, it seems useful to record the facts here.

The overall degree to which a country relies on foreign savings for growth can be roughly measured by the ratio of the current payments deficit to domestic investment. In the case of Taiwan, this proportion ranged between one-third and one-half from 1951 to 1959. The figures both for Taiwan and for the other three are given in Table 7.1 for the years 1960–73.

It can be seen that during the period of Taiwan's "miraculous" growth (1963–73), the average value of the ratio was approximately zero. Korea has

32. Frank, Kim, and Westphal, p. 29.
33. See Cole and Lyman, Table 8.2.
34. An exception is U.K. aid in compensation for its withdrawal from the military base.

Table 7.1. Current Deficit as Percentage of Gross Domestic Investment

	1960	1961	1962	1963	1964	1965	1966	1967	1968	1969	1970	1971	1972	1973
Korea	78.3	65.0	63.3	58.0	48.0	42.2	39.0	40.1	43.1	36.9	35.3	44.0	26.7	15.4
Taiwan	37.3	36.0	34.3	4.6	-1.0	15.3	4.1	7.7	11.3	3.9	0.8	-9.8	-27.6	-3.4
Hong Kong	89.5	98.6	93.4	72.7	70.3	39.8	48.7	17.8	10.4	-12.5	-14.9	9.4	-23.5	-17.2
Singapore*	-21.2	-23.8	8.8	8.9	23.3	-6.5	-35.9	-33.5	-44.6	-55.0	-25.9	-14.4	-11.3	-16.9

*But see text.
Source: World Bank, *World Tables 1976* (Washington, D.C., 1976).

been much more dependent on foreign savings, which financed a very high proportion of gross domestic investment (GDI) until after 1963 (averaging nearly three-quarters from 1956 through 1963). Thereafter, there was a declining trend, but in contrast to Taiwan, the proportion remained high on average—over one-third. Until after 1964, an even higher proportion of Hong Kong's investment was financed from abroad (though not by aid); then the proportion fell rapidly so that Hong Kong apparently became a considerable net foreign investor after 1969. Singapore since 1960 has also apparently been a net foreign investor (except for the brief period 1962–64), although she also borrowed considerably from the IBRD, ADB, and other sources. But there is an enormous errors and omissions figure, resulting partly from the omission from the official figures of trade with Indonesia. All that is certain is that Singapore has rapidly built up its short-term foreign currency assets from 1966 to 1973.

It is an obvious fact that all these countries have cultural affinities. Taiwan, Hong Kong, and Singapore are predominantly Chinese. Koreans are Koreans, but most would agree that they have been strongly influenced by China and by Confucian values. The affinities of the Chinese and Japanese cultures must be much less, considering the latter's 225 years of virtually total self-imposed isolation before the Meiji restoration.

The chief personal characteristics that influence development and may be molded by value systems are attitudes to work, to self-improvement through the acquisition of knowledge, and thriftiness. Development-minded governments are fortunate if they rule people who, by nature or tradition, work hard, are thrifty, and want to learn.

No one who visits these countries (or, indeed, Chinese or Japanese communities anywhere) fails to be highly impressed by the evidence of hard and effective work, not merely the long hours (often sixty hours a week), but the apparently untiring concentration and pertinacity with which tasks are performed. It is not for someone as ignorant as myself in the relevant domain to judge how far this remarkable work ethic derives from Chinese, Korean, and Japanese historical antecedents and philosophical outlook; but it does appear to be relatively invariant to the nature of the economic system and even to personal incentives.

Economists often question the relevance of hard work to growth, arguing that hard work will, of course, increase the national income, but that this is a once-and-for-all effect. Quite apart from the fact that a higher national income is likely to produce more savings (whether for static or dynamic reasons), this is surely wrong. The argument may be true of anyone engaged solely on purely routine tasks. But the work of a significant proportion of the population is concerned with change and progress, and their hard work is directly related to progress.[35] Many others, including farmers, may be innovators, and innovation surely needs effort. Much work, again, is involved in self-improvement.

Self-improvement leads to education. We have already seen that all these communities have had relatively high standards of education, even in the early postwar period, and many authors have emphasized the influence of Confucianism in this connection. In Japan, also, relatively high standards of education can be traced back to the Tokugawa era. Education is not, of course, a sufficient condition of success. Other relatively unsuccessful countries also have high levels of educational enrollment—for example, Philippines, Sri Lanka, and Chile. Moreover, available measures of educational attainment tell nothing about the quality and appropriateness of the system. Even so, it is difficult to believe that education was not a very positive factor in these countries.

In connection with education, it is worth mentioning the linguistic and scriptual heterogenity prevailing in the area. Taiwanese and Mandarin are essential for many in Taiwan, and Japanese is still prevalent both there and in Korea. Although Korea has a phonetic script, Hangul, to which she is slowly switching, two thousand Chinese characters are still taught in the schools. In all these countries, literacy needs more work than elsewhere because of the great multiplicity of characters in their scripts.[36] In addition, these countries are high traders and high absorbers of Western techniques, so that for many in Japan, Western languages are important; and in Taiwan and Korea, both Japanese and Western languages. The disadvantage as compared with, say, Latin America is very considerable; far more educational time must be spent in pursuit of literacy and languages than in most other parts of the world.

Thriftiness is not so obvious a prevailing characteristic, despite the remarkable levels of household savings in Japan, averaging around 20 percent of disposable income in recent years, far higher than for any other country. Of course, "household" savings includes unincorporated enterprise, which probably accounts for more than half of such savings.[37] Even so, the savings of wage and salary earners are also high.[38] The reasons for these very high savings rates in Japan are disputable. There is no doubt that the high growth rate of personal disposable income is a factor, but a natural conservatism in consumption expenditure may also contribute. This thriftiness is not, however, yet so clearly in evidence in either Korea or Taiwan, despite their almost equally rapid rates of growth of personal disposable income. In Korea, house-

35. For a convincing statement of this, see M. FG. Scott, "Investment and Growth," *Oxford Economic Papers* 28, no. 3 (November 1976), 317–63.

36. This is generally accepted; reform has often in the past been advocated on the ground that the script helped to confine literacy to a small elite. Though this is no longer the case, the burden remains. But I have not been able to find any quantification of it.

37. Ohkawa and Rosovsky, p. 169, give a figure of 59.8 percent for 1961.

38. Ibid., 14.4 percent for 1961.

hold savings (including unincorporated enterprise) were very small (
negative in most years from 1960 to 1968. From 1969 to 1974 they b
more important, averaging 5.8 percent of disposable income and rea
about 10 percent in 1973 and 1974.[39] For Taiwan, the national income figures
do not distinguish corporate and household savings. But household savings
are estimated by the research department of the Central Bank and included in
the ''Flow of Funds of the Republic of China.''[40] Combining these figures
with those for consumption expenditure in the national income accounts yields
the high average of 16.6 percent savings from disposable income (with no
clear trend) for the years 1967-73. This is far higher than in Korea, and the
Koreans seem to regard themselves as naturally profligate compared to the
Chinese. But the statistical discrepancy is large (which is why the figures are
not included in the national income accounts), and one can therefore say no
more than that there is some evidence that household (including unincorporated enterprise) savings in Taiwan may be high. This would, of course, be
consistent with the view that profitability for small enterprises, as well as
large, was high in these years.[41]

Such cultural factors cannot be more than contributory factors, which may
play their part, but only when other conditions are favorable. Mainland China
clearly shares these factors. Some people greatly admire mainland China,
primarily because they believe that extreme poverty has been largely eliminated—and that in a very poor country. But it is not claimed that mainland
China has achieved very high growth.[42] Korea, Taiwan, and Singapore also
achieved very high growth only in the 1960s, preceded by Hong Kong and
Japan in the 1950s. China, Korea, and Japan endured centuries of stagnation while northern and western Europe progressed from the fifteenth through
the nineteenth century.

Related to the ethnic and cultural spheres is the fact that, except for Singapore, these countries are very cohesive in the sense that there is little or no
ethnic fragmentation or damaging religious rivalry. They have no problems
comparable in these respects to those of India, Sri Lanka, Malaysia, or the
Philippines, nor, of course, the tribal problems indigenous to Africa. Nor do
they have any very severe regional problems like Thailand or Brazil. Undoubtedly this cohesiveness is a favorable factor.

High growth in the region cannot explain itself; but it is worth considering
the extent to which the rapidity of Japanese growth may have conferred a

39. Bank of Korea, *National Income in Korea 1975* (Seoul, 1976), Table 8.
40. In *Taiwan Financial Statistics Monthly,* July 1976.
41. See Chapter 5.
42. With the lack of statistics emanating from the mainland, both the level of income per head
and the rate of growth can only be guesses. The expert consensus seems to put the growth rate of
her per capita income since 1957 at 3.5-4 percent per annum, about the same as in Thailand.

benefit on The Four. The answer is, "not as much as one might have expected." In 1953, Japan took 45.6 percent of Taiwan's exports, in 1975 only 13.1 percent.[43] Over this period the real value of Taiwan's exports rose by nearly 14 percent per annum, but those to Japan rose by only 7.5 percent per annum. The Korean story is similar, the proportion of exports to Japan falling from 63.4 percent in 1960 to 38.5 percent in 1973.[44] The reason for this, of course, has been Japan's protective policies as a result of which she imported very few consumer goods in which Korea and Taiwan came to specialize in the 1960s. In 1965, for instance, manufactured consumer goods accounted for only 3 percent of Japan's imports.[45] Japan has never been an important market for Hong Kong and Singapore. Intertrade between The Four is also relatively unimportant. The largest flow is from Taiwan to Hong Kong, accounting for 6.8 percent of Taiwan's exports in 1975 and consisting largely of textiles.

It is sometimes argued that the Vietnam War, as well as other "easy" exports to the U.S. resident forces, provided an important stimulus to these economies. There is some truth in this for Korea. Receipts from sales to and procurement for U.N. (mostly U.S.) forces in Korea and from U.S. offshore procurement of supplies for the Vietnam War accounted for 48 percent of Korea's foreign exchange receipts in 1961. The absolute amount peaked at $207 million in 1967, when the Vietnam War escalated, but by then this amount accounted for only 19 percent of foreign exchange receipts. By 1972 the proportion was 9 percent.[46] The end of the Vietnam War has made no dent in her rate of growth. No similar figures are available for Taiwan, but any benefit she derived was much less than for Korea. Although she benefited from offshore purchases, there were never many U.S. troops in Taiwan, and Taiwan did not undertake construction work in South Vietnam on the large scale that Korea did.

Let us take stock before moving on to matters which stem more from economic policy, and politics, than from nature, or any deep-seated ethnic or cultural causes. We have briefly reviewed, or at least mentioned, the immediate postwar histories of the five countries; their initial, i.e., 1953 or thereabouts, levels of income and wealth, including human wealth; their size, location, and natural resources relative to population; the external help received; their cultural heritage; and the extent to which they helped each other.

I have found little by way of any explanation of their extraordinary success, which so far has been unmatched elsewhere. They have many disadvantages, including the lack of minerals and the extraordinary scarcity of cultivable land in relation to population. Only Hong Kong and Singapore have the charac-

43. See Chapter 5.
44. Frank, Kim, and Westphal, Table 6-4.
45. Ohkawa and Rosovsky, Table 13.
46. Frank, Kim, and Westphal, Table 11-5.

teristics of well-placed city states. Japan, Korea, and Taiwan are all far away from what has become much their biggest market—the United States—and especially far from its eastern seaboard. Their initial levels of income and wealth—especially human wealth—were above those of Africa and South Asia, but below those of Latin America and most Mediterranean countries. Korea was on a par with Thailand, Philippines, and South Vietnam. Taiwan was better off, falling between these latter and Malaysia. There are other factors which are not common; Taiwan and Korea are virtually compelled, in the face of external threat, to spend a lot on defense, but the others spend notably little.

More intangible, but possibly influential on the plane of the human spirit, is the fact that all suffered occupation or defeat in World War II (and defeated and/or occupied Western countries have done much better since the war than the United States, United Kingdom, or even Canada or Australia). But so also did Burma and the Philippines. Perhaps more important is the fact that they are culturally and ethnically homogeneous within themselves. Finally, there is the well-attested fact of hard work; but no one knows to what extent this has cultural, religious, or genetic roots or stems from education, health, and opportunity. It is surely an important factor, but certainly very far from being a sufficient explanation; probably the Chinese, Koreans, and Japanese were always willing to work well, but they did not always make much progress. The main part of any explanation must come from government and economic policies.

Stable Factors in Government and Economic Policy

Japan, Taiwan, and Hong Kong have enjoyed stable government throughout this period—albeit for different reasons. Japan is a full-fledged democracy, and the Government has been subject to the need to reconcile divergent interests to much the same extent as in any Western democracy. However, her conservative Liberal Democratic government has never appeared to face defeat until very recently; and the nature of the economic system and the style of economic policies have been remarkably invariant for a quarter of a century. Taiwan, like many developing countries, has a one-party system, with no effective opposition. Hong Kong is a Crown Colony, by consensus of the United Kingdom, the People's Republic of China, and its inhabitants.

Korea's and Singapore's political history is more checkered. In Korea, the twelve-year-old increasingly autocratic government of Syngman Rhee collapsed in 1960 in the face of a student revolt. The successor Democratic party government, weak, split by factions, and scarcely able to maintain law and order, fell to the military after only a year. The military ceded power in 1963, and the country returned to the forms of democratic government with General

Park elected president. His stable and strong government, increasingly repressing any opposition, remains in power.[47] In Singapore, stability of government may be said to date from the dissolution of the Federation with Malaysia in August 1965, although the People's Action party (the only self-styled socialist ruling party among The Five), having won the 1963 elections, after splitting off its communist wing, has remained securely in power in Singapore under Prime Minister Lee Kwan Yew since that date. The essential point concerning Korea and Singapore is that the periods of very rapid growth and stable government have been contemporaneous.

Stability and strength go together, but the latter is most important for economic policies and planning. It is useful to be able to look longer ahead than a few years. Good policies may not be immediately popular; and, although they might have been in time, time is not on the side of a government that faces strong opposition and periodic free elections. If, however, the longer run can be realized, without such a political backlash that the effectiveness of the policies is set at naught or the government unseated, then good policies that benefit, or promise to benefit, the mass of the people will confer legitimacy on the government. The governments of Taiwan, Korea, and Singapore have been able to push through changes in policy that might have been very difficult for governments whose power was more easily open to challenge; devaluation (Taiwan and Korea), land reform (Korea and Taiwan),[48] deflationary monetary policy to control inflation (Taiwan), the encouragement of massive foreign investment (Singapore) have elsewhere provoked opposition that proved fatal to the perpetrating government. There is little question but that such radical, conservative, and open-economy measures were successful and increased the legitimacy of the governments in terms of the support of the mass of the people.[49] Anticommunism has also been a cementing force and would be seen by many as itself conferring legitimacy.

Strong government is not enough. Many countries have strong government but very poor economic performance. The government must also be determined to advance economic development. All these governments (except, arguably, that of Hong Kong) have perceived economic development as the primary means of establishing their legitimacy and consolidating their support.[50] Development for these reasons must embrace the mass of the people. But it has not needed to be populist. Such measures as dramatic wage in-

47. On all this through 1967, see Cole and Lyman, Part I.

48. Land reform was greatly facilitated in both countries by the departure of Japanese landlords. Also, in Taiwan, the Kuomintang government was not beholden to Taiwanese landlords.

49. Of course, there is opposition to varying degrees in all these countries. In Korea, Taiwan, and Singapore there is also political repression, but their governments clearly have the support of a very high proportion of the population.

50. For Korea, see Cole and Lyman, chap. 4. For Singapore, Geiger and Geiger, chap. 9.

creases by fiat and the promotion of very visible projects designed to instill in people's minds an idea of the determination of the government to modernize and strengthen the nation have been few by comparison with most developing countries. Taiwan notably lacks the symbols of greatness, contenting herself with the most modest public buildings.

With the exception of Hong Kong, all these governments (including that of Japan) see a considerable role for themselves in promoting and guiding economic advance. That, too, is not enough for government to have a beneficial influence; governments can do, and have done, much harm as well as much good. Hong Kong stands out as having perhaps the only remaining government in the world which firmly believes that, within wide limits, the less it does the better. The following story perhaps typifies its attitude. When a visiting economist asked why Hong Kong did not have a central bank, he received the reply, "We think it would be too expensive."

The broad nature of the economic system is not in doubt as long as these governments survive. The economies are and have been for the whole of the period highly capitalist economies. Public ownership of the means of production is limited. In Taiwan the public sector inherited from the Japanese most industry that remained after the war, as well as the banking system. Four large enterprises were returned to private hands as part of the compensation to landlords under the land reform. The rest were retained. Apart from the banks, some other financial institutions, and the usual utilities, the public enterprise sector consists mainly of some dozen large industrial corporations owned by the central government.[51] Of these latter only the Sugar Corporation can really be said to have been inherited, although most were incorporated in 1946 and hence had their roots in the vestiges of Japanese industry. Sugar apart, they produce heavy chemicals and fertilizers, some machinery, non-ferrous metals and steel, petroleum products and petrochemicals. Only one new central government corporation was established between 1946 and 1969. But now in the 1970s, since Taiwan is going in for steel and more petrochemicals, there are additions to the government sector.

One or more of these new enterprises may be in the public sector because no private entrepreneur would take them on, and the government deems them to be of high priority for development. Otherwise, the philosophy seems to be that a private company should not have a monopoly of intermediates used in further production (despite Taiwan's increasingly open economy, I found no recognition of the argument that imports can effectively break monopoly power, especially in the case of such rather homogeneous products). Also, there may be some fear of excessive private power. One new plant remained

51. The provincial government and the hsien and municipalities own some other enterprises including the tobacco and wine monopolies.

in the public sector, I was told, because the private bidder was already very powerful. There is apparently no longer any investment control for domestic industry, so that government enters the picture only when favors are required for any new industry that has promise of profitability, or where the government has promoted the industry and is seeking private participation. With few exceptions, public industry thus consists of these parts: (1) historical accidents that are not retained in the public sector for any ideological or economic reason, but rather from inertia; (2) utilities, including rail and some air transport; (3) some capital-intensive intermediate production, which is both inevitably monopolistic if imports are kept out and unprofitable without protection or subsidy.

It appears that public industry has until recently been of rapidly declining quantitative importance. Economic Planning Council (EPC) figures show a steadily declining share in industrial value added (at 1971 prices) from 57 percent in 1952 to 23 percent in 1975; for manufacturing only, the figures are 56 percent and 15 percent.[52] These figures imply a growth rate for public and private industry of 8.6 percent and 17.1 percent per annum, respectively, and for manufacturing of 7.0 percent and 18.3 percent, respectively. Public industry's share in fixed capital formation shows, in contrast, no such marked trend. It tended to rise from 1952 to 1958 (from 32 percent to 45 percent), to fall from 1958 to 1965 (45 percent to 21 percent), and then to rise again from 1965 to 1974 (21 percent to 31 percent).[53] It is likely to go on rising with the development of steel, petrochemicals, and some new big infrastructural projects. But nothing has been nationalized.

Korea is not very different from Taiwan. Many enterprises were inherited from the Japanese. Most of the financial sector is public. In 1972, 15 percent of manufacturing was in public enterprises, the same as in Taiwan. About 20 percent of total industrial output was public, again very similar to Taiwan.[54]

Japan is more capitalistic than Taiwan or Korea. For instance, public investment in the postwar period has accounted for well under 10 percent of total investment,[55] less than one-third of the level of Taiwan. The Singapore government has taken a minority interest in many industrial ventures, but ownership appears to be confined mainly to utilities, communications, and transport, such as Singapore Airlines. The Hong Kong government owns

52. Economic Planning Council (EPC), *Taiwan Statistical Data Book, 1976* (Taipei, 1976), Table 5-4. The textual figures are, however, a little difficult to reconcile with the National Income Accounts, Table IV, which shows a rather steady share, averaging 12.7 percent, in the generation of national income for all public corporations and government enterprises at current prices from 1958 to 1974.

53. Ibid., Table 3-8b.

54. See Table 5.8 in Leroy P. Jones, *Public Enterprise and Economic Development: The Korean Case* (Seoul, 1975).

55. See Ohkawa and Rosovsky, Table 6.1.

no industrial venture or bank; and the Hong Kong—based airline, Ca
Pacific, is private.

The nature and degree of planning and the role of the price mechanism have
evolved over time in most of these countries (except for Hong Kong, which
can be taken as an ostensive definition of minimum planning) and are intimately related to those economic policies that are better described in a temporal framework. For want of space, time, and intimate knowledge, I shall
also have to confine myself to Taiwan, with only occasional comparisons with
the other countries where comparison seems most relevant or differences
striking, when I come to discuss planning or policies, or the institutions and
functioning of the economy in any more detail. Here I will mention only one
more feature, the operation of the labor market, because The Five are so
different in this respect from most developing countries.

Except for Singapore, these countries have very free labor markets; the
price of labor is determined by supply and demand, with very little or no
influence from collective bargaining with trade unions, from government
intervention in the determination of wages, or legislation governing conditions of work.

The situation in Taiwan is fully described in Chapter 6. The unions are very
weak, especially in manufacturing, though not actively discouraged by the
Government. Strikes are illegal. There is a minimum wage law, but the
minimum is so low that probably no one is affected. There is a social insurance scheme, with a payroll tax of 8 percent (employer 6 percent, employee 2
percent), covering all enterprises with ten or more workers. There is also
some mild protective legislation governing hours of work and overtime.

In Korea, labor is still less protected. There is, for instance, no minimum
wage. Although there is some trade union activity, it is clear that no militancy
would be tolerated. Employers are free to sack labor without impediment.
Working conditions are bad, worse than in Taiwan, and hours of work are
very long. The better conditions in Taiwan apparently exist chiefly, if not
entirely, because labor has become more scarce.

Hong Kong's labor and union legislation derives from the United Kingdom and is more restrictive for enterprise and permissive for unions than in
Taiwan. In Hong Kong, despite freedom to organize and strike (except for
public services), the unions are fragmented and weak, especially in manufacturing. They pay relatively little attention to wage bargaining and have little or
no influence on the level or structure of manufacturing wages.[56] Hours of
work are regulated by law, except for adult males, and there is some other
mild protective legislation.

Singapore's union legislation was also derived from the United Kingdom.

56. On Hong Kong, see England and Rear and Geiger and Geiger.

The unions became far stronger than in the other three countries and were permeated by communists. Considerable industrial unrest in the early 1960s resulted in enactment of very comprehensive labor and union legislation in the late 1960s. Hours of work are controlled, and enterprises are required to give paid holidays, sick leave, maternity benefits, and redundancy pay. On the other hand, union activities and the scope of collective bargaining are restricted by law. The government has wide powers to settle strikes (which require a secret ballot). There is, in effect, an active incomes policy with control over wage increases seen as one of the most important compoents of macroeconomic policy. Many union leaders are members of the ruling party.[57]

Japan's industrial relations and wage structure are too complex to be outlined here, except for a few salient features relevant to wage determination. Approximately one-third of the labor force is unionized. The movement is fragmented, about one-third of all members belonging to unions which do not themselves belong to any of the four competing federations. A great many unions are limited to a single large enterprise, and the enterprise is overwhelmingly the bargaining unit. Neither the national unions nor employers' groups engage in collective bargaining. Strikes rarely last for more than a day and are demonstrations rather than trials of strength; they are forbidden in the public sector. At least until 1972, Japan never suffered from cost-push inflation with its leap-frogging mechanism. But unionization probably has contributed to the relatively high wages paid in large enterprises.[58]

The Development of Policy, 1953–1973, and Its Effects

Taiwan

Figure 7.1 shows that the rate of growth was declining in the 1950s, as was recognized at the time. With the wisdom of hindsight, one can put the turning point between 1961 and 1962, for the growth trend accelerated from then to 1973. But it was not clear until 1963 that Taiwan had broken out of the previous downward trend.

A manufacturing revolution occurred. The manufacturing production index rose at 10.3 percent per annum from 1953 to 1963 and 21.1 percent per annum from 1963 to 1973. This was closely associated with the rise of manufactured exports. In dollar value, industrial exports (excluding processed food) rose at 28.6 percent per annum from 1953 to 1963, but from the very low level of $11 million. From 1963 to 1973, the value rose from $136 million to $3,794

57. On Singapore, see Geiger and Geiger.
58. For a full account see Walter Galenson, "The Japanese Labor Market," in Patrick and Rosovsky.

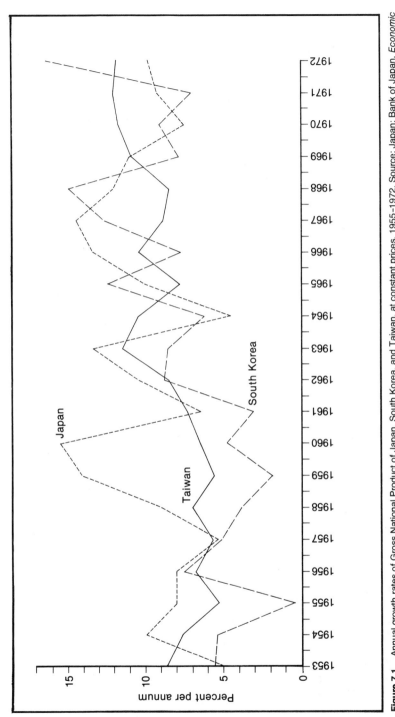

Figure 7.1. Annual growth rates of Gross National Product of Japan, South Korea, and Taiwan, at constant prices, 1955–1972. Source; Japan: Bank of Japan, *Economic Statistics Annual*. Source, South Korea: Bank of Korea, *Economic Statistics Yearbook*. Source, Taiwan: Economic Planning Council, *Taiwan Statistical Data Book, 1976*.

million, a rate of 39.5 percent per annum.[59] The dollar value of exports of agricultural products rose from $18 million in 1953 to $45 million in 1963 (9.6 percent per annum) and thence to a peak of $337 million in 1973 (22.3 percent per annum). Exports of processed foods rose by 4.3 percent per annum and by 8.8 percent per annum in the two periods to a total of $352 million.

This rise in exports resulted in a dramatic change in the structure of production and exports, which is shown in Table 7.2. Columns 1 and 2 consist almost entirely of tradeable products. Column 3, which includes construction, utilities, and all services, consists almost entirely of nontradeables. The proportion, about one-half, that the latter bear to the total product hardly changes. Agriculture plus mining grew at about 3 and 4 percent in the two periods; manufacturing at about 12.5 and 16 percent. As a result, the output of manufacturing rose from 11 to 17 to 32 percent of total output—the acceleration in the second half was marked. Agricultural output fell from 40 to 31 to 16 percent. In relative terms, industry was taking the place of agriculture very rapidly.

Total exports rose from 11 to 16 to 58 percent of net national product; industrial exports from 1 to 7 to 49 percent, with the agricultural-based exports maintaining a proportion of 9–10 percent. Industrial exports by 1973 were much greater than manufacturing production. This is explained by the fact that the total value of exports are compared to value added in production.

Table 7.2 also shows clearly the acceleration in growth after 1963 and that this was more than wholly accounted for by manufacturing growth. Manufacturing growth can be ascribed to the growth in exports and in the home demand for manufactures (import substitution was negative for manufacturing as a whole, probably in both periods).[60] Such statistical ascription is not, however, very interesting. Exports themselves cause an increase in the domestic demand for manufactures, not only because they generate income, but also through backward linkages, which rob statistical accounting of any causative significance. The point is that manufactured exports were clearly the leading sector, especially in the second period. In fact, their acceleration started earlier than 1963, very soon after the reforms of 1959–60. Thus the growth rates (from almost negligible levels) in the four-year subperiods 1952–56, 1956–60, and 1960–64 were 22 percent, 28 percent, and 37 percent.

59. These figures are from EPC, *Taiwan Statistical Data Book, 1976*. Scott gives figures in Chapter 5 adjusted to a Standard International Trade Classification (SITC) basis. His figures yield an almost equal rate of growth for the two periods of 39–40 percent, but starting from a level of only $4.8 million. High rates of growth from such a low level are not, of course, hard to achieve. What is amazing is that the growth rate did not decline as the volume rapidly mounted.

60. See, for example, Shirley W. Y. Kuo, "A Study of Factors Contributing to Labor Absorption in Taiwan, 1954–1971," Institute of Economics, Academia Sinica, *Conference on Population and Economic Development in Taiwan* (Taipei, 1976), and Ho, chap. 10.

Table 7.2. Indices of Total Production and Exports,* Taiwan

	Production				Exports			
	Agriculture and mining (1)	Manufacturing (2)	Other (3)	Total (4)	Total (5)	Industrial products (6)	Processed agricultural products (7)	Agriculture (8)
1953	40(40)	11(11)	49(49)	100	11(11)	1(1)	8(8)	2(2)
	3.0	*12.5*	*7.2*	*6.5*	*10.6*	*29.2*	*4.8*	*10.1*
1963	53(28)	36(19)	98(52)	187	31(16)	13(7)	14(7)	4(2)
	3.9	*15.7*	*9.1*	*10.0*	*24.9*	*34.2*	*4.8*	*17.7*
1973	78(16)	157(32)	235(52)	484	282(58)	239(49)	22(5)	21(4)

*Constant 1971 prices—total production 1953 = 100. Annual growth rates between superior and inferior figures are given in italics. Figures in parentheses are percentages of total product of the same year.

Sources: Total production refers to real net national product and is from Directorate-General of Budget, Accounting, and Statistics (DGBAS), *National Income of the Republic of China, 1975* (Taipei, 1975), Table 7. The distribution of production is from Table 12 (net domestic product). Total real exports are calculated from Table 2. The composition of exports (using current dollar values) comes from Economic Planning Council, *Taiwan Statistical Data Book 1976*, Table 10.8. Clearly, these figures are not perfectly comparable, but they suffice to show the orders of magnitude. Exports of industrial products include some minerals, but this portion is very small.

There can be no doubt whatever that the main cause of the acceleration was the series of changes in trade and exchange rate policies. These changes started tentatively in 1955 with rebates of indirect taxes for exports and a devaluation; and were further consolidated in 1958–60 with the exchange rate unification, further devaluation, and a freeing of many material imports from control. They continued in the 1960s with further liberalization, the creation of the Export Processing Zones and bonded factories, and some streamlining of export incentives, until in the 1970s Taiwan was virtually free of trade controls.[61] There can be few such clear cases in economic history of cause and effect. I shall say more below, however, as to why the economy responded so explosively to these changes.

It is interesting to ask the question why the change of policy was made. There are some obvious explanations arising out of the logic of events in the 1950s. Growth was slowing down. The economy was still highly dependent on U.S. aid for imports, which were severely controlled. Taiwan could not expect, with her rapidly growing population and poor resource base, much, if any, improvement in the primary product balance. Import substitution in such things as beverages, tobacco, textiles and clothing, paper, and cement had been virtually completed. Taiwan in the middle 1950s was indeed in a situation which is by now very familiar. She had a heavily overvalued currency, supported by complete import control. Often the import control resulted in excess profits for importers, rather than cheap inputs for producers. Private industry had little or no incentive to export. There was excess capacity in manufacturing. Controls and irregularity of supply resulted in industrial inefficiency. Investment was virtually stagnant from 1953 to 1957, and the government was promoting the domestic production of things, such as nonferrous metals, which were surely not in Taiwan's comparative advantage to make. The really successful element in Taiwan's policies in the 1950s lay in agriculture, which is described in Chapter 2.

But the logic of the situation is often not enough. Many other countries have been, and still are, in essentially similar situations. A growing number is now realizing the benefit of open policies, and a growing number of economists is advocating them. But in the 1950s there was no example to follow, except that of Hong Kong. Very few believed that Hong Kong was relevant, though fortunately some of these very few were in Taiwan. Almost all development economists were then emphasizing industrialization through protection, the necessity of controlling imports, the particular irrelevance of equilibrium exchange rates and the price mechanism in general, and the dangers of relying on trade with the imperialist powers. Some fears were genuine. Taiwan had experienced an explosive inflation and had only recent-

61. This is described in more detail in Chapter 5.

ly begun to control it (thanks largely to U.S. aid), and no one could have dreamed how great the benefits might be to offset the dangers of again increasing inflation by devaluing. Not only this, but the whole Chinese tradition was against laisser-faire and free trade. Indeed, I am told that the last era of something like laissez-faire in China was during the Han dynasty (around the time of Christ). Moreover, most high officials and ministers had been in government during World War II and were accustomed to controls and afraid that dispensing with them could result only in a loss of reserves and inflation.

In these circumstances, it seems that one must look to personalities as probably playing a major role. Although the U.S. AID mission was arguing for some decontrol, it is not clear that it was very influential in general policies (it certainly failed to get the government to reduce military expenditure). Much credit must go to T. C. Liu and T. S. Tsiang (then part of the International Monetary Fund [IMF] mission), who first advocated in 1954 and continued to advocate on subsequent visits the policies that were at last largely put into effect in 1959. But most credit must go to K. Y. Yin, who was evidently the chief advocate and architect of the reforms, and to K. C. Yeh, who supported and assisted him.[62]

The effect of the new policies was not to create laissez-faire conditions for the whole of industry, let alone the whole economy. They created a kind of dual economy in which exports, but only exports, could be manufactured under virtually free trade conditions—a policy soon copied by Korea (and much less completely and more recently by a number of other developing countries). An exporter can buy his imports at world prices because indirect taxes, including import duties, are rebated. Similarly, the final exporter can buy inputs, which he might have imported, from a domestic producer, who is then entitled to claim the amount of import duty which the exporter would have paid if he had imported instead. The effect is that the domestic producer of the inputs remains protected despite selling to the exporter at world prices. Moreover, the domestic producer is forced to sell to an exporter at around cif prices because the latter has the alternative of importing. This procedure, however, reaches only one link back in the productive chain. The system is evidently effective, but very complicated since a very large number of input coefficients have to be agreed with the authorities.

---

62. This view is based partly on conversations with T. S. Tsiang and K. T. Li, but also on the article "The Man Who Led in the Economic Development of Taiwan," by K. T. Li, in *Industry of Free China,* February 1963, and on Yin's own articles in the same journal. Tsiang told me that he believed the deal was clinched by his giving to Yin a copy of James Meade's *Planning and the Price Mechanism* (London, 1948). But, of course, K. Y. Yin had other advisers, especially C. Y. Wang, who was his chief economist and editor of Yin's collected essays (only in Chinese). K. Y. Yin was minister of economic affairs and chairman of the Foreign Exchange and Control Commission and of the Bank of Taiwan. K. T. Li subsequently became minister of economic affairs and later minister of finance. Fuller details of their careers are given in Chapter 5.

Rebates of indirect taxes are, by convention as well as economic logic, not regarded as subsidies. But there are some subsidies for exports, in the shape of relatively low interest rates; however some industries that primarily serve the domestic market also enjoy relatively low interest rates, as do farmers. There is no way of saying whether such subsidies more than compensate for the fact that the value of the N.T. dollar probably remains higher than it would be if the domestic market were unprotected, and for the delays in getting tax rebates and the cost of the paper work involved. But it is probably fair to say that the Taiwan exporter's situation cannot be very different from what it would be under a free trade regime. In other words, there is probably on balance no discrimination against exports.

As described in Chapter 5, the above system was not fully realized at one blow. It came into being during the 1960s and was supplemented by the Export Processing Zones[63] and bonded factories, where perfect freedom to import existed from the start. The domestic market remains potentially quite heavily protected by tariffs[64] and was until recently also partly protected by import controls (and still is for cars). I shall return to the problem of whether this is beneficial, when discussing an apparent tendency to revert to import-substitution policies in the late 1960s and 1970s. All I need say here is that the apparently sluggish trend of private investment in the late 1950s was dramatically reversed by the profitable export opportunities opened up by the trade policy reforms.[65]

Everything seemed to fall into place from 1963 to 1973. Gross national savings, as a proportion of GNP, which hovered around 9 percent from 1952 to 1956, rising to 12.3 percent in 1962, jumped to 16.9 percent in 1963 and then rose rather steadily to 33 percent in 1973.[66] This performance came more from the private than the public sector. From 1963 to 1973 gross private domestic savings rose at 22.6 percent per annum (in current N.T. dollars); public enterprise savings rose by 16.0 percent per annum. Government savings turned from negative in all years from 1953 through 1963 to positive thereafter, rising strongly until the government was accounting for 20 percent of domestic savings in 1973 (the private sector for 70 percent and public enterprise for 10 percent). After having covered between about one-half and

63. Total employment in the zones was 78,000 in August 1976. Their importance is further discussed in Chapter 5.

64. Much of the tariff protection is redundant, that is, domestic prices are often lower than c.i.f. plus duty. Taking account of this, the effective rate of protection (Corden measure) of the domestic market for manufactures, given the existing exchange rate, has been estimated at 16.8 percent for 1969. See T. H. Lee, K. S. Liang, Chi Shive, and R. S. Yeh, "The Structure of Effective Protection and Subsidy in Taiwan" (forthcoming as part of a World Bank study, organized by B. Balassa, *Development Strategies in Semi-industrial Countries*).

65. Another benefit was the resulting increase in capacity use. See Ho, chap. 10.

66. EPC, *Taiwan Statistical Data Book, 1976*, Table 3-10.

two-thirds of gross investment before 1963, thereafter domestic savings were never less than 85 percent of domestic investment and as much as 127 percent in 1972.

Inflation had already been brought down to low figures by 1961, despite the devaluation of 1958. Between 1961 and 1963, the Consumer Price Index rose at 2.3 percent per annum. From 1963 to 1972 it rose at 3.0 percent per annum, but rapid inflation reoccurred in 1973 with the rise in world commodity prices. The dollar exchange rate, after the unification of 1960, remained unchanged until 1973. Real interest rates were maintained at high levels throughout the period (see Chapter 4). Employment in manufacturing rose by 10.1 percent per annum from 1966 to 1973.[67] There is a break in the figures which precludes giving a figure for the whole period 1963–73. Also, no figure is available for manufacturing in the earlier decade. For industry as a whole, the rate of growth of employment was 4.6 percent per annum from 1953 to 1963.[68] Real manufacturing earnings rose at 4.8 percent per annum from 1963 to 1973, compared with 3.3 percent from 1953 to 1963.[69] Real wages for unskilled workers rose at 2.3 percent per annum from 1953 to 1963 and 4.4 percent per annum from 1963 to 1973.[70] From 1961 to 1973 money wages in industry rose by 9.7 percent per annum, but productivity rose by 10.8 percent per annum, so that unit labor costs fell slightly.[71] Labor supply conditions were such that the very rapid rise in demand for labor resulted in wages rising about as fast as did average productivity. The fact that unit labor costs did not rise is perhaps a good definition of there having been no *excess* demand for labor.

What is the explanation of this extraordinary noninflationary boom, during which investment in manufacturing rose at over 20 percent per annum in real terms? It is clear that the reforms of 1958–60 made exporting a profitable enough business for entrepreneurs to seize the opportunity with alacrity. Taxation was also very favorable to enterprises. The 1958–60 reforms included a statute for the encouragement of investment, with tax holidays, accelerated depreciation, a ceiling on the corporate income tax rate, and other remissions. No good figures for profits are available, but evidence of high profitability is given in Chapters 4 and 5. Without high profits it would be difficult to explain the remarkable rise in private savings. At the same time, the government

67. See Chapter 6, Table 6.4.
68. This figure is, however, probably very unreliable. The source, EPC, *Taiwan Statistical Data Book, 1976,* Tables 2–5(a) and 2–5(b), yields a growth rate for manufacturing employment from 1967 to 1973 of 17.2 percent per annum, which compares with a figure derived from the Galenson source of 8.9 percent per annum. The former source shows total industrial employment rising by 15.1 percent per annum.
69. See Chapter 6, Table 6.19.
70. Derived from Chapter 6, Table 6.20.
71. See Chapter 4, Table 4.11.

behaved with considerable restraint. Government expenditure fell from 19.6 percent of GNP in 1963 to 16 percent in 1973, whereas current revenue rose from 21 percent to 22.4 percent. Taxes, especially direct taxes, remained low, so that the incentives to make money were very high.

Although the boom was extraordinary, it is not really surprising. The great increases in exports came in clothing, textiles, light electrical machinery, radio and television, electronic components, and shoes. All these (except synthetic textiles, fiber, and yarn) are labor-intensive activities. Taiwan had a disciplined, hard-working labor force, working for a small fraction of the wages prevalent in developed countries. The labor supply was also very elastic, although never perfectly elastic. Because construction costs are low, factories can usually be set up at a lower cost than in developed countries (the low construction costs more than compensating for transport costs on imported equipment).

There seems to have been little or no problem arising from the need to use imported technology, which, as a result of being designed in high labor-cost countries, was inappropriately capital-intensive. By using obsolete and often secondhand machinery (largely from Japan), by not mechanizing operations that did not require mechanization for quality reasons (for example, leaving out transfer machinery), by working long hours and in multishifts, operations could be and were made extremely labor-intensive. High real interest rates (even the concessionary rates were not very low) undoubtedly favored economy in the use of capital.

World markets in the kind of products described above proved to be highly price-elastic. As Erik Lundberg remarks in Chapter 4, the growth was remarkably insensitive to world market conditions; this was possibly because Taiwan's products were substituting for others at such a rate that minor fluctuations in the overall growth of world consumption of these products was scarcely noticed. Marketing was hardly necessary in some cases—foreign buyers came. In other cases, Japanese trading houses and other foreign agents were used, and, in yet other cases, the Chinese entrepreneurs themselves learned foreign marketing skills (as also production skills) extremely fast.

For the most part, the Taiwanese surmounted obstacles themselves. But the role of foreign private investment must be mentioned, especially as some foreign critics have wanted to believe that foreign firms were largely responsible for the great export success and that Taiwan gained little from it. Private foreign investment was negligible in the 1950s, and from 1960 to 1966 it still averaged only about U.S.$4 million per annum.[72] From 1967 through 1975 it averaged U.S.$47 million (including overseas Chinese investment, which

---

72. Lamp Li, "Private Foreign Investment in Taiwan," in *Conference on Economic Development in Taiwan* (Taipei, 1967).

may be about 30 percent of the total). This represents 6.5 percent of average fixed capital formation in manufacturing. Judging by approvals,[73] 43 percent of the cumulative total has gone into electrical machinery and electronics, followed by chemicals, nonelectrical machinery and instruments, and the rest nowhere. The multinational company making goods for export to itself or its own sales organization was important only in electronics (as is also true of Korea). Another fact that helps to put foreign investment in perspective is that in 1976, 21 out of the 321 largest industrial corporations were foreign.[74]

Foreign direct investment enjoys the same tax benefits as local industry. Remittances are not restricted, there are no requirements to employ Chinese, and the investments are guaranteed against expropriation for twenty years. There is no restriction on the percentage of foreign ownership, but in fact joint ventures are the most common form. The high concentration in electronics means that foreign investment has followed the signals of the market and has been labor- and export-intensive. It can also be credited with spin-offs in the electronics field, enabling the Taiwanese to develop the electronics industry earlier than would otherwise have been the case. Private foreign investment has thus been a positive factor. It has helped, but not crucially.

It may be argued that the buoyant agriculture of the 1950s and early 1960s set the scene for the boom in manufactures, and that the foreign trade reforms would have been much less successful if agriculture had been stagnant. Without in any way wishing to diminish the importance of agriculture so far as overall growth and equity are concerned, it seems to me likely that the kind of industrial development pursued by Taiwan and the members of the group of Four after 1960 was rather independent of what happened to agriculture.[75] If agricultural productivity had risen more slowly, industry might have got its labor even more cheaply. On the other hand, less food would have been produced, probably therefore requiring more food imports (although the demand for food would have been lower). There would, therefore, have been less import of industrial equipment, unless industry itself exported more (in place of its lower sales to the less thriving agricultural sector) and unless Taiwan had borrowed more. In reality, agricultural growth did slow up after 1965. Industry no doubt exported more than it otherwise would have done. Investment continued to rise fast, output grew at 20 percent per annum, and there was no balance-of-payments problem. It is also true that Korean agricultural productivity started from a lower level, grew more slowly, and never

73. EPC, *Taiwan Statistical Data Book, 1976*, Table 12-3.

74. Only eighty-nine of the top three hundred corporations are owned by mainlanders. See China Credit Information Service, ''The Largest Industrial Corporations in the Republic of China'' (Taipei, 1976). The split between mainlander and indigenous ownership was provided by the EPC.

75. This is perhaps an overcautious statement regarding Hong Kong and Singapore.

developed the surpluses of Taiwan agriculture. Although it can be argued that Taiwan's overall development has been healthier than that of Korea in this respect,[76] it also seems to be true that exports are a good substitute for a thriving agriculture as far as industrial development is concerned.

Apart from the creation of a virtual free trade regime for exports, the conservative government budgeting, high interest rates, and a free labor market—a set of features that, in the past, many development economists would have held to be a certain recipe for stagnation and inequality—it is hard to find any good explanation for the sustained industrial boom of 1963-73. Indeed, this outburst of activity occurred despite a number of prima facie unfavorable institutional features.

Although import controls were being reduced, there was no reform of the tariff structure, which remained, potentially, highly and erratically protective.[77] But the tariff structure is not the only irrational feature of the tax system, which has rightly been described as antiquated. Perhaps the most antiquated feature has been the commodity taxes on intermediate goods and services. (The Diamond-Mirrlees doctrine that, as far as possible, producers' goods should be untaxed, has as yet had no effect.) These include taxes on textile yarns (20 percent), leather (15 percent), plastics (23 percent), cement (30 percent), paper (5 percent), glass (23 percent), sewing machines (10 percent), and steel (10 percent). There is also a cascading turnover tax (the "Business Tax"), with different rates for four different categories of business ranging from .6 percent to 6.0 percent.[78] Traders, manufacturers, publishers, and farmers are in the lowest grade; followed by contractors, printers, restaurants, and public utilities; followed by repairers, subcontractors, hotels, and many services; with financial institutions and those providing technical services and designs in the most penalized category. It would be hard indeed to find any sense in all this, except perhaps to increase bureaucracy and encourage vertical integration. At the same time, there are good theoretical grounds for believing such taxes to be unnecessarily distorting and productive of inefficiency. These features of the tax structure are inherited from prerevolutionary China. The redeeming feature, however, is that the overall burden on business is low.

The proportion of taxes to national income is modest (17 percent in fiscal 1974). The proportion of this proportion which is indirect was very high (83 percent in the same period). This was the situation even after the reforms

76. See John Fei and Gustav Ranis, "A Model of Growth and Employment in the Open Dualistic Economy: The Cases of Korea and Taiwan," *Journal of Development Studies* (January 1975).

77. As we have seen, however, effective protection became quite low, much of the potential protection of the tariff being unused.

78. Rates are as of 1974.

implemented as a result of the Tax Reform Commission of 1969. The range of marginal rates for personal income tax had been previously 3–70 percent. The very low starting rate had made it impossible to collect reasonable amounts from middle-income groups. The range was changed to 6–60 percent—still a very low starting rate. Since the reform, however, income tax receipts have risen by 33 percent per annum, whereas previously they had done little more than keep pace with GNP. This increase has been assisted by computerizing the system (making cross-checks feasible) and the setting up of a Special Audit Group, drawn from nontax officials. Both these later measures have been important in reducing evasion and corruption, although, as elsewhere, there is probably still very considerable evasion by businesses. Whatever the consequences for equity and income distribution, there is no presumption that growth was retarded as a consequence of low direct taxation.

The financial system is described in Chapter 4. It does not appear to be noticeably better than those in most developing countries, except that even the most favored businesses have had to pay positive real interest rates, whereas private savers have been able to obtain high rates on bank deposits (the main savings medium). The country is extensively banked. The banking system is almost wholly public owned, and until recently it was precluded from giving term loans in excess of five years maturity. Selective credit controls and differential interest rates are used, not only to promote exports, but to favor certain import-substituting industries, including farming.

It is very difficult for enterprises to obtain long-term funds. The stock market is still rudimentary, though efforts are being made to encourage it. As to debentures, corporations cannot easily compete with the government, which offers high interest bonds tax-free to savers. Short-term credit instruments are also not well developed, and the postdated check is the main credit instrument. Little effort has been made to reach out to small-scale enterprises, which must rely almost entirely on the curb market or on family and friends for external resources. The China Development Corporation (promoted by the World Bank in 1959) appears to be very conservative and does not generally lend to businesses with less than one hundred employees. A Small and Medium Industries Bank was created only in 1976. Several developing countries, especially India, have done far more to promote small-scale enterprises. Since most successful firms in Taiwan have grown from small beginnings in the past twenty years, it could be questioned whether, at least in a country where the tax system is highly favorable to the reinvestment of profits, financial institutions which specially serve small enterprises are really necessary.

I have explained the industrial boom as largely accounted for by Taiwan's taking advantage of her one cheap resource—labor. The social advantage of a highly labor-demanding development is another matter, to which I return below. I have in turn explained that the reasons why Taiwan took this advantage were (1) tradable commodity inputs into manufacturing could be got at world prices, and without restraint, so that the advantage of cheap labor was not counteracted by the high local price or the unobtainability of intermediate products; and (2) manufacturers were not inhibited from employing more labor by any wage regulation, industrial disorder, or restriction on sacking workers; in short, labor really was cheap; at the same time, (3) capital for large and medium-sized enterprises was more expensive than in most developing countries; the exchange rate was not significantly overvalued, so that foreign machinery was not too cheap; furthermore, even concessional interest rates were around 5 percent in real terms. In short, factor prices, like commodity prices, were not seriously distorted.

Korea, Hong Kong, and Singapore

One's confidence that the above is the main explanation of Taiwan's success is increased by the similar results following from similar changes in policy in Korea and Singapore and by the rapid development of manufacturing in Hong Kong, which has always pursued free trade policies. That Korea's growth of GNP entered, like Taiwan's, a different ball park from 1963 on is evident from Figure 7.1. The rapid growth of Korea's manufactured exports started in 1961 from the very low level of $9.4 million (Taiwan had reached this figure about a decade earlier), when the value of Taiwan's exports of industrial products was $71 million.[79] Exports were mainly plywood, silk yarn, and cotton fabrics. Clothing, footwear, and electrical apparatus were not yet exported; these items spearheaded the advance that came later. Starting from 1963, when the total was still only $43.6 million but export of the above-mentioned items had begun, manufactured exports grew at an average rate of 52 percent per annum until 1973, even faster than Taiwan's, which, however, started from the higher level of $129 million in that year. In 1973, Taiwan's manufactured exports were $3,680 million against Korea's $2,879 million. Manufactures by then accounted for 82 percent and 88 percent of exports in the two cases.

It is a little more difficult in Korea's case than in Taiwan's to relate the emergence of labor-intensive manufactured exports to any precise change of policy, mainly because the changes were more spread out in time. One of the most important measures to make exporting profitable despite protection of the home market was introduced in 1959—the exemption from tariffs on materials and components. Exports were also exempted from internal indirect taxes in 1961. There was a major reform in 1964, involving a massive devaluation and reunification of exchange rates (they had been previously unified for

---

79. This latter figure is from Chapter 5 and is on a SITC basis. I do not know if the Korean figures are strictly comparable.

about two years, from 1961 to 1962); at the same time there was some liberalization of controls, and the system by which suppliers of intermediates to exporters could obtain tax and tariff relief was introduced for the first time.[80] The upshot was that a system very similar to that of Taiwan had emerged by 1965. Interest rates were also raised in 1964. From 1965 to 1971 time deposit rates varied around 15 percent in real terms; the rate on loans was similarly high, but there was a concessionary rate for export credit.

Korea has never achieved the price stability of Taiwan, and consequently the won, which was periodically devalued but not floating, became overvalued from time to time. The authorities offset this overvaluation by varying export incentives so that the effective exchange rate on exports, after allowing for changes in both internal prices and those of competing countries, remained remarkably steady from 1964 until 1973.[81] Effective protection of the home market is now very low, and consequently there is no discrimination against exports. Although the detail is hard to follow, the general picture is clear. There was, as in Taiwan, a quite rapid and eventually massive response to a series of measures that made the production and export of labor-intensive manufactures profitable.

Like Hong Kong, Singapore had a free trade regime in the 1950s; but, unlike Hong Kong, there was very little manufacturing development. The communist menace, general political uncertainty, and bad labor relations may be sufficient causes for this divergence. Protection began in the 1960s, but was limited to very few products until 1965. There was a shift from this limited import substitution toward export-promotion measures beginning with political independence and the collapse of the union with Malaysia in 1965. Exports, as in the rest of The Four, became subject to a virtual free trade regime. Protection of the home market, however, continued to increase until 1969, but was never high and, except for a brief interlude, was by tariff only and not quotas. Effective protection of the home market has been estimated at 8.6 percent for 1966 and 18 percent for 1969,[82] when protection peaked. Since then almost all quotas have been eliminated and tariffs reduced. Until 1965, growth of income per head was erratic, but from 1965 to 1973 it never fell below 7 percent per annum (see Figure 7.2). The growth of manufacturing output and the U.S. dollar value of manufactured exports, has been sensational. They grew respectively by 26 percent per annum and 33 percent per

80. This system differs from that in Taiwan. The domestic suppliers to exporters obtain their own imports duty-free; they do not in Taiwan, but instead are protected even while supplying at cif prices. The effects, however, are very similar.

81. Frank, Kim, and Westphal, Tables 5-9 and 5-10.

82. For 1966, Augustine Tan and Ow Chin Hock, "Singapore," in *Development Strategies in Semi-Industrial Countries*, World Bank study (forthcoming); and for 1969, Chia Siow Yue, "Size of Market and Import-Oriented Industrialization in Singapore," Institute of Developing Economies (Tokyo, 1974).

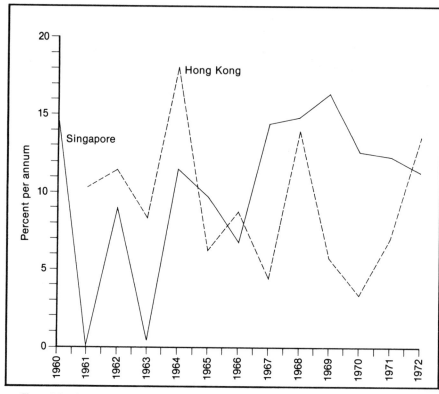

Figure 7.2. Annual growth rates of Gross Domestic Product of Hong Kong and Singapore, at constant prices, 1960–1972. Source, Hong Kong: Census and Statistics Department, estimates of Gross Domestic Product. Source, Singapore: World Bank, *World Tables,* 1976 (GNP).

annum from 1965 to 1972. While Singapore thus exhibited a pattern very similar to Korea and Taiwan, as soon as it achieved political and labor market stability, and concentrated on export markets, there is one important difference. Singapore has relied on foreign firms to a far greater extent than the others. This is only partly because she has become an oil-refining center, an activity based almost entirely on foreign capital. Her clothing and furniture industries were largely established by Hong Kong entrepreneurs, and the electronics industry by Japanese, Americans, and Europeans. Wholly foreign firms accounted for 65 percent of exports in 1972, and joint ventures for another 22 percent.[83] Apart from oil, however, foreign capital flowed into the labor-intensive sectors, and full employment was reached in the early 1970s.

I have not analyzed changes of trade policy in Hong Kong because there have been none. The success of The Four together in exporting manufactures

83. Yue, Tables 6 and 10.

has been so sensational that they now account for half the total exports of manufactures from the developing world.

A large number of other developing countries now give export incentives to greater or lesser degree to counteract the adverse effects on exports of high protection of the domestic market, with varying success. It is, however, remarkable that not one has created the virtual free trade regime for exports that exists in The Four. Tariffs and taxes may be rebated and some subsidies given, but exporters are not in general free to buy imports when domestic products are available, and there is no system which in effect requires and permits domestic producers to supply intermediates at world prices. The other recently most successful countries in expanding manufactured exports have been Argentina, Brazil, and Colombia (with real growth rates of 33.5, 38.5, and 27.5 percent, respectively, from 1966 to 1973). These rates are still below those of Korea, Taiwan, and Singapore for the same period. More significant, however, is the fact that the proportion of their manufactured output which the former export is tiny compared to the latter. For Argentina, Brazil, and Colombia, this share was in 1973 only 3.6 percent, 4.4 percent, and 7.5 percent, which compares with 49.9 percent, 40.5 percent, and 42.6 percent for Taiwan, Korea, and Singapore.[84]

The Role of Planning

The Taiwan boom has thus far been explained largely in terms of the uninhibited private response to the set of policy changes that made exporting manufactures profitable, together with (1) the restraint of government which resulted in a falling proportion of public consumption to GNP, (2) the favorable climate for private savings—low taxes and high interest rates, and (3) the rather elastic supply of labor to the industrial sector. These three factors permitted the extraordinary rapid rises in industrial investment.

We must not neglect the fact, however, that there is a large home market for manufactures, although on my interpretation it would have been much smaller if incomes had not risen as a result of the export success. Nor must we neglect the needs of manufacturing for physical or financial infrastructure. I shall approach these questions by examining the role of planning in Taiwan.

This is a difficult subject to deal with briefly, first because it is unclear what planning means, and second because, whatever it means, it shades into the formulation of economic policies. Depending on the precise meaning, the same person can reasonably be both a fervent opponent of and an ardent

---

84. This paragraph is based on Bela Balassa, "Export Incentives and Export Performance in Developing Countries: A Comparative Analysis" (Paper presented at an Economic Commission for Latin America/International Bank for Resettlement and Development seminar in Santiago, November 1976).

believer in planning. Without wading into a slough of definitions, from which we might not escape for many pages, I will try to explain what the central authorities do in Taiwan, over and above the "normal" processes of influencing the economy through monetary and fiscal management, and planning government expenditure.

Some mechanism for central planning has existed most of the time since 1953, when the Economic Stabilization Board (ESB) was created. This board formulated the first two of the six four-year Plans, covering the years 1953–60. These Plans were autarchic in conception, used the technique of commodity balances, and did not add up to a comprehensive, integrated picture of the economy. They were largely concerned with presenting projects and programs for economic assistance to the aid authorities, who in Taiwan, as in most other developing countries, almost inevitably furthered the cause of central planning.[85] In 1958 the ESB was disbanded, and the planning function was decentralized. Despite the lack of any central planning mechanism, a plan (for 1961–64) was produced by a coordinating committee (with K. T. Li as chairman), which incorporated the Nineteen-Point Program of Economic and Financial Reform (including the trade and exchange rate reforms described). This program of reform overshadowed the plan. For the Fourth Plan, there was again centralization. The Council for U.S. Aid (CUSA) was reorganized into the Council of International Economic Cooperation and Development (CIECD), which absorbed the various decentralized planning groups and formulated the Fourth and Fifth Plans (1965–72). But its role was more that of policy coordination than overall comprehensive planning. It consisted mainly of senior ministers, but included the governor of the Central Bank and some officials. For the Sixth Plan (1973–76) there was again a move toward decentralization. The CIECD had had a development function in that it generated and selected projects and oversaw sectoral planning and employed the engineering staff required. This function was now returned to the ministries, and the new Economic Planning Council, answering to the prime minister, became mainly responsible for forecasting the normal macroeconomic magnitudes, for compiling and revising the Plans, and for regional planning and economic research. It clearly retains a role in helping to sort out projected inconsistencies, but is only one among several voices. Whether there is, in practice, less coordination than with the more centralized arrangement is difficult to say. In short, much the same functions have been catered for throughout, but with considerable changes of organization.

The Plan documents (at least until the Seventh Plan, which now covers six years) are not very different from many found elsewhere in developing coun-

85. On the other hand, Jacoby states, "The Chinese government did not produce detailed plans for development, but left a maximum scope for market guidance to investment. AID wisely refrained from pushing the government into more elaborate planning" (p. 244).

tries. The core consists of the macroeconomic projections. These are not based on any sophisticated model, although some attempts at modeling are made. Many physical production targets for particular commodities are retained in the bulky sectoral chapters, and commodity balances are worked out. This latter seems futile in most cases because they have neither planning force—being unsupported by controls—nor credibility as projections, nor importance, since any imbalances are quickly rectified by trade.

The objectives are stated in the usual high-sounding terms. Where quantified, as in the overall growth goal, they have been far surpassed. It is notable, but not unusual, to find rather little about full employment as an objective and no serious analysis of the supply and demand for labor. But, in recent Plans, there is much talk about the need for more capital-intensity. Taiwan has achieved full employment, but not by planning.

One good feature, especially of the later Plans, is that policies are discussed to a greater extent than in many Plans, and the actual measures to be taken are sometimes adumbrated. Where such phrases as "will be encouraged" and "will be promoted" are used, it is understood that backup plans exist in the ministries. To a large extent, apart from the projections, the Plans have been a compendium of what has been decided. Inclusion of a policy statement in the Plan does not make implementation mandatory, but reasons for change would have to be given.

It is very difficult, especially for an outsider, to assess the benefits of planning of this loose, noncommand style. Any attempt to peer ahead should help policy making, provided the picture is not frozen. This proviso seems to be met in Taiwan, for annual plans are made that frequently revise the four-year Plans. The need for the government to make a periodic public statement of where it sees the economy to be going and of its broad policies may help to create a sense of confidence among decision makers in the economy at large and may even help to preserve some stability in policy making by the government itself.

Such planning is often taken to be "indicative," and it is held that private investment decisions will be more harmonious if taken in the light of a common view as to the growth rate of the economy as a whole and even of particular sectors. Also, if the public sector is large, the private sector in principle needs to know what its demands are likely to be. Fortunately, Taiwan's planning has not been indicative, or anyway not very. For instance, in 1967 the national income was 10.3 percent higher than estimated in 1965; exports were 30 percent higher and imports 60 percent higher. In 1964, exports were 80 percent higher than predicted in 1961. The production detail is as bad, with underestimates prevailing. Of course, in an open economy this was of no importance for tradeable goods, as events proved. Even where there were import controls, they could be quickly relaxed.

It could be argued that Taiwan planning has not even been intended to be indicative. The mechanism usually associated with indicative planning is lacking. There are no standing consultative committees with private industry; any consultations are ad hoc. There are virtually no teeth either. Thus, the textile industry was apparently rightly warned that it was overinvesting in 1973, but it went ahead anyway.

The one area where counterindicative planning might have done harm is in the nontradeable infrastructure (mostly public sector). One might expect that there would have been an underprovision. Indeed, there is some evidence of this. One reads of complaints that the power, transport, and communications networks were overstrained. Certainly they handled far more demand than the plans predicted. For instance, Keelung (the main port) handled 32 percent more cargo than anticipated, and Taipei International Airport 33 percent more passengers.[86] The actual turn of events suggests, however, that power supply and transport can have been only marginally inadequate. It seems probable that the power and possibly other authorities did not regard the target of around 7 percent growth as indicative, but used their own assumptions, so that sectoral planning was not coordinated by the central projections. Furthermore, if there had been "correct" indicative planning and a target growth of 10 percent had been taken seriously, it is quite likely that there would have been wasteful overprovision of infrastructure. I can say this because I have observed a tendency to greatly underestimate the capacity of infrastructural facilities to meet demand (partly because of an unwillingness to even out a fluctuating demand either by peak pricing or by more dirigiste methods). This has to be set against the temptation to argue that nontradeable services should be a little overplanned because they can become bottlenecks. There is no easy answer to these problems. A balanced infrastructure can result in more waste than an unbalanced one. Perhaps one can argue only for better investment and production planning at the sectoral and project levels, with provision for flexibility whenever possible.

Leaving aside agriculture, where Taiwan planning under the Joint Commission on Rural Reconstruction (JCRR) is much admired and where annual is more the reality than quadrennial planning (but which is covered fully in Chapter 2), I gathered the impression from interviews with several officials and ministers in Taiwan that sectoral and project planning in these nontraded fields is weak except in the power supply sector. Sectoral planning is done very much project by project. I was not able to obtain any project plan. Although cost-benefit analysis was occasionally mentioned, I did not get the impression that it was taken very seriously; certainly shadow pricing is not used systematically.

86. The figures of prediction versus performance are taken from Shirley W. Y. Kuo, "Annual Economic Planning in the Republic of China," *Journal of Social Science* (Taipei, July 1969).

The Ministry of Economic Affairs exercises considerable influence over industrialization for the home market, especially with respect to the promotion of mainly import-substituting manufacture of capital-intensive intermediates—synthetic fibers, petroleum products and petrochemicals, steel, and nonferrous metals. In earlier years the CIECD performed the same function. This backward integration strategy may or may not be considered as part of planning. Projects for the production of these things do not emerge from any optimal planning process. The Plan adapts to such projects, not vice versa, and they are rife in those developing countries where any economist would say that planning was almost nonexistent. But if planning includes any promotion of industries that would not be likely to start in response to price signals, then there was considerable industrial planning in the 1950s, and again in the late 1960s and 1970s. We return later to the economic or engineering philosophy which underlies this kind of planning, and to its desirability.

Spatial planning was largely neglected until the late 1960s. There were, of course, city plans with zoning, but the regulations were very loosely applied. The result has been that industry is widely scattered within the towns and cities. At least for light industry, this may be reckoned an advantage because it reduces intraurban travel needs. No regional plans extending beyond a city administration were made before the 1960s. For various reasons it was becoming difficult for industry to buy land for development, and the government took the lead in developing industrial estates. Nevertheless, industry has noticeably straggled into the countryside, in "ribbon" development along highways (rural electrification is virtually complete). On the western side of the island (where for topographical reasons almost everything is located), no farm is very far from a factory, and rural roads are good. This has contributed to the fact that part-time farming is now the rule rather than the exception. Seventy percent of farms were so classified in 1970, and this inevitable development, with farm ownership limited to three hectares and an average of under one hectare, has been facilitated by industrial dispersion.[87] Only recently has a start been made toward spatial planning for the whole island, with the institution in 1970 of the Urban Development Department, first in the CIECD and now in the EPC.

How shall we sum up? It is clear that the first three Plans were admittedly rather rudimentary, but they were probably essential counterparts to the provision of U.S. aid. After that, it is also clear that the main dynamic of Taiwan's growth developed regardless of any planning—unless one rather misleadingly calls the 1959-60 policy reforms part of planning. Whether the actual planning which emerged during the 1960s and early 1970s nevertheless helped

87. The reasons for the industrial dispersion and the benefits deriving from it are further discussed in Chapter 3.

development is a futile question—there is no possible counterfactual (that is, no planning) with which to compare it—and any answer would also depend on one's definition of planning. What one can perhaps say is that some of the planning exercises seem rather redundant, and that planning in other areas, where planning is prima facie most necessary, is weak. One would think that a clearer conception of what planning is supposed to do in such an open, mainly private enterprise, economy would be helpful. Where planning serves no purpose, because it is beyond the wit of man, or is impossible to implement, or even undesirable, then it should be abandoned, and effort be concentrated on improving it where it might yield the greatest returns. This would appear to be in the field of infrastructure (material and educational); but also for public-sector projects in the industrial field, as long as the prevailing economic philosophy determines the further development of such projects. More attention to spatial planning and the environment may also be desirable. Taipei is among the most polluted cities in the world.

I have not mentioned the latest Plan, for the six years 1976–81, which is of a rather different character to the four-year Plans. I shall refer to this in my final section.

The degree of planning in Korea is probably greater than in Taiwan. There the Economic Planning Board controls the budget, unlike the Economic Planning Council in Taiwan. Taiwan has no equivalent to the Korean Development Institute, a parastatal body concerned with economic research and planning. There is the same promotion of capital-intensive intermediate industry. Import controls have probably been more extensive, still persist, and are used selectively to promote favored domestic industries such as recently the machine tool industry. but it is questionable whether indicative planning has been more of a reality. There has been the same underestimation of growth. For instance, export targets are regularly agreed for industries and in cooperation with them and are normally exceeded. Observers disagree as to whether this targetry serves any purpose.

The importance of indicative planning in Japan for our purposes stems from the fact that both Korea and Taiwan to some extent regard Japan as a model. But, for indicative purposes, the Plans seem to suffer much the same defects of those in Taiwan: they are wildly inaccurate, and have always greatly underestimated the growth that was to be achieved. As in Taiwan, they have no binding force, not even on the public sector, where public investment is decided as part of the annual budgeting process, which is influenced only remotely, if at all, by the Plan.[88] Probably the famous Ministry of Trade and

---

88. See Philip H. Trezise and Yukio Suzuki, ''Politics, Government, and Economic Growth in Japan,'' in Patrick and Rosovsky.

Industry (MITI) is more of a model, at least for some people in Taiwan, with its systematic encouragement of capital-intensive import-substituting industry. It has to be remembered in this connection that Japan has had one hundred years of industrial development, has for years had a much higher rate of investment than Taiwan, and has a very low rate of population growth. The beneficial, paternal role of MITI has had wide acclaim, but some of the accounts are perhaps rather romantic. When I once discussed the role of MITI with a gathering of Japanese economists and officials, one of them remarked, "Without MITI Japan would have grown at 15 percent per annum." What seems to be a very balanced account can be found in Philip Trezise and Yukio Suzuki's article.

The Benefits of a Labor-Intensive Development

Export Orientation and Labor Demand

Wherever there is very low marginal productivity in agriculture and many people scratch a bare living in peripheral urban activities, conditions that existed in Taiwan in the 1950s as in most developing countries today, the human benefits of a highly labor-demanding development are obvious. This sort of development is probably the only way in which the benefits of growth can be widely spread. From the production point of view, a highly labor-demanding development is also efficient. The real cost to the economy of supplying labor is low, and there is an advantage in making things which are easily made in relatively labor-intensive ways and also in making everything that is made in relatively labor-intensive ways.

The growth of nonagricultural employment in Taiwan has been high and accelerating. From 1952 to 1962 it increased at 4.7 percent per annum and from 1963 to 1973 at 7.1 percent per annum. In these two periods the population of (official) working age (15–59 years) increased at 2.7 percent per annum and 3.7 percent per annum, respectively. Agricultural-sector employment rose at about 1 percent per annum in the first period and fell slightly in the second.[89] In very few other countries has the growth of demand for labor been so fast.

Under this influence, real manufacturing earnings have risen almost continuously, but faster in the second half of the period, by 3.4 percent per annum from 1953 to 1963 and 4.8 percent per annum from 1963 to 1973. The participation rate for men fell between 1964 and 1973, but this was almost wholly caused by greater enrollment in education; that for women rose con-

89. Figures from Chi-ming Hou and Yu-chu Hsu, "The Supply of Labour in Taiwan: Unlimited or Limited?" in Institute of Economics, Academia Sinica, *Conference on Population and Economic Development in Taiwan.*

siderably, to about 41 percent. Unemployment was stationary at about 6 percent from 1953 to 1963, but then fell to 2.2 percent in 1973.[90] There is, of course, no precise criterion for full employment. But by the early 1970s, Taiwan appears to have been as fully employed as most developed countries, indeed more so, for participation rates are higher than in many, and working hours much longer.

It is interesting, both for Taiwan and other countries, to analyze how far this exceptionally adequate growth in labor demand has been due to policy changes that encouraged manufactured exports. Some work on this subject has been done by Shirley W. Y. Kuo and by Kuo-shu Liang and Ching-ing Hou Liang on which I shall draw.[91]

Kuo examines four labor-intensive industries, food processing, textiles, footwear, and electrical machinery (including electronics and components), which together were responsible for about half of the total extra employment in manufacturing over the whole period 1954–71. Because food processing has had a checkered history and actually shed labor after 1966, I shall first concentrate on the other three and on the third period analyzed in the article cited, 1966–71, when export expansion was in full swing.

During this period, 62.6 percent of the increased production of textiles and footwear was exported and 32.7 percent of the increased production of electrical machinery (in terms of constant 1971 dollars), and they accounted for 33.1 percent and 17.4 percent of the labor absorbed into manufacturing—50.5 percent in total (and 44.4 percent of the increment in manufacturing value added). Manufacturing in total accounted for 42.9 percent of total extra nonagricultural employment.[92] From these figures it is easily calculated that these industries accounted for 11.3 percent of total extra nonagricultural employment—or, since agricultural employment scarcely changed (declining a little on some estimates, rising a little according to others), for, say, 11–12 percent of the total employment increment. However, this assumes that exports of these industries have the same output-labor ratio as production for the home market. Since only about 15 percent of the capital-intensive synthetic fiber production was exported in 1973 and more than half of clothing output, this was surely not the case (see Table 7.3). In other words, further disaggregation would raise the estimate. At a guess, direct labor absorption by these mostly labor-intensive industries could have accounted for, say, 15 percent of total increased employment.

90. See Chapter 6, Table 6.19, column 4; Table 6.1, and Table 6.13.

91. Kuo, "Study," and Kuo-shu Liang and Ching-ing Hou Liang, "Exports and Employment in Taiwan," both in Institute of Economics, Academica Sinica, *Conference on Population and Economic Development in Taiwan.*

92. In 1966, textiles, clothing, leather products, and electrical machinery accounted for 26.6 percent of manufacturing employment, and this is a somewhat wider classification (cf. Chapter 6, Table 6.4). Thus the marginal absorption rate was about double the average.

Table 7.3. Capital-Labor Ratios in Export Industries, $1,000 Per Man (1971 prices)

	1966 Total capital-labor (1)	1971 Total capital-labor (2)	1966 Direct capital-labor (3)	1971 Direct capital-labor (4)	1971 Exports (5)	1971 Direct exports/production (%) (6)	Export weighted average of column 2 (7)
Artificial fibers	3.8	20.9	11.9	42.0	16,300	(14.7)	
Artificial fabrics	2.4	6.8	1.8	4.3	75,675	(26.5)	
Cotton fabrics	1.6	4.0	2.2	3.3	89,350	(22.8)	
Woolen fabrics	2.2	3.9	2.4	3.5	19,625	(24.1)	4.5
Clothing (including misc. fabrics)	1.1	3.0	0.5	1.8	267,150	(51.9)	
Total					468,100		
Leather products*	5.5†	2.2	13.6†	1.9	11,550	(25.0)	
Rubber products*	1.5	2.9	0.9	2.4	50,100	(54.7)	
Total					61,650		2.8
Household electrical appliances	1.9	1.8	1.5	1.1	29,050	(21.5)	
Communications equipment	1.1	2.0	0.7	1.6	242,750	(67.4)	
Other electrical equipment	1.9	2.8	1.4	2.1	22,625	(14.3)	
Total					294,425		2.0
Plastics and products	2.2	2.6	2.0	2.0	110,050	(30.3)	
Misc. manufacturing	1.4	2.0	0.8	1.2	104,300	(60.7)	
Plywood	1.9	2.5	1.5	1.8	93,900	(74.3)	
Other wood products	1.1	2.4	0.3	1.6	35,025	(33.3)	
Total					343,275		2.4
Production weighted average for manufacturing (excluding tobacco and beverage)	1.8	4.0				—	3.2

*There is no heading for footwear in the input/output tables, but leather and rubber products consist mainly of footwear.
†The 1966 figures for leather and its products seem highly suspect.
Sources: Columns 1, 2, and 3 calculated from Kuo-shu Liang and Ching-ing Hou Liang, "Exports and Employment in Taiwan," Institute of Economics, Academia Sinica, Conference on Population and Economic Development in Taiwan. 1966 figures have been multiplied by 1.2182 (the implicit investment deflator) to make them more comparable with the 1971 figures. Columns 4 and 5 from 1971 input/output table. Columns 1 and 2 give direct and indirect capital-labor ratios. Columns 3 and 4 give the direct capital-labor ratio.

The above industries accounted for 63 percent of the rise in exports of manufactures. All other manufacturing, 23.7 percent of the extra output of which was exported (compare 62.8 percent for textiles and footwear and 32.7 percent for electrical machinery), accounted for 49.5 percent of labor absorption in manufacturing (and 55.6 percent of incremental value added). The same calculation as for the three industries yields a figure of 5 percent for total labor absorption accounted for by these exports. Thus, exports of manufactures probably provided between one-fifth and one-sixth of total extra employment between 1966 and 1971.

A higher figure for incremental employment results if employment is included in the industries supplying inputs for manufactured exports. The figure can be calculated and is 30.5 percent for all manufacturing when the backward manufacturing linkages are included.[93] But it is doubtful whether such a figure is of much interest. Any manufacturing, whether for the home market or the export market, requires inputs. The importance of manufactured exports for employment depends on the answer to two questions. The first is whether they are, at the margin, directly *and* indirectly more labor-intensive than the manufactures for home use. The second is whether they generate, directly and indirectly, more real income.[94] The answer to the first question emerges from Table 7.3, where the first three blocks of industries correspond closely to those analyzed above. The fourth block adds four more high-exporting labor-intensive industries.

Textile exports in 1971 were more capital-intensive (directly and indirectly) than manufacturing as a whole. The reverse would have been true in 1966, when there was much less production and export of artificial fibers and fabrics. The increasing use of domestically produced synthetic fiber, which is highly capital-intensive, has also raised the direct plus indirect capital-labor ratio in clothing from half to three-quarters of the average for manufacturing. The effects of synthetic fiber production can also be seen by observing that the total capital-labor ratio for artificial fabrics and clothing is much higher than the direct capital-labor ratio (it was also higher for cotton and woolen fabrics in 1971, but much less so). Artificial fibers must be considered as an import substitute (or as competing with imports) since direct exports account for less than 15 percent of production; moreover, they are not highly labor-absorbing. They are included in the table only because they are textiles and therefore presumably included in the analysis by Kuo given above. While in the 1960s textile and clothing exports were contributing to the labor-intensity of production, this was not true in the 1970s.

93. Calculated from Shirley W. Y. Kuo, ''Labor Absorption in Taiwan, 1954–1971,'' in *Economic Essays* (1977), Table 19.
94. For some discussion of the second question, see pp. 496–7.

Footwear remains well below the manufacturing average in capital-intensity. However, it is the electrical and electronic equipment which is most labor-intensive, capital-intensity being only half the manufacturing average. The increase in capital-intensity between 1966 and 1971 was also less than for industry as a whole.

The last four categories in the table (plastic products, plywood and other wood products, and miscellaneous manufactures) were not included in Kuo's discussion; I cannot therefore give labor-absorption figures, nor the percentage of their increased output that was exported between 1966 and 1971. But it is notable that these categories are important for the value of exports and for the percentage exported. They are also well below the average capital-intensity for manufacturing as a whole.

There are a few other important exports, but which are closely linked to agriculture. These are not included in Table 7.3 because their total capital-labor ratios (as given in Liang and Liang) are misleading, both because the value of land is excluded from assets employed and because the assignments of assets as between different crops is admittedly arbitrary.

It is also the case that food processing ceased to be labor-absorbing in the period 1966–71, although it was so in earlier years. Figures given in Table 7.4 use direct capital-labor ratios only.

The products given in Tables 7.3 and 7.4 accounted for 77.3 percent of exports in 1971, reckoning exports at producers' prices (excluding trade and transport margins) and for 83 percent of manufactured exports. Of the final value of total gross domestic production, 14.3 percent was directly exported; and 24.3 percent of the value of manufactures (these figures also exclude trade and transport margins).

Manufactured tradeables that are predominantly import-competing, (that is, less than 10 percent exported) have total capital-labor ratios around double the average for manufacturing; the production-weighted average is $7,900. But this high average ratio is accounted for by only five products that had total capital-labor ratios in 1971 significantly higher than the manufacturing average of $4,000—artificial fibers ($21,000), fertilizers ($8,000), petroleum

Table 7.4. Capital-Labor Ratios in Food-Processing Export Industries (U.S. $1,000)

	Capital-labor 1971	Capital-labor 1966	Exports 1971	Percent production exported 1971
Sugar	4.5	6.1	62,650	49.1
Canned foods	0.8	0.4	110,750	65.5
Miscellaneous food	3.5	1.1	58,800	18.0
Total			232,200	

Source: Liang and Liang.

products ($12,500), industrial chemicals ($8,500), and aluminum ($13,000). The rest were all relatively labor-intensive (it should be remembered in this context that Taiwan had no integrated steel plant in 1971).[95]

To sum up, Taiwan has a high ratio of exports to GNP—35.1 percent in 1971 and 40.7 percent in 1975. But this corresponded to a ratio of exports (excluding trade and transport margins) of 14.3 percent of the gross value of final output in 1971. Value added in exports as a proportion of GDP (that is, total value added) was probably of the same order of magnitude.[96] No exact figures are available for the numbers of people employed in direct connection with exports. Although exports were clearly more labor-intensive than total production (and much more labor-intensive than import-substituting production), the proportion of the labor force working directly to produce, service, and carry total exports is unlikely to be higher than 15 percent.[97] The direct contribution of increased exports to the increase in employment in 1966–71, a period during which the export quantum rose at 26.6 percent per annum, was higher. As a minimum, the calculations quoted yield a figure of 16.3 percent for manufactures alone. The true figure is probably nearer 20 percent.

This is, however, mere accountancy. The real influence of an export-oriented development to growth and employment is more complicated. First, given the amount of investment, the increased demand for labor can be assessed only by comparing the total demand for labor associated with investing in exports with that associated with investing in production for the home market—more import substitution and/or more growth in nontraded services. Exports were more labor-intensive than manufacturing output as a whole and much more labor-intensive than import-substituting production.[98]

But the total effect, and this brings us to the second question raised above, cannot be quantified without formulating an alternative scenario, which would have to allow not merely for a different pattern of production, but also for a different quantity of production. If, as seems reasonably certain, exports were very profitable, then savings and investment and the growth of output would also have been higher than with more concentration on the home market. Of course, production for the home market can also be highly profitable—indeed, it may in fact have been more profitable for business. But there is an important difference where profitability is a result of high tariffs or import controls. Such profits are achieved by a transfer from consumers, including

95. All these figures are calculated from Liang and Liang.

96. The export-induced (direct and indirect) value added by total exports has been estimated at 24.9 percent of GDP in 1971 and that of manufactured exports, excluding associated services, at 13.1 percent. See Kuo, ''Labor Absorption,'' Table 23.

97. The direct plus indirect employment attributable to total exports has been calculated to have been 24 percent in 1971. See Kuo, ''Labor Absorption,'' Table 19.

98. See Chapter 5 for an alternative analysis that indicates that Taiwan did indeed trade in accordance with her comparative advantage.

the government, who pay higher prices than if inputs were free of tax. Although a high proportion of such profits may also be ploughed back, they would have been achieved at the expense of lower real incomes, and hence savings, elsewhere in the economy. Production for the home market, where high protection is needed, is often good for the businessmen, but yields little overall growth and little or no benefit for the people as a whole. It is very doubtful whether industrialization at Taiwan's great speed could have been achieved at all without massive exports.

The examples given of the production of some capital-intensive tradeables show that Taiwan's industrialization could probably have been even more labor-intensive. In countries where the real cost of labor is still low, the aim, for reasons of both efficiency and equity, should surely be to spread capital fairly evenly over the potential work force and avoid giving to a few very large amounts of capital to work with.[99] One way of achieving this is to import the capital-intensive manufactures. A significant part of the reason for both the high growth and the wide spread of benefits as a result of a high demand for labor is that Taiwan did not put very much investment into the capital-intensive intermediates like steel, petrochemicals, and synthetic fibers. (Even so, as pointed out in Chapter 5, it was somewhat anomalous that Taiwan, with her considerably lower real wages, should be exporting synthetic fiber and fabrics to Hong Kong.) The tremendous success of exports undoubtedly prevented her going very far along this treacherous path.

Some critics like to argue that Taiwan's industrialization (like that of all The Four) is shallow, by which they mean that there is relatively little backward integration. A glance at Table 7.3 shows that backward integration usually raises capital-intensity (the reason why a few products whose direct capital-labor ratio is very high have a lower total capital-labor ratio is the relative labor-intensity of the services they use). This is especially true of economies with few natural resources, where steel, nonferrous metals, and chemicals are produced from imported ores, coal, and oil. Shallowness is surely a great virtue for labor-abundant economies.

Achieving a reasonably labor-intensive development path is not only, not even mainly, a matter of trade policy. In most economies, production for the home market will dominate, even if all good trading opportunities are taken. I believe that Taiwan's policies of high interest rates and a free labor market and possibly a tendency in the past to underprovide infrastructure (allied to her conservative budgetary and low taxation policies) together with reasonably high electricity and rail tariffs (for these are very capital-intensive) must have contributed much to this end. To some extent Taiwan's compactness and high

99. Of course, a more precise statement is to say that investments should be determined by social profitability where inputs and outputs are properly shadow priced.

population density probably also contributed to economy in infrastructure per head and per unit of final output.

Labor-Intensity and Equality

By reference to data compiled by the World Bank, Taiwan is the most equal of developing countries, the poorest 40 percent of households having 21.7 percent of pretax incomes in 1972.[100] This puts it ahead even of most developed countries and only a little behind some countries in Eastern Europe. Such figures, however, have to be regarded with suspicion. In Taiwan's case, in the years 1964-68, there was a single sample of three thousand families for the whole country, and in this period the average share of the lowest 40 percent was 20.2 percent—also showing extraordinary equality for a poor country. Since then separate surveys have been carried out for Taipei and the rest of the country, but the results have been amalgamated in the source cited, and it appears that the later figures are comparable with the earlier. Regular (biennial from 1964 to 1970 and then annual) sampling on this scale exists in no other developing country, which implies that Taiwan's figures are exceptionally good, even if not very good.

The source states that the samples do not have an appropriate number of rich families. Furthermore, Simon Kuznets, by comparing the sample results with national income figures, shows large discrepancies, especially in property incomes. However, understatement of property incomes is probably true of most surveys, especially in developing countries, and correction for this would be unlikely to disturb the conclusion that Taiwan's income is exceptionally equally distributed for a developing country. Figures for many developing countries suggest an income share for the lowest 40 percent that is closer to 10 percent than to 20 percent. On the other hand, such omissions and discrepancies are bound to cast doubt on the validity of small changes over time.

Personal observation is the only check on the finding that Taiwan is, if not the most equal, certainly in a tiny class of very equal developing countries. Of course, one observes consumption and its effects rather than income. But with that reservation, my own observation (and that of all observers I have talked with) confirms the figures. Although the figures and observation also suggest that Korea is a relatively equal country, most would probably say that they got a greater impression of equality in Taiwan.

Taiwan has been growing rapidly through a range of income per head where cross-sectional data suggest a tendency for family income distribution to be

---

100. Wan-yung Kuo, "Income Distribution by Size in Taiwan Area—Changes and Causes," in *Income Distribution, Employment and Economic Development in South East and South Asia,* Council for Asian Manpower Studies (Manila, 1975). The World Bank study by J. Jain and A. Tiemann, *Size Ditribution of Income—A Compilation of Data,* shows only Surinam equaling this (in 1962).

less equal.[101] There is a suggestion that Taiwan is an exception to this rule. The case deserves brief examination.

Figures for 1953 and 1960, based on small samples (301 and 812 families), show, when compared with those for 1964, a very large gain in equity, with the share of the lowest 40 percent rising from 11.3 percent in 1953 to 20.3 percent in 1964 (with 1960 intermediate). The figures are admittedly suspect, but there was probably some corresponding reality. One of the obvious reasons for inequality to increase with growth from low levels is a country's need to acquire a multitude of inevitably highly paid skills in government, defense, education, health, and enterprises. Compared with most other low-income countries, Taiwan had a high education level, and she had acquired many of the needed skills by transfer from the mainland before 1953. A second reason is that a considerable part of per capita income growth is often absorbed by relatively few people entering protected labor markets with a large gain in income. This duality hardly existed in Taiwan, and a larger number of people gained smaller amounts. A third reason why Taiwan is exceptional as compared with most countries was the land reform. Reduction of rents was initiated in 1949, and the transfer of ownership occurred from 1953 through 1957. Thus, although much of the effect must have been felt before 1953, there was some continuing influence through 1957.

There was no change in the inequality measured from 1964 to 1968, nor from 1970 to 1973, that looks significant. However, the average Gini coefficient for the earlier period was 33.1 and for the latter 30.5 (and the average share of the lowest 40 percent as 20.2 percent and 21.5 percent). But it is doubtful whether the quality of the figures permits an unqualified assertion that there has been a further increase in equality since 1964. There can, for instance, be little doubt that a considerable number of large fortunes have been made and that these would escape the samples. But Taiwan seems to have remained rather equal after 1964, during a period of extremely rapid growth of private industry.

There can also be little doubt that the main reason for this equality must have been the rapid rise in demand for nonfarm labor. The result was fewer people in extremely low-productivity jobs, higher participation for women, and rising real wages, despite the rapid rise in the potential labor force.

Table 7.5 shows the shares of different sources of income. The most striking feature is, of course, the fall in farm income. The share of nonfarm employment income rose throughout, whereas that of nonfarm property income also rose until 1974 and 1975, when the recession hit profits (interest and dividends fell absolutely in 1975). Employment income rose faster than property income, especially from 1963 to 1966, after which the relationship

101. See for example, M. S. Ahluwalia, "Income Inequality: Some Dimensions of the Problem," in Hollis Chenery et al., *Redistribution with Growth* (London, 1974).

Table 7.5. Percentage Distribution of National Income

	1960	1964	1968	1972	1975
Nonfarm employment income	45.6	46.4	51.2	54.8	58.8
Nonfarm private property income	20.5	21.9	22.7	23.6	18.2
Farm income	25.4	21.8	15.6	9.8	11.5
Other private income undivided between employment and property	1.3	1.4	1.6	2.0	1.7
Government income	7.2	8.5	8.9	9.8	9.8

Source: DGBAS, *National Income of the Republic of China, 1976* (Taipei, 1976), Table V.

between the two was almost constant until 1974 and 1975, when relative employment income shot ahead in the recession.

No very good theory exists to explain family (let alone personal) income distribution in the face of such large structural and functional shifts. Several points can be made, however. First, income from earnings more than held its own. Industrial capital was increasing faster than employment, but it was deployed in a labor-intensive way, and the demand for labor was great enough to result in higher real wages. Second, within the category of employment income, equality increased as between occupations in a manner that is clearly attributable to a high demand for unskilled and semiskilled labor. Families with a laborer as head increased their money incomes by 123 percent between 1964 and 1972. This compares with increases of 74 percent for the families of salaried workers and professionals, 69 percent for those of small businessmen, and 33 percent for those of managers.[102] Third, earnings of farm families from nonfarm activities have greatly increased. The share of off-farm earnings in farm family income had reached about 24 percent in 1967.[103] Moreover, these earnings were inversely related to farm size. By 1972, 47 percent of the income of farm families with less than half a hectare was from off-farm sources. As the holding size rises to 3–4 hectares, the percentage falls to 13 percent. The demand for off-farm labor has clearly contributed to equality among farm households and has been helped by the dispersion of industrial activity in Taiwan, which has permitted many workers to commute without migrating.[104]

I believe that it is clear that all the factors cited as contributing to high labor-intensive growth can also be seen as contributing to equality.[105]

102. See Kuo, "Income Distribution," Table 15. The basic source for these figures is the household surveys already referred to.
103. JCRR, *Taiwan Farm Income Survey of 1967: With a Brief Comparison with 1952, 1957 and 1962,* JCRR Economic Digest Series, no. 20 (Taipei, January 1970), quoted in Chapter 2.
104. Samuel P. S. Ho, "The Rural Non-Farm Sector in Taiwan," World Bank Studies in Employment and Rural Development, no. 32 (mimeo, Washington, D.C., September 1976), Table 15 and Figure 2.
105. The Taiwan distribution of income and its changes have been intensively analyzed in John C. H. Fei, Gustav Ranis, and Shirley W. Y. Kuo, "Equity with Growth: The Taiwan Case"

1973–1976, the Six-Year Plan, and Current Thinking

Rising commodity prices during 1973, the oil price rises of that autumn and in 1974, followed by a recession in the developed countries, stopped the great ten-year boom.

Inflation became rampant during the latter half of 1973. But deflationary measures in the first quarter of 1974, both fiscal and monetary, together with the large turn around from surplus to deficit in the balance of payments, stopped it in its tracks within a few weeks in March 1974. Wholesale prices have not risen since February 1974, yet unemployment rose only to 3.7 percent in 1975.

A few figures comparing the behavior of Taiwan, Korea, Hong Kong, and Japan—all countries among the most affected by the rise in oil prices—are given in Table 7.6. All came close to a standstill, except Korea which blazed ahead. Korea did not try to stop her inflation, devalued the won by 21.25 percent against the dollar in December 1974, and borrowed extremely heavily. Her exports suffered, but less than the others, and recovered earlier. To some extent this may have been at the expense of the others; the N.T. dollar was revalued by about 5 percent against the U.S. dollar in February 1973, and the Hong Kong dollar also floated up slightly.

Taiwan, Korea, and Hong Kong all did better in real terms than Japan, and indeed better than almost all developed countries, despite their being such open economies. Taiwan's performance was not as good as that of either Korea or Hong Kong. If we give both inflation and real growth some weight, then Hong Kong might be said to have done the best of all.

I have unfortunately neither time nor space to analyze the reasons for the remarkable behavior of these countries in the face of world recession and a sharp deterioration in their terms of trade. The facts are given only as background to a discussion of how things looked to the Taiwan authorities in the summer of 1976.[106] But we shall also include in our discussion much that had already been decided even before the shock of 1973. It is convenient to start with some account of the Six-Year Plan.

This plan contains less analysis and policy discussion than did previous plan documents, possibly because the previous plan became obviously and quickly irrelevant because of the events of 1973, though this hardly explains the retention of production targets nor the switch to a Six-Year Plan. The reason given, that major projects have a long gestation period, is not convincing. A consequence of taking such a long period is that no ministry can

---

(mimeo, prepared under the auspices of the World Bank, 1976). Except for the fact that these authors discuss a break which they see in the trends in 1968, my views expressed here do not seem to be at variance with theirs. But they do discuss some other influences not mentioned here.

106. See also Economic Planning Council, *Taiwan's Economic Situation 1974* (Taipei, February 1976).

Table 7.6. GNP, Investment, Exports, Inflation, 1973–1976 (percentages per annum)

	Taiwan			Korea			Hong Kong*			Japan		
	1974/73	1975/74	1976/75†	1974/73	1975/74	1976/75	1974/73	1975/74	1976/75	1974/73	1975/74	1976/75
Real GNP	0.6	3.0	11.9	8.7	8.3	15.2	2.2	3.3	16.2	−1.3	2.4	n.a.
Real fixed investment	9.9	15.5	9.4	10.2	12.4	16.0	0.0	0.0	29.0	−10.2	−2.8	n.a.
Exports: (1) quantum index	−4.4	−1.1	n.a.	9.2	23.0	35.9	−9.4	5.9	26.9	17.1	2.0	23.3
(2) U.S.$ value	25.8	−5.9	52.2	38.0	10.8	56.2	18.2	2.2	39.4	50.4	0.3	20.6
Inflation of CPI (average year on year)	47.5	5.2	2.5	24.3	25.3	15.3	14.8	0.6	2.8	24.5	11.8	9.3

*Figures for Hong Kong are particularly unreliable, especially for investment.
†Preliminary.
Sources: Taiwan: National Income of the Republic of China 1976, Table XIII; Statistical Yearbook; China Development Corporation, Annual Reports. Korea: Bank of Korea, Economics Statistics Yearbook, 1977. Hong Kong: Census and Statistics Department, Estimates of Gross Domestic Product; and 1977/8 Budget. Japan: Bank of Japan, Economic Statistics Annual, 1976.

foresee even public investments in its sector so far ahead. There is really no question of consistency planning, the investment totals containing large unplanned residuals or gaps to be filled.

The projected rate of growth of GNP is 7.5 percent per annum and that of exports 12.25 percent per annum. Once again the authorities distrust their past success and point to rising wages, increasing competition and protection in world markets, and a declining rate of growth of agricultural productivity. The population of working age will continue to rise by nearly 3 percent per annum,[107] and investment is projected to rise from 29.1 percent to 32.9 percent of national income. Moreover, 1975 was still a relatively depressed year for output in Taiwan, whereas fixed investment, as Table 7.6 shows, had continued to rise fast through the recession. Six months after it was dated, the Plan could already be seen to be far off course, so far as exports were concerned.

Table 7.6 shows the amazing recovery in exports from Korea, Taiwan, and Hong Kong in 1976, when markets in industrialized countries were far from buoyant. Taiwan's exports reached over $8 billion in 1976. The Plan's 1981 target is $12 billion. Even allowing for the fact that this is in 1975 prices, it will need, from 1976 on, a rate of growth of only about 9 percent per annum to reach it—about one-third of what was achieved from 1963 to 1973. Although there are plenty of reasons why one might anticipate some slowdown, this is pessimism indeed.

One of the main features of the Plan, as well as one of the matters with which I was impressed in talking to ministers and civil servants, is the emphasis given to the need to increase capital-intensity and raise technological and skill levels. This determination predates this Plan and was much mentioned in the previous Plan. It is accordingly said that "industry's absorption of the labour force will slow down because of the emphasis on development of capital-intensive industries."[108] The projected rate of increase of industrial employment is 3.6 percent per annum,[109] which compares with over 10 percent from 1966 to 1973.[110] Since I have attributed much of both the high growth rate and the equity of Taiwan's development to the very rapid growth of industrial employment in the past, I believe so great a slowing down to be undesirable. With a continued fall in agricultural employment, the target rate

107. See Hou and Hsu, p. 42. The Plan says that the labor force will rise by 2.8 percent per annum. This is evidently a revision from the Draft Plan, which also gave the figure of 3.0 percent per annum. See Chapter 6, Table 6.17.

108. Economic Planning Council, *A Summary of the Republic of China's Six Year Plan for Economic Development in Taiwan 1976–1981* (Taipei, October 1976), p. 45.

109. This is implied by the statement that total employment will rise by 3 percent per annum and that industry's share in employment will rise from 35.5 percent in 1975 to 36.6 percent in 1981. See ibid., Chapter 6, para. 3.

110. See Chapter 6, Table 6.3.

of growth of 3 percent per annum overall is achieved only by projecting that the proportion of the labor force in services will rise from 34.8 percent in 1975 to 39.2 percent in 1981. Since no such upward trend appears to be discernible in the past, one suspects that this is really a residual and that the true logic of the calculations points to rising unemployment or underemployment.

Why the insistence on creating more public, highly capital-intensive industry, which is also partly reflected in the rising proportion of public-sector investment? Over the Plan period the latter is projected to be 49.7 percent; from 1968 to 1973 it was about 40 percent.

Taiwan has a highly competent and highly technocratic government. I believe that the style of thinking of scientists and engineers tends to convince them of the efficacy of forward and backward linkages. They are more familiar with what is basically engineering than with rates of return, and some structural economists are of the same bent.

However this position is, of course, supported by certain arguments. Wages are rising. Other poorer countries will start succeeding with very labor-intensive products. There is the danger of increased protection. All this is very true. But the question remains whether the price mechanism will not achieve greater capital-intensity more efficiently and more equitably than deliberate industrial engineering. For Taiwan industry has been becoming more capital-intensive for years. Table 7.3 shows it. A more extended version (not reproduced) shows that fifty-two out of fifty-eight sectors increased their direct capital-labor ratios between 1966 and 1971. Every one of about a dozen firms I visited in Taiwan in 1976 had plans to increase capital-intensity under the influence of rising wages.[111]

There is a lot of discussion of a shortage of labor. Industrialists often talk of this, everywhere. But the "shortage" of labor is measured by wage rates, which are still very low. Capital-intensity, which comes *in response* to rising wages, does not prevent wages from rising. Social engineers, who try to anticipate rising wages by using up a lot of capital to employ few men, run the risk of preventing real wages rising for the mass of workers and of leaving a long tail of low-productivity employment, with much of industry left in a situation where capital is very scarce and wages remain low. In fact, they run the risk of creating that duality of the wage structure which Taiwan has so far avoided to a remarkable extent.

The fear of increasing protectionism abroad is unfortunately justified. There is also a threat of increasing competition from some other and now lower wage-cost countries. These are arguments for further import substitution, but preferably not in the most capital-intensive sectors, and for seeking

---

111. This suggests that the celebrated Cambridge (England) reswitching argument can be safely assumed away by applied economists.

out new and more sophisticated export products, whose markets in developed countries have not yet been invaded to the extent they have been in clothing and some electrical goods.

Thus Taiwan will need to increase the range and quality of the consumer goods it makes and exports, as well as producing far more light engineering producers' goods, including machinery of all kinds, both for the home market and for export. These products are relatively labor-intensive and relatively economical in power use. This also is recognized, and skill-intensity is, at least on paper, emphasized as much as capital-intensity. Some believed that Denmark and Switzerland might be better models in this respect than Japan. There is plenty of room and need for the government to encourage skill formation, but steel, aluminum, petroleum, basic petrochemicals and their derivatives, including synthetic fibers, seem to be stealing the show.[112] One petrochemical plant I visited had a capital-labor ratio of U.S.$167,000.

Apart from the above arguments, there is the usual fear of relying on foreigners for inputs. Foreigners in Taiwanese eyes are mostly Japanese, who are thought to have taken advantage of Taiwan when materials were scarce, especially in 1973, and some could not be obtained. It is also said that the Japanese sell too cheap in order to prevent Taiwan from developing basic industries. There seems to be inadequate recognition that the basic inter-mediates are purchasable from many countries; that years like 1973 will seldom if ever recur; and that there is no good substitute for taking a hard look at what the average future prices of such products are likely to be on the world market. The sources of supply of fabricated ores and fuels and their deriva-tives are more diverse than the ores and fuels themselves and from a strategic point of view require less shipping. Apparently, this latter argument con-vinced President Chiang Kai-shek for many years that Taiwan should not have an integrated steel plant. Dependency is surely increased by having basic metal- and petroleum-based industries when one has no ores and no oil.

The arguments for making the highly capital-intensive intermediates would have less credibility if high social profitability were recognized as a criterion. Taiwan's performance suggests that world-price rates of return on investments of 20 percent or more should be widely achievable.[113] Instead, a widely accepted philosophy is that if the home market is large enough to support a reasonably large plant, then these capital-intensive intermediates should be made; there is no thought of exporting such products, except marginally, presumably because it is recognized that Taiwan does not really have any comparative advantage. Yet, if such things are worth making at all, then it

112. Taiwan plans to spend about U.S.$3 billion on investment in these products in the six-year period (at 1975 prices).

113. This guess is based on general knowledge and work in other countries; I have seen no such calculations for Taiwan.

may well be best to go for the largest size, and export in order to realize all the economies of scale. But the main point is that even if it can be shown that the steel plant is likely to be just financially viable (by selling, say, half its output to nonexporters at the protected price), it is virtually certain that its unprotected or world-price rate of return is not much above zero.

The identical arguments are to be heard in Korea, which was planning much the same industrial developments. But Korea has recently reduced this element in her latest Plan and is also in the process of setting up a system for project appraisal.

Finally, we turn to consider the Ten Major Development Projects. Although some of these date back several years, most having been decided around 1971, they are made a great feature of the Six-Year Plan. This is new, for previously the Plans have not chosen to highlight particular projects in this way.[114] Three are in manufacturing, steel, petrochemicals, and shipbuilding, and I say no more about these. Another is construction of the first two nuclear power plants, which are estimated to cost U.S.$.7 billion.[115] The other six are all in transport and will cost U.S.$1.75 billion. Having seen no project report, I can have no personal views about most of them. I can record only that I heard a lot of criticism of them, and it was clear that a number of observers were convinced that their systems of project identification, formulation, and appraisal were inadequate. There is no doubt that more investment in transport is needed, but there is a question about whether demands have been well estimated and will be satisfied in the most economical way.

The new international airport, first planned in 1970 and now due to be opened in 1978, may be a case in point. From a purely traffic point of view there can be little doubt that the existing airport would have been adequate into the 1990s. Traffic growth in terms of passengers has, in the world at large, often been underestimated in the past, but the capacity of airports to deal with that traffic has been underestimated to a greater extent. The reasons have been failure to allow (1) for the increasing size of aircraft, (2) improvements in air traffic control (which now permit movements at a rate of 35–40 per hour on one runway), and (3) the possibility of smoothing demand over the course of the day by peak-load pricing and agreements between the airport and the airlines. It is believed that the Taiwan authorities were advised that the capacity of the old airport was 3.5 million passengers a year. Recent opinion suggests that a one-runway airport may be able to handle 25 million passengers with the prevalence of wide-bodied aircraft that can be expected. It is said, however, that there were also nontraffic reasons for the choice made, and I cannot judge the soundness of these.

114. They are not the ten biggest projects, although size is one criterion; their possible public impact seems to be relevant in singling them out.
115. A third is planned to be ready in 1984.

I have emphasized in this concluding section my fear that Taiwan is reneging on its past success and turning back, to an unnecessary extent, toward policies that have in most countries failed to produce either rapid growth or to preserve a reasonable degree of equality. Japan is an exception. But Japan, even fifteen years ago, was a giant with a higher level of income per head and a higher rate of investment than Taiwan now. Moreover, her population grew at only 1 percent per annum. She could thus afford to continue the capital-intensive development, which was begun in the 1930s largely for military reasons and could realize economies of scale without a very high reliance on exports. Even so, Japan has not avoided a considerable duality of economic structure. One suspects that Japan is taken too much as an economic model to be copied. It could be argued that Taiwan and Korea have had a more desirable pattern of development than Japan at a similar stage. These are, of course, personal views arrived at after all too superficial a study, with many loose ends. But I am convinced that the dangers, for both growth and equality, of promoting a premature and excessive reversion to highly capital-intensive import substitution need to be appreciated.

Index

Library of Congress Cataloging in Publication Data
(For library cataloging purposes only)

Main entry under title:
Economic growth and structural change in Taiwan.

Includes bibliographical references and index.
1. Taiwan—Economic conditions—Addresses, essays,
lectures. I. Galenson, Walter, 1914–
HC430.5.E36   330.9′51′24905   78–10877
ISBN 0-8014-1157-2